INSTITUTES

OF

THE CHRISTIAN RELIGION

By

JOHN CALVIN

Translated by

HENRY BEVERIDGE

VOLUME I

1957

WM. B. EERDMANS PUBLISHING COMPANY

Grand Rapids, Michigan

This printing 1957

PHOTOLITHOPRINTED BY CUSHING - MALLOY, INC.
ANN ARBOR, MICHIGAN, UNITED STATES OF AMERICA
1957

T 46

OUTLINE OF THE INSTITUTES

Introduction

By THE REV. JOHN MURRAY, M.A., TH.M.

THE publication in English of another edition of the *opus magnum* of Christian theology is an event fraught with much encouragement. Notwithstanding the decadence so patent in our present-day world and particularly in the realm of Christian thought and life, the publishers have confidence that there is sufficient interest to warrant such an undertaking. If this faith is justified we have reason for thanksgiving to God. For what would be a better harbinger of another Reformation than widespread recourse to the earnest and sober study of the Word of God which would be evinced by the readiness carefully to peruse *The Institutes of the Christian Religion*.

Dr. B. B. Warfield in his admirable article, "On the Literary History of the *Institutes*," has condensed for us the appraisal accorded Calvin's work by the critics who have been most competent to judge. Among these tributes none expresses more adequately, and none with comparable terseness, the appraisal which is Calvin's due than that of the learned Joseph Scaliger, "Solus inter theologos Calvinus."

It would be a presumptuous undertaking to try to set forth all the reasons why Calvin holds that position of eminence in the history of Christian theology. By the grace and in the overruling providence of God there was the convergence of multiple factors, and all of these it would be impossible to trace in their various interrelations and interactions. One of these, however, calls for special mention. Calvin was an exegete and biblical theologian of the first rank. No other one factor comparably served to equip Calvin for the successful prosecution of his greatest work which in 1559 received its definitive edition.

The attitude to Scripture entertained by Calvin and the principles which guided him in its exposition are nowhere stated with more simplicity and fervor than in the Epistle Dedicatory to his first commentary, the commentary on the epistle to the Romans. "Such veneration," he says, "we ought indeed to entertain for the Word of God, that we ought not to pervert it in the least degree by varying expositions; for its majesty is diminished, I know not how much, especially when not expounded with great discretion and with great sobriety. And if it be deemed a great wickedness to contaminate any thing that is dedicated to God, he surely cannot be endured, who, with impure, or even with unprepared hands, will handle that very thing, which of all things is the most sacred on earth. It is therefore an audacity, closely allied to a sacrilege, rashly to turn Scripture in any way we please, and to indulge our fancies as in sport; which has been done by many in former times" (English Translation, Grand Rapids, 1947, p. xxvii).

It was Calvin preeminently who set the pattern for the exercise of that sobriety which guards the science of exegesis against those distortions and perversions to which allegorizing methods are ever prone to subject the interpretation and application of Scripture. The debt we owe to Calvin in establishing sound canons of interpretation and in thus directing the future course of exegetical study is incalculable. It is only to be lamented that too frequently the preaching of Protestant and even Reformed communions has not been sufficiently grounded in the hermeneutical principles which Calvin so nobly exemplified.

One feature of Calvin's exegetical work is his concern for the analogy of Scripture. He is always careful to take account of the unity and harmony of Scripture teaching. His expositions are not therefore afflicted with the vice of expounding particular passages without respect to the teaching of Scripture elsewhere and without respect to the system of truth set forth in the Word of God. His exegesis, in a word, is theologically oriented. It is this quality that lies close to that which was *par excellence* his genius.

However highly we assess Calvin's exegetical talent and product, his eminence as an exegete must not be allowed to overshadow what was, after all, his greatest gift. He was *par excellence* a theologian. It was his systematizing genius preeminently that equipped him for the prosecution and completion of his masterpiece.

When we say that he was *par excellence* a theologian we must dissociate from our use of this word every notion that is suggestive of the purely speculative. No one has ever fulminated with more passion and eloquence against "vacuous and meteoric speculation" than has Calvin. And no one has ever been more keenly conscious that the theologian's task was the humble and, at the same time, truly noble one of being a disciple of the Scripture. "No man," he declares, "can have the least knowledge of true and sound doctrine, without having been a disciple of the Scripture. Hence originates all true wisdom, when we embrace with reverence the testimony which God hath been pleased therein to deliver concerning himself. For obedience is the source, not only of an absolutely perfect and complete faith, but of all right knowledge of God" (*Inst.* I, vi, 2). In the words of William Cunningham: "In theology there is, of course, no room for originality properly so called, for its whole materials are contained in the actual statements of God's word; and he is the greatest and best theologian who has most accurately apprehended the meaning of the statements of Scripture — who, by comparing and combining them, has most fully and correctly brought out the whole mind of God on all the topics on which the Scriptures give us information — who classifies and digests the truths of Scripture in the way best fitted to commend them to the apprehension and acceptance of men — and who can most clearly and forcibly bring out their scriptural evidence, and most skillfully and effectively defend them against the assaults of adversaries . . . . Calvin was far above the weakness of aiming at the invention of novelties in theology, or of wishing to be regarded as the discoverer of new opinions" (*The Reformers and the Theology of the Reformation*, Edinburgh, 1866, p. 296). As we bring even elementary understanding to bear upon our reading of the *Institutes* we shall immediately discover the profound sense of the majesty of God, veneration for the Word of God, and the jealous care for faithful exposition and systematization which were marked features of the author. And because of this we shall find the *Institutes* to be suffused with the warmth of godly fear. The *Institutes* is not only the classic of Christian theology; it is also a model of Christian devotion. For what Calvin sought to foster was that "pure and genuine religion" which consists in "faith united with the serious fear of God, such fear as may embrace voluntary reverence and draw along with it legitimate worship such as is prescribed in the law" (*Inst.* I, ii, 2).

* * *

The present edition is from the translation made by Henry Beveridge in 1845 for the Calvin Translation Society. The reader may be assured that the translation faithfully reflects the teaching of Calvin but must also bear in mind that no translation can perfectly convey the thought of the original. It may also be added that a more adequate translation of Calvin's *Institutes* into English is a real *desideratum*. In fulfilling this need the translator or translators would perform the greatest service if the work of translation were supplemented by footnotes in which at crucial points, where translation is difficult or most accurate translation impossible, the Latin text would be reproduced and comment made on its more exact import. Furthermore, footnotes which would supply the reader with references to other places in Calvin's writings where he deals with the same subject would be an invaluable help to students of Calvin and to the cause of truth. Admittedly such work requires linguistic skill of the highest order, thorough knowledge of Calvin's writings, and deep sympathy with his theology. It would also involve prodigious labour. We may hope that the seed being sown by the present venture on the part of the Wm. B. Eerdmans Publishing Company may bear fruit some day in such a harvest.

JOHN MURRAY,
Professor of Systematic Theology,
Westminster Theological Seminary.

PHILADELPHIA, PENNA.

CONTENTS OF THE FIRST VOLUME

⁎ THE DIVISION AND ARRANGEMENT OF THE CHAPTERS OF THE INSTITUTES will be found under No. VI.

THE SECTIONS are introduced at the commencement of each Chapter

TABLES

INSTITUTES OF THE CHRISTIAN RELIGION.

TABLE I.

OF PASSAGES FROM THE HOLY SCRIPTURES, AND FROM THE APOCRYPHA, WHICH ARE QUOTED, OR INCIDENTALLY ILLUSTRATED, IN THE INSTITUTES.

Chap.	GENESIS.	Vol.	Chap.	GENESIS.	Vol.	Chap.	GENESIS.	Vol.
i. 2,	...	i. 30	xviii. 23,	...	ii. 162	xlviii. 14,	...	ii. 326
i. 3,	...	i. 116	xx. 3,	...	i. 196	xlviii. 16,	i. 145;	ii. 172
i. 26,	...	i. 134, 163	xx. 3, 18,	...	i. 332	xlix. 5, 6,	...	i. 77
i. 27,	..	i. 102, 406	xx. 7,	...	i. 196	xlix. 18,	...	i. 379
i. 31,	...	ii. 570	xxi. 1,	...	ii. 18	l. 20.	...	i. 190
ii. 7,	...	i. 165, 423	xxi. 10,	....	ii. 307	l. 25,	...	i. 379
ii. 17,	...	i. 474	xxi. 12,	...	ii. 18			
ii. 18,	...	ii. 475	xxii 8,	...	i. 175		EXODUS.	
ii. 23,	i. 407;	ii. 648	xxii. 16. 18,	...	ii. 121	ii. 12,	...	ii. 660
iii. 9,	...	i. 537	xxiii. 4,	...	ii. 271	iii. 14,	...	i. 182
iii. 15,	...	i. 154, 412	xxiii. 19,	...	ii. 271	iii. 21,	...	i. 189
iii. 22,	...	ii. 499	xxiv. 7,	...	i. 150	iv. 11,	...	i. 123
iv. 4,	...	ii. 79	xxvii. 38, 39,	...	i. 589	iv. 21,	i. 201, 268;	ii. 252
iv. 7,	...	i. 288	xxviii. 12,	...	i. 150	iv. 25,	...	ii. 525
iv. 10,	...	i. 474	xxviii. 20,	...	ii. 476	vi. 7,	...	i. 374
vi. 5,	...	i. 244	xxx. 2,	...	i. 178	vii. 1,	...	i. 117
vi. 6,	...	i. 195	xxxi. 19,	...	i. 97	xi. 3,	...	i. 269
vi. 18,	...	ii. 494	xxxii. 10,	...	ii. 174	xii. 5,	...	ii. 553
viii. 21,	... i. 246;	ii. 74	xxxii. 29, 30,	...	i. 118	xii. 26,	...	ii. 550
ix. 9,	...	ii. 494	xxxiv. 25,	...	ii. 300	xii. 43,	...	ii. 575
xii. 17,	...	i. 332	xxxv. 22,	...	ii. 300	xiii. 12,	...	ii. 553
xiv. 18,	...	ii. 608	xxxvii. 18,	...	ii. 300	xiv. 31,	...	ii. 390
xv. 1,	i. 389;	ii. 273	xxxvii. 28,	...	ii. 300	xvi. 7,	...	i. 78
xv. 5,	...	ii. 121	xxxvii. 33,	...	i. 378	xvii. 6,	...	ii. 620
xv. 17,	...	ii. 505	xxxviii. 16,	..	ii. 300	xvii. 15,	...	i. 117
xvii. 2,	...	ii. 494	xxxviii. 18	...	i. 378	xviii. 16,	...	ii. 445
xvii. 7,	... i. 333, 374		xliii. 14,	...	i. 270	xix. 5,	..	ii. 537
xvii. 10,	...	ii. 530	xlv. 5,	...	i. 190	xix. 6,	..	i. 301
xvii. 13,	...	ii. 575	xlvii. 9,	...	i. 378	xx. 2. 3,	...	i. 326
xvii. 15,	...	ii. 535	xlvii. 29, 30,	...	i. 379	xx. 3,	...	i. 328

Chap.	MICAH.	Vol.	Chap.	MATTHEW.	Vol.	Chap.	MATTHEW.	Vol.
ii. 13,	...	i. 296	v. 19,	...	i. 362	xiii. 28,	...	i. 152
iii. 6,	...	ii. 406	v. 22,	...	i. 321, 346	xiii. 29,	...	ii. 460
v. 2,	...	i. 421	v. 28, 24,	...	i. 545	xiii. 31,	...	ii. 647
vii. 9,	...	i. 563	v. 25, 26,	...	i. 577	xiii. 33,	...	ii. 647
			v. 84,	...	i. 336	xiii. 47,	...	ii. 551
	HABAKKUK.		v. 37,	...	i. 336	xv. 3,	...	ii. 420
i. 12,	...	i. 374	v. 39, 40,	...	ii. 667	xv. 4,	...	i. 345
ii. 3,	...	i. 506	v. 44, 45,	...	i. 360	xv. 9,	...	ii. 424. 431
ii. 4,	...	ii. 54, 81	v. 45,	...	ii. 257	xv. 13	i. 259;	ii. 226, 246
ii. 18,	...	i. 61, 94	v. 46,	...	i. 360	xv. 14,	...	ii. 138, 409
ii. 20,	...	i. 61, 89	vi. 2,	...	ii. 8	xv. 24,	...	i. 897
iii. 2,	...	i. 563	vi. 6,	...	ii. 179	xvi. 6,	...	ii. 433
iii. 13,	...	i. 295	vi. 7,	...	ii. 178	xvi. 16,	...	ii. 357
			vi. 9,	...	ii. 184, 187	xvi. 17,		i. 239, 466, 499
	ZEPHANIAH.		vi. 10,	...	ii. 188, 190	xvi. 18,	...	ii. 355, 356
i. 4, 5,	...	i 335	vi. 11,	...	ii. 191	xvi.19,	i.544;	ii.298,355,439
iii. 11, 12,	...	ii. 65	vi. 12,	i. 569;	ii. 193, 299	xvi. 23,	...	ii. 386
			vi. 13,	...	ii. 197	xvi. 24,	...	ii. 8, 16
	HAGGAI.		vi. 21,	...	ii. 124, 260	xvii. 5,		ii. 198, 390, 393
ii. 11, 14,	...	ii. 78	vi. 23,	...	i. 491	xviii. 11,	...	i. 403
			vii. 7,	...	ii. 159	xviii. 15,	...	ii. 454
	ZECHARIAH.		vii. 11,	...	ii. 185	xviii. 17,	...	ii, 400, 454
i. 3,	i. 280;	ii. 256	vii. 12,	...	i. 358	xviii. 17, 18,	...	ii. 441
ii. 8,	...	i. 189	vii. 15,	...	ii. 409	xviii. 18,	i. 544,	547, 551
iii. 9, 10,	...	ii. 72	viii. 4,	...	i. 587			ii. 298, 459
vii 13,	...	i. 530	viii. 10,	...	i. 481	xviii. 20,	...	ii. 180, 289
ix. 9,	...	i. 297, 458	viii. 11,	i. 385;	ii. 537	xviii. 22,	...	ii. 300
ix. 11,	...	i. 442	viii. 12,	...	ii. 275	xix. 11,	...	ii. 486
xii. 4,	...	ii. 405	viii. 25,	...	i. 487	xix. 12,	...	i. 349
xiii. 9,	...	ii. 159	viii. 29,	...	i. 155	xix. 13,	...	ii. 533
			ix. 2,	i. 481,	546, 567	xix. 14,	...	ii. 547
	MALACHI.		ix. 12,	...	i. 403	xix. 15,	...	ii. 826
i. 2, 3,	...	ii. 209	ix. 13,	...	ii. 66, 77	xix. 16,	...	i. 357
i. 6,	...	i. 327, 492	ix. 15,	i. 523;	ii. 464	xix. 16, 17,	...	ii. 127
i. 11,	...	ii. 610, 618	ix. 29,	...	i. 507, 554	xix. 17,	...	i. 133
ii. 4,	...	ii. 307, 890	ix. 35,	...	i. 365	xix. 18, 19,	...	i. 357
ii. 7,	ii. 390,	392, 404	x. 5, 6,	...	i. 397	xix. 19,	...	i. 326
ii. 8, 9,	...	ii. 387	x. 18,	...	i. 538	xix. 21,	...	ii. 482
iii. 1,	...	i. 119, 149	x. 20,	...	ii. 629	xix. 25, 26,	...	i. 304
iii. 17,	...	ii. 133	x. 28,	...	ii. 269	xix. 28,	i. 451;	ii. 274
iv. 2,	...	i. 868	x. 29,	...	i. 177	xix. 29,	...	ii. 274
iv. 4,	...	ii. 393	x. 30,	...	i. 173	xx. 25, 26,	...	ii. 445
iv. 5,	...	i. 367	xi. 10,	...	i. 525	xx. 28,	...	i. 437
iv. 6,	...	ii. 287	xi. 11,	...	i. 867	xxi. 9,	...	i. 297
			xi. 18,	...	i. 392, 395	xxi. 22,	...	ii. 156
	MATTHEW.		xi. 21,	...	i. 524	xxi. 25,	...	ii. 626
i. 5,	...	i. 413	xi. 25,	...	i. 499	xxi. 31,	...	ii, 8
i. 16,	...	i. 415	xi. 27,	...	ii. 392	xxii. 12,	...	ii. 601
i. 21,	...	i. 434	xi. 28,	...	ii. 66	xxii. 13,	...	ii. 274
iii. 2,	...	i. 510, 525	xi. 28, 29,	...	ii. 128	xxii. 14,	...	ii. 246, 247
iii. 11,	...	ii. 517, 546	xii. 24,	...	i. 529	xxii. 23,	...	i. 375
iii. 17,	...	ii. 244	xii. 28,	...	i. 367	xxii. 30,	i. 164;	ii. 283
iv. 4,	...	ii. 193	xii. 31,	...	i. 528	xxii. 32,	i. 327;	ii. 530
iv. 10,	...	i. 106	xii. 32,	...	i. 528	xxii. 37,	...	i. 324
iv. 17,	...	i. 510	xii. 41,	...	ii. 254	xxiii. 3,	...	ii. 433
iv. 19,	...	ii. 551	xii. 48,	...	i. 155	xxiii. 4,	...	ii. 414
iv. 23,	...	i. 865	xiii. 4,	...	ii. 498	xxiii. 8, 10,	...	ii. 394
v. 4,	...	ii. 22	xiii. 7,	...	ii. 590	xxiii. 9,	...	ii. 186
v. 10,	...	ii. 20	xiii. 9,	...	ii. 236	xxiii. 23,	...	i. 357
v. 12,	...	ii. 120	xiii. 11,	...	ii. 252	xxiii. 37,	...	ii. 256
v. 13, 14,	...	ii. 818, 891	xiii. 16, 17,	...	i. 364	xxiv. 14,	...	i. 538
v. 17,	...	i. 311	xiii. 17,	...	i. 892	xxiv. 24,	...	i. 9

TABLE II.

OF HEBREW WORDS EXPLAINED.

TABLE III.

OF GREEK WORDS EXPLAINED.

INDEX

TO

THE AUTHORS QUOTED IN THE INSTITUTES.

INSTITUTIONS

OF

THE CHRISTIAN RELIGION.

A

PREFATORY ADDRESS

TO

HIS MOST CHRISTIAN MAJESTY,

THE MOST MIGHTY AND ILLUSTRIOUS MONARCH,

FRANCIS, KING OF THE FRENCH,

HIS SOVEREIGN ;[1]

JOHN CALVIN PRAYS PEACE AND SALVATION IN CHRIST.[2]

SIRE,—When I first engaged in this work, nothing was farther from my thoughts than to write what should afterwards be presented to your Majesty. My intention was only to furnish a kind of rudiments, by which those who feel some interest in religion might be trained to true godliness. And I toiled at the task chiefly for the sake of my countrymen the French, multitudes of whom I perceived to be hungering and thirsting after Christ, while very few seemed to have been duly imbued with even a slender knowledge of him. That this was the object which I had in view is apparent from the work itself, which is written in a simple and elementary form adapted for instruction.

But when I perceived that the fury of certain bad men had risen to such a height in your realm, that there was no place in it for sound doctrine, I thought it might be of service if I were in the same work both to give instruction to my countrymen, and also lay before your Majesty a Confession, from which you may learn what the doctrine is that so inflames the rage of those madmen who are this day, with fire and sword, troubling your kingdom. For I fear not to declare, that what I have here given may be regarded as a summary of the very doctrine which, they vociferate, ought to be punished

---

[1] In the last edition by Calvin, the words are, as here translated, simply, " Principi suo." In the edition published at Basle in 1536, the words are, " Principi ac Domino suo sibiobservando."
[2] Ed. 1536. " In Domino."

with confiscation, exile, imprisonment, and flames, as well as exterminated by land and sea.

I am aware, indeed, how, in order to render our cause as hateful to your Majesty as possible, they have filled your ears and mind with atrocious insinuations; but you will be pleased, of your clemency, to reflect, that neither in word nor deed could there be any innocence, were it sufficient merely to accuse. When any one, with the view of exciting prejudice, observes that this doctrine, of which I am endeavouring to give your Majesty an account, has been condemned by the suffrages of all the estates, and was long ago stabbed again and again by partial sentences of courts of law, he undoubtedly says nothing more than that it has sometimes been violently oppressed by the power and faction of adversaries, and sometimes fraudulently and insidiously overwhelmed by lies, cavils, and calumny. While a cause is unheard, it is violence to pass sanguinary sentences against it; it is fraud to charge it, contrary to its deserts, with sedition and mischief.

That no one may suppose we are unjust in thus complaining, you yourself, most illustrious Sovereign, can bear us witness with what lying calumnies it is daily traduced in your presence, as aiming at nothing else than to wrest the sceptres of kings out of their hands, to overturn all tribunals and seats of justice, to subvert all order and government, to disturb the peace and quiet of society, to abolish all laws, destroy the distinctions of rank and property, and, in short, turn all things upside down. And yet, that which you hear is but the smallest portion of what is said; for among the common people are disseminated certain horrible insinuations—insinuations which, if well founded, would justify the whole world in condemning the doctrine with its authors to a thousand fires and gibbets. Who can wonder that the popular hatred is inflamed against it, when credit is given to those most iniquitous accusations? See, why all ranks unite with one accord in condemning our persons and our doctrine!

Carried away by this feeling, those who sit in judgment merely give utterance to the prejudices which they have imbibed at home, and think they have duly performed their part if they do not order punishment to be inflicted on any one until convicted, either on his own confession, or on legal evidence. But of what crime convicted? "Of that condemned doctrine," is the answer. But with what justice condemned? The very essence of the defence was, not to abjure the doctrine itself, but to maintain its truth. On this subject, however, not a whisper is allowed!

Justice, then, most invincible Sovereign, entitles me to demand that you will undertake a thorough investigation of this cause, which has hitherto been tossed about in any kind of way, and handled in the most irregular manner, without any order of law, and with passionate heat rather than judicial gravity.

Let it not be imagined that I am here framing my own private defence, with the view of obtaining a safe return to my native land. Though I cherish towards it the feelings which become me as a man, still, as matters now are, I can be absent from it without regret. The cause which I plead is the common cause of all the godly, and therefore the very cause of Christ—a cause which, throughout your realm, now lies, as it were, in despair, torn and trampled upon in all kinds of ways, and that more through the tyranny of certain Pharisees than any sanction from yourself. But it matters not to inquire how the thing is done ; the fact that it is done cannot be denied. For so far have the wicked prevailed, that the truth of Christ, if not utterly routed and dispersed, lurks as if it were ignobly buried ; while the poor Church, either wasted by cruel slaughter or driven into exile, or intimidated and terror-struck, scarcely ventures to breathe. Still her enemies press on with their wonted rage and fury over the ruins which they have made, strenuously assaulting the wall, which is already giving way. Meanwhile, no man comes forth to offer his protection against such furies. Any who would be thought most favourable to the truth, merely talk of pardoning the error and imprudence of ignorant men. For so those modest personages[1] speak ; giving the name of *error and imprudence* to that which they know to be[2] the infallible truth of God, and of *ignorant men* to those whose intellect they see that Christ has not despised, seeing he has deigned to intrust them with the mysteries of his heavenly wisdom.[3] Thus all are ashamed of the Gospel.

Your duty, most serene Prince, is, not to shut either your ears or mind against a cause involving such mighty interests as these : how the glory of God is to be maintained on the earth inviolate, how the truth of God is to preserve its dignity, how the kingdom of Christ is to continue amongst us compact and secure. The cause is worthy of your ear, worthy of your investigation, worthy of your throne.

The characteristic of a true sovereign is, to acknowledge that, in the administration of his kingdom, he is a minister of God. He who does not make his reign subservient to the divine glory, acts the part not of a king, but a robber. He, moreover, deceives himself who anticipates long prosperity to any kingdom which is not ruled by the sceptre of God, that is, by his divine word. For the heavenly oracle is infallible which has declared, that " where there is no vision the people perish" (Prov. xxix. 18).

Let not a contemptuous idea of our insignificance dissuade you from the investigation of this cause. We, indeed, are perfectly conscious how poor and abject we are : in the presence of God we are miserable sinners, and in the sight of men most despised—we are (if you will) the mere dregs and off-scourings of the world, or worse, if

---

1 "Modesti homines," not in Ed. 1536.
2 "Quam norunt," not in Ed. 1536.
3 The words, " Quorum ingenium non adeo despicabile Christi fuisse vident," not in Ed. 1536.

worse can be named : so that before God there remains nothing of which we can glory save only his mercy, by which, without any merit of our own, we are admitted to the hope of eternal salvation :[1] and before men not even this much remains,[2] since we can glory only in our infirmity, a thing which, in the estimation of men, it is the greatest ignominy even tacitly[3] to confess. But our doctrine must stand sublime above all the glory of the world, and invincible by all its power, because it is not ours, but that of the living God and his Anointed, whom the Father has appointed King, that he may rule from sea to sea, and from the rivers even to the ends of the earth ; and so rule as to smite the whole earth and its strength of iron and brass, its splendour of gold and silver, with the mere rod of his mouth, and break them in pieces like a potter's vessel ; according to the magnificent predictions of the prophets respecting his kingdom (Dan. ii. 34 ; Isaiah xi. 4 ; Psalm ii. 9.)

Our adversaries, indeed, clamorously maintain that our appeal to the word of God is a mere pretext,—that we are, in fact, its worst corrupters. How far this is not only malicious calumny, but also shameless effrontery, you will be able to decide, of your own know-ledge, by reading our Confession. Here, however, it may be necessary to make some observations which may dispose, or at least assist, you to read and study it with attention.

When Paul declared that all prophecy ought to be according to the analogy of faith (Rom. xii. 6), he laid down the surest rule for deter-mining the meaning of Scripture. Let our doctrine be tested by this rule and our victory is secure. For what accords better and more aptly with faith than to acknowledge ourselves divested of all virtue that we may be clothed by God, devoid of all goodness that we may be filled by Him, the slaves of sin that he may give us freedom, blind that he may enlighten, lame that he may cure, and feeble that he may sustain us ; to strip ourselves of all ground of glorying that he alone may shine forth glorious, and we be glorified in him ? When these things, and others to the same effect, are said by us, they interpose, and querulously complain, that in this way we overturn some blind light of nature, fancied preparatives, free will, and works meritorious of eternal salvation, with their own supererogations also ;[4] because they cannot bear that the entire praise and glory of all goodness, virtue, justice, and wisdom, should remain with God. But we read not of any having been blamed for drinking too much of the fountain of living water ; on the contrary, those are severely reprimanded who " have hewed them out cisterns, broken cisterns, that can hold no water " (Jer. ii. 13). Again, what more agreeable to faith than to feel assured that God is a propitious Father when Christ is acknow-

---

1 The words stand thus in the Ed. 1536 : " Qua salvi nullo nostro merito facti sumus."
2 " Non ita multum," not in Ed. 1536.
3 " Cum nutu," not in Ed. 1536.
4 The only word in the Ed. 1536 after "free will," is " merita."

ledged as a brother and propitiator, than confidently to expect all prosperity and gladness from Him, whose ineffable love towards us was such that He " spared not his own Son, but delivered him up for us all" (Rom. viii. 32), than to rest in the sure hope of salvation and eternal life whenever Christ, in whom such treasures are hid, is conceived to have been given by the Father? Here they attack us, and loudly maintain that this sure confidence is not free from arrogance and presumption. But as nothing is to be presumed of ourselves, so all things are to be presumed of God; nor are we stript of vainglory for any other reason than that we may learn to glory in the Lord. Why go farther? Take but a cursory view, most valiant King, of all the parts of our cause, and count us of all wicked men the most iniquitous, if you do not discover plainly, that " therefore we both labour and suffer reproach because we trust in the living God" (1 Tim. iv. 10); because we believe it to be " life eternal" to know " the only true God, and Jesus Christ," whom he has sent (John xvii. 3). For this hope some of us are in bonds, some beaten with rods, some made a gazing-stock, some proscribed, some most cruelly tortured, some obliged to flee; we are all pressed with straits, loaded with dire execrations, lacerated by slanders, and treated with the greatest indignity.

Look now to our adversaries (I mean the priesthood, at whose beck and pleasure others ply their enmity against us), and consider with me for a little by what zeal they are actuated. The true religion which is delivered in the Scriptures, and which all ought to hold, they readily permit both themselves and others to be ignorant of, to neglect and despise; and they deem it of little moment what each man believes concerning God and Christ, or disbelieves, provided he submits to the judgment of the Church with what they call[1] implicit faith; nor are they greatly concerned though they should see the glory of God dishonoured by open blasphemies, provided not a finger is raised against the primacy of the Apostolic See and the authority of holy mother Church.[2] Why, then, do they war for the mass, purgatory, pilgrimage, and similar follies, with such fierceness and acerbity, that though they cannot prove one of them from the word of God, they deny godliness can be safe without faith in these things—faith drawn out, if I may so express it, to its utmost stretch? Why? just because their belly is their God, and their kitchen their religion; and they believe, that if these were away they would not only not be Christians, but not even men. For although some wallow in luxury, and others feed on slender crusts, still they all live by the same pot, which without that fuel might not only cool, but altogether freeze. He, accordingly, who is most anxious about his stomach, proves the fiercest champion of his faith. In short, the object on which all to a man are bent, is to

---

[1] Ut aiunt," not in Ed. 1536.
[2] No part of this sentence from "provided" is in the Ed. 1536.

keep their kingdom safe or their belly filled ; not one gives even the smallest sign of sincere zeal.

Nevertheless, they cease not to assail our doctrine, and to accuse and defame it in what terms they may, in order to render it either hated or suspected. They call it new, and of recent birth ; they carp at it as doubtful and uncertain ; they bid us tell by what miracles it has been confirmed ; they ask if it be fair to receive it against the consent of so many holy Fathers and the most ancient custom ; they urge us to confess either that it is schismatical in giving battle to the Church, or that the Church must have been without life during the many centuries in which nothing of the kind was heard. Lastly, they say there is little need of argument, for its quality may be known by its fruits, namely, the large number of sects, the many seditious disturbances, and the great licentiousness which it has produced. No doubt, it is a very easy matter for them, in presence of an ignorant and credulous multitude, to insult over an undefended cause ; but were an opportunity of mutual discussion afforded, that acrimony which they now pour out upon us in frothy torrents, with as much license as impunity,[1] would assuredly boil dry.

1. First, in calling it new, they are exceedingly injurious to God, whose sacred word deserved not to be charged with novelty. To them, indeed, I very little doubt it is new, as Christ is new, and the Gospel new ; but those who are acquainted with the old saying of Paul, that Christ Jesus " died for our sins, and rose again for our justification" (Rom. iv. 25), will not detect any novelty in us. That it long lay buried and unknown is the guilty consequence of man's impiety ; but now when, by the kindness of God, it is restored to us, it ought to resume its antiquity just as the returning citizen resumes his rights.

2. It is owing to the same ignorance that they hold it to be doubtful and uncertain ; for this is the very thing of which the Lord complains by his prophet, " The ox knoweth his owner, and the ass his master's crib ; but Israel doth not know, my people doth not consider" (Isaiah i. 3). But however they may sport with its uncertainty, had they to seal their own doctrine with their blood, and at the expense of life, it would be seen what value they put upon it. Very different is our confidence—a confidence which is not appalled by the terrors of death, and therefore not even by the judgment-seat of God.

3. In demanding miracles from us, they act dishonestly ; for we have not coined some new gospel, but retain the very one the truth of which is confirmed by all the miracles which Christ and the apostles ever wrought. But they have a peculiarity which we have not—they can confirm their faith by constant miracles down to the present day ! Nay rather, they allege miracles which might produce wavering in minds otherwise well disposed ; they are so frivolous and ridiculous,

---

[1] " Tam licenter quam impune," not in Ed. 1536.

so vain and false. But were they even exceedingly wonderful, they could have no effect against the truth of God, whose name ought to be hallowed always, and everywhere, whether by miracles, or by the natural course of events. The deception would perhaps be more specious if Scripture did not admonish us of the legitimate end and use of miracles. Mark tells us (Mark xvi. 20) that the signs which followed the preaching of the apostles were wrought in confirmation of it ; so Luke also relates that the Lord " gave testimony to the word of his grace, and granted signs and wonders to be done" by the hands of the apostles (Acts xiv. 3). Very much to the same effect are those words of the apostle, that salvation by a preached gospel was confirmed, " the Lord bearing witness with signs and wonders, and with divers miracles" (Heb. ii. 4). Those things which we are told are seals of the gospel, shall we pervert to the subversion of the gospel ? what was destined only to confirm the truth, shall we misapply to the confirmation of lies ? The proper course, therefore, is, in the first instance, to ascertain and examine the doctrine which is said by the Evangelist to precede ; then after it has been proved, but not till then, it may receive confirmation from miracles. But the mark of sound doctrine given by our Saviour himself is its tendency to promote the glory not of men, but of God (John vii. 18 ; viii. 50). Our Saviour having declared this to be test of doctrine, we are in error if we regard as miraculous, works which are used for any other purpose than to magnify the name of God.[1] And it becomes us to remember that Satan has his miracles, which, although they are tricks rather than true wonders, are still such as to delude the ignorant and unwary. Magicians and enchanters have always been famous for miracles, and miracles of an astonishing description have given support to idolatry : these, however, do not make us converts to the superstitions either of magicians or idolaters. In old times, too, the Donatists used their power of working miracles as a battering-ram, with which they shook the simplicity of the common people. We now give to our opponents the answer which Augustine then gave to the Donatists (in Joan. Tract. 23), " The Lord put us on our guard against those wonder-workers, when he foretold that false prophets would arise, who, by lying signs and divers wonders, would, if it were possible, deceive the very elect" (Matth. xxiv. 24). Paul, too, gave warning that the reign of antichrist would be " withall power, and signs, and lying wonders" (2 Thess. ii. 9).

But our opponents tell us that their miracles are wrought not by idols, not by sorcerers, not by false prophets, but by saints : as if we did not know it to be one of Satan's wiles to transform himself " into an angel of light" (2 Cor. xi. 14). The Egyptians, in whose neighbourhood Jeremiah was buried, anciently sacrificed and paid other divine honours to him (Hieron. in Præf. Jerem). Did they not

---

[1] No part of the passage, beginning above, " The deception," &c., is in Ed 1536.

make an idolatrous abuse of the holy prophet of God? and yet, in recompense for so venerating his tomb, they thought [1] that they were cured of the bite of serpents. What, then, shall we say but that it has been, and always will be, a most just punishment of God, to send on those who do not receive the truth in the love of it, "strong delusion, that they should believe a lie"? (2 Thess. ii. 11). We, then, have no lack of miracles, sure miracles, that cannot be gainsaid; but those to which our opponents lay claim are mere delusions of Satan, inasmuch as they draw off the people from the true worship of God to vanity.

4. It is a calumny to represent us as opposed to the Fathers (I mean the ancient writers of a purer age), as if the Fathers were supporters of their impiety. Were the contest to be decided by such authority (to speak in the most moderate terms), the better part of the victory would be ours.[2] While there is much that is admirable and wise in the writings of those Fathers, and while in some things it has fared with them as with ordinary men; these pious sons, forsooth, with the peculiar acuteness of intellect, and judgment, and soul, which belongs to them, adore only their slips and errors, while those things which are well said they either overlook, or disguise, or corrupt; so that it may be truly said their only care has been to gather dross among gold. Then, with dishonest clamour, they assail us as enemies and despisers of the Fathers. So far are we from despising them, that if this were the proper place, it would give us no trouble to support the greater part of the doctrines which we now hold by their suffrages. Still, in studying their writings, we have endeavoured to remember (1 Cor. iii. 21–23; see also Augustin. Ep. 28), that all things are ours, to serve, not lord it over us, but that we are Christ's only, and must obey him in all things without exception. He who does not draw this distinction will not have any fixed principles in religion; for those holy men were ignorant of many things, are often opposed to each other, and are sometimes at variance with themselves.

It is not without cause (remark our opponents) we are thus warned by Solomon, "Remove not the ancient landmarks which thy fathers have set" (Prov. xxii. 28). But the same rule applies not to the measuring of fields and the obedience of faith. The rule applicable to the latter is, "Forget also thine own people, and thy father's house" (Ps. xlv. 10). But if they are so fond of allegory, why do they not understand the apostles, rather than any other class of Fathers, to be meant by those whose landmarks it is unlawful to remove? This is the interpretation of Jerome, whose words they have quoted in their canons. But as regards those to whom they apply

---

[1] Instead of "thought they were cured," the Ed. 1536 says simply, "they were cured" (curarentur).

[2] "Ut modestissime etiam loquar," not in the Ed. 1536.

the passage, if they wish the landmarks to be fixed, why do they, whenever it suits their purpose, so freely overleap them?

Among the Fathers there were two, the one of whom said,[1] " Our God neither eats nor drinks, and therefore has no need of chalices and salvers;" and the other,[2] " Sacred rites do not require gold, and things which are not bought with gold, please not by gold." They step beyond the boundary, therefore, when in sacred matters they are so much delighted with gold, silver, ivory, marble, gems, and silks, that unless everything is overlaid with costly show, or rather insane luxury[3], they think God is not duly worshipped.

It was a Father who said,[4] " He ate flesh freely on the day on which others abstained from it, because he was a Christian." They overleap the boundaries, therefore, when they doom to perdition every soul that, during Lent, shall have tasted flesh.

There were two Fathers, the one of whom said,[5] " A monk not labouring with his own hands is no better than a violent man and a robber;" and the other,[6] " Monks, however assiduous they may be in study, meditation, and prayer, must not live by others." This boundary, too, they transgressed, when they placed lazy gormandising monks in dens and stews, to gorge themselves on other men's substance.

It was a Father who said,[7] " It is a horrid abomination to see in Christian temples a painted image either of Christ or of any saint." Nor was this pronounced by the voice of a single individual; but an Ecclesiastical Council also decreed,[8] " Let nought that is worshipped be depicted on walls."[9] Very far are they from keeping within these boundaries when they leave not a corner without images.

Another Father counselled,[10] " That after performing the office of humanity to the dead in their burial, we should leave them at rest." These limits they burst through when they keep up a perpetual anxiety about the dead.

It is a Father who testifies,[11] " That the substance of bread and wine in the Eucharist does not cease but remains, just as the nature and substance of man remains united to the Godhead in the Lord Jesus Christ." This boundary they pass in pretending that, as soon as the words of our Lord are pronounced, the substance of bread and wine ceases, and is transubstantiated into body and blood.

---

[1] i. Acatius in lib. xi. cap 16, F. Triport. Hist.
[2] ii. Ambr. lib. ii. De Officiis, cap. 28.
[3] Instead of the words here translated—viz. " exquisito splendore vel potius insanc luxu," the Ed. 1536 has only the word "luxu."
[4] iii. Spiridion. Trip. Hist. lib. i. cap. 10.
[5] iv. Trip. Hist. lib. viii. cap 1.
[6] August. De Opere Monach cap 7.
[7] vi. Epiph. Epist. ab Hieron. versa.   [8] vii. Conc. Elibert. can. 36.
[9] No part of this sentence is in Ed 1536.
[10] viii. Ambr de Abraha. lib. i. c. 7.
[11] ix. Gelasius Papa in Conc. Rom.

They were Fathers, who, as they exhibited only one Eucharist to
the whole Church,[1] and kept back from it the profane and flagitious;
so they, in the severest terms, censured all those[2] who, being present,
did not communicate How far have they removed these landmarks,
in filling not churches only, but also private houses, with their masses,
admitting all and sundry to be present, each the more willingly the
more largely he pays, however wicked and impure he may be,—not
inviting any one to faith in Christ and faithful communion in the
sacraments, but rather vending their own work for the grace and
merits of Christ![3]

There were two Fathers, the one of whom decided that those were
to be excluded altogether from partaking of Christ's sacred supper,[4]
who, contented with communion in one kind, abstained from the
other; while the other Father strongly contends[5] that the blood of
the Lord ought not to be denied to the Christian people, who, in confessing him, are enjoined to shed their own blood. These landmarks,
also, they removed, when, by an unalterable law, they ordered the
very thing which the former Father punished with excommunication,
and the latter condemned for a valid reason.

It was a Father who pronounced it rashness,[6] in an obscure question,
to decide in either way without clear and evident authority from
Scripture. They forgot this landmark when they enacted so many
constitutions, so many canons, and so many dogmatical decisions,
without sanction from the word of God.

It was a Father who reproved Montanus, among other heresies,[7]
for being the first who imposed laws of fasting. They have gone far
beyond this landmark also in enjoining fasting under the strictest
laws.

It was a Father who denied[8] that the ministers of the Church
should be interdicted from marrying, and pronounced married life to
be a state of chastity; and there were other Fathers who assented to
his decision. These boundaries they overstepped in rigidly binding
their priests to celibacy.

It was a Father who thought[9] that Christ only should be listened
to, from its being said, "hear him;" and that regard is due not to
what others before us have said or done, but only to what Christ, the

1 x. Chrys. in 1. cap. Ephes.
2 xi. Calixt. Papa, De Consecrat. dist. 2.
3 Instead of the whole passage, beginning at bottom of p. 11, "It is a Father who
testifies," &c., the Ed. 1536 has the following sentence: "Ex patribus erat qui negavit
in sacramento cœnæ esse verum corpus sed mysterium duntaxat corporis; sic enim ad
verbum loquitur." On the margin, reference is made to the author of an unfinished
Tract on Matthew, forming the 11th Homil. among the works of Chrysostom.
4 xii. Gelas. can. Comperimus, De Consec. dist. 2.
5 xiii. Cypr. Epist. 2, lib. i. De Lapsis.
6 xiv. August. lib. ii. De Peccat. Mer. cap. ult.
7 xv. Apollon. De quo Eccles. Hist. lib. v. cap. 12.
8 xvi. Paphnut. Tripart. Hist. lib. ii. cap 14.
9 xvii. Cypr. Epist. 2, lib. ii.

head of all, has commanded. This landmark they neither observe themselves nor allow to be observed by others, while they subject themselves and others to any master whatever, rather than Christ.

There is a Father who contends[1] that the Church ought not to prefer herself to Christ, who always judges truly, whereas ecclesiastical judges, who are but men, are generally deceived. Having burst through this barrier also, they hesitate not to suspend the whole authority of Scripture on the judgment of the Church.[2]

All the Fathers with one heart execrated, and with one mouth protested[3] against, contaminating the word of God with the subtleties of sophists, and involving it in the brawls of dialecticians. Do they keep within these limits when the sole occupation of their lives is to entwine and entangle the simplicity of Scripture with endless disputes, and worse than sophistical jargon? So much so, that were the Fathers to rise from their graves, and listen to the brawling art which bears the name of speculative theology, there is nothing they would suppose it less to be than a discussion of a religious nature.

But my discourse would far exceed its just limits were I to show, in detail, how petulantly those men shake off the yoke of the Fathers, while they wish to be thought their most obedient sons. Months, nay, years would fail me; and yet so deplorable and desperate is their effrontery, that they presume to chastise us for overstepping the ancient landmarks!

5. Then, again, it is to no purpose they call us to the bar of custom. To make everything yield to custom would be to do the greatest injustice. Were the judgments of mankind correct, custom would be regulated by the good. But it is often far otherwise in point of fact; for, whatever the many are seen to do, forthwith obtains the force of custom. But human affairs have scarcely ever been so happily constituted as that the better course pleased the greater number. Hence the private vices of the multitude have generally resulted in public error, or rather that common consent in vice which these worthy men would have to be law. Any one with eyes may perceive that it is not one flood of evils which has deluged us; that many fatal plagues have invaded the globe; that all things rush headlong; so that either the affairs of men must be altogether despaired of, or we must not only resist, but boldly attack prevailing evils. The cure is prevented by no other cause than the length of time during which we have been accustomed to the disease. But be it so that public error must have a place in human society, still, in the kingdom of God, we must look and listen only to his eternal truth, against which no series of years, no custom, no conspiracy, can plead prescription. Thus Isaiah for-

---

[1] xviii Aug. cap. 2, Cont. Cresconium Grammat.
[2] No part of this passage is in Ed. 1536.
[3] xix. Calv. De Scholast. Doctor. Judicium. Vid. Book II. cap. ii. sec. 6; Book III. cap. iv. sec. 1, 2, 7, 13, 14, 26–29; Book III. cap. xi. sec. 14, 15; Book IV. cap xviii. sec. 1; and cap. xix. sec. 10, 11, 22, 23.

merly taught the people of God, "Say ye not, A confederacy, to all to whom this people shall say, A confederacy;" *i.e.* do not unite with the people in an impious consent; "neither fear ye their fear, nor be afraid. Sanctify the Lord of hosts himself; and let him be your fear, and let him be your dread" (Is. viii. 12). Now, therefore, let them, if they will, object to us both past ages and present examples; if we sanctify the Lord of hosts, we shall not be greatly afraid. Though many ages should have consented to like ungodliness, He is strong who taketh vengeance to the third and fourth generation; or the whole world should league together in the same iniquity. He taught experimentally what the end is of those who sin with the multitude, when He destroyed the whole human race with a flood, saving Noah with his little family, who, by putting his faith in Him alone, "condemned the world" (Heb. xi. 7). In short, depraved custom is just a kind of general pestilence in which men perish not the less that they fall in a crowd. It were well, moreover, to ponder the observation of Cyprian,[1] that those who sin in ignorance, though they cannot be entirely exculpated, seem, however, to be, in some sense, excusable; whereas those who obstinately reject the truth, when presented to them by the kindness of God, have no defence to offer.[2]

6. Their dilemma does not push us so violently as to oblige us to confess, either that the Church was a considerable time without life, or that we have now a quarrel with the Church. The Church of Christ assuredly has lived, and will live, as long as Christ shall reign at the right hand of the Father. By his hand it is sustained, by his protection defended, by his mighty power preserved in safety. For what he once undertook he will undoubtedly perform, he will be with his people always, "even to the end of the world" (Matth. xxviii. 20). With the Church we wage no war, since, with one consent, in common with the whole body of the faithful, we worship and adore one God, and Christ Jesus the Lord, as all the pious have always adored him. But they themselves err not a little from the truth in not recognising any church but that which they behold with the bodily eye, and in endeavouring to circumscribe it by limits, within which it cannot be confined.

The hinges on which the controversy turns are these: first, in their contending that the form of the Church is always visible and apparent; and, secondly, in their placing this form in the see of the Church of Rome and its hierarchy. We, on the contrary, maintain, both that the Church may exist without any apparent form, and, moreover, that the form is not ascertained by that external splendour which they foolishly admire, but by a very different mark, namely, by the pure preaching of the word of God, and the due administration of

---

1 Epist. 3, lib. ii.; et in Epist ad Julian. De Hæret. Baptiz.
2 No part of this sentence is in ed. 1536.

the sacraments. They make an outcry whenever the Church cannot be pointed to with the finger. But how oft was it the fate of the Church among the Jews to be so defaced that no comeliness appeared? What do we suppose to have been the splendid form when Elijah complained that he was left alone? (1 Kings xix. 14). How long after the advent of Christ did it lie hid without form? How often since has it been so oppressed by wars, seditions, and heresies, that it was nowhere seen in splendour? Had they lived at that time, would they have believed there was any Church? But Elijah learned that there remained seven thousand men who had not bowed the knee to Baal; nor ought we to doubt that Christ has always reigned on earth ever since he ascended to heaven. Had the faithful at that time required some discernible form, must they not have forthwith given way to despondency? And, indeed, Hilary accounted it a very great fault in his day, that men were so possessed with a foolish admiration of Episcopal dignity as not to perceive the deadly hydra lurking under that mask. His words are (Cont. Auxentium), " One advice I give: Beware of Antichrist; for, unhappily, a love of walls has seized you; unhappily, the Church of God which you venerate exists in houses and buildings; unhappily, under these you find the name of peace. Is it doubtful that in these Antichrist will have his seat? Safer to me are mountains, and woods, and lakes, and dungeons, and whirlpools; since in these prophets, dwelling or immersed, did prophesy."

And what is it at the present day that the world venerates in its horned bishops, unless that it imagines those who are seen presiding over celebrated cities to be holy prelates of religion? Away, then, with this absurd mode of judging![1] Let us rather reverently admit, that as God alone knows who are his, so he may sometimes withdraw the external manifestation of his Church from the view of men. This, I allow, is a fearful punishment which God sends on the earth; but if the wickedness of men so deserves, why do we strive to oppose the just vengeance of God?[2] It was thus that God, in past ages, punished the ingratitude of men; for after they had refused to obey his truth, and had extinguished his light, he allowed them, when blinded by sense, both to be deluded by lying vanities and plunged in thick darkness, so that no face of a true Church appeared. Meanwhile, however, though his own people were dispersed and concealed amidst errors and darkness, he saved them from destruction. No wonder; for he knew how to preserve them even in the confusion of Babylon and the flame of the fiery furnace.

But as to the wish that the form of the Church should be ascertained by some kind of vain pomp, how perilous it is I will briefly indicate, rather than explain, that I may not exceed all bounds.

---

[1] No part of the passage beginning above is in the Ed. 1536.
[2] In the last Ed., "justæ Dei ultionis;" in Ed. 1536, "divinæ zustitiæ."

What they say is, that the Pontiff,[1] who holds the apostolic see, and
the priests who are anointed and consecrated by him,[2] provided they
have the insignia of fillets and mitres, represent the Church, and
ought to be considered as in the place of the Church, and therefore
cannot err. Why so? because they are pastors of the Church, and
consecrated to the Lord. And were not Aaron and other prefects of
Israel pastors? But Aaron and his sons, though already set apart
to the priesthood, erred notwithstanding when they made the calf
(Exod. xxxii. 4). Why, according to this view, should not the four
hundred prophets who lied to Ahab represent the Church? (1 Kings
xxii. 11, &c.) The Church, however, stood on the side of Micaiah.
He was alone, indeed, and despised, but from his mouth the truth
proceeded. Did not the prophets also exhibit both the name and
face of the Church, when, with one accord, they rose up against
Jeremiah, and with menaces boasted of it as a thing impossible that
the law should perish from the priest, or counsel from the wise, or
the word from the prophet? (Jer. xviii. 18). In opposition to the
whole body of the prophets, Jeremiah is sent alone to declare from
the Lord (Jer. iv. 9), that a time would come when the law would
perish from the priest, counsel from the wise, and the word from the
prophet. Was not like splendour displayed in that council when the
chief priests, scribes, and Pharisees assembled to consult how they
might put Jesus to death? Let them go, then, and cling to the
external mask, while they make Christ and all the prophets of God
schismatics, and, on the other hand, make Satan's ministers the
organs of the Holy Spirit!

But if they are sincere, let them answer me in good faith,—in what
place, and among whom, do they think the Church resided, after the
Council of Basle degraded and deposed Eugenius from the popedom,
and substituted Amadeus in his place? Do their utmost, they cannot
deny that that Council was legitimate as far as regards external forms,
and was summoned not only by one Pontiff, but by two. Eugenius,
with the whole herd of cardinals and bishops who had joined him in
plotting the dissolution of the Council, was there condemned of contumacy, rebellion, and schism. Afterwards, however, aided by the
favour of princes, he got back his popedom safe. The election of
Amadeus, duly made by the authority of a general holy synod, went
to smoke; only he himself was appeased with a cardinal's cap, like a
piece of offal thrown to a barking dog. Out of the lap of these rebellious and contumacious schismatics proceeded all future popes,
cardinals, bishops, abbots, and presbyters. Here they are caught,
and cannot escape. For, on which party will they bestow the name of
Church? Will they deny it to have been a general Council, though
it lacked nothing as regards external majesty, having been solemnly

---

1 "Papa Romanus," in the Ed. 1536.
2 Instead of the words, "qui ab eo instites inuncti et consecrati, infulis modo et
lituis insigniti sunt," the Ed. 1536 has only "episcopi alii."

called by two bulls, consecrated by the legate of the Roman See as its president, constituted regularly in all respects, and continuing in possession of all its honours to the last? Will they admit that Eugenius, and his whole train, through whom they have all been consecrated, were schismatical? Let them, then, either define the form of the Church differently, or, however numerous they are, we will hold them all to be schismatics in having knowingly and willingly received ordination from heretics. But had it never been discovered before that the Church is not tied to external pomp, we are furnished with a lengthened proof in their own conduct, in proudly vending themselves to the world under the specious title of Church, notwithstanding that they are the deadly pests of the Church. I speak not of their manners and of those tragical atrocities with which their whole life teems, since it is said that they are Pharisees who should be heard, not imitated. By devoting some portion of your leisure to our writings, you will see, not obscurely, that their doctrine—the very doctrine to which they say it is owing that they are the Church—is a deadly murderer of souls, the firebrand, ruin, and destruction of the Church.

7. Lastly, they are far from candid when they invidiously number up the disturbances, tumults, and disputes, which the preaching of our doctrine has brought in its train, and the fruits which, in many instances, it now produces; for the doctrine itself is undeservedly charged with evils which ought to be ascribed to the malice of Satan. It is one of the characteristics of the divine word, that whenever it appears, Satan ceases to slumber and sleep. This is the surest and most unerring test for distinguishing it from false doctrines which readily betray themselves, while they are received by all with willing ears, and welcomed by an applauding world. Accordingly, for several ages, during which all things were immersed in profound darkness, almost all mankind[1] were mere jest and sport to the god of this world, who, like any Sardanapalus, idled and luxuriated undisturbed. For what else could he do but laugh and sport while in tranquil and undisputed possession of his kingdom? But when light beaming from above somewhat dissipated the darkness—when the strong man arose and aimed a blow at his kingdom—then, indeed, he began to shake off his wonted torpor, and rush to arms. And first he stirred up the hands of men, that by them he might violently suppress the dawning truth; but when this availed him not, he turned to snares, exciting dissensions and disputes about doctrine by means of his Catabaptists, and other portentous miscreants, that he might thus obscure, and, at length, extinguish the truth. And now he persists in assailing it with both engines, endeavouring to pluck up the true seed by the violent hand of man, and striving, as much as in him lies, to choke it with his tares, that it may not grow and bear fruit. But it will be in vain, if we listen to the admonition of the Lord, who long ago disclosed his

---

[1] For "cuncti fere mortales" the Ed. 1536 has only "homines."

wiles, that we might not be taken unawares, and armed us with full protection against all his machinations. But how malignant to throw upon the word of God itself the blame either of the seditions which wicked men and rebels, or of the sects which impostors stir up against it! The example, however, is not new. Elijah was interrogated whether it were not he that troubled Israel. Christ was seditious, according to the Jews; and the apostles were charged with the crime of popular commotion. What else do those who, in the present day, impute to us all the disturbances, tumults, and contentions which break out against us? Elijah, however, has taught us our answer (1 Kings xviii. 17, 18). It is not we who disseminate errors or stir up tumults, but they who resist the mighty power of God.

But while this single answer is sufficient to rebut the rash charges of these men, it is necessary, on the other hand, to consult for the weakness of those who take the alarm at such scandals, and not unfrequently waver in perplexity. But that they may not fall away in this perplexity, and forfeit their good degree, let them know that the apostles in their day experienced the very things which now befall us. There were then unlearned and unstable men who, as Peter tells us (2 Pet. iii. 16), wrested the inspired writings of Paul to their own destruction. There were despisers of God, who, when they heard that sin abounded in order that grace might more abound, immediately inferred, "We will continue in sin that grace may abound" (Rom. vi. 1); when they heard that believers were not under the law, but under grace, forthwith sung out, "We will sin because we are not under the law, but under grace" (Rom. vi. 15). There were some who charged the apostle with being the minister of sin. Many false prophets entered in privily to pull down the churches which he had reared. Some preached the gospel through envy and strife, not sincerely (Phil. i. 15)—maliciously even—thinking to add affliction to his bonds. Elsewhere the gospel made little progress. All sought their own, not the things which were Jesus Christ's. Others went back like the dog to his vomit, or the sow that was washed to her wallowing in the mire. Great numbers perverted their spiritual freedom to carnal licentiousness. False brethren crept in to the imminent danger of the faithful. Among the brethren themselves various quarrels arose. What, then, were the apostles to do? Were they either to dissemble for the time, or rather lay aside and abandon that gospel which they saw to be the seed-bed of so many strifes, the source of so many perils, the occasion of so many scandals? In straits of this kind, they remembered that "Christ was a stone of stumbling, and a rock of offence," "set up for the fall and rising again of many," and "for a sign to be spoken against" (Luke ii. 34); and, armed with this assurance, they proceeded boldly through all perils from tumults and scandals. It becomes us to be supported by the same consideration, since Paul declares that it is a never-failing characteristic of the gospel to be a "savour of death unto death in them that perish" (2 Cor. ii. 16), although rather destined to us for the purpose of being a savour of life unto life, and the power of God for the salvation of believers. This we should certainly experience it to be, did we not by our ingratitude corrupt this unspeakable gift of God, and turn to our destruction what ought to be our only saving defence.[1]

But to return, Sire.[2] Be not moved by the absurd insinuations with which our adversaries are striving to frighten you into the belief that nothing else is wished and aimed at by this new gospel (for so they term it), than opportunity for sedition and impunity for all kinds of vice. Our God[3] is not the author of division, but of peace ; and the Son of God, who came to destroy the works of the devil, is not the minister of sin. We, too, are undeservedly charged with desires of a kind for which we have never given even the smallest suspicion. We, forsooth, meditate the subversion of kingdoms ; we, whose voice was never heard in faction, and whose life, while passed under you, is known to have been always quiet and simple ; even now, when exiled from our home, we nevertheless cease not to pray for all prosperity to your person and your kingdom. We, forsooth, are aiming after an unchecked indulgence in vice, in whose manners, though there is much to be blamed, there is nothing which deserves such an imputation ; nor (thank God) have we profited so little in the gospel that our life may not be to these slanderers an example of chastity, kindness, pity, temperance, patience, moderation, or any other virtue. It is plain, indeed, that we fear God sincerely, and worship him in truth, since, whether by life or by death, we desire his name to be hallowed ; and hatred herself has been forced to bear testimony to the innocence and civil integrity of some of our people on whom death was inflicted for the very thing which deserved the highest praise. But if any, under pretext of the gospel, excite tumults (none such have as yet been detected in your realm), if any use the liberty of the grace of God as a cloak for licentiousness (I know of numbers who do), there are laws and legal punishments by which they may be punished up to the measure of their deserts— only, in the mean time, let not the gospel of God be evil spoken of because of the iniquities of evil men.

Sire,[4] That you may not lend too credulous an ear to the accusations of our enemies, their virulent injustice has been set before you at sufficient length ; I fear even more than sufficient, since this preface has grown almost to the bulk of a full apology. My object, however, was not to frame a defence, but only with a view to the hearing

---

1 Instead of the concluding part of the sentence beginning "though rather," &c., and stopping at the reference, the Ed. 1536 simply continues the quotation "odor vitæ in vitam iis qui salvi sunt."
2 Instead of " Rex." simply, the Ed. 1536 has "magnanime Rex.'
3 Instead of " Deus noster," the Ed. 1536 has only " Deus."
4 In Ed. 1536, " Rex magnificentissime "

of our cause, to mollify your mind, now indeed turned away and estranged from us—I add, even inflamed against us—but whose good will, we are confident, we should regain, would you but once, with calmness and composure, read this our Confession, which we desire your Majesty to accept instead of a defence. But if the whispers of the malevolent so possess your ear, that the accused are to have no opportunity of pleading their cause; if those vindictive furies, with your connivance, are always to rage with bonds, scourgings, tortures, maimings, and burnings, we, indeed, like sheep doomed to slaughter, shall be reduced to every extremity; yet so that, in our patience, we will possess our souls, and wait for the strong hand of the Lord, which, doubtless, will appear in its own time, and show itself armed, both to rescue the poor from affliction, and also take vengeance on the despisers, who are now exulting so securely.[1]

Most illustrious King, may the Lord, the King of kings, establish your throne in righteousness, and your sceptre in equity.

BASLE, 1st *August* 1536.

1 The words, " qui tanta securitate nunc exsultant," not in Ed. 1536.

THE EPISTLE TO THE READER.

[PREFIXED TO THE SECOND EDITION, PUBLISHED AT STRASBURG IN 1539.]

IN the First Edition of this work, having no expectation of the success which God has, in his goodness, been pleased to give it, I had, for the greater part, performed my office perfunctorily, as is usual in trivial undertakings. But when I perceived that almost all the godly had received it with a favour which I had never dared to wish, far less to hope for, being sincerely conscious that I had received much more than I deserved, I thought I should be very ungrateful if I did not endeavour, at least according to my humble ability, to respond to the great kindness which had been expressed towards me, and which spontaneously urged me to diligence. I therefore ask no other favour from the studious for my new work than that which they have already bestowed upon me beyond my merits. I feel so much obliged, that I shall be satisfied if I am thought not to have made a bad return for the gratitude I owe. This return I would have made much earlier, had not the Lord, for almost two whole years, exercised me in an extraordinary manner. But it is soon enough if well enough. I shall think it has appeared in good season when I perceive that it produces some fruit to the Church of God. I may add, that my object in this work was to prepare and train students of theology for the study of the sacred volume, so that they might both have an easy introduction to it, and be able to proceed in it, with unfaltering step, seeing I have endeavoured to give such a summary of religion in all its parts, and have digested it into such an order as may make it not difficult for any one, who is rightly acquainted with it, to ascertain both what he ought principally to look for in Scripture, and also to what head he ought to refer whatever is contained in it. Having thus, as it were, paved the way, I shall not feel it necessary, in any Commentaries on Scripture which I may afterwards publish, to enter into long discussions of doctrine, or dilate on common places, and will, therefore, always compress them. In this way the pious reader will be saved much trouble and weariness, provided he comes furnished with a knowledge of the present work as an essential prerequisite. As my Commentary on the Epistle to the Romans will give a specimen of this plan, I would much rather let it speak for itself than declare it in words. Farewell, dear reader, and if you derive any fruit from my labours, give me the benefit of your prayers to the Lord.

STRASBURG, 1st *August* 1539

SUBJECT OF THE PRESENT WORK.

[PREFIXED TO THE FRENCH EDITION, PUBLISHED AT GENEVA IN 1545.]

IN order that my readers may be the better able to profit by the present work, I am desirous briefly to point out the advantage which they may derive from it. For by so doing I will show them the end at which they ought to aim, and to which they ought to give their attention in reading it.

Although the Holy Scriptures contain a perfect doctrine, to which nothing can be added—our Lord having been pleased therein to unfold the infinite treasures of his wisdom—still every person, not intimately acquainted with them, stands in need of some guidance and direction, as to what he ought to look for in them, that he may not wander up and down, but pursue a certain path, and so attain the end to which the Holy Spirit invites him.

Hence it is the duty of those who have received from God more light than others to assist the simple in this matter, and, as it were, lend them their hand to guide and assist them in finding the sum of what God has been pleased to teach us in his word. Now, this cannot be better done in writing than by treating in succession of the principal matters which are comprised in Christian philosophy. For he who understands these will be prepared to make more progress in the school of God in one day than any other person in three months, inasmuch as he, in a great measure, knows to what he should refer each sentence, and has a rule by which to test whatever is presented to him.

Seeing, then, how necessary it was in this manner to aid those who desire to be instructed in the doctrine of salvation, I have endeavoured, according to the ability which God has given me, to employ myself in so doing, and with this view have composed the present book. And first I wrote it in Latin, that it might be serviceable to all studious persons, of what nation soever they might be; afterwards, desiring to communicate any fruit which might be in it to my French countrymen, I translated it into our own tongue. I dare not bear too strong a testimony in its favour, and declare how profitable the reading of it will be, lest I should seem to prize my own work too highly. However, I may promise this much, that it will be a kind of key opening up to all the children of God a right and ready access to the understanding of the sacred volume. Wherefore, should our Lord give me henceforth means and opportunity of composing some Commentaries, I will use the greatest possible brevity, as there will be no occasion to make long digressions, seeing that I have in a manner deduced at length all the articles which pertain to Christianity.

And since we are bound to acknowledge that all truth and sound doctrine proceed from God, I will venture boldly to declare what I think of this work, acknowledging it to be God's work rather than mine. To him, indeed, the praise due to it must be ascribed. My opinion of the work then is this : I exhort all who reverence the word of the Lord, to read it, and diligently imprint it on their memory, if they would, in the first place, have a summary of Christian doctrine, and, 'n the second place, an introduction to the profitable reading both of the Old and New Testament. When they shall have done so, they will know by experience that I have not wished to impose upon them with words. Should any one be unable to comprehend all that is contained in it, he must not, however, give it up in despair ; but continue always to read on, hoping that one passage will give him a more familiar exposition of another. Above all things, I would recommend that recourse be had to Scripture in considering the proofs which I adduce from it.

EPISTLE TO THE READER.

[PREFIXED TO THE LAST EDITION, REVISED BY THE AUTHOR.]

In the first edition of this work, having not the least expectation of the success which God, in his boundless goodness, has been pleased to give it, I had, for the greater part, performed my task in a perfunctory manner (as is usual in trivial undertakings) ; but when I understood that it had been received, by almost all the pious, with a favour which I had never dared to ask, far less to hope for, the more I was sincerely conscious that the reception was beyond my deserts, the greater I thought my gratitude would be, if, to the very kind wishes which had been expressed towards me, and which seemed of their own accord to invite me to diligence, I did not endeavour to respond, at least according to my humble ability. This I attempted not only in the second edition, but in every subsequent one the work has received some improvement. But though I do not regret the labour previously expended, I never felt satisfied until the work was arranged in the order in which it now appears. Now I trust it will approve itself to the judgment of all my readers. As a clear proof of the diligence with which I have laboured to perform this service to the Church of God, I may be permitted to mention, that last winter, when I thought I was dying of quartan ague, the more the disorder increased, the less I spared myself, in order that I might leave this book behind me, and thus make some return to the pious for their kind urgency. I could have wished to give it sooner, but it is soon enough if good enough. I shall think it has appeared in good time when I see it more productive of benefit than formerly to the Church of God. This is my only wish.

And truly it would fare ill with me if, not contented with the approbation of God alone, I were unable to despise the foolish and perverse censures of ignorant, as well as the malicious and unjust censures of ungodly men. For although, by the blessing of God, my most ardent desire has been to advance his kingdom, and promote the public good,—although I feel perfectly conscious, and take

God and his angels to witness, that ever since I began to discharge
the office of teacher in the Church, my only object has been to do
good to the Church, by maintaining the pure doctrine of godliness ;
yet I believe there never was a man more assailed, stung, and torn
by calumny—[as well by the declared enemies of the truth of God,
as by many worthless persons who have crept into his Church—as
well by monks who have brought forth their frocks from their cloisters
to spread infection wherever they come, as by other miscreants not
better than they[1]]. After this letter to the reader was in the press,
I had undoubted information that, at Augsburg, where the Imperial
Diet was held, a rumour of my defection to the papacy was circulated,
and entertained in the courts of the princes more readily than might
have been expected.[2] This, forsooth, is the return made me by those
who certainly are not unaware of numerous proofs of my constancy—
proofs which, while they rebut the foul charge, ought to have defended
me against it, with all humane and impartial judges. But the devil,
with all his crew, is mistaken if he imagines that, by assailing me
with vile falsehoods, he can either cool my zeal or diminish my exertions. I trust that God, in his infinite goodness, will enable me
to persevere with unruffled patience in the course of his holy vocation.
Of this I give the pious reader a new proof in the present edition.

I may further observe, that my object in this work has been, so to
prepare and train candidates for the sacred office, for the study of the
sacred volume, that they may both have an easy introduction to it,
and be able to prosecute it with unfaltering step ; for, if I mistake
not, I have given a summary of religion in all its parts, and digested
it in an order which will make it easy for any one, who rightly comprehends it, to ascertain both what he ought chiefly to look for in
Scripture, and also to what head he ought to refer whatever is contained in it. Having thus, as it were, paved the way, as it will be
unnecessary, in any Commentaries on Scripture which I may afterwards publish, to enter into long discussions of doctrinal points, and
enlarge on commonplaces, I will compress them into narrow compass.
In this way much trouble and fatigue will be spared to the pious
reader, provided he comes prepared with a knowledge of the present
work as an indispensable prerequisite. The system here followed
being set forth as in a mirror in all my Commentaries, I think it
better to let it speak for itself than to give any verbal explanation
of it.

---

1 The passage in brackets occurs only in the French original. The words are as
follows : " Tant des ennemis manifestes de la vérité de Dieu, que de beaucoup de canail-
les qui se sont fourrez en son Eglise : tant des Moines qui ont apporté leurs frocs hors
de leurs cloistres pour infecter le lieu où ils venoyent, que d'autres vilains qui ne valent
pas mieux qu'eux."
2 The words in the French are, " Avec trop grande facilité ; ce qui monstroit que
beaucoup de meschans hypocrites, faisans profession de l'Evangile, eussent bien voulu
qu'ainsi fust." With too great facility ; showing that many wicked hypocrites, making
profession of the gospel, would have been very glad it had been so.

Farewell, kind reader : if you derive any benefit from my labours, aid me with your prayers to our heavenly Father.

GENEVA, 1st *August* 1559.

> The zeal of those whose cause I undertook,
> Has swelled a short defence into a book.

"I profess to be one of those who, by profiting, write, and by writing profit."—*Augustine*, Epist. vii.

METHOD AND ARRANGEMENT,

OR SUBJECT OF THE WHOLE WORK.

[FROM AN EPITOME OF THE INSTITUTIONS, BY GASPAR OLEVIAN.]

THE subject handled by the author of these Christian Institutes is twofold : the former, the knowledge of God, which leads to a blessed immortality; and the latter (which is subordinate to the former), the knowledge of ourselves. With this view the author simply adopts the arrangement of the Apostles' Creed, as that with which all Christians are most familiar. For as the Creed consists of four parts, the first relating to God the Father, the second to the Son, the third to the Holy Spirit, and the fourth to the Church, so the author, in fulfilment of his task, divides his Institutes into four parts, corresponding to those of the Creed. Each of these parts it will now be proper to explain separately.

I. The first article of the Apostles' Creed is concerning *God the Father*, the creation, preservation, and government of the universe, as implied in his omnipotence. Accordingly, the First Book of the Institutes treats of the knowledge of God, considered as the Creator, Preserver, and Governor of the world, and of everything contained in it. It shows both wherein the true knowledge of the Creator consists, and what the end of this knowledge is, chap. i. and ii. ; that it is not learned at school, but that every one is self-taught it from the womb, chap. iii. Such, however, is man's depravity, that he stifles and corrupts this knowledge, partly by ignorance, partly by wicked design ; and hence does not by means of it either glorify God as he ought, or attain to happiness, chap. iv. This inward knowledge is aided from without, namely, by the creatures in which, as in a mirror, the perfections of God may be contemplated. But man does not properly avail himself of this assistance ; and hence to those to whom God is pleased to make himself more intimately known for salvation, he communicates his written word. This leads to a consideration of the Holy Scriptures, in which God has revealed that not the Father only, but along with the Father, the Son, and Holy Spirit, is that Creator of heaven and earth whom, in consequence of our innate depravity, we were unable, either from innate natural knowledge or the beautiful mirror of the world, to know so as to glorify. Here the author treats of the manifestation of God in Scripture; and in connection with it, of the one divine essence in three persons. But, lest man should lay the blame of his voluntary blindness on God, the author shows in what state man was created at first, introducing dissertations on the image of God, free will, and original righteousness. The subject of Creation being thus disposed of, the preservation and government of the world is considered in the three last chapters, which contain a very full discussion of the doctrine of Divine Providence.

II. As man, by sinning, forfeited the privileges conferred on him at his creation, recourse must be had to Christ. Accordingly, the next article in the Creed is, *And in Jesus Christ his only Son, &c.* In like manner, the Second Book of the Institutes treats of the knowledge of God considered as a Redeemer in Christ, and, showing man his fall, conducts him to Christ the Mediator. Here the subject of original sin is considered, and it is shown that man has no means within himself by which he can escape from guilt and the impending curse: that, on the contrary, until he is reconciled and renewed, everything that proceeds from him is of the nature of sin. This subject is considered as far as the vi. chapter. Man being thus utterly undone in himself, and incapable of working out his own cure by thinking a good thought, or doing what is acceptable to God, must seek redemption without himself—viz. in Christ. The end for which the Law was given, was not to secure worshippers for itself, but to conduct them unto Christ. This leads to an exposition of the Moral Law. Christ was known to the Jews under the Law as the author of salvation, but is more fully revealed under the Gospel in which he was manifested to the world. Hence arises the doctrine concerning the similarity and difference of the two Testaments, the Old and the New, the Law and the Gospel. These topics occupy as far as the xii. chapter. It is next shown that, in order to secure a complete salvation, it was necessary that the eternal Son of God should become man, and assume a true human nature. It is also shown in what way these two natures constitute one person. In order to purchase a full salvation by his own merits, and effectually apply it, Christ was appointed to the offices of Prophet, Priest, and King. The mode in which Christ performs these offices is considered, and also whether in point of fact he did accomplish the work of redemption. Here an exposition is given of the articles relating to Christ's death, resurrection, and ascension into heaven. In conclusion, it is proved that Christ is rightly and properly said to have merited divine grace and salvation for us.

III. So long as Christ is separated from us we have no benefit from him. We must be ingrafted in him like branches in the vine. Hence the Creed, after treating of Christ, proceeds in its third article, *I believe in the Holy Spirit,*—the Holy Spirit being the bond of union between us and Christ. In like manner, the Third Book of the Institutes treats of the Holy Spirit which unites us to Christ, and, in connection with it, of faith, by which we embrace Christ with a double benefit—viz. that of gratuitous righteousness, which he imputes to us, and regeneration, which he begins in us by giving us repentance. In order to show the worthlessness of a faith which is not accompanied with a desire of repentance, the author, before pro ceeding to a full discussion of justification, treats at length from chapter iii.-x. of repentance, and the constant study of it—repentance which Christ, when apprehended by faith, begets in us by his Spirit. Chapter xi. treats of the primary and peculiar benefit of Christ when united to us by the Holy Spirit—viz. justification. This subject is continued to the xx. chapter; which treats of prayer, the hand, as it were, to receive the blessings which faith knows to be treasured up for it with God, according to the word of promise. But, as the Holy Spirit, who creates and preserves our faith, does not unite all men to Christ, who is the sole author of salvation, chapter xxi. treats of the eternal election of God, to which it is owing that we, in whom he foresaw no good which he had not previously bestowed, are given to Christ, and united to him by the effectual calling of the Gospel. This subject is continued to the xxv. chapter, which treats of complete regeneration and felicity, namely, the final resurrection to which we must raise our eyes, seeing that, in regard to fruition, the happiness of the godly is only begun in this world.

IV. Since the Holy Spirit does not ingraft all men into Christ, or endue them with faith, and those whom he does so endue he does not ordinarily endue without means, but uses for that purpose the preaching of the Gospel and the dispensation of the Sacraments, together with the administration of all kinds of discipline, the Creed contains the following article, *I believe in the Holy Catholic Church,* namely, that Church which, when lying in eternal death, the Father, by gratuitous election, freely reconciled to himself in Christ and endued with the Holy Spirit, that, being ingrafted into Christ, it might have communion with him as its proper head ; whence flow perpetual remission of sins, and full restoration to eternal life. Accordingly, the Church is treated of in the first fourteen chapters of the Fourth Book, which thereafter treats of the means which the Holy Spirit employs in calling us effectually from spiritual death, and preserving the Church, in other words, Baptism and the Lord's Supper. These means are, as it were, the royal sceptre of Christ, by which, through the efficacy of his Spirit, he commences his spiritual reign in the Church, advances it from day to day, and after this life, without the use of means, finally perfects it. This subject is continued to the xx. chapter.

And because civil governments are, in this life, the hospitable entertainers (*hospitia*) of the Church (though civil government is distinct from the spiritual kingdom of Christ), the author shows how great blessings they are, blessings which the Church is bound gratefully to acknowledge, until we are called away from this tabernacle to the heavenly inheritance, where God will be all in all.

Such is the arrangement of the Institutes, which may be thus summed up: Man being at first created upright, but afterwards being not partially but totally ruined, finds his entire salvation out of himself in Christ, to whom being united by the Holy Spirit freely given, without any foresight of future works, he thereby obtains a double blessing—viz. full imputation of righteousness, which goes along with us even to the grave, and the commencement of sanctification, which daily advances till at length it is perfected in the day of regeneration or resurrection of the body, and this, in order that the great mercy of God may be celebrated in the heavenly mansions throughout eternity.

GENERAL INDEX OF CHAPTERS.

BOOK FIRST.

OF THE KNOWLEDGE OF GOD THE CREATOR.

Eighteen Chapters.

BOOK SECOND.

OF THE KNOWLEDGE OF GOD THE REDEEMER, IN CHRIST, AS FIRST MANIFESTED TO THE FATHERS UNDER THE LAW, AND THEREAFTER TO US UNDER THE GOSPEL.

Seventeen Chapters.

BOOK THIRD.

**THE MODE OF OBTAINING THE GRACE OF CHRIST.
THE BENEFITS IT CONFERS, AND THE EFFECTS RESULTING FROM IT.**

Twenty-Five Chapters.

INSTITUTES

OF

THE CHRISTIAN RELIGION.

BOOK FIRST.

OF THE KNOWLEDGE OF GOD THE CREATOR.

ARGUMENT.

THE First Book treats of the knowledge of God the Creator. But as it is in the creation of man that the divine perfections are best displayed, so man also is made the subject of discourse. Thus the whole book divides itself into two principal heads—the former relating to the knowledge of God, and the latter to the knowledge of man. In the first chapter, these are considered jointly; and in each of the following chapters, separately: occasionally, however, intermingled with other matters which refer to one or other of the heads; e.g., the discussions concerning Scripture and images falling under the former head, and the other three, concerning the creation of the world, the holy angels, and devils, falling under the latter. The last point discussed—viz. the method of the divine government—relates to both.

With regard to the former head—viz. the knowledge of God—it is shown, in the first place, what the kind of knowledge is which God requires, Chap. II. And, in the second place (Chap. III.—IX.), where this knowledge must be sought, namely, not in man; because, although naturally implanted in the human mind, it is stifled, partly by ignorance, partly by evil intent, Chap. III. and IV.; not in the frame of the world: because, although it shines most clearly there, we are so stupid that these manifestations, however perspicuous, pass away without any beneficial result, Chap. V.; but in Scripture (Chap. VI.), which is treated of, Chap. VII.—IX. In the third place, it is shown what the character of God is, Chap. X. In the fourth place, how impious it is to give a visible form to God (here images, the worship of them, and its origin, are considered), Chap. XI. In the fifth place, it is shown that God is to be solely and wholly worshipped, Chap. XII. Lastly, Chap. XIII. treats of the unity of the divine essence, and the distinction of three persons.

With regard to the latter head—viz. the knowledge of man—first, Chap. XIV. treats of the creation of the world, and of good and bad angels (these all having reference to man). And then Chap. XV., taking up the subject of man himself, examines his nature and his powers.

The better to illustrate the nature both of God and man, the three remaining Chapters—viz. XVI.—XVIII.—proceed to treat of the general government of the world, and particularly of human actions, in opposition to fortune and fate, explaining both the doctrine and its use. In conclusion, it is shown, that though God employs the instrumentality of the wicked, he is pure from sin and from taint of every kind.

INSTITUTES

OF

THE CHRISTIAN RELIGION.

BOOK FIRST.

OF THE KNOWLEDGE OF GOD THE CREATOR:

CHAPTER I.

THE KNOWLEDGE OF GOD AND OF OURSELVES MUTUALLY CONNECTED. —NATURE OF THE CONNECTION.

Sections.

1. The sum of true wisdom—viz. the knowledge of God and of ourselves. Effects of the latter.
2. Effects of the knowledge of God, in humbling our pride, unveiling our hypocrisy, demonstrating the absolute perfections of God, and our own utter helplessness.
3. Effects of the knowledge of God illustrated by the examples, 1. of holy patriarchs; 2. of holy angels; 3. of the sun and moon.

1. OUR wisdom, in so far as it ought to be deemed true and solid wisdom, consists almost entirely of two parts: the knowledge of God and of ourselves. But as these are connected together by many ties, it is not easy to determine which of the two precedes, and gives birth to the other. For, in the first place, no man can survey himself without forthwith turning his thoughts towards the God in whom he lives and moves; because it is perfectly obvious, that the endowments which we possess cannot possibly be from ourselves; nay, that our very being is nothing else than subsistence in God alone. In the second place, those blessings which unceasingly distil to us from heaven, are like streams conducting us to the fountain. Here, again, the infinitude of good which resides in God becomes more apparent from our poverty. In particular, the miserable ruin into which the revolt of the first man has plunged us, compels us to turn our eyes upwards; not only that while hungry and famishing we may thence ask what we want, but being aroused by fear may learn

humility. For as there exists in man something like a world of
misery, and ever since we were stript of the divine attire our naked
shame discloses an immense series of disgraceful properties, every
man, being stung by the consciousness of his own unhappiness, in
this way necessarily obtains at least some knowledge of God. Thus,
our feeling of ignorance, vanity, want, weakness, in short, depravity
and corruption, reminds us (see Calvin on John iv. 10) that in the
Lord, and none but He, dwell the true light of wisdom, solid virtue,
exuberant goodness. We are accordingly urged by our own evil
things to consider the good things of God; and, indeed, we cannot
aspire to Him in earnest until we have begun to be displeased with
ourselves. For what man is not disposed to rest in himself? Who,
in fact, does not thus rest, so long as he is unknown to himself; that
is, so long as he is contented with his own endowments, and unconscious or unmindful of his misery? Every person, therefore, on
coming to the knowledge of himself, is not only urged to seek God,
but is also led as by the hand to find him.

2. On the other hand, it is evident that man never attains to a
true self-knowledge until he have previously contemplated the face of
God, and come down after such contemplation to look into himself.
For (such is our innate pride) we always seem to ourselves just, and
upright, and wise, and holy, until we are convinced, by clear evidence,
of our injustice, vileness, folly, and impurity. Convinced, however,
we are not, if we look to ourselves only, and not to the Lord also—
He being the only standard by the application of which this conviction can be produced. For, since we are all naturally prone to hypocrisy, any empty semblance of righteousness is quite enough to
satisfy us instead of righteousness itself. And since nothing appears
within us or around us that is not tainted with very great impurity,
so long as we keep our mind within the confines of human pollution,
anything which is in some small degree less defiled, delights us as if
it were most pure: just as an eye, to which nothing but black had
been previously presented, deems an object of a whitish, or even of a
brownish hue, to be perfectly white. Nay, the bodily sense may
furnish a still stronger illustration of the extent to which we are deluded in estimating the powers of the mind. If, at mid-day, we
either look down to the ground, or on the surrounding objects which
lie open to our view, we think ourselves endued with a very strong
and piercing eyesight; but when we look up to the sun, and gaze at
it unveiled, the sight which did excellently well for the earth, is in
stantly so dazzled and confounded by the refulgence, as to oblige us
to confess that our acuteness in discerning terrestrial objects is mere
dimness when applied to the sun. Thus, too, it happens in estimating our spiritual qualities. So long as we do not look beyond the
earth, we are quite pleased with our own righteousness, wisdom, and
virtue; we address ourselves in the most flattering terms, and seem
only less than demigods. But should we once begin to raise our

thoughts to God, and reflect what kind of Being he is, and how absolute the perfection of that righteousness, and wisdom, and virtue, to which, as a standard, we are bound to be conformed, what formerly delighted us by its false show of righteousness, will become polluted with the greatest iniquity; what strangely imposed upon us under the name of wisdom, will disgust by its extreme folly; and what presented the appearance of virtuous energy, will be condemned as the most miserable impotence. So far are those qualities in us, which seem most perfect, from corresponding to the divine purity.

3. Hence that dread and amazement with which, as Scripture uniformly relates, holy men were struck and overwhelmed whenever they beheld the presence of God. When we see those who previously stood firm and secure so quaking with terror, that the fear of death takes hold of them, nay, they are, in a manner, swallowed up and annihilated, the inference to be drawn is, that men are never duly touched and impressed with a conviction of their insignificance, until they have contrasted themselves with the majesty of God. Frequent examples of this consternation occur both in the Book of Judges and the Prophetical Writings;[1] so much so, that it was a common expression among the people of God, " We shall die, for we have seen the Lord." Hence the Book of Job, also, in humbling men under a conviction of their folly, feebleness, and pollution, always derives its chief argument from descriptions of the divine wisdom, virtue, and purity. Nor without cause: for we see Abraham the readier to acknowledge himself but dust and ashes, the nearer he approaches to behold the glory of the Lord, and Elijah unable to wait with unveiled face for His approach, so dreadful is the sight. And what can man do, man who is but rottenness and a worm, when even the Cherubim themselves must veil their faces in very terror? To this, undoubtedly, the Prophet Isaiah refers, when he says (Isaiah xxiv. 23), " The moon shall be confounded, and the sun ashamed, when the Lord of Hosts shall reign;" i.e., when he shall exhibit his refulgence, and give a nearer view of it, the brightest objects will, in comparison, be covered with darkness.

But though the knowledge of God and the knowledge of ourselves are bound together by a mutual tie, due arrangement requires that we treat of the former in the first place, and then descend to the latter.

1 Judges xiii. 22; Isaiah vi. 5; Ezek. i. 28, iii. 14; Job ix. 4, &c.; Gen. xviii. 27; 1 Kings xix. 18.

[margin note: Men never realize their own insignificance until they have beheld God.]

CHAPTER II.

WHAT IT IS TO KNOW GOD.—TENDENCY OF THIS KNOWLEDGE.

Sections.

1. The knowledge of God the Creator defined. The substance of this knowledge, and the use to be made of it.
2. Further illustration of the use, together with a necessary reproof of vain curiosity, and refutation of the Epicureans. The character of God as it appears to the pious mind, contrasted with the absurd views of the Epicureans. Religion defined.

1. By the knowledge of God, I understand that by which we not only conceive that there is some God, but also apprehend what it is for our interest, and conducive to his glory, what, in short, it is befitting to know concerning him. For, properly speaking, we cannot say that God is known where there is no religion or piety. I am not now referring to that species of knowledge by which men, in themselves lost and under curse, apprehend God as a Redeemer in Christ the Mediator. I speak only of that simple and primitive knowledge, to which the mere course of nature would have conducted us, had Adam stood upright. For although no man will now, in the present ruin of the human race, perceive God to be either a father, or the author of salvation, or propitious in any respect, until Christ interpose to make our peace; still it is one thing to perceive that God our Maker supports us by his power, rules us by his providence, fosters us by his goodness, and visits us with all kinds of blessings, and another thing to embrace the grace of reconciliation offered to us in Christ. Since, then, the Lord first appears, as well in the creation of the world as in the general doctrine of Scripture, simply as a Creator, and afterwards as a Redeemer in Christ,—a twofold knowledge of him hence arises: of these the former is now to be considered, the latter will afterwards follow in its order. But although our mind cannot conceive of God, without rendering some worship to him, it will not, however, be sufficient simply to hold that he is the only being whom all ought to worship and adore, unless we are also persuaded that he is the fountain of all goodness, and that we must seek everything in him, and in none but him. My meaning is: we must be persuaded not only that as he once formed the world, so he sustains it by his boundless power, governs it by his wisdom, preserves it by his goodness, in particular, rules the human race with justice and judgment, bears with them in mercy, shields them by his protection; but also that not a particle of light, or wisdom, or justice, or power, or rectitude, or genuine truth, will anywhere be found, which does not flow

[Margin annotations:]
No man can know God without Christ.

We must learn that God is the Creator and Preserver of all men and learn to expect and ask all things from Him.

from him, and of which he is not the cause; in this way we must *Sense* learn to expect and ask all things from him, and thankfully ascribe *of divine* to him whatever we receive. For this sense of the divine perfections *perfection* is the proper master to teach us piety, out of which religion springs. *yields* By piety I mean that union of reverence and love to God which the *piety* knowledge of his benefits inspires. For, until men feel that they owe everything to God, that they are cherished by his paternal care, and that he is the author of all their blessings, so that nought is to be looked for away from him, they will never submit to him in voluntary obedience; nay, unless they place their entire happiness in him, they will never yield up their whole selves to him in truth and sincerity.

3. Those, therefore, who, in considering this question, propose to inquire what the essence of God is, only delude us with frigid specu- lations,—it being much more our interest to know what kind of being God is, and what things are agreeable to his nature. For, of what use is it to join Epicurus in acknowledging some God who has cast off the care of the world, and only delights himself in ease? What avails it, in short, to know a God with whom we have nothing to do? *The* The effect of our knowledge rather ought to be, *first*, to teach us re- *effect of* verence and fear; and, *secondly*, to induce us, under its guidance and *our knowled-* teaching, to ask every good thing from him, and, when it is received, *ge of* ascribe it to him. For how can the idea of God enter your mind *God should* without instantly giving rise to the thought, that since you are his *be reverance* workmanship, you are bound, by the very law of creation, to submit *and faith.* to his authority?—that your life is due to him?—that whatever you do ought to have reference to him? If so, it undoubtedly follows that your life is sadly corrupted, if it is not framed in obedience to him, since his will ought to be the law of our lives. On the other hand, your idea of his nature is not clear unless you acknowledge him to be the origin and fountain of all goodness. Hence would arise both confidence in him, and a desire of cleaving to him, did not the depravity of the human mind lead it away from the proper course of investigation.

For, first of all, the pious mind does not devise for itself any kind of God, but looks alone to the one true God; nor does it feign for *One who* him any character it pleases, but is contented to have him in the *truly* character in which he manifests himself, always guarding, with the *knows* utmost diligence, against transgressing his will, and wandering, with *God trust* daring presumption, from the right path. He by whom God is thus *Him in* known, perceiving how he governs all things, confides in him as his *every* guardian and protector, and casts himself entirely upon his faithful- *extremity* ness,—perceiving him to be the source of every blessing, if he is in any strait or feels any want, he instantly recurs to his protection and trusts to his aid,—persuaded that he is good and merciful, he reclines upon him with sure confidence, and doubts not that, in the divine clemency, a remedy will be provided for his every time of need,— acknowledging him as his Father and his Lord, he considers himself bound to have respect to his authority in all things, to reverence his majesty, aim at the advancement of his glory, and obey his commands, —regarding him as a just judge, armed with severity to punish crimes, he keeps the judgment-seat always in his view. Standing in awe of it, he curbs himself, and fears to provoke his anger. Nevertheless, he is not so terrified by an apprehension of judgment as to wish he could withdraw himself, even if the means of escape lay before him; nay, he embraces him not less as the avenger of wickedness than as the rewarder of the righteous; because he perceives that it equally appertains to his glory to store up punishment for the one, and eternal life for the other. Besides, it is not the mere fear of punishment that restrains him from sin. Loving and revering God as his father, honouring and obeying him as his master, although there were no hell, he would revolt at the very idea of offending him.

Love of God the proper motive for obedience to the commands of God.

Such is pure and genuine religion, namely, confidence in God coupled with serious fear—fear, which both includes in it willing reverence, and brings along with it such legitimate worship as is prescribed by the law. And it ought to be more carefully considered, that all men promiscuously do homage to God, but very few truly reverence him. On all hands there is abundance of ostentatious ceremonies, but sincerity of heart is rare.

CHAPTER III.

THE KNOWLEDGE OF GOD NATURALLY IMPLANTED IN THE HUMAN MIND.

Sections.

1. The knowledge of God being manifested to all makes the reprobate without excuse· Universal belief and acknowledgment of the existence of God.
2. Objection — that religion and the belief of a Deity are the inventions of crafty politicians. Refutation of the objection. This universal belief confirmed by the examples of wicked men and Atheists.
3. Confirmed also by the vain endeavours of the wicked to banish all fear of God from their minds. Conclusion, that the knowledge of God is naturally implanted in the human mind.

1. THAT there exists in the human mind, and indeed by natural instinct, some sense of Deity, we hold to be beyond dispute, since God himself, to prevent any man from pretending ignorance, has endued all men with some idea of his Godhead, the memory of which he constantly renews and occasionally enlarges, that all to a man, being aware that there is a God, and that he is their Maker, may be condemned by their own conscience when they neither worship him nor consecrate their lives to his service. Certainly, if there is any quarter where it may be supposed that God is unknown, the most likely for such an instance to exist is among the dullest tribes farthest removed from civilisation. But, as a heathen tells us,[1] there is no nation so barbarous, no race so brutish, as not to be imbued with the conviction that there is a God. Even those who, in other respects, seem to differ least from the lower animals, constantly retain some sense of religion ; so thoroughly has this common conviction possessed the mind, so firmly is it stamped on the breasts of all men. Since, then, there never has been, from the very first, any quarter of the globe, any city, any household even, without religion, this amounts to a tacit confession, that a sense of Deity is inscribed on every heart. Nay, even idolatry is ample evidence of this fact. For we know how reluctant man is to lower himself, in order to set other creatures above him. Therefore, when he chooses to worship wood and stone rather than be thought to have no God, it is evident how very strong this impression of a Deity must be ; since it is more difficult to obliterate it from the

[margin note: Admits the existance of natural Knowledge of God.]

---

1 "Intelligi necesse est deos, quoniam insitas eorum vel potius innatas cognitiones habemus.—Quæ nobis natura informationem deorum ipsorum dedit, eadem insculpsit in mentibus ut eos æternos et beatos haberemus."—Cic. de Nat. Deor. lib. i. c. 17.— "Itaque inter omnes omnium gentium summa constat ; omnibus enim innatum est, et in animo quasi insculptum esse deos."—Lib. ii. c. 4. See also Lact. Inst. Div. lib. iii. c. 10.

mind of man, than to break down the feelings of his nature,—these certainly being broken down, when, in opposition to his natural haughtiness, he spontaneously humbles himself before the meanest object as an act of reverence to God.

2. It is most absurd, therefore, to maintain, as some do, that religion was devised by the cunning and craft of a few individuals, as a means of keeping the body of the people in due subjection, while there was nothing which those very individuals, while teaching others to worship God, less believed than the existence of a God. I readily acknowledge, that designing men have introduced a vast number of fictions into religion, with the view of inspiring the populace with reverence or striking them with terror, and thereby rendering them more obsequious; but they never could have succeeded in this, had the minds of men not been previously imbued with that uniform belief in God, from which, as from its seed, the religious propensity springs. And it is altogether incredible that those who, in the matter of religion, cunningly imposed on their ruder neighbours, were altogether devoid of a knowledge of God. For though in old times there were some, and in the present day not a few are found[1] who deny the being of a God, yet, whether they will or not, they occasionally feel the truth which they are desirous not to know. We do not read of any man who broke out into more unbridled and audacious contempt of the Deity than C. Caligula,[2] and yet none showed greater dread when any indication of divine wrath was manifested. Thus, however unwilling, he shook with terror before the God whom he professedly studied to contemn. You may every day see the same thing happening to his modern imitators. The most audacious despiser of God is most easily disturbed, trembling at the sound of a falling leaf. How so, unless in vindication of the divine majesty, which smites their consciences the more strongly the more they endeavour to flee from it. They all, indeed, look out for hiding-places, where they may conceal themselves from the presence of the Lord, and again efface it from their mind; but after all their efforts they remain caught within the net. Though the conviction may occasionally seem to vanish for a moment, it immediately returns, and rushes in with new impetuosity, so that any interval of relief from the gnawings of conscience is not unlike the slumber of the intoxicated or the insane, who have no quiet rest in sleep, but are continually haunted with dire horrific dreams. Even the wicked themselves, therefore, are an example of the fact that some idea of God always exists in every human mind.

3. All men of sound judgment will therefore hold, that a sense of Deity is indelibly engraven on the human heart. And that this belief is naturally engendered in all, and thoroughly fixed as it were

The charge that religion is an invention of evil men cannot be so, for even evil men can't be everywhere, and belief in God is universal.

Even Atheists are not successful in denying God.

---

[1] As to some Atheists of the author's time, see Calvinus De Scandalis.
[2] Suet. Calig. c. 51.

in our very bones, is strikingly attested by the contumacy of the wicked, who, though they struggle furiously, are unable to extricate themselves from the fear of God.   Though Diagoras,[1] and others of like stamp, make themselves merry with whatever has been believed in all ages concerning religion, and Dionysius scoffs at the judgment of heaven, it is but a Sardonian grin; for the worm of conscience, keener than burning steel, is gnawing them within.   I do not say with Cicero, that errors wear out by age, and that religion increases and grows better day by day.   For the world (as will be shortly seen) labours as much as it can to shake off all knowledge of God, and corrupts his worship in innumerable ways.   I only say, that, when the stupid hardness of heart, which the wicked eagerly court as a means of despising God, becomes enfeebled, the sense of Deity, which of all things they wished most to be extinguished, is still in vigour, and now and then breaks forth.   Whence we infer, that this is not a doctrine which is first learned at school, but one as to which every man is, from the womb, his own master; one which nature herself allows no individual to forget, though many, with all their might, strive to do so.   Moreover, if all are born and live for the express purpose of learning to know God, and if the knowledge of God, in so far as it fails to produce this effect, is fleeting and vain, it is clear that all those who do not direct the whole thoughts and actions of their lives to this end fail to fulfil the law of their being.   This did not escape the observation even of philosophers.   For it is the very thing which Plato meant (in *Phæd. et Theact.*) when he taught, as he often does, that the chief good of the soul consists in resemblance to God; *i.e.*, when, by means of knowing him, she is wholly transformed into him.   Thus Gryllus, also, in Plutarch (*lib. quod bruta anim. ratione utantur*), reasons most skilfully, when he affirms that, if once religion is banished from the lives of men, they not only in no respect excel, but are, in many respects, much more wretched than the brutes, since, being exposed to so many forms of evil, they continually drag on a troubled and restless existence: that the only thing, therefore, which makes them superior is the worship of God, through which alone they aspire to immortality.

(margin note: This innate knowledge of God does not, however, imply limitless increase in the understanding of the Divine will)

[1] Cic. De Nat. Deor. lib. i. c. 23.   Valer. Max. lib. i. c. 1.

CHAPTER IV.

THE KNOWLEDGE OF GOD STIFLED OR CORRUPTED, IGNORANTLY OR MALICIOUSLY.

Sections.

1. The knowledge of God suppressed by ignorance, many falling away into superstition. Such persons, however, inexcusable, because their error is accompanied with pride and stubbornness.
2. Stubbornness the companion of impiety.
3. No pretext can justify superstition. This proved, first, from reason; and, secondly, from Scripture.
4. The wicked never willingly come into the presence of God. Hence their hypocrisy. Hence, too, their sense of Deity leads to no good result.

This innate knowledge of God does not lead to salvation.

1. BUT though experience testifies that a seed of religion is divinely sown in all, scarcely one in a hundred is found who cherishes it in his heart, and not one in whom it grows to maturity, so far is it from yielding fruit in its season. Moreover, while some lose themselves in superstitious observances, and others, of set purpose, wickedly revolt from God, the result is that, in regard to the true knowledge of him, all are so degenerate, that in no part of the world can genuine godliness be found. In saying that some fall away into superstition, I mean not to insinuate that their excessive absurdity frees them from guilt; for the blindness under which they labour is almost invariably accompanied with vain pride and stubbornness. Mingled vanity and pride appear in this, that when miserable men do seek after God, instead of ascending higher than themselves, as they ought to do, they measure him by their own carnal stupidity, and, neglecting solid inquiry, fly off to indulge their curiosity in vain speculation. Hence, they do not conceive of him in the character in which he is manifested, but imagine him to be whatever their own rashness has devised. This abyss standing open, they cannot move one footstep without rushing headlong to destruction. With such an idea of God, nothing which they may attempt to offer in the way of worship or obedience can have any value in his sight, because it is not him they worship, but, instead of him, the dream and figment of their own heart. This corrupt procedure is admirably described by Paul, when he says, that "thinking to be wise, they became fools" (Rom. i. 22). He had previously said that "they became vain in their imaginations," but lest any should suppose them blameless, he afterwards adds, that they were deservedly blinded, because, not contented with sober inquiry, because, arrogating to themselves more than they have any title to

Without Christ, men fashion Gods after themselves. The Gods become as degenerate as men.

do, they of their own accord court darkness, nay, bewitch themselves with perverse, empty show. Hence it is that their folly, the result not only of vain curiosity, but of licentious desire and overweening confidence in the pursuit of forbidden knowledge, cannot be excused.

2. The expression of David (Psalm xiv 1, liii. 1), "The fool hath said in his heart, There is no God," is primarily applied to those who, as will shortly farther appear, stifle the light of nature, and intentionally stupify themselves. We see many, after they have become hardened in a daring course of sin, madly banishing all remembrance of God, though spontaneously suggested to them from within, by natural sense. To show how detestable this madness is, the Psalmist introduces them as distinctly denying that there is a God, because, although they do not disown his essence, they rob him of his justice and providence, and represent him as sitting idly in heaven. Nothing being less accordant with the nature of God than to cast off the government of the world, leaving it to chance, and so to wink at the crimes of men that they may wanton with impunity in evil courses; it follows, that every man who indulges in security, after extinguishing all fear of divine judgment, virtually denies that there is a God. As a just punishment of the wicked, after they have closed their own eyes, God makes their hearts dull and heavy, and hence, seeing, they see not. David, indeed, is the best interpreter of his own meaning, when he says elsewhere, the wicked has "no fear of God before his eyes" (Psalm xxxvi. 1); and, again, "He hath said in his heart, God hath forgotten; he hideth his face; he will never see it." Thus, although they are forced to acknowledge that there is some God, they however, rob him of his glory by denying his power. For, as Paul declares, "If we believe not, he abideth faithful, he cannot deny himself" (2 Tim. ii. 13); so those who feign to themselves a dead and dumb idol, are truly said to deny God It is, moreover, to be observed, that though they struggle with their own convictions, and would fain not only banish God from their minds, but from heaven also, there stupefaction is never so complete as to secure them from being occasionally dragged before the divine tribunal. Still, as no fear restrains them from rushing violently in the face of God, so long as they are hurried on by that blind impulse, it cannot be denied that their prevailing state of mind in regard to him is brutish oblivion.

3. In this way, the vain pretext which many employ to clothe their superstition is overthrown. They deem it enough that they have some kind of zeal for religion, how preposterous soever it may be, not observing that true religion must be conformable to the will of God as its unerring standard; that he can never deny himself, and is no spectre or phantom, to be metamorphosed at each individual's caprice. It is easy to see how superstition, with its false glosses, mocks God, while it tries to please him. Usually fastening merely on things on which he has declared he sets no value, it either contemptuously overlooks, or even undisguisedly rejects, the things which he expressly

Man's perversion of God is equivalent to madness.

Men rob God of his glory by denying His power.

enjoins, or in which we are assured that he takes pleasure. Those, therefore, who set up a fictitious worship, merely worship and adore their own delirious fancies; indeed, they would never dare so to trifle with God, had they not previously fashioned him after their own childish conceits. Hence that vague and wandering opinion of Deity is declared by an apostle to be ignorance of God: "Howbeit, then, when ye knew not God, ye did service unto them which by nature are no gods." And he elsewhere declares, that the Ephesians were "without God" (Eph. ii. 12) at the time when they wandered without any correct knowledge of him. It makes little difference, at least in this respect, whether you hold the existence of one God, or a plurality of gods, since, in both cases alike, by departing from the true God, you have nothing left but an execrable idol. It remains, therefore, to conclude with Lactantius (*Instit. Div.* lib. i. 2, 6), "No religion is genuine that is not in accordance with truth."

4. To this fault they add a second—viz. that when they do think of God it is against their will; never approaching him without being dragged into his presence, and when there, instead of the voluntary fear flowing from reverence of the divine majesty, feeling only that forced and servile fear which divine judgment extorts—judgment which, from the impossibility of escape, they are compelled to dread, but which, while they dread, they at the same time also hate. To impiety, and to it alone, the saying of Statius properly applies: "Fear first brought gods into the world" (*Theb.* lib. i.). Those whose inclinations are at variance with the justice of God, knowing that his tribunal has been erected for the punishment of transgression, earnestly wish that that tribunal were overthrown. Under the influence of this feeling they are actually warring against God, justice being one of his essential attributes. Perceiving that they are always within reach of his power, that resistance and evasion are alike impossible, they fear and tremble. Accordingly, to avoid the appearance of contemning a majesty by which all are overawed, they have recourse to some species of religious observance, never ceasing meanwhile to defile themselves with every kind of vice, and add crime to crime, until they have broken the holy law of the Lord in every one of its requirements, and set his whole righteousness at nought; at all events, they are not so restrained by their semblance of fear as not to luxuriate and take pleasure in iniquity, choosing rather to indulge their carnal propensities than to curb them with the bridle of the Holy Spirit. But since this shadow of religion (it scarcely even deserves to be called a shadow) is false and vain, it is easy to infer how much this confused knowledge of God differs from that piety which is instilled into the breasts of believers, and from which alone true religion springs. And yet hypocrites would fain, by means of tortuous windings, make a show of being near to God at the very time they are fleeing from him. For while the whole life ought to be one perpetual course of obedience, they rebel without fear in almost all their actions, and seek to appease

[margin: Natural fear of God does not bring man to worship God voluntarily.

Through fear, men come actually to hate God.]

him with a few paltry sacrifices; while they ought to serve him with integrity of heart and holiness of life, they endeavour to procure his favour by means of frivolous devices and punctilios of no value. Nay, they take greater license in their grovelling indulgencies, because they imagine that they can fulfil their duty to him by preposterous expiations; in short, while their confidence ought to have been fixed upon him, they put him aside, and rest in themselves or the creatures. At length they bewilder themselves in such a maze of error, that the darkness of ignorance obscures, and ultimately extinguishes, those sparks which were designed to show them the glory of God. Still, however, the conviction that there is some Deity continues to exist, like a plant which can never be completely eradicated, though so corrupt that it is only capable of producing the worst of fruit. Nay, we have still stronger evidence of the proposition for which I now contend—viz. that a sense of Deity is naturally engraven on the human heart, in the fact, that the very reprobate are forced to acknowledge it. When at their ease, they can jest about God, and talk pertly and loquaciously in disparagement of his power; but should despair, from any cause, overtake them, it will stimulate them to seek him, and dictate ejaculatory prayers, proving that they were not entirely ignorant of God, but had perversely suppressed feelings which ought to have been earlier manifested.

Hypocrites make a show of being near God while actually floeing from Him.

CHAPTER V.

THE KNOWLEDGE OF GOD CONSPICUOUS IN THE CREATION AND CONTINUAL GOVERNMENT OF THE WORLD.

This chapter consists of two parts: 1. The former, which occupies the first ten sections, divides all the works of God into two great classes, and elucidates the knowledge of God as displayed in each class. The one class is treated of in the first six, and the other in the four following sections: 2. The latter part of the chapter shows, that, in consequence of the extreme stupidity of men, those manifestations of God, however perspicuous, lead to no useful result. This latter part, which commences at the eleventh section, is continued to the end of the chapter.

Sections.

1. The invisible and incomprehensible essence of God, to a certain extent, made visible in his works
2. This declared by the first class of works—viz. the admirable motions of the heavens and the earth, the symmetry of the human body, and the connection of its parts; in short, the various objects which are presented to every eye.
3. This more especially manifested in the structure of the human body.
4. The shameful ingratitude of disregarding God, who, in such a variety of ways, is manifested within us. The still more shameful ingratitude of contemplating the endowments of the soul, without ascending to Him who gave them. No objection can be founded on any supposed organism in the soul.
5. The powers and actions of the soul, a proof of its separate existence from the body. Proofs of the soul's immortality. Objection that the whole world is quickened by one soul. Reply to the objection. Its impiety.
6. Conclusion from what has been said—viz. that the omnipotence, eternity, and goodness of God, may be learned from the first class of works, *i.e.*, those which are in accordance with the ordinary course of nature.
7. The second class of works—viz. those above the ordinary course of nature—afford clear evidence of the perfections of God, especially his goodness, justice, and mercy.
8. Also his providence, power, and wisdom.
9. Proofs and illustrations of the divine Majesty. The use of them—viz. the acquisition of divine knowledge in combination with true piety.
10. The tendency of the knowledge of God to inspire the righteous with the hope of future life and remind the wicked of the punishments reserved for them. Its tendency, moreover, to keep alive in the hearts of the righteous a sense of the divine goodness.
11. The second part of the chapter, which describes the stupidity both of learned and unlearned, in ascribing the whole order of things, and the admirable arrangements of divine Providence, to fortune.
12. Hence Polytheism, with all its abominations, and the endless and irreconcilable opinions of the philosophers concerning God.
13. All guilty of revolt from God, corrupting pure religion, either by following general custom, or the impious consent of antiquity.
14. Though irradiated by the wondrous glories of creation, we cease not to follow our own ways.
15. Our conduct altogether inexcusable, the dulness of perception being attributable to ourselves, while we are fully reminded of the true path, both by the structure and the government of the world.

1. SINCE the perfection of blessedness consists in the knowledge of God, he has been pleased, in order that none might be excluded from the means of obtaining felicity, not only to deposit in our minds that seed of religion of which we have already spoken, but so to manifest his perfections in the whole structure of the universe, and daily place himself in our view, that we cannot open our eyes without being compelled to behold him.　His essence, indeed, is incomprehensible, utterly transcending all human thought; but on each of his works his glory is engraven in characters so bright, so distinct, and so illustrious, that none, however dull and illiterate, can plead ignorance as their excuse.　Hence, with perfect truth, the Psalmist exclaims, "He covereth himself with light as with a garment" (Psalm civ. 2); as if he had said, that God for the first time was arrayed in visible attire when, in the creation of the world, he displayed those glorious banners, on which, to whatever side we turn, we behold his perfections visibly portrayed.　In the same place, the Psalmist aptly compares the expanded heavens to his royal tent, and says, "He layeth the beams of his chambers in the waters, maketh the clouds his chariot, and walketh upon the wings of the wind," sending forth the winds and lightnings as his swift messengers.　And because the glory of his power and wisdom is more refulgent in the firmament, it is frequently designated as his palace.　And, first, wherever you turn your eyes, there is no portion of the world, however minute, that does not exhibit at least some sparks of beauty; while it is impossible to contemplate the vast and beautiful fabric as it extends around, without being overwhelmed by the immense weight of glory.　Hence, the author of the Epistle to the Hebrews elegantly describes the visible worlds as images of the invisible (Heb. xi. 3), the elegant structure of the world serving us as a kind of mirror, in which we may behold God, though otherwise invisible.　For the same reason, the Psalmist attributes language to celestial objects, a language which all nations understand (Psalm xix. 1); the manifestation of the Godhead being too clear to escape the notice of any people, however obtuse.　The apostle Paul, stating this still more clearly, says, "That which may be known of God is manifest in them, for God hath showed it unto them.　For the invisible things of him from the creation of the world are clearly seen, being understood by the things that are made, even his eternal power and Godhead" (Rom. i. 20).

2. In attestation of his wondrous wisdom, both the heavens and the earth present us with innumerable proofs, not only those more recondite proofs which astronomy, medicine, and all the natural sciences, are designed to illustrate, but proofs which force themselves on the notice of the most illiterate peasant, who cannot open his eyes without beholding them.　It is true, indeed, that those who are more or less intimately acquainted with those liberal studies are thereby assisted and enabled to obtain a deeper insight into the secret workings of divine wisdom.　No man, however, though he be ignorant of these,

[margin note:] God, besides implanting a seed of knowledge of Himself in all men, also reveals Himself unmistakably in His works.

is incapacitated for discerning such proofs of creative wisdom as may well cause him to break forth in admiration of the Creator. To investigate the motions of the heavenly bodies, to determine their positions, measure their distances, and ascertain their properties, demands skill, and a more careful examination ; and where these are so employed, as the providence of God is thereby more fully unfolded, so it is reasonable to suppose that the mind takes a loftier flight, and obtains brighter views of his glory.[1] Still, none who have the use of their eyes can be ignorant of the divine skill manifested so conspicuously in the endless variety, yet distinct and well-ordered array, of the heavenly host; and, therefore, it is plain that the Lord has furnished every man with abundant proofs of his wisdom. The same is true in regard to the structure of the human frame. To determine the connection of its parts, its symmetry and beauty, with the skill of a Galen (Lib. De Usu Partium), requires singular acuteness; and yet all men acknowledge that the human body bears on its face such proofs of ingenious contrivance as are sufficient to proclaim the admirable wisdom of its Maker.

3. Hence certain of the philosophers[2] have not improperly called man a *microcosm* (*miniature world*), as being a rare specimen of divine power, wisdom, and goodness, and containing within himself wonders sufficient to occupy our minds, if we are willing so to employ them. Paul, accordingly, after reminding the Athenians that they "might feel after God and find him," immediately adds, that "he is not far from every one of us" (Acts xvii. 27) ; every man having within himself undoubted evidence of the heavenly grace by which he lives, and moves, and has his being. But if, in order to apprehend God, it is unnecessary to go farther than ourselves, what excuse can there be for the sloth of any man who will not take the trouble of descending into himself that he may find Him ? For the same reason, too, David, after briefly celebrating the wonderful name and glory of God, as everywhere displayed, immediately exclaims, " What is man, that thou art mindful of him?" and again, "Out of the mouths of babes and sucklings thou hast ordained strength" (Psalm viii. 2, 4). Thus he declares not only that the human race are a bright mirror of the Creator's works, but that infants hanging on their mothers' breasts have tongues eloquent enough to proclaim his glory without the aid of other orators. Accordingly, he hesitates not to bring them forward as fully instructed to refute the madness of those who, from devilish pride, would fain extinguish the name of God. Hence, too, the passage which Paul quotes from Aratus, "We are his offspring" (Acts xvii. 28), the excellent gifts with which he has endued us attesting that he is our Father. In the same way, also, from natural instinct, and, as it were, at the dictation of experience, heathen poets

---

[1] Augustinus : Astrologia magnum religiosis argumentum, tormentumque curiosis.
[2] See Aristot. Hist. Anim. lib. i. c. 17; Macrob. in Somn. Scip. lib. ii. c. 12; Boeth. De Definitione.

[Marginal notes:]
Proof of the existence of God found in the beauty & order of the universe.

What excuse has man for failing to make use of even those proofs of God which lie within himself.

call him the father of men. No one, indeed, will voluntarily and willingly devote himself to the service of God unless he has previously tasted his paternal love, and been thereby allured to love and reverence Him.

4. But herein appears the shameful ingratitude of men. Though they have in their own persons a factory where innumerable operations of God are carried on, and a magazine stored with treasures of inestimable value—instead of bursting forth in his praise, as they are bound to do, they, on the contrary, are the more inflated and swelled with pride. They feel how wonderfully God is working in them, and their own experience tells them of the vast variety of gifts which they owe to his liberality. Whether they will or not, they cannot but know that these are proofs of his Godhead, and yet they inwardly suppress them. They have no occasion to go farther than themselves, provided they do not, by appropriating as their own that which has been given them from heaven, put out the light intended to exhibit God clearly to their minds. At this day, however, the earth sustains on her bosom many monster minds—minds which are not afraid to employ the seed of Deity deposited in human nature as a means of suppressing the name of God. Can anything be more detestable than this madness in man, who, finding God a hundred times both in his body and his soul, makes his excellence in this respect a pretext for denying that there is a God? He will not say that chance has made him differ from the brutes that perish; but, substituting nature as the architect of the universe, he suppresses the name of God. The swift motions of the soul, its noble faculties and rare endowments, bespeak the agency of God in a manner which would make the suppression of it impossible, did not the Epicureans, like so many Cyclops, use it as a vantage-ground, from which to wage more audacious war with God. Are so many treasures of heavenly wisdom employed in the guidance of such a worm as man, and shall the whole universe be denied the same privilege? To hold that there are organs in the soul corresponding to each of its faculties, is so far from obscuring the glory of God, that it rather illustrates it. Let Epicurus tell what concourse of atoms, cooking meat and drink, can form one portion into refuse and another portion into blood, and make all the members separately perform their office as carefully as if they were so many souls acting with common consent in the superintendence of one body.

5. But my business at present is not with that stye: I wish rather to deal with those who, led away by absurd subtleties, are inclined, by giving an indirect turn to the frigid doctrine of Aristotle, to employ it for the purpose both of disproving the immortality of the soul and robbing God of his rights. Under the pretext that the faculties of the soul are organised, they chain it to the body as if it were incapable of a separate existence, while they endeavour as much as in them lies, by pronouncing eulogiums on nature, to suppress the

Rather than accepting these proofs for what they are, man insists on worshipping the creation rather than the Creator.

The Aristotilians wish to show that the body is inextricably tied to the soul.

Calvin cites astronomy as an occupation at which the soul has no need for the body.

name of God. But there is no ground for maintaining that the powers of the soul are confined to the performance of bodily functions. What has the body to do with your measuring the heavens, counting the number of the stars, ascertaining their magnitudes, their relative distances, the rate at which they move, and the orbits which they describe? I deny not that Astronomy has its use; all I mean to show is, that these lofty investigations are not conducted by organised symmetry, but by the faculties of the soul itself apart altogether from the body. The single example I have given will suggest many others to the reader. The swift and versatile movements of the soul in glancing from heaven to earth, connecting the future with the past, retaining the remembrance of former years, nay, forming creations of its own—its skill, moreover, in making astonishing discoveries, and inventing so many wonderful arts, are sure indications of the agency of God in man. What shall we say of its activity when the body is asleep, its many revolving thoughts, its many useful suggestions, its many solid arguments, nay, its presentiment of things yet to come? What shall we say but that man bears about with him a stamp of immortality which can never be effaced? But how is it possible for man to be divine, and yet not acknowledge his Creator? Shall we, by means of a power of judging implanted in our breast, distinguish between justice and injustice, and yet there be no judge in heaven? Shall some remains of intelligence continue with us in sleep, and yet no God keep watch in heaven? Shall we be deemed the inventors of so many arts and useful properties that God may be defrauded of his praise, though experience tells us plainly enough, that whatever we possess is dispensed to us in unequal measures by another hand? The talk of certain persons concerning a secret inspiration quickening the whole world, is not only silly, but altogether profane. Such persons are delighted with the following celebrated passage of Virgil:[1]—

> " Know, first, that heaven, and earth's compacted frame,
> And flowing waters, and the starry flame,
> And both the radiant lights, one common soul
> Inspires and feeds—and animates the whole.
> This active mind, infused through all the space,
> Unites and mingles with the mighty mass:
> Hence, men and beasts the breath of life obtain,
> And birds of air, and monsters of the main.
> Th' ethereal vigour is in all the same,
> And every soul is filled with equal flame."[2]

The meaning of all this is, that the world, which was made to display the glory of God, is its own creator. For the same poet has in another place,[3] adopted a view common to both Greeks and Latins:—

---

1 Æneid, vi. 724, sq. See Calvin on Acts xvii. 28. Manil. lib. i. Astron.
2 Dryden's Virgil, Æneid, Book vi. l. 980–990.
3 Georgic iv. 220. Plat. in Tim. Arist. lib. i. De Animo. See also Metaph. lib. 1.
Merc. Trismegr. in Pimandro.

> " Hence to the bee some sages have assigned
> A portion of the God, and heavenly mind ;
> For God goes forth, and spreads throughout the whole,
> Heaven, earth, and sea, the universal soul ;
> Each, at its birth, from him all beings share,
> Both man and brute, the breath of vital air ;
> To him return, and, loosed from earthly chain,
> Fly whence they sprang, and rest in God again
> Spurn at t'₂ grave, and, fearless of decay,
> Dwell in high heaven, and star th' ethereal way."[1]

Here we see how far that jejune speculation, of a universal mind animating and invigorating the world, is fitted to beget and foster piety in our minds. We have a still clearer proof of this in the profane verses which the licentious Lucretius has written as a deduction from the same principle.[2] The plain object is to form an unsubstantial deity, and thereby banish the true God whom we ought to fear and worship. I admit, indeed, that the expression, " Nature is God," may be piously used, if dictated by a pious mind ; but as it is inaccurate and harsh (Nature being more properly the order which has been established by God), in matters which are so very important, and in regard to which special reverence is due, it does harm to confound the Deity with the inferior operations of his hands.

6. Let each of us, therefore, in contemplating his own nature, remember that there is one God who governs all natures, and, in governing, wishes us to have respect to himself, to make him the object of our faith, worship, and adoration. Nothing, indeed, can be more preposterous than to enjoy those noble endowments which bespeak the divine presence within us, and to neglect him who, of his own good pleasure, bestows them upon us. In regard to his power, how glorious the manifestations by which he urges us to the contemplation of himself ; unless, indeed, we pretend not to know whose energy it is that by a word sustains the boundless fabric of the universe—at one time making heaven reverberate with thunder, sending forth the scorching lightning, and setting the whole atmosphere in a blaze ; at another, causing the raging tempests to blow, and forthwith, in one moment, when it so pleases him, making a perfect calm ; keeping the sea, which seems constantly threatening the earth with devastation, suspended as it were in air ; at one time, lashing it into fury by the impetuosity of the winds ; at another, appeasing its rage, and stilling all its waves. Here we might refer to those glowing descriptions of divine power, as illustrated by natural events, which occur throughout Scripture ; but more especially in the book of Job and the prophecies of Isaiah. These, however, I purposely omit, because a better opportunity of introducing them will be found when

[Marginal note: Rejects the use of the phrase, "Nature is God." although not entirely.]

---

1 Dryden's Virgil, Book iv. l. 252–262.
2 He maintains, in the beginning of the First Book, that nothing is produced of nothing, but that all things are formed out of certain primitive materials. He also perverts the ordinary course of generation into an argument against the existence of God. In the Fifth Book, however, he admits that the world was born and will die.

I come to treat of the Scriptural account of the creation. (*Infra*, chap. xiv. s. 1, 2, 20, *sq.*) I only wish to observe here, that this method of investigating the divine perfections, by tracing the lineaments of his countenance as shadowed forth in the firmament and on the earth, is common both to those within and to those without the pale of the Church. From the power of God we are naturally led to consider his eternity, since that from which all other things derive their origin must necessarily be self-existent and eternal. Moreover, if it be asked what cause induced him to create all things at first, and now inclines him to preserve them, we shall find that there could be no other cause than his own goodness. But if this is the only cause, nothing more should be required to draw forth our love towards him; every creature, as the Psalmist reminds us, participating in his mercy. "His tender mercies are over all his works" (Ps. cxlv. 9).

Contemplation of God's power leads to His eternity.

God's goodness the cause of His creative impulse.

7. In the second class of God's works, namely, those which are above the ordinary course of nature, the evidence of his perfections are in every respect equally clear. For in conducting the affairs of men, he so arranges the course of his providence, as daily to declare, by the clearest manifestations, that though all are in innumerable ways the partakers of his bounty, the righteous are the special objects of his favour, the wicked and profane the special objects of his severity. It is impossible to doubt his punishment of crimes; while at the same time he, in no unequivocal manner, declares that he is the protector, and even the avenger of innocence, by shedding blessings on the good, helping their necessities, soothing and solacing their griefs, relieving their sufferings, and in all ways providing for their safety. And though he often permits the guilty to exult for a time with impunity, and the innocent to be driven to and fro in adversity, nay, even to be wickedly and iniquitously oppressed, this ought not to produce any uncertainty as to the uniform justice of all his procedure. Nay, an opposite inference should be drawn. When any one crime calls forth visible manifestations of his anger, it must be because he hates all crimes; and, on the other hand, his leaving many crimes unpunished, only proves that there is a judgment in reserve, when the punishment now delayed shall be inflicted. In like manner, how richly does he supply us with the means of contemplating his mercy, when, as frequently happens, he continues to visit miserable sinners with unwearied kindness, until he subdues their depravity, and woos them back with more than a parent's fondness?

God exhibits his justice in nature by the way that He blesses innocence and punishes evil

8. To this purpose the Psalmist (Ps. cvii.), mentioning how God, in a wondrous manner, often brings sudden and unexpected succour to the miserable when almost on the brink of despair, whether in protecting them when they stray in deserts, and at length leading them back into the right path, or supplying them with food when famishing for want, or delivering them when captive from iron fetters and foul dungeons, or conducting them safe into harbour after shipwreck, or bringing them back from the gates of death by curing

their diseases, or, after burning up the fields with heat and drought, fertilising them with the river of his grace, or exalting the meanest of the people, and casting down the mighty from their lofty seats:— the Psalmist, after bringing forward examples of this description, infers that those things which men call fortuitous events, are so many proofs of divine providence, and more especially of paternal clemency, furnishing ground of joy to the righteous, and at the same time stopping the mouths of the ungodly. But as the greater part of mankind, enslaved by error, walk blindfold in this glorious theatre, he exclaims that it is a rare and singular wisdom to meditate carefully on these works of God, which many, who seem most sharp-sighted in other respects, behold without profit. It is indeed true, that the brightest manifestation of divine glory finds not one genuine spectator among a hundred. Still, neither his power nor his wisdom is shrouded in darkness. His power is strikingly displayed when the rage of the wicked, to all appearance irresistible, is crushed in a single moment; their arrogance subdued, their strongest bulwarks overthrown, their armour dashed to pieces, their strength broken, their schemes defeated without an effort, and audacity which set itself above the heavens is precipitated to the lowest depths of the earth. On the other hand, the poor are raised up out of the dust, and the needy lifted out of the dunghill (Ps. cxiii. 7), the oppressed and afflicted are rescued in extremity, the despairing animated with hope, the unarmed defeat the armed, the few the many, the weak the strong. The excellence of the divine wisdom is manifested in distributing everything in due season, confounding the wisdom of the world, and taking the wise in their own craftiness (1 Cor. iii. 19); in short, conducting all things in perfect accordance with reason.

9. We see there is no need of a long and laborious train of argument in order to obtain proofs which illustrate and assert the Divine Majesty. The few which we have merely touched, show them to be so immediately within our reach in every quarter, that we can trace them with the eye, or point to them with the finger. And here we must observe again (see chap. ii. s. 2), that the knowledge of God which we are invited to cultivate is not that which, resting satisfied with empty speculation, only flutters in the brain, but a knowledge which will prove substantial and fruitful wherever it is duly perceived, and rooted in the heart. The Lord is manifested by his perfections. When we feel their power within us, and are conscious of their benefits, the knowledge must impress us much more vividly than if we merely imagined a God whose presence we never felt. Hence it is obvious that, in seeking God, the most direct path and the fittest method is, not to attempt with presumptuous curiosity to pry into his essence, which is rather to be adored than minutely discussed, but to contemplate him in his works, by which he draws near, becomes familiar, and in a manner communicates himself to us. To this the Apostle referred when he said, that we need not go far in

The earth "a glorious theater" of the nature to those with eyes to behold it.

The excellence of the divine wisdom shown by God's management of His universe in perfect accord with the dictates of reason.

True knowledge of God to be perceived and rooted in the heart.

search of him (Acts xvii. 27), because, by the continual working of his power he dwells in every one of us. Accordingly, David (Psalm cxlv.), after acknowledging that his greatness is unsearchable, proceeds to enumerate his works, declaring that his greatness will thereby be unfolded. It therefore becomes us also diligently to prosecute that investigation of God which so enraptures the soul with admiration as, at the same time, to make an efficacious impression on it. And, as Augustine expresses it (in Psalm cxliv.), since we are unable to comprehend Him, and are, as it were, overpowered by his greatness, our proper course is to contemplate his works, and so refresh ourselves with his goodness.

10. By the knowledge thus acquired, we ought not only to be stimulated to worship God, but also aroused and elevated to the hope of future life. For, observing that the manifestations which the Lord gives both of his mercy and severity are only begun and incomplete, we ought to infer that these are doubtless only a prelude to higher manifestations, of which the full display is reserved for another state. Conversely, when we see the righteous brought into affliction by the ungodly, assailed with injuries, overwhelmed with calumnies, and lacerated by insult and contumely, while, on the contrary, the wicked flourish, prosper, acquire ease and honour, and all these with impunity, we ought forthwith to infer, that there will be a future life in which iniquity shall receive its punishment and righteousness its reward. Moreover, when we observe that the Lord often lays his chastening rod on the righteous, we may the more surely conclude, that far less will the unrighteous ultimately escape the scourges of his anger. There is a well-known passage in Augustine (De Civitat. Dei, lib. i. c. 8), "Were all sin now visited with open punishment, it might be thought that nothing was reserved for the final judgment; and, on the other hand, were no sin now openly punished, it might be supposed there was no divine providence." It must be acknowledged, therefore, that in each of the works of God, and more especially in the whole of them taken together, the divine perfections are delineated as in a picture, and the whole human race thereby invited and allured to acquire the knowledge of God, and, in consequence of this knowledge, true and complete felicity. Moreover, while his perfections are thus most vividly displayed, the only means of ascertaining their practical operation and tendency is to descend into ourselves, and consider how it is that the Lord there manifests his wisdom, power, and energy,—how he there displays his justice, goodness, and mercy. For although David (Psalm xcii. 6) justly complains of the extreme infatuation of the ungodly in not pondering the deep counsels of God, as exhibited in the government of the human race, what he elsewhere says (Psalm xl.) is most true, that the wonders of the divine wisdom in this respect are more in number than the hairs of our head. But I leave this topic at present, as it will be more fully considered afterwards in its own place (Book I. c. 16, sec. 6–9).

The vicissitudes and injustices of earthly life point beyond to a time of retribution in a life after death.

11. Bright, however, as is the manifestation which God gives both of himself and his immortal kingdom in the mirror of his works, so great is our stupidity, so dull are we in regard to these bright manifestations, that we derive no benefit from them.   For in regard to the fabric and admirable arrangement of the universe, how few of us are there who, in lifting our eyes to the heavens, or looking abroad on the various regions of the earth, ever think of the Creator?   Do we not rather overlook Him, and sluggishly content ourselves with a view of his works?   And then in regard to supernatural events, though these are occurring every day, how few are there who ascribe them to the ruling providence of God—how many who imagine that they are casual results produced by the blind evolutions of the wheel of chance? Even when, under the guidance and direction of these events, we are in a manner forced to the contemplation of God (a circumstance which all must occasionally experience), and are thus led to form some impressions of Deity, we immediately fly off to carnal dreams and depraved fictions, and so by our vanity corrupt heavenly truth. This far, indeed, we differ from each other, in that every one appropriates to himself some peculiar error ; but we are all alike in this, that we substitute monstrous fictions for the one living and true God —a disease not confined to obtuse and vulgar minds, but affecting the noblest, and those who, in other respects, are singularly acute.   How lavishly in this respect have the whole body of philosophers betrayed their stupidity and want of sense ?   To say nothing of the others whose absurdities are of a still grosser description, how completely does Plato, the soberest and most religious of them all, lose himself in his round globe ?[1]   What must be the case with the rest, when the leaders, who ought to have set them an example, commit such blunders, and labour under such hallucinations?   In like manner, while the government of the world places the doctrine of providence beyond dispute, the practical result is the same as if it were believed that all things were carried hither and thither at the caprice of chance; so prone are we to vanity and error.   I am still referring to the most distinguished of the philosophers, and not to the common herd, whose madness in profaning the truth of God exceeds all bounds.

12. Hence that immense flood of error with which the whole world is overflowed.   Every individual mind being a kind of labyrinth, it is not wonderful, not only that each nation has adopted a variety of fictions, but that almost every man has had his own god.   To the darkness of ignorance have been added presumption and wantonness, and hence there is scarcely an individual to be found without some idol or phantom as a substitute for Deity.   Like water gushing forth from a large and copious spring, immense crowds of gods have issued from the human mind, every man giving himself full license, and

[Margin note: Man's stupidity is such that all of these evidences of the existence and nature of God do Him no good]

[1] Plato in Timæos.   See also Cic. De Nat. Deorum, lib. i ; Plut. De Philos Placitis, lib. i.

devising some peculiar form of divinity, to meet his own views. It is unnecessary here to attempt a catalogue of the superstitions with which the world was overspread. The thing were endless; and the corruptions themselves, though not a word should be said, furnish abundant evidence of the blindness of the human mind. I say nothing of the rude and illiterate vulgar; but among the philosophers[1] who attempted, by reason and learning, to pierce the heavens, what shameful disagreement! The higher any one was endued with genius, and the more he was polished by science and art, the more specious was the colouring which he gave to his opinions. All these, however, if examined more closely, will be found to be vain show. The Stoics plumed themselves on their acuteness, when they said[2] that the various names of God might be extracted from all the parts of nature, and yet that his unity was not thereby divided: as if we were not already too prone to vanity, and had no need of being presented with an endless multiplicity of gods, to lead us further and more grossly into error. The mystic theology of the Egyptians shows how sedulously they laboured to be thought rational on this subject.[3] And, perhaps, at the first glance, some show of probability might deceive the simple and unwary; but never did any mortal devise a scheme by which religion was not foully corrupted. This endless variety and confusion emboldened the Epicureans, and other gross despisers of piety, to cut off all sense of God. For when they saw that the wisest contradicted each other, they hesitated not to infer from their dissensions, and from the frivolous and absurd doctrines of each, that men foolishly, and to no purpose, brought torment upon themselves by searching for a God, there being none: and they thought this inference safe, because it was better at once to deny God altogether than to feign uncertain gods, and thereafter engage in quarrels without end. They, indeed, argue absurdly, or rather weave a cloak for their impiety out of human ignorance; though ignorance surely cannot derogate from the prerogatives of God. But since all confess that there is no topic on which such difference exists, both among learned and unlearned, the proper inference is, that the human mind, which thus errs in inquiring after God, is dull and blind in heavenly mysteries. Some praise the answer of Simonides, who being asked by King Hiero what God was, asked a day to consider. When the king next day repeated the question, he asked two days; and after repeatedly doubling the number of days, at length replied, "The longer I consider, the darker the subject appears."[4] He, no doubt, wisely suspended his opinion, when he did not see clearly:

[margin note:] The theology of the Greeks and Egyptians show how far afield natural knowledge can lead even wise men.

---

[1] Cicero: Qui deos esse dixerunt tanta sunt in varietate ac dissensione, ut eorum molestum sit enumerare sententias.—Cicero, De Nat Deorum, lib. i. and ii. Lactant Inst. Div. lib. i. &c.

[2] Seneca, De Benef., lib. iv. c. 7, et Natural. Quæst, lib. i. in Præf., et lib. ii, c 45.

[3] Plutarch. lib. De Iside et Osiride.

[4] Cicero. De Nat. Deor. lib. i.

still his answer shows, that if men are only naturally taught, instead of having any distinct, solid, or certain knowledge, they fasten only on contradictory principles, and, in consequence, worship an unknown God.

13. Hence we must hold, that whosoever adulterates pure religion (and this must be the case with all who cling to their own views), make a departure from the one God. No doubt, they will allege that they have a different intention ; but it is of little consequence what they intend or persuade themselves to believe, since the Holy Spirit pronounces all to be apostates who, in the blindness of their minds, substitute demons in the place of God. For this reason Paul declares that the Ephesians were "without God" (Eph. ii. 12), until they had learned from the gospel what it is to worship the true God. Nor must this be restricted to one people only, since, in another place, he declares in general, that all men "became vain in their imaginations," after the majesty of the Creator was manifested to them in the structure of the world. Accordingly, in order to make way for the only true God, he condemns all the gods celebrated among the Gentiles as lying and false, leaving no Deity anywhere but in Mount Zion, where the special knowledge of God was professed (Hab. ii. 18, 20). Among the Gentiles in the time of Christ, the Samaritans undoubtedly made the nearest approach to true piety ; yet we hear from his own mouth that they worshipped they knew not what (John iv. 22); whence it follows that they were deluded by vain errors. In short, though all did not give way to gross vice, or rush headlong into open idolatry, there was no pure and authentic religion founded merely on common belief. A few individuals may not have gone all insane lengths with the vulgar ; still Paul's declaration remains true, that the wisdom of God was not apprehended by the princes of this world (1 Cor. ii. 8). But if the most distinguished wandered in darkness, what shall we say of the refuse ? No wonder, therefore, that all worship of man's device is repudiated by the Holy Spirit as degenerate. Any opinion which man can form in heavenly mysteries, though it may not beget a long train of errors, is still the parent of error. And though nothing worse should happen, even this is no light sin—to worship an unknown God at random. Of this sin, however, we hear from our Saviour's own mouth (John iv. 22), that all are guilty who have not been taught out of the law who the God is whom they ought to worship. Nay, even Socrates in Xenophon (lib. i. Memorabilia) lauds the response of Apollo enjoining every man to worship the gods according to the rites of his country, and the particular practice of his own city. But what right have mortals thus to decide of their own authority in a matter which is far above the world ; or who can so acquiesce in the will of his forefathers, or the decrees of the people, as unhesitatingly to receive a god at their hands ? Every one will adhere to his own judgment sooner than submit to the dictation of others. Since, therefore, in regulating the worship of God, the custom of a city, or

[margin note:] Though all did not give way to gross vice, or rush headlong into open idolatry, there was no pure and authentic religion founded on common belief.

[margin note:] Since men are too frail, God has no choice but to reveal Himself.

the consent of antiquity, is a too feeble and fragile bond of piety: it remains that God himself must bear witness to himself from heaven.

14. In vain for us, therefore, does Creation exhibit so many bright lamps lighted up to show forth the glory of its Author. Though they beam upon us from every quarter, they are altogether insufficient of themselves to lead us into the right path. Some sparks, undoubtedly, they do throw out; but these are quenched before they can give forth a brighter effulgence. Wherefore, the apostle, in the very place where he says that the worlds are images of invisible things, adds that it is *by faith* we understand that they were framed by the word of God (Heb. xi. 3); thereby intimating that the invisible Godhead is indeed represented by such displays, but that we have no eyes to perceive it until they are enlightened through faith by internal revelation from God. When Paul says that that which may be known of God is manifested by the creation of the world, he does not mean such a manifestation as may be comprehended by the wit of man (Rom. i. 19); on the contrary, he shows that it has no further effect than to render us inexcusable (Acts xvii. 27). And though he says, elsewhere, that we have not far to seek for God, inasmuch as he dwells within us, he shows, in another passage, to what extent this nearness to God is availing. God, says he, " in times past, suffered all nations to walk in their own ways. Nevertheless, he left not himself without witness, in that he did good, and gave us rain from heaven, and fruitful seasons, filling our hearts with food and gladness" (Acts xiv. 16, 17). But though God is not left without a witness, while, with numberless varied acts of kindness, he woos men to the knowledge of himself, yet they cease not to follow their own ways, in other words, deadly errors.

15. But though we are deficient in natural powers which might enable us to rise to a pure and clear knowledge of God, still, as the dulness which prevents us is within, there is no room for excuse. We cannot plead ignorance, without being at the same time convicted by our own consciences both of sloth and ingratitude. It were, indeed, a strange defence for man to pretend that he has no ears to hear the truth, while dumb creatures have voices loud enough to declare it; to allege that he is unable to see that which creatures without eyes demonstrate; to excuse himself on the ground of weakness of mind, while all creatures without reason are able to teach. Wherefore, when we wander and go astray, we are justly shut out from every species of excuse, because all things point to the right path. But while man must bear the guilt of corrupting the seed of divine knowledge so wondrously deposited in his mind, and preventing it from bearing good and genuine fruit, it is still most true that we are not sufficiently instructed by that bare and simple, but magnificent testimony which the creatures bear to the glory of their Creator. For no sooner do we, from a survey of the world, obtain some slight know-

Natural knowledge is not enough to give a saving knowledge of God.

Man's stupidity does not excuse him.

ledge of Deity, than we pass by the true God, and set up in his stead the dream and phantom of our own brain, drawing away the praise of justice, wisdom, and goodness from the fountain-head, and transferring it to some other quarter.   Moreover, by the erroneous estimate we form, we either so obscure or pervert his daily works, as at once to rob them of their glory, and the author of them of his just praise.

CHAPTER VI.

THE NEED OF SCRIPTURE, AS A GUIDE AND TEACHER, IN COMING TO GOD AS A CREATOR.

Sections.

1. God gives his elect a better help to the knowledge of himself—viz. the Holy Scriptures. This he did from the very first.
2. First. By oracles and visions, and the ministry of the Patriarchs. Secondly, By the promulgation of the Law, and the preaching of the Prophets. Why the doctrines of religion are committed to writing.
3. This view confirmed, 1. By the depravity of our nature making it necessary in every one who would know God to have recourse to the word; 2. From those passages of the Psalms in which God is introduced as reigning.
4. Another confirmation from certain direct statements in the Psalms. Lastly, From the words of our Saviour.

1. THEREFORE, though the effulgence which is presented to every eye, both in the heavens and on the earth, leaves the ingratitude of man without excuse, since God, in order to bring the whole human race under the same condemnation, holds forth to all, without exception, a mirror of his Deity in his works, another and better help must be given to guide us properly to God as a Creator. Not in vain, therefore, has he added the light of his Word in order that he might make himself known unto salvation, and bestowed the privilege on those whom he was pleased to bring into nearer and more familiar relation to himself. For, seeing how the minds of men were carried to and fro, and found no certain resting-place, he chose the Jews for a peculiar people, and then hedged them in that they might not, like others, go astray. And not in vain does he, by the same means, retain us in his knowledge, since but for this, even those who, in comparison of others, seem to stand strong, would quickly fall away. For as the aged, or those whose sight is defective, when any book, however fair, is set before them, though they perceive that there is something written, are scarcely able to make out two consecutive words, but, when aided by glasses, begin to read distinctly, so Scripture, gathering together the impressions of Deity, which, till then, lay confused in their minds, dissipates the darkness, and shows us the true God clearly. God therefore bestows a gift of singular value, when, for the instruction of the Church, he employs not dumb teachers merely, but opens his own sacred mouth; when he not only proclaims that some God must be worshipped, but at the same time declares that He is the God to whom worship is due; when he not

God not only tells us that some God must be worshipped but tells us that He is God to whom worship is due.

only teaches his elect to have respect to God, but manifests himself as the God to whom this respect should be paid.

The course which God followed towards his Church from the very first, was to supplement these common proofs by the addition of his Word, as a surer and more direct means of discovering himself. And there can be no doubt that it was by this help, Adam, Noah, Abraham, and the other patriarchs, attained to that familiar knowledge which, in a manner, distinguished them from unbelievers. I am not now speaking of the peculiar doctrines of faith by which they were elevated to the hope of eternal blessedness. It was necessary, in passing from death unto life, that they should know God, not only as a Creator, but as a Redeemer also; and both kinds of knowledge they certainly did obtain from the Word. In point of order, however, the knowledge first given was that which made them acquainted with the God by whom the world was made and is governed. To this first knowledge was afterwards added the more intimate knowledge which alone quickens dead souls, and by which God is known, not only as the Creator of the world, and the sole author and disposer of all events, but also as a Redeemer, in the person of the Mediator. But as the fall and the corruption of nature have not yet been considered, I now postpone the consideration of the remedy (for which, see Book II. c. vi., &c.). Let the reader then remember, that I am not now treating of the covenant by which God adopted the children of Abraham, or of that branch of doctrine by which, as founded in Christ, believers have, properly speaking, been in all ages separated from the profane heathen. I am only showing that it is necessary to apply to Scripture, in order to learn the sure marks which distinguish God, as the Creator of the world, from the whole herd of fictitious gods. We shall afterward, in due course, consider the work of Redemption. In the mean time, though we shall adduce many passages from the New Testament, and some also from the Law and the Prophets, in which express mention is made of Christ, the only object will be to show that God, the Maker of the world, is manifested to us in Scripture, and his true character expounded, so as to save us from wandering up and down, as in a labyrinth, in search of some doubtful deity.

2. Whether God revealed himself to the fathers by oracles and visions,[1] or, by the instrumentality and ministry of men, suggested what they were to hand down to posterity, there cannot be a doubt that the certainty of what he taught them was firmly engraven on their hearts, so that they felt assured and knew that the things which they learnt came forth from God, who invariably accompanied his word with a sure testimony, infinitely superior to mere opinion. At length, in order that, while doctrine was continually enlarged,

---

1 The French adds, " C'est à dire, temoignages celestes ;"—that is to say, messages from heaven.

its truth might subsist in the world during all ages, it was his pleasure that the same oracles which he had deposited with the fathers should be consigned, as it were, to public records. With this view the law was promulgated, and prophets were afterwards added to be its interpreters. For though the uses of the law were manifold (Book II. c. 7 and 8), and the special office assigned to Moses and all the prophets was to teach the method of reconciliation between God and man (whence Paul calls Christ "the end of the law," Rom. x. 4); still I repeat that, in addition to the proper doctrine of faith and repentance in which Christ is set forth as a Mediator, the Scriptures employ certain marks and tokens to distinguish the only wise and true God, considered as the Creator and Governor of the world, and thereby guard against his being confounded with the herd of false deities. Therefore, while it becomes man seriously to employ his eyes in considering the works of God, since a place has been assigned him in this most glorious theatre that he may be a spectator of them, his special duty is to give ear to the Word, that he may the better profit.[1] Hence it is not strange that those who are born in darkness become more and more hardened in their stupidity; because the vast majority, instead of confining themselves within due bounds by listening with docility to the Word, exult in their own vanity. If true religion is to beam upon us, our principle must be, that it is necessary to begin with heavenly teaching, and that it is impossible for any man to obtain even the minutest portion of right and sound doctrine without being a disciple of Scripture. Hence the first step in true knowledge is taken, when we reverently embrace the testimony which God has been pleased therein to give of himself. For not only does faith, full and perfect faith, but all correct knowledge of God, originate in obedience. And surely in this respect God has with singular Providence provided for mankind in all ages.

No knowledge of true doctrine can be obtained without a thorough knowledge of the Scriptures.

3. For if we reflect how prone the human mind is to lapse into forgetfulness of God, how readily inclined to every kind of error, how bent every now and then on devising new and fictitious religions, it will be easy to understand how necessary it was to make such a depository of doctrine as would secure it from either perishing by the neglect, vanishing away amid the errors, or being corrupted by the presumptuous audacity of men. It being thus manifest that God, foreseeing the inefficiency of his image imprinted on the fair form of the universe, has given the assistance of his Word to all whom he has ever been pleased to instruct effectually, we, too, must pursue this straight path, if we aspire in earnest to a genuine contemplation of God;—we must go, I say, to the Word, where the character of God, drawn from his works, is described accurately and to the life;

---

[1] Tertullian, Apologet. adv. Gentes: "Quæ plenius et impressius tam ipsum quam dispositiones ejus et voluntates adiremus, instrumentum adjecit literaturæ," &c.

these works being estimated, not by our depraved judgment, but by the standard of eternal truth. If, as I lately said, we turn aside from it, how great soever the speed with which we move, we shall never reach the goal, because we are off the course. We should consider that the brightness of the Divine countenance, which even an apostle declares to be inaccessible (1 Tim. vi. 16), is a kind of labyrinth,—a labyrinth to us inextricable, if the Word do not serve us as a thread to guide our path; and that it is better to limp in the way, than run with the greatest swiftness out of it. Hence the Psalmist, after repeatedly declaring (Psalm xciii. xcvi. xcvii. xcix. &c.) that superstition should be banished from the world in order that pure religion may flourish, introduces God as *reigning;* meaning by the term, not the power which he possesses and which he exerts in the government of universal nature, but the doctrine by which he maintains his due supremacy : because error never can be eradicated from the heart of man until the true knowledge of God has been implanted in it.

4. Accordingly, the same prophet, after mentioning that the heavens declare the glory of God, that the firmament showeth forth the works of his hands, that the regular succession of day and night proclaim his Majesty, proceeds to make mention of the Word:—"The law of the Lord," says he, "is perfect, converting the soul; the testimony of the Lord is sure, making wise the simple. The statutes of the Lord are right, rejoicing the heart; the commandment of the Lord is pure, enlightening the eyes" (Psalm xix. 1—9). For though the law has other uses besides (as to which, see Book II. c. 7, sec. 6, 10, 12), the general meaning is, that it is the proper school for training the children of God; the invitation given to all nations, to behold him in the heavens and earth, proving of no avail. The same view is taken in the xxix. Psalm, where the Psalmist, after discoursing on the dreadful voice of God, which, in thunder, wind, rain, whirlwind, and tempest, shakes the earth, makes the mountains tremble, and breaks the cedars, concludes by saying, "that in his temple doth every one speak of his glory," unbelievers being deaf to all God's words when they echo in the air. In like manner another Psalm, after describing the raging billows of the sea, thus concludes, "Thy testimonies are very sure; holiness becometh thine house for ever" (Psalm xciii. 5). To the same effect are the words of our Saviour to the Samaritan woman, when he told her that her nation and all other nations worshipped they knew not what; and that the Jews alone gave worship to the true God (John iv. 22). Since the human mind, through its weakness, was altogether unable to come to God if not aided and upheld by his sacred word, it necessarily followed that all mankind, the Jews excepted, inasmuch as they sought God without the Word, were labouring under vanity and error.

The Jews alone among the nations worshipped God without error, for they had God's Word.

CHAPTER VII.

THE TESTIMONY OF THE SPIRIT NECESSARY TO GIVE FULL AUTHOR-
ITY TO SCRIPTURE. THE IMPIETY OF PRETENDING THAT THE
CREDIBILITY OF SCRIPTURE DEPENDS ON THE JUDGMENT
OF THE CHURCH.

Sections.

1. The authority of Scripture derived not from men, but from the Spirit of God. Objection, That Scripture depends on the decision of the Church. Refutation, I.
The truth of God would thus be subjected to the will of man. II. It is insulting
to the Holy Spirit. III. It establishes a tyranny in the Church. IV. It forms a
mass of errors. V. It subverts conscience. VI. It exposes our faith to the scoffs
of the profane.
2. Another reply to the objection drawn from the words of the Apostle Paul. Solution
of the difficulties started by opponents. A second objection refuted.
3 A third objection founded on a sentiment of Augustine considered.
4. Conclusion, That the authority of Scripture is founded on its being spoken by God.
This confirmed by the conscience of the godly, and the consent of all men of the
least candour. A fourth objection common in the mouths of the profane. Refutation.
5. Last and necessary conclusion, That the authority of Scripture is sealed on the
hearts of believers by the testimony of the Holy Spirit. The certainty of this testimony. Confirmation of it from a passage of Isaiah, and the experience of believers.
Also, from another passage of Isaiah.

1. BEFORE proceeding farther, it seems proper to make some observations on the authority of Scripture, in order that our minds may
not only be prepared to receive it with reference, but be divested of
all doubt.

When that which professes to be the Word of God is acknowledged
to be so, no person, unless devoid of common sense and the feelings
of a man, will have the desperate hardihood to refuse credit to the
speaker. But since no daily responses are given from heaven, and
the Scriptures are the only records in which God has been pleased to
consign his truth to perpetual remembrance, the full authority which
they ought to possess with the faithful is not recognised, unless they
are believed to have come from heaven, as directly as if God had
been heard giving utterance to them. This subject well deserves to
be treated more at large, and pondered more accurately. But my
readers will pardon me for having more regard to what my plan
admits than to what the extent of this topic requires.

A most pernicious error has very generally prevailed—viz. that
Scripture is of importance only in so far as conceded to it by the suffrage of the Church ; as if the eternal and inviolable truth of God
could depend on the will of men. With great insult to the Holy

Spirit, it is asked, Who can assure us that the Scriptures proceeded from God; who guarantee that they have come down safe and unimpaired to our times; who persuade us that *this* book is to be received with reverence, and *that one* expunged from the list, did not the Church regulate all these things with certainty? On the determination of the Church, therefore, it is said, depend both the reverence which is due to Scripture and the books which are to be admitted into the canon. Thus profane men, seeking, under the pretext of the Church, to introduce unbridled tyranny, care not in what absurdities they entangle themselves and others, provided they extort from the simple this one acknowledgment—viz. that there is nothing which the Church cannot do. But what is to become of miserable consciences in quest of some solid assurance of eternal life, if all the promises with regard to it have no better support than man's judgment? On being told so, will they cease to doubt and tremble? On the other hand, to what jeers of the wicked is our faith subjected—into how great suspicion is it brought with all, if believed to have only a precarious authority lent to it by the good-will of men?

2. These ravings are admirably refuted by a single expression of an apostle. Paul testifies that the Church is "built on the foundation of the apostles and prophets" (Eph. ii. 20). If the doctrine of the apostles and prophets is the foundation of the Church, the former must have had its certainty before the latter began to exist. Nor is there any room for the cavil, that though the Church derives her first beginning from thence, it still remains doubtful what writings are to be attributed to the apostles and prophets, until her judgment is interposed. For if the Christian Church was founded at first on the writings of the prophets, and the preaching of the apostles, that doctrine, wheresoever it may be found, was certainly ascertained and sanctioned antecedently to the Church, since, but for this, the Church herself never could have existed.[1] Nothing, therefore, can be more absurd than the fiction, that the power of judging Scripture is in the Church, and that on her nod its certainty depends. When the Church receives it, and gives it the stamp of her authority, she does not make that authentic which was otherwise doubtful or controverted, but, acknowledging it as the truth of God, she, as in duty bound, shows her reverence by an unhesitating assent. As to the question, How shall we be persuaded that it came from God without recurring to a decree of the Church? it is just the same as if it were asked, How shall we learn to distinguish light from darkness, white from black, sweet from bitter? Scripture bears upon the face of it as clear evidence of its truth, as white and black do of their colour, sweet and bitter of their taste.

3. I am aware it is usual to quote a sentence of Augustine, in which

[1] The French adds, "Comme le fondement va deuant l'edifice;"—as the foundation goes before the house.

he says that he would not believe the gospel, were he not moved by the authority of the Church (Aug. Cont. Epist. Fundament. c. v.). But it is easy to discover from the context, how inaccurate and unfair it is to give it such a meaning. He was reasoning against the Manichees, who insisted on being implicitly believed, alleging that they had the truth, though they did not show they had. But as they pretended to appeal to the gospel in support of Manes, he asks what they would do if they fell in with a man who did not even believe the gospel—what kind of argument they would use to bring him over to their opinion. He afterwards adds, " But I would not believe the gospel," &c. ; meaning, that were he a stranger to the faith, the only thing which could induce him to embrace the gospel would be the authority of the Church. And is it anything wonderful, that one who does not know Christ should pay respect to men ?

Augustine did not hold the approval of the Scriptures as necessary for its validation.

Augustine, therefore, does not here say that the faith of the godly is founded on the authority of the Church ; nor does he mean that the certainty of the gospel depends upon it; he merely says that unbelievers would have no certainty of the gospel, so as thereby to win Christ, were they not influenced by the consent of the Church. And he clearly shows this to be his meaning, by thus expressing himself a little before : " When I have praised my own creed, and ridiculed yours, who do you suppose is to judge between us; or what more is to be done than to quit those who, inviting us to certainty, afterwards command us to believe uncertainty, and follow those who invite us, in the first instance, to believe what we are not yet able to comprehend, that waxing stronger through faith itself, we may become able to understand what we believe—no longer men, but God himself internally strengthening and illuminating our minds?" These unquestionably are the words of Augustine (August. Cont. Epist. Fundament. cap. iv.) ; and the obvious inference from them is, that this holy man had no intention to suspend our faith in Scripture on the nod or decision of the Church,[1] but only to intimate (what we too admit to be true) that those who are not yet enlightened by the Spirit of God, become teachable by reverence for the Church, and thus submit to learn the faith of Christ from the gospel. In this way, though the authority of the Church leads us on, and prepares us to believe in the gospel, it is plain that Augustine would have the certainty of the godly to rest on a very different foundation.[2]

At the same time, I deny not that he often presses the Manichees with the consent of the whole Church, while arguing in support of

---

[1] The French adds, " La destournant du seul fondement qu'elle a en l'Escriture ;"—diverting it from the only foundation which it has in Scripture.

[2] Augustin. De Ordine, lib. ii. c. 9. " Ad discendum dupliciter movemur, auctoritate atque ratione : tempore auctoritas, re autem ratio prior est," &c. " Itaque quamquam bonorum auctoritas imperitæ multitudini videatur esse salubrior, ratio vero aptior eruditis : tamen quia nullus hominum nisi ex imperito peritus fit, &c., evenit ut omnibus bona, magna, occulta discere cupientibus, non aperiat nisi auctoritas januam," &c. He has many other excellent things to the same effect.

the Scriptures, which they rejected.   Hence he upbraids Faustus (Lib. xxxii.) for not submitting to evangelical truth—truth so well founded, so firmly established, so gloriously renowned, and handed down by sure succession from the days of the apostles.   But he nowhere insinuates that the authority which we give to the Scriptures depends on the definitions or devices of men.   He only brings forward the universal judgment of the Church, as a point most pertinent to the cause, and one, moreover, in which he had the advantage of his opponents.   Any one who desires to see this more fully proved may read his short treatise, *De Utilitate Credendi* (The Advantages of Believing), where it will be found that the only facility of believing which he recommends is that which affords an introduction, and forms a fit commencement to inquiry; while he declares that we ought not to be satisfied with opinion, but to strive after substantial truth.

4. It is necessary to attend to what I lately said, that our faith in doctrine is not established until we have a perfect conviction that God is its author.   Hence, the highest proof of Scripture is uniformly taken from the character of him whose word it is.   The prophets and apostles boast not their own acuteness, or any qualities which win credit to speakers, nor do they dwell on reasons; but they appeal to the sacred name of God, in order that the whole world may be compelled to submission.   The next thing to be considered is, how it appears not probable merely, but certain, that the name of God is neither rashly nor cunningly pretended.   If, then, we would consult most effectually for our consciences, and save them from being driven about in a whirl of uncertainty, from wavering, and even stumbling at the smallest obstacle, our conviction of the truth of Scripture must be derived from a higher source than human conjectures, judgments, or reasons; namely, the secret testimony of the Spirit.   It is true, indeed, that if we choose to proceed in the way of argument, it is easy to establish, by evidence of various kinds, that if there is a God in heaven, the Law, the Prophecies, and the Gospel, proceeded from him. Nay, although learned men, and men of the greatest talent, should take the opposite side, summoning and ostentatiously displaying all the powers of their genius in the discussion; if they are not possessed of shameless effrontery, they will be compelled to confess that the Scripture exhibits clear evidence of its being spoken by God, and, consequently, of its containing his heavenly doctrine.   We shall see a little farther on, that the volume of sacred Scripture very far surpasses all other writings.   Nay, if we look at it with clear eyes and unbiassed judgment, it will forthwith present itself with a divine majesty which will subdue our presumptuous opposition, and force us to do it homage.

Still, however, it is preposterous to attempt, by discussion, to rear up a full faith in Scripture.   True, were I called to contend with the craftiest despisers of God, I trust, though I am not possessed of the highest ability or eloquence, I should not find it difficult to stop their obstreperous mouths; I could, without much ado, put down the boastings which they mutter in corners, were anything to be gained by refuting their cavils. But although we may maintain the sacred Word of God against gainsayers, it does not follow that we shall forthwith implant the certainty which faith requires in their hearts. Profane men think that religion rests only on opinion, and, therefore, that they may not believe foolishly, or on slight grounds desire and insist to have it proved by reason that Moses and the prophets were divinely inspired. But I answer, that the testimony of the Spirit is superior to reason. For as God alone can properly bear witness to his own words, so these words will not obtain full credit in the hearts of men, until they are sealed by the inward testimony of the Spirit. The same Spirit, therefore, who spoke by the mouth of the prophets, must penetrate our hearts, in order to convince us that they faithfully delivered the message with which they were divinely intrusted. This connection is most aptly expressed by Isaiah in these words, "My Spirit that is upon thee, and my words which I have put in thy mouth, shall not depart out of thy mouth, nor out of the mouth of thy seed, nor out of the mouth of thy seed's seed, saith the Lord, from henceforth and for ever" (Isa. lix. 21). Some worthy persons feel disconcerted, because, while the wicked murmur with impunity at the word of God, they have not a clear proof at hand to silence them, forgetting that the Spirit is called an earnest and seal to confirm the faith of the godly, for this very reason, that, until he enlightens their minds, they are tossed to and fro in a sea of doubts.

5. Let it therefore be held as fixed, that those who are inwardly taught by the Holy Spirit acquiesce implicitly in Scripture; that Scripture, carrying its own evidence along with it, deigns not to submit to proofs and arguments, but owes the full conviction with which we ought to receive it to the testimony of the Spirit.[1] Enlightened by him, we no longer believe, either on our own judgment or that of others, that the Scriptures are from God; but, in a way superior to human judgment, feel perfectly assured—as much so as if we beheld the divine image visibly impressed on it—that it came to us, by the instrumentality of men, from the very mouth of God. We ask not for proofs or probabilities on which to rest our judgment, but we subject our intellect and judgment to it as too transcendent for us to estimate. This, however, we do, not in the manner in which some are wont to fasten on an unknown object, which, as soon as known, displeases, but because we have a thorough conviction that, in holding it, we hold unassailable truth; not like miserable men, whose minds are enslaved by superstition, but because we feel a divine

Those who are taught inwardly by the spirit acquiesce implicitly in Scripture.

---

1 The French adds, "Car jaçoit qu'en sa propre majesté elle ait assez de quoy estre reuerée, neantmoins elle commence lors à nous vrayement toucher, quand elle est scellée en nos cœurs par le Sainct Esprit."—For though in its own majesty it has enough to command reverence, nevertheless, it then begins truly to touch us when it is sealed in our hearts by the Holy Spirit.

energy living and breathing in it—an energy by which we are drawn
and animated to obey it, willingly indeed, and knowingly, but more
vividly and effectually than could be done by human will or knowledge.   Hence, God most justly exclaims by the mouth of Isaiah,
"Ye are my witnesses, saith the Lord, and my servant whom I have
chosen, that ye may know and believe me, and understand that I am
he" (Isa. xliii. 10).

Such, then, is a conviction which asks not for reasons; such, a
knowledge which accords with the highest reason, namely, knowledge
in which the mind rests more firmly and securely than in any reasons;
such, in fine, the conviction which revelation from heaven alone can
produce.   I say nothing more than every believer experiences in himself, though my words fall far short of the reality.   I do not dwell
on this subject at present, because we will return to it again: only
let us now understand that the only true faith is that which the
Spirit of God seals on our hearts.   Nay, the modest and teachable
reader will find a sufficient reason in the promise contained in Isaiah,
that all the children of the renovated Church "shall be taught of the
Lord" (Isaiah liv. 13).   This singular privilege God bestows on his
elect only, whom he separates from the rest of mankind.   For what
is the beginning of true doctrine but prompt alacrity to hear the
word of God?   And God, by the mouth of Moses, thus demands to
be heard: "It is not in heaven, that thou shouldst say, Who shall
go up for us to heaven, and bring it unto us, that we may hear and
do it?   But the word is very nigh unto thee, in thy mouth and in
thy heart" (Deut. xxx. 12, 14).   God having been pleased to reserve
the treasure of intelligence for his children, no wonder that so much
ignorance and stupidity is seen in the generality of mankind.   In the
generality, I include even those specially chosen, until they are ingrafted into the body of the Church.   Isaiah, moreover, while reminding us that the prophetical doctrine would prove incredible not only
to strangers, but also to the Jews, who were desirous to be thought
of the household of God, subjoins the reason, when he asks, "To
whom hath the arm of the Lord been revealed?" (Isaiah liii. 1.)   If
at any time, then, we are troubled at the small number of those who
believe, let us, on the other hand, call to mind, that none comprehend
the mysteries of God save those to whom it is given.

CHAPTER VIII.

THE CREDIBILITY OF SCRIPTURE SUFFICIENTLY PROVED, IN SO FAR AS NATURAL REASON ADMITS.

This chapter consists of four parts. The first contains certain general proofs which may be easily gathered out of the writings both of the Old and New Testament—viz. the arrangement of the sacred volume, its dignity, truth, simplicity, efficacy, and majesty, sec. 1, 2. The second part contains special proofs taken from the Old Testament—viz the antiquity of the books of Moses, their authority, his miracles and prophecies, sec. 3–7; also, the predictions of the other prophets and their wondrous harmony, sec. 8. There is subjoined a refutation of two objections to the books of Moses and the Prophets, sec. 9, 10. The third part exhibits proof gathered out of the New Testament, *e.g.*, the harmony of the Evangelists in their account of heavenly mysteries, the majesty of the writings of John, Peter, and Paul, the remarkable calling of the Apostles and conversion of Paul, sec. 11. The last part exhibits the proofs drawn from ecclesiastical history, the perpetual consent of the Church in receiving and preserving divine truth, the invincible force of the truth in defending itself, the agreement of the godly (though otherwise differing so much from one another), the pious profession of the same doctrine by many illustrious men ; in fine, the more than human constancy of the martyrs, sec. 12, 13. This is followed by a conclusion of the particular topic discussed.

Sections.

1. Secondary helps to establish the credibility of Scripture. I. The arrangement of the sacred volume. II. Its dignity. III. Its truth. IV. Its simplicity. V. Its efficacy.
2. The majesty conspicuous in the writings of the Prophets.
3. Special proofs from the Old Testament. I. The antiquity of the Books of Moses.
4. This antiquity contrasted with the dreams of the Egyptians. II. The majesty of the Books of Moses.
5. The miracles and prophecies of Moses. A profane objection refuted
6. Another profane objection refuted.
7. The prophecies of Moses as to the sceptre not departing from Judah, and the calling of the Gentiles.
8. The predictions of other prophets. The destruction of Jerusalem ; and the return from the Babylonish captivity. Harmony of the Prophets. The celebrated prophecy of Daniel.
9. Objection against Moses and the Prophets. Answer to it.
10. Another objection and answer. Of the wondrous Providence of God in the preservation of the sacred books. The Greek Translation. The carefulness of the Jews.
11. Special proofs from the New Testament. I. The harmony of the Evangelists, and the sublime simplicity of their writings. II. The majesty of John, Paul, and Peter. III. The calling of the Apostles. IV. The conversion of Paul.
12 Proofs from Church history. I. Perpetual consent of the Church in receiving and preserving the truth. II. The invincible power of the truth itself. III. Agreement among the godly, notwithstanding of their many differences in other respects.
13. The constancy of the martyrs. Conclusion. Proofs of this description only of use after the certainty of Scripture has been established in the heart by the Holy Spirit.

1. In vain were the authority of Scripture fortified by argument, or supported by the consent of the Church, or confirmed by any other

helps, if unaccompanied by an assurance higher and stronger than human judgment can give. Till this better foundation has been laid, the authority of Scripture remains in suspense. On the other hand, when recognising its exemption from the common rule, we receive it reverently, and according to its dignity, those proofs which were not so strong as to produce and rivet a full conviction in our minds, become most appropriate helps. For it is wonderful how much we are confirmed in our belief, when we more attentively consider how admirably the system of divine wisdom contained in it is arranged—how perfectly free the doctrine is from everything that savours of earth—how beautifully it harmonises in all its parts—and how rich it is in all the other qualities which give an air of majesty to composition. Our hearts are still more firmly assured when we reflect that our admiration is excited more by the dignity of the matter than by the graces of style. For it was not without an admirable arrangement of Providence, that the sublime mysteries of the kingdom of heaven have for the greater part been delivered with a contemptible meanness of words. Had they been adorned with a more splendid eloquence, the wicked might have cavilled, and alleged that this constituted all their force. But now, when an unpolished simplicity, almost bordering on rudeness, makes a deeper impression than the loftiest flights of oratory, what does it indicate if not that the Holy Scriptures are too mighty in the power of truth to need the rhetorician's art?

Hence there was good ground for the Apostle's declaration, that the faith of the Corinthians was founded not on " the wisdom of men," but on " the power of God" (1 Cor. ii. 5),—his speech and preaching among them having been, " not with enticing words of man's wisdom, but in demonstration of the Spirit and of power" (1 Cor. ii. 5). For the truth is vindicated in opposition to every doubt, when, unsupported by foreign aid, it has its sole sufficiency in itself. How peculiarly this property belongs to Scripture appears from this, that no human writings, however skilfully composed, are at all capable of affecting us in a similar way. Read Demosthenes or Cicero, read Plato, Aristotle, or any other of that class: you will, I admit, feel wonderfully allured, pleased, moved, enchanted; but turn from them to the reading of the sacred volume, and whether you will or not, it will so affect you, so pierce your heart, so work its way into your very marrow, that, in comparison of the impression so produced, that of orators and philosophers will almost disappear; making it manifest that in the sacred volume there is a truth divine, a something which makes it immeasurably superior to all the gifts and graces attainable by man.

2. I confess, however, that in elegance and beauty, nay, splendour, the style of some of the prophets is not surpassed by the eloquence of heathen writers. By examples of this description, the Holy Spirit was pleased to show that it was not from want of eloquence he in

other instances used a rude and homely style.   But whether you read
David, Isaiah, and others of the same class, whose discourse flows
sweet and pleasant; or Amos the herdsman, Jeremiah and Zechariah,
whose rougher idiom savours of rusticity; that majesty of the Spirit to
which I adverted appears conspicuous in all.   I am not unaware, that
as Satan often apes God, that he may by a fallacious resemblance the
better insinuate himself into the minds of the simple, so he craftily
disseminated the impious errors with which he deceived miserable
men in an uncouth and semi-barbarous style, and frequently employed obsolete forms of expression in order to cloak his impostures.
None possessed of any moderate share of sense need be told how vain
and vile such affectation is.   But in regard to the Holy Scriptures,
however petulant men may attempt to carp at them, they are replete
with sentiments which it is clear that man never could have conceived.   Let each of the prophets be examined, and not one will be
found who does not rise far higher than human reach.   Those who
feel their works insipid must be absolutely devoid of taste.

3. As this subject has been treated at large by others, it will be
sufficient here merely to touch on its leading points.   In addition to
the qualities already mentioned, great weight is due to the antiquity
of Scripture (Euseb. Prepar. Evang. lib. ii. c. i.).   Whatever fables
Greek writers may retail concerning the Egyptian Theology, no
monument of any religion exists which is not long posterior to the
age of Moses.   But Moses does not introduce a new Deity.   He only
sets forth that doctrine concerning the eternal God which the Israelites had received by tradition from their fathers, by whom it had
been transmitted, as it were, from hand to hand, during a long series
of ages.   For what else does he do than lead them back to the covenant which had been made with Abraham?   Had he referred to matters of which they had never heard, he never could have succeeded;
but their deliverance from the bondage in which they were held must
have been a fact of familiar and universal notoriety, the very mention
of which must have immediately aroused the attention of all.   It is,
moreover, probable, that they were intimately acquainted with the
whole period of four hundred years.   Now, if Moses (who is so much
earlier than all other writers) traces the tradition of his doctrine
from so remote a period, it is obvious how far the Holy Scriptures
must, in point of antiquity, surpass all other writings.

4. Some perhaps may choose to credit the Egyptians in carrying
back their antiquity to a period of six thousand years before the
world was created.   But their garrulity, which even some profane
authors have held up to derision, it cannot be necessary for me to refute.   Josephus, however, in his work against Appion, produces important passages from very ancient writers, implying that the doctrine
delivered in the law was celebrated among all nations from the
remotest ages, though it was neither read nor accurately known.
And then, in order that the malignant might have no ground for

the majesty of the Spirit is evident in all the books of Scripture.

Great weight is due to the antiquity of Scripture

suspicion, and the ungodly no handle for cavil, God has provided, in the most effectual manner, against both dangers. When Moses relates the words which Jacob, under Divine inspiration, uttered concerning his posterity almost three hundred years before, how does he ennoble his own tribe? He stigmatises it with eternal infamy in the person of Levi. "Simeon and Levi," says he, "are brethren; instruments of cruelty are in their habitations. O my soul, come not thou into their secret; unto their assembly mine honour be not thou united" (Gen. xlix. 5, 6). This stigma he certainly might have passed in silence, not only that he might spare his own ancestor, but also save both himself and his whole family from a portion of the disgrace. How can any suspicion attach to him, who, by voluntarily proclaiming that the first founder of his family was declared detestable by a Divine oracle, neither consults for his own private interest, nor declines to incur obloquy among his tribe, who must have been offended by his statement of the fact? Again, when he relates the wicked murmuring of his brother Aaron, and his sister Miriam (Numb. xii. 1), shall we say that he spoke his own natural feelings, or that he obeyed the command of the Holy Spirit? Moreover, when invested with supreme authority, why does he not bestow the office of High Priest on his sons, instead of consigning them to the lowest place? I only touch on a few points out of many; but the Law itself contains throughout numerous proofs, which fully vindicate the credibility of Moses, and place it beyond dispute, that he was in truth a messenger sent forth from God.

5. The many striking miracles which Moses relates are so many sanctions of the law delivered, and the doctrine propounded, by him.[1] His being carried up into the mount in a cloud; his remaining there forty days separated from human society; his countenance glistening during the promulgation of the law, as with meridian effulgence; the lightnings which flashed on every side; the voices and thunderings which echoed in the air; the clang of the trumpet blown by no human mouth; his entrance into the tabernacle, while a cloud hid him from the view of the people; the miraculous vindication of his authority, by the fearful destruction of Korah, Dathan, and Abiram, and all their impious faction; the stream instantly gushing forth from the rock when struck with his rod; the manna which rained from heaven at his prayer;—did not God by all these proclaim aloud that he was an undoubted prophet? If any one object that I am taking debatable points for granted, the cavil is easily answered, Moses published all these things in the assembly of the people. How, then, could he possibly impose on the very eyewitnesses of what was done? Is it conceivable that he would have come forward, and, while accusing the people of unbelief, obstinacy, ingratitude, and other crimes, have boasted that his doctrine had been confirmed in their own presence by miracles which they never saw?

[1] Exod. xxiv. 18; xxxiv. 29; xix. 16; xl. 34. Numb. xvi. 24; xx. 10; xi. 9.

The disagreeable circumstances surrounding Moses' miracles would surely have arroused comment if untrue

6. For it is also worthy of remark, that the miracles which he relates are combined with disagreeable circumstances, which must have provoked opposition from the whole body of the people, if there had been the smallest ground for it. Hence it is obvious that they were induced to assent, merely because they had been previously convinced by their own experience. But because the fact was too clear to leave it free for heathen writers to deny that Moses did perform miracles, the father of lies suggested a calumny, and ascribed them to magic (Exod. ix. 11). But with what probability is a charge of magic brought against him, who held it in such abhorrence, that he ordered every one who should consult soothsayers and magicians to be stoned? (Lev. xxx. 6.) Assuredly, no impostor deals in tricks, without studying to raise his reputation by amazing the common people. But what does Moses do? By crying out, that he and Aaron his brother are nothing (Exod. xvi. 7), that they merely execute what God has commanded, he clears himself from every approach to suspicion. Again, if the facts are considered in themselves, what kind of incantation could cause manna to rain from heaven every day, and in sufficient quantity to maintain a people, while any one, who gathered more than the appointed measure, saw his incredulity divinely punished by its turning to worms? To this we may add, that God then suffered his servant to be subjected to so many serious trials, that the ungodly cannot now gain anything by their clamour. When (as often happened) the people proudly and petulantly rose up against him, when individuals conspired, and attempted to overthrow him, how could any impostures have enabled him to elude their rage? The event plainly shows that by these means his doctrine was attested to all succeeding ages.

Prophetic prediction of the kingship of the House of Judah.

7. Moreover, it is impossible to deny that he was guided by a prophetic spirit in assigning the first place to the tribe of Judah in the person of Jacob, especially if we take into view the fact itself, as explained by the event. Suppose that Moses was the inventor of the prophecy, still, after he committed it to writing, four hundred years pass away, during which no mention is made of a sceptre in the tribe of Judah. After Saul is anointed, the kingly office seems fixed in the tribe of Benjamin (1 Sam. xi. 15; xvi. 13). When David is anointed by Samuel, what apparent ground is there for the transference? Who could have looked for a king out of the plebeian family of a herdsman? And out of seven brothers, who could have thought that the honour was destined for the youngest? And then by what means did he afterwards come within reach of the throne? Who dare say that his anointing was regulated by human art, or skill, or prudence, and was not rather the fulfilment of a divine prophecy? In like manner, do not the predictions, though obscure, of the admission of the Gentiles into the divine covenant, seeing they were not fulfilled till almost two thousand years after, make it palpable that Moses spoke under divine inspiration? I omit other predictions which so

plainly betoken divine revelation, that all men of sound mind must
see they were spoken by God.   In short, his Song itself (Deut. xxxii.)
is a bright mirror in which God is manifestly seen.

8. In the case of the other prophets the evidence is even clearer.
I will only select a few examples, for it were too tedious to enumerate
the whole.   Isaiah, in his own day, when the kingdom of Judah was
at peace, and had even some ground to confide in the protection of
the Chaldeans, spoke of the destruction of the city and the captivity
of the people (Isaiah xlv. 1).   Supposing it not to be sufficient evidence of divine inspiration to foretell, many years before, events which,
at the time, seemed fabulous, but which ultimately turned out to be
true, whence shall it be said that the prophecies which he uttered
concerning their return proceeded, if it was not from God ? He names
Cyrus, by whom the Chaldeans were to be subdued and the people
restored to freedom.   After the prophet thus spoke, more than a
hundred years elapsed before Cyrus was born, that being nearly the
period which elapsed between the death of the one and the birth of
the other.   It was impossible at that time to guess that some Cyrus
would arise to make war on the Babylonians, and after subduing their
powerful monarchy, put an end to the captivity of the children of
Israel.   Does not this simple, unadorned narrative plainly demonstrate that what Isaiah spoke was not the conjecture of man, but the
undoubted oracle of God?   Again, when Jeremiah, a considerable
time before the people were led away, assigned seventy years as the
period of captivity, and fixed their liberation and return, must not his
tongue have been guided by the Spirit of God ?   What effrontery
were it to deny that, by these evidences, the authority of the prophets
is established, the very thing being fulfilled to which they appeal in
support of their credibility !   " Behold, the former things are come
to pass, and new things do I declare ; before they spring forth I tell
you of them" (Isaiah xlii. 9).   I say nothing of the agreement between Jeremiah and Ezekiel, who, living so far apart, and yet prophesying at the same time, harmonise as completely in all they say as
if they had mutually dictated the words to one another.   What shall
I say of Daniel ?   Did not he deliver prophecies embracing a future
period of almost six hundred years, as if he had been writing of past
events generally known ?   (Dan. ix. &c.)   If the pious will duly
meditate on these things, they will be sufficiently instructed to silence
the cavils of the ungodly.   The demonstration is too clear to be
gainsayed.

9. I am aware of what is muttered in corners by certain miscreants, when they would display their acuteness in assailing divine
truth.   They ask, how do we know that Moses and the prophets
wrote the books which now bear their names ?   Nay, they even dare
to question whether there ever was a Moses.   Were any one to question whether there ever was a Plato, or an Aristotle, or a Cicero,
would not the rod or the whip be deemed the fit chastisement of such

Bases belief in the writings of the Prophets on the accuracy of their predict-ions.

Preser-
vation
of the
Law
through
the centur-
ies, and
its rediscov-
ery by
Josiah

folly? The law of Moses has been wonderfully preserved, more by divine providence than by human care; and though, owing to the negligence of the priests, it lay for a short time buried,—from the time when it was found by good King Josiah (2 Kings xxii. 8; 2 Chron. xxxiv. 15),—it has continued in the hands of men, and been transmitted in unbroken succession from generation to generation. Nor, indeed, when Josiah brought it forth, was it as a book unknown or new, but one which had always been matter of notoriety, and was then in full remembrance. The original writing had been deposited in the temple, and a copy taken from it had been deposited in the royal archives (Deut. xvii. 18, 19); the only thing which had occurred was, that the priests had ceased to publish the law itself in due form, and the people also had neglected the wonted reading of it. I may add, that scarcely an age passed during which its authority was not confirmed and renewed. Were the books of Moses unknown to those who had the Psalms of David in their hands? To sum up the whole in one word, it is certain beyond dispute, that these writings passed down, if I may so express it, from hand to hand, being transmitted in an unbroken series from the fathers, who either with their own ears heard them spoken, or learned them from those who had, while the remembrance of them was fresh.

10. An objection taken from the history of the Maccabees (1 Maccab. i. 57, 58) to impugn the credibility of Scripture, is, on the contrary, fitted the best possible to confirm it. First, however, let us clear away the gloss which is put upon it: having done so, we shall turn the engine which they erect against us upon themselves. As Antiochus ordered all the books of Scripture to be burnt, it is asked, where did the copies we now have come from? I, in my turn, ask, In what workshop could they have been so quickly fabricated? It is certain that they were in existence the moment the persecution ceased, and that they were acknowledged without dispute by all the pious who had been educated in their doctrine, and were familiarly acquainted with them. Nay, while all the wicked so wantonly insulted the Jews as if they had leagued together for the purpose, not one ever dared to charge them with having introduced spurious books. Whatever, in their opinion, the Jewish religion might be, they acknowledged that Moses was the founder of it. What, then, do those babblers, but betray their snarling petulance in falsely alleging the spuriousness of books whose sacred antiquity is proved by the consent of all history? But not to spend labour in vain in refuting these vile calumnies, let us rather attend to the care which the Lord took to preserve his Word, when against all hope he rescued it from the truculence of a most cruel tyrant as from the midst of the flames—inspiring pious priests and others with such constancy that they hesitated not, though it should have been purchased at the expense of their lives, to transmit this treasure to posterity, and defeating the keenest search of prefects and their satellites.

Who does not recognise it as a signal and miraculous work of God, that those sacred monuments which the ungodly persuaded themselves had utterly perished, immediately returned to resume their former rights, and, indeed, in greater honour? For the Greek translation appeared to disseminate them over the whole world. Nor does it seem so wonderful that God rescued the tables of his covenant from the sanguinary edicts of Antiochus, as that they remained safe and entire amid the manifold disasters by which the Jewish nation was occasionally crushed, devastated, and almost exterminated. The Hebrew language was in no estimation, and almost unknown; and assuredly, had not God provided for religion, it must have utterly perished. For it is obvious from the prophetical writings of that age, how much the Jews, after their return from the captivity, had lost the genuine use of their native tongue. It is of importance to attend to this, because the comparison more clearly establishes the antiquity of the Law and the Prophets. And whom did God employ to preserve the doctrine of salvation contained in the Law and the Prophets, that Christ might manifest it in its own time? The Jews, the bitterest enemies of Christ; and hence Augustine justly calls them the librarians of the Christian Church, because they supplied us with books of which they themselves had not the use.

11. When we proceed to the New Testament, how solid are the pillars by which its truth is supported! Three evangelists give a narrative in a mean and humble style. The proud often eye this simplicity with disdain, because they attend not to the principal heads of doctrine; for from these they might easily infer that these evangelists treat of heavenly mysteries beyond the capacity of man. Those who have the least particle of candour must be ashamed of their fastidiousness when they read the first chapter of Luke. Even our Saviour's discourses, of which a summary is given by these three evangelists, ought to prevent every one from treating their writings with contempt. John, again, fulminating in majesty, strikes down more powerfully than any thunderbolt the petulance of those who refuse to submit to the obedience of faith. Let all those acute censors, whose highest pleasure it is to banish a reverential regard of Scripture from their own and other men's hearts, come forward; let them read the Gospel of John, and, willing or unwilling, they will find a thousand sentences which will at least arouse them from their sloth; nay, which will burn into their consciences as with a hot iron, and check their derision. The same thing may be said of Peter and Paul, whose writings, though the greater part read them blindfold, exhibit a heavenly majesty, which in a manner binds and rivets every reader. But one circumstance, sufficient of itself to exalt their doctrine above the world, is, that Matthew, who was formerly fixed down to his money-table, Peter and John, who were employed with their little boats, being all rude and illiterate, had never learned in any human school that which they delivered to others. Paul, more-

[Marginal notes:]
The Septuagint.
Jews, the librarians of the Christian Church.
Against Text-critics.
The apostles never learned in any school that which they delivered to others

over, who had not only been an avowed but a cruel and bloody foe, being changed into a new man, shows, by the sudden and unhoped-for change, that a heavenly power had compelled him to preach the doctrine which once he destroyed. Let those dogs deny that the Holy Spirit descended upon the apostles, or, if not, let them refuse credit to the history, still the very circumstances proclaim that the Holy Spirit must have been the teacher of those who, formerly contemptible among the people, all of a sudden began to discourse so magnificently of heavenly mysteries.

The Holy Spirit must have been their teacher

12. Add, moreover, that, for the best of reasons, the consent of the Church is not without its weight. For it is not to be accounted of no consequence, that, from the first publication of Scripture, so many ages have uniformly concurred in yielding obedience to it, and that, notwithstanding of the many extraordinary attempts which Satan and the whole world have made to oppress and overthrow it, or completely efface it from the memory of men, it has flourished like the palm-tree and continued invincible. Though in old times there was scarcely a sophist or orator of any note who did not exert his powers against it, their efforts proved unavailing. The powers of the earth armed themselves for its destruction, but all their attempts vanished into smoke. When thus powerfully assailed on every side, how could it have resisted if it had trusted only to human aid? Nay, its divine origin is more completely established by the fact, that when all human wishes were against it, it advanced by its own energy. Add that it was not a single city or a single nation that concurred in receiving and embracing it. Its authority was recognised as far and as wide as the world extends—various nations who had nothing else in common entering for this purpose into a holy league. Moreover, while we ought to attach the greatest weight to the agreement of minds so diversified, and in all other things so much at variance with each other—an agreement which a Divine Providence alone could have produced—it adds no small weight to the whole when we attend to the piety of those who thus agree; not of all of them indeed, but of those in whom as lights God was pleased that his Church should shine.

Continuous veneration for the biblical message a reason for belief

Agreement of diverse minds a proof.

13. Again, with what confidence does it become us to subscribe to a doctrine attested and confirmed by the blood of so many saints? They, when once they had embraced it, hesitated not boldly and intrepidly, and even with great alacrity, to meet death in its defence. Being transmitted to us with such an earnest, who of us shall not receive it with firm and unshaken conviction? It is therefore no small proof of the authority of Scripture, that it was sealed with the blood of so many witnesses, especially when it is considered that in bearing testimony to the faith, they met death not with fanatical enthusiasm (as erring spirits are sometimes wont to do), but with a firm and constant, yet sober godly zeal. There are other reasons, neither few nor feeble, by which the dignity and majesty of

Martyrdom a proof of the virtue of the biblical message.

the Scriptures may be not only proved to the pious, but also completely vindicated against the cavils of slanderers. These, however, cannot of themselves produce a firm faith in Scripture until our heavenly Father manifest his presence in it, and thereby secure implicit reverence for it. Then only, therefore, does Scripture suffice to give a saving knowledge of God when its certainty is founded on the inward persuasion of the Holy Spirit. Still the human testimonies which go to confirm it will not be without effect, if they are used in subordination to that chief and highest proof, as secondary helps to our weakness. But it is foolish to attempt to prove to infidels that the Scripture is the Word of God. This it cannot be known to be, except by faith. Justly, therefore, does Augustine remind us, that every man who would have any understanding in such high matters must previously possess piety and mental peace.

[margin handwritten note: Witness of the Holy Spirit only valid proof of the excellency of Scripture. Human proofs merely auxiliary aids.]

CHAPTER IX.

ALL THE PRINCIPLES OF PIETY SUBVERTED BY FANATICS, WHO SUBSTITUTE REVELATIONS FOR SCRIPTURE.

Sections.

1. The temper and error of the Libertines, who take to themselves the name of spiritual, briefly described. Their refutation. 1. The Apostles and all true Christians have embraced the written Word. This confirmed by a passage in Isaiah; also by the example and words of Paul. 2. The Spirit of Christ seals the doctrine of the written Word on the minds of the godly.
2. Refutation continued. 3. The impositions of Satan cannot be detected without the aid of the written Word. First objection. The Answer to it.
3. Second Objection from the words of Paul as to the *letter and spirit.* The Answer, with an explanation of Paul's meaning. How the Spirit and the written Word are indissolubly connected:

There have arisen those who deride Scripture at the expense of the Spirit.

This is contrary to the historical witness of the Church.

1. THOSE who, rejecting Scripture, imagine that they have some peculiar way of penetrating to God, are to be deemed not so much under the influence of error as madness. For certain giddy men[1] have lately appeared, who, while they make a great display of the superiority of the Spirit, reject all reading of the Scriptures themselves, and deride the simplicity of those who only delight in what they call the dead and deadly letter. But I wish they would tell me what spirit it is whose inspiration raises them to such a sublime height that they dare despise the doctrine of Scripture as mean and childish. If they answer that it is the Spirit of Christ, their confidence is exceedingly ridiculous; since they will, I presume, admit that the apostles and other believers in the primitive Church were not illuminated by any other Spirit. None of these thereby learned to despise the Word of God, but every one was imbued with greater reverence for it, as their writings most clearly testify. And, indeed, it had been so foretold by the mouth of Isaiah. For when he says, " My Spirit that is upon thee, and my words which I have put in thy mouth, shall not depart out of thy mouth, nor out of the mouth of thy seed, nor out of the mouth of thy seed's seed, saith the Lord, from henceforth and for ever," he does not tie down the ancient Church to external doctrine, as he were a mere teacher of elements;[2] he rather shows that, under the reign of Christ, the true and full felicity of the new Church will consist in their being ruled not less by the Word than by the Spirit of God. Hence we infer that these miscreants are guilty of fearful sacrilege in tearing asunder what the prophet joins in indissoluble union. Add to this, that Paul, though carried up even to the third heaven, ceased not to profit by the doctrine of the law and the prophets, while, in like manner, he exhorts Timothy, a

---

1 Lactantius: Cœlestes literas corruperunt, ut novam sibi doctrinam sine ulla radice ac stabilitate componerent. *Vide* Calvin in Instruct. adv. Libertinos, cap. ix. and x.
2 For the Latin, " ac si elementarius esset," the French has, " comme s'ils eussent étépetis enfans a l'A, B, C;"—as if they were little children at their A, B, C.

teacher of singular excellence, to give attention to reading (1 Tim. iv. 13). And the eulogium which he pronounces on Scripture well deserves to be remembered—viz., that "it is profitable for doctrine, for reproof, for correction, and for instruction in righteousness, that the man of God may be perfect" (2 Tim. iii. 16). What an infatuation of the devil, therefore, to fancy that Scripture, which conducts the sons of God to the final goal, is of transient and temporary use? Again, I should like those people to tell me whether they have imbibed any other Spirit than that which Christ promised to his disciples. Though their madness is extreme, it will scarcely carry them the length of making this their boast. But what kind of Spirit did our Saviour promise to send? One who should not speak of himself (John xvi. 13), but suggest and instil the truths which he himself had delivered through the word. Hence the office of the Spirit promised to us, is not to form new and unheard-of revelations, or to coin a new form of doctrine, by which we may be led away from the received doctrine of the gospel, but to seal on our minds the very doctrine which the gospel recommends.

2. Hence it is easy to understand that we must give diligent heed both to the reading and hearing of Scripture, if we would obtain any benefit from the Spirit of God (just as Peter praises those who attentively study the doctrine of the prophets (2 Pet. i. 19), though it might have been thought to be superseded after the gospel light arose), and, on the contrary, that any spirit which passes by the wisdom of God's Word, and suggests any other doctrine, is deservedly suspected of vanity and falsehood. Since Satan transforms himself into an angel of light, what authority can the Spirit have with us if he be not ascertained by an infallible mark? And assuredly he is pointed out to us by the Lord with sufficient clearness; but these miserable men err as if bent on their own destruction, while they seek the Spirit from themselves rather than from Him. But they say that it is insulting to subject the Spirit, to whom all things are to be subject, to the Scripture: as if it were disgraceful to the Holy Spirit to maintain a perfect resemblance throughout, and be in all respects without variation consistent with himself. True, if he were subjected to a human, an angelical, or to any foreign standard, it might be thought that he was rendered subordinate, or, if you will, brought into bondage; but so long as he is compared with himself, and considered in himself, how can it be said that he is thereby injured? I admit that he is brought to a test, but the very test by which it has pleased him that his majesty should be confirmed. It ought to be enough for us when once we hear his voice; but lest Satan should insinuate himself under his name, he wishes us to recognise him by the image which he has stamped on the Scriptures. The author of the Scriptures cannot vary, and change his likeness. Such as he there appeared at first, such he will perpetually remain. There is nothing contumelious to him in this, unless we are to think it would be honourable for him to degenerate, and revolt against himself.

3. Their cavil about our cleaving to the dead letter carries with it the punishment which they deserve for despising Scripture. It is clear that Paul is there arguing against false apostles (2 Cor. iii. 6), who, by recommending the law without Christ, deprived the people of the benefit of the New Covenant, by which the Lord engages that he will write his law on the hearts of believers, and engrave it on their inward parts. The letter therefore is dead, and the law of the Lord kills its readers when it is dissevered from the grace of Christ, and only sounds in the ear without touching the heart. But if it is effectually impressed on the heart by the Spirit; if it exhibits Christ, it is the word of life converting the soul, and making wise the simple. Nay, in the very same passage, the apostle calls his own preaching the ministration of the Spirit (2 Cor. iii. 8), intimating that the Holy Spirit so cleaves to his own truth, as he has expressed it in Scripture, that he then only exerts and puts forth his strength when the word is received with due honour and respect.

There is nothing repugnant here to what was lately said (chap. vii.) that we have no great certainty of the word itself, until it be confirmed by the testimony of the Spirit. For the Lord has so knit together the certainty of his word and his Spirit, that our minds are duly imbued with reverence for the word when the Spirit shining upon it enables us there to behold the face of God; and, on the other hand, we embrace the Spirit with no danger of delusion when we recognise him in his image, that is, in his word. Thus, indeed, it is. God did not produce his word before men for the sake of sudden display, intending to abolish it the moment the Spirit should arrive; but he employed the same Spirit, by whose agency he had administered the word, to complete his work by the efficacious confirmation of the word. In this way Christ explained to the two disciples (Luke xxiv. 27), not that they were to reject the Scriptures and trust to their own wisdom, but that they were to understand the Scriptures. In like manner, when Paul says to the Thessalonians, "Quench not the Spirit," he does not carry them aloft to empty speculation apart from the word; he immediately adds, "Despise not prophesyings" (1 Thess. v. 19, 20). By this, doubtless, he intimates that the light of the Spirit is quenched the moment prophesyings fall into contempt. How is this answered by those swelling enthusiasts, in whose idea the only true illumination consists, in carelessly laying aside, and bidding adieu to the Word of God, while, with no less confidence than folly, they fasten upon any dreaming notion which may have casually sprung up in their minds? Surely a very different sobriety becomes the children of God. As they feel that without the Spirit of God they are utterly devoid of the light of truth, so they are not ignorant that the word is the instrument by which the illumination of the Spirit is dispensed. They know of no other Spirit than the one who dwelt and spake in the apostles—the Spirit by whose oracles they are daily invited to the hearing of the Word.

CHAPTER X.

IN SCRIPTURE, THE TRUE GOD OPPOSED, EXCLUSIVELY, TO ALL THE GODS OF THE HEATHEN.

Sections.

1. Explanation of the knowledge of God resumed. God as manifested in Scripture, the same as delineated in his works.
2. The attributes of God as described by Moses, David, and Jeremiah. Explanation of the attributes. Summary. Uses of this knowledge.
3. Scripture, in directing us to the true God, excludes the gods of the heathen, who, however, in some sense, held the unity of God.

1. WE formerly observed that the knowledge of God, which, in other respects, is not obscurely exhibited in the frame of the world, and in all the creatures, is more clearly and familiarly explained by the word. It may now be proper to show, that in Scripture the Lord represents himself in the same character in which we have already seen that he is delineated in his works. A full discussion of this subject would occupy a large space. But it will here be sufficient to furnish a kind of index, by attending to which the pious reader may be enabled to understand what knowledge of God he ought chiefly to search for in Scripture, and be directed as to the mode of conducting the search. I am not now adverting to the peculiar covenant by which God distinguished the race of Abraham from the rest of the nations. For when by gratuitous adoption he admitted those who were enemies to the rank of sons, he even then acted in the character of a Redeemer. At present, however, we are employed in considering that knowledge which stops short at the creation of the world, without ascending to Christ the Mediator. But though it will soon be necessary to quote certain passages from the New Testament (proofs being there given both of the power of God the Creator, and of his providence in the preservation of what he originally created), I wish the reader to remember what my present purpose is, that he may not wander from the proper subject. Briefly, then, it will be sufficient for him at present to understand how God, the Creator of heaven and earth, governs the world which was made by him. In every part of Scripture we meet with descriptions of his paternal kindness and readiness to do good, and we also meet with examples of severity which show that he is the just punisher of the wicked, especially when they continue obstinate notwithstanding of all his forbearance.

2. There are certain passages which contain more vivid descriptions

of the divine character, setting it before us as if his genuine countenance were visibly portrayed. Moses, indeed, seems to have intended briefly to comprehend whatever may be known of God by man, when he said, "The Lord, The Lord God, merciful and gracious, long-suffering, and abundant in goodness and truth, keeping mercy for thousands, forgiving iniquity and transgression and sin, and that will by no means clear the guilty; visiting the iniquity of the fathers upon the children, and upon the children's children, unto the third and to the fourth generation" (Ex. xxxiv. 6, 7). Here we may observe, *first*, that his eternity and self-existence are declared by his magnificent name twice repeated; and, *secondly*, that in the enumeration of his perfections, he is described not as he is in himself, but in relation to us, in order that our acknowledgment of him may be more a vivid actual impression than empty visionary speculation. Moreover, the perfections thus enumerated are just those which we saw shining in the heavens, and on the earth—compassion, goodness, mercy, justice, judgment, and truth. For power and energy are comprehended under the name Jehovah. Similar epithets are employed by the prophets when they would fully declare his sacred name. Not to collect a great number of passages, it may suffice at present to refer to one Psalm (cxlv.), in which a summary of the divine perfections is so carefully given, that not one seems to have been omitted. Still, however, every perfection there set down may be contemplated in creation; and, hence, such as we feel him to be when experience is our guide, such he declares himself to be by his word. In Jeremiah, where God proclaims the character in which he would have us to acknowledge him, though the description is not so full, it is substantially the same. "Let him that glorieth," says he, "glory in this, that he understandeth and knoweth me, that I am the Lord which exercise loving-kindness, judgment, and righteousness, in the earth" (Jerem. ix. 24). Assuredly, the attributes which it is most necessary for us to know are these three: Loving-kindness, on which alone our entire safety depends; Judgment, which is daily exercised on the wicked, and awaits them in a severer form, even for eternal destruction; Righteousness, by which the faithful are preserved, and most benignly cherished. The prophet declares, that when you understand these, you are amply furnished with the means of glorying in God. Nor is there here any omission of his truth, or power, or holiness, or goodness. For how could this knowledge of his loving-kindness, judgment, and righteousness, exist, if it were not founded on his inviolable truth? How, again, could it be believed that he governs the earth with judgment and righteousness, without presupposing his mighty power? Whence, too, his loving-kindness, but from his goodness? In fine, if all his ways are loving-kindness, judgment, and righteousness, his holiness also is thereby conspicuous. Moreover, the knowledge of God, which is set before us in the Scriptures, is designed for the same purpose as that which shines in creation—viz.

(margin notes):
Attributes
of God
1. eternal
2. self-existant
3. compassionate
4. Good
5. Merciful
6. Just
7. Truthful
See Ps. 145
for biblical
summary

Three
Most
Essential
Attributes
1. Loving
kindness
2. Judgment
3. Righteous

These
3 attributes
cause a
fourth to
stand out:
Holiness.

that we may thereby learn to worship him with perfect integrity of heart and unfeigned obedience, and also to depend entirely on his goodness.

Purpose of the Scriptures.

3. Here it may be proper to give a summary of the general doctrine. First, then, let the reader observe that the Scripture, in order to direct us to the true God, distinctly excludes and rejects all the gods of the heathen, because religion was universally adulterated in almost every age. It is true, indeed, that the name of one God was everywhere known and celebrated. For those who worshipped a multitude of gods, whenever they spoke the genuine language of nature, simply used the name god, as if they had thought one god sufficient. And this is shrewdly noticed by Justin Martyr, who, to the same effect, wrote a treatise, entitled, On the Monarchy of God, in which he shows, by a great variety of evidence, that the unity of God is engraven on the hearts of all. Tertullian also proves the same thing from the common forms of speech.[1] But as all, without exception, have in the vanity of their minds rushed or been dragged into lying fictions, these impressions, as to the unity of God, whatever they may have naturally been, have had no further effect than to render men inexcusable. The wisest plainly discover the vague wanderings of their minds when they express a wish for any kind of Deity, and thus offer up their prayers to unknown gods. And then, in imagining a manifold nature in God, though their ideas concerning Jupiter, Mercury, Venus, Minerva, and others, were not so absurd as those of the rude vulgar, they were by no means free from the delusions of the devil. We have elsewhere observed, that however subtle the evasions devised by philosophers, they cannot do away with the charge of rebellion, in that all of them have corrupted the truth of God. For this reason, Habakkuk (ii. 20), after condemning all idols, orders men to seek God in his temple, that the faithful may acknowledge none but Him, who has manifested himself in his word.

Scripture rejects all the gods of the heathen.

---

1 In his book, De Idolatria. See also in Augustine, a letter by one Maximus, a grammarian of Medaura, jesting at his gods, and scoffing at the true religion. See, at the same time, Augustine's grave and admirable reply. Ep. xliii. xliv.

CHAPTER XI.

IMPIETY OF ATTRIBUTING A VISIBLE FORM TO GOD.—THE SETTING UP OF IDOLS A DEFECTION FROM THE TRUE GOD.

There are three leading divisions in this chapter. The first contains a refutation of those who ascribe a visible form to God (s. 1 and 2), with an answer to the objection of those who, because it is said that God manifested his presence by certain symbols, use it as a defence of their error (s. 3 and 4). Various arguments are afterwards adduced, disposing of the trite objection from Gregory's expression, that images are the books of the unlearned (s. 5–7). The second division of the chapter relates to the origin of idols or images, and the adoration of them, as approved by the Papists (s. 8–10). Their evasion refuted (s. 11). The third division treats of the use and abuse of images (s. 12). Whether it is expedient to have them in Christian Churches (s. 13). The concluding part contains a refutation of the second Council of Nice, which very absurdly contends for images in opposition to divine truth, and even to the disparagement of the Christian name.

Sections.

1. God is opposed to idols, that all may know he is the only fit witness to himself. He expressly forbids any attempt to represent him by a bodily shape
2. Reasons fort his prohibition from Moses, Isaiah, and Paul. The complaint of a heathen. It should put the worshippers of idols to shame.
3. Consideration of an objection taken from various passages in Moses. The Cherubim and Seraphim show that images are not fit to represent divine mysteries. The Cherubim belonged to the tutelage of the Law.
4. The materials of which idols are made, abundantly refute the fiction of idolaters. Confirmation from Isaiah and others. Absurd precaution of the Greeks.
5. Objection,—That images are the books of the unlearned. Objection answered, 1. Scripture declares images to be teachers of vanity and lies.
6. Answer continued,—2. Ancient Theologians condemn the formation and worship of idols.
7. Answer continued,—3. The use of images condemned by the luxury and meretricious ornaments given to them in Popish Churches. 4. The Church must be trained in true piety by another method.
8. The second division of the chapter. Origin of idols or images. Its rise shortly after the flood. Its continual progress.
9. Of the worship of images. Its nature. A pretext of idolaters refuted. Pretexts of the heathen. Genius of idolaters.
10. Evasion of the Papists. Their agreement with ancient idolaters.
11. Refutation of another evasion or sophism,—viz. the distinction of *dulia* and *latria*.
12. Third division of the chapter—viz. the use and abuse of images.
13. Whether it is expedient to have images in Christian temples.
14. Absurd defence of the worship of images by the second so-called Council of Nice. Sophisms or perversions of Scripture in defence of images in churches.
15. Passages adduced in support of the worship of images.
16. The blasphemous expressions of some ancient idolaters approved by not a few of the more modern, both in word and deed.

1. As Scripture, in accommodation to the rude and gross intellect of man, usually speaks in popular terms, so whenever its object is to

discriminate between the true God and false deities, it opposes him in particular to idols; not that it approves of what is taught more elegantly and subtilely by philosophers, but that it may the better expose the folly, nay madness, of the world in its inquiries after God, so long as every one clings to his own speculations. This exclusive definition, which we uniformly meet with in Scripture, annihilates every deity which men frame for themselves of their own accord— God himself being the only fit witness to himself. Meanwhile, seeing that this brutish stupidity has overspread the globe, men longing after visible forms of God, and so forming deities of wood and stone, silver and gold, or of any other dead and corruptible matter, we must hold it as a first principle, that as often as any form is assigned to God, his glory is corrupted by an impious lie. In the Law, accordingly, after God had claimed the glory of divinity for himself alone, when he comes to show what kind of worship he approves and rejects, he immediately adds, "Thou shalt not make unto thee any graven image, or any likeness of anything that is in heaven above, or in the earth beneath, or in the water under the earth" (Exod. xx. 4). By these words he curbs any licentious attempt we might make to represent him by a visible shape, and briefly enumerates all the forms by which superstition had begun, even long before, to turn his truth into a lie. For we know that the Sun was worshipped by the Persians. As many stars as the foolish nations saw in the sky, so many gods they imagined them to be. Then to the Egyptians, every animal was a figure of God.[1] The Greeks, again, plumed themselves on their superior wisdom in worshipping God under the human form, (Maximus Tyrius Platonic. Serm. 38). But God makes no comparison between images, as if one were more, and another less befitting; he rejects, without exception, all shapes and pictures, and other symbols by which the superstitious imagine they can bring him near to them.

2. This may easily be inferred from the reasons which he annexes to his prohibition. First, it is said in the books of Moses, (Deut. iv. 15), "Take ye therefore good heed unto yourselves; for ye saw no manner of similitude in the day that the Lord spake unto you in Horeb, out of the midst of the fire, lest ye corrupt yourselves, and make you a graven image, the similitude of any figure," &c. We see how plainly God declares against all figures, to make us aware that all longing after such visible shapes is rebellion against him. Of the prophets, it will be sufficient to mention Isaiah, who is the most copious on this subject (Isaiah xl. 18; xli. 7, 29; xlv. 9; xlvi. 5), in order to show how the majesty of God is defiled by an absurd and indecorous fiction, when he who is incorporeal is assimilated to corporeal matter; he who is invisible to a visible image; he who is a spirit to an inanimate object; and he who fills all space to a bit of

---

[1] The French adds, "voire jusques aux oignons et porreaux;"—they have gone even to onions and leeks.

paltry wood, or stone, or gold. Paul, too, reasons in the same way, "Forasmuch, then, as we are the offspring of God, we ought not to think that the Godhead is like unto gold, or silver, or stone, graven by art and man's device" (Acts xvii. 29). Hence it is manifest, that whatever statues are set up or pictures painted to represent God, are utterly displeasing to him, as a kind of insults to his majesty. And is it strange that the Holy Spirit thunders such responses from heaven, when he compels even blind and miserable idolaters to make a similar confession on the earth ? Seneca's complaint, as given by Augustine, De Civit. Dei, c. 10, is well known. He says, " The sacred, immortal, and invisible gods, they exhibit in the meanest and most ignoble materials, and dress them in the clothing of men and beasts; some confound the sexes, and form a compound out of different bodies, giving the name of deities to objects, which, if they were met alive, would be deemed monsters." Hence, again, it is obvious, that the defenders of images resort to a paltry quibbling evasion, when they pretend that the Jews were forbidden to use them on account of their proneness to superstition ; as if a prohibition which the Lord founds on his own eternal essence, and the uniform course of nature, could be restricted to a single nation. Besides, when Paul refuted the error of giving a bodily shape to God, he was addressing not Jews, but Athenians.

3. It is true that the Lord occasionally manifested his presence by certain signs, so that he was said to be seen face to face ; but all the signs he ever employed were in apt accordance with the scheme of doctrine, and, at the same time, gave plain intimation of his incomprehensible essence. For the cloud, and smoke, and flame, though they were symbols of heavenly glory (Deut. iv. 11), curbed men's minds as with a bridle, that they might not attempt to penetrate farther. Therefore, even Moses (to whom, of all men, God manifested himself most familiarly) was not permitted, though he prayed for it, to behold that face, but received for answer, that the refulgence was too great for man (Exod. xxxiii. 20). The Holy Spirit appeared under the form of a dove, but as it instantly vanished, who does not see that in this symbol of a moment, the faithful were admonished to regard the Spirit as invisible, to be contented with his power and grace, and not call for any external figure ? God sometimes appeared in the form of a man, but this was in anticipation of the future revelation in Christ, and, therefore, did not give the Jews the least pretext for setting up a symbol of Deity under the human form. The mercy-seat, also (Exod. xxv. 17, 18, 21), where, under the Law, God exhibited the presence of his power, was so framed, as to intimate that God is best seen when the mind rises in admiration above itself : the Cherubim with outstretched wings shaded, and the veil covered it, while the remoteness of the place was in itself a sufficient concealment. It is therefore mere infatuation to attempt to defend images of God and the saints by the example of the Cherubim. For

what, pray, did these figures mean, if not that images are unfit to
represent the mysteries of God, since they were so formed as to cover
the mercy-seat with their wings, thereby concealing the view of God,
not only from the eye, but from every human sense, and curbing presumption ?   To this we may add, that the prophets depict the Seraphim, who are exhibited to us in vision, as having their faces veiled ;
thus intimating, that the refulgence of the divine glory is so great,
that even the angels cannot gaze upon it directly, while the minute
beams which sparkle in the face of angels are shrouded from our
view.   Moreover, all men of sound judgment acknowledge that the
Cherubim in question belonged to the old tutelage of the law.   It is
absurd, therefore, to bring them forward as an example for our age.
For that period of puerility, if I may so express it, to which such
rudiments were adapted, has passed away.   And surely it is disgraceful that heathen writers should be more skilful interpreters of Scripture than the Papists.   Juvenal (Sat. xiv.) holds up the Jews to
derision for worshiping the thin clouds and firmament.   This he
does perversely and impiously ; still, in denying that any visible shape
of deity existed among them, he speaks more accurately than the
Papists, who prate about there having been some visible image.   In
the fact that the people every now and then rushed forth with boiling
haste in pursuit of idols, just like water gushing forth with violence
from a copious spring, let us learn how prone our nature is to idolatry, that we may not, by throwing the whole blame of a common vice
upon the Jews, be led away by vain and sinful enticements to sleep
the sleep of death.

4. To the same effect are the words of the Psalmist (Psalms cxv.
4, cxxxv. 15), "Their idols are silver and gold, the work of men's
hands."   From the materials of which they are made, he infers that
they are not gods, taking it for granted that every human device concerning God is a dull fiction.   He mentions silver and gold rather
than clay or stone, that neither splendour nor cost may procure reverence to idols.   He then draws a general conclusion, that nothing is
more unlikely than that gods should be formed of any kind of inanimate matter.   Man is forced to confess that he is but the creature of
a day (see Book III. c. ix. s. 2), and yet would have the metal which
he has deified to be regarded as God.   Whence had idols their origin,
but from the will of man ?   There was ground, therefore, for the sar-
casm of the heathen poet (Hor. Sat. I. 8), " I was once the trunk of
a fig-tree, a useless log, when the tradesman, uncertain whether he
should make me a stool, &c., chose rather that I should be a god."   In
other words, an earth-born creature, who breathes out his life almost
every moment, is able by his own device to confer the name and
honour of deity on a lifeless trunk.   But as that Epicurean poet, in
indulging his wit, had no regard for religion, without attending to his
jeers or those of his fellows, let the rebuke of the prophet sting, nay,
cut us to the heart, when he speaks of the extreme infatuation of

those who take a piece of wood to kindle a fire to warm themselves, bake bread, roast or boil flesh, and out of the residue make a god, before which they prostrate themselves as suppliants (Isaiah xliv. 16). Hence the same prophet, in another place, not only charges idolaters as guilty in the eye of the law, but upbraids them for not learning from the foundations of the earth, nothing being more incongruous than to reduce the immense and incomprehensible Deity to the stature of a few feet. And yet experience shows that this monstrous proceeding, though palpably repugnant to the order of nature, is natural to man. It is, moreover, to be observed, that by the mode of expression which is employed, every form of superstition is denounced. Being works of men, they have no authority from God (Isa. ii. 8, 31; vii. 57; Hos. xiv. 4; Mic. v. 13); and, therefore, it must be regarded as a fixed principle, that all modes of worship devised by man are detestable. The infatuation is placed in a still stronger light by the Psalmist (Psalm cxv. 8), when he shows how aid is implored from dead and senseless objects, by beings who have been endued with intelligence for the very purpose of enabling them to know that the whole universe is governed by Divine energy alone. But as the corruption of nature hurries away all mankind collectively and individually into this madness, the Spirit at length thunders forth a dreadful imprecation, "They that make them are like unto them, so is every one that trusteth in them."[1] And it is to be observed, that the thing forbidden is *likeness*, whether sculptured or otherwise. This disposes of the frivolous precaution taken by the Greek Church. They think they do admirably, because they have no sculptured shape of Deity, while none go greater lengths in the licentious use of pictures. The Lord, however, not only forbids any image of himself to be erected by a statuary, but to be formed by any artist whatever, because every such image is sinful and insulting to his majesty.

5. I am not ignorant, indeed, of the assertion, which is now more than threadbare, "that images are the books of the unlearned." So said Gregory:[2] but the Holy Spirit gives a very different decision; and had Gregory got his lesson in this matter in the Spirit's school, he never would have spoken as he did. For when Jeremiah declares that "the stock is a doctrine of vanities" (Jer. x. 8), and Habakkuk, "that the molten image" is "a teacher of lies," the general doctrine to be inferred certainly is, that everything respecting God which is learned from images is futile and false. If it is objected that the censure of the prophets is directed against those who perverted images to purposes of impious superstition, I admit it to be so; but I add (what must be obvious to all), that the prophets utterly condemn

---

[1] Calvin translates the words of the Psalmist as an imprecation, "Similes illis fiant qui faciunt ea;"—Let those who make them be like unto them.

[2] See Gregory, Ep. ad Serenum Massiliens, Ep. cix. lib. vii.; and Ep. ix. lib. ix.; also Ep. liii. et cxxvi. lib. ii., where Gregory, while wishing to excuse the worship of images, rather accuses it.

what the Papists hold to be an undoubted axiom—viz. that images
are substitutes for books. For they contrast images with the true
God, as if the two were of an opposite nature, and never could be
made to agree. In the passages which I lately quoted, the conclusion
drawn is, that seeing there is one true God whom the Jews worshipped, visible shapes made for the purpose of representing him are false
and wicked fictions; and all, therefore, who have recourse to them
for knowledge are miserably deceived. In short, were it not true that
all such knowledge is fallacious and spurious, the prophets would not
condemn it in such general terms. This at least I maintain, that
when we teach that all human attempts to give a visible shape to
God are vanity and lies, we do nothing more than state *verbatim*
what the prophets taught.

6. Moreover, let Lactantius and Eusebius [1] be read on this subject. [2]
These writers ass me it as an indisputable fact, that all the beings
whose images were erected were originally men. In like manner,
Augustine distinctly declares, that it is unlawful not only to worship
images, but to dedicate them. And in this he says no more than had
been long before decreed by the Elibertine Council, the thirty-sixth
Canon of which is, "There must be no pictures used in churches:
Let nothing which is adored or worshipped be painted on walls."
But the most memorable passage of all is that which Augustine quotes
in another place from Varro, and in which he expressly concurs:—
"Those who first introduced images of the gods both took away fear
and brought in error." Were this merely the saying of Varro, it might
perhaps be of little weight, though it might well make us ashamed
that a heathen, groping as it were in darkness, should have attained
to such a degree of light, as to see that corporeal images are unworthy of the majesty of God, and that, because they diminish reverential fear and encourage error. The sentiment itself bears witness
that it was uttered with no less truth than shrewdness. But Augustine, while he borrows it from Varro, adduces it as conveying his own
opinion. At the outset, indeed, he declares that the first errors into
which men fell concerning God did not originate with images, but
increased with them, as if new fuel had been added. Afterwards,
he explains how the fear of God was thereby extinguished or impaired,
his presence being brought into contempt by foolish, and childish,
and absurd representations. [3] The truth of this latter remark I wish
we did not so thoroughly experience. Whosoever, therefore, is desirous of being instructed in the true knowledge of God must apply
to some other teacher than images.

1 The French adds, "deux des plus anciens Docteurs de l'Eglise;"—two of the most
ancient Doctors of the Church.
2 Lact. Inst. Div. lib. i c. 15; Euseb. Præf. Evang. lib. iii. c. 3, 4; also August. De
Civitate Dei, lib. iv. c. 9, 31.
3 The French is, "Pourceque la gloire de sa Divinite est vilipendée en une chose
si sotte et lourde comme est un marmouset;"—because the glory of his Divinity is degraded into an object so silly and stupid as a marmoset.

7. Let Papists, then, if they have any sense of shame, henceforth desist from the futile plea, that images are the books of the unlearned —a plea so plainly refuted by innumerable passages of Scripture. And yet were I to admit the plea, it would not be a valid defence of their peculiar idols. It is well known what kind of monsters they obtrude upon us as divine. For what are the pictures or statues to which they append the names of saints, but exhibitions of the most shameless luxury or obscenity? Were any one to dress himself after their model, he would deserve the pillory. Indeed, brothels exhibit their inmates more chastely and modestly dressed than churches do images intended to represent virgins. The dress of the martyrs is is in no respect more becoming. Let Papists then have some little regard to decency in decking their idols, if they would give the least plausibility to the false allegation, that they are books of some kind of sanctity. But even then we shall answer, that this is not the method in which the Christian people should be taught in sacred places. Very different from these follies is the doctrine in which God would have them to be there instructed. His injunction is, that the doctrine common to all should there be set forth by the preaching of the Word, and the administration of the sacraments,—a doctrine to which little heed can be given by those whose eyes are carried to and fro gazing at idols. And who are the unlearned, whose rudeness admits of being taught by images only? Just those whom the Lord acknowledges for his disciples; those whom he honours with a revelation of his celestial philosophy, and desires to be trained in the saving mysteries of his kingdom. I confess, indeed, as matters now are, there are not a few in the present day who cannot want such books. But, I ask, whence this stupidity, but just because they are defrauded of the only doctrine which was fit to instruct them? The simple reason why those who had the charge of churches resigned the office of teaching to idols was, because they themselves were dumb. Paul declares, that by the true preaching of the gospel Christ is portrayed and in a manner crucified before our eyes (Gal. iii. 1). Of what use, then, were the erection in churches of so many crosses of wood and stone, silver and gold, if this doctrine were faithfully and honestly preached—viz., Christ died that he might bear our curse upon the tree, that he might expiate our sins by the sacrifice of his body, wash them in his blood, and, in short, reconcile us to God the Father? From this one doctrine the people would learn more than from a thousand crosses of wood and stone. As for crosses of gold and silver, it may be true that the avaricious give their eyes and minds to them more eagerly than to any heavenly instructor.

8. In regard to the origin of idols, the statement contained in the Book of Wisdom has been received with almost universal consent— viz., that they originated with those who bestowed this honour on the dead, from a superstitious regard to their memory. I admit that this perverse practice is of very high antiquity, and I deny not that

it was a kind of torch by which the infatuated proneness of mankind to idolatry was kindled into a greater blaze. I do not, however, admit that it was the first origin of the practice. The idols that were in use before the prevalence of that ambitious consecration of the images of the dead, frequently adverted to by profane writers, is evident from the words of Moses (Gen. xxxi. 19). When he relates that Rachel stole her father's images, he speaks of the use of idols as a common vice. Hence we may infer, that the human mind is, so to speak, a perpetual forge of idols. There was a kind of renewal of the world at the deluge, but before many years elapse, men are forging gods at will. There is reason to believe, that in the holy Patriarch's lifetime his grandchildren were given to idolatry: so that he must with his own eyes, not without the deepest grief, have seen the earth polluted with idols—that earth whose iniquities God had lately purged with so fearful a judgment. For Joshua testifies (Josh. xxiv. 2), that Terah and Nachor, even before the birth of Abraham, were the worshippers of false gods. The progeny of Shem having so speedily revolted, what are we to think of the posterity of Ham, who had been cursed long before in their father? Thus, indeed, it is. The human mind, stuffed as it is with presumptuous rashness, dares to imagine a god suited to its own capacity; as it labours under dulness, nay, is sunk in the grossest ignorance, it substitutes vanity and an empty phantom in the place of God. To these evils another is added. The god whom man has thus conceived inwardly he attempts to embody outwardly. The mind, in this way, conceives the idol, and the hand gives it birth. That idolatry has its origin in the idea which men have, that God is not present with them unless his presence is carnally exhibited, appears from the example of the Israelites: "Up," said they, "make us gods, which shall go before us; for as for this Moses, the man that brought us up out of the land of Egypt, we wot not what is become of him" (Exod. xxxii. 1). They knew, indeed, that there was a God whose mighty power they had experienced in so many miracles, but they had no confidence of his being near to them, if they did not with their eyes behold a corporeal symbol of his presence, as an attestation to his actual government. They desired, therefore, to be assured, by the image which went before them, that they were journeying under Divine guidance. And daily experience shows, that the flesh is always restless until it has obtained some figment like itself, with which it may vainly solace itself as a representation of God. In consequence of this blind passion men have, almost in all ages since the world began, set up signs on which they imagined that God was visibly depicted to their eyes.

9. After such a figment is formed, adoration forthwith ensues; for when once men imagined that they beheld God in images, they also worshipped him as being there. At length their eyes and minds becoming wholly engrossed by them, they began to grow more and

more brutish, gazing and wondering as if some divinity were actually before them. It hence appears that men do not fall away to the worship of images until they have imbibed some idea of a grosser description : not that they actually believe them to be gods, but that the power of divinity somehow or other resides in them. Therefore, whether it be God or a creature that is imaged, the moment you fall prostrate before it in veneration, you are so far fascinated by superstition. For this reason, the Lord not only forbad the erection of statues to himself, but also the consecration of titles and stones which might be set up for adoration. For the same reason, also, the second commandment has an additional part concerning adoration. For as soon as a visible form is given to God, his power also is supposed to be annexed to it. So stupid are men, that wherever they figure God, there they fix him, and by necessary consequence proceed to adore him. It makes no difference whether they worship the idol simply, or God in the idol ; it is always idolatry when divine honours are paid to an idol, be the colour what it may. And because God wills not to be worshipped superstitiously, whatever is bestowed upon idols is so much robbed from him.

Let those attend to this who set about hunting for miserable pretexts in defence of the execrable indolatry in which for many past ages true religion has been buried and sunk. It is said that the images are not accounted gods. Nor were the Jews so utterly thoughtless as not to remember that there was a God whose hand led them out of Egypt before they made the calf. Indeed, Aaron saying that these were the gods which had brought them out of Egypt, they intimated, in no ambiguous terms, that they wished to retain God, their deliverer, provided they saw him going before them in the calf. Nor are the heathen to be deemed to have been so stupid as not to understand that God was something else than wood and stone. For they changed the images at pleasure, but always retained the same gods in their minds ;[1] besides, they daily consecrated new images without thinking they were making new gods. Read the excuses which Augustine tells us were employed by the idolaters of his time (*August. in Ps.* cxiii.). The vulgar, when accused, replied that they did not worship the visible object, but the Deity which dwelt in it invisibly. Those, again, who had what he calls a more refined religion, said, that they neither worshipped the image, nor any inhabiting Deity, but by means of the corporeal image beheld a symbol of that which it was their duty to worship. What then ? All idolaters, whether Jewish or Gentile, were actuated in the very way which has been described. Not contented with spiritual understanding, they thought that images would give them a surer and nearer impression. When once this preposterous representation of God was adopted, there was

---

[1] The French is, " Neantmoins ils ne disoyent point pour cela qu'un Dieu fut divisé :" —nevertheless, they did not therefore say that the unity of God was divided.

no limit until, deluded every now and then by new impostures, they came to think that God exerted his power in images.[1] Still the Jews were persuaded, that, under such images, they worshipped the eternal God, the one true Lord of heaven and earth; and the Gentiles, also, in worshipping their own false gods, supposed them to dwell in heaven.

10. It is an impudent falsehood to deny that the thing which was thus anciently done is also done in our day. For why do men prostrate themselves before images? Why, when in the act of praying, do they turn towards them as to the ears of God? It is indeed true, as Augustine says (in Ps. cxiii.), that no person thus prays or worships, looking at an image, without being impressed with the idea that he is heard by it, or without hoping that what he wishes will be performed by it. Why are such distinctions made between different images of the same God, that while one is passed by, or receives only common honour, another is worshipped with the highest solemnities? Why do they fatigue themselves with votive pilgrimages to images, while they have many similar ones at home?[2] Why at the present time do they fight for them to blood and slaughter, as for their altars and hearths, showing more willingness to part with the one God than with their idols? And yet I am not now detailing the gross errors of the vulgar—errors almost infinite in number, and in possession of almost all hearts. I am only referring to what those profess who are most desirous to clear themselves of idolatry. They say, we do not call them our gods. Nor did either the Jews or Gentiles of old so call them; and yet the prophets never ceased to charge them with their adulteries with wood and stone for the very acts which are daily done by those who would be deemed Christians, namely, for worshipping God carnally in wood and stone.

11. I am not ignorant, however, and I have no wish to disguise the fact, that they endeavour to evade the charge by means of a more subtle distinction, which shall afterwards be fully considered (see *infra*, s. 16, and chap. xii. s. 2). The worship which they pay to their images they cloak with the name of εἰδωλοδυλεία (*idolodulia*), and deny to be εἰδωλολατρεία (*idolatria*). So they speak, holding that the worship which they call *dulia* may, without insult to God, be paid to statues and pictures. Hence, they think themselves blameless if they are only the *servants*, and not the *worshippers*, of idols; as if it were not a lighter matter to *worship* than *to serve*. And yet,

---

1 French, " Ne vouloit monstrer sa vertu que sous les images;"—would only show his power under the form of images.
2 The two last sentences in French are, " Car laissans là un crucifix, ou une image de leur nostre-dame, ou n'en tenans point grand comte, ils mettent leur devotion à un autre. Pourquoy est-ce qu'ils trotent si loin en pelerinage pour voir un marmouset, duquel ils ont le semblable à leur porte?"—For there passing by a crucifix, or an image of what they call " Our Lady," or making no great account of them, they pay their devotion to another. Why is it that they trot so far on a pilgrimage to see a marmoset, when they have one like it at their door?

while they take refuge in a Greek term, they very childishly contradict themselves. For the Greek word λατρεύειν having no other meaning than *to worship*, what they say is just the same as if they were to confess that they worship their images without worshipping them. They cannot object that I am quibbling upon words. The fact is, that they only betray their ignorance while they attempt to throw dust in the eyes of the simple. But how eloquent soever they may be, they will never prove by their eloquence that one and the same thing makes two. Let them show how the things differ if they would be thought different from ancient idolaters. For as a murderer or an adulterer will not escape conviction by giving some adventitious name to his crime, so it is absurd for them to expect that the subtle device of a name will exculpate them, if they, in fact, differ in nothing from idolaters whom they themselves are forced to condemn. But so far are they from proving that their case is different, that the source of the whole evil consists in a preposterous rivalship with them, while they with their minds devise, and with their hands execute, symbolical shapes of God.

12. I am not, however, so superstitious as to think that all visible representations of every kind are unlawful. But as sculpture and painting are gifts of God, what I insist for is, that both shall be used purely and lawfully,—that gifts which the Lord has bestowed upon us, for his glory and our good, shall not be preposterously abused, nay, shall not be perverted to our destruction. We think it unlawful to give a visible shape to God, because God himself has forbidden it, and because it cannot be done without, in some degree, tarnishing his glory. And lest any should think that we are singular in this opinion, those acquainted with the productions of sound divines will find that they have always disapproved of it. If it be unlawful to make any corporeal representation of God, still more unlawful must it be to worship such a representation instead of God, or to worship God in it. The only things, therefore, which ought to be painted or sculptured, are things which can be presented to the eye; the majesty of God, which is far beyond the reach of any eye, must not be dishonoured by unbecoming representations. Visible representations are of two classes—viz. historical, which give a representation of events, and pictorial, which merely exhibit bodily shapes and figures. The former are of some use for instruction or admonition. The latter, so far as I can see, are only fitted for amusement. And yet it is certain, that the latter are almost the only kind which have hitherto been exhibited in churches. Hence we may infer, that the exhibition was not the result of judicious selection, but of a foolish and inconsiderate longing. I say nothing as to the improper and unbecoming form in which they are presented, or the wanton license in which sculptors and painters have here indulged (a point to which I alluded a little ago, *supra*, s. 7). I only say, that though they were otherwise faultless, they could not be of any utility in teaching.

13. But, without reference to the above distinction, let us here consider, whether it is expedient that churches should contain representations of any kind, whether of events or human forms. First, then, if we attach any weight to the authority of the ancient Church, let us remember, that for five hundred years, during which religion was in a more prosperous condition, and a purer doctrine flourished, Christian churches were completely free from visible representations (see Preface, and Book IV., c. ix. s. 9). Hence their first admission as an ornament to churches took place after the purity of the ministry had somewhat degenerated. I will not dispute as to the rationality of the grounds on which the first introduction of them proceeded, but if you compare the two periods, you will find that the latter had greatly declined from the purity of the times when images were unknown. What then? Are we to suppose that those holy fathers, if they had judged the thing to be useful and salutary, would have allowed the Church to be so long without it? Undoubtedly, because they saw very little or no advantage, and the greatest danger in it, they rather rejected it intentionally and on rational grounds, than omitted it through ignorance or carelessness. This is clearly attested by Augustine in these words (Ep. xlix. See also De Civit. Dei, lib. iv. c. 31). "When images are thus placed aloft in seats of honour, to be beheld by those who are praying or sacrificing, though they have neither sense nor life, yet from appearing as if they had both, they affect weak minds just as if they lived and breathed," &c. And again, in another passage (in Ps. cxii.), he says, "The effect produced, and in a manner extorted, by the bodily shape, is, that the mind, being itself in a body, imagines that a body which is so like its own must be similarly affected," &c. A little farther on he says, "Images are more capable of giving a wrong bent to an unhappy soul, from having mouth, eyes, ears, and feet, than of correcting it, as they neither speak, nor see, nor hear, nor walk." This undoubtedly is the reason why John (1 John v. 21) enjoins us to beware, not only of the worship of idols, but also of idols themselves. And from the fearful infatuation under which the world has hitherto laboured, almost to the entire destruction of piety, we know too well from experience that the moment images appear in churches, idolatry has as it were raised its banner; because the folly of manhood cannot moderate itself, but forthwith falls away to superstitious worship. Even were the danger less imminent, still, when I consider the proper end for which churches are erected, it appears to me more unbecoming their sacredness than I well can tell, to admit any other images than those living symbols which the Lord has consecrated by his own word: I mean Baptism and the Lord's Supper, with the other ceremonies. By these our eyes ought to be more steadily fixed, and more vividly impressed, than to require the aid of any images which the wit of man may devise. Such, then, is the incomparable blessing of images—a

blessing, the want of which, if we believe the Papists, cannot possibly be compensated![1]

14. Enough, I believe, would have been said on this subject, were I not in a manner arrested by the Council of Nice; not the celebrated Council which Constantine the Great assembled, but one which was held eight hundred years ago by the orders and under the auspices of the Empress Irene.[2] This Council decreed not only that images were to be used in churches, but also that they were to be worshipped. Everything, therefore, that I have said, is in danger of suffering great prejudice from the authority of this Synod. To confess the truth, however, I am not so much moved by this consideration, as by a wish to make my readers aware of the lengths to which the infatuation has been carried by those who had a greater fondness for images than became Christians. But let us first dispose of this matter. Those who defend the use of images appeal to that Synod for support. But there is a refutation extant which bears the name of Charlemagne, and which is proved by its style to be a production of that period. It gives the opinions delivered by the bishops who were present, and the arguments by which they supported them. John, deputy of the Eastern Churches, said, "God created man in his own image," and thence inferred that images ought to be used. He also thought there was a recommendation of images in the following passage, "Show me thy face, for it is beautiful." Another, in order to prove that images ought to be placed on altars, quoted the passage, "No man, when he hath lighted a candle, putteth it under a bushel." Another, to show the utility of looking at images, quoted a verse of the Psalms, "The light of thy countenance, O Lord, has shone upon us." Another laid hold of this similitude: As the Patriarchs used the sacrifices of the Gentiles, so ought Christians to use the images of saints instead of the idols of the Gentiles. They also twisted to the same effect the words, "Lord, I have loved the beauty of thy house." But the most ingenious interpretation was the following, "As we have heard, so also have we seen;" therefore, God is known not merely by the hearing of the word, but also by the seeing of images. Bishop Theodore was equally acute: "God," says he, "is to be admired in his saints;" and it is elsewhere said, "To the saints who are on earth;" therefore this must refer to images. In short, their absurdities are so extreme that it is painful even to quote them.

15. When they treat of adoration, great stress is laid on the worship of Pharaoh, the staff of Joseph, and the inscription which Jacob set up. In this last case they not only pervert the meaning of Scripture, but quote what is nowhere to be found. Then the passages,

---

The French is, " qu'il n'y ait nulle recompense qui vaille un marmouset guignant à travers et faisant la mine tortue;"—that no compensation can equal the value of a marmoset looking askance and twisting its face.

2 The French is, " une mechante Proserpine nommée Irene;"—a wicked Proserpine named Irene.

"Worship at his footstool"—"Worship in his holy mountain"—"The rulers of the people will worship before thy face," seem to them very solid and apposite proofs.   Were one, with the view of turning the defenders of images into ridicule, to put words into their mouths, could they be made to utter greater and grosser absurdities?   But to put an end to all doubt on the subject of images, Theodosius Bishop of Mira confirms the propriety of worshipping them by the dreams of his archdeacon, which he adduces with as much gravity as if he were in possession of a response from heaven.   Let the patrons of images now go and urge us with the decree of this Synod, as if the venerable Fathers did not bring themselves into utter discredit by handling Scripture so childishly, or wresting it so shamefully and profanely.

16. I come now to monstrous impieties, which it is strange they ventured to utter, and twice strange that all men did not protest against with the utmost detestation.[1]   It is right to expose this frantic and flagitious extravagance, and thereby deprive the worship of images of that gloss of antiquity in which Papists seek to deck it.   Theodosius, Bishop of Amora, fires off an anathema at all who object to the worship of images.   Another attributes all the calamities of Greece and the East to the crime of not having worshipped them.   Of what punishment then are the Prophets, Apostles, and Martyrs worthy, in whose day no images existed?   They afterwards add, that if the statue of the Emperor is met with odours and incense, much more are the images of saints entitled to the honour.   Constantius, Bishop of Constantia in Cyprus, professes to embrace images with reverence, and declares that he will pay them the respect which is due to the ever blessed Trinity : every person refusing to do the same thing he anathematises and classes with Marcionites and Manichees.   Lest you should think this the private opinion of an individual, they all assent.   Nay, John the Eastern legate, carried still farther by his zeal, declares it would be better to allow a city to be filled with brothels than be denied the worship of images.   At last it is resolved with one consent that the Samaritans are the worst of all heretics, and that the enemies of images are worse than the Samaritans.   But that the play may not pass off without the accustomed *Plaudite*, the whole thus concludes, " Rejoice and exult, ye who, having the image of Christ, offer sacrifice to it."   Where is now the distinction of *latria* and *dulia* with which they would throw dust in all eyes, human and divine ?   The Council unreservedly relies as much on images as on the living God.[2]

[1] The French adds, " et qu'il ne se soit trouvé gens qui leur crachassent au visage ;" —and that people were not found to spit in their face.
[2] See Calvin, De Vitandis Superstitionibus, where also see Resp. Pastorum, Tigurin. adver. Nicodem itas.   See also Calvin, De Fugiendis Illicitis Sacris.

CHAPTER XII.

GOD DISTINGUISHED FROM IDOLS, THAT HE MAY BE THE EXCLUSIVE OBJECT OF WORSHIP.

Sections.

1. Scripture, in teaching that there is but one God, does not make a dispute about words, but attributes all honour and religious worship to him alone. This proved, 1st, By the etymology of the term. 2d, By the testimony of God himself, when he declares that he is a jealous God, and will not allow himself to be confounded with any fictitious Deity.
2. The Papists, in opposing this pure doctrine, gain nothing by their distinction of *dulia* and *latria*.
3. Passages of Scripture subversive of the Papistical distinction, and proving that religious worship is due to God alone. Perversions of Divine worship.

1. WE said at the commencement of our work (chap. ii.), that the knowledge of God consists not in frigid speculation, but carries worship along with it ; and we touched by the way (chap. v. s. 6, 9, 10) on what will be more copiously treated in other places (Book II. chap. viii.)—viz. how God is duly worshipped.   Now I only briefly repeat, that whenever Scripture asserts the unity of God, it does not contend for a mere name, but also enjoins that nothing which belongs to Divinity be applied to any other ; thus making it obvious in what respect pure religion differs from superstition.   The Greek word εὐσέβεια means " right worship ;" for the Greeks, though groping in darkness, were always aware that a certain rule was to be observed, in order that God might not be worshipped absurdly.   Cicero truly and shrewdly derives the name *religion* from *relego*, and yet the reason which he assigns is forced and far-fetched—viz. that honest worshippers *read* and *read again*, and ponder what is true.[1]   I rather think the name is used in opposition to *vagrant license*—the greater part of mankind rashly taking up whatever first comes in their way, whereas piety, that it may stand with a firm step, confines itself within due bounds.   In the same way superstition seems to take its name from its not being contented with the measure which reason prescribes, but accumulating a superfluous mass of vanities.   But to say nothing more of words, it has been universally admitted in all ages, that religion is vitiated and perverted whenever false opinions are introduced into it, and hence it is inferred, that whatever is allowed to be done from inconsiderate zeal, cannot be defended by any pretext with which

---

[1] Cic. De Nat. Deor. lib. ii. c. 28.   See also Lactant. Inst. Div. lib. iv. c. 28.

the superstitious may choose to cloak it.   But although this confession is in every man's mouth, a shameful stupidity is forthwith manifested, inasmuch as men neither cleave to the one God, nor use any selection in their worship, as we have already observed.

But God, in vindicating his own right, first proclaims that he is a jealous God, and will be a stern avenger if he is confounded with any false god; and thereafter defines what due worship is, in order that the human race may be kept in obedience.   Both of these he embraces in his Law when he first binds the faithful in allegiance to him as their only Lawgiver, and then prescribes a rule for worshipping him in accordance with his will.   The Law, with its manifold uses and objects, I will consider in its own place; at present I only advert to this one, that it is designed as a bridle to curb men, and prevent them from turning aside to spurious worship.   But it is necessary to attend to the observation with which I set out—viz. that unless everything peculiar to divinity is confined to God alone, he is robbed of his honour, and his worship is violated.

It may be proper here more particularly to attend to the subtleties which superstition employs.   In revolting to strange gods, it avoids the appearance of abandoning the Supreme God, or reducing him to the same rank with others.   It gives him the highest place, but at the same time surrounds him with a tribe of minor deities, among whom it portions out his peculiar offices.   In this way, though in a dissembling and crafty manner, the glory of the Godhead is dissected, and not allowed to remain entire.   In the same way the people of old, both Jews and Gentiles, placed an immense crowd in subordination to the father and ruler of the gods, and gave them, according to their rank, to share with the supreme God in the government of heaven and earth.   In the same way, too, for some ages past, departed saints have been exalted to partnership with God, to be worshipped, invoked, and lauded in his stead.   And yet we do not even think that the majesty of God is obscured by this abomination, whereas it is in a great measure suppressed and extinguished—all that we retain being a frigid opinion of his supreme power.   At the same time, being deluded by these entanglements, we go astray after divers gods.

2. The distinction of what is called *dulia* and *latria* was invented for the very purpose of permitting divine honours to be paid to angels and dead men with apparent impunity.   For it is plain that the worship which Papists pay to saints differs in no respect from the worship of God: for this worship is paid without distinction; only when they are pressed they have recourse to the evasion, that what belongs to God is kept unimpaired, because they leave him *latria*.   But since the question relates not to the word, but the thing, how can they be allowed to sport at will with a matter of the highest moment?   But not to insist on this, the utmost they will obtain by their distinction is, that they give worship to God, and service to the others.   For λατρεία in Greek has the same meaning as *worship* in Latin; whereas

δουλεία properly means *service*, though the words are sometimes used in Scripture indiscriminately. But granting that the distinction is invariably preserved, the thing to be inquired into is the meaning of each. Δουλεία unquestionably means service, and λατρεία worship. But no man doubts that to *serve* is something higher than to *worship*. For it were often a hard thing to serve him whom you would not refuse to reverence. It is, therefore, an unjust division to assign the greater to the saints and leave the less to God. But several of the ancient fathers observed this distinction. What if they did, when all men see that it is not only improper, but utterly frivolous?

3. Laying aside subtleties, let us examine the thing. When Paul reminds the Galatians of what they were before they came to the knowledge of God, he says, that they " did service unto them which by nature are no gods" (Gal. iv. 8). Because he does not say *latria*, was their superstition excusable? This superstition, to which he gives the name of *dulia*, he condemns as much as if he had given it the name of *latria*. When Christ repels Satan's insulting proposal with the words, " It is written, Thou shalt worship the Lord thy God, and him only shalt thou serve" (Matth. viii. 10), there was no question of *latria*. For all that Satan asked was προσκύνησις (obeisance). In like manner, when John is rebuked by the angel for falling on his knees before him (Rev. xix. 10; xxii. 8, 9), we ought not to suppose that John had so far forgotten himself as to have intended to transfer the honour due to God alone to an angel. But because it was impossible that a worship connected with religion should not savour somewhat of divine worship, he could not προσκύνειν (do obeisance to) the angel without derogating from the glory of God. True, we often read that men were worshipped; but that was, if I may so speak, civil honour. The case is different with religious honour, which, the moment it is conjoined with worship, carries profanation of the divine honour along with it. The same thing may be seen in the case of Cornelius (Acts x. 25). He had not made so little progress in piety as not to confine supreme worship to God alone. Therefore, when he prostrates himself before Peter, he certainly does it not with the intention of adoring him instead of God. Yet Peter sternly forbids him. And why, but just because men never distinguish so accurately between the worship of God and the creatures as not to transfer promiscuously to the creature that which belongs only to God. Therefore, if we would have one God, let us remember that we can never appropriate the minutest portion of his glory without retaining what is his due. Accordingly, when Zechariah discourses concerning the repairing of the Church, he distinctly says not only that there would be one God, but also that he would have only one name—the reason being, that he might have nothing in common with idols. The nature of the worship which God requires will be seen in its own place (Book II., c. vii. and viii.). He has been pleased to prescribe in his Law what is lawful and right, and thus astrict men to a certain rule,

lest any should allow themselves to devise a worship of their own. But as it is inexpedient to burden the reader by mixing up a variety of topics, I do not now dwell on this one. Let it suffice to remember, that whatever offices of piety are bestowed anywhere else than on God alone, are of the nature of sacrilege. First, superstition attached divine honours to the sun and stars, or to idols : afterwards ambition followed—ambition which, decking man in the spoils of God, dared to profane all that was sacred. And though the principle of worshipping a supreme Deity continued to be held, still the practice was to sacrifice promiscuously to genii and minor gods, or departed heroes : so prone is the descent to this vice of communicating to a crowd that which God strictly claims as his own peculiar right !

CHAPTER XIII.

THE UNITY OF THE DIVINE ESSENCE IN THREE PERSONS TAUGHT, IN SCRIPTURE, FROM THE FOUNDATION OF THE WORLD.

This chapter consists of two parts. The former delivers the orthodox doctrine concerning the Holy Trinity. This occupies from sec. 1–21, and may be divided into four heads; the first, treating of the meaning of Person, including both the term and the thing meant by it, sec. 2–6; the second, proving the deity of the Son, sec. 7–13; the third, the deity of the Holy Spirit, sec, 14 and 15; and the fourth, explaining what to be held concerning the Holy Trinity. The second part of the chapter refutes certain heresies which have arisen, particularly in our age, in opposition to this orthodox doctrine. This occupies from sec. 21 to the end.

Sections.

1. Scripture, in teaching that the essence of God is immense and spiritual, refutes not only idolaters and the foolish wisdom of the world, but also the Manichees and Anthropomorphites. These latter briefly refuted.
2. In this one essence are three persons, yet so that neither is there a triple God, nor is the simple essence of God divided. Meaning of the word Person in this discussion. Three hypostases in God, or the essence of God.
3. Objection of those who, in this discussion, reject the use of the word Person. Answer 1. That it is not a foreign term, but is employed for the explanation of sacred mysteries.
4. Answer continued, 2. The orthodox compelled to use the terms, Trinity, Subsistence, and Person. Examples from the case of the Arians and Sabellians.
5. Answer continued, 3. The ancient Church, though differing somewhat in the explanation of these terms, agree in substance. Proofs from Hilary, Jerome, Augustine, in their use of the words Essence, Substance, Hypostasis. 4. Provided the orthodox meaning is retained, there should be no dispute about mere terms. But those who object to the terms usually favour the Arian and Sabellian heresy.
6. After the definition of the term follows a definition and explanation of the thing meant by it. The distinction of Persons.
7. Proofs of the eternal Deity of the Son. The Son the λόγος of the Eternal Father, and, therefore, the Son Eternal God. Objection. Reply.
8. Objection, that the λόγος began to be when the creating God spoke. Answer confirmed by Scripture and argument.
9. The Son called God and Jehovah. Other names of the Eternal Father applied to him in the Old Testament. He is, therefore, the Eternal God. Another objection refuted. Case of the Jews explained.
10. The angel who appeared to the fathers under the Law asserts that he is Jehovah. That angel was the λόγος of the Eternal Father. The Son being that λόγος is Eternal God. Impiety of Servetus refuted. Why the Son appeared in the form of an angel.
11. Passages from the New Testament in which the Son is acknowledged to be the Lord of Hosts, the Judge of the world, the God of glory, the Creator of the world, the Lord of angels, the King of the Church, the eternal λόγος, God blessed for ever, God manifest in the flesh, the equal of God, the true God and eternal life, the Lord and God of all believers. Therefore, the Eternal God.
12. Christ the Creator, Preserver, Redeemer, and Searcher of hearts. Therefore, the Eternal God.
13. Christ, by his own inherent power, wrought miracles, and bestowed the power of

working them on others. Out of the Eternal God there is no salvation, no righteousness, no life. All these are in Christ. Christ, consequently, is the Eternal
God. He in whom we believe and hope, to whom we pray, whom the Church
acknowledges as the Saviour of the faithful, whom to know is life eternal, in whom
the pious glory, and through whom eternal blessings are communicated, is the
Eternal God. All these Christ is, and, therefore, he is God.

14. The Divinity of the Spirit proved. I. He is the Creator and Preserver of the world.
II. He sent the Prophets. III. He quickeneth all things. IV, He is everywhere
present. V. He renews the saints, and fits them for eternal life. VI. All the
offices of Deity belong to him.

15. The Divinity of the Spirit continued. VII. He is called God. VIII. Blasphemy
against him is not forgiven.

16. What view to be taken of the Trinity. The form of Christian baptism proves that
there are three persons in one essence. The Arian and Macedonian heresies.

17. Of the distinction of Persons. They are distinct, but not divided. This proved.

18. Analogies taken from human affairs to be cautiously used. Due regard to be paid
to those mentioned by Scripture.

19. How the Three Persons not only do not destroy, but constitute the most perfect
unity.

20. Conclusion of this part of the chapter, and summary of the true doctrine concerning the unity of Essence and the Three Persons.

21. Refutation of Arian, Macedonian, and Antitrinitarian heresies. Caution to be
observed.

22. The more modern Antitrinitarians, and especially Servetus, refuted.

23. Other Antitrinitarians refuted. No good objection that Christ is called the Son of
God, since he is also called God. Impious absurdities of some heretics.

24. The name of God sometimes given to the Son absolutely as to the Father. Same
as to other attributes. Objections refuted.

25. Objections further refuted. Caution to be used.

26. Previous refutations further explained.

27. Reply to certain passages produced from Irenæus. The meaning of Irenæus.

28. Reply to certain passages produced from Tertullian. The meaning of Tertullian.

29. Antitrinitarians refuted by ancient Christian writers ; *e g.*, Justin, Hilary. Objections drawn from writings improperly attributed to Ignatius. Conclusion of
the whole discussion concerning the Trinity.

1. THE doctrine of Scripture concerning the immensity and the
spirituality of the essence of God, should have the effect not only of
dissipating the wild dreams of the vulgar, but also of refuting the
subtleties of a profane philosophy. One of the ancients thought he
spake shrewdly when he said that everything we see and everything
we do not see is God (Senec. Præf. lib. i. Quæst. Nat.). In this way
he fancied that the Divinity was transfused into every separate portion
of the world. But although God, in order to keep us within the
bounds of soberness, treats sparingly of his essence, still, by the two
attributes which I have mentioned, he at once suppresses all gross
imaginations, and checks the audacity of the human mind. His immensity surely ought to deter us from measuring him by our sense,
while his spiritual nature forbids us to indulge in carnal or earthly
speculation concerning him. With the same view he frequently represents heaven as his dwelling-place. It is true, indeed, that as he
is incomprehensible, he fills the earth also, but knowing that our
minds are heavy and grovel on the earth, he raises us above the
world, that he may shake off our sluggishness and inactivity. And
here we have a refutation of the error of the Manichees, who, by
adopting two first principles, made the devil almost the equal of God.

The greatness of God checks the audacity of the human mind.

God
speaks
in
anthro-
pomorphic
language
that man
may
understand
Him.

This, assuredly, was both to destroy his unity and restrict his immensity. Their attempt to pervert certain passages of Scripture proved their shameful ignorance, as the very nature of the error did their monstrous infatuation. The Anthropomorphites also, who dreamed of a corporeal God, because mouth, ears, eyes, hands, and feet are often ascribed to him in Scripture, are easily refuted. For who is so devoid of intellect as not to understand that God, in so speaking, lisps with us as nurses are wont to do with little children? Such modes of expression, therefore, do not so much express what kind of a being God is, as accommodate the knowledge of him to our feebleness. In doing so, he must of course stoop far below his proper height.

God's
unity
exists
in three
persons.

2. But there is another special mark by which he designates himself, for the purpose of giving a more intimate knowledge of his nature. While he proclaims his unity, he distinctly sets it before us as existing in three persons. These we must hold, unless the bare and empty name of Deity merely is a flutter in our brain without any genuine knowledge. Moreover, lest any one should dream of a threefold God, or think that the simple essence is divided by the three Persons, we must here seek a brief and easy definition which may effectually guard us from error. But as some strongly inveigh against the term Person as being merely of human invention, let us first consider how far they have any ground for doing so.

When the Apostle calls the Son of God " the express image of his person" (Heb. i. 3), he undoubtedly does assign to the Father some subsistence in which he differs from the Son. For to hold with some interpreters that the term is equivalent to essence (as if Christ represented the substance of the Father like the impression of a seal upon wax), were not only harsh but absurd. For the essence of God being simple and undivided, and contained in himself entire, in full perfection, without partition or diminution, it is improper, nay, ridiculous, to call it his express image (χαρακτηρ). But because the Father, though distinguished by his own peculiar properties, has expressed himself wholly in the Son, he is said with perfect reason to have rendered his person (hypostasis) manifest in him. And this aptly accords with what is immediately added—viz. that he is "the brightness of his glory." The fair inference from the Apostle's words is, that there is a proper subsistence (hypostasis) of the Father, which shines refulgent in the Son. From this, again, it is easy to infer that there is a subsistence (hypostasis) of the Son which distinguishes him from the Father. The same holds in the case of the Holy Spirit; for we will immediately prove both that he is God, and that he has a separate subsistence from the Father. This, moreover, is not a distinction of essence, which it were impious to multiply. If credit, then, is given to the Apostle's testimony, it follows that there are three persons (hypostases) in God. The Latins having used the word Persona to express the same thing as the Greek ὑποστασις, it betrays excessive fastidiousness and even perverseness to quarrel with the term. The most literal translation would be *subsistence*. Many have used *substance* in the same sense. Nor, indeed, was the use of the term Person confined to the Latin Church. For the Greek Church in like manner, perhaps for the purpose of testifying their consent, have taught that there are three πρόσωπα (*aspects*) in God. All these, however, whether Greeks or Latins, though differing as to the word, are perfectly agreed in substance.

3. Now, then, though heretics may snarl and the excessively fastidious carp at the word Person as inadmissible, in consequence of its human origin, since they cannot displace us from our position that three are named, each of whom is perfect God, and yet that there is no plurality of gods, it is most uncandid to attack the terms which do nothing more than explain what the Scriptures declare and sanction. " It were better," they say, "to confine not only our meanings but our words within the bounds of Scripture, and not scatter about foreign terms to become the future seed-beds of brawls and dissensions. In this way, men grow tired of quarrels about words ; the truth is lost in altercation, and charity melts away amid hateful strife." If they call it a *foreign* term, because it cannot be pointed out in Scripture in so many syllables, they certainly impose an unjust law—a law which would condemn every interpretation of Scripture that is not composed of other words of Scripture. But if by *foreign* they mean that which, after being idly devised, is superstitiously defended,—which tends more to strife than edification,—which is used either out of place, or with no benefit,—which offends pious ears by its harshness, and leads them away from the simplicity of God's Word, I embrace their soberness with all my heart. For I think we are bound to speak of God as reverently as we are bound to think of him. As our own thoughts respecting him are foolish, so our own language respecting him is absurd. Still, however, some medium must be observed. The unerring standard both of thinking and speaking must be derived from the Scriptures : by it all the thoughts of our minds, and the words of our mouths, should be tested. But in regard to those parts of Scripture which, to our capacities, are dark and intricate, what forbids us to explain them in clearer terms —terms, however, kept in reverent and faithful subordination to Scripture truth, used sparingly and modestly, and not without occasion? Of this we are not without many examples. When it has been proved that the Church was impelled, by the strongest necessity, to use the words Trinity and Person, will not he who still inveighs against novelty of terms be deservedly suspected of taking offence at the light of truth, and of having no other ground for his invective, than that the truth is made plain and transparent?

4. Such novelty (if novelty it should be called) becomes most requisite, when the truth is to be maintained against calumniators who evade it by quibbling. Of this, we of the present day have too much

[marginal note: Those who object to the term, 'υποστασις do so on the grounds that it is not found in scripture. This is an unfair limitation of interpretation.]

experience in being constantly called upon to attack the enemies of pure and sound doctrine.   These slippery snakes escape by their swift and tortuous windings, if not strenuously pursued, and when caught, firmly held.   Thus the early Christians, when harassed with the disputes which heresies produced, were forced to declare their sentiments in terms most scrupulously exact in order that no indirect subterfuges might remain to ungodly men, to whom ambiguity of expression was a kind of hiding-place.   Arius confessed that Christ was God, and the Son of God; because the passages of Scripture to this effect were too clear to be resisted, and then, as if he had done well, pretended to concur with others.   But, meanwhile, he ceased not to give out that Christ was created, and had a beginning like other creatures.   To drag this man of wiles out of his lurking-places, the ancient Church took a further step, and declared that Christ is the eternal Son of the Father, and consubstantial with the Father.   The impiety was fully disclosed when the Arians began to declare their hatred and utter detestation of the term ὁμοουσίος.   Had their first confession—viz. that Christ was God—been sincere and from the heart, they would not have denied that he was consubstantial with the Father.   Who dare charge those ancient writers as men of strife and contention, for having debated so warmly, and disturbed the quiet of the Church for a single word?   That little word distinguished between Christians of pure faith and the blasphemous Arians.   Next Sabellius arose, who counted the names of Father, Son, and Holy Spirit, as almost nonentities; maintaining that they were not used to mark out some distinction, but that they were different attributes of God, like many others of a similar kind.   When the matter was debated, he acknowledged his belief that the Father was God the Son God, the Spirit God; but then he had the evasion ready, that he had said nothing more than if he had called God powerful, and just, and wise.   Accordingly, he sang another note—viz. that the Father was the Son, and the Holy Spirit the Father, without order or distinction.   The worthy doctors who then had the interests of piety at heart, in order to defeat this man's dishonesty, proclaimed that three subsistences were to be truly acknowledged in the one God.   That they might protect themselves against tortuous craftiness by the simple open truth, they affirmed that a Trinity of Persons subsisted in the one God, or (which is the same thing) in the unity of God.

5. Where names have not been invented rashly, we must beware lest we become chargeable with arrogance and rashness in rejecting them.   I wish, indeed, that such names were buried, provided all would concur in the belief that the Father, Son, and Spirit, are one God, and yet that the Son is not the Father, nor the Spirit the Son, but that each has his peculiar subsistence.   I am not so minutely precise as to fight furiously for mere words.   For I observe, that the writers of the ancient Church, while they uniformly spoke with great reverence on these matters, neither agreed with each other, nor were

always consistent with themselves.   How strange the formulæ used by Councils, and defended by Hilary!   How extravagant the view which Augustine sometimes takes!   How unlike the Greeks are to the Latins!   But let one example of variance suffice.   The Latins, in translating ὁμοουσίος, used *consubstantialis* (consubstantial), intimating that there was one substance of the Father and the Son, and thus using the word Substance for Essence.   Hence Jerome, in his Letter to Damascus, says it is profane to affirm that there are three Substances in God.   But in Hilary you will find it said more than a hundred times that there are three substances in God.   Then how greatly is Jerome perplexed with the word Hypostasis!   He suspects some lurking poison, when it is said that there are three Hypostases in God.   And he does not disguise his belief that the expression, though used in a pious sense, is improper; if, indeed, he was sincere in saying this, and did not rather designedly endeavour, by an unfounded calumny, to throw odium on the Eastern bishops whom he hated.   He certainly shows little candour in asserting, that in all heathen schools οὐσία is equivalent to Hypostasis—an assertion completely refuted by trite and common use.

More courtesy and moderation is shown by Augustine (De Trinit. lib. v. c. 8 and 9), who, although he says that Hypostasis in this sense is new to Latin ears, is still so far from objecting to the ordinary use of the term by the Greeks, that he is even tolerant of the Latins, who had imitated the Greek phraseology.   The purport of what Socrates says of the term, in the Sixth Book of the Tripartite History, is, that it had been improperly applied to this purpose by the unskilful.   Hilary (De Trinitat. lib. ii.) charges it upon the heretics as a great crime, that their misconduct had rendered it necessary to subject to the peril of human utterance, things which ought to have been reverently confined within the mind, not disguising his opinion that those who do so, do what is unlawful, speak what is ineffable, and pry into what is forbidden.   Shortly after, he apologises at great length for presuming to introduce new terms. For, after putting down the natural names of Father, Son, and Spirit, he adds, that all further inquiry transcends the significancy of words, the discernment of sense, and the apprehension of intellect.   And in another place (De Conciliis), he congratulates the Bishops of France in not having framed any other confession, but received, without alteration, the ancient and most simple confession received by all Churches from the days of the Apostles.   Not unlike this is the apology of Augustine, that the term had been wrung from him by necessity, from the poverty of human language in so high a matter: not that the reality could be thereby expressed, but that he might not pass on in silence without attempting to show how the Father, Son, and Spirit are three.

The modesty of these holy men should be an admonition to us not instantly to dip our pen in gall, and sternly denounce those who may be unwilling to swear to the terms which we have devised, provided they do not in this betray pride, or petulance, or unbecoming heat, but are willing to ponder the necessity which compels us so to speak, and may thus become gradually accustomed to a useful form of expression. Let men also studiously beware, that in opposing the Arians on the one hand, and the Sabellians on the other, and eagerly endeavouring to deprive both of any handle for cavil, they do not bring themselves under some suspicion of being the disciples of either Arius or Sabellius. Arius says, that *Christ is God*, and then mutters that *he was made, and had a beginning*. He says, that *he is one with the Father ;* but secretly whispers in the ears of his party, *made one*, like other believers, though with special privilege. Say, *he is consubstantial*, and you immediately pluck the mask from this chameleon, though you add nothing to Scripture. Sabellius says, that *the Father, Son, and Spirit, indicate some distinction in God.* Say, *they are three*, and he will bawl out that you are making three Gods. Say, that *there is a Trinity of persons in one Divine essence*, you will only express in one word what the Scriptures say, and stop his empty prattle. Should any be so superstitiously precise as not to tolerate these terms, still do their worst, they will not be able to deny that when *one* is spoken of, a unity of substance must be understood, and when *three* in one essence, the persons in this Trinity are denoted. When this is confessed without equivocation, we dwell not on words. But I was long ago made aware, and indeed, on more than one occasion, that those who contend pertinaciously about words are tainted with some hidden poison ; and, therefore, that it is more expedient to provoke them purposely, than to court their favour by speaking obscurely.

6. But to say nothing more of words, let us now attend to the thing signified. By *person*, then, I mean a subsistence in the Divine essence,—a subsistence which, while related to the other two, is distinguished from them by incommunicable properties. By *subsistence* we wish something else to be understood than *essence*. For if the Word were God simply, and had not some property peculiar to himself, John could not have said correctly that he had always been with God. When he adds immediately after, that the Word was God, he calls us back to the one essence. But because he could not be with God without dwelling in the Father, hence arises that subsistence, which, though connected with the essence by an indissoluble tie, being incapable of separation, yet has a special mark by which it is distinguished from it. Now, I say that each of the three subsistences while related to the others, is distinguished by its own properties. Here relation is distinctly expressed, because, when God is mentioned simply and indefinitely, the name belongs not less to the Son and Spirit than to the Father. But whenever the Father is compared with the Son, the peculiar property of each distinguishes the one from the other. Again, whatever is proper to each I affirm

to be incommunicable, because nothing can apply or be transferred to the Son which is attributed to the Father as a mark of distinction. I have no objections to adopt the definition of Tertullian, provided it is properly understood, "that there is in God a certain arrangement or economy, which makes no change on the unity of essence." —Tertull. Lib. contra Praxeam.

7. Before proceeding farther, it will be necessary to prove the Divinity of the Son and the Holy Spirit. Thereafter, we shall see how they differ from each other. When the Word of God is set before us in the Scriptures, it were certainly most absurd to imagine that it is only a fleeting and evanescent voice, which is sent out into the air, and comes forth beyond God himself, as was the case with the communications made to the patriarchs, and all the prophecies. The reference is rather to the wisdom ever dwelling with God, and by which all oracles and prophecies were inspired. For, as Peter testifies (1 Pet. i. 11), the ancient prophets spake by the Spirit of Christ just as did the apostles, and all who after them were ministers of the heavenly doctrine. But as Christ was not yet manifested, we necessarily understand that the Word was begotten of the Father before all ages. But if that Spirit, whose organs the prophets were, belonged to the Word, the inference is irresistible, that the Word was truly God. And this is clearly enough shown by Moses in his account of the creation, where he places the Word as intermediate. For why does he distinctly narrate that God, in creating each of his works, said, Let there be this—let there be that, unless that the unsearchable glory of God might shine forth in his image? I know prattlers would easily evade this, by saying that *Word* is used for *order* or *command;* but the apostles are better expositors, when they tell us that the worlds were created by the Son, and that he sustains all things by his mighty word (Heb. i. 2). For we here see that *word* is used for the nod or command of the Son, who is himself the eternal and essential Word of the Father. And no man of sane mind can have any doubt as to Solomon's meaning, when he introduces Wisdom as begotten by God, and presiding at the creation of the world, and all other divine operations (Prov. viii. 22). For it were trifling and foolish to imagine any temporary command at a time when God was pleased to execute his fixed and eternal counsel, and something more still mysterious. To this our Saviour's words refer, "My Father worketh hitherto, and I work" (John v. 17). In thus affirming, that from the foundation of the world he constantly worked with the Father, he gives a clearer explanation of what Moses simply touched. The meaning therefore is, that God spoke in such a manner as left the Word his peculiar part in the work, and thus made the operation common to both. But the clearest explanation is given by John, when he states that the Word which was from the beginning, God and with God, was, together with God the Father, the maker of all things. For he both attributes a substantial and permanent

essence to the Word, assigning to it a certain peculiarity, and distinctly showing how God spoke the world into being. Therefore, as all revelations from heaven are duly designated by the title of the Word of God, so the highest place must be assigned to that substantial Word, the source of all inspiration, which, as being liable to no variation, remains for ever one and the same with God, and is God.

8. Here an outcry is made by certain men, who, while they dare not openly deny his divinity, secretly rob him of his eternity. For they contend that the Word only began to be when God opened his sacred mouth in the creation of the world. Thus, with excessive temerity, they imagine some change in the essence of God. For as the names of God, which have respect to external work, began to be ascribed to him from the existence of the work (as when he is called the Creator of heaven and earth), so piety does not recognise or admit any name which might indicate that a change had taken place in God himself. For if anything adventitious took place, the saying of James would cease to be true, that " every good gift, and every perfect gift, is from above, and cometh down from the Father of lights, with whom is no variableness, neither shadow of turning" (James i. 17). Nothing, therefore, is more intolerable than to fancy a beginning to that Word which was always God, and afterwards was the Creator of the world. But they think they argue acutely, in maintaining that Moses, when he says that God then spoke for the first time, must be held to intimate that till then no Word existed in him. This is the merest trifling. It does not surely follow, that because a thing begins to be manifested at a certain time, it never existed previously. I draw a very different conclusion. Since at the very moment when God said, "Let there be light," the energy of the Word was immediately exerted, it must have existed long before. If any inquire how long, he will find it was without beginning. No certain period of time is defined, when he himself says, "Now, O Father, glorify thou me with thine own self, with the glory which I had with thee before the world was" (John xvii. 5). Nor is this omitted by John : for before he descends to the creation of the world, he says, that " in the beginning was the Word, and the Word was with God." We, therefore, again conclude, that the Word was eternally begotten by God, and dwelt with him from everlasting. In this way, his true essence, his eternity, and divinity, are established.

9. But though I am not now treating of the office of the Mediator having deferred it till the subject of redemption is considered, yet because it ought to be clear and incontrovertible to all, that Christ is that Word become incarnate, this seems the most appropriate place to introduce those passages which assert the Divinity of Christ. When it is said in the forty-fifth Psalm, " Thy throne, O God, is for ever and ever," the Jews quibble that the name Elohim is applied to angels and sovereign powers. But no passage is to be found in Scripture, where an eternal throne is set up for a creature. For he

is not called God simply, but also the eternal Ruler. Besides, the title is not conferred on any man, without some addition, as when it is said that Moses would be a God to Pharaoh (Exod. vii. 1). Some read as if it were in the genitive case, but this is too insipid. I admit, that anything possessed of singular excellence is often called divine, but it is clear from the context, that this meaning here were harsh and forced, and totally inapplicable. But if their perverseness still refuses to yield, surely there is no obscurity in Isaiah, where Christ is introduced both as God, and as possessed of supreme power, one of the peculiar attributes of God, "His name shall be called the Mighty God, the Everlasting Father, the Prince of Peace (Isa. xi. 6). Here, too, the Jews object, and invert the passage thus, This is the name by which the mighty God, the Everlasting Father, will call him; so that all which they leave to the Son is, "Prince of Peace." But why should so many epithets be here accumulated on God the Father, seeing the prophet's design is to present the Messiah with certain distinguished properties which may induce us to put our faith in him? There can be no doubt, therefore, that he who a little before was called Immanuel, is here called the Mighty God. Moreover, there can be nothing clearer than the words of Jeremiah, "This is the name whereby he shall be called, THE LORD OUR RIGHTEOUSNESS" (Jer. xxiii. 6). For as the Jews themselves teach that the other names of God are mere epithets, whereas this, which they call the ineffable name, is substantive, and expresses his essence, we infer, that the only begotten Son is the eternal God, who elsewhere declares, "My glory will I not give to another" (Isa. xlii. 8). An attempt is made to evade this from the fact, that this name is given by Moses to the altar which he built, and by Ezekiel to the New Jerusalem. But who sees not that the altar was erected as a memorial to show that God was the exalter of Moses, and that the name of God was applied to Jerusalem, merely to testify the Divine presence? For thus the prophet speaks, "The name of the city from that day shall be, The Lord is there" (Ezek. xlviii. 35). In the same way, "Moses built an altar, and called the name of it JEHOVAH-nissi" (Jehovah my exaltation). But it would seem the point is still more keenly disputed as to another passage in Jeremiah, where the same title is applied to Jerusalem in these words, "In those days shall Judah be saved, and Jerusalem shall dwell safely; and this is the name wherewith she shall be called, The Lord our Righteousness." But so far is this passage from being adverse to the truth which we defend, that it rather supports it. The prophet having formerly declared that Christ is the true Jehovah from whom righteousness flows, now declares that the Church would be made so sensible of this as to be able to glory in assuming his very name. In the former passage, therefore, the fountain and cause of righteousness is set down; in the latter, the effect is described.

10. But if this does not satisfy the Jews, I know not what cavils

will enable them to evade the numerous passages in which Jehovah is said to have appeared in the form of an Angel (Judges vi. vii. xiii. 16—23, &c.). This angel claims for himself the name of the Eternal God. Should it be alleged that this is done in respect of the office which he bears, the difficulty is by no means solved. No servant would rob God of his honour, by allowing sacrifice to be offered to himself. But the Angel, by refusing to eat bread, orders the sacrifice due to Jehovah to be offered to him. Thus the fact itself proves that he was truly Jehovah. Accordingly, Manoah and his wife infer from the sign, that they had seen not only an angel, but God. Hence Manoah's exclamation, "We shall die; for we have seen the Lord." When the woman replies, "If Jehovah had wished to slay us, he would not have received the sacrifice at our hand," she acknowledges that he who is previously called an angel was certainly God. We may add, that the angel's own reply removes all doubt, "Why do ye ask my name, which is wonderful?" Hence the impiety of Servetus was the more detestable, when he maintained that God was never manifested to Abraham and the Patriarchs, but that an angel was worshipped in his stead. The orthodox doctors of the Church have correctly and wisely expounded, that the Word of God was the supreme angel, who then began, as it were by anticipation, to perform the office of Mediator. For though he were not clothed with flesh, yet he descended as in an intermediate form, that he might have more familiar access to the faithful. This closer intercourse procured for him the name of the Angel; still, however, he retained the character which justly belonged to him—that of the God of ineffable glory. The same thing is intimated by Hosea, who, after mentioning the wrestling of Jacob with the angel, says, "Even the Lord God of hosts; the Lord is his memorial" (Hosea xii. 5). Servetus again insinuates that God personated an angel; as if the prophet did not confirm what had been said by Moses, "Wherefore is it that thou dost ask after my name?" (Gen. xxxii. 29, 30). And the confession of the holy Patriarch sufficiently declares that he was not a created angel, but one in whom the fulness of the Godhead dwelt, when he says, "I have seen God face to face." Hence also Paul's statement, that Christ led the people in the wilderness (1 Cor. x. 4. See also Calvin on Acts vii. 30, and infra, chap. xiv., s. 9). Although the time of humiliation had not yet arrived, the eternal Word exhibited a type of the office which he was to fulfil. Again, if the first chapter of Zechariah (ver. 9, &c.) and the second (ver. 3, &c.) be candidly considered, it will be seen that the angel who sends the other angel is immediately after declared to be the Lord of hosts, and that supreme power is ascribed to him. I omit numberless passages in which our faith rests secure, though they may not have much weight with the Jews. For when it is said in Isaiah, "Lo, this is our God; we have waited for him, and he will save us: this is the Lord; we have waited for him, we will be glad and rejoice in his

salvation" (Isa. xxv. 9), even the blind may see that the God referred
to is he who again rises up for the deliverance of his people. And
the emphatic description, twice repeated, precludes the idea that reference is made to any other than to Christ. Still clearer and stronger
is the passage of Malachi, in which a promise is made that the messenger who was then expected would come to his own temple (Mal.
iii. 1). The temple certainly was dedicated to Almighty God only,
and yet the prophet claims it for Christ. Hence it follows, that he
is the God who was always worshipped by the Jews.

11. The New Testament teems with innumerable passages, and
our object must therefore be, the selection of a few, rather than an
accumulation of the whole. But though the Apostles spoke of him
after his appearance in the flesh as Mediator, every passage which I
adduce will be sufficient to prove his eternal Godhead. And the
first thing deserving of special observation is, that predictions concerning the eternal God are applied to Christ, as either already fulfilled in him, or to be fulfilled at some future period. Isaiah
prophesies, that "the Lord of Hosts" shall be "for a stone of
stumbling, and for a rock of offence" (Isa. viii. 14). Paul asserts
that this prophecy was fulfilled in Christ (Rom. ix. 33), and therefore declares that Christ is that Lord of Hosts. In like manner, he
says in another passage, "We shall all stand before the judgment-
seat of Christ. For it is written, As I live, saith the Lord, every
knee shall bow to me, and every tongue shall confess to God." Since
in Isaiah God predicts this of himself (Isa. xlv. 23), and Christ exhibits the reality fulfilled in himself, it follows that he is the very
God, whose glory cannot be given to another. It is clear also, that
the passage from the Psalms (Ps. lxviii. 19) which he quotes in the
Epistle to the Ephesians, is applicable only to God, "When he ascended up on high, he led captivity captive" (Eph. iv. 8). Understanding that such an ascension was shadowed forth when the Lord
exerted his power, and gained a glorious victory over heathen nations,
he intimates that what was thus shadowed was more fully manifested
in Christ. So John testifies that it was the glory of the Son which
was revealed to Isaiah in a vision (John xii. 41; Isa. vi. 4), though
Isaiah himself expressly says that what he saw was the Majesty of
God. Again, there can be no doubt that those qualities which, in
the Epistle to the Hebrews, are applied to the Son, are the brightest
attributes of God, "Thou, Lord, in the beginning hast laid the
foundation of the earth," &c., and, "Let all the angels of God worship him" (Heb. i. 10, 6). And yet he does not pervert the passages
in thus applying them to Christ, since Christ alone performed the
things which these passages celebrate. It was he who arose and
pitied Zion—he who claimed for himself dominion over all nations
and islands. And why should John have hesitated to ascribe the
Majesty of God to Christ, after saying in his preface that the Word
was God? (John i. 14). Why should Paul have feared to place

Christ on the judgment-seat of God (2 Cor. v. 10), after he had so openly proclaimed his divinity, when he said that he was God over all, blessed for ever? And to show how consistent he is in this respect, he elsewhere says that "God was manifest in the flesh" (1 Tim. iii. 16). If he is God blessed for ever, he therefore it is to whom alone, as Paul affirms in another place, all glory and honour is due. Paul does not disguise this, but openly exclaims, that "being in the form of God, (he) thought it not robbery to be equal with God, but made himself of no reputation" (Phil. ii. 6). And lest the wicked should clamour and say that he was a kind of spurious God, John goes farther, and affirms, "This is the true God, and eternal life." Though it ought to be enough for us that he is called God, especially by a witness who distinctly testifies that we have no more gods than one, Paul says, "Though there be that are called gods, whether in heaven or in earth (as there be gods many, and lords many), but to us there is but one God" (1 Cor. viii. 5, 6). When we hear from the same lips that God was manifest in the flesh, that God purchased the Church with his own blood, why do we dream of any second God, to whom he makes not the least allusion? And there is no room to doubt that all the godly entertained the same view. Thomas, by addressing him as his Lord and God, certainly professes that he was the only God whom he had ever adored (John xx. 28).

12. The divinity of Christ, if judged by the works which are ascribed to him in Scripture, becomes still more evident. When he said of himself, "My Father worketh hitherto, and I work," the Jews, though most dull in regard to his other sayings, perceived that he was laying claim to divine power. And, therefore, as John relates (John v. 17), they sought the more to kill him, because he not only broke the Sabbath, but also said that God was his Father, making himself equal with God. What, then, will be our stupidity if we do not perceive from the same passage that his divinity is plainly instructed? To govern the world by his power and providence, and regulate all things by an energy inherent in himself (this an Apostle ascribes to him, Heb. 1. 3), surely belongs to none but the Creator. Nor does he merely share the government of the world with the Father, but also each of the other offices, which cannot be communicated to creatures. The Lord proclaims by his prophet, "I, even I, am he that blotteth out thy transgressions for mine own sake" (Isa. xliii. 25). When, in accordance with this declaration, the Jews thought that injustice was done to God when Christ forgave sins, he not only asserted, in distinct terms, that this power belonged to him, but also proved it by a miracle (Matth. ix. 6). We thus see that he possessed in himself not the ministry of forgiving sins, but the inherent power which the Lord declares he will not give to another. What! Is it not the province of God alone to penetrate and interrogate the secret thoughts of the heart? But Christ also had this power, and therefore we infer that Christ is God.

13. How clearly and transparently does this appear in his miracles? I admit that similar and equal miracles were performed by the prophets and apostles; but there is this very essential difference, that they dispensed the gifts of God as his ministers, whereas he exerted his own inherent might. Sometimes, indeed, he used prayer, that he might ascribe glory to the Father, but we see that for the most part his own proper power is displayed. And how should not he be the true author of miracles, who, of his own authority, commissions others to perform them? For the Evangelist relates that he gave power to the apostles to cast out devils, cure the lepers, raise the dead, &c. And they, by the mode in which they performed this ministry, showed plainly that their whole power was derived from Christ. "In the name of Jesus Christ of Nazareth," says Peter, (Acts iii. 6), "rise up and walk." It is not surprising, then, that Christ appealed to his miracles in order to subdue the unbelief of the Jews, inasmuch as these were performed by his own energy, and therefore bore the most ample testimony to his divinity.

Again, if out of God there is no salvation, no righteousness, no life, Christ, having all these in himself, is certainly God. Let no one object that life or salvation is transfused into him by God. For it is said not that he received, but that he himself is salvation. And if there is none good but God, how could a mere man be pure, how could he be, I say not good and just, but goodness and justice? Then what shall we say to the testimony of the Evangelist, that from the very beginning of the creation "in him was life, and this life was the light of men?" Trusting to such proofs, we can boldly put our hope and faith in him, though we know it is blasphemous impiety to confide in any creature.[1]   "Ye believe in God,"[2] says he, "believe also in me" (John xiv. 1). And so Paul (Rom. x. 11, and xv. 12) interprets two passages of Isaiah, "Whoso believeth in him shall not be confounded" (Isa. xxviii. 16); and, "In that day there shall be a root of Jesse, which shall stand for an ensign of the people; to it shall the Gentiles seek" (Isa. xi. 10). But why adduce more passages of Scripture on this head, when we so often meet with the expression, "He that believeth in me hath eternal life"?

Again the prayer of faith is addressed to him—prayer, which specially belongs to the divine majesty, if anything so belongs. For the prophet Joel says, "And it shall come to pass, that whosoever shall call on the name of the Lord (Jehovah) shall be delivered" (Joel ii. 32). And another says, "The name of the Lord (Jehovah) is a strong tower; the righteous runneth into it and is safe" (Prov. xviii. 10). But the name of Christ is invoked for salvation, and therefore it follows that he is Jehovah. Moreover, we have an example of invocation in Stephen, when he said, "Lord Jesus, receive my spirit;"

---

1 The French adds, " Et ne faisons point cela témérairement, mais selon sa parole." —And let us not do this rashly, but in accordance with his Word.
2 Calvin translates interrogatively, " Do ye believe in God?"

and thereafter in the whole Church, when Ananias says in the same book, " Lord, I have heard by many of this man, how much evil he hath done to thy saints at Jerusalem ; and here he hath authority from the chief priests to bind all that call on thy name" (Acts ix. 13, 14). And to make it more clearly understood that in Christ dwelt the whole fulness of the Godhead bodily, the Apostle declares that the only doctrine which he professed to the Corinthians, the only doctrine which he taught, was the knowledge of Christ (1 Cor. ii. 2). Consider what kind of thing it is, and how great, that the name of the Son alone is preached to us, though God command us to glory only in the knowledge of himself (Jer. ix. 24). Who will dare to maintain that he, whom to know forms our only ground of glorying, is a mere creature ? To this we may add, that the salutations prefixed to the Epistles of Paul pray for the same blessings from the Son as from the Father. By this we are taught, not only that the blessings which our heavenly Father bestows come to us through his intercession, but that by a partnership in power, the Son himself is their author. This practical knowledge is doubtless surer and more solid than any idle speculation. For the pious soul has the best view of God, and may almost be said to handle him, when it feels that it is quickened, enlightened, saved, justified, and sanctified by him.

14. In asserting the divinity of the Spirit, the proof must be derived from the same sources. And it is by no means an obscure testimony which Moses bears in the history of the creation, when he says that the Spirit of God was expanded over the abyss or shapeless matter ; for it shows not only that the beauty which the world displays is maintained by the invigorating power of the Spirit, but that even before this beauty existed the Spirit was at work cherishing the confused mass.[1] Again, no cavils can explain away the force of what Isaiah says, " And now the Lord God, and his Spirit, hath sent me " (Isa. xlviii. 16), thus ascribing a share in the sovereign power of sending the prophets to the Holy Spirit. (Calvin in Acts xx. 28.) In this his divine majesty is clear.

But, as I observed, the best proof to us is our familiar experience. For nothing can be more alien from a creature, than the office which the Scriptures ascribe to him, and which the pious actually feel him discharging,—his being diffused over all space, sustaining, invigorating, and quickening all things, both in heaven and on the earth. The mere fact of his not being circumscribed by any limits raises him above the rank of creatures, while his transfusing vigour into all things, breathing into them being, life, and motion, is plainly divine. Again, if regeneration to incorruptible life is higher, and much more excellent than any present quickening, what must be thought of him by whose energy it is produced? Now, many passages of Scripture show that he is the author of regeneration, not by a borrowed, but

[1] The French adds, " à ce qu'elle ne fust point aneantie incontinent ; "—-so as to prevent its being instantly annihilated.

by an intrinsic energy ; and not only so, but that he is also the author of future immortality.   In short, all the peculiar attributes of the Godhead are ascribed to him in the same way as to the Son.   He searches the deep things of God, and has no counsellor among the creatures ; he bestows wisdom and the faculty of speech, though God declares to Moses (Exod. iv. 11) that this is his own peculiar province.   In like manner, by means of him we become partakers of the divine nature, so as in a manner to feel his quickening energy within us.   Our justification is his work ; from him is power, sanctification, truth, grace, and every good thought, since it is from the Spirit alone that all good gifts proceed.   Particular attention is due to Paul's expression, that though there are diversities of gifts, " all these worketh that one and the self-same Spirit " (1 Cor. xii. 11), he being not only the beginning or origin, but also the author ;[1] as is even more clearly expressed immediately after, in these words, " dividing to every man severally as he will."   For were he not something subsisting in God, will and arbitrary disposal would never be ascribed to him.   Most clearly, therefore, does Paul ascribe divine power to the Spirit, and demonstrate that he dwells hypostatically in God.

15. Nor does the Scripture, in speaking of him, withhold the name of God.   Paul infers that we are the temple of God, from the fact that " the Spirit of God dwelleth in us " (1 Cor. iii. 16 ; vi. 19 ; and 2 Cor. vi. 16).   Now, it ought not to be slightly overlooked, that all the promises which God makes of choosing us to himself as a temple, receive their only fulfilment by his Spirit dwelling in us.   Surely, as it is admirably expressed by Augustine (Ad Maximinum, Ep. 66), " were we ordered to make a temple of wood and stone to the Spirit, inasmuch as such worship is due to God alone, it would be a clear proof of the Spirit's divinity ; how much clearer a proof in that we are not to make a temple to him, but to be ourselves that temple." And the Apostle says at one time that we are the temple of God, and at another time, in the same sense, that we are the temple of the Holy Spirit.   Peter, when he rebuked Ananias for having lied to the Holy Spirit, said, that he had not lied unto men, but unto God.   And when Isaiah had introduced the Lord of Hosts as speaking, Paul says, it was the Holy Spirit that spoke (Acts xxviii. 25, 26).   Nay, words uniformly said by the prophets to have been spoken by the Lord of Hosts, are by Christ and his apostles ascribed to the Holy Spirit. Hence it follows that the Spirit is the true Jehovah, who dictated the prophecies.   Again, when God complains that he was provoked to anger by the stubbornness of the people, in place of Him, Isaiah says that his Holy Spirit was grieved (Isa. lxiii. 10).   Lastly, while blasphemy against the Spirit is not forgiven, either in the present life or that which is to come, whereas he who has blasphemed against the

---

[1] The French adds, " Sainct Paul n'eust jamais ainsi parlé, s'il n'eust cognu la vraie Divinité du Sainct Esprit "—St Paul would never have so spoken, if he had not known the divinity of the Holy Spirit.

Son may obtain pardon, that majesty must certainly be divine which it is an inexpiable crime to offend or impair. I designedly omit several passages which the ancient fathers adduced. They thought it plausible to quote from David, "By the word of the Lord were the heavens made, and all the host of them by the breath (Spirit) of his mouth" (Ps. xxxiii. 6), in order to prove that the world was not less the work of the Holy Spirit than of the Son. But seeing it is usual in the Psalms to repeat the same thing twice, and in Isaiah the *spirit* (breath) of the mouth is equivalent to *word*, that proof was weak ; and, accordingly, my wish has been to advert briefly to those proofs on which pious minds may securely rest.

16. But as God has manifested himself more clearly by the advent of Christ, so he has made himself more familiarly known in three persons. Of many proofs let this one suffice. Paul connects together these three, God, Faith, and Baptism, and reasons from the one to the other—viz. because there is one faith, he infers that there is one God ; and because there is one baptism, he infers that there is one faith. Therefore, if by baptism we are initiated into the faith and worship of one God, we must of necessity believe that he into whose name we are baptised is the true God. And there cannot be a doubt that our Saviour wished to testify, by a solemn rehearsal, that the perfect light of faith is now exhibited, when he said, "Go and teach all nations, baptising them in the name of the Father, and of the Son, and of the Holy Spirit" (Matth. xxviii. 19), since this is the same thing as to be baptised into the name of the one God, who has been fully manifested in the Father, the Son, and the Spirit. Hence it plainly appears, that the three persons, in whom alone God is known, subsist in the Divine essence. And since faith certainly ought not to look hither and thither, or run up and down after various objects, but to look, refer, and cleave to God alone, it is obvious that were there various kinds of faith, there behoved also to be various gods. Then, as the baptism of faith is a sacrament, its unity assures us of the unity of God. Hence, also, it is proved that it is lawful only to be baptised into one God, because we make a profession of faith in him in whose name we are baptised. What, then, is our Saviour's meaning in commanding baptism to be administered in the name of the Father, and the Son, and the Holy Spirit, if it be not that we are to believe with one faith in the name of the Father, and the Son, and the Holy Spirit?[1] But is this anything else than to declare that the Father, Son, and Spirit, are one God? Wherefore, since it must be held certain that there is one God, not more than one, we conclude that the Word and Spirit are of the very essence of God. Nothing could be more stupid than the trifling of the Arians, who, while acknowledging the divinity of the Son, denied his divine essence. Equally extravagant were the ravings of the Macedonians, who insisted that by the

---

[1] The French entirely omits the three previous sentences, beginning, " Then, as," &c.

Spirit were only meant the gifts of grace poured out upon men. For as wisdom, understanding, prudence, fortitude, and the fear of the Lord, proceed from the Spirit, so he is the one Spirit of wisdom, prudence, fortitude, and piety. He is not divided according to the distribution of his gifts, but, as the Apostle assures us (1 Cor. xii. 11), however they be divided, he remains one and the same.

17. On the other hand, the Scriptures demonstrate that there is some distinction between the Father and the Word, the Word and the Spirit; but the magnitude of the mystery reminds us of the great reverence and soberness which ought to be employed in discussing it. It seems to me, that nothing can be more admirable than the words of Gregory Nanzianzen: " Ὀυ φθάνω το ἒι νοῆσαι, καὶ τοῖς τρισὶ περιλάμπομαι· οὐ φθάνω τὰ τρία διελεῖν καὶ εἰς τὸ ἓν ἀναφέρομαι" (Greg. Nanzian. in Serm. de Sacro Baptis.). " I cannot think of the unity without being irradiated by the Trinity : I cannot distinguish between the Trinity without being carried up to the unity." [1] Therefore, let us beware of imagining such a Trinity of persons as will distract our thoughts, instead of bringing them instantly back to the unity. The words, Father, Son, and Holy Spirit, certainly indicate a real distinction, not allowing us to suppose that they are merely epithets by which God is variously designated from his works. Still they indicate distinction only, not division. The passages we have already quoted show that the Son has a distinct subsistence from the Father, because the Word could not have been with God unless he were distinct from the Father ; nor but for this could he have had his glory with the Father. In like manner, Christ distinguishes the Father from himself, when he says that there is another who bears witness of him (John v. 32 ; viii. 16). To the same effect is it elsewhere said, that the Father made all things by the Word. This could not be, if he were not in some respect distinct from him. Besides, it was not the Father that descended to the earth, but he who came forth from the Father ; nor was it the Father that died and rose again, but he whom the Father had sent. This distinction did not take its beginning at the incarnation : for it is clear that the only begotten Son previously existed in the bosom of the Father (John i. 18). For who will dare to affirm that the Son entered his Father's bosom for the first time, when he came down from heaven to assume human nature ? Therefore, he was previously in the bosom of the Father, and had his glory with the Father. Christ intimates the distinction between the Holy Spirit and the Father, when he says that the Spirit proceedeth from the Father, and between the Holy Spirit and himself, when he speaks of him as another, as he does when he declares that he will send another

---

1 Bernard, De Consider. lib. v. " Cum dico unum, non me trinitatis turbat numerus, qui essentiam non multiplicat, non variat, nec partitur. Rursum, quum, dico tria, non me arguit intuitus unitatis, quia illa quæcunque tria, seu illos tres, nec in confusionem cogit, nec in singularitatem redigit."—See also Bernard, Serm. 71, in Cantica.

Comforter; and in many other passages besides (John xiv. 6; xv. 26; xiv. 16).

18. I am not sure whether it is expedient to borrow analogies from human affairs to express the nature of this distinction. The ancient fathers sometimes do so, but they at the same time admit, that what they bring forward as analogous is very widely different. And hence it is that I have a great dread of anything like presumption here, lest some rash saying may furnish an occasion of calumny to the malicious, or of delusion to the unlearned. It were unbecoming, however, to say nothing of a distinction which we observe that the Scriptures have pointed out. This distinction is, that to the Father is attributed the beginning of action, the fountain and source of all things; to the Son, wisdom, counsel, and arrangement in action, while the energy and efficacy of action is assigned to the Spirit. Moreover, though the eternity of the Father is also the eternity of the Son and Spirit, since God never could be without his own wisdom and energy; and though in eternity there can be no room for first or last, still the distinction of order is not unmeaning or superfluous, the Father being considered first, next the Son from him, and then the Spirit from both. For the mind of every man naturally inclines to consider, first, God, secondly, the wisdom emerging from him, and, lastly, the energy by which he executes the purposes of his counsel. For this reason, the Son is said to be of the Father only; the Spirit of both the Father and the Son. This is done in many passages, but in none more clearly than in the eighth chapter to the Romans, where the same Spirit is called indiscriminately the Spirit of Christ, and the Spirit of him who raised up Christ from the dead. And not improperly. For Peter also testifies (1 Pet. i. 21), that it was the Spirit of Christ which inspired the prophets, though the Scriptures so often say that it was the Spirit of God the Father.

19. Moreover, this distinction is so far from interfering with the most perfect unity of God, that the Son may thereby be proved to be one God with the Father, inasmuch as he constitutes one Spirit with him, and that the Spirit is not different from the Father and the Son, inasmuch as he is the Spirit of the Father and the Son. In each hypostasis the whole nature is understood, the only difference being that each has his own peculiar subsistence. The whole Father is in the Son, and the whole Son in the Father, as the Son himself also declares (John xiv. 10), "I am in the Father, and the Father in me;" nor do ecclesiastical writers admit that the one is separated from the other by any difference of essence. "By those names which denote distinction," says Augustine, "is meant the relation which they mutually bear to each other, not the very substance by which they are one." In this way, the sentiments of the Fathers, which might sometimes appear to be at variance with each other, are to be reconciled. At one time they teach that the Father is the beginning of the Son, at another they assert that the Son has both di-

[margin notes:]
Distinction among the persons of the Trinity

1. Father: Beginning of all action.

2. Son Wisdom of all action

3. Spirit Energy of action.

The persons of the Trinity to be considered in this order.

vinity and essence from himself, and therefore is one beginning with the Father. The cause of this discrepancy is well and clearly explained by Augustine, when he says,[1] "Christ, as to himself, is called God, as to the Father he is called Son." And again, "The Father, as to himself, is called God, as to the Son he is called Father. He who, as to the Son, is called Father, is not Son; and he who, as to himself, is called Father, and he who, as to himself, is called Son, is the same God." Therefore, when we speak of the Son simply, without reference to the Father, we truly and properly affirm that he is of himself, and, accordingly, call him the only beginning; but when we denote the relation which he bears to the Father, we correctly make the Father the beginning of the Son. Augustine's fifth book on the Trinity is wholly devoted to the explanation of this subject. But it is far safer to rest contented with the relation as taught by him than get bewildered in vain speculation by subtle prying into a sublime mystery.

20. Let those, then, who love soberness, and are contented with the measure of faith, briefly receive what is useful to be known. It is as follows: When we profess to believe in one God, by the name God is understood the one simple essence, comprehending three persons or hypostases; and, accordingly, whenever the name of God is used indefinitely, the Son and Spirit, not less than the Father, is meant. But when the Son is joined with the Father, relation comes into view, and so we distinguish between the Persons. But as the Personal subsistences carry an order with them, the principle and origin being in the Father, whenever mention is made of the Father and Son, or of the Father and Spirit together, the name of God is specially given to the Father. In this way the unity of essence is retained, and respect is had to the order, which, however, derogates in no respect from the divinity of the Son and Spirit. And surely since we have already seen how the apostles declare the Son of God to have been He whom Moses and the prophets declared to be Jehovah, we must always arrive at an unity of essence. We, therefore hold it detestable blasphemy to call the Son a different God from the Father, because the simple name God admits not of relation, nor can God, considered in himself, be said to be this or that. Then, that the name Jehovah, taken indefinitely, may be applied to Christ, is clear from the words of Paul, "For this thing I besought the Lord thrice." After giving the answer, "My grace is sufficient for thee," he subjoins, "that the power of Christ may rest upon me" (2 Cor. xii. 8, 9). For it is certain that the name of Lord (Κύριου) is there put for Jehovah, and, therefore, to restrict it to the person of the Mediator, were puerile and frivolous, the words being used absolutely, and not with the view of comparing the Father and the Son, And

---

1 August. Homil. De Temp. 38, De Trinitate. See also Ad Pascentium Epist. 174 Cyrill. De Trinit. lib. vii.; Idem, lib. iii. Dialog.; Aug. in Psal. cix.; et Tract. in Joann 89; Idem, in Psal. lxviii.

we know that, in accordance with the received usage of the Greeks, the apostles uniformly substitute the word Κυριος for Jehovah. Not to go far for an example, Paul besought the Lord in the same sense in which Peter quotes the passage of Joel, " Whosoever shall call upon the name of the Lord shall be saved" (Acts ii. 21 ; Joel ii. 28). Where this name is specially applied to the Son, there is a different ground for it, as will be seen in its own place ; at present it is sufficient to remember that Paul, after praying to God absolutely, immediately subjoins the name of Christ. Thus, too, the Spirit is called God absolutely by Christ himself. For nothing prevents us from holding that he is the entire spiritual essence of God, in which are comprehended Father, Son, and Spirit. This is plain from Scripture. For as God is there called a Spirit, so the Holy Spirit also, in so far as he is a hypostasis of the whole essence, is said to be both of God and from God.

21. But since Satan, in order to pluck up our faith by the roots, has always provoked fierce disputes, partly concerning the divine essence of the Son and Spirit, and partly concerning the distinction of persons ; since in almost every age he has stirred up impious spirits to vex the orthodox doctors on this head, and is attempting in the present day to kindle a new flame out of the old embers, it will be proper here to dispose of some of these perverse dreams. Hitherto our chief object has been to stretch out our hand for the guidance of such as are disposed to learn, not to war with the stubborn and contentious ; but now the truth which was calmly demonstrated must be vindicated from the calumnies of the ungodly. Still, however, it will be our principal study to provide a sure footing for those whose ears are open to the word of God. Here, if anywhere, in considering the hidden mysteries of Scripture, we should speculate soberly and with great moderation, cautiously guarding against allowing either our mind or our tongue to go a step beyond the confines of God's word. For how can the human mind, which has not yet been able to ascertain of what the body of the sun consists, though it is daily presented to the eye, bring down the boundless essence of God to its little measure ? Nay, how can it, under its own guidance, penetrate to a knowledge of the substance of God while unable to understand its own ? Wherefore, let us willingly leave to God the knowledge of himself. In the words of Hilary (De Trinit. lib. i.), " He alone is a fit witness to himself who is known only by himself." This knowledge, then, if we would leave to God, we must conceive of him as he has made himself known, and in our inquiries make application to no other quarter than his word. On this subject we have five homilies of Chrysostom against the Anomœi (De Incomprehensit. Dei Natura), in which he endeavoured, but in vain, to check the presumption of the Sophists, and curb their garrulity. They showed no more modesty here than they are wont to do in everything else. The very unhappy results of their temerity should be a warning to us to bring more docility than acumen to the discussion of this question, never to at-

tempt to search after God anywhere but in his sacred word, and never to speak or think of him farther than we have it for our guide.　But if the distinction of Father, Son, and Spirit, subsisting in the one Godhead (certainly a subject of great difficulty), gives more trouble and annoyance to some intellects than is meet, let us remember that the human mind enters a labyrinth whenever it indulges its curiosity, and thus submit to be guided by the divine oracles, how much soever the mystery may be beyond our reach.

22. It were tedious, and to no purpose toilsome, to form a catalogue of the errors by which, in regard to this branch of doctrine, the purity of the faith has been assailed.　The greater part of heretics have with their gross deliriums made a general attack on the glory of God, deeming it enough if they could disturb and shake the unwary. ·From a few individuals numerous sects have sprung up, some of them rending the divine essence, and others confounding the distinction of persons.　But if we hold, what has already been demonstrated from Scripture, that the essence of the one God, pertaining to the Father, Son, and Spirit, is simple and indivisible, and again, that the Father differs in some special property from the Son, and the Son from the Spirit, the door will be shut against Arius and Sabellius, as well as the other ancient authors of error.　But as in our day have arisen certain frantic men, such as Servetus and others, who, by new devices, have thrown everything into confusion, it may be worth while briefly to discuss their fallacies.

The name of Trinity was so much disliked, nay, detested, by Servetus, that he charged all whom he called Trinitarians with being Atheists.　I say nothing of the insulting terms in which he thought proper to make his charges.　The sum of his speculations was, that a threefold Deity is introduced wherever three Persons are said to exist in his essence, and that this Triad was imaginary, inasmuch as it was inconsistent with the unity of God.　At the same time, he would have it that the Persons are certain external ideas which do not truly subsist in the Divine essence, but only figure God to us under this or that form : that at first, indeed, there was no distinction in God, because originally the Word was the same as the Spirit, but ever since Christ came forth God of God, another Spirit, also a God, had proceeded from him.　But although he sometimes cloaks his absurdities in allegory, as when he says that the eternal Word of God was the Spirit of Christ with God, and the reflection of the idea, likewise that the Spirit was a shadow of Deity, he at last reduces the divinity of both to nothing ; maintaining that, according to the mode of distribution, there is a part of God as well in the Son as in the Spirit, just as the same spirit substantially is a portion of God in us, and also in wood and stone.　His absurd babbling concerning the person of the Mediator will be seen in its own place.[1]

[1] See Calvin. Defensio Orthodox. Fid. S. Trinit. Adv. Prod. Error. M. Serveti

The monstrous fiction that a person is nothing else than a visible appearance of the glory of God, needs not a long refutation. For when John declares that before the world was created the Logos was God (John i. 1), he shows that he was something very different from an idea. But if even then, and from the remotest eternity, that Logos, who was God, was with the Father, and had his own distinct and peculiar glory with the Father (John xvii. 5), he certainly could not be an external or figurative splendour, but must necessarily have been a hypostasis which dwelt inherently in God himself. But although there is no mention made of the Spirit antecedent to the account of the creation, he is not there introduced as a shadow, but as the essential power of God, where Moses relates that the shapeless mass was upborne by him (Gen. i. 2). It is obvious that the eternal Spirit always existed in God, seeing he cherished and sustained the confused materials of heaven and earth before they possessed order or beauty. Assuredly he could not then be an image or representation of God, as Servetus dreams. But he is elsewhere forced to make a more open disclosure of his impiety when he says, that God by his eternal reason decreeing a Son to himself, in this way assumed a visible appearance. For if this be true, no other Divinity is left to Christ than is implied in his having been ordained a Son by God's eternal decree. Moreover, those phantoms which Servetus substitutes for the hypostases he so transforms as to make new changes in God. But the most execrable heresy of all is his confounding both the Son and Spirit promiscuously with all the creatures. For he distinctly asserts, that there are parts and partitions in the essence of God, and that every such portion is God. This he does especially when he says, that the spirits of the faithful are co-eternal and consubstantial with God, although he elsewhere assigns a substantial divinity, not only to the soul of man, but to all created things.

23. This pool has bred another monster not unlike the former. For certain restless spirits, unwilling to share the disgrace and obloquy of the impiety of Servetus, have confessed that there were indeed three Persons, but added, as a reason, that the Father, who alone is truly and properly God, transfused his Divinity into the Son and Spirit when he formed them. Nor do they refrain from expressing themselves in such shocking terms as these: that the Father is essentially distinguished from the Son and Spirit by this; that he is the only *essentiator*. Their first pretext for this is, that Christ is uniformly called the Son of God. From this they infer that there is no proper God but the Father. But they forget that, although the name of God is common also to the Son, yet it is sometimes, by way of excellence, ascribed to the Father, as being the source and principle of Divinity; and this is done in order to mark the simple unity of essence. They object, that if the Son is truly God, he must be deemed the Son of a person: which is absurd. I answer, that both are true; namely, that he is the Son of God, because he is the Word, begotten of the Father before

all ages (for we are not now speaking of the Person of the Mediator) ; and yet, that for the purpose of explanation, regard must be had to the Person, so that the name God may not be understood in its absolute sense, but as equivalent to Father. For if we hold that there is no other God than the Father, this rank is clearly denied to the Son.

In every case where the Godhead is mentioned, we are by no means to admit that there is an antithesis between the Father and the Son, as if to the former only the name of God could competently be applied. For assuredly, the God who appeared to Isaiah was the one true God, and yet John declares that he was Christ (Isa. vi. ; John xii. 41). He who declared, by the mouth of Isaiah, that he was to be " for a stone of stumbling" to the Jews, was the one God ; and yet Paul declares that he was Christ (Isa. viii. 14 ; Rom. ix. 33). He who proclaims by Isaiah, " Unto me every knee shall bow," is the one God ; yet Paul again explains that he is Christ (Isa. xlv. 23 ; Rom. xiv. 11). To this we may add the passages quoted by an Apostle, " Thou, Lord, hast laid the foundations of the earth ;" " Let all the angels of God worship him" (Heb. i. 10; x. 6; Ps. cii. 26 ; xcvii. 7). All these apply to the one God ; and yet the Apostle contends that they are the proper attributes of Christ. There is nothing in the cavil, that what properly applies to God is transferred to Christ, because he is the brightness of his glory. Since the name of Jehovah is everywhere applied to Christ, it follows that, in regard to Deity, he is of himself. For if he is Jehovah, it is impossible to deny that he is the same God who elsewhere proclaims by Isaiah, " I am the first, and I am the last ; and besides me there is no God" (Isa xliv. 6). We would also do well to ponder the words of Jeremiah, " The gods that have not made the heavens and the earth, even they shall perish from the earth, and from under these heavens" (Jer. x. 11) ; whence it follows conversely, that He whose divinity Isaiah repeatedly proves from the creation of the world, is none other than the Son of God. And how is it possible that the Creator, who gives to all, should not be of himself, but should borrow his essence from another ? Whosoever says that the Son was *essentiated* by the Father,[1] denies his self-existence. Against this, however, the Holy Spirit protests, when he calls him Jehovah. On the supposition, then, that the whole essence is in the Father only, the essence becomes divisible, or is denied to the Son, who, being thus robbed of his essence, will be only a titular God. If we are to believe these triflers, divine essence belongs to the Father only, on the ground that he is sole God, and *essentiator* of the Son. In this way, the divinity of the Son will be something abstracted[2] from the essence of God, or the derivation of a part from the whole. On the same principle it must

---

[1] The French adds, "puisque tels abuseurs forgent des noms contre nature ;"— for these perverters forge names against nature.

[2] The French is, " tiré comme par un alambic ;"—extracted as by an alembic.

also be conceded, that the Spirit belongs to the Father only. For if the derivation is from the primary essence which is proper to none but the Father, the Spirit cannot justly be deemed the Spirit of the Son. This view, however, is refuted by the testimony of Paul, when he makes the Spirit common both to Christ and the Father. Moreover, if the Person of the Father is expunged from the Trinity, in what will he differ from the Son and Spirit, except in being the only God? They confess that Christ is God, and that he differs from the Father. If he differs, there must be some mark of distinction between them. Those who place it in the essence, manifestly reduce the true divinity of Christ to nothing, since divinity cannot exist without essence, and indeed without entire essence.[1] The Father certainly cannot differ from the Son, unless he have something peculiar to himself, and not common to him with the Son. What, then, do these men show as the mark of distinction? If it is in the essence, let them tell whether or not he communicated essence to the Son. This he could not do in part merely, for it were impious to think of a divided God. And besides, on this supposition, there would be a rending of the Divine essence. The whole entire essence must therefore be common to the Father and the Son; and if so, in respect of essence there is no distinction between them. If they reply that the Father, while essentiating, still remains the only God, being the possessor of the essence, then Christ will be a figurative God, one in name or semblance only, and not in reality, because no property can be more peculiar to God than essence, according to the words, "I AM hath sent me unto you" (Ex. iii. 4).

24. The assumption, that whenever God is mentioned absolutely, the Father only is meant, may be proved erroneous by many passages. Even in those which they quote in support of their views they betray a lamentable inconsistency, because the name of Son occurs there by way of contrast, showing that the other name God is used relatively, and in that way confined to the person of the Father. Their objection may be disposed of in a single word. Were not the Father alone the true God, he would, say they, be his own Father. But there is nothing absurd in the name of God being specially applied, in respect of order and degree, to him who not only of himself begat his own wisdom, but is the God of the Mediator, as I will more fully show in its own place. For ever since Christ was manifested in the flesh he is called the Son of God, not only because begotten of the Father before all worlds he was the Eternal Word, but because he undertook the person and office of the Mediator that he might unite us to God. Seeing they are so bold in excluding the Son from the honour of God, I would fain know whether, when he declares that there is "none good but one, that is, God," he deprives himself of

[1] See Bernard, Serm. 80, super Cantica., on the heresy of Gilbert, Bishop of Poictiers.

goodness. I speak not of his human nature, lest perhaps they should object, that whatever goodness was in it was derived by gratuitous gift: I ask whether the Eternal Word of God is good, yes or no? If they say no, their impiety is manifest; if yes, they refute themselves. Christ's seeming at the first glance to disclaim the name of good (Matth. xix. 17), rather confirms our view. Goodness being the special property of God alone, and yet being at the time applied to him in the ordinary way of salutation, his rejection of false honour intimates that the goodness in which he excels is Divine. Again, I ask whether, when Paul affirms that God alone is "immortal," "wise, and true" (1 Tim. i. 17), he reduces Christ to the rank of beings mortal, foolish, and false. Is not he immortal, who, from the beginning, had life so as to bestow immortality on angels? Is not he wise who is the eternal wisdom of God? Is not he true who is truth itself?

I ask, moreover, whether they think Christ should be worshipped. If he claims justly, that every knee shall bow to him, it follows that he is the God who, in the law, forbade worship to be offered to any but himself. If they insist on applying to the Father only the words of Isaiah, "I am, and besides me there is none else" (Isa. xliv. 6), I turn the passage against themselves, since we see that every property of God is attributed to Christ.[1] There is no room for the cavil that Christ was exalted in the flesh in which he humbled himself, and in respect of which all power is given to him in heaven and on earth. For although the majesty of King and Judge extends to the whole person of the Mediator, yet had he not been God manifested in the flesh, he could not have been exalted to such a height without coming into collision with God. And the dispute is admirably settled by Paul, when he declares that he was equal with God before he humbled himself, and assumed the form of a servant (Phil. ii. 6, 7). Moreover, how could such equality exist, if he were not that God whose name is Jah and Jehovah, who rides upon 'the cherubim, is King of all the earth, and King of ages? Let them clamour as they may, Christ cannot be robbed of the honour described by Isaiah, "Lo, this is our God; we have waited for him" (Isa. xxv. 9); for these words describe the advent of God the Redeemer, who was not only to bring back the people from Babylonish captivity, but restore the Church, and make her completely perfect.

Nor does another cavil avail them, that Christ was God in his Father. For though we admit that, in respect of order and gradation, the beginning of divinity is in the Father, we hold it a detestable fiction to maintain that essence is proper to the Father alone, as if he were the deifier of the Son. On this view either the essence is manifold, or Christ is God only in name and imagination. If they

---

1 The French is expressed somewhat differently, "veu que l'Apostre en l'allegant de Christ, lui attribue tout ce qui est de Dieu;"—seeing the Apostle, by applying it to Christ, attributes to him everything belonging to God.

grant that the Son is God, but only in subordination to the Father, the essence which in the Father is unformed and unbegotten will in him be formed and begotten. I know that many who would be thought wise deride us for extracting the distinction of persons from the words of Moses when he introduces God as saying, "Let us make man in our own image" (Gen. i. 26). Pious readers, however, see how frigidly and absurdly the colloquy were introduced by Moses, if there were not several persons in the Godhead. It is certain that those whom the Father addresses must have been uncreated. But nothing is uncreated except the one God. Now then, unless they concede that the power of creating was common to the Father, Son, and Spirit, and the power of commanding common, it will follow that God did not speak thus inwardly with himself, but addressed other extraneous architects. In fine, there is a single passage which will at once dispose of these two objections. The declaration of Christ, that "God is a Spirit" (John iv. 24), cannot be confined to the Father only, as if the Word were not of a spiritual nature. But if the name Spirit applies equally to the Son as to the Father, I infer that under the indefinite name of God the Son is included. He adds immediately after, that the only worshippers approved by the Father are those who worship him in spirit and in truth; and hence I also infer, that because Christ performs the office of teacher under a head, he applies the name God to the Father, not for the purpose of destroying his own Divinity, but for the purpose of raising us up to it as it were step by step.

25. The hallucination consists in dreaming of individuals, each of whom possesses a part of the essence. The Scriptures teach that there is essentially but one God, and therefore that the essence both of the Son and Spirit is unbegotten; but inasmuch as the Father is first in order, and of himself begat his own Wisdom, he, as we lately observed, is justly regarded as the principle and fountain of all the Godhead. Thus God, taken indefinitely, is unbegotten, and the Father, in respect of his person, is unbegotten. For it is absurd to imagine that our doctrine gives any ground for alleging that we establish a quaternion of gods. They falsely and calumniously ascribe to us the figment of their own brain, as if we virtually held that three persons emanate from one essence,[1] whereas it is plain, from our writings, that we do not disjoin the persons from the essence, but interpose a distinction between the persons residing in it. If the persons were separated from the essence, there might be some plausibility in their argument; as in this way there would be a trinity of Gods, not of persons comprehended in one God. This affords an answer to their futile question—whether or not the essence concurs in forming the Trinity; as if we imagined that three Gods were derived from it. Their objection, that there would thus be a Trinity without a God,

---

1 The French adds, " Comme trois ruisseaux;"—like three streams.

originates in the same absurdity. Although the essence does not contribute to the distinction, as if it were a part or member, the persons are not without it, or external to it; for the Father, if he were not God, could not be the Father; nor could the Son possibly be Son unless he were God. We say, then, that the Godhead is absolutely of itself. And hence also we hold that the Son, regarded as God, and without reference to person, is also of himself; though we also say that, regarded as Son, he is of the Father. Thus his essence is without beginning, while his person has its beginning in God. And, indeed, the orthodox writers who in former times spoke of the Trinity, used this term only with reference to the Persons. To have included the essence in the distinction, would not only have been an absurd error, but gross impiety. For those who class the three thus— Essence, Son, and Spirit [1]—plainly do away with the essence of the Son and Spirit; otherwise the parts being intermingled would merge into each other—a circumstance which would vitiate any distinction.[2] In short, if God and Father were synonymous terms, the Father would be deifier in a sense which would leave the Son nothing but a shadow; and the Trinity would be nothing more than the union of one God with two creatures.

26. To the objection, that if Christ be properly God, he is improperly called the Son of God, it has been already answered, that when one person is compared with another, the name God is not used indefinitely, but is restricted to the Father, regarded as the beginning of the Godhead, not by *essentiating*, as fanatics absurdly express it, but in respect of order. In this sense are to be understood the words which Christ addressed to the Father, "This is life eternal, that they might know thee the only true God, and Jesus Christ whom thou hast sent" (John xvii. 3). For speaking in the person of the Mediator, he holds a middle place between God and man; yet so that his majesty is not diminished thereby. For though he humbled (emptied) himself, he did not lose the glory which he had with the Father, though it was concealed from the world. So in the Epistle to the Hebrews (Heb. i. 10; ii. 9), though the apostle confesses that Christ was made a little lower than the angels, he at the same time hesitates not to assert that he is the eternal God who founded the earth. We must hold, therefore, that as often as Christ, in the character of Mediator, addresses the Father, he, under the term God, includes his own divinity also. Thus, when he says to the apostles, "It is expedient for you that I go away," "My Father is greater than I," he does not attribute to himself a secondary divinity merely, as if in regard

1 The French adds, "Comme si l'essence étoit au lieu de la personne du Pére;"—as if the essence were in place of the person of the Father.

2 The French is somewhat differently expressed: "Car le Fils a quelque l'estre, ou il n'en a point. S'il en a, voila deux essences pour jouster l'un contre autre; s'il n'en a point, ce ne seroit qu'une ombre." For the Son has some being, or he has none. If some, here are two essences to tilt with each other: if none, he is only a shadow.

to eternal essence he were inferior to the Father; but having obtained celestial glory, he gathers together the faithful to share it with him. He places the Father in the higher degree, inasmuch as the full perfection of brightness conspicuous in heaven, differs from that measure of glory which he himself displayed when clothed in flesh. For the same reason Paul says, that Christ will restore "the kingdom to God, even the Father," "that God may be all in all" (1 Cor. xv. 24, 28). Nothing can be more absurd than to deny the perpetuity of Christ's divinity. But if he will never cease to be the Son of God, but will ever remain the same that he was from the beginning, it follows that under the name of Father the one divine essence common to both is comprehended. And assuredly Christ descended to us for the very purpose of raising us to the Father, and thereby, at the same time, raising us to himself, inasmuch as he is one with the Father. It is therefore erroneous and impious to confine the name of God to the Father, so as to deny it to the Son. Accordingly, John, declaring that he is the true God, has no idea of placing him beneath the Father in a subordinate rank of divinity. I wonder what these fabricators of new gods mean, when they confess that Christ is truly God, and yet exclude him from the godhead of the Father, as if there could be any true God but the one God, or as if transfused divinity were not a mere modern fiction.

27. In the many passages which they collect from Irenæus, in which he maintains that the Father of Christ is the only eternal God of Israel, they betray shameful ignorance, or very great dishonesty. For they ought to have observed, that that holy man was contending against certain frantic persons, who, denying that the Father of Christ was that God who had in old times spoken by Moses and the prophets, held that he was some phantom or other produced from the pollution of the world. His whole object, therefore, is to make it plain, that in the Scriptures no other God is announced but the Father of Christ; that it is wicked to imagine any other. Accordingly, there is nothing strange in his so often concluding that the God of Israel was no other than he who is celebrated by Christ and the apostles. Now, when a different heresy is to be resisted, we also say with truth, that the God who in old times appeared to the fathers, was no other than Christ. Moreover, if it is objected that he was the Father, we have the answer ready, that while we contend for the divinity of the Son, we by no means exclude the Father. When the reader attends to the purpose of Irenæus, the dispute is at an end. Indeed, we have only to look to lib. iii. c. 6, where the pious writer insists on this one point, "that he who in Scripture is called God absolutely and indefinitely, is truly the only God; and that Christ is called God absolutely." Let us remember (as appears from the whole work, and especially from lib. ii. c. 46), that the point under discussion was, that the name of Father is not applied enigmatically and parabolically to one who was not truly God. We may add, that in lib. iii. c. 9, he contends that

the Son as well as the Father united was the God proclaimed by the prophets and apostles. He afterwards explains (lib. iii. c. 12) how Christ, who is Lord of all, and King and Judge, received power from him who is God of all, namely, in respect of the humiliation by which he humbled himself, even to the death of the cross. At the same time he shortly after affirms (lib. iii. c. 16), that the Son is the maker heaven and earth, who delivered the law by the hand of Moses, and appeared to the fathers. Should any babbler now insist that, according to Irenæus, the Father alone is the God of Israel, I will refer him to a passage in which Irenæus distinctly says (lib. iii. c. 18, 23), that Christ is ever one and the same, and also applies to Christ the words of the prophecy of Habakkuk, " God cometh from the south." To the same effect he says (lib. iv. c. 9), " Therefore, Christ himself, with the Father, is the God of the living." And in the 12th chapter of the same book he explains that Abraham believed God, because Christ is the maker of heaven and earth, and very God.

28. With no more truth do they claim Tertullian as a patron. Though his style is sometimes rugged and obscure, he delivers the doctrine which we maintain in no ambiguous manner, namely, that while there is one God, his Word, however, is with dispensation or economy ; that there is only one God, in unity of substance ; but that nevertheless, by the mystery of dispensation, the unity is arranged into Trinity ; that there are three, not in state, but in degree—not in substance, but in form—not in power, but in order.[1] He says, indeed, that he holds the Son to be second to the Father ; but he means that the only difference is by distinction. In one place he says the Son is visible ; but after he has discoursed on both views, he declares that he is invisible regarded as the Word. In fine, by affirming that the Father is characterised by his own Person, he shows that he is very far from countenancing the fiction which we refute. And although he does not acknowledge any other God than the Father, yet explaining himself in the immediate context, he shows that he does not speak exclusively in respect of the Son, because he denies that he is a different God from the Father ; and, accordingly, that the one supremacy is not violated by the distinction of Person. And it is easy to collect his meaning from the whole tenor of his discourse. For he contends against Praxeas, that although God has three distinct Persons, yet there are not several gods, nor is unity divided.

---

[1] Tertullianus, lib. adv. Praxeam:—"Perversitas hæc (Praxeæ scil.) se existimat meram veritatem possidere, dum unicum Deum non alias putat credendum, quam si ipsum eundemque et Patrem et Filium et Spiritum sanctum dicat : quasi non sic quoque unus sit omnia, dum ex uno omnia, per substantiæ scilicet unitatem, et nihilominus custodiatur οἰκονομίας sacramentum, quæ unitatem in trinitatem disponit, tres dirigens, Patrem, Filium, et Spiritum sanctum. Tres autem non statu, sed gradu : nec substantia, sed forma : nec potestate, sed specie : unius autem substantiæ, et unius status, et unius potestatis : quia unus Deus, ex quo et gradus isti, formæ et species, in nomine Patris, et Filii, et Spiritus sancti deputantur. Quomodo numerum sine divisione patiuntur, procedentes tractatus demonstrabunt," &c.

According to the fiction of Praxeas, Christ could not be God without being the Father also ; and this is the reason why Tertullian dwells so much on the distinction.   When he calls the Word and Spirit a portion of the whole, the expression, though harsh, may be allowed, since it does not refer to the substance, but only (as Tertullian himself testifies) denotes arrangement and economy which applies to the persons only.   Accordingly, he asks, " How many persons, Praxeas, do you think there are, but just as many as there are names for ?" In the same way, he shortly after says, " That they may believe the Father and the Son, each in his own name and person." These things, I think, sufficiently refute the effrontery of those who endeavour to blind the simple by pretending the authority of Tertullian.

29. Assuredly, whosoever will compare the writings of the ancient fathers with each other, will not find anything in Irenæus different from what is taught by those who come after him.   Justin is one of the most ancient, and he agrees with us out and out.   Let them object that, by him and others, the Father of Christ is called the one God.   The same thing is taught by Hilary, who uses the still harsher expression, that Eternity is in the Father.   Is it that he may withhold divine essence from the Son ?   His whole work is a defence of the doctrine which we maintain ; and yet these men are not ashamed to produce some kind of mutilated excerpts for the purpose of persuading us that Hilary is a patron of their heresy.   With regard to what they pretend as to Ignatius, if they would have it to be of the least importance, let them prove that the apostles enacted laws concerning Lent, and other corruptions.   Nothing can be more nauseating than the absurdities which have been published under the name of Ignatius ; and, therefore, the conduct of those who provide themselves with such masks for deception is the less entitled to toleration.

Moreover, the consent of the ancient fathers clearly appears from this, that in the Council of Nice, no attempt was made by Arius to cloak his heresy by the authority of any approved author ; and no Greek or Latin writer apologises as dissenting from his predecessors.   It cannot be necessary to observe how carefully Augustine, to whom all these miscreants are most violently opposed, examined all ancient writings, and how reverently he embraced the doctrine taught by them (August. lib. de Trinit. &c.).   He is most scrupulous in stating the grounds on which he is forced to differ from them, even in the minutest point.   On this subject, too, if he finds anything ambiguous or obscure in other writers, he does not disguise it.[1]   And he assumes it as an acknowledged fact, that the doctrine opposed by the Arians was received without dispute from the earliest antiquity.   At the same time, he was not ignorant of what some others had previously taught.   This is obvious from a

---

1 Athanasius expresses himself thus learnedly and piously :—" On this subject, though you cannot explain yourself, you are not therefore to distrust the Holy Scriptures.   It is better, while hesitating through ignorance, to be silent and believe, than not to believe because you hesitate "

single expression. When he says (De Doct. Christ. lib. i.) that "unity is in the Father," will they pretend that he then forgot himself? In another passage, he clears away every such charge, when he calls the Father the beginning of the Godhead, as being from none —thus wisely inferring that the name of God is specially ascribed to the Father, because, unless the beginning were from him, the simple unity of essence could not be maintained. I hope the pious reader will admit that I have now disposed of all the calumnies by which Satan has hitherto attempted to pervert or obscure the pure doctrine of faith. The whole substance of the doctrine has, I trust, been faithfully expounded, if my readers will set bounds to their curiosity, and not long more eagerly than they ought for perplexing disputation. I did not undertake to satisfy those who delight in speculative views, but I have not designedly omitted anything which I thought adverse to me. At the same time, studying the edification of the Church, I have thought it better not to touch on various topics, which could have yielded little profit, while they must have needlessly burdened and fatigued the reader. For instance, what avails it to discuss, as Lombard does at length (lib. i. dist. 9), whether or not the Father always generates? This idea of continual generation becomes an absurd fiction from the moment it is seen, that from eternity there were three persons in one God.

CHAPTER XIV.

IN THE CREATION OF THE WORLD, AND ALL THINGS IN IT, THE TRUE
GOD DISTINGUISHED BY CERTAIN MARKS FROM FICTITIOUS GODS.

In this chapter commences the second part of Book First—viz., the knowledge of
man. Certain things premised. I. The creation of the world generally (s. 1 and 2);
II. The subject of angels considered (s. 3-13); III. Of bad angels or devils (s. 13-20);
and, IV. The practical use to be made of the history of the creation (s. 20-22).

Sections.

1. The mere fact of creation should lead us to acknowledge God, but to prevent our
   falling away to Gentile fictions, God has been pleased to furnish a history of the
   creation. An impious objection, Why the world was not created sooner? Answer
   to it. Shrewd saying of an old man.
2. For the same reason, the world was created, not in an instant, but in six days. The
   order of creation described, showing that Adam was not created until God had,
   with infinite goodness, made ample provision for him.
3. The doctrine concerning angels expounded. 1. That we may learn from them also
   to acknowledge God. 2. That we may be put on our guard against the errors of
   the worshippers of angels and the Manichees. Manicheeism refuted. Rule of
   piety.
4. The angels created by God. At what time and in what order it is inexpedient to
   inquire. The garrulity of the Pseudo-Dionysius.
5. The nature, offices, and various names of angels.
6. Angels the dispensers of the divine beneficence to us.
7. A kind of prefects over kingdoms and provinces, but specially the guardians of the
   elect. Not certain that every believer is under the charge of a single angel.
   Enough, that all angels watch over the safety of the Church.
8. The number and orders of angels not defined. Why angels said to be winged.
9. Angels are ministering spirits and spiritual essences.
10. The heathen error of placing angels on the throne of God refuted. 1. By passages
    of Scripture.
11. Refutation continued. 2. By inferences from other passages. Why God employs
    the ministry of angels.
12. Use of the doctrine of Scripture concerning the holy angels.
13. The doctrine concerning bad angels or devils reduced to four heads. 1. That we
    may guard against their wiles and assaults.
14. That we may be stimulated to exercises of piety. Why one angel in the singular
    number often spoken of.
15. The devil being described as the enemy of man, we should perpetually war against
    him.
16. The wickedness of the devil not by creation but by corruption. Vain and useless
    to inquire into the mode, time, and character of the fall of angels.
17. Though the devil is always opposed in will and endeavour to the will of God, he can
    do nothing without his permission and consent.
18. God so overrules wicked spirits as to permit them to try the faithful, and rule over
    the wicked.
19. The nature of bad angels. They are spiritual essences endued with sense and
    intelligence.
20. The latter part of the chapter briefly embracing the history of creation, and showing
    what it is of importance for us to know concerning God.

21. The special object of this knowledge is to prevent us, through ingratitude or thoughtlessness, from overlooking the perfections of God. Example of this primary knowledge.
22. Another object of this knowledge—viz., that perceiving how these things were created for our use, we may be excited to trust in God, pray to him, and love him.

1. ALTHOUGH Isaiah justly charges the worshippers of false gods with stupidity, in not learning from the foundations of the earth, and the circle of the heavens, who the true God is (Isa. xl. 21) ; yet so sluggish and grovelling is our intellect, that it was necessary he should be more clearly depicted, in order that the faithful might not fall away to Gentile fictions. The idea that God is the soul of the world, though the most tolerable that philosophers have suggested, is absurd ; and, therefore, it was of importance to furnish us with a more intimate knowledge in order that we might not wander to and fro in uncertainty. Hence God was pleased that a history of the creation should exist—a history on which the faith of the Church might lean without seeking any other God than Him whom Moses sets forth as the Creator and Architect of the world. First, in that history, the period of time is marked so as to enable the faithful to ascend by an unbroken succession of years to the first origin of their race and of all things. This knowledge is of the highest use not only as an antidote to the monstrous fables which anciently prevailed both in Egypt and the other regions of the world, but also as a means of giving a clearer manifestation of the eternity of God as contrasted with the birth of creation, and thereby inspiring us with higher admiration. We must not be moved by the profane jeer, that it is strange how it did not sooner occur to the Deity to create the heavens and the earth, instead of idly allowing an infinite period to pass away, during which thousands of generations might have existed, while the present world is drawing to a close before it has completed its six thousandth year. Why God delayed so long it is neither fit nor lawful to inquire. Should the human mind presume to do it, it could only fail in the attempt, nor would it be useful for us to know what God, as a trial of the modesty of our faith, has been pleased purposely to conceal. It was a shrewd saying of a good old man, who when some one pertly asked in derision what God did before the world was created, answered he made a hell for the inquisitive (August. Confess., lib. xi. c. 12). This reproof, not less weighty than severe, should repress the tickling wantonness which urges many to indulge in vicious and hurtful speculation.

In fine, let us remember that that invisible God, whose wisdom, power, and justice, are incomprehensible, is set before us in the history of Moses as in a mirror, in which his living image is reflected. For as an eye, either dimmed by age or weakened by any other cause, sees nothing distinctly without the aid of glasses, so (such is our imbecility) if Scripture does not direct us in our inquiries after God, we immediately turn vain in our imaginations. Those who now indulge their petulance, and refuse to take warning, will learn, when too late, how much better it had been reverently to regard the secret counsels of God, than to belch forth blasphemies which pollute the face of heaven. Justly does Augustine complain that God is insulted whenever any higher reason than his will is demanded (Lib. de Gent.). He also in another place wisely reminds us that it is just as improper to raise questions about infinite periods of time as about infinite space (De Civit. Dei.). However wide the circuit of the heavens may be, it is of some definite extent. But should any one expostulate with God that vacant space remains exceeding creation by a hundred-fold, must not every pious mind detest the presumption? Similar is the madness of those who charge God with idleness in not having pleased them by creating the world countless ages sooner than he did create it. In their cupidity they affect to go beyond the world, as if the ample circumference of heaven and earth did not contain objects numerous and resplendent enough to absorb all our senses; as if, in the period of six thousand years, God had not furnished facts enough to exercise our minds in ceaseless meditation. Therefore, let us willingly remain hedged in by those boundaries within which God has been pleased to confine our persons, and, as it were, enclose our minds, so as to prevent them from losing themselves by wandering unrestrained.

Let us remain within the limitations of our own understanding.

2. With the same view Moses relates that the work of creation was accomplished not in one moment, but in six days. By this statement we are drawn away from fiction to the one God who thus divided his work into six days, that we may have no reluctance to devote our whole lives to the contemplation of it. For though our eyes, in what direction soever they turn, are forced to behold the works of God, we see how fleeting our attention is, and how quickly pious thoughts, if any arise, vanish away. Here, too, objection is taken to these progressive steps as inconsistent with the power of God, until human reason is subdued to the obedience of faith, and learns to welcome the calm quiescence to which the sanctification of the seventh day invites us. In the very order of events, we ought diligently to ponder on the paternal goodness of God toward the human race, in not creating Adam until he had liberally enriched the earth with all good things. Had he placed him on an earth barren and unfurnished; had he given life before light, he might have seemed to pay little regard to his interest. But now that he has arranged the motions of the sun and stars for man's use, has replenished the air, earth, and water, with living creatures, and produced all kinds of fruit in abundance for the supply of food, by performing the office of a provident and industrious head of a family, he has shown his wondrous goodness toward us. These subjects, which I only briefly touch, if more attentively pondered, will make it manifest that Moses was a sure witness and herald of the one only Creator. I do not repeat what I have

already explained—viz. that mention is here made not of the bare essence of God, but that his eternal Wisdom and Spirit are also set before us, in order that we may not dream of any other God than Him who desires to be recognised in that express image.

3. But before I begin to treat more fully of the nature of man (chap. xv. and B. II. c. 1), it will be proper to say something of angels. For although Moses, in accommodation to the ignorance of the generality of men, does not in the history of the creation make mention of any other works of God than those which meet our eye, yet, seeing he afterwards introduces angels as the ministers of God, we easily infer that he for whom they do service is their Creator. Hence, though Moses, speaking in popular language, did not at the very commencement enumerate the angels among the creatures of God, nothing prevents us from treating distinctly and explictly of what is delivered by Scripture concerning them in other places. For if we desire to know God by his works, we surely cannot overlook this noble and illustrious specimen. We may add that this branch of doctrine is very necessary for the refutation of numerous errors. The minds of many are so struck with the excellence of angelic natures, that they would think them insulted in being subjected to the authority of God, and so made subordinate. Hence a fancied divinity has been assigned them. Manes, too, has arisen with his sect, fabricating to himself two principles—God and the devil, attributing the origin of good things to God, but assigning all bad natures to the devil as their author. Were this delirium to take possession of our minds, God would be denied his glory in the creation of the world. For, seeing there is nothing more peculiar to God than eternity and αὐτουσία, *i.e.* self-existence, or existence of himself, if I may so speak, do not those who attribute it to the devil in some degree invest him with the honour of divinity? And where is the omnipotence of God, if the devil has the power of executing whatever he pleases against the will, and notwithstanding of the opposition of God? But the only good ground which the Manichees have—viz. that it were impious to ascribe the creation of anything bad to a good God, militates in no degree against the orthodox faith, since it is not admitted that there is anything naturally bad throughout the universe ; the depravity and wickedness, whether of man or of the devil, and the sins thence resulting, being not from nature, but from the corruption of nature ; nor, at first, did anything whatever exist that did not exhibit some manifestation of the divine wisdom and justice. To obviate such perverse imaginations, we must raise our minds higher than our eyes can penetrate. It was probably with this view that the Nicene Creed, in calling God the creator of all things, makes express mention of things invisible. My care, however, must be to keep within the bounds which piety prescribes, lest by indulging in speculations beyond my reach, I bewilder the reader, and lead him away from the simplicity of the faith. And since the Holy Spirit

always instructs us in what is useful, but altogether omits, or only touches cursorily on matters which tend little to edification, of all such matters, it certainly is our duty to remain in willing ignorance.

4. Angels being the ministers appointed to execute the commands of God, must of course be admitted to be his creatures; but to stir up questions concerning the time or order in which they were created (see Lombard, lib. ii. dist. 2, sqq.), bespeaks more perverseness than industry. Moses relates that the heavens and the earth were finished, with all their host; what avails it anxiously to inquire at what time other more hidden celestial hosts than the stars and planets also began to be? Not to dwell on this, let us here remember that on the whole subject of religion one rule of modesty and soberness is to be observed, and it is this,—in obscure matters not to speak or think, or even long to know, more than the Word of God has delivered. A second rule is, that in reading the Scriptures we should constantly direct our inquiries and meditations to those things which tend to edification, not indulge in curiosity, or in studying things of no use. And since the Lord has been pleased to instruct us, not in frivolous questions, but in solid piety, in the fear of his name, in true faith, and the duties of holiness, let us rest satisfied with such knowledge. Wherefore, if we would be duly wise, we must renounce those vain babblings of idle men, concerning the nature, ranks, and number of angels, without any authority from the Word of God. I know that many fasten on these topics more eagerly, and take greater pleasure in them than in those relating to daily practice. But if we decline not to be the disciples of Christ, let us not decline to follow the method which he has prescribed. In this way, being contented with him for our master, we will not only refrain from, but even feel averse to, superfluous speculations which he discourages. None can deny that Dionysius (whoever he may have been) has many shrewd and subtle disquisitions in his Celestial Hierarchy; but on looking at them more closely, every one must see that they are merely idle talk. The duty of a Theologian, however, is not to tickle the ear, but confirm the conscience, by teaching what is true, certain, and useful. When you read the work of Dionysius, you would think that the man had come down from heaven, and was relating not what he had learned, but what he had actually seen. Paul, however, though he was carried to the third heaven, so far from delivering anything of the kind, positively declares that it was not lawful for man to speak the secrets which he had seen. Bidding adieu, therefore, to that nugatory wisdom, let us endeavour to ascertain from the simple doctrine of Scripture what it is the Lord's pleasure that we should know concerning angels.

5. In Scripture, then, we uniformly read that angels are heavenly spirits, whose obedience and ministry God employs to execute all the purposes which he has decreed, and hence their name as being a kind of intermediate messengers to manifest his will to men. The names by which several of them are distinguished have reference to the same

office. They are called hosts, because they surround their Prince as his court,—adorn and display his majesty,—like soldiers, have their eyes always turned to their leader's standard, and are so ready and prompt to execute his orders, that the moment he gives the nod, they prepare for, or rather are actually at work. In declaring the magnificence of the divine throne, similar representations are given by the prophets, and especially by Daniel, when he says, that when God stood up to judgment, "thousand thousands ministered unto him, and ten thousand times ten thousand stood before him" (Dan. vii. 10). As by these means the Lord wonderfully exerts and declares the power and might of his hand, they are called Virtues. Again, as his government of the world is exercised and administered by them, they are called at one time Principalities, at another Powers, at another Dominions (Col. i. 16 ; Eph. i. 21). Lastly, as the glory of God in some measure dwells in them, they are also termed Thrones ; though as to this last designation I am unwilling to speak positively, as a different interpretation is equally, if not more congruous. To say nothing, therefore, of the name of Thrones, the former names are often employed by the Holy Spirit in commendation of the dignity of angelic service. Nor is it right to pass by unhonoured those instruments by whom God specially manifests the presence of his power. Nay, they are more than once called Gods, because the Deity is in some measure represented to us in their service, as in a mirror. I am rather inclined, however, to agree with ancient writers, that in those passages [1] wherein it is stated that the angel of the Lord appeared to Abraham, Jacob, and Moses, Christ was that angel. Still it is true, that when mention is made of all the angels, they are frequently so designated. Nor ought this to seem strange. For if princes and rulers have this honour given them, because in their office they are vicegerents of God, the supreme King and Judge, with far greater reason may it be given to angels, in whom the brightness of the divine glory is much more conspicuously displayed.

6. But the point on which the Scriptures specially insist is that which tends most to our comfort, and to the confirmation of our faith, namely, that angels are the ministers and dispensers of the divine bounty towards us. Accordingly, we are told how they watch for our safety, how they undertake our defence, direct our path, and take heed that no evil befall us. There are whole passages which relate, in the first instance, to Christ, the Head of the Church, and after him to all believers. "He shall give his angels charge over thee, to keep thee in all thy ways. They shall bear thee up in their hands, lest thou dash thy foot against a stone." Again, "The angel of the Lord encampeth round about them that fear him, and delivereth them."[2]

[1] Gen. xviii. 2; xxxii. 1, 28; Josh. v. 14; Judges vi. 14; xiii. 10, 22.

[2] Ps. xci. 11; xxxiv. 8; Gen. xvi. 9; xxiv. 7; xlviii. 16; Ex. xiv. 19, 23, 29; Judges ii. 1, 20; vi. 11; xiii. 10; Matth. iv. 11; Luke xxii. 43; Matth. xxviii. 5; Luke xxiv. 5; Acts i. 10; 2 Kings xix. 35; Isa. xxxvii. 36.

By these passages the Lord shows that the protection of those whom he has undertaken to defend he has delegated to his angels. Accordingly, an angel of the Lord consoles Hagar in her flight, and bids her be reconciled to her mistress. Abraham promises to his servant that an angel will be the guide of his journey. Jacob, in blessing Ephraim and Manasseh, prays, "The angel which redeemed me from all evil bless the lads." So an angel was appointed to guard the camp of the Israelites ; and as often as God was pleased to deliver Israel from the hands of his enemies, he stirred up avengers by the ministry of angels. Thus, in fine (not to mention more), angels ministered to Christ, and were present with him in all straits. To the women they announced his resurrection ; to the disciples they foretold his glorious advent. In discharging the office of our protectors, they war against the devil and all our enemies, and execute vengeance upon those who afflict us. Thus we read that an angel of the Lord, to deliver Jerusalem from siege, slew one hundred and eighty-five thousand men in the camp of the king of Assyria in a single night.

7. Whether or not each believer has a single angel assigned to him for his defence, I dare not positively affirm. When Daniel introduces the angel of the Persians and the angel of the Greeks, he undoubtedly intimates that certain angels are appointed as a kind of presidents over kingdoms and provinces.[1] Again, when Christ says that the angels of children always behold the face of his Father, he insinuates that there are certain angels to whom their safety has been intrusted. But I know not if it can be inferred from this, that each believer has his own angel. This, indeed, I hold for certain, that each of us is cared for, not by one angel merely, but that all with one consent watch for our safety. For it is said of all the angels collectively, that they rejoice " over one sinner that repenteth, more than over ninety and nine just persons, which need no repentance." It is also said, that the angels (meaning more than one) carried the soul of Lazarus into Abraham's bosom. Nor was it to no purpose that Elisha showed his servant the many chariots of fire which were specially allotted him.

There is one passage which seems to intimate somewhat more clearly that each individual has a separate angel. When Peter, after his deliverance from prison, knocked at the door of the house where the brethren were assembled, being unable to think it could be himself, they said that it was his angel. This idea seems to have been suggested to them by a common belief that every believer has a single angel assigned to him. Here, however, it may be alleged, that there is nothing to prevent us from understanding it of any one of the angels to whom the Lord might have given the charge of Peter at that particular time, without implying that he was to be his perpetual guardian,

---

[1] Dan. x. 13, 20; xii. 1 ; Matth. xviii. 20 ; Luke xv. 7 ; xvi. 22 ; 2 Kings xvi. 17; Acts xii. 15.

according to the vulgar imagination (see Calvin on Mark v. 9), that two angels, a good and a bad, as a kind of genii, are assigned to each individual. After all, it is not worth while anxiously to investigate a point which does not greatly concern us. If any one does not think it enough to know that all the orders of the heavenly host are perpetually watching for his safety, I do not see what he could gain by knowing that he has one angel as a special guardian. Those, again, who limit the care which God takes of each of us to a single angel, do great injury to themselves and to all the members of the Church, as if there were no value in those promises of auxiliary troops, who on every side encircling and defending us, embolden us to fight more manfully.

8. Those who presume to dogmatise on the ranks and numbers of angels, would do well to consider on what foundation they rest. As to their rank, I admit that Michael is described by David as a mighty Prince, and by Jude as an Archangel.[1] Paul also tells us, that an archangel will blow the trumpet which is to summon the world to judgment. But how is it possible from such passages to ascertain the gradations of honour among the angels, to determine the insignia, and assign the place and station of each? Even the two names, Michael and Gabriel, mentioned in Scripture, or a third, if you choose to add it from the history of Tobit, seem to intimate by their meaning that they are given to angels, in accommodation to the weakness of our capacity, though I rather choose not to speak positively on the point. As to the number of angels, we learn from the mouth of our Saviour that there are many legions, and from Daniel that there are many myriads. Elisha's servant saw a multitude of chariots, and their vast number is declared by the fact, that they encamp round about those that fear the Lord. It is certain that spirits have no bodily shape, and yet Scripture, in accommodation to us, describes them under the form of winged Cherubim and Seraphim; not without cause, to assure us that when occasion requires, they will hasten to our aid with incredible swiftness, winging their way to us with the speed of lightning. Farther than this, in regard both to the ranks and numbers of angels, let us class them among those mysterious subjects, the full revelation of which is deferred to the last day, and accordingly refrain from inquiring too curiously, or talking presumptuously.

9. There is one point, however, which, though called into doubt by certain restless individuals, we ought to hold for certain—viz. that angels are ministering spirits (Heb. i. 14); whose service God employs for the protection of his people, and by whose means he distributes his favours among men, and also executes other works. The Sadducees of old maintain, that by angels nothing more was meant

---

[1] Dan. xii. 1; Jude 9; 1 Thess. iv. 16; Dan. x. 13, 21; Luke i. 19, 26; Tobit iii. 17 v. 5; Matth. xxvi. 53; Dan. vii. 10; 2 Kings vi. 17; Ps. xxxiv. 7.

than the movements which God impresses on men, or manifestations which he gives of his own power (Acts xxiii. 8). But this dream is contradicted by so many passages of Scripture, that it seems strange how such gross ignorance could have had any countenance among the Jews. To say nothing of the passages I have already quoted, passages which refer to thousands and legions of angels, speak of them as rejoicing, as bearing up the faithful in their hands, carrying their souls to rest, beholding the face of their Father, and so forth :[1] there are other passages which most clearly prove that they are real beings possessed of spiritual essence. Stephen and Paul say that the Law was enacted in the hands of angels. Our Saviour, moreover, says, that at the resurrection the elect will be like angels ; that the day of judgment is known not even to the angels ; that at that time he himself will come with the holy angels. However much such passages may be twisted, their meaning is plain. In like manner, when Paul beseeches Timothy to keep his precepts as before Christ and his elect angels, it is not qualities or inspirations without substance that he speaks of, but true spirits. And when it is said, in the Epistle to the Hebrews, that Christ was made more excellent than the angels, that the world was not made subject to them, that Christ assumed not their nature, but that of man, it is impossible to give a meaning to the passages without understanding that angels are blessed spirits, as to whom such comparisons may competently be made. The author of that Epistle declares the same thing when he places the souls of believers and the holy angels together in the kingdom of heaven. Moreover, in the passages we have already quoted, the angels of children are said to behold the face of God, to defend us by their protection, to rejoice in our salvation, to admire the manifold grace of God in the Church, to be under Christ their head. To the same effect is their frequent appearance to the holy patriarchs in human form, their speaking, and consenting to be hospitably entertained. Christ, too, in consequence of the supremacy which he obtains as Mediator, is called the Angel (Mal. iii. 1). It was thought proper to touch on this subject in passing, with the view of putting the simple upon their guard against the foolish and absurd imaginations which, suggested by Satan many centuries ago, are ever and anon starting up anew.

10. It remains to give warning against the superstition which usually begins to creep in, when it is said that all blessings are ministered and dispensed to us by angels. For the human mind is apt immediately to think that there is no honour which they ought not to receive, and hence the peculiar offices of Christ and God are bestowed upon them. In this way, the glory of Christ was for several former ages greatly obscured, extravagant eulogiums being pronounced on

---

[1] Luke xv. 10; Ps. xci. 11; Matth. iv. 6; Luke iv. 10, 16, 22; Matth. xviii. 10; Acts vii. 55; Gal. iii. 19; Matth. xxii. 30; xxiv. 36; Eph. iii. 10; 1 Peter i. 12; Heb. i. 6; Ps. xcvii. 7.

angels without any authority from Scripture. Among the corruptions which we now oppose, there is scarcely any one of greater antiquity. Even Paul appears to have had a severe contest with some who so exalted angels as to make them almost the superiors of Christ. Hence he so anxiously urges in his Epistle to the Colossians (Col. i. 16, 20), that Christ is not only superior to all angels, but that all the endowments which they possess are derived from him ; thus warning us against forsaking him, by turning to those who are not sufficient for themselves, but must draw with us at a common fountain. As the refulgence of the Divine glory is manifested in them, there is nothing to which we are more prone than to prostrate ourselves before them in stupid adoration, and then ascribe to them the blessings which we owe to God alone. Even John confesses in the Apocalypse (Rev. xix. 10 ; xxii. 8, 9), that this was his own case, but he immediately adds the answer which was given to him, " See thou do it not : I am thy fellow-servant ; worship God."

11. This danger we will happily avoid, if we consider why it is that God, instead of acting directly without their agency, is wont to employ it in manifesting his power, providing for the safety of his people, and imparting the gifts of his beneficence. This he certainly does not from necessity, as if he were unable to dispense with them. Whenever he pleases, he passes them by, and performs his own work by a single nod : so far are they from relieving him of any difficulty. Therefore, when he employs them, it is as a help to our weakness, that nothing may be wanting to elevate our hopes or strengthen our confidence. It ought, indeed, to be sufficient for us that the Lord declares himself to be our protector. But when we see ourselves beset by so many perils, so many injuries, so many kinds of enemies, such is our frailty and effeminacy, that we might at times be filled with alarm, or driven to despair, did not the Lord proclaim his gracious presence by some means in accordance with our feeble capacities. For this reason, he not only promises to take care of us, but assures us that he has numberless attendants, to whom he has committed the charge of our safety,—that whatever dangers may impend, so long as we are encircled by their protection and guardianship, we are placed beyond all hazard of evil. I admit that after we have a simple assurance of the divine protection, it is improper in us still to look round for help. But since for this our weakness the Lord is pleased, in his infinite goodness and indulgence, to provide, it would ill become us to overlook the favour. Of this we have an example in the servant of Elisha (2 Kings vi. 17), who, seeing the mountain encompassed by the army of the Assyrians, and no means of escape, was completely overcome with terror, and thought it all over with himself and his master. Then Elisha prayed to God to open the eyes of the servant, who forthwith beheld the mountain filled with horses and chariots of fire ; in other words, with a multitude of angels, to whom he and the prophet had been given in charge. Confirmed by the vision he re-

ceived courage, and could boldly defy the enemy, whose appearance previously filled him with dismay.

12. Whatever, therefore, is said as to the ministry of angels, let us employ for the purpose of removing all distrust, and strengthening our confidence in God. Since the Lord has provided us with such protection, let us not be terrified at the multitude of our enemies, as if they could prevail notwithstanding of his aid, but let us adopt the sentiment of Elisha, that more are for us than against us. How preposterous, therefore, is it to allow ourselves to be led away from God by angels who have been appointed for the very purpose of assuring us of his more immediate presence to help us ? But we are so led away, if angels do not conduct us directly to him—making us look to him, invoke and celebrate him as our only defender—if they are not regarded merely as hands moving to our assistance just as he directs—if they do not direct us to Christ as the only Mediator on whom we must wholly depend and recline, looking towards him, and resting in him. Our minds ought to give thorough heed to what Jacob saw in his vision (Gen. xxviii. 12),—angels descending to the earth to men, and again mounting up from men to heaven, by means of a ladder, at the head of which the Lord of Hosts was seated, intimating that it is solely by the intercession of Christ that the ministry of angels extends to us, as he himself declares, " Hereafter ye shall see heaven open, and the angels of God ascending and descending upon the Son of man" (John i. 51). Accordingly, the servant of Abraham, though he had been commended to the guardianship of an angel (Gen. xxiv. 7), does not therefore invoke that angel to be present with him, but trusting to the commendation, pours out his prayers before the Lord, and entreats him to show mercy to Abraham. As God does not make angels the ministers of his power and goodness, that he may share his glory with them, so he does not promise his assistance by their instrumentality, that we may divide our confidence between him and them. Away, then, with that Platonic philosophy of seeking access to God by means of angels, and courting them with the view of making God more propitious (*Plat. in Epinomide et Cratylo*),—a philosophy which presumptuous and superstitious men attempted at first to introduce into our religion, and which they persist in even to this day.

13. The tendency of all that Scripture teaches concerning devils is to put us on our guard against their wiles and machinations, that we may provide ourselves with weapons strong enough to drive away the most formidable foes. For when Satan is called the god and ruler of this world, the strong man armed, the prince of the power of the air, the roaring lion,[1] the object of all these descriptions is to make us more cautious and vigilant, and more prepared for the contest. This is sometimes stated in distinct terms. For Peter, after describing the

---

[1] 2 Cor. iv. 4; John xii. 31; Matth. xii. 29; Eph. ii. 2.

devil as a roaring lion, going about seeking whom he may devour, immediately adds the exhortation, "whom resist steadfast in the faith" (1 Pet. v. 8). And Paul, after reminding us that we wrestle not against flesh and blood, but against principalities, against powers, against the rulers of the darkness of this world, against spiritual wickedness in high places, immediately enjoins us to put on armour equal to so great and perilous a contest (Ephes. vi. 12). Wherefore, let this be the use to which we turn all these statements. Being forewarned of the constant presence of an enemy the most daring, the most powerful, the most crafty, the most indefatigable, the most completely equipped with all the engines, and the most expert in the science of war, let us not allow ourselves to be overtaken by sloth or cowardice, but, on the contrary, with minds aroused and ever on the alert, let us stand ready to resist; and, knowing that this warfare is terminated only by death, let us study to persevere. Above all, fully conscious of our weakness and want of skill, let us invoke the help of God, and attempt nothing without trusting in him, since it is his alone to supply counsel, and strength, and courage, and arms.

14. That we may feel the more strongly urged to do so, the Scripture declares that the enemies who war against us are not one or two, or few in number, but a great host. Mary Magdalene is said to have been delivered from seven devils by which she was possessed; and our Saviour assures us that it is an ordinary circumstance, when a devil has been expelled, if access is again given to it, to take seven other spirits, more wicked than itself, and resume the vacant possession. Nay, one man is said to have been possessed by a whole legion.[1] By this, then, we are taught that the number of enemies with whom we have to war is almost infinite, that we may not, from a contemptuous idea of the fewness of their numbers, be more remiss in the contest, or from imagining that an occasional truce is given us, indulge in sloth. In one Satan or devil being often mentioned in the singular number, the thing denoted is that domination of iniquity which is opposed to the reign of righteousness. For, as the Church and the communion of saints has Christ for its head, so the faction of the wicked, and wickedness itself, is portrayed with its prince exercising supremacy. Hence the expression, "Depart, ye cursed, into everlasting fire, prepared for the devil and his angels" (Matth. xxv. 41).

15. One thing which ought to animate us to perpetual contest with the devil is, that he is everywhere called both our adversary and the adversary of God. For, if the glory of God is dear to us, as it ought to be, we ought to struggle with all our might against him who aims at the extinction of that glory. If we are animated with proper zeal to maintain the kingdom of Christ, we must wage irreconcilable war with him who conspires its ruin. Again, if we have any anxiety about our own salvation, we ought to make no peace nor truce with him who

---

[1] Mark xvi. 9; Matth. xii. 43; Luke viii. 30.

is continually laying schemes for its destruction. But such is the character given to Satan in the third chapter of Genesis, where he is seen seducing man from his allegiance to God, that he may both deprive God of his due honour, and plunge man headlong in destruction. Such, too, is the description given of him in the Gospels (Matth. xiii. 28), where he is called the enemy, and is said to sow tares in order to corrupt the seed of eternal life. In one word, in all his actions we experience the truth of our Saviour's description, that he was "a murderer from the beginning, and abode not in the truth' (John viii. 44). Truth he assails with lies, light he obscures with darkness. The minds of men he involves in error; he stirs up hatred, inflames strife and war, and all in order that he may overthrow the kingdom of God, and drown men in eternal perdition with himself. Hence it is evident that his whole nature is depraved, mischievous, and malignant. There must be extreme depravity in a mind bent on assailing the glory of God and the salvation of man. This is intimated by John in his Epistle, when he says that he "sinneth from the beginning" (1 John iii. 8), implying that he is the author, leader, and contriver of all malice and wickedness.

16. But as the devil was created by God, we must remember that this malice which we attribute to his nature is not from creation, but from depravation. Everything damnable in him he brought upon himself, by his revolt and fall. Of this Scripture reminds us, lest, by believing that he was so created at first, we should ascribe to God what is most foreign to his nature. For this reason, Christ declares, (John viii. 44), that Satan, when he lies, "speaketh of his own," and states the reason, "because he abode not in the truth." By saying that he abode not in the truth, he certainly intimates that he once was in the truth, and by calling him the father of lies, he puts it out of his power to charge God with the depravity of which he was himself the cause. But although the expressions are brief and not very explicit, they are amply sufficient to vindicate the majesty of God from every calumny. And what more does it concern us to know of devils? Some murmur because the Scripture does not in various passages give a distinct and regular exposition of Satan's fall, its cause, mode, date, and nature. But as these things are of no consequence to us, it was better, if not entirely to pass them in silence, at least only to touch lightly upon them. The Holy Spirit could not deign to feed curiosity with idle, unprofitable histories. We see it was the Lord's purpose to deliver nothing in his sacred oracles which we might not learn for edification. Therefore, instead of dwelling on superfluous matters, let it be sufficient for us briefly to hold, with regard to the nature of devils, that at their first creation they were the angels of God, but by revolting they both ruined themselves and became the instruments of perdition to others. As it was useful to know this much, it is clearly taught by Peter and Jude: "God," they say, "spared not the angels that sinned, but cast them down to

hell, and delivered them into chains of darkness to be reserved unto judgment" (2 Pet. ii. 4 ; Jude ver. 6). And Paul, by speaking of the elect angels, obviously draws a tacit contrast between them and reprobate angels.

17. With regard to the strife and war which Satan is said to wage with God, it must be understood with this qualification, that Satan cannot possibly do anything against the will and consent of God. For we read in the history of Job, that Satan appears in the presence of God to receive his commands, and dares not proceed to execute any enterprise until he is authorised. In the same way, when Ahab was to be deceived, he undertook to be a lying spirit in the mouth of all the prophets ; and on being commissioned by the Lord, proceeds to do so. For this reason, also, the spirit which tormented Saul is said to be an evil spirit from the Lord, because he was, as it were, the scourge by which the misdeeds of the wicked king were punished. In another place it is said that the plagues of Egypt were inflicted by God through the instrumentality of wicked angels. In conformity with these particular examples, Paul declares generally that unbelievers are blinded by God, though he had previously described it as the doing of Satan.[1] It is evident, therefore, that Satan is under the power of God, and is so ruled by his authority that he must yield obedience to it. Moreover, though we say that Satan resists God, and does works at variance with His works, we at the same time maintain that this contrariety and opposition depend on the permission of God. I now speak not of Satan's will and endeavour, but only of the result. For the disposition of the devil being wicked, he has no inclination whatever to obey the divine will, but, on the contrary, is wholly bent on contumacy and rebellion. This much, therefore, he has of himself, and his own iniquity, that he eagerly, and of set purpose, opposes God, aiming at those things which he deems most contrary to the will of God. But as God holds him bound and fettered by the curb of his power, he executes those things only for which permission has been given him, and thus, however unwilling, obeys his Creator, being forced, whenever he is required, to do Him service.

18. God thus turning the unclean spirits hither and thither at his pleasure, employs them in exercising believers by warring against them, assailing them with wiles, urging them with solicitations, pressing close upon them, disturbing, alarming, and occasionally wounding, but never conquering or oppressing them ; whereas they hold the wicked in thraldom, exercise dominion over their minds and bodies, and employ them as bond-slaves in all kinds of iniquity. Because believers are disturbed by such enemies, they are addressed in such exhortations as these; "Neither give place to the devil;" "Your adversary the devil, as a roaring lion, walketh about seeking

---

[1] Job i. 6; ii. 1; 1 Kings xxii. 20; 1 Sam. xvi. 14; xviii. 10; 2 Thess. ii. 9, 11.

whom he may devour; whom resist steadfast in the faith" (Eph. iv. 27; 1 Pet. v. 8). Paul acknowledges that he was not exempt from this species of contest when he says, that for the purpose of subduing his pride, a messenger of Satan was sent to buffet him (2 Cor. xii. 7). This trial, therefore, is common to all the children of God. But as the promise of bruising Satan's head (Gen. iii. 15) applies alike to Christ and to all his members, I deny that believers can ever be oppressed or vanquished by him. They are often, indeed, thrown into alarm, but never so thoroughly as not to recover themselves. They fall by the violence of the blows, but they get up again; they are wounded, but not mortally. In fine, they labour on through the whole course of their lives, so as ultimately to gain the victory, though they meet with occasional defeats. We know how David, through the just anger of God, was left for a time to Satan, and by his instigation numbered the people (2 Sam. xxiv. 1); nor without cause does Paul hold out a hope of pardon in case any should have become ensnared by the wiles of the devil (2 Tim. ii. 26). Accordingly, he elsewhere shows that the promise above quoted commences in this life where the struggle is carried on, and that it is completed after the struggle is ended. His words are, "The God of peace shall bruise Satan under your feet shortly" (Rom. xvi. 20). In our Head, indeed, this victory was always perfect, because the prince of the world "had nothing" in him (John xiv. 30); but in us, who are his members, it is now partially obtained, and will be perfected when we shall have put off our mortal flesh, through which we are liable to infirmity, and shall have been filled with the energy of the Holy Spirit. In this way, when the kingdom of Christ is raised up and established, that of Satan falls, as our Lord himself expresses it, "I beheld Satan as lightning fall from heaven" (Luke x. 18). By these words, he confirmed the report which the apostles gave of the efficacy of their preaching. In like manner he says, "When a strong man armed keepeth his palace, his goods are in peace. But when a stronger than he shall come upon him, and overcome him, he taketh from him all his armour wherein he trusted, and divideth his spoils" (Luke xi. 21, 22). And to this end Christ, by dying, overcame Satan, who had the power of death (Heb. ii. 14), and triumphed over all his hosts, that they might not injure the Church, which otherwise would suffer from them every moment. For (such being our weakness, and such his raging fury) how could we withstand his manifold and unintermitted assaults for any period, however short, if we did not trust to the victory of our leader? God, therefore, does not allow Satan to have dominion over the souls of believers, but only gives over to his sway the impious and unbelieving, whom he deigns not to number among his flock. For the devil is said to have undisputed possession of this world until he is dispossessed by Christ. In like manner, he is said to blind all who do not believe the Gospel, and to do his own work in the children of disobedience. And justly; for all the wicked are vessels of wrath, and, accordingly, to whom should they be subjected but to the minister of the divine vengeance? In fine, they are said to be of their father the devil.[1] For as believers are recognised to be the sons of God by bearing his image, so the wicked are properly regarded as the children of Satan, from having degenerated into his image.

19. Having above refuted that nugatory philosophy concerning the holy angels, which teaches that they are nothing but good motions or inspirations which God excites in the minds of men, we must here likewise refute those who foolishly allege that devils are nothing but bad affections or perturbations suggested by our carnal nature. The brief refutation is to be found in passages of Scripture on this subject, passages neither few nor obscure. First, when they are called unclean spirits and apostate angels (Matth. xii. 43; Jude, verse 6), who have degenerated from their original, the very terms sufficiently declare that they are not motions or affections of the mind, but truly, as they are called, minds or spirits endued with sense and intellect. In like manner, when the children of God are contrasted by John, and also by our Saviour, with the children of the devil, would not the contrast be absurd if the term devil meant nothing more than evil inspirations? And John adds still more emphatically, that the devil sinneth from the beginning (1 John iii. 8). In like manner, when Jude introduces the archangel Michael contending with the devil (Jude, verse 9), he certainly contrasts a wicked and rebellious with a good angel. To this corresponds the account given in the Book of Job, that Satan appeared in the presence of God with the holy angels. But the clearest passages of all are those which make mention of the punishment which, from the judgment of God, they already begin to feel, and are to feel more especially at the resurrection, " What have we to do with thee, Jesus, thou Son of God? art thou come hither to torment us before the time?" (Matth. viii. 29); and again, " Depart, ye cursed, into everlasting fire, prepared for the devil and his angels" (Matth. xxv. 41). Again, "If God spared not the angels that sinned, but cast them down to hell, and delivered them into chains of darkness to be reserved unto judgment," &c. (2 Act. ii. 4). How absurd the expressions, that devils are doomed to eternal punishment, that fire is prepared for them, that they are even now excruciated and tormented by the glory of Christ, if there were truly no devils at all? But as all discussion on this subject is superfluous for those who give credit to the Word of God, while little is gained by quoting Scripture to those empty speculators whom nothing but novelty can please, I believe I have already done enough for my purpose, which was to put the pious on their guard against the delirious dreams with which restless men harass themselves and the simple. The subject, however, deserved to be touched upon, lest any, by embracing that error,

1 2 Cor. iv. 4; Eph. ii. 2; Rom. ix. 22; John viii. 44; 1 John iii. 8.

Let us delight in the manifest works of God

should imagine they have no enemy, and thereby be more remiss or less cautious in resisting.

20. Meanwhile, being placed in this most beautiful theatre, let us not decline to take a pious delight in the clear and manifest works of God. For, as we have elsewhere observed, though not the chief, it is, in point of order, the first evidence of faith, to remember to which side soever we turn, that all which meets the eye is the work of God, and at the same time to meditate with pious care on the end which God had in view in creating it. Wherefore, in order that we may apprehend with true faith what it is necessary to know concerning God, it is of importance to attend to the history of the creation, as briefly recorded by Moses, and afterwards more copiously illustrated by pious writers, more especially by Basil and Ambrose. From this history we learn that God, by the power of his Word and his Spirit, created the heavens and the earth out of nothing; that thereafter he produced things inanimate and animate of every kind, arranging an innumerable variety of objects in admirable order, giving each kind its proper nature, office, place, and station; at the same time, as all things were liable to corruption, providing for the perpetuation of each single species, cherishing some by secret methods, and, as it were, from time to time instilling new vigour into them, and bestowing on others a power of continuing their race, so preventing it from perishing at their own death. Heaven and earth being thus most richly adorned, and copiously supplied with all things, like a large and splendid mansion gorgeously constructed and exquisitely furnished, at length man was made—man, by the beauty of his person and his many noble endowments, the most glorious specimen of the works of God. But, as I have no intention to give the history of creation in detail, it is sufficient to have again thus briefly touched on it in passing. I have already reminded my reader, that the best course for him is to derive his knowledge of the subject from Moses and others, who have carefully and faithfully transmitted an account of the creation.

From God's history of the creation, we find that God created the world out of nothing

Man, the most glorious specimen of the works of God.

21. It is unnecessary to dwell at length on the end that should be aimed at in considering the works of God. The subject has been in a great measure explained elsewhere, and in so far as required by our present work, may now be disposed of in a few words. Undoubtedly, were one to attempt to speak in due terms of the inestimable wisdom, power, justice, and goodness of God, in the formation of the world, no grace or splendour of diction could equal the greatness of the subject. Still there can be no doubt that the Lord would have us constantly occupied with such holy meditation, in order that, while we contemplate the immense treasures of wisdom and goodness exhibited in the creatures, as in so many mirrors, we may not only run our eye over them with a hasty, and, as it were, evanescent glance, but dwell long upon them, seriously and faithfully turn them in our minds, and every now and then bring them to recollection.

God would have us thoughtfully and greatfully behold the works of His hands.

But as the present work is of a didactic nature, we cannot fittingly enter on topics which require lengthened discourse. Therefore, in order to be compendious, let the reader understand that he has a genuine apprehension of the character of God as the Creator of the world; first, if he attends to the general rule, never thoughtlessly or obliviously to overlook the glorious perfections which God displays in his creatures; and, secondly, if he makes a self-application of what he sees, so as to fix it deeply on his heart. The former is exemplified when we consider how great the Architect must be who framed and ordered the multitude of the starry host so admirably, that it is impossible to imagine a more glorious sight, so stationing some, and fixing them to particular spots that they cannot move; giving a fixer course to others, yet setting limits to their wanderings; so tempering the movement of the whole as to measure out day and night, months, years, and seasons, and at the same time so regulating the inequality of days as to prevent everything like confusion. The former course is, moreover, exemplified when we attend to his power in sustaining the vast mass, and guiding the swift revolutions of the heavenly bodies, &c. These few examples sufficiently explain what is meant by recognising the divine perfections in the creation of the world. Were we to attempt to go over the whole subject we should never come to a conclusion, there being as many miracles of divine power, as many striking evidences of wisdom and goodness, as there are classes of objects, nay, as there are individual objects, great or small, throughout the universe.

22. The other course, which has a closer relation to faith, remains to be considered—viz. that while we observe how God has destined all things for our good and salvation, we at the same time feel his power and grace, both in ourselves and in the great blessings which he has bestowed upon us; thence stirring up ourselves to confidence in him, to invocation, praise, and love. Moreover, as I lately observed, the Lord himself, by the very order of creation, has demonstrated that he created all things for the sake of man. Nor is it unimportant to observe, that he divided the formation of the world into six days, though it had been in no respect more difficult to complete the whole work, in all its parts, in one moment than by a gradual progression. But he was pleased to display his providence and paternal care towards us in this, that before he formed man, he provided whatever he foresaw would be useful and salutary to him. How ungrateful, then, were it to doubt whether we are cared for by this most excellent Parent, who we see cared for us even before we were born! How impious were it to tremble in distrust, lest we should one day be abandoned in our necessity by that kindness which, antecedent to our existence, displayed itself in a complete supply of all good things! Moreover, Moses tells us that everything which the world contains is liberally placed at our disposal. This God certainly did not that he might delude us with an empty form of dona-

Genuine apprehension of God as Creator
1. Never thoughtless overlook God's perfect creation
2. Fix in one's heart what one sees.

The apprehension of God's goodness through His creation should lead us to confidence in Him and praise.

Nothing, therefore, which concerns our safety will ever be wanting

tion. <u>Nothing, therefore, which concerns our safety will ever be wanting.</u> To conclude, in one word; as often as we call God the Creator of heaven and earth, let us remember that the distribution of all the things which he created are in his hand and power, but that we are his sons, whom he has undertaken to nourish and bring up in allegiance to him, that we may expect the substance of all good from him alone, and have full hope that he will never suffer us to be in want of things necessary to salvation, so as to leave us dependent on some other scource; that in everything we desire we may address our prayers to him, and in every benefit we receive acknowledge his hand and give him thanks; that thus allured by his great goodness and beneficence, we may study with our whole heart to love and serve him.

CHAPTER XV.

STATE IN WHICH MAN WAS CREATED.   THE FACULTIES OF THE SOUL—
THE IMAGE OF GOD—FREE WILL—ORIGINAL RIGHTEOUSNESS.

This chapter is thus divided :—I. The necessary rules to be observed in considering
the state of man before the fall being laid down, the point first considered is the creation of the body, and the lesson taught by its being formed out of the earth, and made
alive, sec. 1.   II. The immortality of the human soul is proved by various solid arguments, sec. 2.   III. The image of God (the strongest proof of the soul's immortality)
is considered, and various absurd fancies are refuted, sec. 3.   IV. Several errors which
obscure the light of truth being dissipated, follows a philosophical and theological consideration of the faculties of the soul before the fall.

Sections.

1. A twofold knowledge of God—viz. before the fall and after it.   The former here
considered.   Particular rules or precautions to be observed in this discussion.
What we are taught by a body formed out of the dust, and tenanted by a spirit.
2. The immortality of the soul proved from, 1. The testimony of conscience.   2. The
knowledge of God.   3. The noble faculties with which it is endued.   4. Its activity
and wondrous fancies in sleep.   5. Innumerable passages of Scripture.
3. The image of God one of the strongest proofs of the immortality of the soul.
What meant by this image.   The dreams of Osiander concerning the image of
God refuted.   Whether any difference between " image " and " likeness."   Another
objection of Osiander refuted.   The image of God conspicuous in the whole Adam.
4. The image of God is in the soul.   Its nature may be learnt from its renewal by
Christ.   What comprehended under this renewal.   What the image of God in man
before the fall.   In what things it now appears.   When and where it will be seen
in perfection.
5. The dreams of the Manichees and of Servetus, as to the origin of the soul, refuted.
Also of Osiander, who denies that there is any image of God in man without essential righteousness.
6. The doctrine of philosophers as to the faculties of the soul generally discordant,
doubtful, and obscure.   The excellence of the soul described.   Only one soul in
each man.   A brief review of the opinion of philosophers as to the faculties of the
soul.   What to be thought of this opinion.
7. The division of the faculties of the soul into intellect and will, more agreeable to
Christian doctrine.
8. The power and office of the intellect and will in man before the fall.   Man's free
will.   This freedom lost by the fall—a fact unknown to philosophers.   The delusion of Pelagians and Papists.   Objection as to the fall of man when free, refuted.

1. WE have now to speak of the creation of man, not only because
of all the works of God it is the noblest, and most admirable specimen
of his justice, wisdom, and goodness, but, as we observed at the outset, we cannot clearly and properly know God unless the knowledge
of ourselves be added.   This knowledge is twofold,—relating, first,
to the condition in which we were at first created; and, secondly, to
our condition such as it began to be immediately after Adam's fall.
For it would little avail us to know how we were created if we remained

ignorant of the corruption and degradation of our nature in consequence of the fall. At present, however, we confine ourselves to a consideration of our nature in its original integrity. And, certainly, before we descend to the miserable condition into which man has fallen, it is of importance to consider what he was at first. For there is need of caution, lest we attend only to the natural ills of man, and thereby seem to ascribe them to the Author of nature; impiety deeming it a sufficient defence if it can pretend that everything vicious in it proceeded in some sense from God, and not hesitating, when accused, to plead against God, and throw the blame of its guilt upon Him. Those who would be thought to speak more reverently of the Deity catch at an excuse for their depravity from nature, not considering that they also, though more obscurely, bring a charge against God, on whom the dishonour would fall if anything vicious were proved to exist in nature. Seeing, therefore, that the flesh is continually on the alert for subterfuges, by which it imagines it can remove the blame of its own wickedness from itself to some other quarter, we must diligently guard against this depraved procedure, and accordingly treat of the calamity of the human race in such a way as may cut off every evasion, and vindicate the justice of God against all who would impugn it. We shall afterwards see, in its own place (Book II. chap. i. sec. 3), how far mankind now are from the purity originally conferred on Adam. And, first, it is to be observed, that when he was formed out of the dust of the ground a curb was laid on his pride—nothing being more absurd than that those should glory in their excellence who not only dwell in tabernacles of clay, but are themselves in part dust and ashes. But God having not only deigned to animate a vessel of clay, but to make it the habitation of an immortal spirit, Adam might well glory in the great liberality of his Maker.[1]

2. Moreover, there can be no question that man consists of a body and a soul; meaning by soul, an immortal though created essence, which is his nobler part. Sometimes he is called a spirit. But though the two terms, while they are used together, differ in their meaning, still when spirit is used by itself it is equivalent to soul, as when Solomon speaking of death says, that the spirit returns to God who gave it (Eccles. xii. 7). And Christ, in commending his spirit to the Father, and Stephen his to Christ, simply mean, that when the soul is freed from the prison-house of the body, God becomes its perpetual keeper. Those who imagine that the soul is called a spirit because it is a breath or energy divinely infused into bodies, but devoid of essence, err too grossly, as is shown both by the nature of

---

[1] On man's first original, see *Calvin against Pighius;* and on the immortality of the soul, see *Calvin's Psychopannychia* and *Instructio adv. Libertinos,* c. ix. 11, 12. It is curious to see how widely the opinion of Pliny differs from the Christian doctrine: " Omnibus a suprema die eadem quæ ante primam; hic magis a morte sensus ullus aut corpori aut animæ quam ante natales. Eadem enim vanitas in futurum etiam se propagat et in mortis quoque tempora ipsa sibi vitam mentitur."—*Plin. Hist. Nat.* lib. vii. c. 56.

[Margin notes, handwritten:]

It would do us little good to know how we were created if we did not also know of our degredation and fall.

Man consists of a body and a soul.

the thing, and the whole tenor of Scripture. It is true, indeed, that men cleaving too much to the earth are dull of apprehension, nay, being alienated from the Father of Lights, are so immersed in darkness as to imagine that they will not survive the grave ; still the light is not so completely quenched in darkness that all sense of immortality is lost. Conscience, which, distinguishing between good and evil, responds to the judgment of God, is an undoubted sign of an immortal spirit. How could motion devoid of essence penetrate to the judgment-seat of God, and under a sense of guilt strike itself with terror ? The body cannot be affected by any fear of spiritual punishment. This is competent only to the soul, which must therefore be endued with essence. Then the mere knowledge of a God sufficiently proves that souls which rise higher than the world must be immortal, it being impossible that any evanescent vigour could reach the very fountain of life. In fine, while the many noble faculties with which the human mind is endued proclaim that something divine is engraven on it, they are so many evidences of an immortal essence. For such sense as the lower animals possess goes not beyond the body, or at least not beyond the objects actually presented to it. But the swiftness with which the human mind glances from heaven to earth, scans the secrets of nature, and, after it has embraced all ages, with intellect and memory digests each in its proper order, and reads the future in the past, clearly demonstrates that there lurks in man a something separated from the body. We have intellect by which we are able to conceive of the invisible God and angels—a thing of which body is altogether incapable. We have ideas of rectitude, justice, and honesty—ideas which the bodily senses cannot reach. The seat of these ideas must therefore be a spirit. Nay, sleep itself, which stupifying the man, seems even to deprive him of life, is no obscure evidence of immortality ; not only suggesting thoughts of things which never existed, but foreboding future events. I briefly touch on topics which even profane writers describe with a more splendid eloquence. For pious readers, a simple reference is sufficient. Were not the soul some kind of essence separated from the body, Scripture would not teach [1] that we dwell in houses of clay, and at death remove from a tabernacle of flesh ; that we put off that which is corruptible, in order that, at the last day, we may finally receive according to the deeds done in the body. These, and similar passages which everywhere occur, not only clearly distinguish the soul from the body, but by giving it the name of man, intimate that it is his principal part. Again, when Paul exhorts believers to cleanse themselves from all filthiness of the flesh and the spirit, he shows that there are two parts in which the taint of sin resides. Peter, also, in calling Christ the

The mind bears the imprint of the divine hand which made it.

By mind, Calvin seems to imply intellect.

The soul is some kind of essence separated from the body.

[1] Job iv. 19 ; 2 Cor. v 4 ; 2 Pet. i. 13, 14 ; 2 Cor. v. 10 : vii. 1 ; 1 Pet. ii. 25 ; i. 9 ; ii. 11 ; Heb. xiii 17 ; 2 Cor. i. 23 ; Matth. x. 28 ; Luke xii. 5 ; Heb. xii. 9 ; Luke xvi. 22 ; 2 Cor. v. 6, 8 ; Acts xxiii. 8.

Shepherd and Bishop of souls, would have spoken absurdly if there were no souls towards which he might discharge such an office. Nor would there be any ground for what he says concerning the eternal salvation of souls, or for his injunction to purify our souls, or for his assertion that fleshly lusts war against the soul; neither could the author of the Epistle to the Hebrews say, that pastors watch as those who must give an account for our souls, if souls were devoid of essence. To the same effect Paul calls God to witness upon his soul, which could not be brought to trial before God if incapable of suffering punishment. This is still more clearly expressed by our Saviour, when he bids us fear him who, after he hath killed the body, is able also to cast into hell fire. Again, when the author of the Epistle to the Hebrews distinguishes the fathers of our flesh from God, who alone is the Father of our spirits, he could not have asserted the essence of the soul in clearer terms. Moreover, did not the soul, when freed from the fetters of the body, continue to exist, our Saviour would not have represented the soul of Lazarus as enjoying blessedness in Abraham's bosom, while, on the contrary, that of Dives was suffering dreadful torments. Paul assures us of the same thing when he says, that so long as we are present in the body we are absent from the Lord. Not to dwell on a matter as to which there is little obscurity, I will only add, that Luke mentions among the errors of the Sadducees that they believed neither angel nor spirit.

3. A strong proof of this point may be gathered from its being said, that man was created in the image of God. For though the divine glory is displayed in man's outward appearance, it cannot be doubted that the proper seat of the image is in the soul. I deny not, indeed, that external shape, in so far as it distinguishes and separates us from the lower animals, brings us nearer to God; nor will I vehemently oppose any who may choose to include under the image of God that

> " While the mute creation downward bend
> Their sight, and to their earthly mother tend,
> Man looks aloft, and with erected eyes,
> Beholds his own hereditary skies."[1]

Only let it be understood, that the image of God which is beheld or made conspicuous by these external marks, is spiritual. For Osiander (whose writings exhibit a perverse ingenuity in futile devices), extending the image of God indiscriminately as well to the body as to the soul, confounds heaven with earth. He says that the Father, the Son, and the Holy Spirit placed their image in man, because, even though Adam had stood entire, Christ would still have become man. Thus, according to him, the body which was destined for Christ was a model and type of that corporeal figure which was then formed.

---

[1] Ovid, Metam. Lib. I.—*Dryden's Translation.*

But where does he find that Christ is an image of the Spirit? I admit, indeed, that in the person of the Mediator, the glory of the whole Godhead is displayed: but how can the eternal Word, who in order precedes the Spirit, be called his image? In short, the distinction between the Son and the Spirit is destroyed when the former is represented as the image of the latter. Moreover, I should like to know in what respect Christ in the flesh in which he was clothed resembles the Holy Spirit, and by what marks or lineaments the likeness is expressed. And since the expression, " Let us make man in our own image," is used in the person of the Son also, it follows that he is the image of himself—a thing utterly absurd. Add that, according to the figment of Osiander,[1] Adam was formed after the model or type of the man Christ. Hence Christ, inasmuch as he was to be clothed with flesh, was the idea according to which Adam was formed, whereas the Scriptures teach very differently—viz. that he was formed in the image of God. There is more plausibility in the imagination of those who interpret that Adam was created in the image of God, because it was conformable to Christ, who is the only image of God ; but not even for this is there any solid foundation. The " image " and " likeness " has given rise to no small discussion ; interpreters searching without cause for a difference between the two terms, since " likeness " is merely added by way of exposition. First, we know that repetitions are common in Hebrew, which often gives two words for one thing ; and, secondly, there is no ambiguity in the thing itself, man being called the image of God because of his likeness to God. Hence there is an obvious absurdity in those who indulge in philosophical speculation as to these names, placing the Zelem, that is, the image, in the substance of the soul, and the Demuth, that is, the likeness, in its qualities, and so forth. God having determined to create man in his own image, to remove the obscurity which was in this term, adds, by way of explanation, in *his likeness*, as if he had said, that he would make man, in whom he would, as it were, image himself by means of the marks of resemblance impressed upon him. Accordingly, Moses, shortly after repeating the account, puts down the image of God twice, and makes no mention of the likeness. Osiander frivolously objects that it is not a part of the man, or the soul with its faculties, which is called the image of God, but the whole Adam, who received his name from the dust out of which he was taken. I call the objection frivolous, as all sound readers will judge. For though the whole man is called mortal, the soul is not therefore liable to death, nor when he is called a rational animal is reason or intelligence thereby attributed to the body. Hence, although the soul is not the man, there is no absurdity in holding that he is called the

---

[1] As to Osiander's absurd fancy, see Book II. cap. 12, sec. 5, sq. In Rom. viii. 3, Christ is said to have been sent by the Father in the likeness of sinful flesh, but nowhere is Adam said to have been formed in the likeness of Christ's future flesh, although Tertullian somewhere says so.

The image of God extends to everything in which the nature of man surpasses that of all other animals.

image of God in respect of the soul; though I retain the principle which I lately laid down, that the image of God extends to everything in which the nature of man surpasses that of all other species of animals. Accordingly, by this term is denoted the integrity with which Adam was endued when his intellect was clear, his affections subordinated to reason, all his senses duly regulated, and when he truly ascribed all his excellence to the admirable gifts of his Maker. And though the primary seat of the divine image was in the mind and the heart, or in the soul and its powers, there was no part even of the body in which some rays of glory did not shine. It is certain that in every part of the world some lineaments of divine glory are beheld; and hence we may infer, that when his image is placed in man, there is a kind of tacit antithesis, as it were, setting man apart from the crowd, and exalting him above all the other creatures. But it cannot be denied that the angels also were created in the likeness of God, since, as Christ declares (Matth. xxii. 30), our highest perfection will consist in being like them. But it is not without good cause that Moses commends the favour of God towards us by giving us this peculiar title, the more especially that he was only comparing man with the visible creation.

4. But our definition of the image seems not to be complete until it appears more clearly what the faculties are in which man excels, and in which he is to be regarded as a mirror of the divine glory. This, however, cannot be better known than from the remedy provided for the corruption of nature. It cannot be doubted that when Adam lost his first estate he became alienated from God. Wherefore, although we grant that the image of God was not utterly effaced and destroyed in him, it was, however, so corrupted, that any thing which remains is fearful deformity; and, therefore, our deliverance begins with that renovation which we obtain from Christ, who is, therefore, called the second Adam, because he restores us to true and substantial integrity. For although Paul, contrasting the quickening Spirit which believers receive from Christ, with the living soul which Adam was created (1 Cor. xv. 45), commends the richer measure of grace bestowed in regeneration, he does not, however, contradict the statement, that the end of regeneration is to form us anew in the image of God. Accordingly, he elsewhere shows that the new man is renewed after the image of him that created him (Col. iii. 19). To this corresponds another passage, "Put ye on the new man, who after God is created" (Eph. iv. 24). We must now see what particulars Paul comprehends under this renovation. In the first place, he mentions knowledge; and, in the second, true righteousness and holiness. Hence we infer, that at the beginning the image of God was manifested by light of intellect, rectitude of heart, and the soundness of every part. For though I admit that the forms of expression are elliptical, this principle cannot be overthrown—viz. that the leading feature in the renovation of the divine image must also have held

Image of God not totally destroyed in man, but so defaced as to be useless.

At the beginning, the image of God was manifested by the light of intellect.

the highest place in its creation.   To the same effect Paul elsewhere says that, beholding the glory of Christ with unveiled face, we are transformed into the same image.   We now see how Christ is the most perfect image of God, into which we are so renewed as to bear the image of God in knowledge, purity, righteousness, and true holiness.   This being established, the imagination of Osiander, as to bodily form, vanishes of its own accord.   As to that passage of St Paul (1 Cor. xi. 7), in which the man alone, to the express exclusion of the woman, is called the image and glory of God, it is evident, from the context, that it merely refers to civil order.   I presume it has already been sufficiently proved, that the image comprehends everything which has any relation to the spiritual and eternal life. The same thing, in different terms, is declared by St John when he says, that the light which was from the beginning, in the eternal Word of God, was the light of man (John i. 4).   His object being to extol the singular grace of God in making man excel the other animals, he at the same time shows how he was formed in the image of God, that he may separate him from the common herd, as possessing not ordinary animal existence, but one which combines with it the light of intelligence.   Therefore, as the image of God constitutes the entire excellence of human nature, as it shone in Adam before his fall, but was afterwards vitiated and almost destroyed, nothing remaining but a ruin, confused, mutilated, and tainted with impurity, so it is now partly seen in the elect, in so far as they are regenerated by the Spirit.   Its full lustre, however, will be displayed in heaven. But in order to know the particular properties in which it consists, it will be proper to treat of the faculties of the soul.   For there is no solidity in Augustine's speculation,[1] that the soul is a mirror of the Trinity, inasmuch as it comprehends within itself, intellect, will, and memory.   Nor is there probability in the opinion of those who place likeness to God in the dominion bestowed upon man, as if he only resembled God in this, that he is appointed lord and master of all things.   The likeness must be within, in himself.   It must be something which is not external to him, but is properly the internal good of the soul.

5. But before I proceed farther, it is necessary to advert to the dream of the Manichees, which Servetus has attempted in our day to revive.   Because it is said that God breathed into man's nostrils the breath of life (Gen. ii. 7), they thought that the soul was a transmission of the substance of God; as if some portion of the boundless divinity had passed into man.   It cannot take long time to show how many gross and foul absurdities this devilish error carries in its train.   For if the soul of man is a portion transmitted from the essence of God, the divine nature must not only be liable to passion and change, but also to ignorance, evil desires, infirmity, and all

[1] See Aug. *Lib. de Trin.* 10, et *Lib. de Civit. Dei,* 11.   See farther, Calvin, in *Psycho pannychia et Comment. in Genes.*

kinds of vice. There is nothing more inconstant than man, contrary movements agitating and distracting his soul. He is ever and anon deluded by want of skill, and overcome by the slightest temptations; while every one feels that the soul itself is a receptacle for all kinds of pollution. All these things must be attributed to the divine nature, if we hold that the soul is of the essence of God, or a secret influx of divinity. Who does not shudder at a thing so monstrous? Paul, indeed, quoting from Aratus, tells us we are his offspring (Acts xvii. 28); not in substance, however, but in quality, inasmuch as he has adorned us with divine endowments. Meanwhile, to lacerate the essence of the Creator, in order to assign a portion to each individual, is the height of madness. It must, therefore, be held as certain, that souls, notwithstanding of their having the divine image engraven on them, are created just as angels are. Creation, however, is not a transfusion of essence,[1] but a commencement of it out of nothing. Nor, though the spirit is given by God, and when it quits the flesh again returns to him, does it follow that it is a portion withdrawn from his essence.[2] Here, too, Osiander, carried away by his illusions, entangled himself in an impious error, by denying that the image of God could be in man without his essential righteousness; as if God were unable, by the mighty power of his Spirit, to render us conformable to himself, unless Christ were substantially transfused into us. Under whatever colour some attempt to gloss these delusions, they can never so blind the eyes of intelligent readers, as to prevent them from discerning in them a revival of Manicheism. But from the words of Paul, when treating of the removal of the image (2 Cor. iii. 18), the inference is obvious, that man was conformable to God, not by an influx of substance, but by the grace and virtue of the Spirit. He says, that by beholding the glory of Christ, we are transformed into the same image as by the Spirit of the Lord; and certainly the Spirit does not work in us so as to make us of the same substance with God.

6. It were vain to seek a definition of the soul from philosophers, not one of whom, with the exception of Plato, distinctly maintained its immortality. Others of the school of Socrates, indeed, lean the same way, but still without teaching distinctly a doctrine of which they were not fully persuaded. Plato, however, advanced still further, and regarded the soul as an image of God. Others so attach its powers and faculties to the present life, that they leave nothing external to the body. Moreover, having already shown from Scripture that the substance of the soul is incorporeal, we must now add, that though it is not properly enclosed by space, it however occupies the body as a kind of habitation, not only animating all its parts, and

---

1 The French adds, " comme si on tiroit le vin d'un vaisseau en une bouteille;"—as if one were to draw wine out of a cask into a bottle.

2 The French is, "qu'il le coupe de sa substance comme une branche d'arbre;"—that he cuts it from his substance like a branch from a tree.

rendering the organs fit and useful for their actions, but also holding the first place in regulating the conduct. This it does not merely in regard to the offices of a terrestrial life, but also in regard to the service of God. This, though not clearly seen in our corrupt state, yet the impress of its remains is seen in our very vices. For whence have men such a thirst for glory but from a sense of shame? And whence this sense of shame, but from a respect for what is honourable? Of this, the first principle and source is a consciousness that they were born to cultivate righteousness,—a consciousness akin to religion. But as man was undoubtedly created to meditate on the heavenly life, so it is certain that the knowledge of it was engraven on the soul. And, indeed, man would want the principal use of his understanding if he were unable to discern his felicity, the perfection of which consists in being united to God. Hence, the principal action of the soul is to aspire thither, and, accordingly, the more a man studies to approach to God, the more he proves himself to be endued with reason.

Though there is some plausibility in the opinion of those who maintain that man has more than one soul, namely, a sentient and a rational, yet as there is no soundness in their arguments, we must reject it, unless we would torment ourselves with things frivolous and useless. They tell us (see chap. v. sec. 4), there is a great repugnance between organic movements and the rational part of the soul. As if reason also were not at variance with herself, and her counsels sometimes conflicting with each other like hostile armies. But since this disorder results from the depravation of nature, it is erroneous to infer that there are two souls, because the faculties do not accord so harmoniously as they ought. But I leave it to philosophers to discourse more subtilely of these faculties. For the edification of the pious, a simple definition will be sufficient. I admit, indeed, that what they ingeniously teach on the subject is true, and not only pleasant, but also useful to be known; nor do I forbid any who are inclined to prosecute the study. First, I admit that there are five senses, which Plato (in Theæteto) prefers calling organs, by which all objects are brought into a common sensorium, as into a kind of receptacle:[1] Next comes the imagination (*phantasia*), which distinguishes between the objects brought into the sensorium: Next, reason, to which the general power of judgment belongs: And, lastly, intellect, which contemplates with fixed and quiet look whatever reason discursively revolves. In like manner,[2] to intellect, fancy, and reason, the three cognitive faculties of the soul, correspond

---

[1] The French is, " Et que par iceux comme par canaux, tous objects qui se presentent à la veuë, au goust, ou au flair, ou a l'attouchement 'distillent au sens commun, comme en une cisterne qui reçoit d'un coté et d'autre."—" And that by them as by channels, all objects which present themselves to the sight, taste, smell, or touch, drop into the common sensorium, as into a cistern which receives on either side."

[2] See Arist. lib. i. Ethic. cap. ult.; item, lib. vi. cap. 2.

three appetive faculties—viz. will—whose office is to choose whatever reason and intellect propound; irascibility, which seizes on what is set before it by reason and fancy; and concupiscence, which lays hold of the objects presented by sense and fancy.

Though these things are true, or at least plausible, still, as I fear they are more fitted to entangle, by their obscurity, than to assist us, I think it best to omit them. If any one chooses to distribute the powers of the mind in a different manner, calling one appetive, which, though devoid of reason, yet obeys reason, if directed from a different quarter, and another intellectual, as being by itself participant of reason, I have no great objection. Nor am I disposed to quarrel with the view, that there are three principles of action—viz. sense, intellect, and appetite. But let us rather adopt a division adapted to all capacities—a thing which certainly is not to be obtained from philosophers. For they,[1] when they would speak most plainly, divide the soul into appetite and intellect, but make both double. To the latter they sometimes give the name of *contemplative*, as being contented with mere knowledge, and having no active power—(which circumstance makes Cicero designate it by the name of intellect, *ingenii*) (De Fin. lib. v.). At other times they give it the name of *practical*, because it variously moves the will by the apprehension of good or evil. Under this class is included the art of living well and justly. The former—viz. appetite—they divide into will and concupiscence, calling it βουλησις, whenever the appetite, which they call ὁρμη, obeys the reason. But when appetite, casting off the yoke of reason, runs to intemperance, they call it παθος. Thus they always presuppose in man a reason by which he is able to guide himself aright.

7. From this method of teaching we are forced somewhat to dissent. For philosophers, being unacquainted with the corruption of nature, which is the punishment of revolt, erroneously confound two states of man which are very different from each other. Let us therefore hold, for the purpose of the present work, that the soul consists of two parts, the intellect and the will (Book II. chap. ii. sec. 2, 12)—the office of the intellect being to distinguish between objects, according as they seem deserving of being approved or disapproved; and the office of the will, to choose and follow what the intellect declares to be good, to reject and shun what it declares to be bad (Plato in Phædro). We dwell not on the subtlety of Aristotle, that the mind has no motion of itself; but that the moving power is choice, which he also terms the appetive intellect. Not to lose ourselves in superfluous questions, let it be enough to know that the intellect is to us, as it were, the guide and ruler of the soul; that the will always follows its beck, and waits for its decision, in matters of desire. For which reason Aristotle truly taught, that in the appetite there is a

The soul consists of two parts, intellect and will.

---

[1] See Themist. lib. iii De Anima, 49, De Dupl. Intellectu.

The intellect rules the will.

pursuit and rejection corresponding in some degree to affirmation and negation in the intellect (Aristot. Ethic. lib. vi. c. 2). Moreover, it will be seen in another place (Book II. c. ii. sec. 12—26), how surely the intellect governs the will. Here we only wish to observe, that the soul does not possess any faculty which may not be duly referred to one or other of these members. And in this way we comprehend sense under intellect. Others distinguish thus : They say that sense inclines to pleasure in the same way as the intellect to good ; that hence the appetite of sense becomes concupiscence and lust, while the affection of the intellect becomes will. For the term appetite, which they prefer, I use that of will, as being more common.

8. Therefore, God has provided the soul of man with intellect, by which he might discern good from evil, just from unjust, and might know what to follow or to shun, reason going before with her lamp ; whence philosophers, in reference to her directing power, have called her το ἡγεμονικον. To this he has joined will, to which choice belongs. Man excelled in these noble endowments in his primitive condition, when reason, intelligence, prudence, and judgment, not only sufficed for the government of his earthly life, but also enabled him to rise up to God and eternal happiness. Thereafter choice was added to direct the appetites and temper all the organic motions ; the will being thus perfectly submissive to the authority of reason. In this upright state, man possessed freedom of will, by which, if he chose, he was able to obtain eternal life. It were here unseasonable to introduce the question concerning the secret predestination of God, because we are not considering what might or might not happen, but what the nature of man truly was. Adam, therefore, might have stood if he chose, since it was only by his own will that he fell ; but it was because his will was pliable in either direction, and he had not received constancy to persevere, that he so easily fell. Still he had a free choice of good and evil ; and not only so, but in the mind and will there was the highest rectitude, and all the organic parts were duly framed to obedience, until man corrupted its good properties, and destroyed himself. Hence the great darkness of philosophers who have looked for a complete building in a ruin, and fit arrangement in disorder. The principle they set out with was, that man could not be a rational animal unless he had a free choice of good and evil. They also imagined that the distinction between virtue and vice was destroyed, if man did not of his own counsel arrange his life. So far well, had there been no change in man. This being unknown to them, it is not surprising that they throw everything into confusion. But those who, while they profess to be the disciples of Christ, still seek for free-will in man, notwithstanding of his being lost and drowned in spiritual destruction, labour under manifold delusion, making a heterogeneous mixture of inspired doctrine and philosophical opinions, and so erring as to both. But it will be better to leave these things to their own place (see Book II. chap. ii.). At present

Intellect the means of discerning good and evil

it is necessary only to remember, that man at his first creation, was very different from all his posterity; who, deriving their origin from him after he was corrupted, received a hereditary taint. At first every part of the soul was formed to rectitude. There was soundness of mind and freedom of will to choose the good. If any one objects that it was placed, as it were, in a slippery position, because its power was weak, I answer, that the degree conferred was sufficient to take away every excuse. For surely the Deity could not be tied down to this condition,—to make man such, that he either could not or would not sin. Such a nature might have been more excellent;[1] but to expostulate with God as if he had been bound to confer this nature on man, is more than unjust, seeing He had full right to determine how much or how little He would give. Why He did not sustain him by the virtue of perseverance is hidden in his counsel; it is ours to keep within the bounds of soberness. Man had received the power, if he had the will, but he had not the will which would have given the power; for this will would have been followed by perseverance. Still, after he had received so much, there is no excuse for his having spontaneously brought death upon himself. No necessity was laid upon God to give him more than that intermediate and even transient will, that out of man's fall he might extract materials for his own glory.

[1] See August. lib xi., super Gen. cap. vii. viii. ix., and De Corrept. et Gratia ad Valent., cap. xi.

CHAPTER XVI.

THE WORLD, CREATED BY GOD, STILL CHERISHED AND PROTECTED BY
HIM.　EACH AND ALL OF ITS PARTS GOVERNED BY HIS PROVIDENCE.

The divisions of this chapter are, I. The doctrine of the special providence of God
over all the creatures, singly and collectively, as opposed to the dreams of the Epicureans about fortune and fortuitous causes.　II. The fiction of the Sophists concerning
the omnipotence of God, and the error of philosophers, as to a confused and equivocal
government of the world, sec. 1–5.　All animals, but especially mankind, from the
peculiar superintendence exercised over them, are proofs, evidences, and examples of
the providence of God, sec. 6, 7.　III. A consideration of fate, fortune, chance, contingence, and uncertain events (on which the matter here under discussion turns).

Sections.

1. Even the wicked, under the guidance of carnal sense, acknowledge that God is the
   Creator.　The godly acknowledge not this only, but that he is a most wise and
   powerful governor and preserver of all created objects.　In so doing, they lean on
   the Word of God, some passages from which are produced.
2. Refutation of the Epicureans, who oppose fortune and fortuitous causes to Divine
   Providence, as taught in Scripture.　The sun, a bright manifestation of Divine
   Providence.
3. Figment of the Sophists as to an indolent Providence refuted.　Consideration of the
   Omnipotence as combined with the Providence of God.　Double benefit resulting
   from a proper acknowledgment of the Divine Omnipotence.　Cavils of Infidelity.
4. A definition of Providence refuting the erroneous dogmas of Philosophers.　Dreams
   of the Epicureans and Peripatetics.
5. Special Providence of God asserted and proved by arguments founded on a consideration of the Divine Justice and Mercy.　Proved also by passages of Scripture,
   relating to the sky, the earth, and animals.
6. Special Providence proved by passages relating to the human race, and the more
   especially that for its sake the world was created.
7. Special Providence proved, lastly, from examples taken from the history of the
   Israelites, of Jonah, Jacob, and from daily experience.
8. Erroneous views as to Providence refuted:—I. The sect of the Stoics. II. The fortune and chance of the Heathen.
9. How things are said to be fortuitous to us, though done by the determinate counsel
   of God.　Example.　Error of separating contingency and event from the secret,
   but just, and most wise counsel of God.　Two examples.

1. IT were cold and lifeless to represent God as a momentary
Creator, who completed his work once for all, and then left it.　Here,
especially, we must dissent from the profane, and maintain that the
presence of the divine power is conspicuous, not less in the perpetual
condition of the world than in its first creation.　For, although even
wicked men are forced, by the mere view of the earth and sky, to rise
to the Creator, yet faith has a method of its own in assigning the
whole praise of creation to God.　To this effect is the passage of the
Apostle already quoted, that by faith we understand that the worlds

were framed by the Word of God (Heb. xi. 3) ; because, without proceeding to his Providence, we cannot understand the full force of what is meant by God being the Creator, how much soever we may seem to comprehend it with our mind, and confess it with our tongue. The carnal mind, when once it has perceived the power of God in the creation, stops there, and, at the farthest, thinks and ponders on nothing else than the wisdom, power, and goodness, displayed by the Author of such a work (matters which rise spontaneously, and force themselves on the notice even of the unwilling), or on some general agency on which the power of motion depends, exercised in preserving and governing it. In short, it imagines that all things are sufficiently sustained by the energy divinely infused into them at first. But faith must penetrate deeper. After learning that there is a Creator, it must forthwith infer that he is also a Governor and Preserver, and that, not by producing a kind of general motion in the machine of the globe as well as in each of its parts, but by a special Providence sustaining, cherishing, superintending, all the things which he has made, to the very minutest, even to a sparrow. Thus David, after briefly premising that the world was created by God, immediately descends to the continual course of Providence, " By the word of the Lord were the heavens framed, and all the host of them by the breath of his mouth;" immediately adding, " The Lord looketh from heaven, he beholdeth the children of men" (Ps. xxxiii. 6, 13, &c.). He subjoins other things to the same effect. For although all do not reason so accurately, yet because it would not be credible that human affairs were superintended by God, unless he were the maker of the world, and no one could seriously believe that he is its Creator without feeling convinced that he takes care of his works ; David, with good reason, and in admirable order, leads us from the one to the other. In general, indeed, philosophers teach, and the human mind conceives, that all the parts of the world are invigorated by the secret inspiration of God. They do not, however, reach the height to which David rises, taking all the pious along with him, when he says, " These wait all upon thee, that thou mayest give them their meat in due season. That thou givest them they gather : thou openest thine hand, they are filled with good. Thou hidest thy face, they are troubled : thou takest away their breath, they die, and return to their dust. Thou sendest forth thy Spirit, they are created, and thou renewest the face of the earth" (Ps. civ. 27—30). Nay, though they subscribe to the sentiment of Paul, that in God " we live, and move, and have our being" (Acts xvii. 28), yet they are far from having a serious apprehension of the grace which he commends, because they have not the least relish for that special care in which alone the paternal favour of God is discerned.

2. That this distinction may be the more manifest, we must consider that the Providence of God, as taught in Scripture, is opposed

[marginalia, left margin:] Faith must see God, not in isolation from His Creation, but as active in it.

Though human reason may behold the glory of God, it rarely infers that loving, Fatherly care which is His nature & which makes man uneasy.

to fortune and fortuitous causes.   By an erroneous opinion prevailing
in all ages, an opinion almost universally prevailing in our own day—
viz. that all things happen fortuitously—the true doctrine of Providence has not only been obscured, but almost buried.   If one falls
among robbers, or ravenous beasts ; if a sudden gust of wind at sea
causes shipwreck ; if one is struck down by the fall of a house or a
tree ; if another, when wandering through desert paths, meets with
deliverance ; or, after being tossed by the waves, arrives in port, and
makes some wondrous hairbreadth escape from death—all these
occurrences, prosperous as well as adverse, carnal sense will attribute
to fortune.   But whoso has learned from the mouth of Christ that all
the hairs of his head are numbered (Matth. x. 30), will look farther
for the cause, and hold that all events whatsoever are governed by
the secret counsel of God.   With regard to inanimate objects, again,
we must hold that though each is possessed of its peculiar properties,
yet all of them exert their force only in so far as directed by the
immediate hand of God.   Hence they are merely instruments, into
which God constantly infuses what energy he sees meet, and turns
and converts to any purpose at his pleasure.   No created object makes
a more wonderful or glorious display than the sun.   For, besides
illuminating the whole world with its brightness, how admirably does
it foster and invigorate all animals by its heat, and fertilise the earth
by its rays, warming the seeds of grain in its lap, and thereby calling
forth the verdant blade !   This it supports, increases, and strengthens
with additional nurture, till it rises into the stalk ; and still feeds it
with perpetual moisture, till it comes into flower ; and from flower to
fruit, which it continues to ripen till it attains maturity.   In like
manner, by its warmth trees and vines bud, and put forth first their
leaves, then their blossom, then their fruit.   And the Lord, that he
might claim the entire glory of these things as his own, was pleased
that light should exist, and that the earth should be replenished with
all kinds of herbs and fruits before he made the sun.   No pious man,
therefore, will make the sun either the necessary or principal cause
of those things which existed before the creation of the sun, but only
the instrument which God employs, because he so pleases ; though he
can lay it aside, and act equally well by himself.   Again, when we
read, that at the prayer of Joshua the sun was stayed in its course
(Josh. x. 13) ; that as a favour to Hezekiah, its shadow receded ten
degrees (2 Kings xx. 11) ; by these miracles God declared that the
sun does not daily rise and set by a blind instinct of nature, but is
governed by Him in its course, that he may renew the remembrance
of his paternal favour toward us.   Nothing is more natural than for
spring, in its turn, to succeed winter, summer spring, and autumn
summer ; but in this series the variations are so great and so unequal
as to make it very apparent that every single year, month, and day,
is regulated by a new and special providence of God.

3. And truly God claims omnipotence to himself, and would have us

All events are governed by the secret counsel of God.

What we normally call the "causes" of events are really only the instruments which God uses to accomplish His purposes

God's omnipotence consists not as a vague, abstract first principle, but in the fact that He is intent on individual and special movements.

to acknowledge it,—not the vain, indolent, slumbering omnipotence which sophists feign, but vigilant, efficacious, energetic, and ever active,—not an omnipotence which may only act as a general principle of confused motion, as in ordering a stream to keep within the channel once prescribed to it, but one which is intent on individual and special movements. God is deemed omnipotent, not because he can act though he may cease or be idle, or because by a general instinct, he continues the order of nature previously appointed; but because, governing heaven and earth by his providence, he so overrules all things that nothing happens without his counsel. For when it is said in the Psalms, "He hath done whatsoever he hath pleased" (Ps. cxv. 3), the thing meant is his sure and deliberate purpose. It were insipid to interpret the Psalmist's words in philosophic fashion, to mean that God is the primary agent, because the beginning and cause of all motion. This rather is the solace of the faithful, in their adversity, that everything which they endure is by the ordination and command of God, that they are under his hand. But if the government of God thus extends to all his works, it is a childish cavil to confine it to natural influx.[1] Those, moreover, who confine the providence of God within narrow limits, as if he allowed all things to be borne along freely according to a perpetual law of nature, do not more defraud God of his glory than themselves of a most useful doctrine; for nothing were more wretched than man if he were exposed to all possible movements of the sky, the air, the earth, and the water. We may add, that by this view the singular goodness of God towards each individual is unbecomingly impaired. David exclaims (Ps. viii. 3), that infants hanging at their mothers' breasts are eloquent enough to celebrate the glory of God, because, from the very moment of their birth, they find an aliment prepared for them by heavenly care. Indeed, if we do not shut our eyes and senses to the fact, we must see that some mothers have full provision for their infants, and others almost none, according as it is the pleasure of God to nourish one child more liberally, and another more sparingly. Those who attribute due praise to the omnipotence of God, thereby derive a double benefit. He to whom heaven and earth belong, and whose nod all creatures must obey, is fully able to reward the homage which they pay to him, and they can rest secure in the protection of Him to whose control everything that could do them harm is subject, by whose authority, Satan, with all his furies and engines, is curbed as with a bridle, and on whose will everything adverse to our safety depends. In this way, and in no other, can the immoderate and superstitious fears, excited by the dangers to which we are exposed, be calmed or subdued. I say superstitious fears. For such they are, as often as the dangers threatened by any created objects inspire us with such terror, that we tremble as if they had in themselves a

Everything which befalls the faithful is by the hand and ordination of God.

God can reward and protect those who honor Him.

[1] See Hyperius in Methodo Theologiæ.

power to hurt us, or could hurt at random or by chance ; or as if we had not in God a sufficient protection against them. For example, Jeremiah forbids the children of God "to be dismayed at the signs of heaven, as the heathen are dismayed at them" (Jer. x. 2). He does not, indeed, condemn every kind of fear. But as unbelievers transfer the government of the world from God to the stars, imagining that happiness or misery depends on their decrees or presages, and not on the Divine will, the consequence is, that their fear, which ought to have reference to him only, is diverted to stars and comets. Let him, therefore, who would beware of such unbelief, always bear in mind, that there is no random power, or agency, or motion in the creatures, who are so governed by the secret counsel of God, that nothing happens but what he has knowingly and willingly decreed.[1]

4. First, then, let the reader remember that the providence we mean is not one by which the Deity, sitting idly in heaven, looks on at what is taking place in the world, but one by which he, as it were, holds the helm, and overrules all events. Hence his providence extends not less to the hand than to the eye.[2] When Abraham said to his son, *God will provide* (Gen. xxii. 8), he meant not merely to assert that the future event was foreknown to God, but to resign the management of an unknown business to the will of Him whose province it is to bring perplexed and dubious matters to a happy result. Hence it appears that providence consists in action. What many talk of bare prescience is the merest trifling. Those do not err quite so grossly who attribute government to God, but still, as I have observed, a confused and promiscuous government which consists in giving an impulse and general movement to the machine of the globe and each of its parts, but does not specially direct the action of every creature. It is impossible, however, to tolerate this error. For, according to its abettors, there is nothing in this providence, which they call universal, to prevent all the creatures from being moved contingently, or to prevent man from turning himself in this direction or in that, according to the mere freedom of his own will. In this way, they make man a partner with God,—God, by his energy, impressing man with the movement by which he can act, agreeably to the nature conferred upon him, while man voluntarily regulates his own actions. In short, their doctrine is, that the world, the affairs of men, and men themselves, are governed by the power, but not by the decree of God. I say nothing of the Epicureans (a pest with which the world has always been plagued), who dream of an inert and idle God,[3] and others, not a whit sounder, who of old feigned that God rules the

---

1 See Calvin adversus Astrolog. Judiciariam. August De Ordine, lib. ii. cap. 15.

2 The French adds, "Cest à dire, que non seulement il voit, mais aussi ordonne ce qu'il veut estre fait;"—"that is to say, he not only sees, but ordains what he wills to be done."

3 Plin. lib. ii. c. 7. "Irridendum vero, agere curam rerum humanarum, illud, quicquid est, summum. Anne tam tristi atque multiplici ministerio non pollui credamus dubitemusve?"

[Margin notes:] Providence is not a passive thing, but God at the helm, overruling all events. Providence consists in action. God's action in His universe is not abstract in nature.

upper regions of the air, but leaves the inferior to Fortune. Against such evident madness even dumb creatures lift their voice.

My intention now is, to refute an opinion which has very generally obtained—an opinion which, while it concedes to God some blind and equivocal movement, withholds what is of principal moment—viz. the disposing and directing of everything to its proper end by incomprehensible wisdom. By withholding government, it makes God the ruler of the world in name only, not in reality. For what, I ask, is meant by government, if it be not to preside so as to regulate the destiny of that over which you preside? I do not, however, totally repudiate what is said of an universal providence, provided, on the other hand, it is conceded to me that the world is governed by God, not only because he maintains the order of nature appointed by him, but because he takes a special charge of every one of his works. It is true, indeed, that each species of created objects is moved by a secret instinct of nature, as if they obeyed the eternal command of God, and spontaneously followed the course which God at first appointed. And to this we may refer our Saviour's words, that he and his Father have always been at work from the beginning (John v. 17); also the words of Paul, that "in him we live, and move, and have our being" (Acts xvii. 28), also the words of the author of the Epistle to the Hebrews, who, when wishing to prove the divinity of Christ, says, that he upholdeth "all things by the word of his power" (Heb. i. 3). But some, under pretext of the general, hide and obscure the special providence, which is so surely and clearly taught in Scripture, that it is strange how any one can bring himself to doubt of it. And, indeed, those who interpose that disguise are themselves forced to modify their doctrine, by adding that many things are done by the special care of God. This, however, they erroneously confine to particular acts. The thing to be proved, therefore, is that single events are so regulated by God, and all events so proceed from his determinate counsel, that nothing happens fortuitously.

5. Assuming that the beginning of motion belongs to God, but that all things move spontaneously or casually, according to the impulse which nature gives, the vicissitudes of day and night, summer and winter, will be the work of God; inasmuch as he, in assigning the office of each, appointed a certain law, namely, that they should always with uniform tenor observe the same course, day succeeding night, month succeeding month, and year succeeding year. But, as at one time, excessive heat, combined with drought, burns up the fields; at another time excessive rains rot the crops, while sudden devastation is produced by tempests and storms of hail, these will not be the works of God, unless in so far as rainy or fair weather, heat or cold, are produced by the concourse of the stars, and other natural causes. According to this view, there is no place left either for the paternal favour or the judgments of God. If it is said that God fully manifests his beneficence to the human race, by fur-

nishing heaven and earth with the ordinary power of producing food, the explanation is meagre and heathenish : as if tne fertility of one year were not a special blessing, the penury and dearth of another a special punishment and curse from God.   But as it would occupy too much time to enumerate all the arguments, let the authority of God himself suffice.   In the Law and the Prophets he repeatedly declares, that as often as he waters the earth with dew and rain, he manifests his favour, that by his command the heaven becomes hard as iron, the crops are destroyed by mildew and other evils, that storms and hail, in devastating the fields, are signs of sure and special vengeance. This being admitted, it is certain that not a drop of rain falls without the express command of God.   David, indeed (Ps. cxlvi. 9), extols the general providence of God in supplying food to the young ravens that cry to him, but when God himself threatens living creatures with famine, does he not plainly declare that they are all nourished by him, at one time with scanty, at another with more ample measure ? It is childish, as I have already said, to confine this to particular acts, when Christ says, without reservation, that not a sparrow falls to the ground without the will of his Father (Matth. x. 29).   Surely, if the flight of birds is regulated by the counsel of God, we must acknowledge with the prophet, that while he " dwelleth on high," he " humbleth himself to behold the things that are in heaven and in the earth " (Ps. cxiii. 5, 6).

6. But as we know that it was chiefly for the sake of mankind that the world was made, we must look to this as the end which God has in view in the government of it.   The prophet Jeremiah exclaims, " O Lord, I know that the way of man is not in himself : it is not in man that walketh to direct his steps " (Jer. x. 23).   Solomon again says, " Man's goings are of the Lord : how can a man then understand his own way ? " (Prov. xx. 24.)   Will it now be said that man is moved by God according to the bent of his nature, but that man himself gives the movement any direction he pleases ?   Were it truly so, man would have the full disposal of his own ways.   To this it will perhaps be answered, that man can do nothing without the power of God.   But the answer will not avail, since both Jeremiah and Solomon attribute to God not power only, but also election and decree.   And Solomon, in another place, elegantly rebukes the rashness of men in fixing their plans without reference to God, as if they were not led by his hand.   " The preparations of the heart in man, and the answer of the tongue, is from the Lord " (Prov. xvi. 1).   It is a strange infatuation, surely, for miserable men, who cannot even give utterance except in so far as God pleases, to begin to act without him !   Scripture, moreover, the better to show that everything done in the world is according to his decree, declares that the things which seem most fortuitous are subject to him.   For what seems more attributable to chance than the branch which falls from a tree, and kills the passing traveller ?   But the Lord sees very differently, and

[Margin note:] God provides the power for producing food in general, but expresses his judgement by the abundance of rain or lack thereof. etc., etc..

[Margin note:] What we most frequently attribute to chance is really the work of God.

declares that He delivered him into the hand of the slayer (Exod. xxi. 13). In like manner, who does not attribute the lot to the blindness of Fortune? Not so the Lord, who claims the decision for himself (Prov. xvi. 33). He says not, that by his power the lot is thrown into the lap, and taken out, but declares that the only thing which could be attributed to chance is from him. To the same effect are the words of Solomon, "The poor and the deceitful man meet together; the Lord lighteneth both their eyes" (Prov. xxix. 13). For although rich and poor are mingled together in the world, in saying that the condition of each is divinely appointed, he reminds us that God, who enlightens all, has his own eye always open, and thus exhorts the poor to patient endurance, seeing that those who are discontented with their lot endeavour to shake off a burden which God has imposed upon them. Thus, too, another prophet upbraids the profane, who ascribe it to human industry, or to fortune, that some grovel in the mire, while others rise to honour. "Promotion cometh neither from the east, nor from the west, nor from the south. But God is the judge: he putteth down one, and setteth up another" (Ps. lxxv. 6, 7). Because God cannot divest himself of the office of judge, he infers that to his secret counsel it is owing that some are elevated, while others remain without honour.

7. Nay, I affirm in general, that particular events are evidences of the special providence of God. In the wilderness, God caused a south wind to blow, and brought the people a plentiful supply of birds (Exod. xix. 13). When he desired that Jonah should be thrown into the sea, he sent forth a whirlwind. Those who deny that God holds the reins of government will say that this was contrary to ordinary practice, whereas I infer from it that no wind ever rises or rages without his special command. In no way could it be true that "he maketh the winds his messengers, and the flames of fire his ministers;" that "he maketh the clouds his chariot, and walketh upon the wings of the wind" (Ps. civ. 3, 4), did he not at pleasure drive the clouds and winds, and therein manifest the special presence of his power. In like manner, we are elsewhere taught, that whenever the sea is raised into a storm, its billows attest the special presence of God. "He commandeth and raiseth the stormy wind, which lifteth up the waves." "He maketh the storm a calm, so that the waves thereof are still" (Ps. cvii. 25, 29). He also elsewhere declares, that he had smitten the people with blasting and mildew (Amos iv. 9). Again, while man naturally possesses the power of continuing his species, God describes it as a mark of his special favour, that while some continue childless, others are blessed with offspring: for the fruit of the womb is his gift. Hence the words of Jacob to Rachel, "Am I in God's stead, who hath withheld from thee the fruit of the womb?" (Gen. xxx. 2.) To conclude in one word. Nothing in nature is more ordi-

[Margin notes:]

God cannot divest Himself of the office of judge. Hence, some are elevated while others remain without honor.

The instances in which God uses nature for his special purposes are only examples of the fact that God is always at work in His creation. Nothing out of the ordinary.

nary than that we should be nourished with bread. But the Spirit declares not only that the produce of the earth is God's special gift, but "that man doth not live by bread only" (Deut. viii. 3), because it is not mere fulness that nourishes him, but the secret blessing of God. And hence, on the other hand, he threatens to take away "the stay and the staff, the whole stay of bread, and the whole stay of water" (Is. iii. 1). Indeed, there could be no serious meaning in our prayer for daily bread, if God did not with paternal hand supply us with food. Accordingly, to convince the faithful that God, in feeding them, fulfils the office of the best of parents, the prophet reminds them that he "giveth food to all flesh" (Ps. cxxxvi. 25). In fine, when we hear on the one hand, that "the eyes of the Lord are upon the righteous, and his ears are open unto their cry," and, on the other hand, that "the face of the Lord is against them that do evil, to cut off the remembrance of them from the earth" (Ps. xxxiv. 15, 16), let us be assured that all creatures above and below are ready at his service, that he may employ them in whatever way he pleases. Hence we infer, not only that the general providence of God, continuing the order of nature, extends over the creatures, but that by his wonderful counsel they are adapted to a certain and special purpose.

8. Those who would cast obloquy on this doctrine, calumniate it as the dogma of the Stoics concerning fate. The same charge was formerly brought against Augustine (Lib. ad Bonifac. II., c. vi. et alibi.). We are unwilling to dispute about words; but we do not admit the term Fate, both because it is of the class which Paul teaches us to shun, as profane novelties (1 Tim. vi. 20), and also because it is attempted, by means of an odious term, to fix a stigma on the truth of God. But the dogma itself is falsely and maliciously imputed to us. For we do not with the Stoics imagine a necessity consisting of a perpetual chain of causes, and a kind of involved series contained in nature, but we hold that God is the disposer and ruler of all things,—that from the remotest eternity, according to his own wisdom, he decreed what he was to do, and now by his power executes what he decreed. Hence we maintain that, by his providence, not heaven and earth and inanimate creatures only, but also the counsels and wills of men are so governed as to move exactly in the course which he has destined. What, then, you will say, does nothing happen fortuitously, nothing contingently? I answer, it was a true saying of Basil the Great, that Fortune and Chance are heathen terms; the meaning of which ought not to occupy pious minds. For if all success is blessing from God, and calamity and adversity are his curse, there is no place left in human affairs for Fortune and chance. We ought also to be moved by the words of Augustine (Retract. Lib. i. cap. 1), "In my writings against the Academics," says he, "I regret having so often used the term fortune; although I intended to denote by it not some goddess, but the fortuitous issue of events in external

God uses His creation for His own special purposes

Fortune and fate are heathen terms which ought not to occupy the pious mind.

matters, whether good or evil. Hence, too, those words, Perhaps, Perchance, Fortuitously,[1] which no religion forbids us to use, though everything must be referred to Divine Providence. Nor did I omit to observe this when I said, Although, perhaps, that which is vulgarly called Fortune, is also regulated by a hidden order, and what we call Chance is nothing else than that the reason and cause of which is secret. It is true, I so spoke, but I repent of having mentioned Fortune there as I did, when I see the very bad custom which men have of saying, not as they ought to do, ' So God pleased,' but, ' So Fortune pleased.'" In short, Augustine everywhere teaches, that if anything is left to fortune, the world moves at random. And although he elsewhere declares (Quæstionum, Lib. lxxxiii.), that all things are carried on, partly by the free will of man, and partly by the Providence of God, he shortly after shows clearly enough that his meaning was, that men also are ruled by Providence, when he assumes it as a principle, that there cannot be a greater absurdity than to hold that anything is done without the ordination of God ; because it would happen at random. For which reason, he also excludes the contingency which depends on human will, maintaining a little further on, in clearer terms, that no cause must be sought for but the will of God. When he uses the term permission, the meaning which he attaches to it will best appear from a single passage (De Trinit. Lib. iii. cap. 4), where he proves that the will of God is the supreme and primary cause of all things, because nothing happens without his order or permission. He certainly does not figure God sitting idly in a watch-tower, when he chooses to permit anything. The will which he represents as interposing is, if I may so express it, active (*actualis*), and but for this could not be regarded as a cause.

9. But since our sluggish minds rest far beneath the height of Divine Providence, we must have recourse to a distinction which may assist them in rising. I say then, that though all things are ordered by the counsel and certain arrangement of God, to us, however, they are fortuitous,—not because we imagine that Fortune rules the world and mankind, and turns all things upside down at random (far be such a heartless thought from every Christian breast); but as the order, method, end, and necessity of events, are, for the most part, hidden in the counsel of God, though it is certain that they are produced by the will of God, they have the appearance of being fortuitous, such being the form under which they present themselves to us, whether considered in their own nature, or estimated according to our knowledge and judgment. Let us suppose, for example, that a merchant, after entering a forest in company with trust-worthy individuals, imprudently strays from his companions, and wanders bewildered till he falls into a den of robbers and is murdered. His death was not only foreseen by the eye of God, but had been fixed by his decree. For it is said, not that he foresaw how far the life of each

Because the councils of God are hidden from us, they often have the appearance of being due to fortune.

---

[1] Forte. Forsan. Forsitan. Fortuito.

individual should extend, but that he determined and fixed the bounds, which could not be passed (Job xiv. 5). Still, in relation, to our capacity of discernment, all these things appear fortuitous. How will the Christian feel? Though he will consider that every circumstance which occurred in that person's death was indeed in its nature fortuitous, he will have no doubt that the Providence of God overruled it and guided fortune to his own end. The same thing holds in the case of future contingencies. All future events being uncertain to us, seem in suspense as if ready to take either direction. Still, however, the impression remains seated in our hearts, that nothing will happen which the Lord has not provided. In this sense the term event is repeatedly used in Ecclesiastes, because, at the first glance, men do not penetrate to the primary cause which lies concealed. And yet, what is taught in Scripture of the secret providence of God was never so completely effaced from the human heart, as that some sparks did not always shine in the darkness. Thus the soothsayers of the Philistines, though they waver in uncertainty, attribute the adverse event partly to God and partly to chance. If the ark, say they, " goeth up by the way of his own coast to Bethshemish, then he hath done us this great evil; but if not, then we shall know that it is not his hand that smote us, it was a chance that happened to us" (1 Sam. vi. 9). Foolishly, indeed, when divination fails them they flee to fortune. Still we see them constrained, so as not to venture to regard their disaster as fortuitous. But the mode in which God, by the curb of his Providence, turns events in whatever direction he pleases, will appear from a remarkable example. At the very same moment when David was discovered in the wilderness of Maon, the Philistines make an inroad into the country, and Saul is forced to depart (1 Sam. xxiii. 26, 27). If God, in order to provide for the safety of his servant, threw this obstacle in the way of Saul, we surely cannot say, that though the Philistines took up arms contrary to human expectation, they did it by chance. What seems to us contingence, faith will recognise as the secret impulse of God. The reason is not always equally apparent, but we ought undoubtedly to hold that all the changes which take place in the world are produced by the secret agency of the hand of God. At the same time, that which God has determined, though it must come to pass, is not, however, precisely, or in its own nature, necessary. We have a familiar example in the case of our Saviour's bones. As he assumed a body similar to ours, no sane man will deny that his bones were capable of being broken, and yet it was impossible that they should be broken (John xix. 33, 36). Hence again, we see that there was good ground for the distinction which the Schoolmen made between necessity, *secundum quid*, and necessity absolute, also between the necessity of *consequent* and *of consequence*. God made the bones of his Son frangible, though he exempted them from actual fracture; and thus, in reference to the necessity of his counsel, made that impossible which might have naturally taken place.

[Handwritten marginal notes:] Both the past and the future have the appearance of being under the control of Fortune but, of course, are really in the hand of God.

Divination has shown that man has always had some awareness of the fact that God controls his destiny

CHAPTER XVII.

USE TO BE MADE OF THE DOCTRINE OF PROVIDENCE.

This chapter may be conveniently divided into two parts :—I. A general explanation is given of the doctrine of Divine Providence, in so far as conducive to the solid instruction and consolation of the godly, sect. 1, and specially sect. 2-12. First, however, those are refuted who deny that the world is governed by the secret and incomprehensible counsel of God; those also who throw the blame of all wickedness upon God, and absurdly pretend that exercises of piety are useless, sect. 2-5. Thereafter is added a holy meditation on Divine Providence, which, in the case of prosperity, is painted to the life, sect. 6-11.

II. A solution of two objections from passages of Scripture, which attribute repentance to God, and speak of something like an abrogation of his decrees.

Sections.

1. Summary of the doctrine of Divine Providence. 1. It embraces the future and the past. 2. It works by means, without means, and against means. 3. Mankind, and particularly the Church, the object of special care. 4. The mode of administration usually secret, but always just. This last point more fully considered.
2. The profane denial that the world is governed by the secret counsel of God, refuted by passages of Scripture. Salutary counsel.
3. This doctrine, as to the secret counsel of God in the government of the world, gives no countenance either to the impiety of those who throw the blame of their wickedness upon God, the petulance of those who reject means, or the error of those who neglect the duties of religion.
4. As regards future events, the doctrine of Divine Providence not inconsistent with deliberation on the part of man.
5. In regard to past events, it is absurd to argue that crimes ought not to be punished, because they are in accordance with the divine decrees. 1. The wicked resist the declared will of God. 2. They are condemned by conscience. 3. The essence and guilt of the crime is in themselves, though God uses them as instruments.
6. A holy meditation on Divine Providence. 1. All events happen by the ordination of God. 2. All things contribute to the advantage of the godly. 3. The hearts of men and all their endeavours are in the hand of God. 4. Providence watches for the safety of the righteous. 5. God has a special care of his elect.
7. Meditation on Providence continued. 6. God in various ways curbs and defeats the enemies of the Church. 7. He overrules all creatures, even Satan himself, for the good of his people.
8. Meditation on Providence continued. 8. He trains the godly to patience and moderation. Examples. Joseph, Job, and David. 9. He shakes off their lethargy, and urges them to repentance.
9. Meditation continued. 10. The right use of inferior causes explained. 11. When the godly become negligent or imprudent in the discharge of duty, Providence reminds them of their fault. 12. It condemns the iniquities of the wicked. 13. It produces a right consideration of the future, rendering the servants of God prudent, diligent, and active. 14. It causes them to resign themselves to the wisdom and omnipotence of God, and, at the same time, makes them diligent in their calling.
10. Meditation continued. 15. Though human life is beset with innumerable evils, the righteous, trusting to Divine Providence, feel perfectly secure.
11. The use of the foregoing meditation.
12. The second part of the chapter, disposing of two objections. 1. That Scripture

represents God as changing his purpose, or repenting, and that, therefore, his Providence is not fixed.   Answer to this first objection.   Proof from Scripture that God cannot repent.
13. Why repentance attributed to God.
14. Second objection, that Scripture speaks of an annulment of the divine decrees. Objection answered.   Answer confirmed by an example.

1. MOREOVER, such is the proneness of the human mind to indulge in vain subtleties, that it becomes almost impossible for those who do not see the sound and proper use of this doctrine, to avoid entangling themselves in perplexing difficulties.   It will, therefore, be proper here to advert to the end which Scripture has in view in teaching that all things are divinely ordained.   And it is to be observed, first, that the Providence of God is to be considered with reference both to the past and the future; and, secondly, that in overruling all things, it works at one time with means, at another without means, and at another against means.   Lastly, the design of God is to show that He takes care of the whole human race, but is especially vigilant in governing the Church, which he favours with a closer inspection.   Moreover, we must add, that although the paternal favour and beneficence, as well as the judicial severity of God, is often conspicuous in the whole course of his Providence, yet occasionally as the causes of events are concealed, the thought is apt to rise, that human affairs are whirled about by the blind impulse of Fortune, or our carnal nature inclines us to speak as if God were amusing himself by tossing men up and down like balls.   It is true, indeed, that if with sedate and quiet minds we were disposed to learn, the issue would at length make it manifest that the counsel of God was in accordance with the highest reason, that his purpose was either to train his people to patience, correct their depraved affections, tame their wantonness, inure them to self-denial, and arouse them from torpor ; or, on the other hand, to cast down the proud, defeat the craftiness of the ungodly, and frustrate all their schemes. How much soever causes may escape our notice, we must feel assured that they are deposited with him, and accordingly exclaim with David, "Many, O Lord my God, are thy wonderful works which thou hast done, and thy thoughts which are to us-ward : if I would declare and speak of them, they are more than can be numbered" (Ps. xl. 5). For while our adversities ought always to remind us of our sins, that the punishment may incline us to repentance, we see, moreover, how Christ declares there is something more in the secret counsel of his Father than to chastise every one as he deserves.   For he says of the man who was born blind, "Neither hath this man sinned, nor his parents : but that the works of God should be made manifest in him" (John ix. 3).   Here, where calamity takes precedence even of birth, our carnal sense murmurs as if God were unmerciful in thus afflicting those who have not offended.   But Christ declares that, provided we had eyes clear enough, we should perceive that in this spectacle the

[marginal note:] Temptation to attribute the providence of God to chance

[marginal note:] There is something more in the secret counsel of God than to chastise everyone as he deserves

glory of his Father is brightly displayed. We must use modesty, not as it were compelling God to render an account, but so revering his hidden judgments as to account his will the best of all reasons.[1] When the sky is overcast with dense clouds, and a violent tempest arises, the darkness which is presented to our eye, and the thunder which strikes our ears, and stupifies all our senses with terror, make us imagine that everything is thrown into confusion, though in the firmament itself all continues quiet and serene. In the same way, when the tumultuous aspect of human affairs unfits us for judging, we should still hold that God, in the pure light of his justice and wisdom, keeps all these commotions in due subordination, and conducts them to their proper end. And certainly in this matter many display monstrous infatuation, presuming to subject the works of God to their calculation, and discuss his secret counsels, as well as to pass a precipitate judgment on things unknown, and that with greater license than on the doings of mortal men. What can be more preposterous than to show modesty toward our equals, and choose rather to suspend our judgment than incur the blame of rashness, while we petulantly insult the hidden judgments of God, judgments which it becomes us to look up to and to revere.

2. No man, therefore, will duly and usefully ponder on the providence of God save he who recollects that he has to do with his own Maker, and the Maker of the world, and in the exercise of the humility which becomes him, manifests both fear and reverence. Hence it is, that in the present day so many dogs tear this doctrine with envenomed teeth, or, at least, assail it with their bark, refusing to give more license to God than their own reason dictates to themselves. With what petulance, too, are we assailed for not being contented with the precepts of the Law, in which the will of God is comprehended, and for maintaining that the world is governed by his secret counsels? As if our doctrine were the figment of our own brain, and were not distinctly declared by the Spirit, and repeated in innumerable forms of expression! Since some feeling of shame restrains them from daring to belch forth their blasphemies against heaven, that they may give the freer vent to their rage, they pretend to pick a quarrel with us. But if they refuse to admit that every event which happens in the world is governed by the incomprehensible counsel of God, let them explain to what effect Scripture declares, that "his judments are a great deep" (Ps. xxxvi. 7). For when Moses exclaims that the will of God "is not in heaven that thou shouldest say, Who shall go up for us to heaven, and bring it unto us? Neither is it beyond the sea that thou shouldest say, Who shall go over the sea and bring it unto us?" (Deut. xxx. 12, 13) because it was familiarly expounded in the law, it follows that there must be another hidden will which is compared to "a great deep."

---

1 "Here the words of Cicero admirably apply: Nec si ego quod tu sis sequutus, non perspicio, idcirco minus existimo te nihil sine summa ratione fecisse."

It is of this will Paul exclaims, "O! the depths of the riches of the wisdom and knowledge of God! How unsearchable are his judgments, and his ways past finding out! For who hath known the mind of the Lord, or who hath been his counsellor?" (Rom. xi. 33, 34.) It is true, indeed, that in the law and the gospel are comprehended mysteries which far transcend the measure of our sense; but since God, to enable his people to understand those mysteries which he has deigned to reveal in his word, enlightens their minds with a spirit of understanding, they are now no longer a deep, but a path in which they can walk safely—a lamp to guide their feet—a light of life—a school of clear and certain truth. But the admirable method of governing the world is justly called a deep, because, while it lies hid from us, it is to be reverently adored. Both views Moses has beautifully expressed in a few words. "Secret things," saith he, "belong unto the Lord our God, but those things which are revealed belong unto us and to our children for ever" (Deut. xxix. 29). We see how he enjoins us not only studiously to meditate on the law, but to look up with reverence to the secret Providence of God. The Book of Job also, in order to keep our minds humble, contains a description of this lofty theme. The author of the Book, after taking an ample survey of the universe, and discoursing magnificently on the works of God, at length adds, "Lo, these are parts of his ways: but how little a portion is heard of him?" (Job xxvi. 14.) For which reason he, in another passage, distinguishes between the wisdom which dwells in God, and the measure of wisdom which he has assigned to man (Job xxviii. 21, 28). After discoursing of the secrets of nature, he says that wisdom "is hid from the eyes of all living;" that "God understandeth the way thereof." Shortly after he adds, that it has been divulged that it might be investigated; for "unto man he said, Behold the fear of the Lord, that is wisdom." To this the words of Augustine refer, "As we do not know all the things which God does respecting us in the best order, we ought, with good intention, to act according to the Law, and in some things be acted upon according to the Law, his Providence being a Law immutable" (August. Quæst. Lib. lxxxiii. c. 27). Therefore, since God claims to himself the right of governing the world, a right unknown to us, let it be our law of modesty and soberness to acquiesce in his supreme authority, regarding his will as our only rule of justice, and the most perfect cause of all things,—not that absolute will, indeed, of which sophists prate, when by a profane and impious divorce, they separate his justice from his power, but that universal overruling Providence from which nothing flows that is not right, though the reasons thereof may be concealed.[1]

3. Those who have learned this modesty, will neither murmur against God for adversity in time past, nor charge him with the

---

[1] See Salvian. in Tract. de Vero Judicio et Providentia Dei. Also Bernard. De Interiore Domo, cap. 25. Also Luther in Epist. ad Fratres Antwerpienses.

blame of their own wickedness, as Homer's Agamemnon does.—'Εγω δ' ουκ αίτιός ειμι, αλλα Ζευς και μοῖρα. "*Blame not me, but Jupiter and fate.*" On the other hand, they will not, like the youth in Plautus, destroy themselves in despair, as if hurried away by the Fates. "Unstable is the condition of affairs; instead of doing as they list, men only fulfil their fate: I will hie me to a rock, and there end my fortune with my life." Nor will they, after the example of another, use the name of God as a cloak for their crimes. For in another comedy Lyconides thus expresses himself: "God was the impeller: I believe the gods wished it. Did they not wish it, it would not be done, I know." They will rather inquire and learn from Scripture what is pleasing to God, and then, under the guidance of the Spirit, endeavour to attain it. Prepared to follow whithersoever God may call, they will show by their example that nothing is more useful than the knowledge of this doctrine, which perverse men undeservedly assail, because it is sometimes wickedly abused. The profane make such a bluster with their foolish puerilities, that they almost, according to the expression, confound heaven and earth. If the Lord has marked the moment of our death, it cannot be escaped,—it is vain to toil and use precaution. Therefore, when one ventures not to travel on a road which he hears is infested by robbers; when another calls in the physician, and annoys himself with drugs, for the sake of his health; a third abstains from coarser food, that he may not injure a sickly constitution; and a fourth fears to dwell in a ruinous house; when all, in short, devise, and, with great eagerness of mind, strike out paths by which they may attain the objects of their desire; either these are all vain remedies, laid hold of to correct the will of God, or his certain decree does not fix the limits of life and death, health and sickness, peace and war, and other matters which men, according as they desire and hate, study by their own industry to secure or avoid. Nay, these trifles even infer, that the prayers of the faithful must be perverse, not to say superfluous, since they intreat the Lord to make a provision for things which he has decreed from eternity. And then, imputing whatever happens to the providence of God, they connive at the man who is known to have expressly designed it. Has an assassin slain an honest citizen? He has, say they, executed the counsel of God. Has some one committed theft or adultery? The deed having been provided and ordained by the Lord, he is the minister of his providence. Has a son waited with indifference for the death of his parent, without trying any remedy? He could not oppose God, who had so predetermined from eternity. Thus all crimes receive the name of virtues, as being in accordance with divine ordination.

4. As regards future events, Solomon easily reconciles human deliberation with divine providence. For while he derides the stupidity of those who presume to undertake anything without God, as if they were not ruled by his hand, he elsewhere thus expresses himself:

"A man's heart deviseth his way, but the Lord directeth his steps," (Prov. xvi. 9); intimating that the eternal decrees of God by no means prevent us from proceeding, under his will, to provide for ourselves, and arrange all our affairs. And the reason for this is clear. For he who has fixed the boundaries of our life, has at the same time intrusted us with the care of it, provided us with the means of preserving it, forewarned us of the dangers to which we are exposed, and supplied cautions and remedies, that we may not be overwhelmed unawares. Now, our duty is clear, namely, since the Lord has committed to us the defence of our life,—to defend it; since he offers assistance,—to use it; since he forewarns us of danger—not to rush on heedless; since he supplies remedies,—not to neglect them. But it is said, a danger that is not fatal 'll not hurt us, and one that is fatal cannot be resisted by any precaution. But what if dangers are not fatal, merely because the Lord has furnished you with the means of warding them off, and surmounting them? See how far your reasoning accords with the order of divine procedure: You infer that danger is not to be guarded against, because, if it is not fatal you shall escape without precaution; whereas the Lord enjoins you to guard against it, just because he wills it not to be fatal.[1] These insane cavillers overlook what is plainly before their eyes—viz. that the Lord has furnished men with the arts of deliberation and caution, that they may employ them in subservience to his providence, in the preservation of their life; while, on the contrary, by neglect and sloth, they bring upon themselves the evils which he has annexed to them. How comes it that a provident man, while he consults for his safety, disentangles himself from impending evils; while a foolish man, through unadvised temerity, perishes, unless it be that prudence and folly are, in either case, instruments of divine dispensation? God has been pleased to conceal from us all future events that we may prepare for them as doubtful, and cease not to apply the provided remedies until they have either been overcome, or have proved too much for all our care. Hence, I formerly observed, that the Providence of God does not interpose simply; but, by employing means, assumes, as it were, a visible form.

5. By the same class of persons, past events are referred improperly and inconsiderately to simple providence. As all contingencies whatsoever depend on it, therefore, neither thefts nor adulteries, nor murders, are perpetrated without an interposition of the divine will. Why, then, they ask, should the thief be punished for robbing him whom the Lord chose to chastise with poverty? Why should the murderer be punished for slaying him whose life the Lord had terminated? If all such persons serve the will of God, why should they be punished? I deny that they serve the will of God. For we can-

---

[1] Cic. de Fato. "Recte Chrysippus, tam futile est medicum adhibere, quam convalescere."—See Luther on Genesis xxx. 7, against those who thus abuse the doctrine of Predestination.

not say that he who is carried away by a wicked mind performs service on the order of God, when he is only following his own malignant desires. He obeys God, who, being instructed in his will, hastens in the direction in which God calls him. But how are we so instructed unless by his word? The will declared by his word is, therefore, that which we must keep in view in acting. God requires of us nothing but what he enjoins. If we design anything contrary to his precept, it is not obedience, but contumacy and transgression. But if he did not will it, we could not do it. I admit this. But do we act wickedly for the purpose of yielding obedience to him? This, assuredly, he does not command. Nay, rather we rush on, not thinking of what he wishes, but so inflamed by our own passionate lust, that, with destined purpose, we strive against him. And in this way, while acting wickedly, we serve his righteous ordination, since in his boundless wisdom he well knows how to use bad instruments for good purposes. And see how absurd this mode of arguing is. They will have it that crimes ought not to be punished in their authors, because they are not committed without the dispensation of God. I concede more—that thieves and murderers, and other evil-doers, are instruments of Divine Providence, being employed by the Lord himself to execute the judgments which he has resolved to inflict. But I deny that this forms any excuse for their misdeeds. For how? Will they implicate God in the same iniquity with themselves, or will they cloak their depravity by his righteousness? They cannot exculpate themselves, for their own conscience condemns them: they cannot charge God, since they perceive the whole wickedness in themselves, and nothing in Him save the legitimate use of their wickedness. But it is said he works by their means. And whence, I pray, the fœtid odour of a dead body, which has been uncoffined and putrified by the sun's heat? All see that it is excited by the rays of the sun, but no man therefore says that the fœtid odour is in them. In the same way, while the matter and guilt of wickedness belongs to the wicked man, why should it be thought that God contracts any impurity in using it at pleasure as his instrument? Have done, then, with that dog-like petulance which may, indeed, bay from a distance at the justice of God, but cannot reach it!

6. These calumnies, or rather frenzied dreams, will easily be dispelled by a pure and holy meditation on Divine Providence, meditation such as piety enjoins, that we may thence derive the best and sweetest fruit. The Christian, then, being most fully persuaded that all things come to pass by the dispensation of God, and that nothing happens fortuitously, will always direct his eye to him as the principal cause of events, at the same time paying due regard to inferior causes in their own place. Next, he will have no doubt that a special providence is awake for his preservation, and will not suffer anything to happen that will not turn to his good and safety. But as its business is first with men and then with the other creatures, he will feel

assured that the providence of God reigns over both. In regard to
men, good as well as bad, he will acknowledge that their counsels,
wishes, aims, and faculties, are so under his hand, that he has full
power to turn them in whatever direction, and constrain them as
often as he pleases. The fact that a special providence watches over
the safety of believers, is attested by a vast number of the clearest
promises.[1] "Cast thy burden upon the Lord, and he shall sustain
thee: he shall never suffer the righteous to be moved." "Casting
all your care upon him: for he careth for you." "He that dwelleth
in the secret place of the Most High, shall abide under the shadow
of the Almighty." "He that toucheth you, toucheth the apple of
mine eye." "We have a strong city: salvation will God appoint for
walls and bulwarks." "Can a woman forget her sucking child, that
she should not have compassion on the son of her womb? yea, they
may forget, yet will I not forget thee." Nay, the chief aim of the
historical books of Scripture is to show that the ways of his saints
are so carefully guarded by the Lord, as to prevent them even from
dashing their foot against a stone. Therefore, as we a little ago justly
exploded the opinion of those who feign a universal providence,
which does not condescend to take special care of every creature, so
it is of the highest moment that we should specially recognise this
care towards ourselves. Hence, our Saviour, after declaring that
even a sparrow falls not to the ground without the will of his Father,
immediately makes the application, that being more valuable than
many sparrows, we ought to consider that God provides more carefully for us. He even extends this so far, as to assure us that the
hairs of our head are all numbered. What more can we wish, if not
even a hair of our head can fall, save in accordance with his will? I
speak not merely of the human race in general. God having chosen
the Church for his abode, there cannot be a doubt, that in governing
it, he gives singular manifestations of his paternal care.

7. The servant of God being confirmed by these promises and
examples, will add the passages which teach that all men are under
his power, whether to conciliate their minds, or to curb their wickedness, and prevent it from doing harm. For it is the Lord who gives
us favour, not only with those who wish us well, but also in the eyes
of the Egyptians (Exod. iii. 21), in various ways defeating the malice
of our enemies. Sometimes he deprives them of all presence of mind,
so that they cannot undertake anything soundly or soberly. In this
way, he sends Satan to be a lie in the mouths of all the prophets in
order to deceive Ahab (1 Kings xxii. 22); by the counsel of the
young men he so infatuates Rehoboam, that his folly deprives him of
his kingdom (1 Kings xii. 10, 15). Sometimes when he leaves them
in possession of intellect, he so fills them with terror and dismay, that
they can neither will nor plan the execution of what they had

1 Ps. lv. 23; 1 Pet. v. 7; Ps. xci. 1; Zech. ii. 8; Isaiah xxvi. 1; xxix. 15.

designed. Sometimes, too, after permitting them to attempt what lust and rage suggested, he opportunely interrupts them in their career, and allows them not to conclude what they had begun. Thus the counsel of Ahithophel, which would have been fatal to David, was defeated before its time (2 Sam. xvii. 7, 14). Thus, for the good and safety of his people, he overrules all the creatures, even the devil himself, who, we see, durst not attempt anything against Job without his permission and command. This knowledge is necessarily followed by gratitude in prosperity, patience in adversity, and incredible security for the time to come. Everything, therefore, which turns out prosperous and according to his wish, the Christian will ascribe entirely to God, whether he has experienced his beneficence through the instrumentality of men, or been aided by inanimate creatures. For he will thus consider with himself: Certainly it was the Lord that disposed the minds of these people in my favour, attaching them to me so as to make them the instruments of his kindness. In an abundant harvest he will think that it is the Lord who listens to the heaven, that the heaven may listen to the earth, and the earth herself to her own offspring; in other cases, he will have no doubt that he owes all his prosperity to the divine blessing, and, admonished by so many circumstances, will feel it impossible to be ungrateful.

8. If anything adverse befalls him, he will forthwith raise his mind to God, whose hand is most effectual in impressing us with patience and placid moderation of mind. Had Joseph kept his thoughts fixed on the treachery of his brethren, he never could have resumed fraternal affection for them. But turning toward the Lord, he forgot the injury, and was so inclined to mildness and mercy, that he even voluntarily comforts his brethren, telling them, "Be not grieved nor angry with yourselves that ye sold me hither; for God did send me before you to preserve life." "As for you, ye thought evil against me; but God meant it unto good" (Gen. xlv. 5; l. 20). Had Job turned to the Chaldees, by whom he was plundered, he should instantly have been fired with revenge, but recognising the work of the Lord, he solaces himself with this most beautiful sentiment: "The Lord gave, and the Lord hath taken away; blessed be the name of the Lord" (Job i. 21). So when David was assailed by Shimei with stones and curses, had he immediately fixed his eyes on the man, he would have urged his people to retaliate the injury; but perceiving that he acts not without an impulse from the Lord, he rather calms them. "So let him curse," says he, "because the Lord hath said unto him, Curse David." With the same bridle he elsewhere curbs the excess of his grief, "I was dumb, I opened not my mouth, because thou didst it" (Ps. xxxix. 9). If there is no more effectual remedy for anger and impatience, he assuredly has not made little progress who has learned so to meditate on Divine Providence, as to be able always to bring his mind to this, The Lord willed it, it

must therefore be borne ; not only because it is unlawful to strive with him, but because he wills nothing that is not just and befitting. The whole comes to this. When unjustly assailed by men, over-looking their malice (which could only aggravate our grief, and whet our minds for vengeance), let us remember to ascend to God, and learn to hold it for certain that whatever an enemy wickedly com-mitted against us was permitted, and sent by his righteous dispensa-tion. Paul, in order to suppress our desire to retaliate injuries, wisely reminds us that we wrestle not with flesh and blood, but with our spiritual enemy the devil, that we may prepare for the contest (Eph. vi. 12). But to calm all the impulses of passion, the most useful consideration is, that God arms the devil, as well as all the wicked, for conflict, and sits as umpire, that he may exercise our patience. But if the disasters and miseries which press us happen without the agency of men, let us call to mind the doctrine of the Law (Deut. xxviii. 1), that all prosperity has its source in the blessing of God, that all adversity is his curse. And let us tremble at the dreadful denunciation, "And if ye will not be reformed by these things, but will walk contrary unto me ; then will I also walk con-trary unto you" (Lev. xxvi. 23, 24). These words condemn our torpor, when, according to our carnal sense, deeming that whatever happens in any way is fortuitous, we are neither animated by the kindness of God to worship him, nor by his scourge stimulated to repentance. And it is for this reason that Jeremiah (Lament. iii. 38) and Amos (Amos iii. 6) expostulated bitterly with the Jews, for not believing that good as well as evil was produced by the command of God. To the same effect are the words in Isaiah, " I form the light and create darkness : I make peace and create evil. I the Lord do all these things" (Is. xlv. 7).

9. At the same time, the Christian will not overlook inferior causes. For, while he regards those by whom he is benefited as ministers of the divine goodness, he will not, therefore, pass them by, as if their kindness deserved no gratitude, but feeling sincerely obliged to them, will willingly confess the obligation, and endeavour, according to his ability, to return it. In fine, in the blessings which he receives, he will revere and extol God as the principal author, but will also honour men as his ministers, and perceive, as is the truth, that by the will of God he is under obligation to those, by whose hand God has been pleased to show him kindness. If he sustains any loss through negli-gence or imprudence, he will, indeed, believe that it was the Lord's will it should so be, but at the same time, he will impute it to him-self. If one for whom it was his duty to care, but whom he has treated with neglect, is carried off by disease, although aware that the person had reached a limit beyond which it was impossible to pass, he will not, therefore, extenuate his fault, but, as he had neglected to do his duty faithfully towards him, will feel as if he had perished by his guilty negligence. Far less where, in the case of theft or murder,

[margin note:] Man is under obligation to those by whose hand God has been pleased to show him kindness. Loss is ones own fault.

fraud and preconceived malice have existed, will he palliate it under the pretext of Divine Providence, but in the same crime will distinctly recognise the justice of God, and the iniquity of man, as each is separately manifested. But in future events, especially, will he take account of such inferior causes. If he is not left destitute of human aid, which he can employ for his safety, he will set it down as a divine blessing; but he will not, therefore, be remiss in taking measures, or slow in employing the help of those whom he sees possessed of the means of assisting him. Regarding all the aids which the creatures can lend him, as hands offered him by the Lord, he will avail himself of them as the legitimate instruments of Divine Providence. And as he is uncertain what the result of any business in which he engages is to be (save that he knows, that in all things the Lord will provide for his good), he will zealously aim at what he deems for the best, so far as his abilities enable him. In adopting his measures, he will not be carried away by his own impressions, but will commit and resign himself to the wisdom of God, that under his guidance he may be led into the right path. However, his confidence in external aid will not be such, that the presence of it will make him feel secure, the absence of it fill him with dismay, as if he were destitute. His mind will always be fixed on the Providence of God alone, and no consideration of present circumstances will be allowed to withdraw him from the steady contemplation of it. Thus Joab, while he acknowledges that the issue of the battle is entirely in the hand of God, does not therefore become inactive, but strenuously proceeds with what belongs to his proper calling. "Be of good courage," says he, "and let us play the men for our people, and for the cities of our God; and the Lord do that which seemeth him God" (2 Sam. x. 12). The same conviction keeping us free from rashness and false confidence, will stimulate us to constant prayer, while at the same time filling our minds with good hope, it will enable us to feel secure, and bid defiance to all the dangers by which we are surrounded.

10. Here we are forcibly reminded of the inestimable felicity of a pious mind. Innumerable are the ills which beset human life, and present death in as many different forms. Not to go beyond ourselves, since the body is a receptacle, nay, the nurse, of a thousand diseases, a man cannot move without carrying along with him many forms of destruction. His life is in a manner interwoven with death. For what else can be said where heat and cold bring equal danger? Then, in what direction soever you turn, all surrounding objects not only may do harm, but almost openly threaten and seem to present immediate death. Go on board a ship, you are but a plank's breadth from death. Mount a horse, the stumbling of a foot endangers your life. Walk along the streets, every tile upon the roofs is a source of danger. If a sharp instrument is in your own hand, or that of a friend, the possible harm is manifest. All the savage beasts you see are so many beings armed for your destruction. Even within a high-walled

garden, where everything ministers to delight, a serpent will sometimes lurk. Your house, constantly exposed to fire, threatens you with poverty by day, with destruction by night. Your fields, subject to hail, mildew, drought, and other injuries, denounce barrenness, and thereby famine. I say nothing of poison, treachery, robbery, some of which beset us at home, others follow us abroad. Amid these perils, must not man be very miserable, as one who, more dead than alive, with difficulty draws an anxious and feeble breath, just as if a drawn sword were constantly suspended over his neck? It may be said that these things happen seldom, at least not always, or to all, certainly never all at once. I admit it; but since we are reminded by the example of others, that they may also happen to us, and that our life is not an exception any more than theirs, is it impossible not to fear and dread as if they were to befall us? What can you imagine more grievous than such trepidation? Add that there is something like an insult to God when it is said that man, the noblest of the creatures, stands exposed to every blind and random stroke of fortune. Here, however, we were only referring to the misery which man should feel, were he placed under the dominion of chance.

11. But when once the light of Divine Providence has illumined the believer's soul, he is relieved and set free, not only from the extreme fear and anxiety which formerly oppressed him, but from all care. For as he justly shudders at the idea of chance, so he can confidently commit himself to God. This, I say, is his comfort, that his heavenly Father so embraces all things under his power —so governs them at will by his nod—so regulates them by his wisdom, that nothing takes place save according to his appointment; that received into his favour, and intrusted to the care of his angels, neither fire, not water, nor sword, can do him harm, except in so far as God their master is pleased to permit. For thus sings the Psalm, "Surely he shall deliver thee from the snare of the fowler, and from the noisome pestilence. He shall cover thee with his feathers, and under his wings shalt thou trust; his truth shall be thy shield and buckler. Thou shalt not be afraid for the terror by night; nor for the arrow that flieth by day; nor for the pestilence that walketh in darkness; nor for the destruction that wasteth at noonday," &c. (Ps. xci. 2–6). Hence the exulting confidence of the saints, "The Lord is on my side; I will not fear: what can man do unto me? The Lord taketh my part with them that help me." "Though an host should encamp against me, my heart shall not fear." "Yea, though I walk through the valley of the shadow of death, I will fear no evil" (Ps. cxviii. 6; xxvii. 3; xxiii. 4).

How comes it, I ask, that their confidence never fails, but just that while the world apparently revolves at random, they know that God is everywhere at work, and feel assured that his work will be their safety? When assailed by the devil and wicked men, were they not confirmed by remembering and meditating on Providence, they should, of necessity, forthwith despond. But when they call to mind that the devil, and the whole train of the ungodly, are, in all directions, held in by the hand of God as with a bridle, so that they can neither conceive any mischief, nor plan what they have conceived, nor how much soever they may have planned, move a single finger to perpetrate, unless in so far as he permits, nay, unless in so far as he commands; that they are not only bound by his fetters, but are even forced to do him service,—when the godly think of all these things they have ample sources of consolation. For, as it belongs to the Lord to arm the fury of such foes, and turn and destine it at pleasure, so it is his also to determine the measure and the end, so as to prevent them from breaking loose and wantoning as they list. Supported by this conviction, Paul, who had said in one place that his journey was hindered by Satan (1 Thess. ii. 18), in another resolves, with the permission of God, to undertake it (1 Cor. xvi. 7). If he had only said that Satan was the obstacle, he might have seemed to give him too much power, as if he were able even to overturn the counsels of God; but now, when he makes God the disposer, on whose permission all journeys depend, he shows, that however Satan may contrive, he can accomplish nothing except in so far as He pleases to give the word. For the same reason, David, considering the various turns which human life undergoes as it rolls, and in a manner whirls around, betakes himself to this asylum, "My times are in thy hand" (Ps. xxxi. 15). He might have said the course of life or *time* in the singular number, but by *times* he meant to express, that how unstable soever the condition of man may be, the vicissitudes which are ever and anon taking place are under divine regulation. Hence Rezin and the king of Israel, after they had joined their forces for the destruction of Israel, and seemed torches which had been kindled to destroy and consume the land, are termed by the prophet "smoking firebrands." They could only emit a little smoke (Is. vii. 4). So Pharaoh, when he was an object of dread to all by his wealth and strength, and the multitude of his troops, is compared to the largest of beasts, while his troops are compared to fishes; and God declares that he will take both leader and army with his hooks, and drag them whither he pleases (Exod. xxix. 4). In one word, not to dwell longer on this, give heed, and you will at once perceive that ignorance of Providence is the greatest of all miseries, and the knowledge of it the highest happiness.

12. On the Providence of God, in so far as conducive to the solid instruction and consolation of believers (for, as to satisfying the curiosity of foolish men, it is a thing which cannot be done, and ought not to be attempted), enough would have been said, did not a few passages remain which seem to insinuate, contrary to the view which we have expounded, that the counsel of God is not firm and stable, but varies with the changes of sublunary affairs. First, in reference to the Providence of God, it is said that he repented of

having made man (Gen. vi. 6), and of having raised Saul to the kingdom (1 Sam. xv. 11), and that he will repent of the evil which he had resolved to inflict on his people as soon as he shall have perceived some amendment in them (Jer. xviii. 8). Secondly, his decrees are sometimes said to be annulled. He had by Jonah proclaimed to the Ninevites, "Yet forty days and Nineveh shall be overthrown," but, immediately on their repentance, he inclined to a more merciful sentence (Jonah iii. 4—10). After he had, by the mouth of Isaiah, given Hezekiah intimation of his death, he was moved by his tears and prayers to defer it (Is. xxxviii. 15; 2 Kings xx. 15). Hence many argue that God has not fixed human affairs by an eternal decree, but according to the merits of each individual, and as he deems right and just, disposes of each single year, and day, and hour. As to repentance, we must hold that it can no more exist in God than ignorance, or error, or impotence. If no man knowingly or willingly reduces himself to the necessity of repentance, we cannot attribute repentance to God without saying either that he knows not what is to happen, or that he cannot evade it, or that he rushes precipitately and inconsiderately into a resolution, and then forthwith regrets it. But so far is this from the meaning of the Holy Spirit, that in the very mention of repentance he declares that God is not influenced by any feeling of regret, that he is not a man that he should repent. And it is to be observed that, in the same chapter, both things are so conjoined, that a comparison of the passages admirably removes the appearance of contradiction. When it is said that God repented of having made Saul king, the term *change* is used figuratively. Shortly after, it is added, "The Strength of Israel will not lie nor repent; for he is not a man, that he should repent" (1 Sam. xv. 29). In these words, his immutability is plainly asserted without figure. Wherefore it is certain that, in administering human affairs, the ordination of God is perpetual, and superior to everything like repentance. That there might be no doubt of his constancy, even his enemies are forced to bear testimony to it. For Balaam, even against his will, behoved to break forth into this exclamation, "God is not a man, that he should lie; neither the son of man, that he should repent: hath he said, and shall he not do it? or hath he spoken, and shall he not make it good?" (Num. xxiii. 19).

13. What then is meant by the term repentance? The very same that is meant by the other forms of expression, by which God is described to us humanly. Because our weakness cannot reach his height, any description which we receive of him must be lowered to our capacity in order to be intelligible. And the mode of lowering is to represent him not as he really is, but as we conceive of him. Though he is incapable of every feeling of perturbation, he declares that he is angry with the wicked. Wherefore, as when we hear that God is angry, we ought not to imagine that there is any emotion in

him, but ought rather to consider the mode of speech accommodated to our sense, God appearing to us like one inflamed and irritated whenever he exercises judgment, so we ought not to imagine anything more under the term repentance than a change of action, men being wont to testify their dissatisfaction by such a change. Hence, because every change whatever among men is intended as a correction of what displeases, and the correction proceeds from repentance, the same term applied to God simply means that his procedure is changed. In the mean time, there is no inversion of his counsel or will, no change of his affection. What from eternity he had foreseen, approved, decreed, he prosecutes with unvarying uniformity, how sudden soever to the eye of man the variation may seem to be.

14. Nor does the Sacred History, while it relates that the destruction which had been proclaimed to the Ninevites was remitted, and the life of Hezekiah, after an intimation of death, prolonged, imply that the decrees of God were annulled. Those who think so labour under delusion as to the meaning of *threatenings*, which, though they affirm simply, nevertheless contain in them a tacit condition dependent on the result. Why did the Lord send Jonah to the Ninevites to predict the overthrow of their city? Why did he by Isaiah give Hezekiah intimation of his death? He might have destroyed both them and him without a message to announce the disaster. He had something else in view than to give them a warning of death, which might let them see it at a distance before it came. It was because he did not wish them destroyed but reformed, and thereby saved from destruction. When Jonah prophesies that in forty days Nineveh will be overthrown, he does it in order to prevent the overthrow. When Hezekiah is forbidden to hope for longer life, it is that he may obtain longer life. Who does not now see that, by threatenings of this kind, God wished to arouse those to repentance whom he terrified, that they might escape the judgment which their sins deserved? If this is so, the very nature of the case obliges us to supply a tacit condition in a simple denunciation. This is even confirmed by analogous cases. The Lord rebuking king Abimelech for having carried off the wife of Abraham, uses these words: "Behold, thou art but a dead man, for the woman which thou hast taken; for she is a man's wife." But, after Abimelech's excuse, he thus speaks: "Restore the man his wife, for he is a prophet, and he shall pray for thee, and thou shalt live; and if thou restore her not, know thou that thou shalt surely die, thou and all that art thine" (Gen. xx. 3, 7). You see that, by the first announcement, he makes a deep impression on his mind, that he may render him eager to give satisfaction, and that by the second he clearly explains his will. Since the other passages may be similarly explained, you must not infer from them that the Lord derogated in any respect from his former counsel, because he recalled what he had promulgated. When, by denouncing punishment, he admonishes to repentance those whom he wishes to spare, he paves

the way for his eternal decree, instead of varying it one whit either in will or in language. The only difference is, that he does not express, in so many syllables, what is easily understood. The words of Isaiah must remain true, " The Lord of hosts hath purposed, and who shall disannul it ? And his hand is stretched out, and who shall turn it back ?" (Isaiah xiv. 27.)

CHAPTER XVIII.

THE INSTRUMENTALITY OF THE WICKED EMPLOYED BY GOD, WHILE HE CONTINUES FREE FROM EVERY TAINT.[1]

This last chapter of the First Book consists of three parts: I. It having been said above that God bends all the reprobate, and even Satan himself, at his will, three objections are started. First, that this happens by the permission, not by the will of God. To this objection there is a twofold reply, the one, that angels and men, good and bad, do nothing but what is appointed by God; the second, that all movements are secretly directed to their end by the hidden inspiration of God, sec. 1, 2. II. A second objection is, that there are two contrary wills in God, if by a secret counsel he decrees what he openly prohibits by his law. This objection refuted, sec. 3. III. The third objection is, that God is made the author of all wickedness, when he is said not only to use the agency of the wicked, but also to govern their counsels and affections, and that therefore the wicked are unjustly punished. This objection refuted in the last section.

Sections.

1. The carnal mind the source of the objections which are raised against the Providence of God. A primary objection, making a distinction between the *permission* and the *will* of God, refuted. Angels and men, good and bad, do nought but what has been decreed by God. This proved by examples.
2. All hidden movements directed to their end by the unseen but righteous instigation of God. Examples, with answers to objections.
3. These objections originate in a spirit of pride and blasphemy. Objection, that there must be two contrary wills in God, refuted. Why the one simple will of God seems to us as if it were manifold.
4. Objection, that God is the author of sin, refuted by examples. Augustine's answer and admonition.

1. From other passages, in which God is said to draw or bend Satan himself, and all the reprobate, to his will, a more difficult question arises. For the carnal mind can scarcely comprehend how, when acting by their means, he contracts no taint from their impurity, nay, how, in a common operation, he is exempt from all guilt, and can justly condemn his own ministers. Hence a distinction has been invented between *doing* and *permitting*, because to many it seemed altogether inexplicable how Satan and all the wicked are so under the hand and authority of God, that he directs their malice to whatever end he pleases, and employs their iniquities to execute his judgments. The modesty of those who are thus alarmed at the appearance of absurdity might perhaps be excused, did they not endeavour to vindicate the justice of God from every semblance of stigma by defending an untruth. It seems absurd that man should be

[1] See Calvin, adv. Libertinos, cap. xv. xvi., and Augustin. de Ordine, Lib. i. and ii., where he admirably discusses the question, Whether the order of Divine Providence includes all good and evil?

blinded by the will and command of God, and yet be forthwith punished for his blindness. Hence recourse is had to the evasion that
this is done only by the permission, and not also by the will of God.
He himself, however, openly declaring that he *does* this, repudiates
the evasion. That men do nothing save at the secret instigation of
God, and do not discuss and deliberate on anything but what he has
previously decreed with himself, and brings to pass by his secret direction, is proved by numberless clear passages of Scripture. What we
formerly quoted from the Psalms, to the effect that he does whatever
pleases him, certainly extends to all the actions of men. If God is
the arbiter of peace and war, as is there said, and that without any
exception, who will venture to say that men are borne along at random with a blind impulse, while He is unconscious or quiescent ?
But the matter will be made clearer by special examples. From the
first chapter of Job we learn that Satan appears in the presence of
God to receive his orders, just as do the angels who obey spontaneously. The manner and the end are different, but still the fact
is, that he cannot attempt anything without the will of God. But
though afterwards his power to afflict the saint seems to be only a
bare permission, yet as the sentiment is true, " The Lord gave, and
the Lord hath taken away ; as it pleased the Lord, so it hath been
done," we infer that God was the author of that trial of which Satan
and wicked robbers were merely the instruments. Satan's aim is to
drive the saint to madness by despair. The Sabeans cruelly and
wickedly make a sudden incursion to rob another of his goods. Job
acknowledges that he was deprived of all his property, and brought to
poverty, because such was the pleasure of God. Therefore, whatever
men or Satan himself devise, God holds the helm, and makes all their
efforts contribute to the execution of his judgments. God wills that
the perfidious Ahab should be deceived ; the devil offers his agency
for that purpose, and is sent with a definite command to be a lying
spirit in the mouth of all the prophets (2 Kings xxii. 20). If the
blinding and infatuation of Ahab is a judgment from God, the fiction
of bare permission is at an end ; for it would be ridiculous for a judge
only to permit, and not also to decree, what he wishes to be done at
the very time that he commits the execution of it to his ministers.
The Jews purposed to destroy Christ. Pilate and the soldiers indulged them in their fury ; yet the disciples confess in solemn prayer
that all the wicked did nothing but what the hand and counsel of
God had decreed (Acts iv. 28), just as Peter had previously said in
his discourse, that Christ was delivered to death by the determinate
counsel and foreknowledge of God (Acts ii. 23); in other words, that
God, to whom all things are known from the beginning, had determined what the Jews had executed. He repeats the same thing elsewhere, " Those things, which God before had showed by the mouth
of all his prophets, that Christ should suffer, he hath so fulfilled
(Acts iii. 18). Absalom incestuously defiling his father's bed, per-

petrates a detestable crime. God, however, declares that it was his work; for the words are, "Thou didst it secretly, but I will do this thing before all Israel, and before the sun."[1] The cruelties of the Chaldeans in Judea are declared by Jeremiah to be the work of God. For which reason, Nebuchadnezzar is called the servant of God. God frequently exclaims, that by his hiss, by the clang of his trumpet, by his authority and command, the wicked are excited to war. He calls the Assyrian the rod of his anger, and the axe which he wields in his hand. The overthrow of the city, and downfall of the temple, he calls his own work. David, not murmuring against God, but acknowledging him to be a just judge, confesses that the curses of Shimei are uttered by his orders. "The Lord," says he, "has bidden him curse." Often in sacred history whatever happens is said to proceed from the Lord, as the revolt of the ten tribes, the death of Eli's sons, and very many others of a similar description. Those who have a tolerable acquaintance with the Scriptures see that, with a view to brevity, I am only producing a few out of many passages, from which it is perfectly clear that it is the merest trifling to substitute a bare permission for the providence of God, as if he sat in a watch-tower waiting for fortuitous events, his judgments meanwhile depending on the will of man.

2. With regard to secret movements, what Solomon says of the heart of a king, that it is turned hither and thither, as God sees meet, certainly applies to the whole human race, and has the same force as if he had said, that whatever we conceive in our minds is directed to its end by the secret inspiration of God. And certainly, did he not work internally in the minds of men, it could not have been properly said, that he takes away the lip from the true, and prudence from the aged—takes away the heart from the princes of the earth, that they wander through devious paths. To the same effect, we often read that men are intimidated when He fills their hearts with terror. Thus David left the camp of Saul while none knew of it, because a sleep from God had fallen upon all. But nothing can be clearer than the many passages which declare, that he blinds the minds of men, and smites them with giddiness, intoxicates them with a spirit of stupor, renders them infatuated, and hardens their hearts. Even these expressions many would confine to permission, as if, by deserting the reprobate, he allowed them to be blinded by Satan. But since the Holy Spirit distinctly says, that the blindness and infatuation are inflicted by the just judgment of God, the solution is altogether inadmissible. He is said to have hardened the heart of Pharaoh, to have hardened it yet more, and confirmed it. Some evade these forms of expression by a silly cavil, because Pharaoh is elsewhere said to have hardened his own heart, thus making his will the cause of hardening it; as if the two things did not perfectly agree with each other, though

[1] 2 Sam. xii. 12; Jer. l. 25; Is. v. 26; x. 5: xix. 25; 2 Sam. xvi 10; 1 Kings xi. 31; 1 Sam. ii. 34.

in different senses—viz. that man, though acted upon by God, at the same time also acts. But I retort the objection on those who make it. If to harden means only bare permission, the contumacy will not properly belong to Pharaoh. Now, could anything be more feeble and insipid than to interpret as if Pharaoh had only allowed himself to be hardened? We may add, that Scripture cuts off all handle for such cavils: "I," saith the Lord, "will harden his heart" (Exod. iv. 21). So also, Moses says of the inhabitants of the land of Caanan, that they went forth to battle because the Lord had hardened their hearts (Josh. xi. 20). The same thing is repeated by another prophet, "He turned their hearts to hate his people" (Psalm cv. 25). In like manner, in Isaiah, he says of the Assyrian, "I will send him against a hypocritical nation, and against the people of my wrath will I give him a charge to take the spoil, and to take the prey" (Isaiah x. 6); not that he intends to teach wicked and obstinate man to obey spontaneously, but because he bends them to execute his judgments, just as if they carried their orders engraven on their minds. And hence it appears that they are impelled by the sure appointment of God. I admit, indeed, that God often acts in the reprobate by interposing the agency of Satan; but in such a manner, that Satan himself performs his part, just as he is impelled, and succeeds only in so far as he is permitted. The evil spirit that troubled Saul is said to be from the Lord (1 Sam. xvi. 14), to intimate that Saul's madness was a just punishment from God. Satan is also said to blind the minds of those who believe not (2 Cor. iv. 4). But how so, unless that a spirit of error is sent from God himself, making those who refuse to obey the truth to believe a lie? According to the former view, it is said, "If the prophet be deceived when he hath spoken a thing, I the Lord have deceived that prophet" (Ezek. xiv. 9). According to the latter view, he is said to have given men over to a reprobate mind (Rom. i. 28), because he is the special author of his own just vengeance; whereas Satan is only his minister (see Calv. in Ps. cxli. 4). But as in the Second Book (chap. iv. sec. 3, 4), in discussing the question of man's freedom, this subject will again be considered, the little that has now been said seems to be all that the occasion requires. The sum of the whole is this,—since the will of God is said to be the cause of all things, all the counsels and actions of men must be held to be governed by his providence; so that he not only exerts his power in the elect, who are guided by the Holy Spirit, but also forces the reprobate to do him service.

3. As I have hitherto stated only what is plainly and unambiguously taught in Scripture, those who hesitate not to stigmatise what is thus taught by the sacred oracles, had better beware what kind of censure they employ. If, under a pretence of ignorance, they seek the praise of modesty, what greater arrogance can be imagined than to utter one word in opposition to the authority of God—to say, for instance, "I think otherwise,"—I would not have this subject

touched"? But if they openly blaspheme, what will they gain by assaulting heaven? Such petulance, indeed, is not new. In all ages there have been wicked and profane men, who rabidly assailed this branch of doctrine. But what the Spirit declared of old by the mouth of David (Ps. li. 6), they will feel by experience to be true—God will overcome when he is judged. David indirectly rebukes the infatuation of those whose license is so unbridled, that from their grovelling spot of earth they not only plead against God, but arrogate to themselves the right of censuring him. At the same time, he briefly intimates that the blasphemies which they belch forth against heaven, instead of reaching God, only illustrate his justice, when the mists of their calumnies are dispersed. Even our faith, because founded on the sacred word of God, is superior to the whole world, and is able from its height to look down upon such mists.

Their first objection—that if nothing happens without the will of God, he must have two contrary wills, decreeing by a secret counsel what he has openly forbidden in his law—is easily disposed of. But before I reply to it, I would again remind my readers that this cavil is directed not against me, but against the Holy Spirit, who certainly dictated this confession to that holy man Job, "The Lord gave, and the Lord hath taken away," when, after being plundered by robbers, he acknowledges that their injustice and mischief was a just chastisement from God. And what says the Scripture elsewhere? The sons of Eli "hearkened not unto the voice of their father, because the Lord would slay them" (1 Sam. ii. 25). Another prophet also exclaims, "Our God is in the heavens: he hath done whatsoever he hath pleased" (Ps. cxv. 3). I have already shown clearly enough that God is the author of all those things which, according to these objectors, happen only by his inactive permission. He testifies that he creates light and darkness, forms good and evil (Is. xlv. 7); that no evil happens which he hath not done (Amos iii. 6). Let them tell me whether God exercises his judgments willingly or unwillingly. As Moses teaches that he who is accidentally killed by the blow of an axe, is delivered by God into the hand of him who smites him (Deut. xix. 5), so the Gospel, by the mouth of Luke, declares, that Herod and Pontius Pilate conspired "to do whatsoever thy hand and thy counsel determined before to be done" (Acts iv. 28). And, in truth, if Christ was not crucified by the will of God, where is our redemption? Still, however, the will of God is not at variance with itself. It undergoes no change. He makes no pretence of not willing what he wills, but while in himself the will is one and undivided, to us it appears manifold, because, from the feebleness of our intellect, we cannot comprehend how, though after a different manner, he wills and wills not the very same thing. Paul terms the calling of the Gentiles a hidden mystery, and shortly after adds, that therein was manifested the manifold wisdom of God (Eph. iii. 10). Since, on account of the dulness of our sense, the wisdom of God seems manifold (or, as an old interpreter rendered it, multiform), are we, therefore, to dream of some variation in God, as if he either changed his counsel, or disagreed with himself? Nay, when we cannot comprehend how God can will that to be done which he forbids us to do, let us call to mind our imbecility, and remember that the light in which he dwells is not without cause termed inaccessible (1 Tim. vi. 16), because shrouded in darkness. Hence, all pious and modest men will readily acquiesce in the sentiment of Augustine: "Man sometimes with a good-will wishes something which God does not will, as when a good son wishes his father to live, while God wills him to die. Again, it may happen that man with a bad will wishes what God wills righteously, as when a bad son wishes his father to die, and God also wills it. The former wishes what God wills not, the latter wishes what God also wills. And yet the filial affection of the former is more consonant to the good-will of God, though willing differently, than the unnatural affection of the latter, though willing the same thing; so much does approbation or condemnation depend on what it is befitting in man, and what in God to will, and to what end the will of each has respect. For the things which God rightly wills, he accomplishes by the evil wills of bad men" (*August. Enchirid. ad Laurent.* cap. 101). He had said a little before (cap. 100), that the apostate angels, by their revolt, and all the reprobate, as far as they themselves were concerned, did what God willed not; but, in regard to his omnipotence, it was impossible for them to do so; for, while they act against the will of God, his will is accomplished in them. Hence he exclaims, "Great is the work of God, exquisite in all he wills! so that, in a manner wondrous and ineffable, that is not done without his will which is done contrary to it, because it could not be done if he did not permit; nor does he permit it unwillingly, but willingly; nor would He who is good permit evil to be done, were he not omnipotent to bring good out of evil" (*Augustin. in* Ps. cxi. 2).

4. In the same way is solved, or rather spontaneously vanishes, another objection—viz. If God not only uses the agency of the wicked, but also governs their counsels and affections, he is the author of all their sins; and therefore men, in executing what God has decreed, are unjustly condemned, because they are obeying his will. Here *will* is improperly confounded with *precept*, though it is obvious, from innumerable examples, that there is the greatest difference between them.[1] When Absalom defiled his father's bed, though God was pleased thus to avenge the adultery of David, he did not therefore enjoin an abandoned son to commit incest, unless, perhaps, in respect of David, as David himself says of Shimei's

---

[1] The French is, "Car ils meslent perversement le commandement de Dieu avec son vouloir secret, veu qu'il appert par exemples infinis qu'il y a bien longue distance et diversité de l'un à l'autre;" for they perversely confound the command of God with his secret will, though it appears, by an infinite number of examples, that there is a great distance and diversity between them.

curses. For, while he confesses that Shimei acts by the order of God, he by no means commends the obedience, as if that petulant dog had been yielding obedience to a divine command; but, recognising in his tongue the scourge of God, he submits patiently to be chastised. Thus we must hold, that while by means of the wicked God performs what he had secretly decreed, they are not excusable as if they were obeying his precept, which of set purpose they violate according to their lust.

How these things, which men do perversely, are of God, and are ruled by his secret providence, is strikingly shown in the election of king Jeroboam (1 Kings xii. 20), in which the rashness and infatuation of the people are severely condemned for perverting the order sanctioned by God, and perfidiously revolting from the family of David. And yet we know it was God's will that Jeroboam should be anointed. Hence the apparent contradiction in the words of Hosea (Hosea viii. 4; xiii. 11), because, while God complained that that kingdom was erected without his knowledge, and against his will, he elsewhere declares, that he had given king Jeroboam in his anger. How shall we reconcile the two things,—that Jeroboam's reign was not of God, and yet God appointed him king? In this way: The people could not revolt from the family of David without shaking off a yoke divinely imposed on them, and yet God himself was not deprived of the power of thus punishing the ingratitude of Solomon. We therefore see how God, while not willing treachery, with another view justly wills the revolt; and hence Jeroboam, by unexpectedly receiving the sacred unction, is urged to aspire to the kingdom. For this reason, the sacred history says, that God stirred up an enemy to deprive the nos of Solomon of part of the kingdom (1 Kings xi. 23). Let the reader diligently ponder both points: how, as it was the will of God that the people should be ruled by the hand of one king, their being rent into two parties was contrary to his will; and yet how this same will originated the revolt. For certainly when Jeroboam, who had no such thought, is urged by the prophet verbally, and by the oil of unction, to hope for the kingdom, the thing was not done without the knowledge or against the will of God, who had expressly commanded it; and yet the rebellion of the people is justly condemned, because it was against the will of God that they revolted from the posterity of David. For this reason, it is afterwards added, that when Rehoboam haughtily spurned the prayers of the people, " the cause was from the Lord, that he might perform his saying, which the Lord spake by Ahijah" (1 Kings xii. 15). See how sacred unity was violated against the will of God, while, at the same time, with his will the ten tribes were alienated from the son of Solomon. To this might be added another similar example—viz. the murder of the sons of Ahab, and the extermination of his whole progeny by the consent, or rather the active agency, of the people. Jehu says truly, " There shall fall unto the earth nothing of the word

of the Lord, which the Lord spake concerning the house of Ahab :
for the Lord hath done that which he spake by his servant Elijah"
(2 Kings x. 10). And yet, with good reason, he upbraids the citizens
of Samaria for having lent their assistance. " Ye be righteous : behold, I conspired against my master, and slew him, but who slew all
these ? "

If I mistake not, I have already shown clearly how the same act
at once betrays the guilt of man, and manifests the righteousness of
God.   Modest minds will always be satisfied with Augustine's
answer, " Since the Father delivered up the Son, Christ his own body,
and Judas his Master, how in such a case is God just, and man guilty,
but just because in the one act which they did, the reasons for which
they did it are different ?" (*August. Ep.* 48, *ad Vincentium.*)   If
any are not perfectly satisfied with this explanation—viz. that there
is no concurrence between God and man, when by His righteous impulse man does what he ought not to do—let them give heed to what
Augustine elsewhere observes : " Who can refrain from trembling at
those judgments when God does according to his pleasure even in the
hearts of the wicked, at the same time rendering to them according
to their deeds ?" (*De Grat. et Lib. Arbit. ad Valent.* c. 20.)   And
certainly, in regard to the treachery of Judas, there is just as little
ground to throw the blame of the crime upon God, because He was
both pleased that his Son should be delivered up to death, and did
deliver him, as to ascribe to Judas the praise of our redemption.
Hence Augustine, in another place, truly observes, that when God
makes his scrutiny, he looks not to what men could do, or to what
they did, but to what they wished to do, thus taking account of their
will and purpose.   Those to whom this seems harsh had better consider how far their captiousness is entitled to any toleration, while,
on the ground of its exceeding their capacity, they reject a matter
which is clearly taught by Scripture, and complain of the enunciation
of truths, which, if they were not useful to be known, God never
would have ordered his prophets and apostles to teach.   Our true
wisdom is to embrace with meek docility, and without reservation,
whatever the Holy Scriptures have delivered.   Those who indulge
their petulance, a petulance manifestly directed against God, are un-
deserving of a longer refutation.

END OF THE FIRST BOOK.

INSTITUTES

OF

THE CHRISTIAN RELIGION.

BOOK SECOND.

OF THE KNOWLEDGE OF GOD THE REDEEMER,
IN CHRIST, AS FIRST MANIFESTED
TO THE FATHERS, UNDER THE LAW, AND
THEREAFTER TO US UNDER THE GOSPEL.

SUBJECT.

THE First Part of the Apostles' Creed—viz. the knowledge of God the Creator, being disposed of, we now come to the Second Part, which relates to the knowledge of God as a Redeemer in Christ. The subjects treated of accordingly are, *first*, the Occasion of Redemption—viz. Adam's fall; and, *secondly*, Redemption itself. The first five chapters are devoted to the former subject, and the remainder to the latter.

Under the Occasion of Redemption, the Fall is considered not only in a general way, but also specially in its effects. Hence the first four chapters treat of original sin, free will, the corruption of human nature, and the operation of God in the heart. The fifth chapter contains a refutation of the arguments usually urged in support of free will.

The subject of redemption may be reduced to five particular heads:—

I. The character of him in whom salvation for lost man must be sought, Chap. VI.

II. How he was manifested to the world, namely, in a twofold manner First, under the Law. Here the Decalogue is expounded, and some other points relating to the law discussed, Chap. VII. and VIII. Secondly, under the Gospel. Here the resemblance and difference of the two dispensations are considered, Chap. IX. X. XI.

III. What kind of person Christ was, and behoved to be, in order to perform the office of Mediator—viz. God and man in one person, Chap. XII. XIII. XIV.

IV. For what end he was sent into the world by the Father. Here Christ's prophetical, kingly, and priestly offices are considered, Chap. XV.

V. In what way, or by what successive steps, Christ fulfilled the office of our Redeemer, Chap. XVI. Here are considered his crucifixion, death, burial, descent to hell, resurrection, ascension to heaven, and seat at the right hand of the Father, together with the practical use of the whole doctrine. Chapter XVII. contains an answer to the question, Whether Christ is properly said to have merited the grace of God for us.

INSTITUTES

OF

THE CHRISTIAN RELIGION.

BOOK SECOND.

OF THE KNOWLEDGE OF GOD THE REDEEMER, IN CHRIST, AS FIRST MANIFESTED TO THE FATHERS, UNDER THE LAW, AND THEREAFTER TO US UNDER THE GOSPEL.

CHAPTER I.

THROUGH THE FALL AND REVOLT OF ADAM, THE WHOLE HUMAN RACE MADE ACCURSED AND DEGENERATE. OF ORIGINAL SIN.

I. How necessary the knowledge of ourselves is, its nature, the danger of mistake, its leading parts, sec. 1, 2, 3. II. The causes of Adam's fearful fall, sec. 4. III. The effects of the fall extending to Adam's posterity, and all the creatures, sec. 5, to the end of the Chapter, where the nature, propagation, and effect of original sin are considered.

Sections.

1. The knowledge of ourselves most necessary. To use it properly we must be divested of pride, and clothed with true humility, which will dispose us to consider our fall, and embrace the mercy of God in Christ.
2. Though there is plausibility in the sentiment which stimulates us to self-admiration, the only sound sentiment is that which inclines us to true humbleness of mind. Pretexts for pride. The miserable vanity of sinful man.
3. Different views taken by carnal wisdom and by conscience, which appeals to divine justice as its standard. The knowledge of ourselves, consisting of two parts, the former of which having already been discussed, the latter is here considered.
4. In considering this latter part, two points to be considered : 1. How it happened that Adam involved himself and the whole human race in this dreadful calamity. This the result not of sensual intemperance, but of infidelity (the source of other heinous sins), which led to revolt from God, from whom all true happiness must

be derived. An enumeration of the other sins produced by the infidelity of the first man.

5. The second point to be considered is, the extent to which the contagious influence of the fall extends. It extends, 1. To all the creatures, though unoffending ; and, 2. To the whole posterity of Adam. Hence hereditary corruption, or original sin, and the depravation of a nature which was previously pure and good. This depravation communicated to the whole posterity of Adam, but not in the way supposed by the Pelagians and Celestians.

6. Depravation communicated not merely by imitation, but by propagation. This proved, 1. From the contrast drawn between Adam and Christ. Confirmation from passages of Scripture ; 2. From the general declaration that we are the children of wrath.

7. Objection, that if Adam's sin is propagated to his posterity, the soul must be derived by transmission. Answer. Another objection—viz. that children cannot derive corruption from pious parents. Answer.

8. Definition of original sin. Two parts in the definition. Exposition of the latter part. Original sin exposes us to the wrath of God. It also produces in us the works of the flesh. Other definitions considered.

9. Exposition of the former part of the definition—viz. that hereditary depravity extends to all the faculties of the soul.

10. From the exposition of both parts of the definition it follows that God is not the author of sin, the whole human race being corrupted by an inherent viciousness.

11. This, however, is not from nature, but is an adventitious quality. Accordingly, the dream of the Manichees as to two principles vanishes.

1. It was not without reason that the ancient proverb so strongly recommended to man the knowledge of himself. For if it is deemed disgraceful to be ignorant of things pertaining to the business of life, much more disgraceful is self-ignorance, in consequence of which we miserably deceive ourselves in matters of the highest moment, and so walk blindfold. But the more useful the precept is, the more careful we must be not to use it preposterously, as we see certain philosophers have done. For they, when exhorting man to know himself, state the motive to be, that he may not be ignorant of his own excellence and dignity. They wish him to see nothing in himself but what will fill him with vain confidence, and inflate him with pride. But self-knowledge consists in this, *first*, When reflecting on what God gave us at our creation, and still continues graciously to give, we perceive how great the excellence of our nature would have been had its integrity remained, and, at the same time, remember that we have nothing of our own, but depend entirely on God, from whom we hold at pleasure whatever he has seen it meet to bestow ; *secondly*, When viewing our miserable condition since Adam's fall, all confidence and boasting are overthrown, we blush for shame, and feel truly humble. For as God at first formed us in his own image, that he might elevate our minds to the pursuit of virtue, and the contemplation of eternal life, so to prevent us from heartlessly burying those noble qualities which distinguish us from the lower animals, it is of importance to know that we were endued with reason and intelligence, in order that we might cultivate a holy and honourable life, and regard a blessed immortality as our destined aim. At the same time, it is impossible to think of our primeval dignity without being immediately reminded of the sad spectacle of our ignominy and corruption, ever since we

fell from our original in the person of our first parent. In this way, we feel dissatisfied with ourselves, and become truly humble, while we are inflamed with new desires to seek after God, in whom each may regain those good qualities of which all are found to be utterly destitute.

2. In examining ourselves, the search which divine truth enjoins, and the knowledge which it demands, are such as may indispose us to everything like confidence in our own powers, leave us devoid of all means of boasting, and so incline us to submission. This is the course which we must follow, if we would attain to the true goal, both in speculation and practice. I am not unaware how much more plausible the view is, which invites us rather to ponder on our good qualities than to contemplate what must overwhelm us with shame—our miserable destitution and ignominy. There is nothing more acceptable to the human mind than flattery, and, accordingly, when told that its endowments are of a high order, it is apt to be excessively credulous. Hence it is not strange that the greater part of mankind have erred so egregiously in this matter. Owing to the innate self-love by which all are blinded, we most willingly persuade ourselves that we do not possess a single quality which is deserving of hatred; and hence, independent of any countenance from without, general credit is given to the very foolish idea, that man is perfectly sufficient of himself for all the purposes of a good and happy life. If any are disposed to think more modestly, and concede somewhat to God, that they may not seem to arrogate everything as their own, still, in making the division, they apportion matters so that the chief ground of confidence and boasting always remains with themselves. Then, if a discourse is pronounced which flatters the pride spontaneously springing up in man's inmost heart, nothing seems more delightful. Accordingly, in every age, he who is most forward in extolling the excellence of human nature, is received with the loudest applause. But be this heralding of human excellence what it may, by teaching man to rest in himself, it does nothing more than fascinate by its sweetness, and, at the same time, so delude as to drown in perdition all who assent to it. For what avails it to proceed in vain confidence, to deliberate, resolve, plan, and attempt what we deem pertinent to the purpose, and, at the very outset, prove deficient and destitute both of sound intelligence and true virtue, though we still confidently persist till we rush headlong on destruction? But this is the best that can happen to those who put confidence in their own powers. Whosoever, therefore, gives heed to those teachers who merely employ us in contemplating our good qualities, so far from making progress in self-knowledge, will be plunged into the most pernicious ignorance.

3. While revealed truth concurs with the general consent of mankind in teaching that the second part of wisdom consists in self-knowledge, they differ greatly as to the method by which this

People would much rather near their good qualities extolled than to seem themselves as they really are.

This leads to the most pernicious self-ignorance

knowledge is to be acquired. In the judgment of the flesh man deems his self-knowledge complete, when, with overweening confidence in his own intelligence and integrity, he takes courage, and spurs himself on to virtuous deeds, and when, declaring war upon vice, he uses his utmost endeavour to attain to the honourable and the fair. But he who tries himself by the standard of divine justice, finds nothing to inspire him with confidence; and hence, the more thorough his self-examination, the greater his despondency. Abandoning all dependence on himself, he feels that he is utterly incapable of duly regulating his conduct. It is not the will of God, however, that we should forget the primeval dignity which he bestowed on our first parents—a dignity which may well stimulate us to the pursuit of goodness and justice. It is impossible for us to think of our first original, or the end for which we were created, without being urged to meditate on immortality, and to seek the kingdom of God. But such meditation, so far from raising our spirits, rather casts them down, and makes us humble. For what is our original? One from which we have fallen. What the end of our creation? One from which we have altogether strayed, so that, weary of our miserable lot, we groan, and groaning sigh for a dignity now lost. When we say that man should see nothing in himself which can raise his spirits, our meaning is, that he possesses nothing on which he can proudly plume himself. Hence, in considering the knowledge which man ought to have of himself, it seems proper to divide it thus, *first*, to consider the end for which he was created, and the qualities—by no means contemptible qualities—with which he was endued, thus urging him to meditate on divine worship and the future life; and, *secondly*, to consider his faculties, or rather want of faculties—a want which, when perceived, will annihilate all his confidence, and cover him with confusion. The tendency of the former view is to teach him what his duty is, of the latter, to make him aware how far he is able to perform it. We shall treat of both in their proper order.

4. As the act which God punished so severely must have been not a trivial fault but a heinous crime, it will be necessary to attend to the peculiar nature of the sin which produced Adam's fall, and provoked God to inflict such fearful vengeance on the whole human race. The common idea of sensual intemperance is childish. The sum and substance of all virtues could not consist in abstinence from a single fruit amid a general abundance of every delicacy that could be desired, the earth, with happy fertility, yielding not only abundance, but also endless variety. We must, therefore, look deeper than sensual intemperance. The prohibition to touch the tree of the knowledge of good and evil was a trial of obedience, that Adam, by observing it, might prove his willing submission to the command of God. For the very term shows the end of the precept to have been to keep him contented with his lot, and not allow him arro-

gantly to aspire beyond it. The promise, which gave him hope of eternal life as long as he should eat of the tree of life, and, on the other hand, the fearful denunciation of death the moment he should taste of the tree of the knowledge of good and evil, were meant to prove and exercise his faith. Hence it is not difficult to infer in what way Adam provoked the wrath of God. Augustine, indeed, is not far from the mark, when he says (in Psal. xix.), that pride was the beginning of all evil, because, had not man's ambition carried him higher than he was permitted, he might have continued in his first estate. A further definition, however, must be derived from the kind of temptation which Moses describes. When, by the subtlety of the devil, the woman faithlessly abandoned the command of God, her fall obviously had its origin in disobedience. This Paul confirms, when he says, that, by the disobedience of one man, all were destroyed. At the same time, it is to be observed, that the first man revolted against the authority of God, not only in allowing himself to be ensnared by the wiles of the devil, but also by despising the truth, and turning aside to lies. Assuredly, when the word of God is despised, all reverence for Him is gone. His majesty cannot be duly honoured among us, nor his worship maintained in its integrity, unless we hang as it were upon his lips. Hence infidelity was at the root of the revolt. From infidelity, again, sprang ambition and pride, together with ingratitude; because Adam, by longing for more than was allotted him, manifested contempt for the great liberality with which God had enriched him. It was surely monstrous impiety that a son of earth should deem it little to have been made in the likeness, unless he were also made the equal of God. If the apostacy by which man withdraws from the authority of his Maker, nay, petulantly shakes off his allegiance to him, is a foul and execrable crime, it is in vain to extenuate the sin of Adam. Nor was it simple apostacy. It was accompanied with foul insult to God, the guilty pair assenting to Satan's calumnies when he charged God with malice, envy, and falsehood. In fine, infidelity opened the door to ambition, and ambition was the parent of rebellion, man casting off the fear of God, and giving free vent to his lust. Hence, Bernard truly says, that, in the present day, a door of salvation is opened to us when we receive the gospel with our ears, just as by the same entrance, when thrown open to Satan, death was admitted. Never would Adam have dared to show any repugnance to the command of God if he had not been incredulous as to his word. The strongest curb to keep all his affections under due restraint, would have been the belief that nothing was better than to cultivate righteousness by obeying the commands of God, and that the highest possible felicity was to be loved by him.[1] Man, therefore, when carried away by the blasphemies of Satan, did his very utmost to annihilate the whole glory of God.

Infidelity was the root of Adam's revolt and then it opened the door to ambition and ambition led to lust.

---

[1] The latter clause of this sentence is omitted in the French.

5. As Adam's spiritual life would have consisted in remaining united and bound to his Maker, so estrangement from him was the death of his soul. Nor is it strange that he who perverted the whole order of nature in heaven and earth deteriorated his race by his revolt. "The whole creation groaneth," saith St Paul, "being made subject to vanity, not willingly" (Rom. viii. 20, 22). If the reason is asked, there cannot be a doubt that creation bears part of the punishment deserved by man, for whose use all other creatures were made. Therefore, since through man's fault a curse has extended above and below, over all the regions of the world, there is nothing unreasonable in its extending to all his offspring. After the heavenly image in man was effaced, he not only was himself punished by a withdrawal of the ornaments in which he had been arrayed—viz. wisdom, virtue, justice, truth, and holiness, and by the substitution in their place of those dire pests, blindness, impotence, vanity, impurity, and unrighteousness, but he involved his posterity also, and plunged them in the same wretchedness. This is the hereditary corruption to which early Christian writers gave the name of Original Sin, meaning by the term the depravation of a nature formerly good and pure. The subject gave rise to much discussion, there being nothing more remote from common apprehension, than that the fault of one should render all guilty, and so become a common sin. This seems to be the reason why the oldest doctors of the church only glance obscurely at the point, or, at least, do not explain it so clearly as it required. This timidity, however, could not prevent the rise of a Pelagius with his profane fiction—that Adam sinned only to his own hurt, but did no hurt to his posterity. Satan, by thus craftily hiding the disease, tried to render it incurable. But when it was clearly proved from Scripture that the sin of the first man passed to all his posterity, recourse was had to the cavil, that it passed by imitation, and not by propagation. The orthodox, therefore, and more especially Augustine, laboured to show, that we are not corrupted by acquired wickedness, but bring an innate corruption from the very womb. It was the greatest impudence to deny this. But no man will wonder at the presumption of the Pelagians and Celestians, who has learned from the writings of that holy man how extreme the effrontery of these heretics was. Surely there is no ambiguity in David's confession, "I was shapen in iniquity; and in sin did my mother conceive me" (Ps. li. 5). His object in the passage is not to throw blame on his parents; but the better to commend the goodness of God towards him, he properly reiterates the confession of impurity from his very birth. As it is clear, that there was no peculiarity in David's case, it follows that it is only an instance of the common lot of the whole human race. All of us, therefore, descending from an impure seed, come into the world tainted with the contagion of sin. Nay, before we behold the light of the sun we are in God's sight defiled and polluted. "Who can bring a clean

thing out of an unclean? Not one," says the Book of Job (Job xiv. 4).

6. We thus see that the impurity of parents is transmitted to their children, so that all, without exception, are originally depraved. The commencement of this depravity will not be found until we ascend to the first parent of all as the fountain head. We must, therefore, hold it for certain that, in regard to human nature, Adam was not merely a progenitor, but, as it were, a root, and that accordingly, by his corruption, the whole human race was deservedly vitiated. This is plain from the contrast which the Apostle draws between Adam and Christ, "Wherefore, as by one man sin entered into the world, and death by sin; and so death passed upon all men, for that all have sinned; even so might grace reign through righteousness unto eternal life by Jesus Christ our Lord" (Rom. v. 19—21). To what quibble will the Pelagians here recur? That the sin of Adam was propagated by imitation? Is the righteousness of Christ then available to us only in so far as it is an example held forth for our imitation? Can any man tolerate such blasphemy? But if, out of all controversy, the righteousness of Christ, and thereby life, is ours by communication, it follows that both of these were lost in Adam that they might be recovered in Christ, whereas sin and death were brought in by Adam, that they might be abolished in Christ. There is no obscurity in the words, "As by one man's disobedience many were made sinners, so by the obedience of one shall many be made righteous." Accordingly, the relation subsisting between the two is this, As Adam, by his ruin, involved and ruined us, so Christ, by his grace, restored us to salvation. In this clear light of truth I cannot see any need of a longer or more laborious proof. Thus, too, in the First Epistle to the Corinthians, when Paul would confirm believers in the confident hope of the resurrection, he shows that the life is recovered in Christ which was lost in Adam (1 Cor. xv. 22). Having already declared that all died in Adam, he now also openly testifies that all are imbued with the taint of sin. Condemnation, indeed, could not reach those who are altogether free from blame. But his meaning cannot be made clearer than from the other member of the sentence, in which he shows that the hope of life is restored in Christ. Every one knows that the only mode in which this is done is, when by a wondrous communication Christ transfuses into us the power of his own righteousness, as it is elsewhere said, "The Spirit is life because of righteousness" (1 Cor. xv. 22). Therefore, the only explanation which can be given of the expression, "in Adam all died," is, that he by sinning not only brought disaster and ruin upon himself, but also plunged our nature into like destruction; and that not only in one fault, in a matter not pertaining to us, but by the corruption into which he himself fell, he infected his whole seed. Paul never could have said that all are "by nature the children of wrath" (Eph. ii. 3), if

[Handwritten margin note:] Christ and Adam's cases are not supposed by "Pellagians" to be the same. Salvation by Christ is more than imitation, but we do not claim that it is biologically inherited Christ saves only those who accept Him.

they had not been cursed from the womb. And it is obvious, that the nature there referred to is not nature such as God created, but as vitiated in Adam; for it would have been most incongruous to make God the author of death. Adam, therefore, when he corrupted himself, transmitted the contagion to all his posterity. For a heavenly Judge, even our Saviour himself, declares that all are by birth vicious and depraved, when he says that "that which is born of the flesh is flesh" (John iii. 6), and that therefore the gate of life is closed against all until they have been regenerated.

7. To the understanding of this subject, there is no necessity for an anxious discussion (which in no small degree perplexed the ancient doctors) as to whether the soul of the child comes by transmission from the soul of the parent.[1] It should be enough for us to know that Adam was made the depository of the endowments which God was pleased to bestow on human nature, and that, therefore, when he lost what he had received, he lost not only for himself but for us all. Why feel any anxiety about the transmission of the soul, when we know that the qualities which Adam lost he received for us not less than for himself, that they were not gifts to a single man, but attributes of the whole human race? There is nothing absurd, therefore, in the view, that when he was divested, his nature was left naked and destitute, that he having been defiled by sin, the pollution extends to all his seed. Thus, from a corrupt root corrupt branches proceeding, transmit their corruption to the saplings which spring from them. The children being vitiated in their parent, conveyed the taint to the grandchildren; in other words, corruption commencing in Adam, is, by perpetual descent, conveyed from those preceding to those coming after them. The cause of the contagion is neither in the substance of the flesh nor the soul, but God was pleased to ordain that those gifts which he had bestowed on the first man, that man should lose as well for his descendants as for himself. The Pelagian cavil, as to the improbability of children deriving corruption from pious parents, whereas, they ought rather to be sanctified by their purity, is easily refuted. Children come not by spiritual regeneration but carnal descent.[2] Accordingly, as Augustine says, "Both the condemned unbeliever and the acquitted believer beget offspring not acquitted but condemned, because the nature which begets is corrupt."[3] Moreover, though godly parents do in some measure contribute to the holiness of their offspring, this is by the blessing of God; a blessing,

More on the biological inheritance of Original Sin.

---

[1] The French is, "Assavoir, si l'ame du fils procede de la substance de l'ame paternelle, veu que c'est en l'ame que reside le peché originel." That is, whether the soul of the child is derived from the substance of the soul of the parent, seeing it is in the soul that original sin resides.

[2] The French is, "Les enfans ne descendent point de la generation spirituelle qui les serviteurs de Dieu ont du S. Esprit, mais de la generation charnelle qu'ils ont d'Adam." Children descend not from the spiritual generation which the servants of God have of the Holy Spirit, but the carnal generation which they have of Adam.

[3] Lib. contra Pelag. Cœlest. See also Ep. 157, ad Gregor., Lib. vii. Ep. 53.

however, which does not prevent the primary and universal curse of the whole race from previously taking effect. Guilt is from nature, whereas sanctification is from supernatural grace.

8. But lest the thing itself of which we speak be unknown or doubtful, it will be proper to define original sin (Calvin, in Conc. Trident. I., Dec. Sess. v.). I have no intention, however, to discuss all the definitions which different writers have adopted, but only to adduce the one which seems to me most accordant with truth. Original sin, then, may be defined a hereditary corruption and depravity of our nature, extending to all the parts of the soul, which first makes us obnoxious to the wrath of God, and then produces in us works which in Scripture are termed works of the flesh. This corruption is repeatedly designated by Paul by the term sin[1] (Gal. v. 19); while the works which proceed from it, such as adultery, fornication, theft, hatred, murder, revellings, he terms, in the same way, the fruits of sin, though in various passages of Scripture, and even by Paul himself, they are also termed sins. The two things, therefore, are to be distinctly observed—viz. that being thus perverted and corrupted in all the parts of our nature, we are, merely on account of such corruption, deservedly condemned by God, to whom nothing is acceptable but righteousness, innocence, and purity. This is not liability for another's fault. For when it is said, that the sin of Adam has made us obnoxious to the justice of God, the meaning is not, that we, who are in ourselves innocent and blameless, are bearing his guilt, but that since by his transgression we are all placed under the curse, he is said to have brought us under obligation.[2] Through him, however, not only has punishment been derived, but pollution instilled, for which punishment is justly due. Hence Augustine, though he often terms it another's sin (that he may more clearly show how it comes to us by descent), at the same time asserts that it is each individual's own sin.[3] And the Apostle most distinctly testifies, that " death passed upon all men, for that all have sinned" (Rom. v. 12); that is, are involved in original sin, and polluted by its stain. Hence, even infants bringing their condemnation with them from their mother's womb, suffer not for another's, but for their own defect. For although they have not yet produced the fruits of their own unrighteousness, they have the seed implanted in them. Nay, their whole nature is, as it were, a seed-bed of sin, and therefore cannot

[Marginal notes: "Original Sin Defined"; "Infants are sinful and suffer justly for their own sin."]

---

[1] The French adds, " Sans adjouster Originel : "—without adding Original.

[2] The French is, " Car en ce qui est dit, que par Adam nous sommes fait redevables au jugement de Dieu, ce ne'st pas a dire que nous soyons innocens, et que sans avoir merité aucune peine nous portions la folleenchere de son peché ; mais pourceque par sa transgression nous sommes tous enveloppés de confusion, il est dit nous avoir tous obligez." For when it is said, that by Adam we are made liable to the judgment of God, the meaning is, not that we are innocent, and that without having deserved any punishment, we are made to pay dear for his sin, but because by his transgression we are all covered with confusion, he is said to have bound us.

[3] In many passages, and especially in his treatise, *De Peccatorum Merit. et Remiss.* Lib. iii. cap. 8.

but be odious-and abominable to God. Hence it follows, that it is properly deemed sinful in the sight of God; for there could be no condemnation without guilt. Next comes the other point—viz. that this perversity in us never ceases, but constantly produces new fruits, in other words, those works of the flesh which we formerly described; just as a lighted furnace sends forth sparks and flames, or a fountain without ceasing pours out water. Hence, those who have defined original sin as the want of the original righteousness which we ought to have had, though they substantially comprehend the whole case, do not significantly enough express its power and energy. For our nature is not only utterly devoid of goodness, but so prolific in all kinds of evil, that it can never be idle. Those who term it *concupiscence* use a word not very inappropriate, provided it were added (this, however, many will by no means concede), that everything which is in man, from the intellect to the will, from the soul even to the flesh, is defiled and pervaded with this concupiscence; or, to express it more briefly, that the whole man is in himself nothing else than concupiscence.

The whole man in himself is nothing else than concupiscence.

9. I have said, therefore, that all the parts of the soul were possessed by sin, ever since Adam revolted from the fountain of righteousness. For not only did the inferior appetites entice him, but abominable impiety seized upon the very citadel of the mind, and pride penetrated to his inmost heart (Rom. vii. 12; Book IV., chap. xv., sec. 10–12), so that it is foolish and unmeaning to confine the corruption thence proceeding to what are called sensual motions, or to call it an excitement, which allures, excites, and drags the single part which they call sensuality into sin. Here Peter Lombard has displayed gross ignorance (Lomb., Lib. ii. Dist. 21). When investigating the seat of corruption, he says it is in the flesh (as Paul declares), not properly, indeed, but as being more apparent in the flesh. As if Paul had meant that only a part of the soul, and not the whole nature, was opposed to supernatural grace. Paul himself leaves no room for doubt, when he says, that corruption does not dwell in one part only, but that no part is free from its deadly taint. For, speaking of corrupt nature, he not only condemns the inordinate nature of the appetites, but, in particular, declares that the understanding is subjected to blindness, and the heart to depravity (Eph. iv. 17, 18). The third chapter of the Epistle to the Romans is nothing but a description of original sin. The same thing appears more clearly from the mode of renovation. For the spirit, which is contrasted with the old man, and the flesh, denotes not only the grace by which the sensual or inferior part of the soul is corrected, but includes a complete reformation of all its parts (Eph. iv. 23). And, accordingly, Paul enjoins not only that gross appetites be suppressed, but that we be renewed in the spirit of our mind (Eph. iv. 23), as he elsewhere tells us to be transformed by the renewing of our mind (Rom. xii. 2). Hence it follows, that that part in which the dignity and excellence of the soul

Cure is not enough, there must be a new nature.

are most conspicuous, has not only been wounded, but so corrupted, that mere cure is not sufficient. There must be a new nature. How far sin has seized both on the mind and heart, we shall shortly see. Here I only wish briefly to observe, that the whole man, from the crown of the head to the sole of the foot, is so deluged, as it were, that no part remains exempt from sin, and, therefore, everything which proceeds from him is imputed as sin. Thus Paul says, that all carnal thoughts and affections are enmity against God, and consequently death (Rom. viii. 7).

10. Let us have done, then, with those who dare to inscribe the name of God on their vices, because we say that men are born vicious. The divine workmanship, which they ought to look for in the nature of Adam, when still entire and uncorrupted, they absurdly expect to find in their depravity. The blame of our ruin rests with our own carnality, not with God, its only cause being our degeneracy from our original condition. And let no one here clamour that God might have provided better for our safety by preventing Adam's fall. This objection, which, from the daring presumption implied in it, is odious to every pious mind, relates to the mystery of predestination, which will afterwards be considered in its own place (Tertull. de Præscript. Calvin, Lib. de Predest.). Meanwhile, let us remember that our ruin is attributable to our own depravity, that we may not insinuate a charge against God himself, the Author of nature. It is true that nature has received a mortal wound, but there is a great difference between a wound inflicted from without, and one inherent in our first condition. It is plain that this wound was inflicted by sin ; and, therefore, we have no ground of complaint except against ourselves. This is carefully taught in Scripture. For the Preacher says, " Lo, this only have I found, that God made man upright ; but they have sought out many inventions " (Eccl. vii. 29). Since man, by the kindness of God, was made upright, but by his own infatuation fell away unto vanity, his destruction is obviously attributable only to himself (Athanas. in Orat. Cont. Idola.)

Thus, our ruin is attributable to our own depravity

11. We say, then, that man is corrupted by a natural viciousness, but not by one which proceeded from nature. In saying that it proceeded not from nature, we mean that it was rather an adventitious event which befell man, than a substantial property assigned to him from the beginning.[1] We, however, call it *natural* to prevent any one from supposing that each individual contracts it by depraved habit, whereas all receive it by a hereditary law. And we have authority for so calling it. For, on the same ground, the Apostle says, that we are " by nature the children of wrath " (Eph. ii. 3).

---

[1] The French is, " Nous nions qu'elle soit de nature, afin de monstrer que c'est plutot une qualité survenue à l'homme qu'une proprieté de sa substance, laquelle ait eté, dés le commencément enracinée en lui ; "—we deny that it is of nature, in order to show that it is rather a quality superadded to man than a property of his substance, which has been from the beginning rooted in him.

(marginal handwritten note: The offence is not in God's work itself, but in the corruption of that work.)

How could God, who takes pleasure in the meanest of his works, be offended with the noblest of them all? The offence is not with the work itself, but the corruption of the work. Wherefore, if it is not improper to say that, in consequence of the corruption of human nature, man is naturally hateful to God, it is not improper to say, that he is naturally vicious and depraved. Hence, in the view of our corrupt nature, Augustine hesitates not to call those sins natural which necessarily reign in the flesh wherever the grace of God is wanting. This disposes of the absurd notion of the Manichees, who, imagining that man was essentially wicked, went the length of assigning him a different Creator, that they might thus avoid the appearance of attributing the cause and origin of evil to a righteous God.

CHAPTER II.

MAN NOW DEPRIVED OF FREEDOM OF WILL, AND MISERABLY ENSLAVED.

Having in the first chapter treated of the fall of man, and the corruption of the human race, it becomes necessary to inquire, Whether the sons of Adam are deprived of all liberty; and if any particle of liberty remains, how far its power extends? The four next chapters are devoted to this question. This second chapter may be reduced to three general heads: I. The foundation of the whole discussion. II. The opinions of others on the subject of human freedom, sec. 2–9. III. The true doctrine on the subject, sec. 10–27.

Sections.

1. Connection of the previous with the four following chapters. In order to lay a proper foundation for the discussion of free will, two obstacles in the way to be removed—viz. sloth and pride. The basis and sum of the whole discussion. The solid structure of this basis, and a clear demonstration of it by the argument *à majori ad minus*. Also from the inconveniences and absurdities arising from the obstacle of pride.
2. The second part of the chapter containing the opinions of others. 1. The opinions of philosophers.
3. The labyrinths of philosophers. A summary of the opinion common to all the philosophers.
4. The opinions of others continued—viz. The opinions of the ancient theologians on the subject of free will. These composed partly of Philosophy and partly of Theology. Hence their falsehood, extravagance, perplexity, variety, and contradiction. Too great fondness for philosophy in the Church has obscured the knowledge of God and of ourselves. The better to explain the opinions of philosophers, a definition of Free Will given. Wide difference between this definition and these opinions.
5. Certain things annexed to Free Will by the ancient theologians, especially the Schoolmen. Many kinds of Free Will according to them.
6. Puzzles of scholastic divines in the explanation of this question.
7. The conclusion that so trivial a matter ought not to be so much magnified. Objection of those who have a fondness for new terms in the Church. Objection answered.
8. Another answer. The Fathers, and especially Augustine, while retaining the term Free Will, yet condemned the doctrine of the heretics on the subject, as destroying the grace of God.
9. The language of the ancient writers on the subject of Free Will is, with the exception of that of Augustine, almost unintelligible. Still they set little or no value on human virtue, and ascribe the praise of all goodness to the Holy Spirit.
10. The last part of the chapter, containing a simple statement of the true doctrine. The fundamental principle is, that man first begins to profit in the knowledge of himself when he becomes sensible of his ruined condition. This confirmed, 1. by passages of Scripture.
11. Confirmed, 2. by the testimony of ancient theologians.
12. The foundation being laid, to show how far the power both of the intellect and will now extends, it is maintained in general, and in conformity with the views of Augustine and the Schoolmen, that the natural endowments of man are corrupted, and the supernatural almost entirely lost. A separate consideration of the powers

1. HAVING seen that the dominion of sin, ever since the first man was brought under it, not only extends to the whole race, but has complete possession of every soul, it now remains to consider more closely, whether, from the period of being thus enslaved, we have been deprived of all liberty ; and if any portion still remains, how far its power extends. In order to facilitate the answer to this question, it may be proper in passing to point out the course which our

inquiry ought to take. The best method of avoiding error is to consider the dangers which beset us on either side. Man being devoid of all uprightness, immediately takes occasion from the fact to indulge in sloth, and having no ability in himself for the study of righteousness, treats the whole subject as if he had no concern in it. On the other hand, man cannot arrogate anything, however minute, to himself, without robbing God of his honour, and through rash confidence subjecting himself to a fall. To keep free of both these rocks,[1] our proper course will be, first, to show that man has no remaining good in himself, and is beset on every side by the most miserable destitution; and then teach him to aspire to the goodness of which he is devoid, and the liberty of which he has been deprived: thus giving him a stronger stimulus to exertion than he could have if he imagined himself possessed of the highest virtue. How necessary the latter point is, everybody sees. As to the former, several seem to entertain more doubt than they ought. For it being admitted as incontrovertible that man is not to be denied anything that is truly his own, it ought also to be admitted, that he is to be deprived of everything like false boasting. If man had no title to glory in himself, when, by the kindness of his Maker, he was distinguished by the noblest ornaments, how much ought he to be humbled now, when his ingratitude has thrust him down from the highest glory to extreme ignominy? At the time when he was raised to the highest pinnacle of honour, all which Scripture attributes to him is, that he was created in the image of God, thereby intimating that the blessings in which his happiness consisted were not his own, but derived by divine communication. What remains, therefore, now that man is stript of all his glory, than to acknowledge the God for whose kindness he failed to be grateful, when he was loaded with the riches of his grace? Not having glorified him by the acknowledgment of his blessings, now, at least, he ought to glorify him by the confession of his poverty. In truth, it is no less useful for us to renounce all the praise of wisdom and virtue, than to aim at the glory of God. Those who invest us with more than we possess only add sacrilege to our ruin. For when we are taught to contend in our own strength, what more is done than to lift us up, and then leave us to lean on a reed which immediately gives way? Indeed, our strength is exaggerated when it is compared to a reed. All that foolish men invent and prattle on this subject is mere smoke. Wherefore, it is not without reason that Augustine so often repeats the well-known saying, that free will is more destroyed than established by its defenders (August. in Evang. Joann. Tract. 81). It was necessary to premise this much for the sake of some who, when they hear that human virtue is totally overthrown, in

---

[1] See *Calvin Adv. Theolog. Parisienses*, Art. 2. These two rocks are adverted to by *Augustine, Ep.* 47, *et in Joannem*, cap. 12.

order that the power of God in man may be exalted, conceive an utter dislike to the whole subject, as if it were perilous, not to say superfluous, whereas it is manifestly both most necessary and most useful.[1]

2. Having lately observed that the faculties of the soul are seated in the mind and the heart, let us now consider how far the power of each extends. Philosophers generally maintain that reason dwells in the mind like a lamp, throwing light on all its counsels, and, like a queen, governing the will—that it is so pervaded with divine light as to be able to consult for the best, and so endued with vigour as to be able perfectly to command; that, on the contrary, sense is dull and short-sighted, always creeping on the ground, grovelling among inferior objects, and never rising to true vision; that the appetite, when it obeys reason, and does not allow itself to be subjugated by sense, is borne to the study of virtue, holds a straight course, and becomes transformed into will; but that when enslaved by sense, it is corrupted and depraved so as to degenerate into lust. In a word, since, according to their opinion, the faculties which I have mentioned above—namely, intellect, sense, and appetite, or will (the latter being the term in ordinary use)—are seated in the soul, they maintain that the intellect is endued with reason, the best guide to a virtuous and happy life, provided it duly avails itself of its excellence, and exerts the power with which it is naturally endued; that, at the same time, the inferior movement, which is termed sense, and by which the mind is led away to error and delusion, is of such a nature, that it can be tamed and gradually subdued by the power of reason. To the will, moreover, they give an intermediate place between reason and sense, regarding it as possessed of full power and freedom, whether to obey the former, or yield itself up to be hurried away by the latter.

3. Sometimes, indeed, convinced by their own experience, they do not deny how difficult it is for man to establish the supremacy of reason in himself, inasmuch as he is at one time enticed by the allurements of pleasure; at another, deluded by a false semblance of good; and at another, impelled by unruly passions, and pulled away (to use Plato's expression) as by ropes or sinews (Plato, De Legibus, lib. i.). For this reason, Cicero says, that the sparks given forth by nature are immediately extinguished by false opinions and depraved manners (Cicero, Tusc. Quæst. lib. iii.). They confess that when once diseases of this description have seized upon the mind, their course is too impetuous to be easily checked, and they hesitate not to compare them to fiery steeds, which, having thrown off the charioteer, scamper away without restraint. At the same time, they set it down as beyond

[margin note, handwritten: Philosophers see senses and will as under the guidance of intellect or wisdom]

---

1 The French is, " Laquelle toutefois nous cognoistrons etre très-utile et qui plus est, etre un des fondemens de la religion;"—which, however, we shall know to be very useful, and what is more, to be one of the fundamentals of religion.

dispute, that virtue and vice are in our own power. For (say they), If it is in our choice to do this thing or that, it must also be in our choice not to do it : Again, If it is in our choice nor to act, it must also be in our choice to act : But both in doing and abstaining we seem to act from free choice ; and, therefore, if we do good when we please, we can also refrain from doing it ; if we commit evil, we can also shun the commission of it (Aristot. Ethic. lib. iii. c. 5). Nay, some have gone the length of boasting (Seneca, *passim*), that it is the gift of the gods that we live, but our own that we live well and purely. Hence Cicero says, in the person of Cotta, that as every one acquires virtue for himself, no wise man ever thanked the gods for it. " We are praised," says he, " for virtue, and glory in virtue, but this could not be, if virtue were the gift of God, and not from ourselves" (Cicero, De Nat. Deorum). A little after, he adds, " The opinion of all mankind is, that fortune must be sought from God, wisdom from ourselves." Thus, in short, all philosophers maintain, that human reason is sufficient for right government ; that the will, which is inferior to it, may indeed be solicited to evil by sense, but having a free choice, there is nothing to prevent it from following reason as its guide in all things.

4. Among ecclesiastical writers, although there is none who did not acknowledge that sound reason in man was seriously injured by sin, and the will greatly entangled by vicious desires, yet many of them made too near an approach to the philosophers. Some of the most ancient writers appear to me to have exalted human strength, from a fear that a distinct acknowledgment of its impotence might expose them to the jeers of the philosophers with whom they were disputing, and also furnish the flesh, already too much disinclined to good, with a new pretext for sloth. Therefore, to avoid teaching anything which the majority of mankind might deem absurd, they made it their study, in some measure, to reconcile the doctrine of Scripture with the dogmas of philosophy, at the same time making it their special care not to furnish any occasion to sloth. This is obvious from their words. Chrysostom says, " God having placed good and evil in our power, has given us full freedom of choice ; he does not keep back the unwilling, but embraces the willing" (Homil. de Prodit. Judæ.). Again, " He who is wicked is often, when he so chooses, changed into good, and he who is good falls through sluggishness, and becomes wicked. For the Lord has made our nature free. He does not lay us under necessity, but furnishing apposite remedies, allows the whole to depend on the views of the patient" (Homil. 16, in Genesim.). Again, " As we can do nothing rightly until aided by the grace of God, so, until we bring forward what is our own, we cannot obtain favour from above" (Homil. 52). He had previously said, " As the whole is not done by divine assistance, we ourselves must of necessity bring somewhat. " Accordingly, one of his common expressions is "Let us bring what is our own, God will supply the rest."

In unison with this, Jerome says, "It is ours to begin, God's to finish: it is ours to offer what we can, his to supply what we cannot" (Dialog. iii. Cont. Pelag.).

From these sentences, you see that they have bestowed on man more than he possesses for the study of virtue, because they thought that they could not skake off our innate sluggishness unless they argued that we sin by ourselves alone. With what skill they have thus argued we shall afterwards see. Assuredly we shall soon be able to show that the sentiments just quoted are most inaccurate.[1] Moreover, although the Greek Fathers, above others, and especially Chrysostom, have exceeded due bounds in extolling the powers of the human will, yet all ancient theologians, with the exception of Augustine, are so confused, vacillating, and contradictory on this subject, that no certainty can be obtained from their writings. It is needless, therefore, to be more particular in enumerating every separate opinion. It will be sufficient to extract from each as much as the exposition of the subject seems to require. Succeeding writers (every one courting applause for his acuteness in the defence of human nature) have uniformly, one after the other, gone more widely astray, until the common dogma came to be, that man was corrupted only in the sensual part of his nature, that reason remained entire, and will was scarcely impaired. Still the expression was often on their lips, that man's natural gifts were corrupted, and his supernatural[2] taken away. Of the thing implied by these words, however, scarcely one in a hundred had any distinct idea. Certainly, were I desirous clearly to express what the corruption of nature is, I would not seek for any other expression. But it is of great importance attentively to consider what the power of man now is when vitiated in all the parts of his nature, and deprived of supernatural gifts. Persons professing to be the disciples of Christ have spoken too much like the philosophers on this subject. As if human nature were still in its integrity, the term free will has always been in use among the Latins, while the Greeks were not ashamed to use a still more presumptuous term—viz. αὐτεξούσιον—as if man had still full power in himself.

But since the principle entertained by all, even the vulgar, is, that man is endued with free will, while some, who would be thought more skilful, know not how far its power extends; it will be necessary, first to consider the meaning of the term, and afterwards ascertain, by a simple appeal to Scripture, what man's natural power for good or evil is. The thing meant by free will, though constantly occurring in all writers, few have defined. Origen,[3] however, seems

---

1 The French adds, " Pour en dire franchement ce qui en est ;"—to speak of them frankly as they deserve.

2 The French adds the explanation, "Assavoir ceux qui concernoyent la vie celeste;" that is to say, those which concern the heavenly life.

3 Orig. De Principiis, Lib. iii. It is given by Lombard, Lib. ii. Dist. xxiv. Bernard. de Grat. et Liber Arbit. Anselm, Dialog. de Liber. Arbit. cap. xii. xiii. Lombard, Lib. ii. Dist. xxiv. sec. 5.

to have stated the common opinion when he said, It is a power of reason to discern between good and evil; of will, to choose the one or other. Nor does Augustine differ from him when he says, It is a power of reason and will to choose the good, grace assisting,—to choose the bad, grace desisting. Bernard, while aiming at greater acuteness, speaks more obscurely, when he describes it as consent, in regard to the indestructible liberty of the will, and the inalienable judgment of reason. Anselm's definition is not very intelligible to ordinary understandings. He calls it a power of preserving rectitude on its own account. Peter Lombard and the Schoolmen preferred the definition of Augustine, both because it was clearer, and did not exclude divine grace, without which they saw that the will was not sufficient of itself. They, however, add something of their own, because they deemed it either better or necessary for clearer explanation. First, they agree that the term *will* (arbitrium) has reference to reason, whose office it is to distinguish between good and evil, and that the epithet *free* properly belongs to the will, which may incline either way. Wherefore, since liberty properly belongs to the will, Thomas Aquinas says (Part I. Quæst. 83, Art. 3), that the most congruous definition is to call free will an elective power, combining intelligence and appetite, but inclining more to appetite. We now perceive in what it is they suppose the faculty of free will to consist —viz. in reason and will. It remains to see how much they attribute to each.

5. In general, they are wont to place under the free will of man only intermediate things—viz. those which pertain not to the kingdom of God—while they refer true righteousness to the special grace of God and spiritual regeneration. The author of the work, "De Vocatione Gentium" (On the Calling of the Gentiles),[1] wishing to show this, describes the will as threefold—viz. sensitive, animal, and spiritual. The two former, he says, are free to man, but the last is the work of the Holy Spirit. What truth there is in this will be considered in its own place. Our intention at present is only to mention the opinions of others, not to refute them. When writers treat of free will, their inquiry is chiefly directed not to what its power is in relation to civil or external actions, but to the obedience required by the divine law. The latter I admit to be the great question, but I cannot think the former should be altogether neglected; and I hope to be able to give the best reason for so thinking (sec. 12 to 18). The schools, however, have adopted a distinction which enumerates three kinds of freedom (see Lombard, Lib. ii. Dist. 25): the first, a freedom from necessity; the second, a freedom from sin; and the third, a freedom from misery: the first naturally so inherent in man, that he cannot possibly be deprived of it; while through sin the other two have been lost. I willingly admit this

---

1 The French adds ("qu'en attribue à St Ambroise");—which is attributed to St Ambrose.

distinction, except in so far as it confounds *necessity* with *compulsion*. How widely the things differ, and how important it is to attend to the difference, will appear elsewhere.

6. All this being admitted, it will be beyond dispute, that free will does not enable any man to perform good works, unless he is assisted by grace; indeed, the special grace which the elect alone receive through regeneration. For I stay not to consider the extravagance of those who say that grace is offered equally and promiscuously to all (Lomb. Lib. ii. Dist. 26). But it has not yet been shown whether man is entirely deprived of the power of well-doing, or whether he still possesses it in some, though in a very feeble and limited degree—a degree so feeble and limited, that it can do nothing of itself, but when assisted by grace, is able also to perform its part. The Master of the Sentences (Lombard, ibid.), wishing to explain this, teaches that a twofold grace is necessary to fit for any good work. The one he calls Operating. To it it is owing that we effectually will what is good. The other, which succeeds this good-will, and aids it, he calls Co-operating. My objection to this division (see *infra*, chap. iii. sec. 10, and chap. vii. sec. 9) is, that while it attributes the effectual desire of good to divine grace, it insinuates that man, by his own nature, desires good in some degree, though ineffectually. Thus Bernard, while maintaining that a good-will is the work of God, concedes this much to man—viz. that of his own nature he longs for such a good-will. This differs widely from the view of Augustine, though Lombard pretends to have taken the division from him. Besides, there is an ambiguity in the second division, which has led to an erroneous interpretation. For it has been thought that we co-operate with subsequent grace, inasmuch as it pertains to us either to nullify the first grace, by rejecting it, or to confirm it, by obediently yielding to it. The author of the work De Vocatione Gentium expresses it thus: It is free to those who enjoy the faculty of reason to depart from grace, so that the not departing is a reward, and that which cannot be done without the co-operation of the Spirit is imputed as merit to those whose will might have made it otherwise (Lib ii. cap. iv.). It seemed proper to make these two observations in passing, that the reader may see how far I differ from the sounder of the Schoolmen. Still further do I differ from more modern sophists, who have departed even more widely than the Schoolmen from the ancient doctrine. The division, however, shows in what respect free will is attributed to man. For Lombard ultimately declares (Lib. ii. Dist. 25), that our freedom is not to the extent of leaving us equally inclined to good and evil in act or in thought, but only to the extent of freeing us from compulsion. This liberty is compatible with our being depraved, the servants of sin, able to do nothing but sin.

7. In this way, then, man is said to have free will, not because he has a free choice of good and evil, but because he acts voluntarily,

Man's freedom consists chiefly in the ability voluntarily to choose evil.

and not by compulsion. This is perfectly true: but why should so small a matter have been dignified with so proud a title? An admirable freedom! that man is not forced to be the servant of sin, while he is, however, ἐθελόδουλος (a voluntary slave); his will being bound by the fetters of sin. I abominate mere verbal disputes, by which the Church is harassed to no purpose; but I think we ought religiously to eschew terms which imply some absurdity, especially in subjects where error is of pernicious consequence. How few are there who, when they hear free will attributed to man, do not immediately imagine that he is the master of his mind and will in such a sense, that he can of himself incline himself either to good or evil? It may be said that such dangers are removed by carefully expounding the meaning to the people. But such is the proneness of the human mind to go astray, that it will more quickly draw error from one little word, than truth from a lengthened discourse. Of this, the very term in question furnishes too strong a proof. For the explanation given by ancient Christian writers having been lost sight of, almost all who have come after them, by attending only to the etymology of the term, have been led to indulge a fatal confidence.

8. As to the Fathers (if their authority weighs with us), they have the term constantly in their mouths; but they, at the same time, declare what extent of meaning they attach to it. In particular, Augustine hesitates not to call the will *a slave*.[1] In another passage, he is offended with those who deny free will; but his chief reason for this is explained when he says, "Only, lest any one should presume so to deny freedom of will, from a desire to excuse sin." It is certain, he elsewhere admits, that without the Spirit the will of man is not free, inasmuch as it is subject to lusts which chain and master it. And again, that nature began to want liberty the moment the will was vanquished by the revolt into which it fell. Again, that man, by making a bad use of free will, lost both himself and his will. Again, that free will having been made a captive, can do nothing in the way of righteousness. Again, that no will is free which has not been made so by divine grace. Again, that the righteousness of God is not fulfilled when the law orders, and man acts, as it were, by his own strength, but when the Spirit assists, and the will (not the free will of man, but the will freed by God) obeys. He briefly states the ground of all these observations, when he says, that man at his creation received a great degree of free will, but lost it by sinning. In another place, after showing that free will is established by grace, he strongly inveighs against those who arrogate anything to themselves without grace. His words are, "How much soever miserable men presume to plume themselves on free will before they are made free,

[1] August. Lib. i. cont. Julian. For the subsequent quotations, see Homil. 53, in Joannem; Ad Anast. Epist. 144; De Perf. Just; Eucher. ad Laur. c. 30; Idem ad Bonifac. Lib. iii. c. 8; Ibid. c. 7; Idem ad Bonifac. Lib. i. c. 3; Ibid. Lib. iii. cap. 7; Idem, Lib. de Verbis Apost. Serm. 3; Lib. de Spiritu et Litera. cap. 30.

or on their strength after they are made free, they do not consider that, in the very expression *free will*, liberty is implied. ' Where the Spirit of the Lord is, there is liberty' (2 Cor. iii. 17). If, therefore, they are the servants of sin, why do they boast of free will? He who has been vanquished is the servant of him who vanquished him. But if men have been made free, why do they boast of it as of their own work? Are they so free that they are unwilling to be the servants of Him who has said, 'Without me ye can do nothing'?" (John xv. 5). In another passage he even seems to ridicule the word, when he says,[1] "That the will is indeed free, but not freed—free of righteousness, but enslaved to sin." The same idea he elsewhere repeats and explains, when he says, "That man is not free from righteousness save by the choice of his will, and is not made free from sin save by the grace of the Saviour." Declaring that the freedom of man is nothing else than emancipation or manumission from righteousness, he seems to jest at the emptiness of the name. If any one, then, chooses to make use of this term, without attaching any bad meaning to it, he shall not be troubled by me on that account ; but as it cannot be retained without very great danger, I think the abolition of it would be of great advantage to the Church. I am unwilling to use it myself ; and others, if they will take my advice, will do well to abstain from it.

9. It may, perhaps, seem that I have greatly prejudiced my own view by confessing that all the ecclesiastical writers, with the exception of Augustine, have spoken so ambiguously or inconsistently on this subject, that no certainty is attainable from their writings. Some will interpret this to mean, that I wish to deprive them of their right of suffrage, because they are opposed to me. Truly, however, I have had no other end in view than to consult, simply and in good faith, for the advantage of pious minds, which, if they trust to those writers for their opinion, will always fluctuate in uncertainty. At one time they teach, that man having been deprived of the power of free will must flee to grace alone ; at another, they equip or seem to equip him in armour of his own. It is not difficult, however, to show, that notwithstanding of the ambiguous manner in which those writers express themselves, they hold human virtue in little or no account, and ascribe the whole merit of all that is good to the Holy Spirit. To make this more manifest, I may here quote some passages from them. What, then, is meant by Cyprian in the passage so often lauded by Augustine,[2] "Let us glory in nothing, because nothing is ours," unless it be, that man being utterly destitute, considered in himself, should entirely depend on God? What is meant by Augustine and

---

[1] See August. de Corrept. et Grat. cap. 13. Adv. Lib. Arbit. See also August. Epist. 107. Also the first and last parts of Bernard's Treatise De Gratia et Libero Arbitrio.

[2] August. de Prædest. Sanct. Idem ad Bonifacum, Lib. iv. et alibi. Eucher. Lib. in Genesin. Chrysost. Homil. in Adventu.

Eucherius,[1] when they expound that Christ is the tree of life, and that whoso puts forth his hand to it shall live; that the choice of the will is the tree of the knowledge of good and evil, and that he who, forsaking the grace of God, tastes of it shall die? What is meant by Chrysostom, when he says, "That every man is not only naturally a sinner, but is wholly sin"? If there is nothing good in us; if man, from the crown of the head to the sole of the foot, is wholly sin; if it is not even lawful to try how far the power of the will extends,—how can it be lawful to share the merit of a good work between God and man? I might quote many passages to the same effect from others writers; but lest any caviller should say, that I select those only which serve my purpose, and cunningly pass by those which are against me, I desist. This much however, I dare affirm, that though they sometimes go too far in extolling free will, the main object which they had in view was to teach man entirely to renounce all self-confidence, and place his strength in God alone. I now proceed to a simple exposition of the truth in regard to the nature of man.

10. Here, however, I must again repeat what I premised at the outset of this chapter,[2] that he who is most deeply abased and alarmed, by the consciousness of his disgrace, nakedness, want, and misery, has made the greatest progress in the knowledge of himself. Man is in no danger of taking too much from himself, provided he learns that whatever he wants is to be recovered in God. But he cannot arrogate to himself one particle beyond his due, without losing himself in vain confidence, and, by transferring divine honour to himself, becoming guilty of the greatest impiety. And, assuredly, whenever our minds are seized with a longing to possess a somewhat of our own, which may reside in us rather than in God, we may rest assured that the thought is suggested by no other counsellor than he who enticed our first parents to aspire to be like gods, knowing good and evil.[3] It is sweet, indeed, to have so much virtue of our own as to be able to rest in ourselves; but let the many solemn passages by which our pride is sternly humbled, deter us from indulging this vain confidence: "Cursed be the man that trusteth in man, and maketh flesh his arm" (Jer. xvii. 5). "He delighteth not in the strength of the horse; he taketh not pleasure in the legs of a man. The Lord taketh pleasure in those that fear him, in those that hope in his mercy" (Ps. cxlvii. 10, 11). "He giveth power to the faint; and to them that have no might he increaseth strength. Even the youths shall faint and be weary, and the young men shall utterly fall: But they that wait upon the Lord shall renew their strength"

1 The French adds, "Ancien evesque de Lion;" ancient bishop of Lyons.
2 The French has, "Au commencement de ce traité;" at the commencement of this treatise.
3 The French adds, "Si c'est parole diabolique celle qui exalte homme en soy-mesme, il ne nous lui faut donner lieu, sinon que nous veuillions prendre conseil de nostre ennemi;"—if words which exalt man in himself are devilish, we must not give place to them unless we would take counsel of our enemy.

(Is. xl. 29—31). The scope of all these passages is, that we must not entertain any opinion whatever of our own strength, if we would enjoy the favour of God, who "resisteth the proud, but giveth grace unto the humble" (James iv. 6). Then let us call to mind such promises as these, "I will pour water upon him that is thirsty, and floods upon the dry ground" (Is. xliv. 3); "Ho, every one that thirsteth, come ye to the waters" (Is. lv. 1). These passages declare that none are admitted to enjoy the blessings of God save those who are pining under a sense of their own poverty. Nor ought such passages as the following to be omitted: "The sun shall no more be thy light by day; neither for brightness shall the moon give light unto thee: but the Lord shall be unto thee an everlasting light, and thy God thy glory" (Is. lx. 19). The Lord certainly does not deprive his servants of the light of the sun or moon, but as he would alone appear glorious in them, he dissuades them from confidence even in those objects which they deem most excellent.

11. I have always been exceedingly delighted with the words of Chrysostom, "The foundation of our philosophy is humility;"[1] and still more with those of Augustine, "As the orator,[2] when asked, What is the first precept in eloquence? answered, Delivery: What is the second? Delivery: What the third? Delivery: so, if you ask me in regard to the precepts of the Christian Religion, I will answer, first, second, and third, Humility." By humility, he means not when a man, with a consciousness of some virtue, refrains from pride, but when he truly feels that he has no refuge but in humility. This is clear from another passage,[3] "Let no man," says he, "flatter himself: of himself he is a devil: his happiness he owes entirely to God. What have you of your own but sin? Take your sin which is your own: for righteousness is of God." Again, "Why presume so much on the capability of nature? It is wounded, maimed, vexed, lost. The thing wanted is genuine confession, not false defence." "When any one knows that he is nothing in himself, and has no help from himself, the weapons within himself are broken, and the war is ended." All the weapons of impiety must be bruised, and broken, and burnt in the fire; you must remain unarmed, having no help in yourself. The more infirm you are, the more the Lord will sustain you. So, in expounding the seventieth Psalm, he forbids us to remember our own righteousness, in order that we may recognise the righteousness of God, and shows that God bestows his grace upon us, that we may know that we are nothing; that we stand only by the mercy of God, seeing that in ourselves we are altogether wicked. Let us not contend with God for our right, as if anything attributed to him were

---

1 Chrysost. Homil. de Perf. Evang. August. Epist. 56, ad Discur. As to true humility, see *infra*, chap. vii. sec. 4, and lib. iii. c. 12, sec. 6, 7.
2 The French is, "Demosthene orateur Grec;"—the Greek orator Demosthenes.
3 August. Homil. in Joann. 49, lib. de Natura et Gratia, cap. lii.; and in Psalms xlv. set lxx.

lost to our salvation. As our insignificance is his exaltation, so the confession of our insignificance has its remedy provided in his mercy. I do not ask, however, that man should voluntarily yield without being convinced, or that, if he has any powers, he should shut his eyes to them, that he may thus be subdued to true humility; but that getting quit of the disease of self-love and ambition, φιλαυτία καὶ φιλονεικία, under the blinding influences of which he thinks of himself more highly than he ought to think, he may see himself as he really is, by looking into the faithful mirror of Scripture.

12. I feel pleased with the well-known saying which has been borrowed from the writings of Augustine, that man's natural gifts were corrupted by sin, and his supernatural gifts withdrawn; meaning by supernatural gifts the light of faith and righteousness, which would have been sufficient for the attainment of heavenly life and everlasting felicity. Man, when he withdrew his allegiance to God, was deprived of the spiritual gifts by which he had been raised to the hope of eternal salvation. Hence it follows, that he is now an exile from the kingdom of God, so that all things which pertain to the blessed life of the soul are extinguished in him until he recover them by the grace of regeneration. Among these are faith, love to God, charity towards our neighbour, the study of righteousness and holiness. All these, when restored to us by Christ, are to be regarded as adventitious and above nature. If so, we infer that they were previously abolished. On the other hand, soundness of mind and integrity of heart were, at the same time, withdrawn, and it is this which constitutes the corruption of natural gifts. For although there is still some residue of intelligence and judgment as well as will, we cannot call a mind sound and entire which is both weak and immersed in darkness. As to the will, its depravity is but too well known. Therefore, since reason, by which man discerns between good and evil, and by which he understands and judges, is a natural gift, it could not be entirely destroyed; but being partly weakened and partly corrupted, a shapeless ruin is all that remains. In this sense it is said (John i. 5), that "the light shineth in darkness, and the darkness comprehended it not;" these words clearly expressing both points—viz. that in the perverted and degenerate nature of man there are still some sparks which show that he is a rational animal, and differs from the brutes, inasmuch as he is endued with intelligence, and yet, that this light is so smothered by clouds of darkness, that it cannot shine forth to any good effect. In like manner, the will, because inseparable from the nature of man, did not perish, but was so enslaved by depraved lusts as to be incapable of one righteous desire. The definition now given is complete, but there are several points which require to be explained. Therefore, proceeding agreeably to that primary distinction (Book I. c. xv, sec. 7 and 8), by which we divided the soul into intellect and will, we will now inquire into the power of the intellect.

To charge the intellect with perpetual blindness so as to leave it no intelligence of any description whatever, is repugnant not only to the Word of God, but to common experience. We see that there has been implanted in the human mind a certain desire of investigating truth, to which it never would aspire unless some relish for truth antecedently existed. There is, therefore, now, in the human mind, discernment to this extent, that it is naturally influenced by the love of truth, the neglect of which in the lower animals is a proof of their gross and irrational nature. Still it is true that this love of truth fails before it reaches the goal, forthwith falling away into vanity. As the human mind is unable, from dulness, to pursue the right path of investigation, and, after various wanderings, stumbling every now and then like one groping in darkness, at length gets completely bewildered, so its whole procedure proves how unfit it is to search the truth and find it. Then it labours under another grievous defect, in that it frequently fails to discern what the knowledge is which it should study to acquire. Hence, under the influence of a vain curiosity, it torments itself with superfluous and useless discussions, either not adverting at all to the things necessary to be known, or casting only a cursory and contemptuous glance at them. At all events, it scarcely ever studies them in sober earnest. Profane writers are constantly complaining of this perverse procedure, and yet almost all of them are found pursuing it. Hence Solomon, throughout the Book of Ecclesiastes, after enumerating all the studies in which men think they attain the highest wisdom, pronounces them vain and frivolous.

13. Still, however, man's efforts are not always so utterly fruitless as not to lead to some result, especially when his attention is directed to inferior objects. Nay, even with regard to superior objects, though he is more careless in investigating them, he makes some little progress. Here, however, his ability is more limited, and he is never made more sensible of his weakness than when he attempts to soar above the sphere of the present life. It may therefore be proper, in order to make it more manifest how far our ability extends in regard to these two classes of objects, to draw a distinction between them. The distinction is, that we have one kind of intelligence of earthly things, and another of heavenly things. By earthly things, I mean those which relate not to God and his kingdom, to true righteousness and future blessedness, but have some connection with the present life, and are in a manner confined within its boundaries. By heavenly things, I mean the pure knowledge of God, the method of true righteousness, and the mysteries of the heavenly kingdom. To the former belong matters of policy and economy, all mechanical arts and liberal studies. To the latter (as to which, see the eighteenth and following sections) belong the knowledge of God and of his will, and the means of framing the life in accordance with them. As to the former, the view to be taken is this: Since man is by nature a social animal, he is disposed, from natural instinct, to cherish and preserve society;

and accordingly we see that the minds of all men have impressions of civil order and honesty. Hence it is that every individual understands how human societies must be regulated by laws, and also is able to comprehend the principles of those laws. Hence the universal agreement in regard to such subjects, both among nations and individuals, the seeds of them being implanted in the breasts of all without a teacher or lawgiver. The truth of this fact is not affected by the wars and dissensions which immediately arise, while some, such as thieves and robbers, would invert the rules of justice, loosen the bonds of law, and give free scope to their lust; and while others (a vice of most frequent occurrence) deem that to be unjust which is elsewhere regarded as just, and, on the contrary, hold that to be praiseworthy which is elsewhere forbidden. For such persons do not hate the laws from not knowing that they are good and sacred, but, inflamed with headlong passion, quarrel with what is clearly reasonable, and licentiously hate what their mind and understanding approve. Quarrels of this latter kind do not destroy the primary idea of justice. For while men dispute with each other as to particular enactments, their ideas of equity agree in substance. This, no doubt, proves the weakness of the human mind, which, even when it seems on the right path, halts and hesitates. Still, however, it is true, that some principle of civil order is impressed on all. And this is ample proof that, in regard to the constitution of the present life, no man is devoid of the light of reason.

14. Next come manual and liberal arts, in learning which, as all have some degree of aptitude, the full force of human acuteness is displayed. But though all are not equally able to learn all the arts, we have sufficient evidence of a common capacity in the fact, that there is scarcely an individual who does not display intelligence in some particular art. And this capacity extends not merely to the learning of the art, but to the devising of something new, or the improving of what had been previously learned. This led Plato to adopt the erroneous idea, that such knowledge was nothing but recollection.[1] So cogently does it oblige us to acknowledge that its principle is naturally implanted in the human mind. But while these proofs openly attest the fact of an universal reason and intelligence naturally implanted, this universality is of a kind which should lead every individual for himself to recognise it as a special gift of God. To this gratitude we have a sufficient call from the Creator himself, when, in the case of idiots, he shows what the endowments of the soul would be were it not pervaded with his light. Though natural to all, it is so in such a sense that it ought to be regarded as a gratuitous gift of his beneficence to each. Moreover, the invention, the methodical arrangement, and the more thorough and superior knowledge of the arts, being confined to a few individuals, cannot be

[1] The French adds, " de ce que l'ame savoit avant qu'etre mis dedans le corps;"— of what the soul knew before it was placed within the body.

regarded as a solid proof of common shrewdness. Still, however, as they are bestowed indiscriminately on the good and the bad, they are justly classed among natural endowments.

15. Therefore, in reading profane authors, the admirable light of truth displayed in them should remind us, that the human mind, however much fallen and perverted from its original integrity, is still adorned and invested with admirable gifts from its Creator. If we reflect that the Spirit of God is the only fountain of truth, we will be careful, as we would avoid offering insult to him, not to reject or contemn truth wherever it appears. In despising the gifts, we insult the Giver. How, then, can we deny that truth must have beamed on those ancient lawgivers who arranged civil order and discipline with so much equity? Shall we say that the philosophers, in their exquisite researches and skilful description of nature, were blind? Shall we deny the possession of intellect to those who drew up rules for discourse, and taught us to speak in accordance with reason? Shall we say that those who, by the cultivation of the medical art, expended their industry in our behalf, were only raving? What shall we say of the mathematical sciences? Shall we deem them to be the dreams of madmen? Nay, we cannot read the writings of the ancients on these subjects without the highest admiration; an admiration which their excellence will not allow us to withhold. But shall we deem anything to be noble and praiseworthy, without tracing it to the hand of God? Far from us be such ingratitude; an ingratitude not chargeable even on heathen poets, who acknowledged that philosophy and laws, and all useful arts, were the inventions of the gods. Therefore, since it is manifest that men 'whom the Scriptures term natural, are so acute and clear-sighted in the investigation of inferior things, their example should teach us how many gifts the Lord has left in possession of human nature, notwithstanding of its having been despoiled of the true good.

16. Moreover, let us not forget that there are most excellent blessings which the Divine Spirit dispenses to whom he will for the common benefit of mankind. For if the skill and knowledge required for the construction of the Tabernacle behoved to be imparted to Bezaleel and Aholiab, by the Spirit of God (Exod. xxxi. 2; xxxv. 30), it is not strange that the knowledge of those things which are of the highest excellence in human life is said to be communicated to us by the Spirit. Nor is there any ground for asking what concourse the Spirit can have with the ungodly, who are altogether alienated from God? For what is said as to the Spirit dwelling in believers only, is to be understood of the Spirit of holiness, by which we are consecrated to God as temples. Notwithstanding of this, He fills, moves, and invigorates all things by the virtue of the Spirit, and that according to the peculiar nature which each class of beings has received by the Law of Creation. But if the Lord has been pleased to assist us by the work and ministry of the ungodly in physics, dialectics, mathe-

matics, and other similar sciences, let us avail ourselves of it, lest, by neglecting the gifts of God spontaneously offered to us, we be justly punished for our sloth. Lest any one, however, should imagine a man to be very happy merely because, with reference to the elements of this world, he has been endued with great talents for the investigation of truth, we ought to add, that the whole power of intellect thus bestowed is, in the sight of God, fleeting and vain whenever it is not based on a solid foundation of truth. Augustine (*supra*, sec. 4 and 12), to whom, as we have observed, the Master of Sentences (Lib. ii. Dist. 25) and the Schoolmen are forced to subscribe, says most correctly, that as the gratuitous gifts bestowed on man were withdrawn, so the natural gifts which remained were corrupted after the fall. Not that they can be polluted in themselves in so far as they proceed from God, but that they have ceased to be pure to polluted man, lest he should by their means obtain any praise.

17. The sum of the whole is this: From a general survey of the human race, it appears that one of the essential properties of our nature is reason, which distinguishes us from the lower animals, just as these by means of sense are distinguished from inanimate objects. For although some individuals are born without reason, that defect does not impair the general kindness of God, but rather serves to remind us, that whatever we retain ought justly to be ascribed to the Divine indulgence. Had God not so spared us, our revolt would have carried along with it the entire destruction of nature. In that some excel in acuteness, and some in judgment, while others have greater readiness in learning some peculiar art, God, by this variety, commends his favour toward us, lest any one should presume to arrogate to himself that which flows from his mere liberality. For whence is it that one is more excellent than another, but that in a common nature the grace of God is specially displayed in passing by many, and thus proclaiming that it is under obligation to none. We may add, that each individual is brought under particular influences according to his calling. Many examples of this occur in the Book of Judges, in which the Spirit of the Lord is said to have come upon those whom he called to govern his people (Judges vi. 34). In short, in every distinguished act there is a special inspiration. Thus it is said of Saul, that "there went with him a band of men whose hearts the Lord had touched" (1 Sam. x. 26). And when his inauguration to the kingdom is foretold, Samuel thus addresses him, "The Spirit of the Lord will come upon thee, and thou shalt prophesy with them, and shalt be turned into another man" (1 Sam. x. 6). This extends to the whole course of government, as it is afterwards said of David, "The Spirit of the Lord came upon David from that day forward" (1 Sam. xvi. 13). The same thing is elsewhere said with reference to particular movements. Nay, even in Homer, men are said to excel in genius, not only according as Jupiter has distributed to each, but according as he leads them day by day, οἶον ἐπ ἦμαρ ἄγῃσι. And

certainly experience shows when those who were most skilful and ingenious stand stupified, that the minds of men are entirely under the control of God, who rules them every moment. Hence it is said, that "He poureth contempt upon princes, and causeth them to wander in the wilderness where there is no way" (Ps. cvii. 40). Still, in this diversity we can trace some remains of the divine image distinguishing the whole human race from other creatures.

18. We must now explain what the power of human reason is, in regard to the kingdom of God, and spiritual discernment, which consists chiefly of three things—the knowledge of God, the knowledge of his paternal favour towards us, which constitutes our salvation, and the method of regulating of our conduct in accordance with the Divine Law. With regard to the former two, but more properly the second, men otherwise the most ingenious are blinder than moles. I deny not, indeed, that in the writings of philosophers we meet occasionally with shrewd and apposite remarks on the nature of God, though they invariably savour somewhat of giddy imagination. As observed above, the Lord has bestowed on them some slight perception of his Godhead, that they might not plead ignorance as an excuse for their impiety, and has, at times, instigated them to deliver some truths, the confession of which should be their own condemnation. Still, though seeing, they saw not. Their discernment was not such as to direct them to the truth, far less to enable them to attain it, but resembled that of the bewildered traveller, who sees the flash of lightning glance far and wide for a moment, and then vanish into the darkness of the night, before he can advance a single step. So far is such assistance from enabling him to find the right path. Besides, how many monstrous falsehoods intermingle with those minute particles of truth scattered up and down in their writings as if by chance. In short, not one of them even made the least approach to that assurance of the divine favour, without which the mind of man must ever remain a mere chaos of confusion. To the great truths, What God is in himself, and what he is in relation to us, human reason makes not the least approach. (See Book III. c. ii. sec. 14, 15, 16.)

19. But since we are intoxicated with a false opinion of our own discernment, and can scarcely be persuaded that in divine things it is altogether stupid and blind, I believe the best course will be to establish the fact, not by argument, but by Scripture. Most admirable to this effect is the passage which I lately quoted from John, when he says, "In him was life; and the life was the light of men. And the light shineth in darkness; and the darkness comprehended it not" (John i. 4, 5). He intimates that the human soul is indeed irradiated with a beam of divine light, so that it is never left utterly devoid of some small flame, or rather spark, though not such as to enable it to comprehend God. And why so? Because its acuteness is, in reference to the knowledge of God, mere blindness. When the

[margin notes] Philosophical knowledge gives some vague insights into the nature and will of God, but these are so confused and giddy as only to bring man under condemnation.

Man cannot know God apart from the aid of His Holy Spirit.

Spirit describes men under the term *darkness*, he declares them void of all power of spiritual intelligence. For this reason, it is said that believers, in embracing Christ, are " born, not of blood, nor of the will of the flesh, nor of the will of man, but of God" (John i. 13) ; in other words, that the flesh has no capacity for such sublime wisdom as to apprehend God, and the things of God, unless illumined by his Spirit. In like manner our Saviour, when he was acknowledged by Peter, declared that it was by special revelation from the Father (Matth. xvi. 17).

20. If we were persuaded of a truth which ought to be beyond dispute—viz. that human nature possesses none of the gifts which the elect receive from their heavenly Father through the Spirit of regeneration, there would be no room here for hesitation. For thus speaks the congregation of the faithful, by the mouth of the prophet : " With thee is the fountain of life : in thy light shall we see light " (Ps. xxxvi. 9). To the same effect is the testimony of the apostle Paul, when he declares that " no man can say that Jesus is the Lord, but by the Holy Ghost " (1 Cor. xii. 3). And John the Baptist, on seeing the dulness of his disciples, exclaims, " A man can receive nothing, unless it be given him from heaven " (John iii. 27). That the gift to which he here refers must be understood not of ordinary natural gifts, but of special illumination, appears from this —that he was complaining how little his disciples had profited by all that he had said to them in commendation of Christ. " I see," says he, " that my words are of no effect in imbuing the minds of men with divine things, unless the Lord enlighten their understandings by His Spirit." Nay, Moses also, while upbraiding the people for their forgetfulness, at the same time observes, that they could not become wise in the mysteries of God without his assistance. " Ye have seen all that the Lord did before your eyes in the land of Egypt, unto Pharaoh, and unto all his servants, and unto all his land ; the great temptations which thine eyes have seen, the signs, and these great miracles : yet the Lord hath not given you an heart to perceive, and eyes to see, and ears to hear, unto this day" (Deut. xxix. 2, 4). Would the expression have been stronger had he called us mere blocks in regard to the contemplation of divine things ? Hence the Lord, by the mouth of the prophet, promises to the Israelites as a singular favour, " I will give them an heart to know me" (Jer. xxiv. 7); intimating, that in spiritual things the human mind is wise only in so far as He enlightens it. This was also clearly confirmed by our Saviour when he said, " No man can come to me, except the Father which hath sent me draw him" (John vi. 44). Nay, is not he himself the living image of his Father, in which the full brightness of his glory is manifested to us ? Therefore, how far our faculty of knowing God extends could not be better shown than when it is declared, that though his image is so plainly exhibited, we have not eyes to perceive it. What ? Did not Christ descend into the world

that he might make the will of his Father manifest to men, and did he not faithfully perform the office? True! He did; but nothing is accomplished by his preaching unless the inner teacher, the Spirit, open the way into our minds. Only those, therefore, come to him who have heard and learned of the Father. And in what is the method of this hearing and learning? It is when the Spirit, with a wondrous and special energy, forms the ear to hear and the mind to understand. Lest this should seem new, our Saviour refers to the prophecy of Isaiah, which contains a promise of the renovation of the Church. "For a small moment have I forsaken thee; but with great mercies will I gather thee" (Is. liv. 7). If the Lord here predicts some special blessing to his elect, it is plain that the teaching to which he refers is not that which is common to them with the ungodly and profane.

It thus appears that none can enter the kingdom of God save those whose minds have been renewed by the enlightening of the Holy Spirit. On this subject the clearest exposition is given by Paul, who, when expressly handling it, after condemning the whole wisdom of the world as foolishness and vanity, and thereby declaring man's utter destitution, thus concludes, "The natural man receiveth not the things of the Spirit of God: for they are foolishness unto him: neither can he know them, for they are spiritually discerned" (1 Cor. ii. 14). Whom does he mean by the "natural man"? The man who trusts to the light of nature. Such a man has no understanding in the spiritual mysteries of God. Why so? Is it because through sloth he neglects them? Nay, though he exert himself, it is of no avail; they are "spiritually discerned." And what does this mean? That altogether hidden from human discernment, they are made known only by the revelation of the Spirit; so that they are accounted foolishness wherever the Spirit does not give light. The Apostle had previously declared, that "Eye hath not seen, nor ear heard, neither have entered into the heart of man, the things which God hath prepared for them that love him;" nay, that the wisdom of the world is a kind of veil by which the mind is prevented from beholding God (I Cor. ii. 9). What would we more? The Apostle declares that God hath "made foolish the wisdom of this world" (1 Cor. i. 20); and shall we attribute to it an acuteness capable of penetrating to God, and the hidden mysteries of his kingdom? Far from us be such presumption!

21. What the Apostle here denies to man, he, in another place, ascribes to God alone, when he prays, "that the God of our Lord Jesus Christ, the Father of glory, may give unto you the spirit of wisdom and revelation" (Eph. i. 17). You now hear that all wisdom and revelation is the gift of God. What follows? "The eyes of your understanding being enlightened." Surely, if they require a new enlightening, they must in themselves be blind. The next words are, "that ye may know what is the hope of his calling" (Eph. i. 18). In other words, the minds of men have not capacity enough to know

their calling. Let no prating Pelagian here allege that God obviates this rudeness or stupidity, when, by the doctrine of his word, he directs us to a path which we could not have found without a guide. David had the law, comprehending in it all the wisdom that could be desired, and yet not contented with this, he prays, "Open thou mine eyes, that I may behold wondrous things out of thy law" (Ps. cxix. 18). By this expression, he certainly intimates, that it is like sunrise to the earth when the word of God shines forth ; but that men do not derive much benefit from it until he himself, who is for this reason called the Father of lights (James i. 17), either gives eyes or opens them ; because, whatever is not illuminated by his Spirit is wholly darkness. The Apostles had been duly and amply instructed by the best of teachers. Still, as they wanted the Spirit of truth to complete their education in the very doctrine which they had previously heard, they were ordered to wait for him (John xiv. 26). If we confess that what we ask of God is lacking to us, and He by the very thing promised intimates our want, no man can hesitate to acknowledge that he is able to understand the mysteries of God, only in so far as illuminated by his grace. He who ascribes to himself more understanding than this, is the blinder for not acknowledging his blindness.

22. It remains to consider the third branch of the knowledge of spiritual things—viz. <u>the method of properly regulating the conduct.</u> This is correctly termed the knowledge of the works of righteousness, a branch in which the human mind seems to have somewhat more discernment than in the former two, since an Apostle declares, "When the Gentiles, which have not the law, do by nature the things contained in the law, these, having not the law, are a law unto themselves : which show the work of the law written in their hearts, their conscience also bearing witness, and their thoughts the meantime accusing or else excusing one another" (Rom. ii. 14, 15). If the Gentiles have the righteousness of the law naturally engraven on their minds, we certainly cannot say that they are altogether blind as to the rule of life. <u>Nothing, indeed, is more common, than for man to be sufficiently instructed in a right course of conduct by natural law,</u> of which the Apostle here speaks. Let us consider, however, for what end this knowledge of the law was given to men. For from this it will forthwith appear how far it can conduct them in the way of reason and truth. This is even plain from the words of Paul, if we attend to their arrangement. He had said a little before, that those who had sinned in the law will be judged by the law ; and those who have sinned without the law will perish without the law. As it might seem unaccountable that the Gentiles should perish without any previous judgment, he immediately subjoins, that conscience served them instead of the law, and was therefore sufficient for their righteous condemnation. <u>The end of the natural law, therefore, is to render man inexcusable, and may be not improperly defined—the</u>

[marginal notes:]
The method of properly regulating the conduct.

Commonly, natural man has knowledge of a right course of conduct.

This is only to leave him without excuse.

judgment of conscience distinguishing sufficiently between just and unjust, and by convicting men on their own testimony, depriving them of all pretext for ignorance. So indulgent is man toward himself, that, while doing evil, he always endeavours as much as he can to suppress the idea of sin. It was this, apparently, which induced Plato (in his Protagoras) to suppose that sins were committed only through ignorance. There might be some ground for this, if hypocrisy were so successful in hiding vice as to keep the conscience clear in the sight of God. But since the sinner, when trying to evade the judgment of good and evil implanted in him, is ever and anon dragged forward, and not permitted to wink so effectually as not to be compelled at times, whether he will or not, to open his eyes, it is false to say that he sins only through ignorance.

This is because only thus can man not be said to sin in ignorance

23. Themistius is more accurate in teaching (Paraphr. in Lib. iii. de Anima, cap. xlvi.), that the intellect is very seldom mistaken in the general definition or essence of the matter; but that deception begins as it advances farther—namely, when it descends to particulars. That homicide, putting the case in the abstract, is an evil, no man will deny; and yet one who is conspiring the death of his enemy deliberates on it as if the thing was good. The adulterer will condemn adultery in the abstract, and yet flatter himself while privately committing it. The ignorance lies here; that man, when he comes to the particular, forgets the rule which he had laid down in the general case. Augustine treats most admirably on this subject in his exposition of the first verse of the fifty-seventh Psalm. The doctrine of Themistius, however, does not always hold true: for the turpitude of the crime sometimes presses so on the conscience, that the sinner does not impose upon himself by a false semblance of good, but rushes into sin knowingly and willingly. Hence the expression,—I see the better course, and approve it: I follow the worse (Medea of Ovid.). For this reason, Aristotle seems to me to have made a very shrewd distinction between incontinence and intemperance (Ethic. Lib. vii. cap. iii.). Where incontinence (ἀκρασία) reigns, he says, that through the passion (πάθος) particular knowledge is suppressed: so that the individual sees not in his own misdeed the evil which he sees generally in similar cases; but when the passion is over, repentance immediately succeeds. Intemperance (ἀκολασία), again, is not extinguished or diminished by a sense of sin, but, on the contrary, persists in the evil choice which it has once made.

In the individual case, man forgets his lofty generalizations, and herein exists his ignorance.

Man may, however, sin intentionally. — Intemperance.

24. Moreover, when you hear of an universal judgment in man distinguishing between good and evil, you must not suppose that this judgment is, in every respect, sound and entire. For if the hearts of men are imbued with a sense of justice and injustice, in order that they may have no pretext to allege ignorance, it is by no means necessary for this purpose that they should discern the truth in particular cases. It is even more than sufficient if they understand so far as to be unable to practise evasion without being convicted by

their own conscience, and beginning even now to tremble at the judgment-seat of God.   Indeed, if we would test our reason by the Divine Law, which is a perfect standard of righteousness, we should find how blind it is in many respects.   It certainly attains not to the principal heads in the First Table, such as, trust in God, the ascription to him of all praise in virtue and righteousness, the invocation of his name, and the true observance of his day of rest.   Did ever any soul, under the guidance of natural sense, imagine that these and the like constitute the legitimate worship of God?   When profane men would worship God, how often soever they may be drawn off from their vain trifling, they constantly relapse into it.   They admit, indeed, that sacrifices are not pleasing to God, unless accompanied with sincerity of mind; and by this they testify that they have some conception of spiritual worship, though they immediately pervert it by false devices: for it is impossible to persuade them that everything which the law enjoins on the subject is true.   Shall I then extol the discernment of a mind which can neither acquire wisdom by itself, nor listen to advice?[1]   As to the precepts of the Second Table, there is considerably more knowledge of them, inasmuch as they are more closely connected with the preservation of civil society. Even here, however, there is something defective.   Every man of understanding deems it most absurd to submit to unjust and tyrannical domination, provided it can by any means be thrown off, and there is but one opinion among men, that it is the part of an abject and servile mind to bear it patiently, the part of an honourable and high-spirited mind to rise up against it.   Indeed, the revenge of injuries is not regarded by philosophers as a vice.   But the Lord condemning this too lofty spirit, prescribes to his people that patience which mankind deem infamous.   In regard to the general observance of the law, concupiscence altogether escapes our animadversion.   For the natural man cannot bear to recognise diseases in his lusts.   The light of nature is stifled sooner than take the first step into this profound abyss.   For, when philosophers class immoderate movements of the mind among vices, they mean those which break forth and manifest themselves in grosser forms.   Depraved desires, in which the mind can quietly indulge, they regard as nothing (see *infra*, chap. viii. sect. 49).

25. As we have above animadverted on Plato's error, in ascribing all sins to ignorance, so we must repudiate the opinion of those who hold that all sins proceed from preconceived pravity and malice.   We know too well from experience how often we fall, even when our intention is good.   Our reason is exposed to so many forms of delusion, is liable to so many errors, stumbles on so many obstacles, is entangled by so many snares, that it is ever wandering from the right direc-

---

[1] The French adds, " Or l'entendement humain a eté tel en cest endroit. Nous appercevons donques qu'il est du tout stupide ; " now, the understanding has proved so in this matter. We see, therefore, that it is quite stupid.

tion. Of how little value it is in the sight of God, in regard to all the parts of life, Paul shows, when he says, that we are not "sufficient of ourselves to think anything as of ourselves" (2 Cor. iii. 5). He is not speaking of the will or affection; he denies us the power of thinking aright how anything can be duly performed. Is it indeed true that all thought, intelligence, discernment, and industry, are so defective, that, in the sight of the Lord, we cannot think or aim at anything that is right? To us, who can scarcely bear to part with acuteness of intellect (in our estimation a most precious endowment), it seems hard to admit this, whereas it is regarded as most just by the Holy Spirit, who "knoweth the thoughts of man, that they are vanity" (Ps. xciv. 11), and distinctly declares, that "every imagination of the thoughts of his heart was only evil continually" (Gen. vi. 5 ; viii. 21). If everything which our mind conceives, meditates, plans, and resolves, is always evil, how can it ever think of doing what is pleasing to God, to whom righteousness and holiness alone are acceptable? It is thus plain that our mind, in what direction soever it turns, is miserably exposed to vanity. David was conscious of its weakness when he prayed, "Give me understanding, and I shall keep thy law" (Ps. cxix. 34). By desiring to obtain a new understanding, he intimates that his own was by no means sufficient. This he does not once only, but in one Psalm repeats the same prayer almost ten times, the repetition intimating how strong the necessity which urged him to pray. What he thus asked for himself alone, Paul prays for the churches in general. "For this cause," says he, "we also, since the day we heard it, do not cease to pray for you, and to desire that ye might be filled with the knowledge of his will, in all wisdom and spiritual understanding; that you might walk worthy of the Lord," &c. (Col. i. 9, 10). Whenever he represents this as a blessing from God, we should remember that he at the same time testifies that it is not in the power of man. Accordingly, Augustine, in speaking of this inability of human reason to understand the things of God, says, that he deems the grace of illumination not less necessary to the mind than the light of the sun to the eye (*August. de Peccat. Merit. et Remiss.* lib. ii. cap. v.). And, not content with this, he modifies his expression, adding, that we open our eyes to behold the light, whereas the mental eye remains shut, until it is opened by the Lord. Nor does Scripture say that our minds are illuminated in a single day, so as afterwards to see of themselves. The passage, which I lately quoted from the Apostle Paul, refers to continual progress and increase. David, too, expresses this distinctly in these words: "With my whole heart have I sought thee: O let me not wander from thy commandments" (Ps. cxix. 10). Though he had been regenerated, and so had made no ordinary progress in true piety, he confesses that he stood in need of direction every moment, in order that he might not decline from the knowledge with which he had been endued. Hence, he elsewhere prays for a renewal of a right spirit, which he had lost by his sin [1] (Ps. li. 12). For that which God gave at first, while temporarily withdrawn, it is equally his province to restore.

26. We must now examine the will, on which the question of freedom principally turns, the power of choice belonging to it rather than the intellect, as we have already seen (*supra*, sect. 4). And, at the outset, to guard against its being thought that the doctrine taught by philosophers, and generally received—viz. that all things by natural instinct have a desire of good—is any proof of the rectitude of the human will—let us observe, that the power of free will is not to be considered in any of those desires which proceed more from instinct than mental deliberation. Even the Schoolmen admit (*Thomas*, Part I., *Quæst.* 83, art. 3) that there is no act of free will, unless when reason looks at opposites. By this they mean, that the things desired must be such as may be made the object of choice, and that to pave the way for choice, deliberation must precede. And, undoubtedly, if you attend to what this natural desire of good in man is, you will find that it is common to him with the brutes. They, too, desire what is good; and when any semblance of good capable of moving the sense appears, they follow after it. Here, however, man does not, in accordance with the excellence of his immortal nature, rationally choose, and studiously pursue, what is truly for his good. He does not admit reason to his counsel, nor exert his intellect; but without reason, without counsel, follows the bent of his nature like the lower animals. The question of freedom, therefore, has nothing to do with the fact of man's being led by natural instinct to desire good. The question is, Does man, after determining by right reason what is good, choose what he thus knows, and pursue what he thus chooses? Lest any doubt should be entertained as to this, we must attend to the double misnomer. For this *appetite* is not properly a movement of the will, but natural inclination; and this *good* is not one of virtue or righteousness, but of condition —viz. that the individual may feel comfortable. In fine, how much soever man may desire to obtain what is good, he does not follow it. There is no man who would not be pleased with eternal blessedness; and yet, without the impulse of the Spirit, no man aspires to it. Since, then, the natural desire of happiness in man no more proves the freedom of the will, than the tendency in metals and stones to attain the perfection of their nature, let us consider, in other respects, whether the will is so utterly vitiated and corrupted in every part as to produce nothing but evil, or whether it retains some portion uninjured, and productive of good desires.

27. Those who ascribe our willing effectually, to the primary grace of God (*supra*, sect. 6), seem conversely to insinuate that the soul has in itself a power of aspiring to good, though a power too

Margin note: How much soever man may desire to obtain what is good, he does not follow it; — unless it be by the impulse of the Spirit.

---

[1] Calvin, in his Commentary on the passage, says, " Lost in part or appearance, or deserved to lose."

feeble to rise to solid affection or active endeavour. There is no doubt that this opinion, adopted from Origen and certain of the ancient Fathers, has been generally embraced by the Schoolmen, who are wont to apply to man in his natural state (*in puris naturalibus*, as they express it) the following description of the apostle:—"For that which I do I allow not: for what I would, that do I not; but what I hate, that do I." "To will is present with me; but how to perform that which is good I find not" (Rom. vii. 15, 18). But, in this way, the whole scope of Paul's discourse is inverted. He is speaking of the Christian struggle (touched on more briefly in the Epistle to the Galatians) which believers constantly experience from the conflict between the flesh and the spirit. But the spirit is not from nature, but from regeneration. That the apostle is speaking of the regenerate is apparent from this, that after saying, "in me dwells no good thing," he immediately adds the explanation, "in my flesh." Accordingly, he declares, "It is no more I that do it, but sin that dwelleth in me." What is the meaning of the correction, "in me (that is, in my flesh?") It is just as if he had spoken in this way, No good thing dwells in me, of myself, for in my flesh nothing good can be found. Hence follows the species of excuse, It is not I myself that do evil, but sin that dwelleth in me. This applies to none but the regenerate, who, with the leading powers of the soul, tend towards what is good. The whole is made plain by the conclusion, "I delight in the law of God after the inward man: but I see another law in my members, warring against the law of my mind" (Rom. vii. 22, 23). Who has this struggle in himself, save those who, regenerated by the Spirit of God, bear about with them the remains of the flesh? Accordingly, Augustine, who had at one time thought that the discourse related to the natural man (August. ad Bonifac. Lib. i. c. 10), afterwards retracted his exposition as unsound and inconsistent. And, indeed, if we admit that men, without grace, have any motions to good, however feeble, what answer shall we give to the apostle, who declares that " we are incapable of thinking a good thought"? (2 Cor. iii. 5.) What answer shall we give to the Lord, who declares, by Moses, that "every imagination of man's heart is only evil continually"? (Gen. viii. 21.) Since the blunder has thus arisen from an erroneous view of a single passage, it seems unnecessary to dwell upon it. Let us rather give due weight to our Saviour's words, "Whosoever committeth sin is the servant of sin" (John viii. 34). We are all sinners by nature, therefore we are held under the yoke of sin. But if the whole man is subject to the dominion of sin, surely the will, which is its principal seat, must be bound with the closest chains. And, indeed, if divine grace were preceded by any will of ours, Paul could not have said that "it is God which worketh in us both to will and to do" (Philip. ii. 13). Away, then, with all the absurd trifling which many have indulged in with regard to preparation. Although believers sometimes ask to have

We are
sinners
by nature
and are
bound
under
the yoke
of sin.

their heart trained to the obedience of the divine law, as David does
in several passages (Ps. li. 12), it is to be observed, that even this
longing in prayer is from God.   This is apparent from the language
used.   When he prays, "Create in me a clean heart," he certainly
does not attribute the beginning of the creation to himself.   Let us
therefore rather adopt the sentiment of Augustine, "God will prevent
you in all things, but do you sometimes prevent his anger.   How?
Confess that you have all these things from God, that all the good
you have is from him, all the evil from yourself" (August. De Verbis
Apost. Serm. 10).   Shortly after he says, "Of our own we have
nothing but sin."

Of our own we have nothing but sin.

CHAPTER III.

EVERYTHING PROCEEDING FROM THE CORRUPT NATURE OF MAN DAMNABLE.

The principal matters in this chapter are—I. A recapitulation of the former chapter, proving, from passages of Scripture, that the intellect and will of man are so corrupted, that no integrity, no knowledge or fear of God, can now be found in him, sect. 1 and 2. II. Objections to this doctrine, from the virtues which shone in some of the heathen, refuted, sect. 3 and 4. III. What kind of will remains in man, the slave of sin, sect. 5. The remedy and cure, sect. 6. IV. The opinion of Neo-Pelagian sophists concerning the preparation and efficacy of the will, and also concerning perseverance and co-operating grace, refuted, both by reason and Scripture, sect. 7–12. V. Some passages from Augustine confirming the truth of this doctrine, sect. 13 and 14.

Sections.

1. The intellect and will of the whole man corrupt. The term *flesh* applies not only to the sensual, but also to the higher part of the soul. This demonstrated from Scripture.
2. The heart also involved in corruption, and hence in no part of man can integrity or knowledge, or the fear of God, be found.
3. Objection, that some of the heathen were possessed of admirable endowments, and, therefore, that the nature of man is not entirely corrupt. Answer, Corruption is not entirely removed, but only inwardly restrained. Explanation of this answer.
4. Objection still urged, that the virtuous and vicious among the heathen must be put upon the same level, or the virtuous prove that human nature, properly culti-vated, is not devoid of virtue. Answer, That these are not ordinary properties of human nature, but special gifts of God. These gifts defiled by ambition, and hence the actions proceeding from them, however esteemed by man, have no merit with God.
5. Though man has still the faculty of willing, there is no soundness in it. He falls under the bondage of sin necessarily, and yet voluntarily. Necessity must be distinguished from compulsion. The ancient Theologians acquainted with this necessity. Some passages condemning the vacillation of Lombard.
6. Conversion to God constitutes the remedy or soundness of the human will. This not only begun, but continued and completed; the beginning, continuance, and completion, being ascribed entirely to God. This proved by Ezekiel's description of the stony heart, and from other passages of Scripture.
7. Various Objections.—1. The will is converted by God, but, when once prepared, does its part in the work of conversion. Answer from Augustine. 2. Grace can do nothing without will, nor the will without grace. Answer, Grace itself pro-duces will. God prevents the unwilling, making him willing, and follows up this preventing grace that he may not will in vain. Another answer gathered from various passages of Augustine.
8. Answer to the second Objection continued. No will inclining to good except in the elect. The cause of election out of man. Hence right will, as well as elec-tion, are from the good pleasure of God. The beginning of willing and doing well is of faith; faith again is the gift of God; and hence mere grace is the cause of our beginning to will well. This proved by Scripture.
9. Answer to second Objection continued. That good-will is merely of grace proved by the prayers of saints. Three axioms—1. God does not prepare man's heart,

1. The nature of man, in both parts of his soul—viz. intellect and will—cannot be better ascertained than by attending to the epithets applied to him in Scripture. If he is fully depicted (and it may easily be proved that he is) by the words of our Saviour, " that which is born of the flesh is flesh" (John iii. 6), he must be a very miserable creature. For, as an apostle declares, " to be carnally minded is death" (Rom. viii. 8), " It is enmity against God, and is not subject to the law of God, neither indeed can be." Is it true that the flesh is so perverse, that it is perpetually striving with all its might against God ? that it cannot accord with the righteousness of the divine law ? that, in short, it can beget nothing but the materials of death? Grant that there is nothing in human nature but flesh, and then extract something good out of it if you can. But it will be said, that the word *flesh* applies only to the sensual, and not to the higher part of the soul. This, however, is completely refuted by the words both of Christ and his apostle. The statement of our Lord is, that a man must be born again, because he is flesh. He requires not to be born again, with reference to the body. But a mind is not born again merely by having some portion of it reformed. It must be totally renewed. This is confirmed by the antithesis used in both passages. In the contrast between the Spirit and the flesh, there is nothing left of an intermediate nature. In this way, everything in man, which is not spiritual, falls under the denomination of carnal. But we have nothing of the Spirit except through regeneration. Everything, therefore, which we have from nature is flesh. Any possible doubt which might exist on the subject is removed by the words of Paul (Eph. iv. 23), where, after a description of the old man, who, he says, " is corrupt according to the deceitful lusts," he bids us " be renewed in the spirit" of our mind. You see that he places unlawful and depraved desires not in the sensual part merely, but in the mind itself, and therefore requires that it should be renewed. Indeed, he had a little before drawn a picture of human nature, which shows that there is no part in which it is not perverted and corrupted. For when he says that the " Gentiles walk in the vanity of their mind, having the understanding darkened, being alienated from the life of

God through the ignorance that is in them, because of the blindness of their heart" (Eph. iv. 17, 18), there can be no doubt that his words apply to all whom the Lord has not yet formed anew both to wisdom and righteousness. This is rendered more clear by the comparison which immediately follows, and by which he reminds believers that they " have not so learned Christ;"—these words implying, that the grace of Christ is the only remedy for that blindness and its evil consequences. Thus, too, had Isaiah prophesied of the kingdom of Christ, when the Lord promised to the Church, that though darkness should " cover the earth, and gross darkness the people," yet that he should " arise" upon it, and " his glory" should be seen upon it (Isaiah lx. 2). When it is thus declared that divine light is to arise on the Church alone, all without the Church is left in blindness and darkness. I will not enumerate all that occurs throughout Scripture, and particularly in the Psalms and Prophetical writings, as to the vanity of man. There is much in what David says, " Surely men of low degree are vanity, and men of high degree are a lie : to be laid in the balance, they are altogether lighter than vanity" (Ps. lxii. 9). The human mind receives a humbling blow when all the thoughts which proceed from it are derided as foolish, frivolous, perverse, and insane.

2. In no degree more lenient is the condemnation of the heart, when it is described as " deceitful above all things, and desperately wicked" (Jer. xvii. 9). But as I study brevity, I will be satisfied with a single passage, one, however, in which, as in a bright mirror, we may behold a complete image of our nature. The Apostle, when he would humble man's pride, uses these words : " There is none righteous, no, not one : there is none that understandeth, there is none that seeketh after God. They are all gone out of the way, they are together become unprofitable ; there is none that doeth good, no, not one. Their throat is an open sepulchre ; with their tongues they have used deceit ; the poison of asps is under their lips : Whose mouth is full of cursing and bitterness : their feet are swift to shed blood : destruction and misery are in their ways : and the way of peace have they not known : there is no fear of God before their eyes" (Rom. iii. 10—18). Thus he thunders not against certain individuals, but against the whole posterity of Adam—not against the depraved manners of any single age, but the perpetual corruption of nature. His object in the passage is not merely to upbraid men in order that they may repent, but to teach that all are overwhelmed with inevitable calamity, and can be delivered from it only by the mercy of God. As this could not be proved without previously proving the overthrow and destruction of nature, he produced those passages to show that its ruin is complete.

Let it be a fixed point, then, that men are such as is here described, not by vicious custom, but by depravity of nature. The reasoning of the Apostle, that there is no salvation for man, save in the mercy of God, because in himself he is desperate and undone, could not otherwise stand. I will not here labour to prove that the passages apply, with the view of removing the doubts of any who might think them quoted out of place. I will take them as if they had been used by Paul for the first time, and not taken from the Prophets. First, then, he strips man of righteousness, that is, integrity and purity; and, secondly, he strips him of sound intelligence. He argues, that defect of intelligence is proved by apostacy from God. To seek Him is the beginning of wisdom, and, therefore, such defect must exist in all who have revolted from Him. He subjoins, that all have gone astray, and become as it were mere corruption; that there is none that doeth good. He then enumerates the crimes by which those who have once given loose to their wickedness pollute every member of their bodies. Lastly, he declares that they have no fear of God, according to whose rule all our steps should be directed. If these are the hereditary properties of the human race, it is vain to look for anything good in our nature. I confess, indeed, that all these iniquities do not break out in every individual. Still it cannot be denied that the hydra lurks in every breast. For as a body, while it contains and fosters the cause and matter of disease, cannot be called healthy, although pain is not actually felt; so a soul, while teeming with such seeds of vice, cannot be called sound. This similitude, however, does not apply throughout. In a body, however morbid, the functions of life are performed; but the soul, when plunged into that deadly abyss, not only labours under vice, but is altogether devoid of good.

3. Here, again, we are met with a question very much the same as that which was previously solved. In every age there have been some who, under the guidance of nature, were all their lives devoted to virtue. It is of no consequence, that many blots may be detected in their conduct; by the mere study of virtue, they evinced that there was somewhat of purity in their nature. The value which virtues of this kind have in the sight of God will be considered more fully when we treat of the merit of works. Meanwhile, however, it will be proper to consider it in this place also, in so far as necessary for the exposition of the subject in hand. Such examples, then, seem to warn us against supposing that the nature of man is utterly vicious, since, under its guidance, some have not only excelled in illustrious deeds, but conducted themselves most honourably through the whole course of their lives. But we ought to consider that, notwithstanding of the corruption of our nature, there is some room for divine grace, such grace as, without purifying it, may lay it under internal restraint. For, did the Lord let every mind loose to wanton in its lusts, doubtless there is not a man who would not show that his nature is capable of all the crimes with which Paul charges it (Rom. iii. compared with Ps. xiv. 3, &c.). What? Can you exempt yourself from the number of those whose feet are swift to shed blood; whose hands are foul

with rapine and murder ; whose throats are like open sepulchres ; whose tongues are deceitful ; whose lips are venomous ; whose actions are useless, unjust, rotten, deadly ; whose soul is without God ; whose inward parts are full of wickedness ; whose eyes are on the watch for deception ; whose minds are prepared for insult ; whose every part, in short, is framed for endless deeds of wickedness ? If every soul is capable of such abominations (and the Apostle declares this boldly), it is surely easy to see what the result would be, if the Lord were to permit human passion to follow its bent. No ravenous beast would rush so furiously, no stream, however rapid and violent, so impetuously burst its banks. In the elect, God cures these diseases in the mode which will shortly be explained ; in others, he only lays them under such restraint as may prevent them from breaking forth to a degree incompatible with the preservation of the established order of things. Hence, how much soever men may disguise their impurity, some are restrained only by shame, others by a fear of the laws, from breaking out into many kinds of wickedness. Some aspire to an honest life, as deeming it most conducive to their interest, while others are raised above the vulgar lot, that, by the dignity of their station, they may keep inferiors to their duty. Thus God, by his providence, curbs the perverseness of nature, preventing it from breaking forth into action, yet without rendering it inwardly pure.

4. The objection, however, is not yet solved. For we must either put Cataline on the same footing with Camillus, or hold Camillus to be an example that nature, when carefully cultivated, is not wholly void of goodness. I admit that the specious qualities which Camillus possessed were divine gifts, and appear entitled to commendation when viewed in themselves. But in what way will they be proofs of a virtuous nature ? Must we not go back to the mind, and from it begin to reason thus ? If a natural man possesses such integrity of manners, nature is not without the faculty of studying virtue. But what if his mind was depraved and perverted, and followed anything rather than rectitude ? Such it undoubtedly was, if you grant that he was only a natural man. How then will you laud the power of human nature for good, if, even where there is the highest semblance of integrity, a corrupt bias is always detected ? Therefore, as you would not commend a man for virtue whose vices impose upon you by a show of virtue, so you will not attribute a power of choosing rectitude to the human will while rooted in depravity (see August. Lib. iv., Cont. Julian). Still, the surest and easiest answer to the objection is, that those are not common endowments of nature, but special gifts of God, which he distributes in divers forms, and in a definite measure, to men otherwise profane. For which reason, we hesitate not, in common language, to say, that one is of a good, another of a vicious nature ; though we cease not to hold that both are placed under the universal condition of human depravity. All we mean is, that God has conferred on the one a special grace which

he has not seen it meet to confer on the other. When he was pleased to set Saul over the kingdom, he made him as it were a new man. This is the thing meant by Plato, when, alluding to a passage in the Iliad, he says, that the children of kings are distinguished at their birth by some special qualities—God, in kindness to the human race, often giving a spirit of heroism to those whom he destines for empire. In this way, the great leaders celebrated in history were formed. The same judgment must be given in the case of private individuals. But as those endued with the greatest talents were always impelled by the greatest ambition (a stain which defiles all virtues, and makes them lose all favour in the sight of God), so we cannot set any value on anything that seems praiseworthy in ungodly men. We may add, that the principal part of rectitude is wanting, when there is no zeal for the glory of God, and there is no such zeal in those whom he has not regenerated by his Spirit. Nor is it without good cause said in Isaiah, that on Christ should rest "the spirit of knowledge, and of the fear of the Lord" (Isa. xi. 2); for by this we are taught that all who are strangers to Christ are destitute of that fear of God which is the beginning of wisdom (Ps. cxi. 10). The virtues which deceive us by an empty show may have their praise in civil society and the common intercourse of life, but before the judgment-seat of God they will be of no value to establish a claim of righteousness.

5. When the will is enchained as the slave of sin, it cannot make a movement towards goodness, far less steadily pursue it. Every such movement is the first step in that conversion to God, which in Scripture is entirely ascribed to divine grace. Thus Jeremiah prays, "Turn thou me, and I shall be turned" (Jer. xxxi. 18). Hence, too, in the same chapter, describing the spiritual redemption of believers, the Prophet says, "The Lord hath redeemed Jacob, and ransomed him from the hand of him that was stronger than he" (Jer. xxxi. 11); intimating how close the fetters are with which the sinner is bound, so long as he is abandoned by the Lord, and acts under the yoke of the devil. Nevertheless, there remains a will which both inclines and hastens on with the strongest affection towards sin ; man, when placed under this bondage, being deprived not of will, but of soundness of will. Bernard says not improperly, that all of us have a will ; but to will well is proficiency, to will ill is defect. Thus simply to will is the part of man, to will ill the part of corrupt nature, to will well the part of grace. Moreover, when I say that the will, deprived of liberty, is led or dragged by necessity to evil, it is strange that any should deem the expression harsh, seeing there is no absurdity in it, and it is not at variance with pious use. It does, however, offend those who hnow not how to distinguish between necessity and compulsion. Were any one to ask them, Is not God necessarily good, is not the devil necessarily wicked, what answer would they give? The goodness of God is so connected with his Godhead, that it is

not more necessary to be God than to be good; whereas, the devil, by his fall, was so estranged from goodness, that he can do nothing but evil. Should any one give utterance to the profane jeer (see Calvin Adv. Pighium), that little praise is due to God for a goodness to which he is forced, is it not obvious to every man to reply, It is owing not to violent impulse, but to his boundless goodness, that he cannot do evil? Therefore, if the free will of God in doing good is not impeded, because he necessarily must do good; if the devil, who can do nothing but evil, nevertheless sins voluntarily; can it be said that man sins less voluntarily because he is under a necessity of sinning? This necessity is uniformly proclaimed by Augustine, who, even when pressed by the invidious cavil of Celestius, hesitated not to assert it in the following terms: "Man through liberty became a sinner, but corruption, ensuing as the penalty, has converted liberty into necessity" (August. Lib. de Perf. Justit.). Whenever mention is made of the subject, he hesitates not to speak in this way of the necessary bondage of sin (August. de Natura et Gratia, et alibi). Let this, then, be regarded as the sum of the distinction. Man, since he was corrupted by the fall, sins not forced or unwilling, but voluntarily, by a most forward bias of the mind; not by violent compulsion, or external force, but by the movement of his own passion; and yet such is the depravity of his nature, that he cannot move and act except in the direction of evil. If this is true, the thing not obscurely expressed is, that he is under a necessity of sinning. Bernard, assenting to Augustine, thus writes: "Among animals, man alone is free, and yet sin intervening, he suffers a kind of violence, but a violence proceeding from his will, not from nature, so that it does not even deprive him of innate liberty" (Bernard, Sermo. super Cantica, 81). For that which is voluntary is also free. A little after he adds, "Thus, by some means strange and wicked, the will itself, being deteriorated by sin, makes a necessity; but so that the necessity, inasmuch as it is voluntary, cannot excuse the will, and the will, inasmuch as it is enticed, cannot exclude the necessity." For this necessity is in a manner voluntary. He afterwards says that "we are under a yoke, but no other yoke than that of voluntary servitude; therefore, in respect of servitude, we are miserable, and in respect of will, inexcusable; because the will, when it was free, made itself the slave of sin." At length he concludes, "Thus the soul, in some strange and evil way, is held under this kind of voluntary, yet sadly free necessity, both bond and free; bond in respect of necessity, free in respect of will: and what is still more strange, and still more miserable, it is guilty because free, and enslaved because guilty, and therefore enslaved because free." My readers hence perceive that the doctrine which I deliver is not new, but the doctrine which of old Augustine delivered with the consent of all the godly, and which was afterwards shut up in the cloisters of monks for almost a thousand years. Lombard, by not knowing how to distinguish between necessity and compulsion, gave occasion to a pernicious error.[1]

6. On the other hand, it may be proper to consider what the remedy is which divine grace provides for the correction and cure of natural corruption. Since the Lord, in bringing assistance, supplies us with what is lacking, the nature of that assistance will immediately make manifest its converse—viz. our penury. When the Apostle says to the Philippians, " Being confident of this very thing, that he which hath begun a good work in you, will perform it until the day of Jesus Christ" (Phil. i. 6), there cannot be a doubt that, by the good work thus begun, he means the very commencement of conversion in the will. God, therefore, begins the good work in us by exciting in our hearts a desire, a love, and a study of righteousness, or (to speak more correctly) by turning, training, and guiding our hearts unto righteousness; and he completes this good work by confirming us unto perseverance. But lest any one should cavil that the good work thus begun by the Lord consists in aiding the will, which is in itself weak, the Spirit elsewhere declares what the will, when left to itself, is able to do. His words are, " A new heart also will I give you, and a new spirit will I put within you: and I will take away the stony heart out of your flesh, and I will give you an heart of flesh. And I will put my Spirit within you, and cause you to walk in my statutes, and ye shall keep my judgments, and do them" (Ezek. xxxvi. 26, 27). How can it be said that the weakness of the human will is aided so as to enable it to aspire effectually to the choice of good, when the fact is, that it must be wholly transformed and renovated? If there is any softness in a stone; if you can make it tender, and flexible into any shape, then it may be said, that the human heart may be shaped for rectitude, provided that which is imperfect in it is supplemented by divine grace. But if the Spirit, by the above similitude, meant to show that no good can ever be extracted from our heart until it is made altogether new, let us not attempt to share with Him what He claims for himself alone. If it is like turning a stone into flesh when God turns us to the study of rectitude, everything proper to our own will is abolished, and that which succeeds in its place is wholly of God. I say the will is abolished, but not in so far as it is will, for in conversion everything essential to our original nature remains: I also say, that it is created anew, not because the will then begins to exist, but because it is turned from evil to good. This, I maintain, is wholly the work of God, because, as the Apostle testifies, we are not " sufficient of ourselves to think anything as of ourselves" (2 Cor. iii. 5). Accordingly, he elsewhere says, not merely that God assists the weak or corrects the depraved will, but that he worketh in us to will (Philip. ii. 13). From this it is easily inferred,

1 The French adds, " Qui a esté une peste mortelle à l'Eglise, d'estimer que l'homme pouvoit eviter le peché pource qu'il peche franchement;" which has been a deadly pest to the Church—viz. that man could avoid sin, because he sins frankly.

as I have said, that everything good in the will is entirely the result of grace. In the same sense, the Apostle elsewhere says, "It is the same God which worketh all in all" (1 Cor. xii. 6). For he is not there treating of universal government, but declaring that all the good qualities which believers possess are due to God. In using the term "all," he certainly makes God the author of spiritual life from its beginning to its end. This he had previously taught in different terms, when he said that there is "one Lord Jesus Christ, by whom are all things, and we by him" (1 Cor. viii. 6); thus plainly extolling the new creation, by which everything of our common nature is destroyed. There is here a tacit antithesis between Adam and Christ, which he elsewhere explains more clearly when he says, "We are his workmanship, created in Christ Jesus unto good works, which God hath before ordained that we should walk in them" (Eph. ii. 10). His meaning is to show in this way that our salvation is gratuitous, because the beginning of goodness is from the second creation which is obtained in Christ. If any, even the minutest, ability were in ourselves, there would also be some merit. But to show our utter destitution, he argues, that we merit nothing, because we are created in Christ Jesus unto good works, which God hath prepared; again intimating by these words, that all the fruits of good works are originally and immediately from God. Hence the Psalmist, after saying that the Lord "hath made us," to deprive us of all share in the work, immediately adds, "not we ourselves." That he is speaking of regeneration, which is the commencement of the spiritual life, is obvious from the context, in which the next words are, "we are his people, and the sheep of his pasture" (Psalm c. 3). Not contented with simply giving God the praise of our salvation, he distinctly excludes us from all share in it, just as if he had said that not one particle remains to man as a ground of boasting. The whole is of God.

7. But perhaps there will be some who, while they admit that the will is in its own nature averse to righteousness, and is converted solely by the power of God, will yet hold that, when once it is prepared, it performs a part in acting. This they found upon the words of Augustine, that grace precedes every good work; the will accompanying, not leading; a handmaid, and not a guide (August. ad Bonifac. Ep. 106). The words thus not improperly used by this holy writer, Lombard preposterously wrests to the above effect (Lombard, Lib. ii. Dist. 25). But I maintain that, as well in the words of the Psalmist which I have quoted, as in other passages of Scripture, two things are clearly taught—viz. that the Lord both corrects, or rather destroys, our depraved will, and also substitutes a good will from himself. Inasmuch as it is prevented by grace, I have no objection to your calling it a handmaid; but inasmuch as when formed again, it is the work of the Lord, it is erroneous to say, that it accompanies preventing grace as a voluntary attendant. Therefore, Chrysostom is inaccurate in saying, that grace cannot do anything

without will, nor will anything without grace (Serm. de Invent. Sanct. Crucis); as if grace did not, in terms of the passage lately quoted from Paul, produce the very will itself. The intention of Augustine, in calling the human will the handmaid of grace, was not to assign it a kind of second place to grace in the performance of good works. His object merely was to refute the pestilential dogma of Pelagius, who made human merit the first cause of salvation. As was sufficient for his purpose at the time, he contends that grace is prior to all merit, while, in the mean time, he says nothing of the other question as to the perpetual effect of grace, which, however, he handles admirably in other places. For in saying, as he often does, that the Lord prevents the unwilling in order to make him willing, and follows after the willing that he may not will in vain, he makes Him the sole author of good works. Indeed, his sentiments on this subject are too clear to need any lengthened illustration. "Men," says he, "labour to find in our will something that is our own, and not God's; how they can find it, I wot not" (August. de Remiss. Peccat., Lib. ii. c. 18). In his First Book against Pelagius and Celestius, expounding the saying of Christ, "Every man therefore that hath heard, and hath learned of the Father, cometh unto me" (John vi. 45), he says, "The will is aided not only so as to know what is to be done, but also to do what it knows." And thus, when God teaches not by the letter of the Law, but by the grace of the Spirit, he so teaches, that every one who has learned, not only knowing, sees, but also willing, desires, and acting, performs.

8. Since we are now occupied with the chief point on which the controversy turns, let us give the reader the sum of the matter in a few, and those most unambiguous, passages of Scripture; thereafter, lest any one should charge us with distorting Scripture, let us show that the truth, which we maintain to be derived from Scripture, is not unsupported by the testimony of this holy man (I mean Augustine). I deem it unnecessary to bring forward every separate passage of Scripture in confirmation of my doctrine. A selection of the most choice passages will pave the way for the understanding of all those which lie scattered up and down in the sacred volume. On the other hand, I thought it not out of place to show my accordance with a man whose authority is justly of so much weight in the Christian world. It is certainly easy to prove that the commencement of good is only with God, and that none but the elect have a will inclined to good. But the cause of election must be sought out of man; and hence it follows that a right will is derived not from man himself, but from the same good pleasure by which we were chosen before the creation of the world. Another argument much akin to this may be added. The beginning of right will and action being of faith, we must see whence faith itself is. But since Scripture proclaims throughout that it is the free gift of God, it follows, that when

men, who are with their whole soul naturally prone to evil, begin to have a good will, it is owing to mere grace. Therefore, when the Lord, in the conversion of his people, sets down these two things as requisite to be done—viz. to take away the heart of stone, and give a heart of flesh—he openly declares that, in order to our conversion to righteousness, what is ours must be taken away, and that what is substituted in its place is of himself. Nor does he declare this in one passage only. For he says in Jeremiah, "I will give them one heart, and one way, that they may fear me for ever;" and a little after he says, "I will put my fear in their hearts, that they shall not depart from me" (Jer. xxxii. 39, 40). Again, in Ezekiel, "I will give them one heart, and I will put a new spirit within you; and I will take the stony heart out of their flesh, and will give them an heart of flesh" (Ezek. xi. 19). He could not more clearly claim to himself, and deny to us, everything good and right in our will, than by declaring, that in our conversion there is the creation of a new spirit and a new heart. It always follows, both that nothing good can proceed from our will until it be formed again, and that after it is formed again, in so far as it is good, it is of God, and not of us.

9. With this view, likewise, the prayers of the saints correspond. Thus Solomon prays that the Lord may "incline our hearts unto him, to walk in his ways, and keep his commandments" (1 Kings viii. 58); intimating that our heart is perverse, and naturally indulges in rebellion against the Divine law, until it be turned. Again it is said in the Psalms, "Incline my heart unto thy testimonies" (Ps. cxix. 36). For we should always note the antithesis between the rebellious movement of the heart, and the correction by which it is subdued to obedience. David, feeling for the time that he was deprived of directing grace, prays, "Create in me a clean heart, O God; and renew a right spirit within me" (Ps. li. 10). Is not this an acknowledgment that all the parts of the heart are full of impurity, and that the soul has received a twist, which has turned it from straight to crooked? And then, in describing the cleansing, which he earnestly demands as a thing to be created by God, does he not ascribe the work entirely to Him? If it is objected, that the prayer itself is a symptom of a pious and holy affection, it is easy to reply, that although David had already in some measure repented, he was here contrasting the sad fall which he had experienced with his former state. Therefore, speaking in the person of a man alienated from God, he properly prays for the blessings which God bestows upon his elect in regeneration. Accordingly, like one dead, he desires to be created anew, so as to become, instead of a slave of Satan, an instrument of the Holy Spirit. Strange and monstrous are the longings of our pride. There is nothing which the Lord enjoins more strictly than the religious observance of his Sabbath, in other words, resting from our works; but in nothing do we show greater reluctance than to renounce our own works, and give due place to

the works of God. Did not arrogance stand in the way, we could not overlook the clear testimony which Christ has borne to the efficacy of his grace. "I," said he, "am the true vine, and my Father is the husbandman." "As the branch cannot bear fruit of itself, except it abide in the vine; no more can ye, except ye abide in me" (John xv. 1, 4). If we can no more bear fruit of ourselves than a vine can bud when rooted up and deprived of moisture, there is no longer any room to ask what the aptitude of our nature is for good. There is no ambiguity in the conclusion, "For without me ye can do nothing." He says not that we are too weak to suffice for ourselves; but, by reducing us to nothing, he excludes the idea of our possessing any, even the least ability. If, when engrafted into Christ, we bear fruit like the vine, which draws its vegetative power from the moisture of the ground, and the dew of heaven, and the fostering warmth of the sun, I see nothing in a good work, which we can call our own, without trenching upon what is due to God. It is vain to have recourse to the frivolous cavil, that the sap and the power of producing are already contained in the vine, and that, therefore, instead of deriving everything from the earth or the original root, it contributes something of its own. Our Saviour's words simply mean, that when separated from him, we are nothing but dry, useless wood, because, when so separated, we have no power to do good, as he elsewhere says, "Every plant which my heavenly Father hath not planted, shall be rooted up" (Matth. xv. 13). Accordingly, in the passage already quoted from the Apostle Paul, he attributes the whole operation to God, "It is God which worketh in you both to will and to do of his good pleasure" (Philip. ii. 13). The first part of a good work is the will, the second is vigorous effort in the doing of it.[1] God is the author of both. It is, therefore, robbery from God to arrogate anything to ourselves, either in the will or the act. Were it said that God gives assistance to a weak will, something might be left us; but when it is said that he makes the will, everything good in it is placed without us. Moreover, since even a good will is still weighed down by the burden of the flesh, and prevented from rising, it is added that, to meet the difficulties of the contest, God supplies the persevering effort until the effect it obtained. Indeed, the Apostle could not otherwise have said, as he elsewhere does, that "it is the same God which worketh all in all" (1 Cor. xii. 6); words comprehending, as we have already observed (sec. 6), the whole course of the spiritual life. For which reason, David, after praying, "Teach me thy way, O Lord, I will walk in thy truth," adds, "unite my heart to fear thy name" (Ps. lxxxvi. 11); by these words intimating, that even those who are well-affected are liable to so many distractions that they easily become vain and fall away, if

---

[1] French, "La premiere partie des bonnes œuvres est la volonté; l'autre est de s'efforcer a l'executer et le pouvoir faire."—The first part of good works is the will; the second is the attempt to execute it, and the power to do so.

not strengthened to persevere. And hence, in another passage, after praying, "Order my steps in thy word," he requests that strength also may be given him to carry on the war, "Let not any iniquity have dominion over me" (Ps. cxix. 133). In this way, the Lord both begins and perfects the good work in us, so that it is due to Him, first, that the will conceives a love of rectitude, is inclined to desire, is moved and stimulated to pursue it; secondly, that this choice, desire, and endeavour fail not, but are carried forward to effect; and, lastly, that we go on without interruption, and persevere even to the end.

10. This movement of the will is not of that description which was for many ages taught and believed—viz. a movement which thereafter leaves us the choice to obey or resist it—but one which affects us efficaciously. We must, therefore, repudiate the oft-repeated sentiment of Chrysostom, "Whom he draws, he draws willingly;" insinuating that the Lord only stretches out his hand, and waits to see whether we will be pleased to take his aid. We grant that, as man was originally constituted, he could incline to either side, but since he has taught us by his example how miserable a thing free will is if God works not in us to will and to do, of what use to us were grace imparted in such scanty measure? Nay, by our own ingratitude, we obscure and impair divine grace. The Apostle's doctrine is not, that the grace of a good will is offered to us if we will accept of it, but that God himself is pleased so to work in us as to guide, turn, and govern our heart by his Spirit, and reign in it as his own possession. Ezekiel promises that a new-spirit will be given to the elect, not merely that they may be able to walk in his precepts, but that they may really walk in them (Ezek. xi. 19; xxxvi. 27). And the only meaning which can be given to our Saviour's words, "Every man, therefore, that hath heard and learned of the Father, cometh unto me" (John vi. 45), is, that the grace of God is effectual in itself. This Augustine maintains in his book De Prædestinatione Sancta. This grace is not bestowed on all promiscuously, according to the common brocard (of Occam, if I mistake not), that it is not denied to any one who does what in him lies. Men are indeed to be taught that the favour of God is offered, without exception, to all who ask it; but since those only begin to ask whom heavenly grace inspires, even this minute portion of praise must not be withheld from him. It is the privilege of the elect to be regenerated by the Spirit of God, and then placed under his guidance and government. Wherefore Augustine justly derides some who arrogate to themselves a certain power of willing, as well as censures others who imagine that that which is a special evidence of gratuitous election is given to all (August. de Verbis Apost. Serm. xxi.). He says, "Nature is common to all, but not grace;" and he calls it a showy acuteness "which shines by mere vanity, when that which God bestows on whom he will is attributed generally to all." Elsewhere he says, "How came

you ? By believing. Fear, lest by arrogating to yourself the merit of finding the right way, you perish from the right way. I came, you say, by free choice, came by my own will. Why do you boast ? Would you know that even this was given you ? Hear Christ exclaiming, 'No man cometh unto me, except the Father which hath sent me draw him.'" And from the words of John (vi. 44), he infers it to be an incontrovertible fact, that the hearts of believers are so effectually governed from above, that they follow with undeviating affection. "Whosoever is born of God doth not commit sin ; for his seed remaineth in him" (1 John iii. 9). That intermediate movement which the sophists imagine, a movement which every one is free to obey or to reject, is obviously excluded by the doctrine of effectual perseverance.[1]

11. As to perseverance, it would undoubtedly have been regarded as the gratuitous gift of God, had not the very pernicious error prevailed, that it is bestowed in proportion to human merit, according to the reception which each individual gives to the first grace. This having given rise to the idea that it was entirely in our own power to receive or reject the offered grace of God, that idea is no sooner exploded than the error founded on it must fall. The error, indeed, is twofold. For, besides teaching that our gratitude for the first grace and our legitimate use of it is rewarded by subsequent supplies of grace, its abettors add that, after this, grace does not operate alone, but only co-operates with ourselves. As to the former, we must hold that the Lord, while he daily enriches his servants, and loads them with new gifts of his grace, because he approves of and takes pleasure in the work which he has begun, finds that in them which he may follow up with larger measures of grace. To this effect are the sentences, " To him that hath shall be given." " Well done, good and faithful servant : thou hast been faithful over a few things, I will make thee ruler over many things" (Matth. xxv. 21, 23, 29 ; Luke xix. 17, 26). But here two precautions are necessary. It must not be said that the legitimate use of the first grace is rewarded by subsequent measures of grace, as if man rendered the grace of God effectual by his own industry, nor must it be thought that there is any such remuneration as to make it cease to be the gratuitous grace of God. 1 admit, then, that believers may expect as a blessing from God, that the better the use they make of previous, the larger the supplies they will receive of future grace ; but I say that even

<hr/>

1 The French is, " Nous voyons que ce mouvement sans vertu, lequel imaginent les sophistes, est exclus ; J'entend ce qu'ils disent, que Dieu offre seulement sa grace, a telle condition que chacun la refuse ou accepte selon que bon lui semble. Telle reverie di-je, qui n'est ne chair ne poisson, est exclue, quand il est dit que Dieu nous fait tellement perseverer que nous sommes hors de danger de decliver."—We see that this movement without virtue, which the sophists imagine, I mean their dogma, that God only offers his grace on such conditions that each may refuse or accept it as seems to him good. Such a reverie, I say, which is neither fish nor flesh, is excluded, when it is said that God makes us so persevere that we are in no danger of declining.

this use is of the Lord, and that this remuneration is bestowed freely of mere good-will. The trite distinction of operating and co-operating grace is employed no less siuistrously than unhappily. Augustine, indeed, used it, but softened it by a suitable definition—-viz. that God, by co-operating, perfects what he begins by operating,—that both graces are the same, but obtain different names from the different manner in which they produce their effects. Whence it follows, that he does not make an apportionment between God and man, as if a proper movement on the part of each produced a mutual concurrence. All he does is to mark a multiplication of grace. To this effect, accordingly, he elsewhere says, that in man good will precedes many gifts from God ; but among these gifts is this good will itself. (*August. Enchiridion ad Laurent.* cap. 32). Whence it follows, that nothing is left for the will to arrogate as its own. This Paul has expressly stated. For, after saying, " It is God which worketh in you both to will and to do," he immediately adds, " of his good pleasure " (Phil. ii. 13) ; indicating by this expression, that the blessing is gratuitous. As to the common saying, that after we have given admission to the first grace, our efforts co-operate with subsequent grace, this is my answer :—If it is meant that after we are once subdued by the power of the Lord to the obedience of righteousness, we proceed voluntarily, and are inclined to follow the movement of grace, I have nothing to object. For it is most certain, that where the grace of God reigns, there is also this readiness to obey. And whence this readiness, but just that the Spirit of God being everywhere consistent with himself, after first begetting a principle of obedience, cherishes and strengthens it for perseverance ? If, again, it is meant that man is able of himself to be a fellow-labourer with the grace of God, I hold it to be a most pestilential delusion.

12. In support of this view, some make an ignorant and false application of the Apostle's words : " I laboured more abundantly than they all : yet not I, but the grace of God which was with me" (1 Cor. xv. 10). The meaning they give them is, that as Paul might have seemed to speak somewhat presumptuously in preferring himself to all the other apostles, he corrects the expression so far by referring the praise to the grace of God, but he, at the same time, calls himself a co-operator with grace. It is strange that this should have proved a stumbling-block to so many writers, otherwise respectable. The Apostle says not that the grace of God laboured with him so as to make him a copartner in the labour. He rather transfers the whole merit of the labour to grace alone, by thus modifying his first expression, " It was not I," says he, " that laboured, but the grace of God that was present with me." Those who have adopted the erroneous interpretation have been misled by an ambiguity in the expression, or rather by a preposterous translation, in which the force of the Greek article is overlooked. For to take the words literally, the Apostle does not say that grace was a fellow-worker with him, but

that the grace which was with him was sole worker. And this is taught not obscurely, though briefly, by Augustine when he says, " Good will in man precedes many gifts from God, but not all gifts, seeing that the will which precedes is itself among the number." He adds the reason " for it is written, ' The God of my mercy shall prevent me' (Ps. lix. 10), and ' Surely goodness and mercy shall follow me' (Ps. xxiii. 6) ; it prevents him that is unwilling, and makes him willing ; it follows him that is willing, that he may not will in vain." To this Bernard assents, introducing the Church as praying thus, " Draw me, who am in some measure unwilling, and make me willing ; draw me, who am sluggishly lagging, and make me run" (Serm. II. in Cantic.)

13. Let us now hear Augustine in his own words, lest the Pelagians of our age, I mean the sophists of the Sorbonne, charge us after their wont with being opposed to all antiquity. In this, indeed, they imitate their father Pelagius, by whom of old a similar charge was brought against Augustine. In the second chapter of his Treatise De Correptione et Gratia, addressed to Valentinus, Augustine explains at length what I will state briefly, but in his own words, that to Adam was given the grace of persevering in goodness if he had the will ; to us it is given to will, and by will overcome concupiscence : that Adam, therefore, had the power if he had the will, but did not will to have the power, whereas to us is given both the will and the power ; that the original freedom of man was to be able not to sin, but that we have a much greater freedom—viz. not to be able to sin. And lest it should be supposed, as Lombard erroneously does (Lib. ii. Dist. 25), that he is speaking of the perfection of the future state, he shortly after removes all doubt when he says, " For so much is the will of the saints inflamed by the Holy Spirit that they are able, because they are willing; and willing, because God worketh in them so to will." For if, in such weakness (in which, however, to suppress pride, " strength" must be made " perfect"), their own will is left to them, in such sense that, by the help of God, they are able, if they will, while at the same time God does not work in them so as to make them will; among so many temptations and infirmities the will itself would give way, and, consequently, they would not be able to persevere. Therefore, to meet the infirmity of the human will, and prevent it from failing, how weak soever it might be, divine grace was made to act on it inseparably and uninterruptedly. Augustine (ibid. cap. xiv.) next entering fully into the question, how our hearts follow the movement when God affects them, necessarily says, indeed, that the Lord draws men by their own wills ; wills, however, which he himself has produced. We have now an attestation by Augustine to the truth which we are specially desirous to maintain—viz. that the grace offered by the Lord is not merely one which every individual has full liberty of choosing to receive or reject, but a grace which produces in the heart both choice and will:

so that all the good works which follow after are its fruit and effect ; the only will which yields obedience being the will which grace itself has made. In another place Augustine uses these words, " Every good work in us is performed only by grace" (August. Ep. 105).

14. In saying elsewhere that the will is not taken away by grace, but out of bad is changed into good, and after it is good is assisted, —he only means, that man is not drawn as if by an extraneous impulse[1] without the movement of the heart, but is inwardly affected so as to obey from the heart. Declaring that grace is given specially and gratuitously to the elect, he writes in this way to Boniface : " We know that Divine grace is not given to all men, and that to those to whom it is given, it is not given either according to the merit of works, or according to the merit of the will, but by free grace : in regard to those to whom it is not given, we know that the not giving of it is a just judgment from God " (August. ad Bonifac. Ep. 106). In the same epistle, he argues strongly against the opinion of those who hold that subsequent grace is given to human merit as a reward for not rejecting the first grace. For he presses Pelagius to confess that gratuitous grace is necessary to us for every action, and that merely from the fact of its being truly grace, it cannot be the recompense of works. But the matter cannot be more briefly summed up than in the eighth chapter of his Treatise De Correptione et Gratia, where he shows, *First*, that human will does not by liberty obtain grace, but by grace obtains liberty. *Secondly*, that by means of the same grace, the heart being impressed with a feeling of delight, is trained to persevere, and strengthened with invincible fortitude. *Thirdly*, that while grace governs the will, it never falls ; but when grace abandons it, it falls forthwith. *Fourthly*, that by the free mercy of God, the will is turned to good, and when turned, perseveres. *Fifthly*, that the direction of the will to good, and its constancy after being so directed, depend entirely on the will of God, and not on any human merit. Thus the will (free will, if you choose to call it so), which is left to man, is, as he in another place (Ep. 46) describes it, a will which can neither be turned to God, nor continue in God, unless by grace ; a will which, whatever its ability may be, derives all that ability from grace.

---

1 French, " Comme une pierre ; "—like a stone.

CHAPTER IV.

HOW GOD WORKS IN THE HEARTS OF MEN.

The leading points discussed in this chapter are—I. Whether in bad actions anything is to be attributed to God; if anything, how much. Also, what is to be attributed to the devil and to man, sec. 1—5. II. In indifferent matters, how much is to be attributed to God, and how much is left to man, sec. 6. III. Two objections refuted, sec. 7, 8.

Sections.

1. Connection of this chapter with the preceding. Augustine's similitude of a good and bad rider. Question answered in respect to the devil.
2. Question answered in respect to God and man. Example from the history of Job. The works of God distinguished from the works of Satan and wicked men. 1. By the design or end of acting. How Satan acts in the reprobate. 2. How God acts in them.
3. Old Objection, that the agency of God in such cases is referable to prescience or permission, not actual operation. Answer, showing that God blinds and hardens the reprobate, and this in two ways: 1. By deserting them; 2. By delivering them over to Satan.
4. Striking passages of Scripture, proving that God acts in both ways, and disposing of the objection with regard to prescience. Confirmation from Augustine.
5. A modification of the former answer, proving that God employs Satan to instigate the reprobate, but, at the same time, is free from all taint.
6. How God works in the hearts of men in indifferent matters. Our will in such matters not so free as to be exempt from the overruling providence of God. This confirmed by various examples.
7. Objection, that these examples do not form the rule. An answer, fortified by the testimony of universal experience, by Scripture, and a passage of Augustine.
8. Some, in arguing against the error of free will, draw an argument from the event. How this is to be understood.

1. THAT man is so enslaved by the yoke of sin, that he cannot of his own nature aim at good either in wish or actual pursuit, has, I think, been sufficiently proved. Moreover, a distinction has been drawn between compulsion and necessity, making it clear that man, though he sins necessarily, nevertheless sins voluntarily. But since, from his being brought into bondage to the devil, it would seem that he is actuated more by the devil's will than his own, it is necessary, first, to explain what the agency of each is, and then solve the question,[1] Whether in bad actions anything is to be attributed to God, Scripture intimating that there is some way in which he interferes? Augustine (in Psalm xxxi. and xxxiii.) compares the human will to

---

[1] The French adds, "dont on doute communement;" on which doubts are commonly entertained.

a horse preparing to start, and God and the devil the riders. "If God mounts, he, like a temperate and skilful rider, guides it calmly, urges it when too slow, reins it in when too fast, curbs its forwardness and over-action, checks its bad temper, and keeps it on the proper course; but if the devil has seized the saddle, like an ignorant and rash rider, he hurries it over broken ground, drives it into ditches, dashes it over precipices, spurs it into obstinacy or fury." With this simile, since a better does not occur, we shall for the present be contented. When it is said, then, that the will of the natural man is subject to the power of the devil, and is actuated by him, the meaning is, not that the will, while reluctant and resisting, is forced to submit (as masters oblige unwilling slaves to execute their orders), but that, fascinated by the impostures of Satan, it necessarily yields to his guidance, and does him homage. Those whom the Lord favours, not with the direction of his Spirit, he, by a righteous judgment, consigns to the agency of Satan. Wherefore, the Apostle says, that "the god of this world hath blinded the minds of them which believe not, lest the light of the glorious gospel of Christ, who is the image of God, should shine into them." And, in another passage, he describes the devil as "the spirit that now worketh in the children of disobedience" (Eph. ii. 2). The blinding of the wicked, and all the iniquities consequent upon it, are called the works of Satan; works, the cause of which is not to be sought in anything external to the will of man, in which the root of the evil lies, and in which the foundation of Satan's kingdom, in other words, sin, is fixed.

2. The nature of the divine agency in such cases is very different. For the purpose of illustration, let us refer to the calamities brought upon holy Job by the Chaldeans. They having slain his shepherds, carry off his flocks. The wickedness of their deed is manifest,[1] as is also the hand of Satan, who, as the history informs us, was the instigator of the whole. Job, however, recognises it as the work of God, saying, that what the Chaldeans had plundered, "the Lord" had "taken away." Low can we attribute the same work to God, to Satan, and to man, without either excusing Satan by the interference of God, or making God the author of the crime? This is easily done if we look first to the end, and then to the mode of acting. The Lord designs to exercise the patience of his servant by adversity; Satan's plan is to drive him to despair; while the Chaldeans are bent on making unlawful gain by plunder. Such diversity of purpose makes a wide distinction in the act. In the mode there is not less difference. The Lord permits Satan to afflict his servant; and the Chaldeans, who had been chosen as the ministers to execute the deed, he hands over to the impulses of Satan, who, pricking on the already depraved

---

[1] The French adds, "Car quand nous voyons des voleurs, qui ont commis quelque meurtre ou larrecin, nous ne doutons point de leur imputer la faute, et de les condamner."—For when we see robbers who have committed some murder or robbery, we hesitate not to impute the blame to them, and condemn them.

Chaldeans with his poisoned darts, instigates them to commit the crime. They rush furiously on to the unrighteous deed, and become its guilty perpetrators. Here Satan is properly said to act in the reprobate, over whom he exercises his sway, which is that of wickedness. God also is said to act in his own way; because even Satan, when he is the instrument of divine wrath, is completely under the command of God, who turns him as he will in the execution of his just judgments. I say nothing here of the universal agency of God, which, as it sustains all the creatures, also gives them all their power of acting. I am now speaking only of that special agency which is apparent in every act. We thus see that there is no inconsistency in attributing the same act to God, to Satan, and to man, while, from the difference in the end and mode of action, the spotless righteousness of God shines forth at the same time that the iniquity of Satan and of man is manifested in all its deformity.

3. Ancient writers sometimes manifest a superstitious dread of making a simple confession of the truth in this matter, from a fear of furnishing impiety with a handle for speaking irreverently of the works of God. While I embrace such soberness with all my heart, I cannot see the least danger in simply holding what Scripture delivers. Even Augustine was not always free from this superstition, as when he says, that blinding and hardening have respect not to the operation of God, but to prescience (Lib. de Predestina. et Gratia). But this subtilty is repudiated by many passages of Scripture, which clearly show that the divine interference amounts to something more than prescience. And Augustine himself, in his book against Julian,[1] contends at length that sins are manifestations not merely of divine permission or patience, but also of divine power, that thus former sins may be punished. In like manner, what is said of permission is too weak to stand. God is very often said to blind and harden the reprobate, to turn their hearts, to incline and impel them, as I have elsewhere fully explained (Book I. c. xviii.). The extent of this agency can never be explained by having recourse to prescience or permission. We, therefore, hold that there are two methods in which God may so act. When his light is taken away, nothing remains but blindness and darkness: when his Spirit is taken away, our hearts become hard as stones: when his guidance is withdrawn, we immediately turn from the right path: and hence he is properly said to incline, harden, and blind those whom he deprives of the faculty of seeing, obeying, and rightly executing. The second method, which comes much nearer to the exact meaning of the words, is when executing his judgments by Satan as the minister of his anger, God both directs men's counsels, and excites their wills, and regulates their efforts as he pleases. Thus when Moses relates that Sihon, king of the Amorites, did not give the Israelites a passage, because the Lord

[1] The French adds, "se retractant de l'autre sentence;" retracting the other sentiment.

" had hardened his spirit, and made his heart obstinate," he immediately adds the purpose which God had in view—viz. that he might deliver him into their hand (Deut. ii. 30). As God had resolved to destroy him, the hardening of his heart was the divine preparation for his ruin.

4. In accordance with the former method, it seems to be said,[1] " The law shall perish from the priest, and counsel from the ancients." " He poureth contempt upon princes, and causeth them to wander in the wilderness, where there is no way." Again, " O Lord, why hast thou made us to err from thy ways, and hardened our heart from thy fear ?" These passages rather indicate what men become when God deserts them, than what the nature of his agency is when he works in them. But there are other passages which go farther, such as those concerning tha hardening of Pharaoh : " I will harden his heart, that he shall not let the people go." The same thing is afterwards repeated in stronger terms. Did he harden his heart by not softening it? This is, indeed, true ; but he did something more : he gave it in charge to Satan to confirm him in his obstinacy. Hence he had previously said, " I am sure he will not let you go." The people come out of Egypt, and the inhabitants of a hostile region come forth against them. How were they instigated? Moses certainly declares of Sihon, that it was the Lord who " had hardened his spirit, and made his heart obstinate" (Deut. ii. 30). The Psalmist, relating the same history, says, " He turned their hearts to hate his people" (Psalm cv. 25). You cannot now say that they stumbled merely because they were deprived of divine counsel. For if they are *hardened* and *turned*, they are purposely bent to the very end in view. Moreover, whenever God saw it meet to punish the people for their transgression, in what way did he accomplish his purpose by the reprobate ? In such a way as shows that the efficacy of the action was in him, and that they were only ministers. At one time he declares, " that he will lift an ensign to the nations from far, and will hiss unto them from the end of the earth ;" at another, that he will take a net to ensnare them ; and at another, that he will be like a hammer to strike them. But he specially declared that he was not inactive among them, when he called Sennacherib an axe, which was formed and destined to be wielded by his own hand.[2] Augustine is not far from the mark when he states the matter thus, That men sin, is attributable to themselves : that in sinning they produce this or that result, is owing to the mighty power of God, who divides the darkness as he pleases (August. de Prædest. Sanct.).

5. Moreover, that the ministry of Satan is employed to instigate the reprobate, whenever the Lord, in the course of his providence, has any purpose to accomplish in them, will sufficiently appear from

God hardens the hearts of men that His purposes may be accomplished.

[1] Ezek. vii. 26 ; Psalm cvii. 40 ; Job xii. 20, 24 ; Isaiah lxiii. 17 ; Exod. iv. 21 ; vii. 3 ; x. 1 ; iii. 19.
[2] Isa. v. 26 ; vii. 18 ; Ezek. xii. 13 ; xvii. 20 ; Jer. 1. 23 ; Isa. x. 15.

a single passage. It is repeatedly said in the First Book of Samuel, that an evil spirit from the Lord came upon Saul, and troubled him (1 Sam. xvi. 14 ; xviii. 10 ; xix. 9). It were impious to apply this to the Holy Spirit. An impure spirit must therefore be called a spirit from the Lord, because completely subservient to his purpose, being more an instrument in acting than a proper agent. We should also add what Paul says, " God shall send them strong delusion, that they should believe a lie : that they all might be damned who believed not the truth (2 Thess. ii. 11, 12). But in the same transaction there is always a wide difference between what the Lord does, and what Satan and the ungodly design to do. The wicked instruments which he has under his hand, and can turn as he pleases, he makes subservient to his own justice. They, as they are wicked, give effect to the iniquity conceived in their wicked minds. Everything necessary to vindicate the majesty of God from calumny, and cut off any subterfuge on the part of the ungodly, has already been expounded in the chapters on Providence (Book I. chapter xvi.—xviii.) Here I only meant to show, in a few words, how Satan reigns in the reprobate, and how God works in both.

6. In those actions which in themselves are neither good nor bad, and concern the corporeal rather than the spiritual life, the liberty which man possesses, although we have above touched upon it (*supra*, Chap. ii. sect. 13—17), has not yet been explained. Some have conceded a free choice to man in such actions ; more, I suppose, because they were unwilling to debate a matter of no great moment, than because they wished positively to assert what they were prepared to concede. While I admit that those who hold that man has no ability in himself to do righteousness, hold what is most necessary to be known for salvation, I think it ought not to be overlooked that we owe it to the special grace of God, whenever, on the one hand, we choose what is for our advantage, and whenever our will inclines in that direction ; and on the other, whenever with heart and soul we shun what would otherwise do us harm. And the interference of Divine Providence goes to the extent not only of making events turn out as was foreseen to be expedient, but of giving the wills of men the same direction. If we look at the administration of human affairs with the eye of sense, we will have no doubt that, so far, they are placed at man's disposal ; but if we lend an ear to the many passages of Scripture which proclaim that even in these matters the minds of men are ruled by God, they will compel us to place human choice in subordination to his special influence. Who gave the Israelites such favour in the eyes of the Egyptians, that they lent them all their most valuable commodities ? (Exod. xi. 3.) They never would have been so inclined of their own accord. Their inclinations, therefore, were more overruled by God than regulated by themselves. And surely, had not Jacob been persuaded that God inspires men with divers affections as seemeth

not have said of his son Joseph (whom he thought to be some heathen Egyptian), " God Almighty give you mercy before the man" (Gen. xliii. 14). In like manner, the whole Church confesses that when the Lord was pleased to pity his people, he made them also to be pitied of all them that carried them captives (Ps. cvi. 46). In like manner, when his anger was kindled against Saul, so that he prepared himself for battle, the cause is stated to have been, that a spirit from God fell upon him (1 Sam. xi. 6). Who dissuaded Absolom from adopting the counsel of Ahithophel, which was wont to be regarded as an oracle? (2 Sam. xvii. 14.) Who disposed Rehoboam to adopt the counsel of the young men? (1 Kings xii. 10.) Who caused the approach of the Israelites to strike terror into nations formerly distinguished for valour? Even the harlot Rahab recognised the hand of the Lord. Who, on the other hand, filled the hearts of the Israelites with fear and dread (Lev. xxvi. 36), but He who threatened in the Law that he would give them a " trembling heart"? (Deut. xxviii. 65.)

7. It may be objected, that these are special examples which cannot be regarded as a general rule. They are sufficient, at all events, to prove the point for which I contend—viz. that whenever God is pleased to make way for his providence, he even in external matters so turns and bends the wills of men, that whatever the freedom of their choice may be, it is still subject to the disposal of God. That your mind depends more on the agency of God than the freedom of your own choice, daily experience teaches. Your judgment often fails, and in matters of no great difficulty, your courage flags; at other times, in matters of the greatest obscurity, the mode of explicating them at once suggests itself, while in matters of moment and danger, your mind rises superior to every difficulty.[1] In this way, I interpret the words of Solomon, " The hearing ear, and the seeing eye, the Lord hath made even both of them" (Prov. xx. 12). For they seem to me to refer not to their creation, but to peculiar grace in the use of them. When he says, " The king's heart is in the hand of the Lord as the rivers of water; he turneth it whithersoever he will" (Prov. xxi. 1), he comprehends the whole race under one particular class. If any will is free from subjection, it must be that of one possessed of regal power, and in a manner exercising dominion over other wills. But if it is under the hand of God, ours surely cannot be exempt from it. On this subject there is an admirable sentiment of Augustine, " Scripture, if it be carefully examined, will show not only that the good wills of men are made good by God out of evil, and when so made, are directed to good acts, even to eternal life, but those which retain the elements of the world are in the power of God, to turn them whither he pleases, and when he pleases, either to perform acts of kindness, or by a hidden, indeed, but, at the

[Margin note:] Whatever man's choice, it is still subject to the disposal of God.

---

[1] The French adds, " D'où procede cela sinon que Dieu besongne tant d'une part que d'autre?"— Whence this, but that God interferes thus far in either case?

same time, most just judgment, to inflict punishment" (August. De Gratia et Lib. Arb. ad Valent. cap . xx.).

8. Let the reader here remember, that the power of the human will is not to be estimated by the event, as some unskilful persons are absurdly wont to do. They think it an elegant and ingenious proof of the bondage of the human will, that even the greatest monarchs are sometimes thwarted in their wishes. But the ability of which we speak must be considered as within the man, not measured by outward success. In discussing the subject of free will, the question is not, whether external obstacles will permit a man to execute what he has internally resolved, but whether, in any matter whatever, he has a free power of judging and of willing. If men possess both of these, Attilius Regulus, shut up in a barrel studded with sharp nails, will have a will no less free than Augustus Cæsar ruling with imperial sway over a large portion of the globe.[1]

---

1 The French is simply, " Car si cela pouvoit etre en l'homme, il ne seroit par moins libre enfermé en un prison que dominant par toute la terre." If that could be in man, he would be no less free shut up in a prison than ruling all the earth.

CHAPTER V.

THE ARGUMENTS USUALLY ALLEGED IN SUPPORT OF FREE WILL REFUTED.

Objections reduced to three principal heads:—I. Four absurdities advanced by the opponents of the orthodox doctrine concerning the slavery of the will, stated and refuted, sec. 1—5. II. The passages of Scripture which they pervert in favour of their error, reduced to five heads, and explained, sec. 6—15. III. Five other passages quoted in defence of free will expounded, sec. 16—19.

Sections.

1. Absurd fictions of opponents first refuted, and then certain passages of Scripture explained. Answer by a negative. Confirmation of the answer.
2. Another absurdity of Aristotle and Pelagius. Answer by a distinction. Answer fortified by passages from Augustine, and supported by the authority of an Apostle.
3. Third absurdity borrowed from the words of Chrysostom. Answer by a negative.
4. Fourth absurdity urged of old by the Pelagians. Answer from the works of Augustine. Illustrated by the testimony of our Saviour. Another answer, which explains the use of exhortations.
5. A third answer, which contains a fuller explanation of the second. Objection to the previous answers. Objection refuted. Summary of the previous answers.
6. First class of arguments which the Neo-Pelagians draw from Scripture in defence of free will. 1. The Law demands perfect obedience; and, therefore, God either mocks us, or requires things which are not in our power. Answer by distinguishing precepts into three sorts. The first of these considered in this and the following section.
7. This general argument from the Law of no avail to the patrons of free will. Promises conjoined with precepts, prove that our salvation is to be found in the grace of God. Objection, that the Law was given to the persons living at the time. Answer, confirmed by passages from Augustine.
8. A special consideration of the three classes of precepts of no avail to the defenders of free will. 1. Precepts enjoining us to turn to God. 2. Precepts which simply speak of the observance of the Law. 3. Precepts which enjoin us to persevere in the grace of God.
9. Objection. Answer. Confirmation of the answer from Jeremiah. Another objection refuted.
10. A second class of arguments in defence of free will drawn from the promises of God—viz. that the promises which God makes to those who seek him are vain if it is not in our power to do, or not do, the thing required. Answer, which explains the use of promises, and removes the supposed inconsistency.
11. Third class of arguments drawn from the divine upbraidings—that it is in vain to upbraid us for evils which it is not in our power to avoid. Answer. Sinners are condemned by their own consciences, and, therefore, the divine upbraidings are just. Moreover, there is a twofold use in these upbraidings. Various passages of Scripture explained by means of the foregoing answers.
12. Objection founded on the words of Moses. Refutation by the words of an Apostle. Confirmation by argument.
13. Fourth class of arguments by the defenders of free will. God waits to see whether or not sinners will repent; therefore they can repent. Answer by a dilemma. Passage in Hosea explained.
14. Fifth class of arguments in defence of free will. Good and bad works described as our own, and therefore we are capable of both. Answer by an exposition,

1. ENOUGH would seem to have been said on the subject of man's will, were there not some who endeavour to urge him to his ruin by a false opinion of liberty, and at the same time, in order to support their own opinion, assail ours. First, they gather together some absurd inferences, by which they endeavour to bring odium upon our doctrine, as if it were abhorrent to common sense, and then they oppose it with certain passages of Scripture (*infra*, sec. 6). Both devices we shall dispose of in their order. If sin, say they, is necessary, it ceases to be sin; if it is voluntary, it may be avoided. Such, too, were the weapons with which Pelagius assailed Augustine. But we are unwilling to crush them by the weight of his name, until we have satisfactorily disposed of the objections themselves. I deny, therefore, that sin ought to be the less imputed because it is necessary; and, on the other hand, I deny the inference, that sin may be avoided because it is voluntary. If any one will dispute with God, and endeavour to evade his judgment, by pretending that he could not have done otherwise, the answer already given is sufficient, that it is owing not to creation, but the corruption of nature, that man has become the slave of sin, and can will nothing but evil. For whence that impotence of which the wicked so readily avail themselves as an excuse, but just because Adam voluntarily subjected himself to the tyranny of the devil? Hence, the corruption by which we are held bound as with chains, originated in the first man's revolt from his Maker. If all men are justly held guilty of this revolt, let them not think themselves excused by a necessity in which they see the clearest cause of their condemnation. But this I have fully explained above; and in the case of the devil himself, have given an example of one who sins not less voluntarily that he sins necessarily. I have also shown, in the case of the elect angels, that though their will cannot decline from good, it does not therefore cease to be will. This Bernard shrewdly explains when he says (Serm. 81, in Cantica), that we are the more miserable in this, that the necessity is voluntary; and yet this necessity so binds us who are subject to it, that we are the slaves of sin, as we have already observed. The second step in the reasoning is vicious, because it leaps from *voluntary* to *free*; whereas we have proved above, that a thing may be done voluntarily, though not subject to free choice.

2. They add, that unless virtue and vice proceed from free choice, it is absurd either to punish man or reward him. Although this argument is taken from Aristotle, I admit that it is also used by Chrysostom and Jerome. Jerome, however, does not disguise that it was familiar to the Pelagians. He even quotes their words, " If grace acts in us, grace, and not we who do the work, will be crowned" (*Hieron. in Ep. ad Ctesiphont. et Dialog. 1.*). With regard to punishment, I answer, that it is properly inflicted on those by whom the guilt is contracted. What matters it whether you sin with a free or an enslaved judgment, so long as you sin voluntarily, especially when man is proved to be a sinner because he is under the bondage of sin? In regard to the rewards of righteousness, is there any great absurdity in acknowledging that they depend on the kindness of God rather than our own merits? How often do we meet in Augustine with this expression,—" God crowns not our merits but his own gifts ; and the name of reward is given not to what is due to our merits, but to the recompense of grace previously bestowed?" Some seem to think there is acuteness in the remark, that there is no place at all for the mind, if good works do not spring from free will as their proper source ; but in thinking this so very unreasonable they are widely mistaken. Augustine does not hesitate uniformly to describe as necessary the very thing which they count it impious to acknowledge. Thus he asks, " What is human merit? He who came to bestow not due recompense but free grace, though himself free from sin, and the giver of freedom, found all men sinners" (Augustin. in Psal. xxxi.). Again, " If you are to receive your due, you must be punished. What then is done? God has not rendered you due punishment, but bestows upon you unmerited grace. If you wish to be an alien from grace, boast your merits" (in Psal. lxx.). Again, " You are nothing in yourself, sin is yours, merit God's. Punishment is your due ; and when the reward shall come, God shall crown his own gifts, not your merits" (Ep. lii.). To the same effect he elsewhere says (De Verb. Apostol. Serm. xv.), that grace is not of merit, but merit of grace. And shortly after he concludes, that God by his gifts anticipates all our merit, that he may thereby manifest his own merit, and give what is absolutely free, because he sees nothing in us that can be a ground of salvation. But why extend the list of quotations, when similar sentiments are ever and anon recurring in his works? The abettors of this error would see a still better refutation of it, if they would attend to the source from which the apostle derives the glory of the saints,—" Moreover, whom he did predestinate, them he also called ; and whom he called, them he also justified ; and whom he justified, them he also glorified" (Rom. viii. 30). On what ground, then, the apostle being judge (2 Tim. iv. 8), are believers crowned? Because by the mercy of God, not their own exertions, they are predestinated, called, and justified. Away, then, with the vain fear, that unless free will stand, there will no longer be

any merit ! It is most foolish to take alarm, and recoil from that which Scripture inculcates. " If thou didst receive it, why dost thou glory as if thou hadst not received it ?" (1 Cor. iv. 7.) You see how everything is denied to free will, for the very purpose of leaving no room for merit. And yet, as the beneficence and liberality of God are manifold and inexhaustible, the grace which he bestows upon us, inasmuch as he makes it our own, he recompenses as if the virtuous acts were our own.

3. But it is added, in terms which seem to be borrowed from Chrysostom (Homil. 22, in Genes.), that if our will possesses not the power of choosing good or evil, all who are partakers of the same nature must be alike good or alike bad. A sentiment akin to this occurs in the work De Vocatione Gentium (Lib. iv. c. 4), usually attributed to Ambrose, in which it is argued, that no one would ever decline from faith, did not the grace of God leave us in a mutable state. It is strange that such men should have so blundered. How did it fail to occur to Chrysostom, that it is divine election which distinguishes among men ? We have not the least hesitation to admit what Paul strenuously maintains, that all, without exception, are depraved and given over to wickedness ; but at the same time we add, that through the mercy of God all do not continue in wickedness. Therefore, while we all labour naturally under the same disease, those only recover health to whom the Lord is pleased to put forth his healing hand. The others whom, in just judgment, he passes over, pine and rot away till they are consumed. And this is the only reason why some persevere to the end, and others, after beginning their course, fall away. Perseverance is the gift of God, which he does not lavish promiscuously on all, but imparts to whom he pleases. If it is asked how the difference arises—why some steadily persevere, and others prove deficient in steadfastness—we can give no other reason than that the Lord, by his mighty power, strengthens and sustains the former, so that they perish not, while he does not furnish the same assistance to the latter, but leaves them to be monuments of instability.

4. Still it is insisted, that exhortations are vain, warnings superfluous, and rebukes absurd, if the sinner possesses not the power to obey. When similar objections were urged against Augustine, he was obliged to write his book, De Correptione et Gratia, where he has fully disposed of them. The substance of his answer to his opponents is this : " O, man ! learn from the precept what you ought to do ; learn from correction, that it is your own fault you have not the power ; and learn in prayer, whence it is that you may receive the power." Very similar is the argument of his book, De Spiritu et Litera, in which he shows that God does not measure the precepts of his law by human strength, but, after ordering what is right, freely bestows on his elect the power of fulfilling it. The subject, indeed, does not require a long discussion. For we are not

singular in our doctrine, but have Christ and all his apostles with us. Let our opponents, then, consider how they are to come off victorious in a contest which they wage with such antagonists. Christ declares, "without me ye can do nothing" (John xv. 5). Does he the less censure and chastise those who, without him, did wickedly ? Does he the less exhort every man to be intent on good works ? How severely does Paul inveigh against the Corinthians for want of charity (1 Cor. iii. 3) ; and yet, at the same time, he prays that charity may be given them by the Lord. In the Epistle to the Romans, he declares that "it is not of him that willeth, nor of him that runneth, but of God that showeth mercy" (Rom. ix. 16). Still he ceases not to warn, exhort, and rebuke them. Why then do they not expostulate with God for making sport with men, by demanding of them things which he alone can give, and chastising them for faults committed through want of his grace ? Why do they not admonish Paul to spare those who have it not in their power to will or to run, unless the mercy of God, which has forsaken them, precede ? As if the doctrine were not founded on the strongest reason —reason which no serious inquirer can fail to perceive. The extent to which doctrine, and exhortation, and rebuke, are in themselves able to change the mind, is indicated by Paul when he says, " Neither is he that planteth any thing, neither he that watereth ; but God that giveth the increase" (1 Cor. iii. 7). In like manner, we see that Moses delivers the precepts of the Law under a heavy sanction, and that the prophets strongly urge and threaten transgressors, though they at the same time confess, that men are wise only when an understanding heart is given them ; that it is the proper work of God to circumcise the heart, and to change it from stone into flesh; to write his law on their inward parts ; in short, to renew souls so as give efficacy to doctrine.

5. What purpose, then, is served by exhortations ? It is this: As the wicked, with obstinate heart, despise them, they will be a testimony against them when they stand at the judgment-seat of God ; nay, they even now strike and lash their consciences. For, however they may petulantly deride, they cannot disapprove them. But what, you will ask, can a miserable mortal do, when softness of heart, which is necessary to obedience, is denied him ? I ask, in reply, Why have recourse to evasion, since hardness of heart cannot be imputed to any but the sinner himself ? The ungodly, though they would gladly evade the divine admonitions, are forced, whether they will or not, to feel their power. But their chief use is to be seen in the case of believers, in whom the Lord, while he always acts by his Spirit, also omits not the instrumentality of his word, but employs it, and not without effect. Let this, then, be a standing truth, that the whole strength of the godly consists in the grace of God, according to the words of the prophet, " I will give them one heart, and I will put a new spirit within you : and I will take the stony heart out

of their flesh, and will give them an heart of flesh, that they may walk in my statutes" (Ezek. xi. 19, 20). But it will be asked, why are they now admonished of their duty, and not rather left to the guidance of the Spirit? Why are they urged with exhortations when they cannot hasten any faster than the Spirit impels them? and why are they chastised, if at any time they go astray, seeing that this is caused by the necessary infirmity of the flesh? "O, man! who art thou that repliest against God?" If, in order to prepare us for the grace which enables us to obey exhortation, God sees meet to employ exhortation, what is there in such an arrangement for you to carp and scoff at? Had exhortations and reprimands no other profit with the godly than to convince them of sin, they could not be deemed altogether useless. Now, when, by the Spirit of God acting within, they have the effect of inflaming their desire of good, of arousing them from lethargy, of destroying the pleasure and honeyed sweetness of sin, making it hateful and loathsome, who will presume to cavil at them as superfluous?

Should any one wish a clearer reply, let him take the following:— God works in his elect in two ways: inwardly, by his Spirit; outwardly, by his Word. By his Spirit illuminating their minds, and training their hearts to the practice of righteousness, he makes them new creatures, while, by his Word, he stimulates them to long and seek for this renovation. In both, he exerts the might of his hand in proportion to the measure in which he dispenses them. The Word, when addressed to the reprobate, though not effectual for their amendment, has another use. It urges their consciences now, and will render them more inexcusable on the day of judgment. Thus, our Saviour, while declaring that none can come to him but those whom the Father draws, and that the elect come after they have heard and learned of the Father (John vi. 44, 45), does not lay aside the office of teacher, but carefully invites those who must be taught inwardly by the Spirit before they can make any profit. The reprobate, again, are admonished by Paul, that the doctrine is not in vain; because, while it is in them a savour of death unto death, it is still a sweet savour unto God (2 Cor. ii. 16).

6. The enemies of this doctrine are at great pains in collecting passages of Scripture, as if, unable to accomplish anything by their weight, they were to overwhelm us by their number. But as in battle, when it is come to close quarters, an unwarlike multitude, how great soever the pomp and show they make, give way after a few blows, and take to flight,[1] so we shall have little difficulty here in disposing of our opponents and their host. All the passages which they pervert in opposing us are very similar in their import; and

---

1 The French is, "Mais c'est comme si un capitaine assembloit force gens qui ne fussent nullement duits à la guerre pour espouvanter son ennemi. Avant que les mettre en œuvre, il feroient grande monstre; mais s'il faloit venir en bataille et joindre contre son ennemi on les feroit fuir du premier coup." But it is as if a captain were

hence, when they are arranged under their proper heads, one answer will suffice for several ; it is not necessary to give a separate consideration to each. Precepts seem to be regarded as their stronghold. These they think so accommodated to our abilities, as to make it follow as a matter of course, that whatever they enjoin we are able to perform. Accordingly, they run over all the precepts, and by them fix the measure of our power. For, say they, when God enjoins meekness, submission, love, chastity, piety, and holiness, and when he forbids anger, pride, theft, uncleanness, idolatry, and the like, he either mocks us, or only requires things which are in our power.

All the precepts which they thus heap together may be divided into three classes. Some enjoin a first conversion unto God, others speak simply of the observance of the law, and others inculcate perseverance in the grace which has been received. We shall first treat of precepts in general, and then proceed to consider each separate class. That the abilities of man are equal to the precepts of the divine law, has long been a common idea, and has some show of plausibility. It is founded, however, on the grossest ignorance of the law. Those who deem it a kind of sacrilege to say, that the observance of the law is impossible, insist, as their strongest argument, that, if it is so, the law has been given in vain (*infra*, chap. vii. sec. 5). For they speak just as if Paul had never said anything about the Law. But what, pray, is meant by saying, that the Law " was added because of transgressions ;" " by the law is the knowledge of sin ;" "I had not known sin but by the law ;" " the law entered that the offence might abound "? (Gal. iii. 19 ; Rom. iii. 20 ; vii. 7 ; v. 20.) Is it meant that the Law was to be limited to our strength, lest it should be given in vain ? Is it not rather meant that it was placed far above us, in order to convince us of our utter feebleness ? Paul indeed declares, that charity is the end and fulfilling of the Law (1 Tim. i. 5). But when he prays that the minds of the Thessalonians may be filled with it, he clearly enough acknowledges that the Law sounds in our ears without profit, if God do not implant it thoroughly in our hearts (1 Thess. iii. 12).

7. I admit, indeed, that if the Scripture taught nothing else on the subject than that the Law is a rule of life by which we ought to regulate our pursuits, I should at once assent to their opinion ; but since it carefully and clearly explains that the use of the Law is manifold, the proper course is to learn from that explanation what the power of the Law is in man. In regard to the present question, while it explains what our duty is, it teaches that the power of obeying it is derived from the goodness of God, and it accordingly urges us to pray that this power may be given us. If there were merely a

to assemble a large body of people, in no wise trained to war, to astonish the enemy. Before coming into action they would make a great show ; but if they were to go into battle, and come to close quarters with the enemy, the first stroke would make them fly.

command and no promise, it would be necessary to try whether our strength were sufficient to fulfil the command; but since promises are annexed, which proclaim not only that aid, but that our whole power is derived from divine grace, they at the same time abundantly testify that we are not only unequal to the observance of the law, but mere fools in regard to it. Therefore, let us hear no more of a proportion between our ability and the divine precepts, as if the Lord had accommodated the standard of justice which he was to give in the law to our feeble capacities. We should rather gather from the promises how ill provided we are, having in everything so much need of grace. But say they, Who will believe that the Lord designed his Law for blocks and stones? There is no wish to make any one believe this. The ungodly are neither blocks nor stones,when taught by the Law that their lusts are offensive to God; they are proved guilty by their own confession; nor are the godly blocks or stones, when, admonished of their powerlessness, they take refuge in grace. To this effect are the pithy sayings of Augustine, " God orders what we cannot do, that we may know what we ought to ask of him. There is a great utility in precepts, if all that is given to free will is to do greater honour to divine grace. Faith acquires what the law requires; nay, the law requires, in order that faith may acquire what is thus required; nay, more, God demands of us faith itself, and finds not what he thus demands, until by giving he makes it possible to find it." Again, he says, " Let God give what he orders, and order what he wills."[1]

8. This will be more clearly seen by again attending to the three classes of precepts to which we above referred. Both in the Law and in the Prophets, God repeatedly calls upon us to turn to him.[2] But, on the other hand, a prophet exclaims, "Turn thou me, and I shall be turned; for thou art the Lord my God. Surely, after that I was turned, I repented." He orders us to circumcise the foreskins of our hearts; but Moses declares, that that circumcision is made by his own hand. In many passages he demands a new heart, but in others he declares that he gives it. As Augustine says, " What God promises, we ourselves do not through choice or nature, but he himself does by grace." The same observation is made, when, in enumerating the rules of Tichonius, he states the third in effect to be—that we distinguish carefully between the Law and the promises, or between the commands and grace (Augustin. de Doctrina Christiana, Lib. iii.). Let them now go and gather from precepts what man's power of obedience is, when they would destroy the divine grace by which the precepts themselves are accomplished. The precepts of the second class are simply those which enjoin us to worship God, to

---

[1] August. Enchir. ad Laurent. de Gratia et Liber. Arbit. cap. 16. Homil. 29, in Joann. Ep. 24.
[2] Joel ii. 12; Jer. xxxi. 18; Deut. x. 16; xxx 6; Ezek. xxxvi. 26; Jer. xxxi. 18. Vid. Calvin. adv. Pighium.

obey and adhere to his will, to do his pleasure, and follow his teaching. But innumerable passages testify that every degree of purity, piety, holiness, and justice, which we possess, is his gift. Of the third class of precepts is the exhortation of Paul and Barnabas to the proselytes, as recorded by Luke ; they " persuaded them to continue in the grace of God" (Acts xiii. 43). But the source from which this power of continuance must be sought is elsewhere explained by Paul, when he says, " Finally, my brethren, be strong in the Lord" (Eph. vi. 10). In another passage he says, " Grieve not the Holy Spirit of God, whereby ye are sealed unto the day of redemption" (Eph. iv. 30). But as the thing here enjoined could not be performed by man, he prays in behalf of the Thessalonians, that God would count them " worthy of this calling, and fulfil all the good pleasure of his goodness, and the work of faith with power " (2 Thess. i. 11). In the same way, in the Second Epistle to the Corinthians, when treating of alms, he repeatedly commends their good and pious inclination. A little farther on, however, he exclaims, " Thanks be to God, which put the same earnest care into the heart of Titus for you. For indeed he accepted the exhortation" (2 Cor. viii. 16, 17). If Titus could not even perform the office of being a mouth to exhort others, except in so far as God suggested, how could the others have been voluntary agents in acting, if the Lord Jesus had not directed their hearts ?

9. Some, who would be thought more acute, endeavour to evade all these passages, by the quibble, that there is nothing to hinder us from contributing our part, while God, at the same time, supplies our deficiencies. They, moreover, adduce passages from the Prophets, in which the work of our conversion seems to be shared between God and ourselves ; " Turn ye unto me, saith the Lord of hosts, and I will turn unto you, saith the Lord of hosts " (Zech i. 3). The kind of assistance which God gives us has been shown above (sect. 7, 8), and need not now be repeated. One thing only I ask to be conceded to me, that it is vain to think we have a power of fulfilling the Law, merely because we are enjoined to obey it. Since, in order to our fulfilling the divine precepts, the grace of the Lawgiver is both necessary, and has been promised to us, this much at least is clear, that more is demanded of us than we are able to pay. Nor can any cavil evade the declaration in Jeremiah, that the covenant which God made with his ancient people was broken, because it was only of the letter—that to make it effectual, it was necessary for the Spirit to interpose and train the heart to obedience (Jer. xxxi. 32). The opinion we now combat is not aided by the words, " Turn unto me, and I will turn unto you." The turning there spoken of is not that by which God renews the heart unto repentance ; but that in which, by bestowing prosperity, he manifests his kindness and favour, just in the same way as he sometimes expresses his displeasure by sending adversity. The people complaining under the many calami-

ties which befell them, that they were forsaken by God, he answers, that his kindness would not fail them, if they would return to a right course, and to himself, the standard of righteousness. The passage, therefore, is wrested from its proper meaning when it is made to countenance the idea that the work of conversion is divided between God and man (*supra*, Chap, il. sec. 27). We have only glanced briefly at this subject, as the proper place for it will occur when we come to treat of the Law (Chap. vii. sec. 2 and 3).

10. The second class of objections is akin to the former. They allege the promises in which the Lord makes a paction with our will. Such are the following: "Seek good, and not evil, that ye may live" (Amos v. 14). "If ye be willing and obedient, ye shall eat the good of the land : but if ye refuse and rebel, ye shall be devoured with the sword : for the mouth of the Lord hath spoken it" (Isaiah i. 19, 20). "If thou wilt put away thine abominations out of my sight, then thou shalt not remove" (Jer. iv. 1). "It shall come to pass, if thou shalt hearken diligently unto the voice of the Lord thy God, to observe and do all the commandments which I command thee this day, that the Lord thy God will set thee on high above all nations of the earth" (Deut. xxviii. 1). There are other similar passages (Lev. xxvi. 3, &c.). They think that the blessings contained in these promises are offered to our will absurdly and in mockery, if it is not in our power to secure or reject them. It is, indeed, an easy matter to indulge in declamatory complaint on this subject,—to say that we are cruelly mocked [1] by the Lord when he declares that his kindness depends on our will, if we are not masters of our will,—that it would be a strange liberality on the part of God to set his blessings before us, while we have no power of enjoying them,—a strange certainty of promises, which, to prevent their ever being fulfilled, are made to depend on an impossibility. Of promises of this description, which have a condition annexed to them, we shall elsewhere speak, and make it plain that there is nothing absurd in the impossible fulfilment of them. In regard to the matter in hand, I deny that God cruelly mocks us when he invites us to merit blessings which he knows we are altogether unable to merit. The promises being offered alike to believers and to the ungodly, have their use in regard to both. As God by his precepts stings the consciences of the ungodly, so as to prevent them from enjoying their sins while they have no remembrance of his judgments, so, in his promises, he in a manner takes them to witness how unworthy they are of his kindness. Who can deny that it is most just and most becoming in God to do good to those who worship him, and to punish with due severity those who despise his majesty? God, therefore, proceeds in due order, when, though the wicked are bound

---

1 The French is, " Et de fait cette raison a grande apparence humainement. Car on peut deduire que ce seroit une cruauté de Dieu," &c.—And, in fact, humanly speaking, there is great plausibility in this argument. For, it may be maintained, that it would be cruelty in God, &c.

by the fetters of sin, he lays down the law in his promises, that he will do them good only if they depart from their wickedness. This would be right, though His only object were to let them understand that they are deservedly excluded from the favour due to his true worshippers. On the other hand, as he desires by all means to stir up believers to supplicate his grace, it surely should not seem strange that he attempts to accomplish by promises the same thing which, as we have shown, he to their great benefit accomplishes by means of precepts. Being taught by precepts what the will of God is, we are reminded of our wretchedness in being so completely at variance with that will, and, at the same time, are stimulated to invoke the aid of the Spirit to guide us into the right path. But as our indolence is not sufficiently aroused by precepts, promises are added, that they may attract us by their sweetness, and produce a feeling of love for the precept. The greater our desire of righteousness, the greater will be our earnestness to obtain the grace of God. And thus it is, that in the protestations, *if ye be willing, if thou shalt hearken*, the Lord neither attributes to us a full power of willing and hearkening, nor yet mocks us for our impotence.[1]

11. The third class of objections is not unlike the other two. For they produce passages in which God upbraids his people for their ingratitude, intimating that it was not his fault that they did not obtain all kinds of favour from his indulgence. Of such passages, the following are examples: "The Amalekites and the Canaanites are before you, and ye shall fall by the sword: because ye are turned away from the Lord, therefore the Lord will not be with you" (Num. xiv. 43). "Because ye have done all these works, saith the Lord, and I spake unto you, rising up early and speaking, but ye heard not; and I called you, but ye answered not; therefore will I do unto this house, which is called by my name, wherein ye trust, and unto the place which I gave to you and to your fathers, as I have done to Shiloh" (Jer. vii. 13, 14). "They obeyed not thy voice, neither walked in thy law: they have done nothing of all that thou commandedst them to do; therefore thou hast caused all this evil to come upon them" (Jer. xxxii. 23). How, they ask, can such upbraiding be directed against those who have it in their power immediately to reply,— Prosperity was dear to us: we feared adversity; that we did not, in order to obtain the one and avoid the other, obey the Lord, and listen to his voice, is owing to its not being free for us to do so in consequence of our subjection to the dominion of sin; in vain, therefore, are we upbraided with evils which it was not in our power to escape. But to say nothing of the pretext of necessity, which is but a feeble and flimsy defence of their conduct, can they, I ask, deny their guilt? If they are held convicted of any fault, the Lord is not unjust in upbraiding them for having, by their own perverseness, deprived them-

---

1 The French adds, " Veu qu'en cela il fait le profit de ses serviteurs et rend les iniques plus damnables ;" seeing that by this he promotes the good of his servants, and rend..rs the wicked more deserving of condemnation.

selves of the advantages of his kindness.   Let them say, then, whether they can deny that their own will is the depraved cause of their rebellion.   If they find within themselves a fountain of wickedness, why do they stand declaiming about extraneous causes, with the view of making it appear that they are not the authors of their own destruction?   If it be true that it is not for another's faults that sinners are both deprived of the divine favour, and visited with punishment, there is good reason why they should hear these rebukes from the mouth of God.   If they obstinately persist in their vices, let them learn in their calamities to accuse and detest their own wickedness, instead of charging God with cruelty and injustice.   If they have not manifested docility, let them, under a feeling of disgust at the sins which they see to be the cause of their misery and ruin, return to the right path, and, with serious contrition, confess the very thing of which the Lord by his rebuke reminds them.   Of what use those upbraidings of the prophets above quoted are to believers, appears from the solemn prayer of Daniel, as given in his ninth chapter.   Of their use in regard to the ungodly, we see an example in the Jews, to whom Jeremiah was ordered to explain the cause of their miseries, though the event could not be otherwise than the Lord had foretold.   "Therefore thou shalt speak these words unto them ; but they will not hearken unto thee : thou shalt also call unto them ; but they will not answer thee" (Jer. vii. 27).   Of what use, then, was it to talk to the deaf?   It was, that even against their will they might understand that what they heard was true, and that it was impious blasphemy to transfer the blame of their wickedness to God, when it resided in themselves.

These few explanations will make it very easy for the reader to disentangle himself from the immense heap of passages (containing both precepts and reprimands) which the enemies of divine grace are in the habit of piling up, that they may thereon erect their statue of free will.   The Psalmist upbraids the Jews as "a stubborn and rebellious generation ; a generation that set not their heart aright" (Psalm lxxviii. 8); and in another passage, he exhorts the men of his time, "Harden not your heart" (Psalm xcv. 8).   This implies that the whole blame of the rebellion lies in human depravity.   But it is foolish thence to infer, that the heart, the preparation of which is from the Lord, may be equally bent in either direction.   The Psalmist says, "I have inclined my heart to perform thy statutes alway" (Psalm cxix. 112); meaning, that with willing and cheerful readiness of mind he had devoted himself to God.   He does not boast, however, that he was the author of that disposition, for in the same psalm he acknowledges it to be the gift of God.   We must, therefore, attend to the admonition of Paul, when he thus addresses believers, "Work out your own salvation with fear and trembling.   For it is God which worketh in you both to will and to do of his good pleasure" (Philip. ii. 12, 13).   He ascribes to them a part in acting that they may not indulge in carnal sloth, but by enjoining fear and trembling, he humbles them so as to keep them in remembrance, that the very thing which they are ordered to do is the proper work of God—distinctly intimating, that believers act (if I may so speak) *passively*, inasmuch as the power is given them from heaven, and cannot in any way be arrogated to themselves. Accordingly, when Peter exhorts us to "add to faith virtue" (2 Pet. i. 5), he does not concede to us the possession of a second place, as if we could do anything separately. He only arouses the sluggishness of our flesh, by which faith itself is frequently stifled. To the same effect are the words of Paul. He says, "Quench not the Spirit" (1 Thess. v. 19); because a spirit of sloth, if not guarded against, is ever and anon creeping in upon believers. But should any thence infer that it is entirely in their own power to foster the offered light, his ignorance will easily be refuted by the fact, that the very diligence which Paul enjoins is derived only from God (2 Cor. vii. 1). We are often commanded to purge ourselves of all impurity, though the Spirit claims this as his peculiar office. In fine, that what properly belongs to God is transferred to us only by way of concession, is plain from the words of John, "He that is begotten of God keepeth himself" (1 John v. 18). The advocates of free will fasten upon the expression, as if it implied that we are kept partly by the power of God, partly by our own, whereas the very keeping of which the Apostle speaks is itself from heaven. Hence, Christ prays his Father to keep us from evil (John xvii. 15), and we know that believers, in their warfare against Satan, owe their victory to the armour of God. Accordingly, Peter, after saying, "Ye have purified your souls in obeying the truth," immediately adds by way of correction, "through the Spirit" (1 Pet. i. 22). In fine, the nothingness of human strength in the spiritual contest is briefly shown by John, when he says, that "Whosoever is born of God doth not commit sin ; for his seed remaineth in him" (1 John iii. 9). He elsewhere gives the reason, "This is the victory that overcometh the world, even our faith" (1 John v. 4).

12. But a passage is produced from the Law of Moses, which seems very adverse to the view now given. After promulgating the Law, he takes the people to witness in these terms: "This commandment which I command thee this day, it is not hidden from thee, neither is it far off. It is not in heaven, that thou shouldest say, Who shall go up for us to heaven, and bring it unto us, that we may hear it, and do it ? But the word is very nigh unto thee, in thy mouth, and in thy heart, that thou mayest do it" (Deut. xxx. 11, 12, 14). Certainly, if this is to be understood of mere precepts, I admit that it is of no little importance to the matter in hand. For, though it were easy to evade the difficulty by saying, that the thing here treated of is not the observance of the law, but the facility and readiness of becoming acquainted with it, some scruple, perhaps, would still remain. The Apostle Paul, however, no mean interpreter, removes all doubt when he affirms, that Moses here spoke of the doctrine of the Gospel (Rom.

x. 8). If any one is so refractory as to contend that Paul violently wrested the words in applying them to the Gospel, though his hardihood is chargeable with impiety, we are still able, independently of the authority of the Apostle, to repel the objection. For, if Moses spoke of precepts merely, he was only inflating the people with vain confidence. Had they attempted the observance of the law in their own strength, as a matter in which they should find no difficulty, what else could have been the result than to throw them headlong? Where, then, was that easy means of observing the law, when the only access to it was over a fatal precipice?[1] Accordingly, nothing, is more certain, than that under these words is comprehended the covenant of mercy, which had been promulgated along with the demands of the law. A few verses before, he had said, "The Lord thy God will circumcise thine heart, and the heart of thy seed, to love the Lord thy God with all thine heart, and with all thy soul, that thou mayest live" (Deut. xxx. 6). Therefore, the readiness of which he immediately after speaks was placed not in the power of man, but in the protection and help of the Holy Spirit, who mightily performs his own work in our weakness. The passage, however, is not to be understood of precepts simply, but rather of the Gospel promises, which, so far from proving any power in us to fulfil righteousness, utterly disprove it. This is confirmed by the testimony of Paul, when he observes that the Gospel holds forth salvation to us, not under the harsh, arduous, and impossible terms on which the law treats with us (namely, that those shall obtain it who fulfil all its demands), but on terms easy, expeditious, and readily obtained. This passage, therefore, tends in no degree to establish the freedom of the human will.

13. They are wont also to adduce certain passages in which God is said occasionally to try men, by withdrawing the assistance of his grace, and to wait until they turn to him, as in Hosea, "I will go and return to my place, till they acknowledge their offence, and seek my face" (Hosea v. 15). It were absurd (say they), that the Lord should wait till Israel should seek his face, if their minds were not flexible, so as to turn in either direction of their own accord. As if anything were more common in the prophetical writings than for God to put on the semblance of rejecting and casting off his people until they reform their lives. But what can our opponents extract from such threats? If they mean to maintain that a people, when abandoned by God, are able of themselves to think of turning unto him, they will do it in the very face of Scripture. On the other hand, if they admit that divine grace is necessary to conversion, why do they dispute with us? But while they admit that grace is so far necessary, they insist on reserving some ability for man. How do they

---

[1] The French is, "Où est-ce que sera cette facilité, veu que notre natute succombe en cet endroit, et n'y a celui qui ne trebusche voulant marcher?" Where is this facility, seeing that our nature here gives way, and there is not a man who in wishing to walk does not tumble?

prove it ? Certainly not from this nor any similar passage; for it is one thing to withdraw from man, and look to what he will do when thus abandoned and left to himself, and another thing to assist his powers (whatever they may be), in proportion to their weakness. What, then, it will be asked, is meant by such expressions ? I answer, just the same as if God were to say, Since nothing is gained by admonishing, exhorting, rebuking this stubborn people, I will withdraw for a little, and silently leave them to be afflicted; I shall see whether, after long calamity, any remembrance of me will return, and induce them to seek my face. But by the departure of the Lord to a distance is meant the withdrawal of prophecy. By his waiting to see what men will do is meant that he, while silent, and in a manner hiding himself, tries them for a season with various afflictions. Both he does that he may humble us the more; for we shall sooner be broken than corrected by the strokes of adversity, unless his Spirit train us to docility. Moreover, when the Lord, offended, and, as it were, fatigued with our obstinate perverseness, leaves us for a while (by withdrawing his word, in which he is wont in some degree to manifest his presence), and makes trial of what we will do in his absence, from this it is erroneously inferred, that there is some power of free will, the extent of which is to be considered and tried, whereas the only end which he has in view is to bring us to an acknowledgment of our utter nothingness.

14. Another objection is founded on a mode of speaking which is constantly observed both in Scripture and in common discourse. Good works are said to be ours, and we are said to do what is holy and acceptable to God, just as we are said to commit sin. But if sins are justly imputed to us, as proceeding from ourselves, for the same reason (say they) some share must certainly be attributed to us in works of righteousness. It could not be accordant with reason to say, that we do those things which we are incapable of doing of our own motion, God moving us, as if we were stones. These expressions, therefore, it is said, indicate that while, in the matter of grace, we give the first place to God, a secondary place must be assigned to our agency. If the only thing here insisted on were, that good works are termed *ours*, I, in my turn, would reply, that the bread which we ask God to give us is also termed *ours*. What, then, can be inferred from the title of possession, but simply that, by the kindness and free gift of God, that becomes ours which in other respects is by no means due to us ? Therefore, let them either ridicule the same absurdity in the Lord's Prayer, or let them cease to regard it as absurd, that good works should be called ours, though our only property in them is derived from the liberality of God. But there is something stronger in the fact, that we are often said in Scripture to worship God, do justice, obey the law, and follow good works. These being proper offices of the mind and will, how can they be consistently referred to the Spirit, and, at the same time, attributed to us, unless there be some concur-

rence on our part with the divine agency? This difficulty will be easily disposed of if we attend to the manner in which the Holy Spirit acts in the righteous. The similitude with which they invidiously assail us is foreign to the purpose; for who is so absurd as to imagine that movement in man differs in nothing from the impulse given to a stone? Nor can anything of the kind be inferred from our doctrine. To the natural powers of man we ascribe approving and rejecting, willing and not willing, striving and resisting—viz. approving vanity, rejecting solid good, willing evil and not willing good, striving for wickedness and resisting righteousness. What then does the Lord do? If he sees meet to employ depravity of this description as an instrument of his anger, he gives it whatever aim and direction he pleases, that, by a guilty hand, he may accomplish his own good work. A wicked man thus serving the power of God, while he is bent only on following his own lust, can we compare to a stone, which, driven by an external impulse, is borne along without motion, or sense, or will of its own? We see how wide the difference is. But how stands the case with the godly, as to whom chiefly the question is raised? When God erects his kingdom in them, he, by means of his Spirit, curbs their will, that it may not follow its natural bent, and be carried hither and thither by vagrant lusts; bends, frames, trains, and guides it according to the rule of his justice, so as to incline it to righteousness and holiness, and stablishes it and strengthens it by the energy of his Spirit, that it may not stumble or fall. For which reason Augustine thus expresses himself (De Corrept. et Gratia, cap. ii.), "It will be said we are therefore acted upon, and do not act. Nay, you act and are acted upon, and you then act well when you are acted upon by one that is good. The Spirit of God who actuates you is your helper in acting, and bears the name of helper, because you, too, do something." In the former member of this sentence, he reminds us that the agency of man is not destroyed by the motion of the Holy Spirit, because nature furnishes the will which is guided so as to aspire to good. As to the second member of the sentence, in which he says that the very idea of help implies that we also do something, we must not understand it as if he were attributing to us some independent power of action; but not to foster a feeling of sloth, he reconciles the agency of God with our own agency, by saying, that to wish is from nature, to wish well is from grace. Accordingly, he had said a little before, "Did not God assist us, we should not only not be able to conquer, but not able even to fight."

15. Hence it appears that the grace of God (as this name is used when regeneration is spoken of) is the rule of the Spirit, in directing and governing the human will. Govern he cannot, without correcting, reforming, renovating (hence we say that the beginning of regeneration consists in the abolition of what is ours); in like manner, he cannot govern without moving, impelling, urging, and restraining. Accordingly, all the actions which are afterwards done are truly said

to be wholly his. Meanwhile, we deny not the truth of Augustine's doctrine, that the will is not destroyed, but rather repaired, by grace —the two things being perfectly consistent—viz. that the human will may be said to be renewed when, its vitiosity and perverseness being corrected, it is conformed to the true standard of righteousness, and that, at the same time, the will may be said to be made new, being so vitiated and corrupted that its nature must be entirely changed. There is nothing then to prevent us from saying, that our will does what the Spirit does in us, although the will contributes nothing of itself apart from grace. We must, therefore, remember what we quoted from Augustine, that some men labour in vain to find in the human will some good quality properly belonging to it. Any intermixture which men attempt to make by conjoining the effort of their own will with divine grace is corruption, just as when unwholesome and muddy water is used to dilute wine. But though everything good in the will is entirely derived from the influence of the Spirit, yet, because we have naturally an innate power of willing, we are not improperly said to do the things of which God claims for himself all the praise: first, because everything which his kindness produces in us is our own (only we must understand that it is not of ourselves); and, secondly, because it is our mind, our will, our study, which are guided by him to what is good.

16. The other passages which they gather together from different quarters will not give much trouble to any person of tolerable understanding, who pays due attention to the explanations already given. They adduce the passage of Genesis, "Unto thee shall be his desire, and thou shalt rule over him" (Gen. iv. 7). This they interpret of sin, as if the Lord were promising Cain that the dominion of sin should not prevail over his mind, if he would labour in subduing it. We, however, maintain that it is much more agreeable to the context to understand the words as referring to Abel, it being there the purpose of God to point out the injustice of the envy which Cain had conceived against his brother. And this He does in two ways, by showing, first, that it was vain to think he could, by means of wickedness, surpass his brother in the favour of God, by whom nothing is esteemed but righteousness; and, secondly, how ungrateful he was for the kindness he had already received, in not being able to bear with a brother who had been subjected to his authority. But lest it should be thought that we embrace this interpretation because the other is contrary to our view, let us grant that God does here speak of sin. If so, his words contain either an order or a promise. If an order, we have already demonstrated that this is no proof of man's ability ; if a promise, where is the fulfilment of the promise when Cain yielded to the sin over which he ought to have prevailed? They will allege a tacit condition in the promise, as if it were said that he would gain the victory if he contended. This sul terfuge is altogether unavailing. For, if the dominion spoken of refers to sin,

no man can have any doubt that the form of expression is imperative, declaring not what we are able, but what it is our duty to do, even if beyond our ability. Although both the nature of the case, and the rule of grammatical construction, require that it be regarded as a comparison between Cain and Abel, we think the only preference given to the younger brother was, that the elder made himself inferior by his own wickedness.

17. They appeal, moreover, to the testimony of the Apostle Paul, because he says, "It is not of him that willeth, nor of him that runneth, but of God that showeth mercy" (Rom. ix. 15). From this they infer, that there is something in will and endeavour, which, though weak in themselves, still, being mercifully aided by God, are not without some measure of success. But if they would attend in sober earnest to the subject there handled by Paul, they would not so rashly pervert his meaning. I am aware they can quote Origen and Jerome[1] in support of this exposition. To these I might, in my turn, oppose Augustine. But it is of no consequence what they thought, if it is clear what Paul meant. He teaches that salvation is prepared for those only on whom the Lord is pleased to bestow his mercy—that ruin and death await all whom he has not chosen. He had proved the condition of the reprobate by the example of Pharaoh, and confirmed the certainty of gratuitous election by the passage in Moses, "I will have mercy on whom I will have mercy." Thereafter he concludes, that it is not of him that willeth, nor of him that runneth, but of God that showeth mercy. If these words are understood to mean that the will or endeavour are not sufficient, because unequal to such a task, the apostle has not used them very appropriately. We must therefore abandon this absurd mode of arguing, "It is not of him that willeth, nor of him that runneth;"—therefore, there is some will, some running. Paul's meaning is more simple—there is no will nor running by which we can prepare the way for our salvation—it is wholly of the divine mercy. He indeed says nothing more than he says to Titus, when he writes, "After that the kindness and love of God our Saviour toward man appeared, not by works of righteousness which we have done, but according to his mercy he saved us" (Titus iii. 4, 5). Those who argue that Paul insinuated there was some will and some running when he said, "It is not of him that willeth, nor of him that runneth," would not allow me to argue after the same fashion, that we have done some righteous works, because Paul says that we have attained the divine favour, "not by works of righteousness which we have done." But if they see a flaw in this mode of arguing, let them open their eyes, and they will see that their own mode is not free from a similar fallacy. The argument which Augustine uses is well founded, "If it is said, ' It

[1] Orig. Lib. vii. in Epist. ad Rom.—Hieron. Dial. i in Pelagium.—For the passage in Augustine, see the extract in Book III. chap. xxiv. sec. i.

is not of him that willeth, nor of him that runneth,' because neither will nor running are sufficient ; it may, on the other hand, be retorted, it is not ' of God that showeth mercy,' because mercy does not act alone" (August. Ep. 170, ad Vital. See also Enchirid. ad Laurent. cap. 32). This second proposition being absurd, Augustine justly concludes the meaning of the words to be, that there is no good will in man until it is prepared by the Lord ; not that we ought not to will and run, but that both are produced in us by God. Some, with equal unskilfulness, wrest the saying of Paul, " We are labourers together with God" (1 Cor. iii. 9). There cannot be a doubt that these words apply to ministers only, who are called " labourers with God," not from bringing anything of their own, but because God makes use of their instrumentality after he has rendered them fit, and provided them with the necessary endowments.

18. They appeal also to Ecclesiasticus, who is well known to be a writer of doubtful authority. But, though we might justly decline his testimony, let us see what he says in support of free will. His words are, " He himself made man from the beginning, and left him in the hand of his counsel ; If thou wilt, to keep the commandments, and perform acceptable faithfulness. He hath set fire and water before thee : stretch forth thy hand unto whether thou wilt. Before man is life and death ; and whether him liketh shall be given him" (Ecclesiasticus xv. 14—17). Grant that man received at his creation a power of acquiring life or death ; what, then, if we, on the other hand, can reply that he has lost it ? Assuredly I have no intention to contradict Solomon, who asserts that " God hath made man upright ;" that " they have sought out many inventions" (Eccl. vii. 29). But since man, by degenerating, has made shipwreck of himself and all his blessings, it certainly does not follow, that everything attributed to his nature, as originally constituted, applies to it now when vitiated and degenerate. Therefore, not only to my opponents, but to the author of Ecclesiasticus himself (whoever he may have been), this is my answer : If you mean to tell man that in himself there is a power of acquiring salvation, your authority with us is not so great as, in the least degree, to prejudice the undoubted word of God ; but if only wishing to curb the malignity of the flesh, which, by transferring the blame of its own wickedness to God, is wont to catch at a vain defence, you say that rectitude was given to man, in order to make it apparent he was the cause of his own destruction, I willingly assent. Only agree with me in this, that it is by his own fault he is stript of the ornaments in which the Lord at first attired him, and then let us unite in acknowledging that what he now wants is a physician, and not a defender.

19. There is nothing more frequent in their mouths than the parable of the traveller who fell among thieves, and was left half dead (Luke x. 32). I am aware that it is a common idea with almost all writers, that under the figure of the traveller is represented

the calamity of the human race. Hence our opponents argue that man was not so mutilated by the robbery of sin and the devil as not to preserve some remains of his former endowments ; because it is said he was left half dead. For where is the half living, unless some portion of right will and reason remain ? First, were I to deny that there is any room for their allegory, what could they say ? There can be no doubt that the Fathers invented it contrary to the genuine sense of the parable. Allegories ought to be carried no further than Scripture expressly sanctions : so far are they from forming a sufficient basis to found doctrines upon. And were I so disposed, I might easily find the means of tearing up this fiction by the roots. The Word of God leaves no half life to man, but teaches that, in regard to life and happiness, he has utterly perished. Paul, when he speaks of our redemption, says not that the half dead are cured (Eph. ii. 5, 30 ; v. 14), but that those who were dead are raised up. He does not call upon the half dead to receive the illumination of Christ, but upon those who are asleep and buried. In the same way our Lord himself says, " The hour is coming, and now is, when the dead shall hear the voice of the Son of God" (John v. 25). How can they presume to set up a flimsy allegory in opposition to so many clear statements ? But be it that this allegory is good evidence, what can they extort out of it ?   Man is half dead ; therefore there is some soundness in him. True ! he has a mind capable of understanding, though incapable of attaining to heavenly and spiritual wisdom ; he has some discernment of what is honourable ; he has some sense of the Divinity, though he cannot reach the true knowledge of God. But to what do these amount? They certainly do not refute the doctrine of Augustine—a doctrine confirmed by the common suffrages even of the Schoolmen, that after the fall, the free gifts on which salvation depends were withdrawn, and natural gifts corrupted and defiled (*supra*, chap. ii. sec. 2). Let it stand, therefore, as an indubitable truth, which no engines can shake, that the mind of man is so entirely alienated from the righteousness of God that he cannot conceive, desire, or design anything but what is wicked, distorted, foul, impure, and iniquitous ; that his heart is so thoroughly envenomed by sin, that it can breathe out nothing but corruption and rottenness ; that if some men occasionally make a show of goodness, their mind is ever interwoven with hypocrisy and deceit, their soul inwardly bound with the fetters of wickedness.

CHAPTER VI.

REDEMPTION FOR MAN LOST TO BE SOUGHT IN CHRIST.

The parts of this chapter are, I. The excellence of the doctrine of Christ the Redeemer —a doctrine always entertained by the Church, sec. 1. II. Christ, the Mediator in both dispensations, was offered to the faith of the pious Israelites and people of old, as is plain from the institution of sacrifice, the calling of Abraham's family, and the elevation of David and his posterity, sec. 2. III. Hence the consolation, strength, hope, and confidence of the godly under the Law, Christ being offered to them in various ways by their heavenly Father.

Sections.

1. The knowledge of God the Creator of no avail without faith in Christ the Redeemer. First reason. Second reason strengthened by the testimony of an Apostle. Conclusion. This doctrine entertained by the children of God in all ages from the beginning of the world. Error of throwing open heaven to the heathen, who know nothing of Christ. The pretexts for this refuted by passages of Scripture.
2. God never was propitious to the ancient Israelites without Christ the Mediator. First reason founded on the institution of sacrifice. Second reason founded on the calling of Abraham. Third reason founded on the elevation of David's family to regal dignity, and confirmed by striking passages of Scripture.
3. Christ the solace ever promised to the afflicted; the banner of faith and hope always erected. This confirmed by various passages of Scripture.
4. The Jews taught to have respect to Christ. This teaching sanctioned by our Saviour himself. The common saying, that God is the object of faith, requires to be explained and modified. Conclusion of this discussion concerning Christ. No saving knowledge of God in the heathen.

1. THE whole human race having been undone in the person of Adam, the excellence and dignity of our origin, as already described, is so far from availing us, that it rather turns to our greater disgrace, until God, who does not acknowledge man when defiled and corrupted by sin as his own work, appear as a Redeemer in the person of his only begotten Son. Since our fall from life unto death, all that knowledge of God the Creator, of which we have discoursed, would be useless, were it not followed up by faith, holding forth God to us as a Father in Christ. The natural course undoubtedly was, that the fabric of the world should be a school in which we might learn piety, and from it pass to eternal life and perfect felicity. But after looking at the perfection beheld wherever we turn our eye, above and below, we are met by the divine malediction, which, while it involves innocent creatures in our fault, of necessity fills our own souls with despair. For although God is still pleased in many ways to manifest his paternal favour towards us, we cannot, from a mere survey of the world, infer that he is a Father. Conscience urging us within, and showing that sin is a just ground for our being forsaken, will not allow us to think that God accounts or treats us as sons. In addition

This chapter added in 1559.

to this are our sloth and ingratitude.   Our minds are so blinded that they cannot perceive the truth, and all our senses are so corrupt that we wickedly rob God of his glory.   Wherefore, we must conclude with Paul, "After that in the wisdom of God the world by wisdom knew not God, it pleased God by the foolishness of preaching to save them that believe" (1 Cor. i. 21).   By the "wisdom of God," he designates this magnificent theatre of heaven and earth replenished with numberless wonders, the wise contemplation of which should have enabled us to know God.   But this we do with little profit; and, therefore, he invites us to faith in Christ,—faith which, by a semblance of foolishness, disgusts the unbeliever.   Therefore, although the preaching of the cross is not in accordance with human wisdom, we must, however, humbly embrace it if we would return to God our Maker, from whom we are estranged, that he may again become our Father.   It is certain that after the fall of our first parent, no knowledge of God without a Mediator was effectual to salvation.   Christ speaks not of his own age merely, but embraces all ages, when he says, "This is life eternal, that they might know thee the only true God, and Jesus Christ, whom thou hast sent" (John xvii. 3).   The more shameful, therefore, is the presumption of those who throw heaven open to the unbelieving and profane, in the absence of that grace which Scripture uniformly describes as the only door by which we enter into life.   Should any confine our Saviour's words to the period subsequent to the promulgation of the Gospel, the refutation is at hand; since, on a ground common to all ages and nations, it is declared, that those who are estranged from God, and as such, are under the curse, the children of wrath, cannot be pleasing to God until they are reconciled.   To this we may add the answer which our Saviour gave to the Samaritan woman, "Ye worship ye know not what; we know what we worship: for salvation is of the Jews" (John iv. 22).   By these words, he both charges every Gentile religion with falsehood, and assigns the reason—viz., that under the Law the Redeemer was promised to the chosen people only, and that, consequently, no worship was ever pleasing to God in which respect was not had to Christ.   Hence also Paul affirms, that all the Gentiles were "without God," and deprived of the hope of life.   Now, since John teaches that there was life in Christ from the beginning, and that the whole world had lost it (John i. 4), it is necessary to return to that fountain; and, accordingly, Christ declares that, inasmuch as he is a propitiator, he is life.   And, indeed, the inheritance of heaven belongs to none but the sons of God (John xv. 6).   Now, it were most incongruous to give the place and rank of sons to any who have not been engrafted into the body of the only begotten Son.   And John distinctly testifies that those become the sons of God who believe in his name.   But as it is not my intention at present formally to discuss the subject of faith in Christ, it is enough to have thus touched on it in passing.

[margin note:] Because of the Fall, man's mind became so clouded that not even the witness of His creation could supply man's missing knowledge of God. For this reason, the coming of Christ was necessary—that man's knowledge of God might be restored.

2. Hence it is that God never showed himself propitious to his
ancient people, nor gave them any hope of grace without a Mediator.
I say nothing of the sacrifices of the Law, by which believers were
plainly and openly taught that salvation was not to be found anywhere but in the expiation which Christ alone completed. All I
maintain is, that the prosperous and happy state of the Church was
always founded in the person of Christ. For although God embraced
the whole posterity of Abraham in his covenant, yet Paul properly
argues (Gal. iii. 16), that Christ was truly the seed in which all the
nations of the earth were to be blessed, since we know that all who
were born of Abraham, according to the flesh, were not accounted
the seed. To omit Ishmael and others, how came it that of the two
sons of Isaac, the twin brothers, Esau and Jacob, while yet in the
womb, the one was chosen and the other rejected? Nay, how came
it that the first-born was rejected, and the younger alone admitted?
Moreover, how happens it that the majority are rejected? It is
plain, therefore, that the seed of Abraham is considered chiefly in
one head, and that the promised salvation is not attained without
coming to Christ, whose office it is to gather together those which
were scattered abroad. Thus the primary adoption of the chosen
people depended on the grace of the Mediator. Although it is not
expressed in very distinct terms in Moses, it, however, appears to
have been commonly known to all the godly. For before a king was
appointed over the Israelites, Hannah, the mother of Samuel, describing the happiness of the righteous, speaks thus in her song, " He
shall give strength unto his king, and exalt the horn of his anointed ;"
meaning by these words, that God would bless his Church. To this
corresponds the prediction, which is afterwards added, " I will raise
me up a faithful priest,——and he shall walk before mine anointed
for ever" (1 Sam. ii. 10, 35). And there can be no doubt that our
heavenly Father intended that a living image of Christ should be
seen in David and his posterity. Accordingly, exhorting the righteous to fear Him, he bids them " Kiss the Son" (Psalm ii. 12).
Corresponding to this is the passage in the Gospel, " He that
honoureth not the Son, honoureth not the Father" (John v. 23).
Therefore, though the kingdom was broken up by the revolt of the
ten tribes, yet the covenant which God had made in David and his
successors behoved to stand, as is also declared by his Prophets,
" Howbeit I will not take the whole kingdom out of his hand : but I
will make him prince all the days of his life for David my servant's
sake" (1 Kings xi. 34). The same thing is repeated a second and
third time. It is also expressly said, " I will for this afflict the seed
of David, but not for ever" (1 Kings xi. 39). Some time afterwards
it was said, " Nevertheless, for David's sake did the Lord his God
give him a lamp in Jerusalem, to set up his own after him, and to
establish Jerusalem" (1 Kings xv. 4). And when matters were
bordering on destruction, it was again said, " Yet the Lord would

*[margin note:] Through-
out the
O.T.
appear
the
types
of
Christ.*

uot destroy Judah for David his servant's sake, as he had promised to give him alway a light, and to his children" (2 Kings viii.19).

The sum of the whole comes to this—David, all others being excluded, was chosen to be the person in whom the good pleasure of the Lord should dwell; as it is said elsewhere, "He forsook the tabernacle of Shiloh;" "Moreover, he refused the tabernacle of Joseph, and chose not the tribe of Ephraim;" "But chose the tribe of Judah, the mount Zion which he loved;" "He chose David also his servant, and took him from the sheepfolds: from following the ewes great with young he brought him to feed Jacob his people, and Israel his inheritance" (Ps. lxxviii. 60, 67, 70, 71). In fine, God, in thus preserving his Church, intended that its security and salvation should depend on Christ as its head. Accordingly, David exclaims, "The Lord is their strength, and he is the saving strength of his anointed;" and then prays, "Save thy people, and bless thine inheritance;" intimating, that the safety of the Church was indissolubly connected with the government of Christ. In the same sense he elsewhere says, "Save Lord: let the king hear us when we call" (Ps. xx. 9). These words plainly teach that believers, in applying for the help of God, had their sole confidence in this—that they were under the unseen government of the King. This may be inferred from another psalm, "Save now, I beseech thee, O Lord: Blessed be he that cometh in the name of the Lord" (Ps. cxviii. 25, 26). Here it is obvious that believers are invited to Christ, in the assurance that they will be safe when entirely in his hand. To the same effect is another prayer, in which the whole Church implores the divine mercy, "Let thy hand be upon the Man of thy right hand, upon the Son of man, whom thou madest strong (or hast fitted) for thyself" (Ps. lxxx. 17). For though the author of the psalm laments the dispersion of the whole nation, he prays for its revival in him who is sole Head. After the people were led away into captivity, the land laid waste, and matters to appearance desperate, Jeremiah, lamenting the calamity of the Church, especially complains, that by the destruction of the kingdom the hope of believers was cut off; "The breath of our nostrils, the anointed of the Lord, was taken in their pits, of whom we said, Under his shadow we shall live among the heathen" (Lam. iv. 20). From all this it is abundantly plain, that as the Lord cannot be propitious to the human race without a Mediator, Christ was always held forth to the holy Fathers under the Law as the object of their faith.

3. Moreover, when comfort is promised in affliction, especially when the deliverance of the Church is described, the banner of faith and hope in Christ is unfurled. "Thou wentest forth for the salvation of thy people, even for salvation with thine anointed," says Habakkuk (iii. 13). And whenever mention is made in the Prophets of the renovation of the Church, the people are directed to the promise made to David, that his kingdom would be for ever. And

there is nothing strange in this, since otherwise there would have been no stability in the covenant. To this purpose is the remarkable prophecy in Isaiah vii. 14. After seeing that the unbelieving king Ahaz repudiated what he had testified regarding the deliverance of Jerusalem from siege and its immediate safety, he passes as it were abruptly to the Messiah, " Behold, a Virgin shall conceive and bear a son, and shall call his name Immanuel ;" intimating indirectly, that though the king and his people wickedly rejected the promise offered to them, as if they were bent on causing the faith of God to fail, the covenant would not be defeated—the Redeemer would come in his own time. In fine, all the prophets, to show that God was placable, were always careful to bring forward that kingdom of David, on which redemption and eternal salvation depended. Thus in Isaiah it is said, " I will make an everlasting covenant with you, even the sure mercies of David. Behold, I have given him for a witness to the people" (Isa. lv. 3, 4); intimating, that believers, in calamitous circumstances, could have no hope, had they not this testimony, that God would be ready to hear them. In the same way, to revive their drooping spirits, Jeremiah says, " Behold, the days come, saith the Lord, that I will raise unto David a righteous Branch, and a King shall reign and prosper, and shall execute judgment and justice in the earth. In his days Judah shall be saved, and Israel shall dwell safely" (Jer. xxiii. 5, 6). In Ezekiel also it is said, "I will set up one Shepherd over them, and he shall feed them, even my servant David ; he shall feed them, and he shall be their shepherd. And I the Lord will be their God, and my servant David a prince among them : I the Lord have spoken it. And I will make with them a covenant of peace" (Ezek. xxxiv. 23, 24, 25). And again, after discoursing of this wondrous renovation, he says, " David my servant shall be king over them : and they all shall have one shepherd." " Moreover, I will make a covenant of peace with them ; it shall be an everlasting covenant with them" (Ezek. xxxvii. 24—26). I select a few passages our of many, because I merely wish to impress my readers with the fact, that the hope of believers was ever treasured up in Christ alone. All the other prophets concur in this. Thus Hosea, " Then shall the children of Judah and the children of Israel be gathered together, and appoint themselves one head" (Hosea i. 11). This he afterwards explains in clearer terms, " Afterward shall the childen of Israel return, and seek the Lord their God, and David their king" (Hosea iii. 5). Micah, also speaking of the return of the people, says expressly, " Their king shall pass before them, and the Lord on the head of them" (Micah ii. 13). So Amos, in predicting the renovation of the people, says, " In that day will I raise up the tabernacle of David that is fallen, and close up the breaches thereof; and I will raise up the ruins, and I will build it as in the days of old" (Amos ix. 11); in other words, the only banner of salvation was, the exaltation of the family of David to regal splendour,

Prophets pre-figured Christ.

as fulfilled in Christ. Hence, too, Zechariah, as nearer in time to the manifestation of Christ, speaks more plainly, " Rejoice greatly, O daughter of Zion; shout, O daughter of Jerusalem: behold, thy King cometh unto thee: he is just, and having salvation" (Zech. ix. 9). This corresponds to the passage already quoted from the Psalms, "The Lord is their strength, and he is the saving health of their anointed." Here salvation is extended from the head to the whole body.

4. By familiarising the Jews with these prophecies, God intended to teach them, that in seeking for deliverance, they should turn their eyes directly towards Christ. And though they had sadly degenerated, they never entirely lost the knowledge of this general principle, that God, by the hand of Christ, would be the deliverer of the Church, as he had promised to David; and that in this way only the free covenant by which God had adopted his chosen people would be fulfilled. Hence it was, that on our Saviour's entry into Jerusalem, shortly before his death, the children shouted, "Hosannah to the son of David" (Matth. xxi. 9). For there seems to have been a hymn known to all, and in general use, in which they sang, that the only remaining pledge which they had of the divine mercy was the promised advent of a Redeemer. For this reason, Christ tells his disciples to believe in him, in order that they might have a distinct and complete belief in God, " Ye believe in God, believe also in me" (John xiv. 1). For although, properly speaking, faith rises from Christ to the Father, he intimates, that even when it leans on God, it gradually vanishes away, unless he himself interpose to give it solid strength. The majesty of God is too high to be scaled up to by mortals, who creep like worms on the earth. Therefore, the common saying that God is the object of faith (Lactantius, Lib. iv. c. 16), requires to be received with some modification. When Christ is called the image of the invisible God (Col. i. 15), the expression is not used without cause, but is designed to remind us that we can have no knowledge of our salvation, until we behold God in Christ. For although the Jewish scribes had by their false glosses darkened what the prophets had taught concerning the Redeemer, yet Christ assumed it to be a fact, received, as it were, with public consent, that there was no other remedy in desperate circumstances, no other mode of delivering the Church, than the manifestation of the Mediator. It is true, that the fact adverted to by Paul was not so generally known as it ought to have been—viz. that Christ is the end of the Law (Rom. x. 4), though this is both true, and clearly appears both from the Law and the Prophets. I am not now, however, treating of faith, as we shall elsewhere have a fitter place (Book III. chap. ii.), but what I wish to impress upon my readers in this way is, that the first step in piety is, to acknowledge that God is a Father, to defend, govern, and cherish us, until he brings us to the eternal inheritance of his kingdom; that hence it is plain, as we lately observed, there is no

Jews had a foreknowledge of Christ, but this became perverted

Only by belief in Christ can one gain a distinct and complete belief in God.

First step in piety is to acknowledge God to be a loving Father.

Thus,
No
Know-
ledge of
God
apart
from
Christ.

having knowledge of God without Christ, and that, consequently, from the beginning of the world Christ was held forth to all the elect as the object of their faith and confidence. In this sense, Irenæus says, that the Father, who is boundless in himself, is bounded in the Son, because he has accommodated himself to our capacity, lest our minds should be swallowed up by the immensity of his glory (Irenæus, Lib. iv. cap. 8). Fanatics, not attending to this, distort a useful sentiment into an impious dream,[1] as if Christ had only a share of the Godhead, as a part taken from a whole ; whereas the meaning merely is, that God is comprehended in Christ alone. The saying of John was always true, " Whosoever denieth the Son, the same hath not the Father" (1 John ii. 23). For though in old time there were many who boasted that they worshipped the Supreme Deity, the Maker of heaven and earth, yet as they had no Mediator, it was impossible for them truly to enjoy the mercy of God, so as to feel persuaded that he was their Father. Not holding the head, that is, Christ, their knowledge of God was evanescent ; and hence they at length fell away to gross and foul superstitions, betraying their ignorance, just as the Turks in the present day, who, though proclaiming, with full throat, that the Creator of heaven and earth is their God, yet, by their rejection of Christ, substitute an idol in his place.

1 French, " reverie infernale.

CHAPTER VII.

THE LAW GIVEN, NOT TO RETAIN A PEOPLE FOR ITSELF, BUT TO KEEP ALIVE THE HOPE OF SALVATION IN CHRIST UNTIL HIS ADVENT.

The divisions of this chapter are, I. The Moral and Ceremonial Law a schoolmaster to bring us to Christ, sec. 1, 2. II. This true of the Moral Law, especially its conditional promises. These given for the best reasons. In what respect the observance of the Moral Law is said to be impossible, sec. 3—5. III. Of the threefold office and use of the Moral Law, sec. 6—12. Antinomians refuted, sec. 13. IV. What the abrogation of the Law, Moral and Ceremonial, sec. 14—17.

Sections.

1. The whole system of religion delivered by the hand of Moses, in many ways pointed to Christ. This exemplified in the case of sacrifices, ablutions, and an endless series of ceremonies. This proved, 1. By the declared purpose of God; 2. By the nature of the ceremonies themselves; 3. From the nature of God; 4. From the grace offered to the Jews; 5. From the consecration of the priests.
2. Proof continued. 6. From a consideration of the kingdom erected in the family of David. 7. From the end of the ceremonies. 8. From the end of the Moral Law.
3. A more ample exposition of the last proof. The Moral Law leads believers to Christ. Showing the perfect righteousness required by God, it convinces us of our inability to fulfil it. It thus denies us life, adjudges us to death, and so urges us to seek deliverance in Christ.
4. The promises of the Law, though conditional, founded on the best reason. This reason explained.
5. No inconsistency in giving a law, the observance of which is impossible. This proved from reason, and confirmed by Scripture. Another confirmation from Augustine.
6. A consideration of the office and use of the Moral Law shows that it leads to Christ. The Law, while it describes the righteousness which is acceptable to God, proves that every man is unrighteous.
7. The Law fitly compared to a mirror, which shows us our wretchedness. This derogates not in any degree from its excellence.
8. When the Law discloses our guilt, we should not despond, but flee to the mercy of God. How this may be done.
9. Confirmation of the first use of the Moral Law from various passages in Augustine.
10. A second use of the Law is to curb sinners. This most necessary for the good of the community at large; and this in respect not only of the reprobate, but also of the elect, previous to regeneration. This confirmed by the authority of an Apostle.
11. The Law showing our wretchedness, disposes us to admit the remedy. It also tends to keep us in our duty. Confirmation from general experience.
12. The third and most appropriate use of the Law respects the elect. 1. It instructs and teaches them to make daily progress in doing the will of God. 2. Urges them by exhortation to obedience. Testimony of David. How he is to be reconciled with the Apostle.
13. The profane heresy of the Antinomians must be exploded. Argument founded on a passage in David, and another in Moses.
14. Last part of the chapter treating of the abrogation of the Law. In what respect any part of the Moral Law abrogated.

First four sections added in 1559

15. The curse of the Law how abrogated.
16. Of the abrogation of the Ceremonial Law in regard to the observance only.
17. The reason assigned by the Apostle applicable not to the Moral Law, but to ceremonial observances only. These abrogated, not only because they separated the Jews from the Gentiles, but still more because they were a kind of formal instruments to attest our guilt and impurity. Christ, by destroying these, is justly said to have taken away the handwriting that was against us, and nailed it to his cross.

1. FROM the whole course of the observations now made, we may infer that the Law was not superadded about four hundred years after the death of Abraham in order that it might lead the chosen people away from Christ, but, on the contrary, to keep them in suspense until his advent; to inflame their desire, and confirm their expectation, that they might not become dispirited by the long delay. By the Law, I understand not only the Ten Commandments, which contain a complete rule of life, but the whole system of religion delivered by the hand of Moses. Moses was not appointed as a Lawgiver, to do away with the blessing promised to the race of Abraham; nay, we see that he is constantly reminding the Jews of the free covenant which had been made with their fathers, and of which they were heirs; as if he had been sent for the purpose of renewing it. This is most clearly manifested by the ceremonies. For what could be more vain or frivolous than for men to reconcile themselves to God, by offering him the foul odour produced by burning the fat of beasts? or to wipe away their own impurities by besprinkling themselves with water or blood? In short, the whole legal worship (if considered by itself apart from the types and shadows of corresponding truth) is a mere mockery. Wherefore, both in Stephen's address (Acts vii. 44), and in the Epistle to the Hebrews, great weight is justly given to the passage in which God says to Moses, "Look that thou make them after the pattern which was showed thee in the mount" (Exod. xxv. 40). Had there not been some spiritual end to which they were directed, the Jews, in the observance of them, would have deluded themselves as much as the Gentiles in their vanities. Profane men, who have never made religion their serious study, cannot bear without disgust to hear of such a multiplicity of rites. They not merely wonder why God fatigued his ancient people with such a mass of ceremonies, but they despise and ridicule them as childish toys. This they do, because they attend not to the end; from which, if the legal figures are separated, they cannot escape the charge of vanity. But the type shows that God did not enjoin sacrifice, in order that he might occupy his worshippers with earthly exercises, but rather that he might raise their minds to something higher. This is clear even from His own nature. Being a spirit, he is delighted only with spiritu l worship. The same thing is testified by the many passages in which the Prophets accuse the Jews of stupidity, for imagining that mere sacrifices have any value in the sight of God. Did they by this mean to derogate in any respect from the Law? By

no means; but as interpreters of its true meaning, they wished in this way to turn the attention of the people to the end which they ought to have had in view, but from which they generally wandered. From the grace offered to the Jews, we may certainly infer, that the law was not a stranger to Christ. Moses declared the end of the adoption of the Israelites to be, that they should be " a kingdom of priests, and an holy nation" (Exod. xix. 6). This they could not attain, without a greater and more excellent atonement than the blood of beasts. For what could be less in accordance with reason, than that the sons of Adam, who, from hereditary taint, are all born the slaves of sin, should be raised to royal dignity, and in this way made partakers of the glory of God, if the noble distinction were not derived from some other source? How, moreover, could the priestly office exist in vigour among those whose vices rendered them abominable in the sight of God, if they were not consecrated in a holy head? Wherefore, Peter elegantly transposes the words of Moses, teaching that the fulness of grace, of which the Jews had a foretaste under the Law, is exhibited in Christ, " Ye are a chosen generation, a royal priesthood" (1 Pet. ii. 9). The transposition of the words intimates that those to whom Christ has appeared in the Gospel, have obtained more than their fathers, inasmuch as they are all endued with priestly and royal honour, and can, therefore, trusting to their Mediator, appear with boldness in the presence of God.

2. And it is to be observed, by the way, that the kingdom, which was at length erected in the family of David, is part of the Law, and is comprehended under the dispensation of Moses; whence it follows, that, as well in the whole tribe of Levi as in the posterity of David, Christ was exhibited to the eyes of the Israelites as in a double mirror. For, as I lately observed (sec. i.), in no other way could those who were the slaves of sin and death, and defiled with corruption, be either kings or priests. Hence appears the perfect truth of Paul's statement, " The law was our schoolmaster to bring us unto Christ," " till the seed should come to whom the promise was made" (Gal. iii. 24, 19). For Christ not yet having been made familiarly known to the Jews, they were like children whose weakness could not bear a full knowledge of heavenly things. How they were led to Christ by the ceremonial law has already been adverted to, and may be made more intelligible by several passages in the Prophets. Although they were required, in order to appease God, to approach him daily with new sacrifices, yet Isaiah promises, that all their sins would be expiated by one single sacrifice, and with this Daniel concurs (Is. liii. 5; Dan. ix. 26, 27). The priests appointed from the tribe of Levi entered the sanctuary, but it was once said of a single priest, " The Lord hath sworn, and will not repent, Thou art a priest for ever, after the order of Melchizedek" (Ps. cx. 4). The unction of oil was then visible, but Daniel in vision declares that there will be another unction. Not to dwell on this, the author of the Epistle to

the Hebrews proves clearly, and at length, from the fourth to the eleventh chapter, that ceremonies were vain, and of no value, unless as bringing us to Christ. In regard to the Ten Commandments, we must, in like manner, attend to the statement of Paul, that "Christ is the end of the law for righteousness to every one that believeth" (Rom. x. 4) ; and, again, that ministers of the New Testament were "not of the letter, but of the spirit : for the letter killeth, but the spirit giveth life" (2 Cor. iii. 6). The former passage intimates, that it is in vain to teach righteousness by precept, until Christ bestow it by free imputation, and the regeneration of the Spirit. Hence he properly calls Christ the end or fulfilling of the Law, because it would avail us nothing to know what God demands, did not Christ come to the succour of those who are labouring, and oppressed under an intolerable yoke and burden. In another place, he says that the Law " was added because of transgressions" (Gal. iii. 19), that it might humble men under a sense of their condemnation. Moreover, inasmuch as this is the only true preparation for Christ, the statements, though made in different words, perfectly agree with each other. But because he had to dispute with perverse teachers, who pretended that men merited justification by the works of the Law, he was sometimes obliged, in refuting their error, to speak of the Law in a more restricted sense, merely as law, though, in other respects, the covenant of free adoption is comprehended under it.

3. But in order that a sense of guilt may urge us to seek for pardon, it is of importance to know how our being instructed in the Moral Law renders us more inexcusable. If it is true, that a perfect righteousness is set before us in the Law, it follows, that the complete observance of it is perfect righteousness in the sight of God ; that is, a righteousness by which a man may be deemed and pronounced righteousness at the divine tribunal. Wherefore Moses, after promulgating the Law, hesitates not to call heaven and earth to witness, that he had set life and death, good and evil before the people. Nor can it be denied, that the reward of eternal salvation, as promised by the Lord, awaits the perfect obedience of the Law (Deut. xxx. 19). Again, however, it is of importance to understand in what way we perform that obedience for which we justly entertain the hope of that reward. For of what use is it to see that the reward of eternal life depends on the observance of the Law, unless it moreover appears whether it be in our power in that way to attain to eternal life ? Herein, then, the weakness of the Law is manifested ; for, in none of us is that righteousness of the Law manifested, and, therefore, being excluded from the promises of life, we again fall under the curse. I state not only what happens, but what must necessarily happen. The doctrine of the Law transcending our capacity, a man may indeed look from a distance at the promises held forth, but he cannot derive any benefit from them. The only thing, therefore, remaining for him is, from their excellence to form a better estimate of his own

misery, while he considers that the hope of salvation is cut off, and he is threatened with certain death. On the other hand, those fearful denunciations which strike not at a few individuals, but at every individual without exception, rise up; rise up, I say, and, with inexorable severity, pursue us; so that nothing but instant death is presented by the Law.

4. Therefore, if we look merely to the Law, the result must be despondency, confusion, and despair, seeing that by it we are all cursed and condemned, while we are kept far away from the blessedness which it holds forth to its observers. Is the Lord, then, you will ask, only sporting with us? Is it not the next thing to mockery, to hold out the hope of happiness, to invite and exhort us to it, to declare that it is set before us, while all the while the entrance to it is precluded and quite shut up? I answer, Although the promises, in so far as they are conditional, depend on a perfect obedience of the Law, which is nowhere to be found, they have not, however, been given in vain. For when we have learned, that the promises would be fruitless and unavailing, did not God accept us of his free goodness, without any view to our works, and when, having so learned, we, by faith, embrace the goodness thus offered in the gospel, the promises, with all their annexed conditions, are fully accomplished. For God, while bestowing all things upon us freely, crowns his goodness by not disdaining our imperfect obedience; forgiving its deficiencies, accepting it as if it were complete, and so bestowing upon us the full amount of what the Law has promised. But as this point will be more fully discussed in treating of justification by faith, we shall not follow it further at present.

The Law accomplishes its mission when it shows us that our salvation depends almost soley upon the grace of God. — As taught in the gospel.

5. What has been said as to the impossible observance of the Law, it will be proper briefly to explain and confirm, the general opinion being, that nothing can be more absurd. Hence Jerome has not hesitated to denounce anathema against it.[1] What Jerome thought, I care not; let us inquire what is the truth. I will not here enter into a long and intricate discussion on the various kinds of possibility. By impossible, I mean, that which never was, and, being prevented by the ordination and decree of God, never will be. I say, that if we go back to the remotest period, we shall not find a single saint who, clothed with a mortal body, ever attained to such perfection as to love the Lord with all his heart, and soul, and mind, and strength; and, on the other hand, not one who has not felt the power of concupiscence. Who can deny this? I am aware, indeed, of a kind of saints whom a foolish superstition imagines, and whose purity the angels of heaven scarcely equal. This, however, is repugnant both to Scripture and experience. But I say further, that no saint ever will attain to perfection, so long as he is in the body. Scripture bears clear testimony to this effect: "There is no man that sinneth

---

[1] See among the works of Justin. Quæst. 103; and Hieronymus ad Ctesiphont adv. Pelegianos, where he seems to admit and deny the same proposition.

not," saith Solomon (1 Kings viii. 46). David says, "In thy sight shall no man living be justified" (Psalm cxliii. 2). Job also, in numerous passages, affirms the same thing. But the clearest of all is Paul, who declares that "the flesh lusteth against the Spirit, and the Spirit against the flesh" (Gal. v. 17). And he proves, that "as many as are of the works of the Law are under the curse," for the simple reason, that it is written, "Cursed is every one that continueth not in all things which are written in the book of the law to do them" (Gal. iii. 10; Deut. xxvii. 26); intimating, or rather assuming it as confessed, that none can so continue. But whatever has been declared by Scripture must be regarded as perpetual, and hence necessary. The Pelagians annoyed Augustine with the sophism, that it was insulting to God to hold, that he orders more than believers are able, by his grace, to perform; and he, in order to evade it, acknowledged that the Lord was able, if he chose, to raise a mortal man to angelic purity; but that he had never done, and never would do it, because so the Scripture had declared (Augustine, Lib. de Nat. et Grat.). This I deny not: but I add, that there is no use in absurdly disputing concerning the power of God in opposition to his truth; and therefore there is no ground for cavilling, when it is said that that thing cannot be, which the Scriptures declare will never be. But if it is the word that is objected to, I refer to the answer which our Saviour gave to his disciples when they asked, "Who then can be saved?" "With men," said he, "This is impossible; but with God all things are possible" (Matth. xix. 25). Augustine argues in the most convincing manner, that while in the flesh, we never can give God the love which we owe him. "Love so follows knowledge, that no man can perfectly love God who has not previously a full comprehension of his goodness" (Augustin. de Spiritu et Litera, towards the end and elsewhere). So long as we are pilgrims in the world, we see through a glass darkly, and therefore our love is imperfect. Let it therefore be held incontrovertible, that, in consequence of the feebleness of our nature, it is impossible for us, so long as we are in the flesh, to fulfil the law. This will also be proved elsewhere from the writings of Paul (Rom. viii. 3).[1]

6. That the whole matter may be made clearer, let us take a succinct view of the office and use of the Moral Law. Now, this office and use seems to me to consist of three parts. First, by exhibiting the righteousness of God,—in other words, the righteousness which alone is acceptable to God,—it admonishes every one of his own unrighteousness, certiorates, convicts, and finally condemns him. This is necessary, in order that man, who is blind and intoxicated with self-love, may be brought at once to know and to confess his weakness and impurity. For until his vanity is made perfectly manifest, he is puffed up with infatuated confidence in his own

So long as we are in the flesh, it is impossible for us to fulfill the Law.

Office of the Moral Law —
1. To show the righteousness which alone is acceptable to God.

1 Book II. chap. xii. sec. 4; and Book III. chap. iv. sec. 27; and chap. xi. sec. 23.

powers, and never can be brought to feel their feebleness so long as he measures them by a standard of his own choice. So soon, however, as he begins to compare them with the requirements of the Law, he has something to tame his presumption. How high soever his opinion of his own powers may be, he immediately feels that they pant under the heavy load, then totter and stumble, and finally fall and give way. He, then, who is schooled by the Law, lays aside the arrogance which formerly blinded him. In like manner must he be cured of pride, the other disease under which we have said that he labours. So long as he is permitted to appeal to his own judgment, he substitutes a hypocritical for a real righteousness, and, contented with this, sets up certain factitious observances in opposition to the grace of God. But after he is forced to weigh his conduct in the balance of the Law, renouncing all dependence on this fancied righteousness, he sees that he is at an infinite distance from holiness, and, on the other hand, that he teems with innumerable vices of which he formerly seemed free. The recesses in which concupiscence lies hid are so deep and tortuous that they easily elude our view ; and hence the Apostle had good reason for saying, " I had not known lust, except the law had said, Thou shalt not covet." For, if it be not brought forth from its lurking-places, it miserably destroys in secret before its fatal sting is discerned.

7. Thus the Law is a kind of mirror.. As in a mirror we discover any stains upon our face, so in the Law we behold, first, our impotence ; then, in consequence of it, our iniquity; and, finally, the curse, as the consequence of both. He who has no power of following righteousness is necessarily plunged in the mire of iniquity, and this iniquity is immediately followed by the curse. Accordingly, the greater the transgression of which the Law convicts us, the severer the judgment to which we are exposed. To this effect is the Apostle's declaration, that " by the law is the knowledge of sin" (Rom. iii. 20). By these words, he only points out the first office of the Law as experienced by sinners not yet regenerated. In conformity to this, it is said, " the law entered that the offence might abound ;" and, accordingly, that it is " the ministration of death ;" that it " worketh wrath " and kills (Rom. v. 20 ; 2 Cor. iii. 7 ; Rom. iv. 15). For there cannot be a doubt that the clearer the consciousness of guilt, the greater the increase of sin ; because then to transgression a rebellious feeling against the Lawgiver is added. All that remains for the Law, is to arm the wrath of God for the destruction of the sinner ; for by itself it can do nothing but accuse, condemn, and destroy him. Thus Augustine says, " If the Spirit of grace be absent, the law is present only to convict and slay us."[1] But to say this neither insults the law, nor derogates in any degree from its excellence. Assuredly, if our whole will were formed and disposed to obedience, the

[margin note: Thus, the Law is a kind of Mirror]

---

merc knowledge of the law would be sufficient for salvation ; but since our carnal and corrupt nature is at enmity with the Divine law, and is in no degree amended by its discipline, the consequence is, that the law which, if it had been properly attended to, would have given life, becomes the occasion of sin and death. When all are convicted of transgression, the more it declares the righteousness of God, the more, on the other hand, it discloses our iniquity ; the more certainly it assures us that life and salvation are treasured up as the reward of righteousness, the more certainly it assures us that the un-righteous will perish. So far, however, are these qualities from throw-ing disgrace on the Law, that their chief tendency is to give a brighter display of the divine goodness. For they show that it is only our weakness and depravity that prevents us from enjoying the blessed-ness which the law openly sets before us. Hence additional sweet-ness is given to divine grace, which comes to our aid without the law, and additional loveliness to the mercy which confers it, because they proclaim that God is never weary in doing good, and in loading us with new gifts.

8. But while the unrighteousness and condemnation of all are attested by the law, it does not follow (if we make the proper use of it) that we are immediately to give up all hope and rush headlong on despair. No doubt, it has some such effect upon the reprobate, but this is owing to their obstinacy. With the children of God the effect is different. The Apostle testifies that the law pronounces its sentence of condemnation in order " that every mouth may be stopped, and all the world may become guilty before God" (Rom. iii. 19). In another place, however, the same Apostle declares that "God hath con-cluded them all in unbelief ;" not that he might destroy all, or allow all to perish, but that " he might have mercy upon all" (Rom. xi. 32): in other words, that divesting themselves of an absurd opinion of their own virtue, they may perceive how they are wholly depend-ent on the hand of God ; that feeling how naked and destitute they are, they may take refuge in his mercy, rely upon it, and cover them-selves up entirely with it ; renouncing all righteousness and merit, and clinging to mercy alone, as offered in Christ to all who long and look for it in true faith. In the precepts of the law, God is seen as the rewarder only of perfect righteousness (a righteousness of which all are destitute), and, on the other hand, as the stern avenger of wickedness. But in Christ his countenance beams forth full of grace and gentleness towards poor unworthy sinners.

9. There are many passages in Augustine, as to the utility of the law in leading us to implore Divine assistance. Thus he writes to Hilary,[1] " The law orders, that we, after attempting to do what is ordered, and so feeling our weakness under the law, may learn to implore the help of grace." In like manner, he writes to Assellius,

---

[1] August. Ep. 89, Quæst. 2 ; ad Assell. Ep. 200 ; ad Innocent. Ep. 95 ; Lib. de Cor-rept. et Gratia ad Valent. ; in Ps. lxx. et cxviii. ; Item, Concio. 27.

" The utility of the law is, that it convinces man of his weakness, and compels him to apply for the medicine of grace, which is in Christ." In like manner, he says to Innocentius Romanus, " The law orders ; grace supplies the power of acting." Again, to Valentinus, " God enjoins what we cannot do, in order that we may know what we have to ask of him." Again, " The law was given, that it might make you guilty—being made guilty, might fear ; fearing, might ask indulgence, not presume on your own strength." Again, " The law was given, in order to convert a great into a little man— to show that you have no power of your own for righteousness ; and might thus, poor, needy, and destitute, flee to grace." He afterwards thus addresses the Almighty, " So do, O Lord, so do, O merciful Lord ; command what cannot be fulfilled ; nay, command what cannot be fulfilled, unless by thy own grace : so that when men feel they have no strength in themselves to fulfil it, every mouth may be stopped, and no man seem great in his own eyes. Let all be little ones ; let the whole world become guilty before God." But I am forgetting myself in producing so many passages, since this holy man wrote a distinct treatise, which he entitled *De Spiritu et Litera*. The other branch of this first use he does not describe so distinctly, either because he knew that it depended on the former, or because he was not so well aware of it, or because he wanted words in which he might distinctly and clearly explain its proper meaning. But even in the reprobate themselves, this first office of the law is not altogether wanting. They do not, indeed, proceed so far with the children of God as, after the flesh is cast down, to be renewed in the inner man, and revive again, but stunned by the first terror, give way to despair. Still it tends to manifest the equity of the Divine judgment, when their consciences are thus heaved upon the waves. They would always willingly carp at the judgment of God ; but now, though that judgment is not manifested, still the alarm produced by the testimony of the law and of their conscience bespeaks their deserts.

10. The second office of the Law is, by means of its fearful denunciations and the consequent dread of punishment, to curb those who, unless forced, have no regard for rectitude and justice. Such persons are curbed, not because their mind is inwardly moved and affected, but because, as if a bridle were laid upon them, they refrain their hands from external acts, and internally check the depravity which would otherwise petulantly burst forth. It is true, they are not on this account either better or more righteous in the sight of God. For although restrained by terror or shame, they dare not proceed to what their mind has conceived, nor give full license to their raging lust, their heart is by no means trained to fear and obedience. Nay, the more they restrain themselves, the more they are inflamed, the more they rage and boil, prepared for any act or outbreak whatsoever, were it not for the terror of the law. And not only so, but they thoroughly detest the law itself, and execrate the Lawgiver ; so that

2. To curb those who otherwise would have no regard for rectitude and justice.

if they could, they would most willingly annihilate him, because they cannot bear either his ordering what is right, or his avenging the despisers of his Majesty. The feeling of all who are not yet regenerate, though in some more, in others less lively, is, that in regard to the observance of the law, they are not led by voluntary submission, but dragged by the force of fear. Nevertheless, this forced and extorted righteousness is necessary for the good of society, its peace being secured by a provision but for which all things would be thrown into tumult and confusion. Nay, this tuition is not without its use, even to the children of God, who, previous to their effectual calling, being destitute of the Spirit of holiness, freely indulge the lusts of the flesh. When, by the fear of Divine vengeance, they are deterred from open outbreakings, though, from not being subdued in mind, they profit little at present, still they are in some measure trained to bear the yoke of righteousness, so that when they are called, they are not like mere novices, studying a discipline of which previously they had no knowledge. This office seems to be especially in the view of the Apostle, when he says, " That the law is not made for a righteous man, but for the lawless and disobedient, for the ungodly and for sinners, for unholy and profane, for murderers of fathers and murderers of mothers, for manslayers, for whoremongers, for them that defile themselves with mankind, for men-stealers, for liars, for perjured persons, and if there be any other thing that is contrary to sound doctrine" (1 Tim. i. 9, 10). He thus indicates that it is a restraint on unruly lusts that would otherwise burst all bonds.

11. To both may be applied the declaration of the Apostle in another place, that " The law was our schoolmaster to bring us unto Christ" (Gal. iii. 24); since there are two classes of persons, whom by its training it leads to Christ. Some (of whom we spoke in the first place), from excessive confidence in their own virtue or righteousness, are unfit to receive the grace of Christ, until they are completely humbled. This the law does by making them sensible of their misery, and so disposing them to long for what they previously imagined they did not want. Others have need of a bridle to restrain them from giving full scope to their passions, and thereby utterly losing all desire after righteousness. For where the Spirit of God rules not, the lusts sometimes so burst forth, as to threaten to drown the soul subjected to them in forgetfulness and contempt of God; and so they would, did not God interpose with this remedy. Those, therefore, whom he has destined to the inheritance of his kingdom, if he does not immediately regenerate, he, through the works of the law, preserves in fear, against the time of his visitation, not, indeed, that pure and chaste fear which his children ought to have, but a fear useful to the extent of instructing them in true piety according to their capacity. Of this we have so many proofs, that there is not the least need of an example. For all who have remained for some

time in ignorance of God will confess, as the result of their own experience, that the law had the effect of keeping them in some degree in the fear and reverence of God, till, being regenerated by his Spirit, they began to love him from the heart.

12. The third use of the Law (being also the principal use, and more closely connected with its proper end) has respect to believers in whose hearts the Spirit of God already flourishes and reigns. For although the Law is written and engraven on their hearts by the finger of God, that is, although they are so influenced and actuated by the Spirit, that they desire to obey God, there are two ways in which they still profit in the Law. For it is the best instrument for enabling them daily to learn with greater truth and certainty what that will of the Lord is which they aspire to follow, and to confirm them in this knowledge; just as a servant who desires with all his soul to approve himself to his master, must still observe, and be careful to ascertain his master's dispositions, that he may comport himself in accommodation to them. Let none of us deem ourselves exempt from this necessity, for none have as yet attained to such a degree of wisdom, as that they may not, by the daily instruction of the Law, advance to a purer knowledge of the Divine will. Then, because we need not doctrine merely, but exhortation also, the servant of God will derive this further advantage from the Law: by frequently meditating upon it, he will be excited to obedience, and confirmed in it, and so drawn away from the slippery paths of sin. In this way must the saints press onward, since, however great the alacrity with which, under the Spirit, they hasten toward righteousness, they are retarded by the sluggishness of the flesh, and make less progress than they ought. The Law acts like a whip to the flesh, urging it on as men do a lazy sluggish ass. Even in the case of a spiritual man, inasmuch as he is still burdened with the weight of the flesh, the Law is a constant stimulus, pricking him forward when he would indulge in sloth. David had this use in view when he pronounced this high eulogium on the Law, "The law of the Lord is perfect, converting the soul: the testimony of the Lord is sure, making wise the simple. The statutes of the Lord are right, rejoicing the heart: the commandment of the Lord is pure, enlightening the eyes" (Ps. xix. 7, 8). Again, "Thy word is a lamp unto my feet, and a light unto my path" (Ps. cxix. 105). The whole Psalm abounds in passages to the same effect. Such passages are not inconsistent with those of Paul, which show not the utility of the law to the regenerate, but what it is able of itself to bestow. The object of the Psalmist is to celebrate the advantages which the Lord, by means of his law, bestows on those whom he inwardly inspires with a love of obedience. And he adverts not to the mere precepts, but also to the promise annexed to them, which alone makes that sweet which in itself is bitter. For what is less attractive than the law, when, by its demands and threatenings, it overawes the soul, and

[margin note: 9. To urge on the holy man to the knowledge of God.]

fills it with terror ? David specially shows that in the law he saw the Mediator, without whom it gives no pleasure or delight.

13. Some unskilful persons, from not attending to this, boldly discard the whole law of Moses, and do away with both its Tables, imaging it unchristian to adhere to a doctrine which contains the *we are* ministration of death. Far from our thoughts be this profane notion. *not to* Moses has admirably shown that the Law, which can produce nothing but death in sinners, ought to have a better and more excellent effect *dispise* upon the righteous. When about to die, he thus addressed the *the Law* people, " Set your hearts unto all the words which I testify among you this day, which ye shall command your children to observe to do, *because* all the words of this law. For it is not a vain thing for you ; because *we cannot* it is your life" (Deut. xxxii. 46, 47). If it cannot be denied that it *fulfill it* contains a perfect pattern of righteousness, then, unless we ought not to have any proper rule of life, it must be impious to discard it. There are not various rules of life, but one perpetual and inflexible rule ; and, therefore, when David describes the righteous as spending their whole lives in meditating on the Law (Psalm i. 2), we must not confine to a single age, an employment which is most appropriate to all ages, even to the end of the world. Nor are we to be deterred or to shun its instructions, because the holiness which it prescribes is stricter than we are able to render, so long as we bear about the *Our life* prison of the body. It does not now perform toward us the part of a *is a race,* hard taskmaster, who will not be satisfied without full payment ; but, *and after* in the perfection to which it exhorts us, points out the goal at which, *its end,* during the whole course of our lives, it is not less our interest than *we will* our duty to aim. It is well if we thus press onward. Our whole *reach the* life is a race, and after we have finished our course, the Lord will *goal.* enable us to reach that goal to which, at present, we can only aspire in wish.

14. Since, in regard to believers, the law has the force of exhortation, not to bind their consciences with a curse, but by urging them, from time to time, to shake off sluggishness and chastise imperfection, —many, when they would express this exemption from the curse, say, that in regard to believers the Law (I still mean the Moral Law) is abrogated : not that the things which it enjoins are no longer right to be observed, but only that it is not to believers what it formerly was ; in other words, that it does not, by terrifying and confounding their consciences, condemn and destroy. It is certainly true that Paul shows, in clear terms, that there is such an abrogation of the Law. And that the same was preached by our Lord appears from this, that he would not have refuted the opinion of his destroying the Law, if it had not been prevalent among the Jews. Since such an opinion could not have arisen at random without some pretext, there is reason to presume that it originated in a false interpretation of his doctrine, in the same way in which all errors generally arise from a perversion of the truth. But lest we should stumble against the same

stone, let us distinguish accurately between what has been abrogated in the Law, and what still remains in force. When the Lord declares, that he came not to destroy the Law, but to fulfil (Matth. v. 17), that until heaven and earth pass away, not one jot or tittle shall remain unfulfilled; he shows that his advent was not to derogate, in any degree, from the observance of the Law. And justly, since the very end of his coming was to remedy the transgression of the Law. Therefore, the doctrine of the Law has not been infringed by Christ, but remains, that, by teaching, admonishing, rebuking, and correcting, it may fit and prepare us for every good work.

15. What Paul says, as to the abrogation of the Law, evidently applies not to the Law itself, but merely to its power of constraining the conscience. For the Law not only teaches, but also imperiously demands. If obedience is not yielded, nay, if it is omitted in any degree, it thunders forth its curse. For this reason, the Apostle says, that "as many as are of the works of the law are under the curse: for it is written, Cursed is every one that continueth not in all things which are written in the book of the law to do them" (Gal. iii. 10; Deut. xxvii. 26). Those he describes as under the works of the Law, who do not place righteousness in that forgiveness of sins by which we are freed from the rigour of the Law. He therefore shows, that we must be freed from the fetters of the Law, if we would not perish miserably under them. But what fetters? Those of rigid and austere exaction, which remits not one iota of the demand, and leaves no transgression unpunished. To redeem us from this curse, Christ was made a curse for us: for it is written, Cursed is every one that hangeth on a tree (Deut. xxi. 23, compared with Gal. iii. 13, iv. 4). In the following chapter, indeed, he says, that "Christ was made under the law, in order that he might redeem those who are under the law;" but the meaning is the same. For he immediately adds, "That we might receive the adoption of sons." What does this mean? That we might not be, all our lifetime, subject to bondage, having our consciences oppressed with the fear of death. Meanwhile, it must ever remain an indubitable truth, that the Law has lost none of its authority, but must always receive from us the same respect and obedience.

16. The case of ceremonies is different, these having been abrogated not in effect but in use only. Though Christ by his advent put an end to their use, so far is this from derogating from their sacredness, that it rather commends and illustrates it. For as these ceremonies would have given nothing to God's ancient people but empty show, if the power of Christ's death and resurrection had not been prefigured by them,—so, if the use of them had not ceased, it would, in the present day, be impossible to understand for what purpose they were instituted. Accordingly, Paul, in order to prove that the observance of them was not only superfluous, but pernicious also, says that they "are a shadow of things to come; but the body is of Christ" (Col.

The
Ceremonial
Law was
a type
of the
Salvation
brought
by Christ
and
would
have no
meaning
were it
to be
continued
to the
present
time.

ii. 17). We see, therefore, that the truth is made clearer by their abolition than if Christ, who has been openly manifested, were still figured by them as at a distance, and as under a veil. By the death of Christ, the veil of the temple was rent in twain, the living and express image of heavenly things, which had begun to be dimly shadowed forth, being now brought fully into view, as is described by the author of the Epistle to the Hebrews (Heb. x. 1). To the same effect, our Saviour declares, that " the law and the prophets were until John : since that time the kingdom of God is preached, and every man presseth into it" (Luke xvi. 16); not that the holy fathers were left without the preaching of the hope of salvation and eternal life, but because they only saw at a distance, and under a shadow, what we now behold in full light. Why it behoved the Church to ascend higher than these elements, is explained by John the Baptist, when he says, " The law was given by Moses, but grace and truth came by Jesus Christ" (John i. 17). For though it is true that expiation was promised in the ancient sacrifices, and the ark of the covenant was a sure pledge of the paternal favour of God, the whole would have been elusory had it not been founded on the grace of Christ, wherein true and eternal stability is found. It must be held as a fixed point, that though legal rites ceased to be observed, their end serves to show more clearly how great their utility was before the advent of Christ, who, while he abolished the use, sealed their force and effect by his death.

17. There is a little more difficulty in the following passage of Paul : " You, being dead in your sins and the uncircumcision of your flesh, hath he quickened together with him, having forgiven you all trespasses ; blotting out the handwriting of ordinances that was against us, which was contrary to us, and took it out of the way, nailing it to his cross" &c. (Col. ii. 13, 14). He seems to extend the abolition of the Law considerably farther, as if we had nothing to do with its injunctions. Some err in interpreting this simply of the Moral Law, as implying the abolition not of its injunctions, but of its inexorable rigour. Others examining Paul's words more carefully, see that they properly apply to the Ceremonial Law, and show that Paul repeatedly uses the term *ordinance* in this sense. He thus writes to the Ephesians : " He is our peace, who hath made both one, and hath broken down the middle wall of partition between us ; having abolished in his flesh the enmity, even the law of commandments contained in ordinances ; for to make in himself of twain one new man" (Eph. ii. 14). There can be no doubt that he is there treating of ceremonies, as he speaks of " the middle wall of partition" which separated Jews and Gentiles. I therefore hold that the former view is erroneous ; but, at the same time, it does not appear to me that the latter comes fully up to the Apostle's meaning. For I cannot admit that the two passages are perfectly parallel. As his object was to assure the Ephesians that they were admitted to fellowship with

the Jews, he tells them that the obstacle which formerly stood in the way was removed. This obstacle was in the ceremonies. For the rites of ablution and sacrifice, by which the Jews were consecrated to the Lord, separated them from the Gentiles. But who sees not that, in the Epistle to the Colossians, a sublimer mystery is adverted to? No doubt, a question is raised there as to the Mosaic observances, to which false apostles were endeavouring to bind the Christian people. But as in the Epistle to the Galatians he takes a higher view of this controversy, and in a manner traces it to its fountain, so he does in this passage also. For if the only thing considered in rites is the necessity of observing them, of what use was it to call it a handwriting which was contrary to us? Besides, how could the bringing in of it be set down as almost the whole sum of redemption? Wherefore, the very nature of the case clearly shows that reference is here made to something more internal. I cannot doubt that I have ascertained the genuine interpretation, provided I am permitted to assume what Augustine has somewhere most truly affirmed, nay, derived from the very words of the Apostle—viz. that in the Jewish ceremonies there was more a confession than an expiation of sins. For what more was done in sacrifice by those who substituted purifications instead of themselves, than to confess that they were conscious of deserving death? What did these purifications testify but that they themselves were impure? By these means, therefore, the handwriting both of their guilt and impurity was ever and anon renewed. But the attestation of these things was not the removal of them. Wherefore, the Apostle says that Christ is " the mediator of the new testament,—by means of death, for the redemption of the transgressions that were under the first testament" (Heb. ix. 15). Justly, therefore, does the Apostle describe these handwritings as against the worshippers, and contrary to them, since by means of them their impurity and con-demnation were openly sealed. There is nothing contrary to this in the fact that they were partakers of the same grace with ourselves. This they obtained through Christ, and not through the ceremonies which the Apostle there contrasts with Christ, showing that by the continued use of them the glory of Christ was obscured. We perceive how ceremonies, considered in themselves, are elegantly and appositely termed handwritings, and contrary to the salvation of man, inasmuch as they were a kind of formal instruments which attested his liability. On the other hand, when false apostles wished to bind them on the Christian Church, Paul, entering more deeply into their signification, with good reason warned the Colossians how seriously they would relapse if they allowed a yoke to be in that way imposed upon them. By so doing, they, at the same time, deprived themselves of all benefit from Christ, who, by his eternal sacrifice once offered, had abolished those daily sacrifices, which were indeed powerful to attest sin, but could do nothing to destroy it.

CHAPTER VIII.

EXPOSITION OF THE MORAL LAW.

This chapter consists of four parts. I. Some general observations necessary for the understanding of the subject are made by way of preface, sec. 1—5. II. Three things always to be attended to in ascertaining and expounding the meaning of the Moral Law, sec. 6—12. III. Exposition of the Moral Law, or the Ten Commandments, sec. 13—15. IV. The end for which the whole Law is intended—viz. to teach not only elementary principles, but perfection—sec. 51, to the end of the chapter.

Sections.

1. The Law was committed to writing, in order that it might teach more fully and perfectly that knowledge, both of God and of ourselves, which the law of nature teaches meagrely and obscurely. Proof of this, from an enumeration of the principal parts of the Moral Law; and also from the dictate of natural law, written on the hearts of all, and, in a manner, effaced by sin.
2. Certain general maxims. 1. From the knowledge of God, furnished by the Law, we learn that God is our Father and Ruler. Righteousness is pleasing, iniquity is an abomination in his sight. Hence, how weak soever we may be, our duty is to cultivate the one, and shun the other.
3. From the knowledge of ourselves, furnished by the Law, we learn to discern our own utter powerlessness, we are ashamed; and seeing it is in vain to seek for righteousness in ourselves, are induced to seek it elsewhere.
4. Hence, God has annexed promises and threatenings to his promises. These not limited to the present life, but embrace things heavenly and eternal. They, moreover, attest the spotless purity of God, his love of righteousness, and also his kindness towards us.
5. The Law shows, moreover, that there is nothing more acceptable to God than obedience. Hence, all superstitious and hypocritical modes of worship are condemned. A remedy against superstitious worship and human presumption.
6. The second part of the chapter, containing three observations or rules. First rule, Our life must be formed by the Law, not only to external honesty, but to inward and spiritual righteousness. In this respect the Law of God differs from civil laws, he being a spiritual Lawgiver, man not. This rule of great extent, and not sufficiently attended to.
7. This first rule confirmed by the authority of Christ, and vindicated from the false dogma of Sophists, who say that Christ is only another Moses.
8. Second observation or rule to be carefully attended to—viz. that the end of the command must be inquired into, until it is ascertained what the Lawgiver approves or disapproves. Example. Where the Law approves, its opposite is condemned, and *vice versa.*
9. Full explanation of this latter point. Example.
10. The Law states what is most impious in each transgression, in order to show how heinous the transgression is. Example.
11. Third observation or rule regards the division of the Law into Two Tables: the former comprehending our duty to God; the latter, our duty to our neighbour. The connection between these necessary and inseparable. Their invariable order. Sum of the Law.
12. Division of the Law into Ten Commandments. Various distinctions made with regard to them, but the best distinction that which divides them into Two Tables Four commandments belong to the First, and six to the Second Table.

13. The third part of the chapter, containing an exposition of the Decalogue. The preface vindicates the authority of the Law. This it does in three ways. First, by a declaration of its majesty.

14. The preface to the Law vindicates its authority. Secondly, by calling to mind God's paternal kindness.

15. Thirdly, by calling to mind the deliverance out of the land of Egypt. Why God distinguishes himself by certain epithets. Why mention is made of the deliverance from Egypt. In what way, and how far, the remembrance of this deliverance should still affect us.

16. Exposition of the First Commandment. Its end. What it is to have God, and to have strange gods. Adoration due to God, trust, invocation, thanksgiving, and also true religion, required by the Commandment. Superstition, Polytheism, and Atheism, forbidden. What meant by the words, "before me."

17. Exposition of the Second Commandment. The end and sum of it. Two parts. Short enumeration of forbidden shapes.

18. Why a threatening is added. Four titles applied to God, to make a deeper impression. He is called Mighty, Jealous, an Avenger, Merciful. Why said to be jealous. Reason drawn from analogy.

19. Exposition of the threatening which is added. First, as to visiting the iniquity of the fathers upon the children. A misinterpretation on this head refuted, and the genuine meaning of the threatening explained.

20. Whether this visiting of the sins of parents inconsistent with the divine justice. Apparently conflicting passages reconciled.

21. Exposition of the latter part—viz. the showing mercy to thousands. The use of this promise. Consideration of an exception of frequent occurrence. The extent of this blessing.

22. Exposition of the Third Commandment. The end and sum of it. Three parts. These considered. What it is to use the name of God in vain. Swearing. Distinction between this commandment and the Ninth.

23. An oath defined. It is a species of divine worship. This explained.

24. Many modes in which this commandment is violated. 1. By taking God to witness what we know is false. The insult thus offered.

25. Modes of violation continued. 2. Taking God to witness in trivial matters. Contempt thus shown. When and how an oath should be used. 3. Substituting the servants of God instead of himself when taking an oath.

26. The Anabaptists, who condemn all oaths, refuted. 1. By the authority of Christ, who cannot be opposed in anything to the Father. A passage perverted by the Anabaptists explained. The design of our Saviour in the passage. What meant by his there prohibiting oaths.

27. The lawfulness of oaths confirmed by Christ and the apostles. Some approve of public, but not of private oaths. The lawfulness of the latter proved both by reason and example. Instances from Scripture.

28. Exposition of the Fourth Commandment. Its end. Three purposes.

29. Explanation of the first purpose—viz. a shadowing forth of spiritual rest. This the primary object of the precept. God is therein set forth as our sanctifier; and hence we must abstain from work, that the work of God in us may not be hindered.

30. The number seven denoting perfection in Scripture, this commandment may, in that respect, denote the perpetuity of the Sabbath, and its completion at the last day.

31. Taking a simpler view of the commandment, the number is of no consequence, provided we maintain the doctrine of a perpetual rest from all our works, and at the same time, avoid a superstitious observance of days. The ceremonial part of the commandment abolished by the advent of Christ.

32. The second and third purposes of the Commandment explained. These twofold and perpetual. This confirmed. Of religious assemblies.

33. Of the observance of the Lord's day, in answer to those who complain that the Christian people are thus trained to Judaism. Objection.

34. Ground of this institution. There is no kind of superstitious necessity. The sum of the Commandment.

35. The Fifth Commandment (the first of the Second Table) expounded. Its end and substance. How far honour due to parents. To whom the term *father* applies.

36. It makes no difference whether those to whom this honour is required are worthy

1. I BELIEVE it will not be out of place here to introduce the Ten

Commandments of the Law, and give a brief exposition of them. In this way it will be made more clear, that the worship which God originally prescribed is still in force (a point to which I have already adverted) ; and then a second point will be confirmed—viz. that the Jews not only learned from the law wherein true piety consisted, but from feeling their inability to observe it were overawed by the fear of judgment, and so drawn, even against their will, towards the Mediator. In giving a summary of what constitutes the true knowledge of God,[1] we showed that we cannot form any just conception of the character of God, without feeling overawed by his majesty, and bound to do him service. In regard to the knowledge of ourselves, we showed that it principally consists in renouncing all idea of our own strength, and divesting ourselves of all confidence in our own righteousness, while, on the other hand, under a full consciousness of our wants, we learn true humility and self-abasement. Both of these the Lord accomplishes by his Law, first, when, in assertion of the right which he has to our obedience, he calls us to reverence his majesty, and prescribes the conduct by which this reverence is manifested ; and, secondly, when, by promulgating the rule of his justice (a rule, to the rectitude of which our nature, from being depraved and perverted, is continually opposed, and to the perfection of which our ability, from its infirmity and nervelessness for good, is far from being able to attain), he charges us both with impotence and unrighteousness. Moreover, the very things contained in the two tables are, in a manner, dictated to us by that internal law, which, as has been already said, is in a manner written and stamped on every heart. For conscience, instead of allowing us to stifle our perceptions, and sleep on without interruption, acts as an inward witness and monitor, reminds us of what we owe to God, points out the distinction between good and evil, and therbey convicts us of departure from duty. But man, being immured in the darkness of error, is scarcely able, by means of that natural law, to form any tolerable idea of the worship which is acceptable to God. At all events, he is very far from forming any correct knowledge of it. In addition to this, he is so swollen with arrogance and ambition, and so blinded with self-love, that he is unable to survey, and, as it were, descend into himself, that he may so learn to humble and abase himself, and confess his misery. Therefore, as a necessary remedy, both for our dulness and our contumacy, the Lord has given us his written Law, which, by its sure attestations, removes the obscurity of the law of nature, and also, by shaking off our lethargy, makes a more lively and permanent impression on our minds.

2. It is now easy to understand the doctrine of the law—viz. that God, as our Creator, is entitled to be regarded by us as a Father and Master, and should, accordingly, receive from us fear, love, reverence,

---

[1] This chapter is connected with Book I., chap. i. and ii., and with Book II., chap. i.—vi. See also Book II. chap. ii., sec. 22.

and glory; nay, that we are not our own, to follow whatever course passion dictates, but are bound to obey him implicitly, and to acquiesce entirely in his good pleasure. Again, the Law teaches, that justice and rectitude are a delight, injustice an abomination to him, and, therefore, as we would not with impious ingratitude revolt from our Maker, our whole life must be spent in the cultivation of righteousness. For if we manifest becoming reverence only when we prefer his will to our own, it follows, that the only legitimate service to him is the practice of justice, purity, and holiness. Nor can we plead as an excuse, that we want the power, and, like debtors, whose means are exhausted, are unable to pay. We cannot be permitted to measure the glory of God by our ability; whatever we may be, he ever remains like himself, the friend of righteousness, the enemy of unrighteousness, and whatever his demands from us may be, as he can only require what is right, we are necessarily under a natural obligation to obey. Our inability to do so is our own fault. If lust, in which sin has its dominion, so enthrals us, that we are not free to obey our Father, there is no ground for pleading necessity as a defence, since this evil necessity is within, and must be imputed to ourselves.

3. When, under the guidance of the Law, we have advanced thus far, we must, under the same guidance, proceed to descend into ourselves. In this way, we at length arrive at two results: First, contrasting our conduct with the righteousness of the Law, we see how very far it is from being in accordance with the will of God, and, therefore, how unworthy we are of holding our place among his creatures, far less of being accounted his sons; and, secondly, taking a survey of our powers, we see that they are not only unequal to fulfil the Law, but are altogether null. The necessary consequence must be, to produce distrust of our own ability, and also anxiety and trepidation of mind. Conscience cannot feel the burden of its guilt, without forthwith turning to the judgment of God, while the view of this judgment cannot fail to excite a dread of death. In like manner, the proofs of our utter powerlessness must instantly beget despair of our own strength. Both feelings are productive of humility and abasement, and hence the sinner, terrified at the prospect of eternal death (which he sees justly impending over him for his iniquities), turns to the mercy of God as the only haven of safety. Feeling his utter inability to pay what he owes to the Law, and thus despairing of himself, he bethinks him of applying and looking to some other quarter for help.

4. But the Lord does not count it enough to inspire a reverence for his justice. To imbue our hearts with love to himself, and, at the same time, with hatred to iniquity, he has added promises and threatenings. The eye of our mind being too dim to be attracted by the mere beauty of goodness, our most merciful Father has been pleased, in his great indulgence, to allure us to love and long after it by the hope of

[Margin handwritten notes:] The Law makes us realize how far short we have come of the righteousness demanded by God.

We realize how powerless we are to fulfill the Law

We turn to Lord for help.

God commends the works of the Law by the promise of reward for obedience and of punishment for disobedience.

reward. He accordingly declares that rewards for virtue are treasured up with him. That none who yield obedience to his commands will labour in vain. On the other hand, he proclaims not only that iniquity is hateful in his sight, but that it will not escape with impunity, because he will be the avenger of his insulted majesty. That he may encourage us in every way, he promises present blessings, as well as eternal felicity, to the obedience of those who shall have kept his commands, while he threatens transgressors with present suffering, as well as the punishment of eternal death. The promise, " Ye shall therefore keep my statutes, and my judgments ; which if a man do, he shall live in them" (Lev. xviii. 5), and corresponding to this the threatening, " The soul that sinneth, it shall die" (Ezek. xviii. 4, 20) ; doubtless point to a future life and death, both without end. But though in every passage where the favour or anger of God is mentioned, the former comprehends eternity of life and the latter eternal destruction, the Law, at the same time, enumerates a long catalogue of present blessings and curses (Lev. xxvi. 4 ; Deut. xxviii. 1). The threatenings attest the spotless purity of God, which cannot bear iniquity, while the promises attest at once his infinite love of righteousness (which he cannot leave unrewarded), and his wondrous kindness. Being bound to do him homage with all that we have, he is perfectly entitled to demand everything which he requires of us as a debt ; and as a debt, the payment is unworthy of reward. He therefore foregoes his right, when he holds forth reward for services which are not offered spontaneously, as if they were not due. The amount of these services, in themselves, has been partly described, and will appear more clearly in its own place. For the present, it is enough to remember that the promises of the Law are no mean commendation of righteousness, as they show how much God is pleased with the observance of them, while the threatenings denounced are intended to produce a greater abhorrence of unrighteousness, lest the sinner should indulge in the blandishments of vice, and forget the judgment which the divine Lawgiver has prepared for him.

5. The Lord, in delivering a perfect rule of righteousness, has reduced it in all its parts to his mere will, and in this way has shown that there is nothing more acceptable to him than obedience. There is the more necessity for attending to this, because the human mind, in its wantonness, is ever and anon inventing different modes of worship as a means of gaining his favour. This irreligious affectation of religion being innate in the human mind, has betrayed itself in every age, and is still doing so, men always longing to devise some method of procuring righteousness without any sanction from the Word of God.[1] Hence, in those observances which are generally regarded as good works, the precepts of the Law occupy a narrow space, almost

---

[1] See Calvin, De Vera Ecclesiæ Reformandæ Ratione.

Man has a tendancy to make up new and un-Scriptural means of attaining righteous-ness.

This is disobedien-ce.

Man would do better to stick closely with what God has expressly enjoined

the whole being usurped by this endless host of human inventions. But was not this the very license which Moses meant to curb, when, after the promulgation of the Law, he thus addressed the people: "Observe and hear all these words which I command thee, that it may go well with thee, and with thy children after thee for ever, when thou doest that which is good and right in the sight of the Lord thy God." "What thing soever I command you, observe to do it ; thou shalt not add thereto, nor diminish from it" (Deut. xii. 28 —32). Previously, after asking "what nation is there so great, that hath statutes and judgments so righteous as all this law, which I set before you this day ?" he had added, "Only take heed to thyself, and keep thy soul diligently, lest thou forget the things which thine eyes have seen, and lest they depart from thy heart all the days of thy life" (Deut. iv. 8, 9). God foreseeing that the Israelites would not rest, but after receiving the Law, would, unless sternly prohibited, give birth to new kinds of righteousness, declares that the Law comprehended a perfect righteousness. This ought to have been a most powerful restraint, and yet they desisted not from the presumptuous course so strongly prohibited. How do we act ? We are certainly under the same obligation as they were ; for there cannot be a doubt that the claim of absolute perfection which God made for his Law is perpetually in force. Not contented with it, however, we labour prodigiously in feigning and coining an endless variety of good works, one after another. The best cure for this vice would be a constant and deeply-seated conviction that the Law was given from heaven to teach us a perfect righteousness ; that the only righteousness so taught is that which the divine will expressly enjoins ; and that it is, therefore, vain to attempt, by new forms of worship, to gain the favour of God, whose true worship consists in obedience alone ; or rather, that to go a-wandering after good works which are not prescribed by the Law of God, is an intolerable violation of true and divine righteousness. Most truly does Augustine say in one place, that the obedience which is rendered to God is the parent and guardian ; in another, that it is the source of all the virtues.[1]

6. After we shall have expounded the Divine Law, what has been previously said of its office and use will be understood more easily, and with greater benefit. But before we proceed to the consideration of each separate commandment, it will be proper to take a general survey of the whole. At the outset, it was proved that in the Law human life is instructed not merely in outward decency, but in inward spiritual righteousness. Though none can deny this, yet very few duly attend to it, because they do not consider the Lawgiver, by whose character that of the Law must also be determined. Should a king issue an edict prohibiting murder, adultery, and theft, the

1 See Augustin. De Civitate Dei, Lib. iv. c. 12, and Lib. xiii. c. 20, and Lib. xiv. c. 12. See also Lib. De Bono Conjugali, and Lib. Contra Adversarios Legis et Prophetarum, Lib. i. c. 14.

penalty, I admit, will not be incurred by the man who has only felt a longing in his mind after these vices, but has not actually committed them. The reason is, that a human lawgiver does not extend his care beyond outward order, and, therefore, his injunctions are not violated without outward acts. But God, whose eye nothing escapes, and who regards not the outward appearance so much as purity of heart, under the prohibition of murder, adultery, and theft, includes wrath, hatred, lust, covetousness, and all other things of a similar nature. Being a spiritual Lawgiver, he speaks to the soul not less than the body. The murder which the soul commits is wrath and hatred; the theft, covetousness, and avarice; and the adultery, lust. It may be alleged that human laws have respect to intentions and wishes, and not fortuitous events. I admit this, but then these must manifest themselves externally. They consider the *animus* with which the act was done, but do not scrutinise the secret thoughts. Accordingly, their demand is satisfied when the hand merely refrains from transgression. On the contrary, the law of heaven being enacted for our minds, the first thing necessary to a due observance of the Law is to put them under restraint. But the generality of men, even while they are most anxious to conceal their disregard of the Law, only frame their hands and feet and other parts of their body to some kind of observance, but in the meanwhile keep the heart utterly estranged from everything like obedience. They think it enough to have carefully concealed from man what they are doing in the sight of God. Hearing the commandments, " Thou shalt not kill," " Thou shalt not commit adultery," " Thou shalt not steal," they do not unsheathe their sword for slaughter, nor defile their bodies with harlots, nor put forth their hands to other men's goods. So far well; but with their whole soul they breathe out slaughter, boil with lust, cast a greedy eye at their neighbour's property, and in wish devour it. Here the principal thing which the Law requires is wanting. Whence, then, this gross stupidity, but just because they lose sight of the Lawgiver, and form an idea of righteousness in accordance with their own disposition? Against this Paul strenuously protests, when he declares that the " *law is spiritual* " (Rom. vii. 14); intimating that it not only demands the homage of the soul, and mind, and will, but requires an angelic purity, which, purified from all filthiness of the flesh, savours only of the Spirit.

7. In saying that this is the meaning of the Law, we are not introducing a new interpretation of our own; we are following Christ, the best interpreter of the Law (Matth. v. 22, 28, 44). The Pharisees having instilled into the people the erroneous idea that the Law was fulfilled by every one who did not in external act do anything against the Law, he pronounces this a most dangerous delusion, and declares that an immodest look is adultery, and that hatred of a brother is murder. " Whosoever is angry with his brother without a cause, shall be in danger of the judgment;" whosoever by

whispering or murmuring gives indication of being offended, "shall be in danger of the council;" whosoever by reproaches and evil-speaking gives way to open anger, "shall be in danger of hell-fire." Those who have not perceived this, have pretended that Christ was only a second Moses, the giver of an Evangelical, to supply the deficiency of the Mosaic Law. Hence the common axiom as to the perfection of the Evangelical Law, and its great superiority to that of Moses. This idea is in many ways most pernicious. For it will appear from Moses himself, when we come to give a summary of his precepts, that great indignity is thus done to the Divine Law. It certainly insinuates, that the holiness of the fathers under the Law was little else than hypocrisy, and leads us away from that one unvarying rule of righteousness. It is very easy, however, to confute this error, which proceeds on the supposition that Christ added to the Law, whereas he only restored it to its integrity by maintaining and purifying it when obscured by the falsehood, and defiled by the leaven of the Pharisees.

8. The next observation we would make is, that there is always more in the requirements and prohibitions of the Law than is expressed in words. This, however, must be understood so as not to convert it into a kind of Lesbian code;[1] and thus, by licentiously wresting the Scriptures, make them assume any meaning that we please. By taking this excessive liberty with Scripture, its authority is lowered with some, and all hope of understanding it abandoned by others. We must, therefore, if possible, discover some path which may conduct us with direct and firm step to the will of God. We must consider, I say, how far interpretation can be permitted to go beyond the literal meaning of the words, still making it apparent that no appendix of human glosses is added to the Divine Law, but that the pure and genuine meaning of the Lawgiver is faithfully exhibited. It is true that, in almost all the commandments, there are elliptical expressions, and that, therefore, any man would make himself ridiculous by attempting to restrict the spirit of the Law to the strict letter of the words. It is plain that a sober interpretation of the Law must go beyond these, but how far is doubtful, unless some rule be adopted. The best rule, in my opinion, would be, to be guided by the principle of the commandment—viz. to consider in the case of each what the purpose is for which it was given. For example, every commandment either requires or prohibits; and the nature of each is instantly discerned when we look to the principle of the commandment as its end. Thus, the end of the Fifth Commandment is to render honour to those on whom God bestows it. The sum of the commandment, therefore, is, that it is right in itself, and pleasing to God, to honour those on whom he has conferred some distinction; that to despise and rebel against such persons is offensive to Him. The principle of the First Commandment is, that God only is to be

---

1 "Ne sit nobis Lesbiæ regulæ," omitted in the French.

[Margin notes:]

We must go beyond the purely literal meaning of a commandment if we are to understand its meaning

The best method of interpretation is to consider the purpose for which each was given.

'If this pleases God, its opposite displeases.

worshipped. The sum of the commandment, therefore, is, that true piety, in other words, the worship of the Deity, is acceptable, and impiety is an abomination to him. So in each of the commandments we must first look to the matter of which it treats, and then consider its end, until we discover what it properly is that the Lawgiver declares to be pleasing or displeasing to him. Only, we must reason from the precept to its contrary in this way: If this pleases God, its opposite displeases; if that displeases, its opposite pleases: if God commands this, he forbids the opposite; if he forbids that, he commands the opposite.

9. What is now touched on somewhat obscurely will become perfectly clear as we proceed and get accustomed to the exposition of the Commandments. It is sufficient thus to have adverted to the subject; but perhaps our concluding statement will require to be briefly confirmed, as it might otherwise not be understood, or, though understood, might, perhaps, at the outset appear unsound. There is no need of proving, that when good is ordered, the evil which is opposed to it is forbidden. This every one admits. It will also be admitted, without much difficulty, that when evil is forbidden, its opposite is enjoined. Indeed, it is a common saying, that censure of vice is commendation of virtue. We, however, demand somewhat more than is commonly understood by these expressions. When the particular virtue opposed to a particular vice is spoken of, all that is usually meant is abstinence from that vice. We maintain that it goes farther, and means opposite duties and positive acts. Hence the commandment, "Thou shalt not kill," the generality of men will merely consider as an injunction to abstain from all injury, and all wish to inflict injury. I hold that it moreover means, that we are to aid our neighbour's life by every means in our power. And not to assert without giving my reason, I prove it thus: God forbids us to injure or hurt a brother, because he would have his life to be dear and precious to us; and, therefore, when he so forbids, he, at the same time, demands all the offices of charity which can contribute to his preservation.

This opposite implies not only negative actions, but opposite duties and positive acts (Internalues ala Christ)

10. But why did God thus deliver his commandments, as it were, by halves, using elliptical expressions with a larger meaning than that actually expressed? Other reasons are given, but the following seems to me the best:—As the flesh is always on the alert to extenuate the heinousness of sin (unless it is made, as it were, perceptible to the touch), and to cover it with specious pretexts, the Lord sets forth, by way of example, whatever is foulest and most iniquitous in each species of transgression, that the delivery of it might produce a shudder in the hearer, and impress his mind with a deeper abhorrence of sin. In forming an estimate of sins, we are often imposed upon by imagining that the more hidden the less heinous they are. This delusion the Lord dispels by accustoming us to refer the whole multitude of sins to particular, heads, which admirably show how great a degree of heinousness there is in each. For example, wrath

The Command-
ments take more
innocent sounding
sins and follow
them to their
hideous & ultimate
conclusion

and hatred do not seem so very bad when they are designated by their own names; but when they are prohibited under the name of murder, we understand better how abominable they are in the sight of God, who puts them in the same class with that horrid crime. Influenced by his judgment, we accustom ourselves to judge more accurately of the heinousness of offences which previously seemed trivial.

11. It will now be proper to consider what is meant by the division of the divine Law into Two Tables. It will be judged by all men of sense from the formal manner in which these are sometimes mentioned, that it has not been done at random, or without reason. Indeed, the reason is so obvious as not to allow us to remain in doubt with regard to it. God thus divided his Law into two parts, containing a complete rule of righteousness, that he might assign the first place to the duties of religion which relate especially to His worship, and the second to the duties of charity which have respect to man. The

God divides the law into 2 parts, that he may assign the first place to the duties of religion and the second place to the duties of charity

first foundation of righteousness undoubtedly is the worship of God. When it is subverted, all the other parts of righteousness, like a building rent asunder, and in ruins, are racked and scattered. What kind of righteousness do you call it, not to commit theft and rapine, if you, in the mean time, with impious sacrilege, rob God of his glory? or not to defile your body with fornication, if you profane his holy name with blasphemy? or not to take away the life of man, if you strive to cut off and destroy the remembrance of God? It is vain, therefore, to talk of righteousness apart from religion. Such righteousness has no more beauty than the trunk of a body deprived of its head.[1] Nor is religion the principal part merely: it is the very soul by which the whole lives and breathes. Without the fear of God, men do not even observe justice and charity among themselves. We say, then, that the worship of God is the beginning and foundation of righteousness; and that wherever it is wanting, any degree of equity, or continence, or temperance, existing among men themselves, is empty and frivolous in the sight of God. We call it the source and soul of righteousness, inasmuch as men learn to live together temperately, and without injury, when they revere God as the judge of right and wrong. In the First Table, accordingly, he teaches us how to cultivate piety, and the proper duties of religion in which his worship consists; in the second, he shows how, in the fear of his name, we are to conduct ourselves towards our fellow-men. Hence, as related by the Evangelists (Matth. xxii. 37; Luke x. 27), our Saviour summed up the whole Law in two heads—viz. to love the Lord with all our heart, with all our soul, and with all our strength, and our neighbour as ourselves. You see how, of the two parts under which he comprehends the whole Law, he devotes the one to God, and assigns the other to mankind.

[1] The French is, "Tout ainsi comme si quelcun vouloit faire une belle monstre d'un corps sans teste;" just as if one were to try to make a beautiful monster of a body without a head.

There should be freedo. of judgement in relation to the interpret- ation of the division of the command- ments.

12. But although the whole Law is contained in two heads, yet, in order to remove every pretext for excuse, the Lord has been pleased to deliver more fully and explicitly in Ten Commandments, every-thing relating to his own honour, fear, and love, as well as every-thing relating to the charity which, for his sake, he enjoins us to have towards our fellow-men. Nor is it an unprofitable study to consider the division of the commandments, provided we remember that it is one of those matters in which every man should have full freedom of judgment, and on account of which, difference of opinion should not lead to contention. We are, indeed, under the necessity of making this observation, lest the division which we are to adopt should excite the surprise or derision of the reader, as novel or of recent invention.

There is no room for controversy as to the fact, that the Law is divided into ten heads, since this is repeatedly sanctioned by divine *Catholic* authority. The question, therefore, is not as to the number of the *3* parts, but the method of dividing them. Those who adopt a division *7* which gives three commandments to the First Table, and throws the remaining seven into the Second Table, expunge the commandment *unsound* concerning images from the list, or at least conceal it under the first, though there cannot be a doubt that it was distinctly set down by the *Calvin* Lord as a separate commandment; whereas the tenth, which prohibits *4* the coveting of what belongs to our neighbour, they absurdly break *6* down into two. Moreover, it will soon appear, that this method of dividing was unknown in a purer age. Others count four command-ments in the First Table as we do, but for the first set down the in-troductory promise, without adding the precept. But because I must hold, unless I am convinced by clear evidence to the contrary, that the "ten words" mentioned by Moses are Ten Commandments, and because I see that number arranged in most admirable order, I must, while I leave them to hold their own opinion, follow what appears to me better established—viz. that what they make to be the first com-mandment is of the nature of a preface to the whole Law, that there-after follow four commandments in the First Table, and six in the Second, in the order in which they will here be reviewed. This division Origen adopts without discussion, as if it had been every-where received in his day.[1] It is also adopted by Augustine, in his book addressed to Boniface, where, in enumerating the command-ments, he follows this order, Let one God be religiously obeyed, let no idol be worshipped, let the name of God be not used in vain; while previously he had made separate mention of the typical com-mandment of the Sabbath. Elsewhere, indeed, he expresses appro-bation of the first division, but on too slight grounds, because, by the

---

[1] Origen in Exod. cap. **xx.** Homil. 8; Augustin. contra duas Epist. Pelagii, Lib. iii. cap. 4; Quæst. in Vet. Test. Lib. ii. cap. 74; Epist. cxix. ad Januarium, cap. 11. The opinion of Josephus, and the last-mentioned opinion of Augustine, are briefly refuted by Calvin, in Exod. cap. **xx.**, in expounding the Fifth Commandment.

number three (making the First Table consist of three commandments), the mystery of the Trinity would be better manifested. Even here, however, he does not disguise his opinion, that in other respects, our division is more to his mind. Besides these, we are supported by the author of an unfinished work on Matthew.[1] Josephus, no doubt with the general consent of his age, assigns five commandments to each table. This, while repugnant to reason, inasmuch as it confounds the distinction between piety and charity, is also refuted by the authority of our Saviour, who in Matthew places the command to honour parents in the list of those belonging to the Second Table (Matth. xix. 19). Let us now hear God speaking in his own words.

First Commandment.

I AM THE LORD THY GOD, WHICH BROUGHT THEE OUT OF THE LAND OF EGYPT, OUT OF THE HOUSE OF BONDAGE. THOU SHALT HAVE NO OTHER GODS BEFORE ME.

13. Whether you take the former sentence as a part of the commandment, or read it separately, is to me a matter of indifference, provided you grant that it is a kind of preface to the whole Law. In enacting laws, the first thing to be guarded against is their being forthwith abrogated by contempt. The Lord, therefore, takes care, in the first place, that this shall not happen to the Law about to be delivered, by introducing it with a triple sanction. He claims to himself power and authority to command, that he may impress the chosen people with the necessity of obedience; he holds forth a promise of favour, as a means of alluring them to the study of holiness; and he reminds them of his kindness, that he may convict them of ingratitude, if they fail to make a suitable return. By the name, Lord, are denoted power and lawful dominion. If all things are from him, and by him consist, they ought in justice to bear reference to him, as Paul says (Rom. xi. 36). This name, therefore, is in itself sufficient to bring us under the authority of the divine majesty: for it were monstrous for us to wish to withdraw from the dominion of him, out of whom we cannot even exist.

14. After showing that he has a right to command, and to be obeyed, he next, in order not to seem to drag men by mere necessity, but to allure them, graciously declares, that he is the God of the Church. For the mode of expression implies, that there is a mutual relation included in the promise, " I will be their God, and they shall be my people " (Jer. xxxi. 33). Hence Christ infers the immortality

---

[1] The French is, "Nous avous aussi un autre ancien Pere qui accorde a nostre opinion, celui qui a ecrit les Commentaires imparfaits sur Sainct Matthieu." We have also another ancient Father who agrees with us in our opinion, he who wrote the unfinished Commentaries on St Matthew.

of Abraham, Isaac, and Jacob, from the fact that God had declared himself to be their God (Matth. xxii. 52).   It is, therefore, the same as if he had said, I have chosen you to myself, as a people to whom I shall not only do good in the present life, but also bestow felicity in the life to come.   The end contemplated in this is adverted to in the Law, in various passages.   For when the Lord condescends in mercy to honour us so far as to admit us to partnership with his chosen people, he chooses us, as Moses says, "to be a holy people," "a peculiar people unto himself," to "keep all his commandments" (Deut. vii. 6; xiv. 2; xxvi. 18).   Hence the exhortation, "Ye shall be holy; for I the Lord your God am holy" (Lev. xix. 2).   These two considerations form the ground of the remonstrance, "A son honoureth his father, and a servant his master; if then I be a father, where is mine honour? and if I be a master, where is my fear? saith the Lord of hosts" (Mal. i. 6).

15. Next follows a commemoration of his kindness, which ought to produce upon us an impression strong in proportion to the detestation in which ingratitude is held even among men.   It is true, indeed, he was reminding Israel of a deliverance then recent, but one which, on account of its wondrous magnitude, was to be for ever memorable to the remotest posterity.   Moreover, it is most appropriate to the matter in hand.[1]   For the Lord intimates that they were delivered from miserable bondage, that they might learn to yield prompt submission and obedience to him as the author of their freedom.   In like manner, to keep us to his true worship, he often describes himself by certain epithets which distinguish his sacred Deity from all idols and fictitious gods.   For, as I formerly observed, such is our proneness to vanity and presumption, that as soon as God is named, our minds, unable to guard against error, immediately fly off to some empty delusion. In applying a remedy to this disease, God distinguishes his divinity by certain titles, and thus confines us, as it were, within distinct boundaries, that we may not wander hither and thither, and feign some new deity for ourselves, abandoning the living God, and setting up an idol.   For this reason, whenever the Prophets would bring him properly before us, they invest, and, as it were, surround him with those characters under which he had manifested himself to the people of Israel.   When he is called the God of Abraham, or the God of Israel, when he is stationed in the temple of Jerusalem, between the Cherubim, these, and similar modes of expression,[2] do not confine him to one place or one people, but are used merely for the purpose of fixing our thoughts on that God who so manifested himself in the covenant which he made with Israel, as to make it unlawful on any account to deviate from the strict view there given of his character. Let it be understood, then, that mention is made of deliverance, in

---

[1] "Præsenti causæ."—The French is, "du temps que la loi devoit estre publiée;" to the time when the Law was to be published.

[2] Exod. iii. 6; Amos i. 2; Hab. ii. 20; Psalm lxxx. 2; xcix. 1; Isaiah xxxvii. 16.

order to make the Jews submit with greater readiness to that God who justly claims them as his own. We again, instead of supposing that the matter has no reference to us, should reflect that the bondage of Israel in Egypt was a type of that spiritual bondage, in the fetters of which we are all bound, until the heavenly avenger delivers us by the power of his own arm, and transports us into his free kingdom. Therefore, as in old times, when he would gather together the scattered Israelites to the worship of his name, he rescued them from the intolerable tyranny of Pharaoh, so all who profess him now are delivered from the fatal tyranny of the devil, of which that of Egypt was only a type. There is no man, therefore, whose mind ought not to be aroused to give heed to the Law, which, as he is told, proceeded from the supreme King, from him who, as he gave all their being, justly destines and directs them to himself as their proper end. There is no man, I say, who should not hasten to embrace the Lawgiver, whose commands, he knows, he has been specially appointed to obey, from whose kindness he anticipates an abundance of all good, and even a blessed immortality, and to whose wondrous power and mercy he is indebted for deliverance from the jaws of death.[1]

16. The authority of the Law being founded and established, God delivers his First Commandment—

THOU SHALT HAVE NO OTHER GODS BEFORE ME.

The purport of this commandment is, that the Lord will have himself alone to be exalted in his people, and claims the entire possession of them as his own. That it may be so, he orders us to abstain from ungodliness and superstition of every kind, by which the glory of his divinity is diminished or obscured; and, for the same reason, he requires us to worship and adore him with truly pious zeal. The simple terms used obviously amount to this. For seeing we cannot have God without embracing everything which belongs to him, the prohibition against having strange gods means, that nothing which belongs to him is to be transferred to any other. The duties which we owe to God are innumerable, but they seem to admit of being not improperly reduced to four heads: Adoration, with its accessory spiritual submission of conscience, Trust, Invocation, Thanksgiving.[2] By Adoration, I mean the veneration and worship which we render to him when we do homage to his majesty; and hence I make part of it to consist in bringing our consciences into subjection to his Law.[3] Trust, is secure resting in him under a recognition of his perfections, when, ascribing to him all power, wisdom, justice, goodness, and

---

1 "E faucibus mortis."—French, "du gouffre d'enfer;" from the gulf of hell.

2 Calvin. in Catechismo; De Necessitate Reformandæ Ecclesiæ; Vera Reformandæ Ecclesiæ Ratio.

3 The French adds, "Car c'est un hommage spirituel qui se rend a lui comme souverain Roy, et ayant toute superiorité sur nos ames." For this is a spiritual homage which is rendered to him as sovereign King, having full supremacy over our souls.

truth, we consider ourselves happy in having been brought into intercourse with him. Invocation may be defined the betaking of ourselves to his promised aid as the only resource in every case of need. Thanksgiving is the gratitude which ascribes to him the praise of all our blessings. As the Lord does not allow these to be derived from any other quarter, so he demands that they shall be referred entirely to himself. It is not enough to 'refrain from other gods. We must, at the same time, devote ourselves wholly to him, not acting like certain impious despisers, who regard it as the shortest method, to hold all religious observance in derision. But here precedence must be given to true religion, which will direct our minds to the living God. When duly imbued with the knowledge of him, the whole aim of our lives will be to revere, fear, and worship his majesty, to enjoy a share in his blessings, to have recourse to him in every difficulty, to acknowledge, laud, and celebrate the magnificence of his works, to make him, as it were, the sole aim of all our actions. Next, we must beware of superstition, by which our minds are turned aside from the true God, and carried to and fro after a multiplicity of gods. Therefore, if we are contented with one God, let us call to mind what was formerly observed, that all fictitious gods are to be driven far away, and that the worship which he claims for himself is not to be mutilated. Not a particle of his glory is to be withheld: everything belonging to him must be reserved to him entire. The words, "before me," go to increase the indignity, God being provoked to jealousy whenever we substitute our fictions in his stead ; just as an unfaithful wife stings her husband's heart more deeply when her adultery is committed openly before his eyes. Therefore, God having by his present power and grace declared that he had respect to the people whom he had chosen, now, in order to deter them from the wickedness of revolt, warns them that they cannot adopt strange gods without his being witness and spectator of the sacrilege. To the audacity of so doing is added the very great impiety of supposing that they can mock the eye of God with their evasions. Far from this, the Lord proclaims that everything which we design, plan, or execute, lies open to his sight. Our conscience must, therefore, keep aloof from the most distant thought of revolt, if we would have our worship approved by the Lord. The glory of his godhead must be maintained entire and incorrupt, not merely by external profession, but as under his eye, which penetrates the inmost recesses of his heart.

Second Commandment.

THOU SHALT NOT MAKE UNTO THEE ANY GRAVEN IMAGE, OR ANY
LIKENESS OF ANYTHING THAT IS IN HEAVEN ABOVE, OR THAT IS
IN THE EARTH BENEATH, OR THAT IS IN THE WATER UNDER THE
EARTH: THOU SHALT NOT BOW DOWN THYSELF TO THEM, NOR
SERVE THEM.

17. As in the First Commandment the Lord declares that he is one,
and that besides him no gods must be either worshipped or imagined,
so he here more plainly declares what his nature is, and what the kind
of worship with which he is to be honoured, in order that we may not
presume to form any carnal idea of him. The purport of the commandment, therefore, is, that he will not have his legitimate worship
profaned by superstitious rites. Wherefore, in general, he calls us
entirely away from the carnal frivolous observances which our stupid
minds are wont to devise after forming some gross idea of the divine
nature, while, at the same time, he instructs us in the worship which
is legitimate, namely, spiritual worship of his own appointment. The
grossest vice here prohibited is external idolatry. This commandment consists of two parts. The former curbs the licentious daring
which would subject the incomprehensible God to our senses, or represent him under any visible shape. The latter forbids the worship
of images, on any religious ground. There is, moreover, a brief
enumeration of all the forms by which the Deity was usually represented by heathen and superstitious nations. By "anything which
is in heaven above," is meant the sun, the moon, and the stars, perhaps also birds, as in Deuteronomy, where the meaning is explained,
there is mention of birds as well as stars (Deut. iv. 15). I would
not have made this observation, had I not seen that some absurdly
apply it to the angels. The other particulars I pass, as requiring no
explanation. We have already shown clearly enough (Book I. chap.
xi. xii.) that every visible shape of Deity which man devises is diametrically opposed to the divine nature; and, therefore, that the
moment idols appear, true religion is corrupted and adulterated.

18. The threatening subjoined ought to have no little effect in
shaking off our lethargy. It is in the following terms:—

I THE LORD THY GOD AM A JEALOUS[1] GOD, VISITING THE INIQUITY
OF THE FATHERS UPON THE CHILDREN UNTO THE THIRD AND
FOURTH GENERATION OF THEM THAT HATE ME; AND SHOWING
MERCY UNTO THOUSANDS OF THEM THAT LOVE ME, AND KEEP MY
COMMANDMENTS.

The meaning here is the same as if he had said, that our duty is

[1] Or "Strong," this name being derived from a word denoting strength.

to cleave to him alone. To induce us to this, he proclaims his authority, which he will not permit to be impaired or despised with impunity. It is true, the word used is *El*, which means God; but as it is derived from a word meaning *strength*, I have had no hesitation, in order to express the sense more fully, so to render it as inserted on the margin. Secondly, he calls himself *jealous*, because he cannot bear a partner. Thirdly, he declares that he will vindicate his majesty and glory, if any transfer it either to the creatures or to graven images; and that not by a simple punishment of brief duration, but one extending to the third and fourth generation of such as imitate the impiety of their progenitors. In like manner, he declares his constant mercy and kindness to the remote posterity of those who love him, and keep his Law. The Lord very frequently addresses us in the character of a husband;[1] the union by which he connects us with himself, when he receives us into the bosom of the Church, having some resemblance to that of holy wedlock, because founded on mutual faith. As he performs all the offices of a true and faithful husband, so he stipulates for love and conjugal chastity from us; that is, that we do not prostitute our souls to Satan, to be defiled with foul carnal lusts. Hence, when he rebukes the Jews for their apostacy, he complains that they have cast off chastity, and polluted themselves with adultery. Therefore, as the purer and chaster the husband is, the more grievously he is offended when he sees his wife inclining to a rival; so the Lord, who hath betrothed us to himself in truth, declares that he burns with the hottest jealousy whenever, neglecting the purity of his holy marriage, we defile ourselves with abominable lusts, and especially when the worship of his Deity, which ought to have been most carefully kept unimpaired, is transferred to another, or adulterated with some superstition; since, in this way, we not only violate our plighted troth, but defile the nuptial couch, by giving access to adulterers.

19. In the threatening, we must attend to what is meant when God declares that he will visit the iniquity of the fathers upon the children unto the third and fourth generation. It seems inconsistent with the equity of the divine procedure to punish the innocent for another's fault; and the Lord himself declares, that "the son shall not bear the iniquity of the father" (Ezek. xviii. 20). But still we meet more than once with a declaration as to the postponing of the punishment of the sins of fathers to future generations. Thus Moses repeatedly addresses the Lord as "visiting the iniquity of the fathers upon the children unto the third and fourth generation" (Num. xiv. 18). In like manner, Jeremiah, "Thou showest loving-kindness unto thousands, and recompensest the iniquity of the fathers into the bosom of their children after them" (Jer. xxxii. 18). Some feeling sadly perplexed how to solve this difficulty, think it is to be

---

1 2 Cor. xi. 2; Eph. v. 30; Jer. lxii. 5; Hos. ii. 9; Jer. iii. 1, 2; Hos. ii. 2.

understood of temporal punishments only, which it is said sons may properly bear for the sins of their parents, because they are often inflicted for their own safety. This is indeed true ; for Isaiah declared to Hezekiah, that his children should be stript of the kingdom, and carried away into captivity, for a sin which he had committed (Isa. xxxix. 7) ; and the households of Pharaoh and Abimelech were made to suffer for an injury done to Abraham (Gen. xii. 17 ; xx. 3—18). But the attempt to solve the question in this way is an evasion rather than a true interpretation. For the punishment denounced here and in similar passages is too great to be confined within the limits of the present life. We must therefore understand it to mean, that a curse from the Lord righteously falls not only on the head of the guilty individual, but also on all his lineage. When it has fallen, what can be anticipated but that the father, being deprived of the Spirit of God, will live most flagitiously ; that the son, being in like manner forsaken of the Lord, because of his father's iniquity, will follow the same road to destruction ; and be followed in his turn by succeeding generations, forming a seed of evil-doers ?

20. First, let us examine whether such punishment is inconsistent with the divine justice. If human nature is universally condemned, those on whom the Lord does not bestow the communication of his grace must be doomed to destruction ; nevertheless, they perish by their own iniquity, not by unjust hatred on the part of God. There is no room to expostulate, and ask why the grace of God does not forward their salvation as it does that of others. Therefore, when God punishes the wicked and flagitious for their crimes, by depriving their families of his grace for many generations, who will dare to bring a charge against him for this most righteous vengeance ? But it will be said, the Lord, on the contrary, declares, that the son shall not suffer for the father's sin (Ezek. xviii. 20). Observe the scope of that passage. The Israelites, after being subjected to a long period of uninterrupted calamities, had begun to say, as a proverb, that their fathers had eaten the sour grape, and thus set the children's teeth on edge ; meaning that they, though in themselves righteous and innocent, were paying the penalty of sins committed by their parents, and this more from the implacable anger than the duly tempered severity of God. The prophet declares it was not so : that they were punished for their own wickedness ; that it was not in accordance with the justice of God that a righteous son should suffer for the iniquity of a wicked father ; and that nothing of the kind was exemplified in what they suffered. For, if the visitation of which we now speak is accomplished when God withdraws from the children of the wicked the light of his truth and the other helps to salvation, the only way in which they are accursed for their fathers' wickedness is in being blinded and abandoned by God, and so left to walk in their parents' steps. The misery which they suffer in time, and the destruction to which they are finally doomed, are thus punishments

inflicted by divine justice, not for the sins of others, but for their own iniquity.

21. On the other hand, there is a promise of mercy to thousands—a promise which is frequently mentioned in Scripture, and forms an article in the solemn covenant made with the Church—I will be "a God unto thee, and to thy seed after thee" (Gen. xvii. 7). With reference to this, Solomon says, "The just man walketh in his integrity: his children are blessed after him" (Prov. xx. 7); not only in consequence of a religious education (though this certainly is by no means unimportant), but in consequence of the blessing promised in the covenant—viz. that the divine favour will dwell for ever in the families of the righteous. Herein is excellent consolation to believers, and great ground of terror to the wicked; for if, after death, the mere remembrance of righteousness and iniquity have such an influence on the divine procedure, that his blessing rests on the posterity of the righteous, and his curse on the posterity of the wicked, much more must it rest on the heads of the individuals themselves. Notwithstanding of this, however, the offspring of the wicked sometimes amends, while that of believers degenerates; because the Almighty has not here laid down an inflexible rule which might derogate from his free election. For the consolation of the righteous, and the dismay of the sinner, it is enough that the threatening itself is not vain or nugatory, although it does not always take effect. For, as the temporal punishments inflicted on a few of the wicked are proofs of the divine wrath against sin, and of the future judgment that will ultimately overtake all sinners, though many escape with impunity even to the end of their lives, so, when the Lord gives one example of blessing a son for his father's sake, by visiting him in mercy and kindness, it is a proof of constant and unfailing favour to his worshippers. On the other hand, when, in any single instance, he visits the iniquity of the father on the son, he gives intimation of the judgment which awaits all the reprobate for their own iniquities. The certainty of this is the principal thing here taught. Moreover, the Lord, as it were by the way, commends the riches of his mercy by extending it to thousands, while he limits his vengeance to four generations.

Third Commandment.

THOU SHALT NOT TAKE THE NAME OF THE LORD THY GOD IN VAIN.

22. The purport of this Commandment is, that the majesty of the name of God is to be held sacred. In sum, therefore, it means, that we must not profane it by using it irreverently or contemptuously. This prohibition implies a corresponding precept—viz. that it be our

study and care to treat his name with religious veneration. Wherefore it becomes us to regulate our minds and our tongues, so as never to think or speak of God and his mysteries without reverence and great soberness, and never, in estimating his works, to have any feeling towards him but one of deep veneration. We must, I say, steadily observe the three following things :—*First*, Whatever our mind conceives of him, whatever our tongue-utters, must bespeak his excellence, and correspond to the sublimity of his sacred name; in short, must be fitted to extol its greatness. *Secondly*, We must not rashly and preposterously pervert his sacred word and adorable mysteries to purposes of ambition, or avarice, or amusement, but, according as they bear the impress of his dignity, must always maintain them in due honour and esteem. *Lastly*, We must not detract from or throw obloquy upon his works, as miserable men are wont insultingly to do, but must laud every action which we attribute to him as wise, and just, and good. This is to sanctify the name of God. When we act otherwise, his name is profaned with vain and wicked abuse, because it is applied to a purpose foreign to that to which it is consecrated. Were there nothing worse, in being deprived of its dignity it is gradually brought into contempt. But if there is so much evil in the rash and unseasonable employment of the divine name, there is still more evil in its being employed for nefarious purposes, as is done by those who use it in necromancy, cursing, illicit exorcisms, and other impious incantations. But the Commandment refers especially to the case of oaths, in which a perverse employment of the divine name is particularly detestable ; and this it does the more effectually to deter us from every species of profanation. That the thing here commanded relates to the worship of God, and the reverence due to his name, and not to the equity which men are to cultivate towards each other, is apparent from this, that afterwards, in the Second Table, there is a condemnation of the perjury and false testimony by which human society is injured, and that the repetition would be superfluous, if, in this Commandment, the duty of charity were handled. Moreover, this is necessary even for distinction, because, as was observed, God has, for good reason, divided his Law into two tables. The inference then is, that God here vindicates his own right, and defends his sacred name, but does not teach the duties which men owe to men.

23. In the first place, we must consider what an oath is. An oath, then, is calling God to witness that what we say is true. Execrations being manifestly insulting to God, are unworthy of being classed among oaths. That an oath, when duly taken, is a species of divine worship, appears from many passages of Scripture, as when Isaiah prophesies of the admission of the Assyrians and Egyptians to a participation in the covenant, he says, " In that day shall five cities in the land of Egypt speak the language of Canaan. and swear to the Lord of hosts" (Isaiah xix. 18). Swearing by the name of

the Lord here means, that they will make a profession of religion. In like manner, speaking of the extension of the Redeemer's kingdom, it is said, "He who blesseth himself in the earth shall bless himself in the God of truth : and he that sweareth in the earth shall swear by the God of truth" (Isaiah lxv. 16). In Jeremiah it is said, "If they will diligently learn the ways of my people, to swear by my name, The Lord liveth ; as they taught my people to swear by Baal ; then shall they be built in the midst of my people" (Jer. xii. 16). By appealing to the name of the Lord, and calling him to witness, we are justly said to declare our own religious veneration of him. For we thus acknowledge that he is eternal and unchangeable truth, inasmuch as we not only call upon him, in preference to others, as a fit witness to the truth, but as its only assertor, able to bring hidden things to light, a discerner of the hearts. When human testimony fails, we appeal to God as witness, especially when the matter to be proved lies hid in the conscience. For which reason, the Lord is grievously offended with those who swear by strange gods, and construes such swearing as a proof of open revolt, "Thy children have forsaken me, and sworn by them that are no gods" (Jer. v. 7). The heinousness of the offence is declared by the punishment denounced against it, "I will cut off them that swear by the Lord, and that swear by Malcham" (Zeph. i. 4, 5).

24. Understanding that the Lord would have our oaths to be a species of divine worship, we must be the more careful that they do not, instead of worship, contain insult, or contempt, and vilification. It is no slight insult to swear by him and do it falsely ; hence in the Law this is termed profanation (Lev. xix. 12). For if God is robbed of his truth, what is it that remains ? Without truth he could not be God. But assuredly he is robbed of his truth, when he is made the approver and attester of what is false. Hence, when Joshua is endeavouring to make Achan confess the truth, he says, "My son, give, I pray thee, glory to the Lord God of Israel" (Joshua vii. 19); intimating, that grievous dishonour is done to God when men swear by him falsely. And no wonder ; for, as far as in them lies, his sacred name is in a manner branded with falsehood. That this mode of expression was common among the Jews whenever any one was called upon to take an oath, is evident from a similar obtestation used by the Pharisees, as given in John (John ix. 24). Scripture reminds us of the caution which we ought to use by employing such expressions as the following :—"As the Lord liveth ;" "God do so and more also ;" "I call God for a record upon my soul."[1] Such expressions intimate, that we cannot call God to witness our statement, without imprecating his vengeance for perjury if it is false.

25. The name of God is vulgarised and vilified when used in oaths, which, though true, are superfluous. This, too, is to take his name

1 1 Sam. xiv. 44; 2 Kings vi. 31; 2 Cor. i. 23.

in vain. Wherefore, it is not sufficient to abstain from perjury, unless we, at the same time, remember that an oath is not appointed or allowed for passion or pleasure, but for necessity; and that, therefore, a licentious use is made of it by him who uses it on any other than necessary occasions. Moreover, no case of necessity can be pretended, unless where some purpose of religion or charity is to be served. In this matter, great sin is committed in the present day— sin the more intolerable in this, that its frequency has made it cease to be regarded as a fault, though it certainly is not accounted trivial before the judgment-seat of God. The name of God is everywhere profaned by introducing it indiscriminately in frivolous discourse; and the evil is disregarded, because it has been long and audaciously persisted in with impunity. The commandment of the Lord, however, stands; the penalty also stands, and will one day receive effect. Special vengeance will be executed on those who have taken the name of God in vain. Another form of violation is exhibited, when, with manifest impiety, we, in our oaths, substitute the holy servants of God for God himself,[1] thus conferring upon them the glory of his Godhead. It is not without cause the Lord has, by a special commandment, required us to swear by his name, and, by a special prohibition, forbidden us to swear by other gods.[2] The Apostle gives a clear attestation to the same effect, when he says, that "men verily swear by the greater;" but that, "when God made promise to Abraham, because he could swear by no greater, he sware by himself" (Heb. vi. 16, 13).

26. The Anabaptists, not content with this moderate use of oaths, condemn all, without exception, on the ground of our Saviour's general prohibition, "I say unto you, Swear not at all:" "Let your speech be Yea, yea; Nay, nay: for whatsoever is more than these cometh of evil" (Matth. v. 34; James v. 12). In this way, they inconsiderately make a stumbling-stone of Christ, setting him in opposition to the Father, as if he had descended into the world to annul his decrees. In the Law, the Almighty not only permits an oath as a thing that is lawful (this were amply sufficient), but, in a case of necessity, actually commands it (Exod. xxii. 11). Christ again declares, that he and his Father are one; that he only delivers what was commanded of his Father; that his doctrine is not his own, but his that sent him (John x. 18, 30; vii. 16). What then? Will they make God contradict·himself, by approving and commanding at one time, what he afterwards prohibits and condemns? But as there is some difficulty in what our Saviour says on the subject of swearing, it may be proper to consider it a little. Here, however, we shall never arrive at the true meaning, unless we attend to the design of Christ, and the subject of which he is treating. His pur-

1 The French adds, "jurans par S. Jaques ou S. Antoine;"—swearing by St James or St Anthony.
2 Exod. xxiii. 13; Deut. vi. 13; x. 20; Heb. vi. 18.

pose was, neither to relax nor to curtail the Law, but to restore the true and genuine meaning, which had been greatly corrupted by the false glosses of the Scribes and Pharisees. If we attend to this, we shall not suppose that Christ condemned all oaths, but those only which transgressed the rule of the Law. It is evident, from the oaths themselves, that the people were accustomed to think it enough if they avoided perjury, whereas the Law prohibits not perjury merely, but also vain and superfluous oaths. Therefore our Lord, who is the best interpreter of the Law, reminds them that there is a sin not only in perjury, but in swearing. How in swearing? Namely, by swearing vainly. Those oaths, however, which are authorised by the Law, he leaves safe and free. Those who condemn oaths think their argument invincible when they fasten on the expression, *not at all.* The expression applies not to the word *swear*, but to the subjoined forms of oaths. For part of the error consisted in their supposing, that when they swore by the heaven and the earth, they did not touch the name of God. The Lord, therefore, after cutting off the principal source of prevarication, deprives them of all subterfuges, warning them against supposing that they escape guilt by suppressing the name of God, and appealing to heaven and earth. For it ought here to be observed in passing, that although the name of God is not expressed, yet men swear by him in using indirect forms, as when they swear by the light of life, by the bread they eat, by their baptism, or any other pledges of the divine liberality towards them. Some erroneously suppose that our Saviour in that passage, rebukes superstition, by forbidding men to swear by heaven and earth, and Jerusalem. He rather refutes the sophistical subtlety of those who thought it nothing vainly to utter indirect oaths, imagining that they thus spared the holy name of God, whereas that name is inscribed on each of his mercies. The case is different, when any mortal, living or dead, or an angel, is substituted in the place of God, as in the vile form devised by flattery in heathen nations, *By the life or genius of the king;* for, in this case, the false apotheosis obscures and impairs the glory of the one God. But when nothing else is intended than to confirm what is said by an appeal to the holy name of God, although it is done indirectly, yet his majesty is insulted by all frivolous oaths. Christ strips this abuse of every vain pretext when he says, Swear not at all. To the same effect is the passage in which James uses the words of our Saviour above quoted (James v. 12). For this rash swearing has always prevailed in the world, notwithstanding that it is a profanation of the name of God. If you refer the words, *not at all*, to the act itself, as if every oath, without exception, were unlawful, what will be the use of the explanation which immediately follows—Neither by heaven, neither by the earth, &c.? These words make it clear, that the object in view was to meet the cavils by which the Jews thought they could extenuate their fault.

27. Every person of sound judgment must now see that in that passage our Lord merely condemned those oaths which were forbidden by the Law. For he who in his life exhibited a model of the perfection which he taught, did not object to oaths whenever the occasion required them; and the disciples, who doubtless in all things obeyed their Master, followed the same rule. Who will dare to say that Paul would have sworn (Rom. i. 9; 2 Cor. i. 23) if an oath had been altogether forbidden? But when the occasion calls for it, he adjures without any scruple, and sometimes even imprecates. The question, however, is not yet disposed of. For some think that the only oaths exempted from the prohibition are public oaths, such as those which are administered to us by the magistrate, or independent states employ in ratifying treaties, or the people take when they swear allegiance to their sovereign, or the soldier in the case of the military oath, and others of a similar description. To this class they refer (and justly) those protestations in the writings of Paul, which assert the dignity of the Gospel; since the apostles, in discharging their office, were not private individuals, but the public servants of God. I certainly deny not that such oaths are the safest, because they are most strongly supported by passages of Scripture. The magistrate is enjoined, in a doubtful matter, to put the witness upon oath; and he in his turn to answer upon oath; and an apostle says, that in this way there is an end of all strife (Heb. vi. 16). In this commandment, both parties are fully approved. Nay, we may observe, that among the ancient heathens a public and solemn oath was held in great reverence, while those common oaths which were indiscriminately used were in little or no estimation, as if they thought that, in regard to them, the Deity did not interpose. Private oaths used soberly, sacredly, and reverently, on necessary occasions, it were perilous to condemn, supported as they are by reason and example. For if private individuals are permitted, in a grave and serious matter, to appeal to God as a judge, much more may they appeal to him as a witness. Your brother charges you with perfidy. You, as bound by the duties of charity, labour to clear yourself from the charge. He will on no account be satisfied. If, through his obstinate malice, your good name is brought into jeopardy, you can appeal, without offence, to the judgment of God, that he may in time manifest your innocence. If the terms are weighed, it will be found that it is a less matter to call upon him to be witness; and I therefore see not how it can be called unlawful to do so. And there is no want of examples. If it is pretended that the oath which Abraham and Isaac made with Abimelech was of a public nature, that by which Jacob and Laban bound themselves in mutual league was private. Boaz, though a private man, confirmed his promise of marriage to Ruth in the same way. Obadiah, too, a just man, and one that feared God, though a private individual, in seeking to persuade Elijah, asseverates with an oath.[1] I hold, therefore, that there is no better rule than so to regu-

[1] Gen. xxi. 24; xxvi. 31; xxxi. 63; Ruth iii. 13; 1 Kings xviii. 10.

late our oaths that they shall neither be rash, frivolous, promiscuous, nor passionate, but be made to serve a just necessity; in other words, to vindicate the glory of God, or promote the edification of a brother. This is the end of the Commandment.

Fourth Commandment.

REMEMBER THE SABBATH DAY TO KEEP IT HOLY. SIX DAYS SHALT THOU LABOUR AND DO ALL THY WORK: BUT THE SEVENTH DAY IS THE SABBATH OF THE LORD THY GOD. IN IT THOU SHALT NOT DO ANY WORK, &C.

28. The purport of the commandment is, that being dead to our own affections and works, we meditate on the kingdom of God, and in order to such meditation, have recourse to the means which he has appointed. But as this commandment stands in peculiar circum- *Reasons for* stances apart from the others, the mode of exposition must be some- *the* what different. Early Christian writers are wont to call it typical, *Sabbath* as containing the external observance of a day which was abolished with the other types on the advent of Christ. This is indeed true; but it leaves the half of the matter untouched. Wherefore, we must look deeper for our exposition, and attend to three cases in which it appears to me that the observance of this commandment consists. First, under the rest of the seventh day, the divine Lawgiver meant *1. Spiritual* to furnish the people of Israel with a type of the spiritual rest by *Rest.* which believers were to cease from their own works, and allow God to work in them. Secondly, he meant that there should be a stated *2. Stated* day on which they should assemble to hear the Law, and perform *time for* religious rites, or which, at least, they should specially employ in *worship.* meditating on his works, and be thereby trained to piety. Thirdly, *3. Physical* he meant that servants, and those who lived under the authority of *rest.* others, should be indulged with a day of rest, and thus have some intermission from labour.

29. We are taught in many passages[1] that this adumbration of *The* spiritual rest held a primary place in the Sabbath. Indeed, there is *importance* no commandment the observance of which the Almighty more strictly *of the* enforces. When he would intimate by the prophets that religion *Sabbath* was entirely subverted, he complains that his sabbaths were polluted, *viewed* violated, not kept, not hallowed; as if, after it was neglected, there *as* remained nothing in which he could be honoured. The observance *Spiritual* of it he eulogises in the highest terms, and hence, among other divine *Rest.* privileges, the faithful set an extraordinary value on the revelation of the Sabbath. In Nehemiah, the Levites, in the public assembly,

1 Num. xiii. 22; Ezek. xx. 12; xxii. 8; xxiii. 38; Jer. xvii. 21, 22, 27; Isaiah lvi. 2; Neh. ix. 14.

thus speak : " Thou madest known unto them thy holy sabbath, and commandedst them precepts, statutes, and laws, by the hand of Moses thy servant." You see the singular honour which it holds among all the precepts of the Law. All this tends to celebrate the dignity of the mystery, which is most admirably expressed by Moses and Ezekiel. Thus in Exodus: " Verily my sabbaths shall ye keep: for it is a sign between me and you throughout your generations ; that ye may know that I am the Lord that doth sanctify you. Ye shall keep my sabbath therefore ; for it is holy unto you : every one that defileth it shall surely be put to death : for whosoever doeth any work therein, that soul shall be cut off from among his people. Six days may work be done ; but in the seventh is the sabbath of rest, holy to the Lord : whosoever doeth any work in the sabbath day, he shall surely be put to death. Wherefore the children of Israel shall keep the sabbath, to observe the sabbath throughout their generations, for a perpetual covenant. It is a sign between me and the children of Israel for ever " (Exodus xxxi. 13—17). Ezekiel is still more full, but the sum of what he says amounts to this: that the sabbath is a sign by which Israel might know that God is their sanctifier. If our sanctification consists in the mortification of our own will, the analogy between the external sign and the thing signified is most appropriate. We must rest entirely, in order that God may work in us ; we must resign our own will, yield up our heart, and abandon all the lusts of the flesh. In short, we must desist from all the acts of our own mind, that God working in us, we may rest in him, as the Apostle also teaches (Heb. iii. 13 ; iv. 3, 9).

30. This complete cessation was represented to the Jews by the observance of one day in seven, which, that it might be more religiously attended to, the Lord recommended by his own example. For it is no small incitement to the zeal of man to know that he is engaged in imitating his Creator. Should any one expect some secret meaning in the number seven, this being in Scripture the number for perfection, it may have been selected, not without cause, to denote perpetuity. In accordance with this, Moses concludes his description of the succession of day and night on the same day on which he relates that the Lord rested from his works. Another probable reason for the number may be, that the Lord intended that the Sabbath never should be completed before the arrival of the last day. We here begin our blessed rest in him, and daily make new progress in it ; but because we must still wage an incessant warfare with the flesh, it shall not be consummated until the fulfilment of the prophecy of Isaiah : " From one new moon to another, and from one sabbath to another, shall all flesh come to worship before me, saith the Lord" (Isaiah lxvi. 23) ; in other words, when God shall be " all in all " (1 Cor. xv. 28). It may seem, therefore, that by the seventh day the Lord delineated to his people the future perfection of his sabbath

The importance of the Sabbath being celebrated on the Seventh Day.

on the last day, that by continual meditation on the Sabbath, they might throughout their whole lives aspire to this perfection.

31. Should these remarks on the number seem to any somewhat far-fetched, I have no objection to their taking it more simply: that the Lord appointed a certain day on which his people might be trained, under the tutelage of the Law, to meditate constantly on the spiritual rest, and fixed upon the seventh, either because he foresaw it would be sufficient, or in order that his own example might operate as a stronger stimulus; or, at least, to remind men that the Sabbath was appointed for no other purpose than to render them conformable to their Creator. It is of little consequence which of these be adopted, provided we lose not sight of the principal thing delineated—viz. the mystery of perpetual resting from our works. To the contemplation of this, the Jews were every now and then called by the prophets, lest they should think a carnal cessation from labour sufficient. Beside the passages already quoted, there is the following: "If thou turn away thy foot from the Sabbath, from doing thy pleasure on my holy day; and call the Sabbath a delight, the holy of the Lord, honourable; and shalt honour him, not doing thine own ways, nor finding thine own pleasure, nor speaking thine own words: then shalt thou delight thyself in the Lord" (Isaiah lviii. 13, 14). Still there can be no doubt, that, on the advent of our Lord Jesus Christ, the ceremonial part of the commandment was abolished. He is the truth, at whose presence all the emblems banish; the body, at the sight of which the shadows disappear. He, I say, is the true completion of the Sabbath: "We are buried with him by baptism unto death: that like as Christ was raised up from the dead by the glory of the Father, even so we should walk in newness of life" (Rom. vi. 4). Hence, as the Apostle elsewhere says, "Let no man therefore judge you in meat, or in drink, or in respect of an holyday, or of the new moon, or of the Sabbath days; which are a shadow of things to come; but the body is of Christ" (Col. ii. 16, 17); meaning by body the whole essence of the truth, as is well explained in that passage. This is not contented with one day, but requires the whole course of our lives, until being completely dead to ourselves, we are filled with the life of God. Christians, therefore, should have nothing to do with a superstitious observance of days.

32. The two other cases ought not to be classed with ancient shadows, but are adapted to every age. The Sabbath being abrogated, there is still room among us, first, to assemble on stated days for the hearing of the word, the breaking of the mystical bread, and public prayer: and, secondly, to give our servants and labourers relaxation from labour. It cannot be doubted that the Lord provided for both in the commandment of the Sabbath. The former is abundantly evinced by the mere practice of the Jews. The latter Moses has expressed in Deuteronomy in the following terms: "The seventh day

is the Sabbath of the Lord thy God : in it thou shalt not do any work, thou, nor thy son, nor thy daughter, nor thy man-servant, nor thy maid-servant ;—that thy man-servant and thy maid-servant may rest as well as thou" (Deut. v. 14). Likewise in Exodus, "That thine ox and thine ass may rest, and the son of thy handmaid, and the stranger, may be refreshed" (Exod. xxiii. 12). Who can deny that both are equally applicable to us as to the Jews? Religious meetings are enjoined us by the word of God ; their necessity, experience itself sufficiently demonstrates. But unless these meetings are stated, and have fixed days allotted to them, how can they be held? We must, as the Apostle expresses it, do all things decently and in order (1 Cor. xiv. 40). So impossible, however, would it be to preserve decency and order without this politic arrangement, that the dissolution of it would instantly lead to the disturbance and ruin of the Church. But if the reason for which the Lord appointed a Sabbath to the Jews is equally applicable to us, no man can assert that it is a matter with which we have nothing to do. Our most provident and indulgent Parent has been pleased to provide for our wants not less than for the wants of the Jews. Why, it may be asked, do we not hold daily meetings, and thus avoid the distinction of days? Would that we were privileged to do so! Spiritual wisdom undoubtedly deserves to have some portion of every day devoted to it. But if, owing to the weakness of many, daily meetings cannot be held, and charity will not allow us to exact more of them, why should we not adopt the rule which the will of God has obviously imposed upon us?

33. I am obliged to dwell a little longer on this, because some restless spirits are now making an outcry about the observance of the Lord's day. They complain that Christian people are trained in Judaism, because some observance of days is retained. My reply is, That those days are observed by us without Judaism, because in this matter we differ widely from the Jews. We do not celebrate it with most minute formality, as a ceremony by which we imagine that a spiritual mystery is typified, but we adopt it as a necessary remedy for preserving order in the Church. Paul informs us that Christians are not to be judged in respect of its observance, because it is a shadow of something to come (Col. ii. 16) ; and, accordingly, he expresses a fear lest his labour among the Galatians should prove in vain, because they still observed days (Gal. iv. 10, 11). And he tells the Romans that it is superstitious to make one day differ from another (Rom. xiv. 5). But who, except those restless men, does not see what the observance is to which the Apostle refers ? Those persons had no regard to that politic and ecclesiastical arrangement,[1] but by retaining the days as types of spiritual things, they in so far obscured

---

1 "Finem istum politicum et ecclesiasticum ordinem."—French, "la police et ordre en l'Eglise;" policy and order in the Church.

the glory of Christ, and the light of the Gospel. They did not desist from manual labour on the ground of its interfering with sacred study and meditation, but as a kind of religious observance ; because they dreamed that by their cessation from labour, they were cultivating the mysteries which had of old been committed to them. It was, I say, against this preposterous observance of days that the Apostle inveighs, and not against that legitimate selection which is subservient to the peace of Christian society. For in the churches established by him, this was the use for which the Sabbath was retained. He tells the Corinthians to set the first day apart for collecting contributions for the relief of their brethren at Jerusalem (1 Cor. xvi. 2). If superstition is dreaded, there was more danger in keeping the Jewish Sabbath than the Lord's day as Christians now do. It being expedient to overthrow superstition, the Jewish holyday was abolished ; and as a thing necessary to retain decency, order, and peace, in the Church, another day was appointed for that purpose.

34. It was not, however, without a reason that the early Christians substituted what we call the Lord's day for the Sabbath. The resurrection of our Lord being the end and accomplishment of that true rest which the ancient Sabbath typified, this day, by which types were abolished, serves to warn Christians against adhering to a shadowy ceremony. I do not cling so to the number seven as to bring the Church under bondage to it, nor do I condemn churches for holding their meetings on other solemn days, provided they guard against superstition. This they will do if they employ those days merely for the observance of discipline and regular order. The whole may be thus summed up : As the truth was delivered typically to the Jews, so it is imparted to us without figure ; first, that during our whole lives we may aim at a constant rest from our own works, in order that the Lord may work in us by his Spirit ; secondly, that every individual, as he has opportunity, may diligently exercise himself in private, in pious meditation on the works of God, and, at the same time, that all may observe the legitimate order appointed by the Church, for the hearing of the word, the administration of the sacraments, and public prayer : and, thirdly, that we may avoid oppressing those who are subject to us. In this way, we get quit of the trifling of the false prophets, who in later times instilled Jewish ideas into the people, alleging that nothing was abrogated but what was ceremonial in the commandment [1] (this they term in their language the taxation of the seventh day), while the moral part remains—viz. the observance of one day in seven.[2] But this is nothing else than to

---

[1] As to this liberty, see Socrates, Hist. Trip. Lib. ix. c. 38.

[2] French, " ne discernans entre le Dimanche et le Sabbath autrement, sinon que le septiéme jour estoit abrogé qu'on gardoit pour lors, mais qu'il on faloit neantmoins garder un ; "—making no other distinction between the Sunday and the Sabbath, save that the seventh day, which was kept till then, was abrogated, but that it was nevertheless necessary to keep some one day.

insult tne Jews, by changing the day, and yet mentally attributing to it the same sanctity; thus retaining the same typical distinction of days as had place among the Jews. And of a truth, we see what profit they have made by such a doctrine. Those who cling to their constitutions go thrice as far as the Jews in the gross and carnal superstition of sabbatism; so that the rebukes which we read in Isaiah (Isa. i. 13; lviii. 13) apply as much to those of the present day,[1] as to those to whom the Prophet addressed them. We must be careful, however, to observe the general doctrine—viz. in order that religion may neither be lost nor languish among us, we must diligently attend on our religious assemblies, and duly avail ourselves of those external aids which tend to promote the worship of God.

𝔉𝔦𝔣𝔱𝔥 𝔆𝔬𝔪𝔪𝔞𝔫𝔡𝔪𝔢𝔫𝔱.

HONOUR THY FATHER AND THY MOTHER, THAT THY DAYS MAY BE LONG UPON THE LAND WHICH THE LORD THY GOD GIVETH THEE.

35. The end of this commandment is, that since the Lord takes pleasure in the preservation of his own ordinance, the degrees of dignity appointed by him must be held inviolable. The sum of the commandment, therefore, will be; that we are to look up to those whom the Lord has set over us, yielding them honour, gratitude, and obedience. Hence it follows, that everything in the way of contempt, ingratitude, or disobedience, is forbidden. For the term *honour* has this extent of meaning in Scripture. Thus when the Apostle says, "Let the elders that rule well be counted worthy of double honour" (1 Tim. v. 17), he refers not only to the reverence which is due to them, but to the recompense to which their services are entitled. But as this command to submit is very repugnant to the perversity of the human mind (which, puffed up with ambitious longings, will scarcely allow itself to be subject), that superiority which is most attractive and least invidious is set forth as an example calculated to soften and bend our minds to habits of submission. From that subjection which is most easily endured, the Lord gradually accustoms us to every kind of legitimate subjection, the same principle regulating all. For to those whom he raises to eminence, he communicates his authority, in so far as necessary to maintain their station. The titles of Father, God, and Lord, all meet in him alone; and hence, whenever any one of them is mentioned, our mind should be impressed with the same feeling of reverence. Those, therefore, to whom he imparts such titles, he distinguishes by some small spark of his refulgence, so as to entitle them to honour, each in his own place. In this way, we must consider that our earthly father possesses something of a divine

---

[1] French, "leur conviendroyent mieux;"—would be more applicable to them.

nature in him, because there is some reason for his bearing a divine title, and that he who is our prince and ruler is admitted to some communion of honour with God.

36. Wherefore, we ought to have no doubt that the Lord here lays down this universal rule—viz. that knowing how every individual is set over us by his appointment, we should pay him reverence, gratitude, obedience, and every duty in our power. And it makes no difference whether those on whom the honour is conferred are deserving or not. Be they what they may, the Almighty, by conferring their station upon them, shows that he would have them honoured. The commandment specifies the reverence due to those to whom we owe our being. This Nature herself should in some measure teach us. For they are monsters, and not men, who petulantly and contumeliously violate the paternal authority. Hence, the Lord orders all who rebel against their parents to be put to death, they being, as it were, unworthy of the light in paying no deference to those to whom they are indebted for beholding it. And it is evident, from the various appendices to the Law, that we were correct in stating, that the honour here referred to consists of three parts, reverence, obedience, and gratitude. The first of these the Lord enforces, when he commands that whoso curseth his father or his mother shall be put to death. In this way he avenges insult and contempt. The second he enforces, when he denounces the punishment of death on disobedient and rebellious children. To the third belongs our Saviour's declaration, that God requires us to do good to our parents (Matth. xv.). And whenever Paul mentions this commandment, he interprets it as enjoining obedience.[1]

37. A promise is added by way of recommendation, the better to remind us how pleasing to God is the submission which is here required. Paul applies that stimulus to rouse us from our lethargy, when he calls this the first commandment with promise; the promise contained in the First Table not being specially appropriated to any one commandment, but extended to the whole law. Moreover, the sense in which the promise is to be taken is as follows:—The Lord spoke to the Israelites specially of the land which he had promised them for an inheritance. If, then, the possession of the land was an earnest of the divine favour, we cannot wonder if the Lord was pleased to testify his favour, by bestowing long life, as in this way they were able long to enjoy his kindness. The meaning therefore is: Honour thy father and thy mother, that thou mayst be able, during the course of a long life, to enjoy the possession of the land which is to be given thee in testimony of my favour. But, as the whole earth is blessed to believers, we justly class the present life among the number of divine blessings. Whence this promise has, in like manner, refer-

---

[1] Exod. xxi. 17; Levit. xx. 9; Prov. xx. 20; Deut. xxi. 18; Matth. xv. 4; Eph. vi. 1; Coloss. iii. 20.

ence to us also, inasmuch as the duration of the present life is a proof of the divine benevolence toward us. It is not promised to us, nor was it promised to the Jews, as if in itself it constituted happiness, but because it is an ordinary symbol of the divine favour to the pious. Wherefore, if any one who is obedient to parents happens to be cut off before mature age (a thing which not unfrequently happens), the Lord nevertheless adheres to his promise as steadily as when he bestows a hundred acres of land where he had promised only one. The whole lies in this: We must consider that long life is promised only in so far as it is a blessing from God, and that it is a blessing only in so far as it is a manifestation of divine favour. This, however, he testifies and truly manifests to his servants more richly and substantially by death.

38. Moreover, while the Lord promises the blessing of present life to children who show proper respect to their parents, he, at the same time, intimates that an inevitable curse is impending over the rebellious and disobedient; and, that it may not fail of execution, he, in his Law, pronounces sentence of death upon them, and orders it to be inflicted. If they escape the judgment, he, in some way or other, will execute vengeance. For we see how great a number of this description of individuals fall either in battle or in brawls; others of them are overtaken by unwonted disasters, and almost all are a proof that the threatening is not used in vain. But if any do escape till extreme old age, yet, because deprived of the blessing of God in this life, they only languish on in wickedness, and are reserved for severer punishment in the world to come; they are far from participating in the blessing promised to obedient children. It ought to be observed, by the way, that we are ordered to obey parents only in the Lord. This is clear from the principle already laid down: for the place which they occupy is one to which the Lord has exalted them, by communicating to them a portion of his own honour. Therefore the submission yielded to them should be a step in our ascent to the Supreme Parent, and hence, if they instigate us to transgress the law, they deserve not to be regarded as parents, but as strangers attempting to seduce us from our obedience to our true Father. The same holds in the case of rulers, masters, and superiors of every description. For it were unbecoming and absurd that the honour of God should be impaired by their exaltation—an exaltation which, being derived from him, ought to lead us up to him.[1]

Sixth Commandment.

THOU SHALT NOT KILL.

39. The purport of this commandment is, that since the Lord has

[1] The French adds, "et la doit plustost augmenter, qu'amoindrir confirmer que violer;"—and ought to augment rather than diminish, to confirm rather than violate it.

bound the whole human race by a kind of unity, the safety of all ought to be considered as intrusted to each. In general, therefore, all violence and injustice, and every kind of harm from which our neighbour's body suffers, is prohibited. Accordingly, we are required faithfully to do what in us lies to defend the life of our neighbour, to promote whatever tends to his tranquility, to be vigilant in warding off harm, and, when danger comes, to assist in removing it. Remembering that the Divine Lawgiver thus speaks, consider, moreover, that he requires you to apply the same rule in regulating your mind. It were ridiculous, that he, who sees the thoughts of the heart, and has special regard to them, should train the body only to rectitude. This commandment, therefore, prohibits the murder of the heart, and requires a sincere desire to preserve our brother's life. The hand, indeed, commits the murder, but the mind, under the influence of wrath and hatred, conceives it. How can you be angry with your brother, without passionately longing to do him harm? If you must not be angry with him, neither must you hate him, hatred being nothing but inveterate anger. However you may disguise the fact, or endeavour to escape from it by vain pretexts, where either wrath or hatred is, there is an inclination to do mischief. If you still persist in tergiversation, the mouth of the Spirit has declared, that "whosoever hateth his brother is a murderer" (1 John iii. 15); and the mouth of our Saviour has declared, that "whosoever is angry with his brother without a cause shall be in danger of the judgment: and whosoever shall say to his brother, Raca, shall be in danger of the council: but whosoever shall say, Thou fool, shall be in danger of hell fire" (Matth. v. 22).

40. Scripture notes a twofold equity on which this commandment is founded. Man is both the image of God and our flesh. Wherefore, if we would not violate the image of God, we must hold the person of man sacred—if we would not divest ourselves of humanity, we must cherish our own flesh. The practical inference to be drawn from the redemption and gift of Christ will be elsewhere considered.[1] The Lord has been pleased to direct our attention to these two natural considerations as inducements to watch over our neighbour's preservation—viz. to revere the divine image impressed upon him, and embrace our own flesh. To be clear of the crime of murder, it is not enough to refrain from shedding man's blood. If in act you perpetrate, if in endeavour you plot, if in wish and design you conceive what is adverse to another's safety, you have the guilt of murder. On the other hand, if you do not according to your means and opportunity study to defend his safety, by that inhumanity you violate the law. But if the safety of the body is so carefully provided for, we may hence infer how much care and exertion is due to the safety

---

[1] Book III. Chap. vii. sec. 4—7; Chap. xx. sec. 38, 45; Book IV. Chap. i. sec. 18—19; Chap. xviii. sec. 38, 40.

of the soul, which is of immeasurably higher value in the sight of God.

Seventh Commandment.

THOU SHALT NOT COMMIT ADULTERY.

41. The purport of this commandment is, that as God loves chastity and purity, we ought to guard against all uncleanness. The substance of the commandment therefore is, that we must not defile ourselves with any impurity or libidinous excess. To this corresponds the affirmative, that we must regulate every part of our conduct chastely and continently. The thing expressly forbidden is adultery, to which lust naturally tends, that its filthiness (being of a grosser and more palpable form, inasmuch as it casts a stain even on the body) may dispose us to abominate every form of lust. As the law under which man was created was not to lead a life of solitude, but enjoy a help-meet for him—and ever since he fell under the curse the necessity for this mode of life is increased—the Lord made the requisite provision for us in this respect by the institution of marriage, which, entered into under his authority, he has also sanctified with his blessing. Hence, it is evident, that any mode of cohabitation different from marriage is cursed in his sight, and that the conjugal relation was ordained as a necessary means of preventing us from giving way to unbridled lust. Let us beware, therefore, of yielding to indulgence, seeing we are assured that the curse of God lies on every man and woman cohabiting without marriage.

42. Now, since natural feeling and the passions inflamed by the fall make the marriage tie doubly necessary, save in the case of those whom God has by special grace exempted, let every individual consider how the case stands with himself. Virginity, I admit, is a virtue not to be despised; but since it is denied to some, and to others granted only for a season, those who are assailed by incontinence, and unable successfully to war against it, should betake themselves to the remedy of marriage, and thus cultivate chastity in the way of their calling. Those incapable of self-restraint, if they apply not to the remedy allowed and provided for intemperance, war with God and resist his ordinance. And let no man tell me (as many in the present day do) that he can do all things, God helping! The help of God is present with those only who walk in his ways (Ps. xci. 14), that is, in his calling, from which all withdraw themselves who, omitting the remedies provided by God, vainly and presumptuously strive to struggle with and surmount their natural feelings. That continence is a special gift from God, and of the class of those which are not bestowed indiscriminately on the whole body of the Church, but only on a few of its members, our Lord

affirms (Matth. xix. 12). He first describes a certain class of individuals who have made themselves eunuchs for the kingdom of heaven's sake; that is, in order that they may be able to devote themselves with more liberty and less restraint to the things of heaven. But lest any one should suppose that such a sacrifice was in every man's power, he had shown a little before that all are not capable, but those only to whom it is specially given from above. Hence he concludes, "He that is able to receive it, let him receive it." Paul asserts the same thing still more plainly when he says, "Every man has his proper gift of God, one after this manner, and another after that" (1 Cor. vii. 7).

43. Since we are reminded by an express declaration, that it is not in every man's power to live chaste in celibacy, although it may be his most strenuous study and aim to do so—that it is a special grace which the Lord bestows only on certain individuals, in order that they may be less encumbered in his service, do we not oppose God, and nature as constituted by him, if we do not accommodate our mode of life to the measure of our ability? The Lord prohibits fornication, therefore he requires purity and chastity. The only method which each has of preserving it is to measure himself by his capacity. Let no man rashly despise matrimony as a thing useless or superfluous to him; let no man long for celibacy unless he is able to dispense with the married state. Nor even here let him consult the tranquility or convenience of the flesh, save only that, freed from this tie, he may be the readier and more prepared for all the offices of piety. And since there are many on whom this blessing is conferred only for a time, let every one, in abstaining from marriage, do it so long as he is fit to endure celibacy. If he has not the power of subduing his passion, let him understand that the Lord has made it obligatory on him to marry. The Apostle shows this when he enjoins: "Nevertheless, to avoid fornication, let every man have his own wife, and let every woman have her own husband." "If they cannot contain, let them marry." He first intimates that the greater part of men are liable to incontinence; and then of those so liable, he orders all, without exception, to have recourse to the only remedy by which unchastity may be obviated. The incontinent, therefore, in neglecting to cure their infirmity by this means, sin by the very circumstance of disobeying the Apostle's command. And let not a man flatter himself, that because he abstains from the outward act he cannot be accused of unchastity. His mind may in the meantime be inwardly inflamed with lust. For Paul's definition of chastity is purity of mind, combined with purity of body. "The unmarried woman careth for the things of the Lord, that she may be holy both in body and spirit" (1 Cor. vii. 34). Therefore, when he gives a reason for the former precept, he not only says that it is better to marry than to live in fornication, but that it is better to marry than to burn.

44. Moreover, when spouses are made aware that their union is blessed by the Lord, they are thereby reminded that they must not give way to intemperate and unrestrained indulgence. For though honourable wedlock veils the turpitude of incontinence, it does not follow that it ought forthwith to become a stimulus to it. Wherefore, let spouses consider that all things are not lawful for them. Let there be sobriety in the behaviour of the husband toward the wife, and of the wife in her turn toward the husband ; each so acting as not to do anything unbecoming the dignity and temperance of married life. Marriage contracted in the Lord ought to exhibit measure and modesty—not run to the extreme of wantonness. This excess Ambrose censured gravely, but not undeservedly, when he described the man who shows no modesty or comeliness in conjugal intercourse, as committing adultery with his wife.[1] Lastly, let us consider who the Lawgiver is that thus condemns fornication : even He who, as he is entitled to possess us entirely, requires integrity of body, soul, and spirit. Therefore, while he forbids fornication, he at the same time forbids us to lay snares for our neighbour's chastity by lascivious attire, obscene gestures, and impure conversation. There was reason in the remark made by Archelaus to a youth clothed effeminately and over-luxuriously, that it mattered not in what part his wantonness appeared. We must have respect to God, who abhors all contamination, whatever be the part of soul or body in which it appears. And that there may be no doubt about it, let us remember, that what the Lord here commends is chastity. If he requires chastity, he condemns everything which is opposed to it. Therefore, if you aspire to obedience, let not your mind burn within with evil concupiscence, your eyes wanton after corrupting objects, nor your body be decked for allurement; let neither your tongue by filthy speeches, nor your appetite by intemperance, entice the mind to corresponding thoughts. All vices of this description are a kind of stains which despoil chastity of its purity.

Eight Commandment.

THOU SHALT NOT STEAL.

The purport is, that injustice being an abomination to God, we must render to every man his due. In substance, then, the commandment forbids us to long after other men's goods, and, accordingly, requires every man to exert himself honestly in preserving his own. For we must consider, that what each individual possesses has not fallen to him by chance, but by the distribution of the sovereign

---

[1] See Ambros. Lib. de Philosoph., quoted by Augustine in his book, Contra Julian, Lib. ii.

Lord of all, that no one can pervert his means to bad purposes without committing a fraud on a divine dispensation. There are very many kinds of theft. One consists in violence, as when a man's goods are forcibly plundered and carried off; another in malicious imposture, as when they are fraudulently intercepted; a third in the more hidden craft which takes possession of them with a semblance of justice; and a fourth in sycophancy, which wiles them away under the pretence of donation. But not to dwell too long in enumerating the different classes, we know that all the arts by which we obtain possession of the goods and money of our neighbours, for sincere affection substituting an eagerness to deceive or injure them in any way, are to be regarded as thefts. Though they may be obtained by an action at law, a different decision is given by God. He sees the long train of deception by which the man of craft begins to lay nets for his more simple neighbour, until he entangles him in its meshes—sees the harsh and cruel laws by which the more powerful oppresses and crushes the feeble—sees the enticements by which the more wily baits the hook for the less wary, though all these escape the judgment of man, and no cognisance is taken of them. Nor is the violation of this commandment confined to money, or merchandise, or lands, but extends to every kind of right; for we defraud our neighbours to their hurt if we decline any of the duties which we are bound to perform towards them. If an agent or an indolent steward wastes the substance of his employer, or does not give due heed to the management of his property; if he unjustly squanders or luxuriously wastes the means intrusted to him; if a servant holds his master in derision, divulges his secrets, or in any way is treacherous to his life or his goods; if, on the other hand, a master cruelly torments his household, he is guilty of theft before God; since every one who, in the exercise of his calling, performs not what he owes to others, keeps back, or makes away with what does not belong to him.

46. This commandment, therefore, we shall duly obey, if, contented with our own lot, we study to acquire nothing but honest and lawful gain; if we long not to grow rich by injustice, nor to plunder our neighbour of his goods, that our own may thereby be increased; if we hasten not to heap up wealth cruelly wrung from the blood of others; if we do not, by means lawful and unlawful, with excessive eagerness, scrape together whatever may glut our avarice or meet our prodigality. On the other hand, let it be our constant aim faithfully to lend our counsel and aid to all so as to assist them in retaining their property; or if we have to do with the perfidious or crafty, let us rather be prepared to yield somewhat of our right than to contend with them. And not only so, but let us contribute to the relief of those whom we see under the pressure of difficulties, assisting their want out of our abundance. Lastly, let each of us consider how far he is bound in duty to others, and in good faith pay what we owe. In the same way, let the people pay all due honour to their rulers,

submit patiently to their authority, obey their laws and orders, and decline nothing which they can bear without sacrificing the favour of God. Let rulers, again, take due charge of their people, preserve the public peace, protect the good, curb the bad, and conduct themselves throughout as those who must render an account of their office to God, the Judge of all. Let the ministers of churches faithfully give heed to the ministry of the word, and not corrupt the doctrine of salvation, but deliver it purely and sincerely to the people of God. Let them teach not merely by doctrine, but by example; in short, let them act the part of good shepherds towards their flocks. Let the people, in their turn, receive them as the messengers and apostles of God, render them the honour which their Supreme Master has bestowed on them, and supply them with such things as are necessary for their livelihood. Let parents be careful to bring up, guide, and teach their children as a trust committed to them by God. Let them not exasperate or alienate them by cruelty, but cherish and embrace them with the lenity and indulgence which becomes their character. The regard due to parents from their children has already been adverted to. Let the young respect those advanced in years, as the Lord has been pleased to make that age honourable. Let the aged also, by their prudence and their experience (in which they are far superior), guide the feebleness of youth, not assailing them with harsh and clamorous invectives, but tempering strictness with ease and affability. Let servants show themselves diligent and respectful in obeying their masters, and this not with eye-service, but from the heart, as the servants of God. Let masters also not be stern and disobliging to their servants, nor harass them with excessive asperity, nor treat them with insult, but rather let them acknowledge them as brethren and fellow-servants of our heavenly Master, whom, therefore, they are bound to treat with mutual love and kindness. Let every one, I say, thus consider what in his own place and order he owes to his neighbours, and pay what he owes. Moreover, we must always have a reference to the Lawgiver, and so remember that the law requiring us to promote and defend the interest and convenience of our fellowmen, applies equally to our minds and our hands.

Ninth Commandment.

THOU SHALT NOT BEAR FALSE WITNESS AGAINST THY NEIGHBOUR.

47. The purport of the commandment is, since God, who is truth, abhors falsehood, we must cultivate unfeigned truth towards each other. The sum, therefore, will be, that we must not by calumnies and false accusations injure our neighbour's name, or by falsehood impair his fortunes; in fine, that we must not injure any one from

petulance, or a love of evil speaking.　To this prohibition corresponds the command, that we must faithfully assist every one, as far as in us lies, in asserting the truth, for the maintenance of his good name and his estate.　The Lord seems to have intended to explain the commandment in these words: "Thou shalt not raise a false report: put not thine hand with the wicked to be an unrighteous witness." "Keep thee far from a false matter" (Exod. xxiii. 1, 7).　In another passage, he not only prohibits that species of falsehood which consists in acting the part of tale-bearers among the people, but says, "Neither shalt thou stand against the blood of thy neighbour" (Lev. xix. 16).　Both transgressions are distinctly prohibited.　Indeed, there can be no doubt, that as in the previous commandment he prohibited cruelty, unchastity, and avarice, so here he prohibits falsehood, which consists of the two parts to which we have adverted.　By malignant or vicious detraction, we sin against our neighbour's good name: by lying, sometimes even by casting a slur upon him, we injure him in his estate.　It makes no difference whether you suppose that formal and judicial testimony is here intended, or the ordinary testimony which is given in private conversation.　For we must always recur to the consideration, that for each kind of transgression one species is set forth by way of example, that to it the others may be referred, and that the species chiefly selected, is that in which the turpitude of the transgression is most apparent.　It seems proper, however, to extend it more generally to calumny and sinister insinuations by which our neighbours are unjustly aggrieved.　For falsehood in a court of justice is always accompanied with perjury.　But against perjury, in so far as it profanes and violates the name of God, there is a sufficient provision in the third commandment.　Hence the legitimate observance of this precept consists in employing the tongue in the maintenance of truth, so as to promote both the good name and the prosperity of our neighbour.　The equity of this is perfectly clear. For if a good name is more precious than riches, a man, in being robbed of his good name, is no less injured than if he were robbed of his goods; while, in the latter case, false testimony is sometimes not less injurious than rapine committed by the hand.

48. And yet it is strange, with what supine security men everywhere sin in this respect.　Indeed, very few are found who do not notoriously labour under this disease: such is the envenomed delight we take both in prying into and exposing our neighbour's faults.　Let us not imagine it is a sufficient excuse to say that on many occasions our statements are not false.　He who forbids us to defame our neighbour's reputation by falsehood, desires us to keep it untarnished in so far as truth will permit.　Though the commandment is only directed against falsehood, it intimates that the preservation of our neighbour's good name is recommended.　It ought to be a sufficient inducement to us to guard our neighbour's good name, that God takes an interest in it.　Wherefore, evil-speaking in general is undoubtedly

condemned. Moreover, by evil-speaking, we understand not the
rebuke which is administered with a view of correcting ; not accusa-
tion or judicial decision, by which evil is sought to be remedied ; not
public censure, which tends to strike terror into other offenders ; not
the disclosure made to those whose safety depends on being forewarned, lest unawares they should be brought into danger, but the
odious crimination which springs from a malicious and petulant love
of slander. Nay, the commandment extends so far as to include that
scurrilous affected urbanity, instinct with invective, by which the
failings of others, under an appearance of sportiveness, are bitterly
assailed, as some are wont to do, who court the praise of wit, though
it should call forth a blush, or inflict a bitter pang. By petulance of
this description, our brethren are sometimes grievously wounded.[1]
But if we turn our eye to the Lawgiver, whose just authority extends
over the ears and the mind, as well as the tongue, we cannot fail to
perceive that eagerness to listen to slander, and an unbecoming proneness to censorious judgment, are heie forbidden. It were absurd to
suppose that God hates the disease of evil-speaking in the tongue,
and yet disapproves not of its malignity in the mind. Wherefore, if
the true fear and love of God dwell in us, we must endeavour, as far
as is lawful and expedient, and as far as charity admits, neither to
listen nor give utterance to bitter and acrimonious charges, nor rashly
entertain sinister suspicions. As just interpreters of the words and
actions of other men, let us candidly maintain the honour due to
them by our judgment, our ear, and our tongue.

Tenth Commandment.

THOU SHALT NOT COVET THY NEIGHBOUR'S HOUSE, THOU SHALT NOT
COVET THY NEIGHBOUR'S WIFE, NOR HIS MAN-SERVANT, NOR HIS
MAID-SERVANT, NOR HIS OX, NOR HIS ASS, NOR ANY THING THAT
IS. THY NEIGHBOUR'S.

The purport is : Since the Lord would have the whole soul pervaded with love, any feeling of an adverse nature must be banished
from our minds. The sum, therefore, will be, that no thought be
permitted to insinuate itself into our minds, and inflame them with
a noxious concupiscence tending to our neighbour's loss. To this

---

1 The French is, " D'avantage ce precepte s'estend jusques là, que nous n'affections
point une plaisanterie d'honnesteté et une grace de brocarder et mordre en riant les
uns et les autres, comme sont aucuns, qui se bagnent quand ils peuvent faire vergogne
à quelqu'un : car par telle intemperance souventes fois quelque marque demeure sur
l'homme qu'on a ainsi noté."—Moreover, the commandment extends thus far : we must
not affect a good-humoured pleasantry and grace in nicknaming, and with a smile say
cutting things of others, as some persons do, who are delighted when they can make
another blush : by such intemperance a stigma is often fastened on the individual thus
attacked.

corresponds the contrary precept, that everything which we conceive, deliberate, will, or design, be conjoined with the good and advantage of our neighbour. But here it seems we are met with a great and perplexing difficulty. For if it was correctly said above, that under the words adultery and theft, lust and an intention to injure and deceive are prohibited, it may seem superfluous afterwards to employ a separate commandment to prohibit a covetous desire of our neighbour's goods. The difficulty will easily be removed by distinguishing between *design* and *covetousness*.[1] Design, such as we have spoken of in the previous commandments, is a deliberate consent of the will, after passion has taken possession of the mind. Covetousness may exist without such deliberation and assent, when the mind is only stimulated and tickled by vain and perverse objects. As, therefore, the Lord previously ordered that charity should regulate our wishes, studies, and actions, so he now orders us to regulate the thoughts of the mind in the same way, that none of them may be depraved and distorted, so as to give the mind a contrary bent. Having forbidden us to turn and incline our mind to wrath, hatred, adultery, theft, and falsehood, he now forbids us to give our thoughts the same direction.

50. Nor is such rectitude demanded without reason. For who can deny the propriety of occupying all the powers of the mind with charity? If it ceases to have charity for its aim, who can question that it is diseased? How comes it that so many desires of a nature hurtful to your brother enter your mind, but just because, disregarding him, you think only of yourself? Were your mind wholly imbued with charity, no portion of it would remain for the entrance of such thoughts. In so far, therefore, as the mind is devoid of charity, it must be under the influence of concupiscence. Some one will object that those fancies which casually rise up in the mind, and forthwith vanish away, cannot properly be condemned as concupiscences, which have their seat in the heart. I answer, That the question here relates to a description of fancies which, while they present themselves to our thoughts, at the same time impress and stimulate the mind with cupidity, since the mind never thinks of making some choice, but the heart is excited and tends towards it. God therefore commands a strong and ardent affection, an affection not to be impeded by any portion, however minute, of concupiscence. He requires a mind so admirably arranged as not to be prompted in the slightest degree contrary to the law of love. Lest you should imagine that this view is not supported by any grave authority, I may mention that it was first suggested to me by Augustine.[2] But although it was the intention of God to prohibit every kind of perverse desire, he, by way of

[Margin notes, handwritten: The Commandment not to covet is an internalization of the previous ones listed above. God demands a mind so arranged that it absolutely cannot be prompted contrary to the law of love.]

---

[1] See *supra*, chap. ii., end of sec. 24; and Book III. chap. iii. sec. 11, 12, 13; and Book IV. chap. xv. sec. 11, 12.

[2] See August. Ep. 200, ad Asellicum, et Quæstio, Lib. lxxxiii., sub fin. Quæst. 66; but especially Conscio. 8, in Ps. cxviii. The subject is also touched on in Ps. cxliii. und De Temp. Serm. 45, and Retract. Lib. i. cap. 5, and De Continentia, cap. 8.

example, sets before us those objects which are generally regarded as most attractive : thus leaving no room for cupidity of any kind, by the interdiction of those things in which it especially delights and loves to revel.

Such, then, is the Second Table of the Law, in which we are sufficiently instructed in the duties which we owe to man for the sake of God, on a consideration of whose nature the whole system of love is founded. It were vain, therefore, to inculcate the various duties taught in this table, without placing your instructions on the fear and reverence to God as their proper foundation. I need not tell the considerate reader, that those who make two precepts out of the prohibition of covetousness, perversely split one thing into two. There is nothing in the repetition of the words, " Thou shalt not covet." The " house" being first put down, its different parts are afterwards enumerated, beginning with the " wife ;" and hence it is clear, that the whole ought to be read consecutively, as is properly done by the Jews. The sum of the whole commandment, therefore, is, that whatever each individual possesses remain entire and secure, not only from injury, or the wish to injure, but also from the slightest feeling of covetousness which can spring up in the mind.

51. It will not now be difficult to ascertain the general end contemplated by the whole Law—viz. the fulfilment of righteousness, that man may form his life on the model of the divine purity. For therein God has so delineated his own character, that any one exhibiting in action what is commanded, would in some measure exhibit a living image of God. Wherefore Moses, when he wished to fix a summary of the whole in the memory of the Israelites, thus addressed them, " And now, Israel, what doth the Lord thy God require of thee, but to fear the Lord thy God, to walk in all his ways, and to love him, and to serve the Lord thy God with all thy heart, and with all thy soul, to keep the commandments of the Lord and his statutes which I command thee this day for thy good ?" (Deut. x. 12, 13.) And he ceased not to reiterate the same thing, whenever he had occasion to mention the end of the Law. To this the doctrine of the Law pays so much regard, that it connects man, by holiness of life, with his God ; and, as Moses elsewhere expresses it (Deut. vi. 5 ; xi. 13), and makes him cleave to him. Moreover, this holiness of life is comprehended under the two heads above mentioned. " Thou shalt love the Lord thy God with all thy heart, and with all thy soul, and with all thy mind, and with all thy strength, and thy neighbour as thyself." First, our mind must be completely filled with love to God, and then this love must forthwith flow out toward our neighbour. This the Apostle shows when he says, " The end of the commandment is charity out of a pure heart, and a good conscience, and of faith unfeigned " (1 Tim. i. 5). You see that conscience and faith unfeigned are placed at the head, in other words, true piety ; and that from this charity is derived. It is a mistake then to suppose, that merely

[margin note: Prohibition of covetousness ought not perversely to be split in two.]

the rudiments and first principles of righteousness are delivered in the Law, to form, as it were, a kind of introduction to good works, and not to guide to the perfect performance of them. For complete perfection, nothing more can be required than is expressed in these passages of Moses and Paul. How far, pray, would he wish to go, who is not satisfied with the instruction which directs man to the fear of God, to spiritual worship, practical obedience ; in fine, purity of conscience, faith unfeigned, and charity ? This confirms that interpretation of the Law which searches out, and finds in its precepts, all the duties of piety and charity. Those who merely search for dry and meagre elements, as if it taught the will of God only by halves, by no means understand its end, the Apostle being witness.

52. As, in giving a summary of the Law, Christ and the Apostles sometimes omit the First Table, very many fall into the mistake of supposing that their words apply to both tables. In Matthew, Christ calls "judgment, mercy, and faith," the "weightier matters of the Law." I think it clear, that by *faith* is here meant veracity towards men. But in order to extend the words to the whole Law, some take it for piety towards God. This is surely to no purpose. For Christ is speaking of those works by which a man ought to approve himself as just. If we attend to this, we will cease to wonder why elsewhere, when asked by the young man, " What good thing shall I do, that I may have eternal life ?" he simply answers, that he must keep the commandments, " Thou shalt do no murder, Thou shalt not commit adultery, Thou shalt not steal, Thou shalt not bear false witness, Honour thy father and thy mother : and, Thou shalt love thy neighbour as thyself" (Matth. xix. 16, 18). For the obedience of the First Table consisted almost entirely either in the internal affection of the heart, or in ceremonies. The affection of the heart was not visible, and hypocrites were diligent in the observance of ceremonies ; but the works of charity were of such a nature as to be a solid attestation of righteousness. The same thing occurs so frequently in the Prophets, that it must be familiar to every one who has any tolerable acquaintance with them.[1] For, almost on every occasion, when they exhort men to repentance, omitting the First Table, they insist on faith, judgment, mercy, and equity. Nor do they, in this way, omit the fear of God. They only require a serious proof of it from its signs. It is well known, indeed, that when they treat of the Law, they generally insist on the Second Table, because therein the cultivation of righteousness and integrity is best manifested. There is no occasion to quote passages. Every one can easily for himself perceive the truth of my observation.

53. Is it then true, you will ask, that it is a more complete summary of righteousness to live innocently with men, than piously towards God ? By no means ; but because no man, as a matter of

[1] Is. i. 17; lviii. 6; Jer. vii. 5, 6; Ezek. xviii. 7, 8; Hosea vi. 6; Zech. vii. 9, 10.

course, observes charity in all respects, unless he seriously fear God, such observance is a proof of piety also.   To this we may add, that the Lord, well knowing that none of our good deeds can reach him (as the Psalmist declares, Psalm xvi. 2), does not demand from us duties towards himself, but exercises us in good works towards our neighbour.   Hence the Apostle, not without cause, makes the whole perfection of the saints to consist in charity (Eph. iii. 19 ; Col. iii. 14).   And in another passage, he not improperly calls it the " fulfilling of the law," adding, that " he that loveth another hath fulfilled the law " (Rom. xiii. 8).   And again, "All the law is fulfilled in this : Thou shalt love thy neighbour as thyself " (Gal. v. 14).   For this is the very thing which Christ himself teaches when he says, " All things whatsoever ye would that men should do to you, do ye even so to them : fo this is the law and the prophets " (Matth. vii. 12).   It is certain that, in the law and the prophets, faith, and whatever pertains to the du worship of God, holds the first place, and that to this charity is made subordinate; but our Lord means, that in the Law the observance of justice and equity towards men is prescribed as the means which we are to employ in testifying a pious fear of God, if we truly possess it.

54.   Let us therefore hold, that our life will be framed in best accordance with the will of God, and the requirements of his Law, when it is, in every respect, most advantageous to our brethren.   But in the whole Law, there is not one syllable which lays down a rule as to what man is to do or avoid for the advantage of his own carnal nature. And, indeed, since men are naturally prone to excessive self-love, which they always retain, how great soever their departure from the truth may be, there was no need of a law to inflame a love already existing in excess.   Hence it is perfectly plain,[1] that the observance of the Commandments consists not in the love of ourselves, but in the love of God and our neighbour ; and that he leads the best and holiest life who as little as may be studies and lives for himself; and that none lives worse and more unrighteously than he who studies and lives only for himself, and seeks and thinks only of his own.   Nay, the better to express how strongly we should be inclined to love our neighbour, the Lord has made self-love as it were the standard, there being no feeling in our nature of greater strength and vehemence. The force of the expression ought to be carefully weighed.   For he does not (as some sophists have stupidly dreamed) assign the first place to self-love, and the second to charity.   He rather transfers to others the love which we naturally feel for ourselves.   Hence the Apostle declares, that charity "seeketh not her own" (1 Cor. xiii. 5). Nor is the argument worth a straw, That the thing regulated must always be inferior to the rule.   The Lord did not make self-love the rule, as if love towards others was subordinate to it ; but whereas,

[1] See Book III. chap. vii. sec. 4.   Also August. de Doctrina Christiana, Lib. i. chap. xxiii. et seq.

through natural pravity, the feeling of love usually rests on ourselves, he shows that it ought to diffuse itself in another direction—that we should be prepared to do good to our neighbour with no less alacrity, ardour, and solicitude, than to ourselves.

55. Our Saviour having shown, in the parable of the Samaritan (Luke x. 36), that the term *neighbour* comprehends the most remote stranger, there is no reason for limiting the precept of love to our own connections. I deny not that the closer the relation the more frequent our offices of kindness should be. For the condition of humanity requires that there be more duties in common between those who are more nearly connected by the ties of relationship, or friendship, or neighbourhood. And this is done without any offence to God, by whose providence we are in a manner impelled to do it. But I say that the whole human race, without exception, are to be embraced with one feeling of charity: that here there is no distinction of Greek or Barbarian, worthy or unworthy, friend or foe, since all are to be viewed not in themselves, but in God. If we turn aside from this view, there is no wonder that we entangle ourselves in error. Wherefore, if we would hold the true course in love, our first step must be to turn our eyes not to man, the sight of whom might oftener produce hatred than love, but to God, who requires that the love which we bear to him be diffused among all mankind, so that our fundamental principle must ever be, Let a man be what he may, he is still to be loved, because God is loved.

56. Wherefore, nothing could be more pestilential than the ignorance or wickedness of the Schoolmen in converting the precepts respecting revenge and the love of enemies (precepts which had formerly been delivered to all the Jews, and were then delivered universally to all Christians) into counsels which it was free to obey or disobey, confining the necessary observance of them to the monks, who were made more righteous than ordinary Christians, by the simple circumstance of voluntarily binding themselves to obey counsels. The reason they assign for not receiving them as laws, is that they seem too heavy and burdensome, especially to Christians, who are under the law of grace. Have they, indeed, the hardihood to remodel the eternal law of God concerning the love of our neighbour? Is there a page of the Law in which any such distinction exists; or rather, do we not meet in every page with commands which, in the strictest terms, require us to love our enemies? What is meant by commanding us to feed our enemy if he is hungry, to bring back his ox or his ass if we meet it going astray, or help it up if we see it lying under its burden? (Prov. xxv. 21 ; Exod. xxiii. 4.) Shall we show kindness to cattle for man's sake, and have no feeling of goodwill to himself? What? Is not the word of the Lord eternally true: "Vengeance is mine, I will repay?" (Deut. xxxii. 35). This is elsewhere more explicitly stated: "Thou shalt not avenge, nor bear any grudge against the children of thy people" (Lev. xix. 18). Let

them either erase these passages from the Law, or let them acknowledge the Lord as a Lawgiver, not falsely feign him to be merely a counsellor.

57. And what, pray, is meant by the following passage, which they have dared to insult with this absurd gloss? " Love your enemies, bless them that curse you, do good to them that hate you, and pray for them which despitefully use you, and persecute you ; that ye may be the children of your Father which is in heaven" (Matth. v. 44, 45). Who does not here concur in the reasoning of Chrysostom (Lib. de Compunctione Cordis, et ad Rom. vii.), that the nature of the motive makes it plain that these are not exhortations, but precepts ? For what is left to us if we are excluded from the number of the children of God? According to the Schoolmen, monks alone will be the children of our Father in heaven—monks alone will dare to invoke God as their Father. And in the mean time, how will it fare with the Church ? By the same rule, she will be confined to heathens and publicans. For our Saviour says, " If ye love them which love you, what reward have ye ? do not even the publicans the same?" It will truly be well with us if we are left only the name of Christians, while we are deprived of the inheritance of the kingdom of heaven! Nor is the argument of Augustine less forcible: " When the Lord forbids adultery, he forbids it in regard to the wife of a foe not less than the wife of a friend ; when he forbids theft, he does not allow stealing of any description, whether from a friend or an enemy" (August. Lib. de Doctr. Christ.). Now, these two commandments, " Thou shalt not steal, Thou shalt not commit adultery,". Paul brings under the rule of love ; nay, he says that they are briefly comprehended in this saying, " Thou shalt love thy neighbour as thyself" (Rom. xiii. 9). Therefore, Paul must either be a false interpreter of the Law, or we must necessarily conclude, that under this precept we are bound to love our enemies just as our friends. Those, then, show themselves to be in truth the children of Satan who thus licentiously shake off a yoke common to the children of God. It may be doubted whether, in promulgating this dogma, they have displayed greater stupidity or impudence. There is no ancient writer who does not hold it as certain that these are pure precepts. It was not even doubted in the age of Gregory, as is plain from his decided assertion ; for he holds it to be incontrovertible that they are precepts. And how stupidly they argue! The burden, say they, were too difficult for Christians to bear! As if anything could be imagined more difficult than to love the Lord with all the heart, and soul, and strength. Compared with this Law, there is none which may not seem easy, whether it be to love our enemy, or to banish every feeling of revenge from our minds. To our weakness, indeed, everything, even to the minutest tittle of the Law, is arduous and difficult. In the Lord we have strength. It is his to give what he orders, and to order what he wills. That Christians are under the law of grace, means not that

they are to wander unrestrained without law, but that they are engrafted into Christ, by whose grace they are freed from the curse of
the Law, and by whose Spirit they have the Law written in their
hearts. This grace Paul has termed, but not in the proper sense of
the term, a law, alluding to the Law of God, with which he was contrasting it. The Schoolmen, laying hold of the term *Law*, make it
the ground-work of their vain speculations.[1]

58. The same must be said of their application of the term, venial
sin, both to the hidden impiety which violates the First Table, and
the direct transgression of the last commandment of the Second
Table[2] They define venial sin to be, desire unaccompanied with
deliberate assent, and not remaining long in the heart. But I maintain that it cannot even enter the heart unless through a want of
those things which are required in the Law. We are forbidden to
have strange gods. When the mind, under the influence of distrust,
looks elsewhere, or is seized with some sudden desire to transfer its
blessedness to some other quarter, whence are these movements, however evanescent, but just because there is some empty corner in the
soul to receive such temptations? And, not to lengthen out the
discussion, there is a precept to love God with the whole heart, and
mind, and soul; and, therefore, if all the powers of the soul are not
directed to the love of God, there is a departure from the obedience
of the Law; because those internal enemies which rise up against the
dominion of God, and countermand his edicts, prove that his throne
is not well established in our consciences. It has been shown that
the last commandment goes to this extent. Has some undue longing
sprung up in our mind? Then we are chargeable with covetousness,
and stand convicted as transgressors of the Law. For the Law forbids us not only to meditate and plan our neighbour's loss, but to be
stimulated and inflamed with covetousness. But every transgression
of the Law lays us under the curse, and therefore even the slightest
desires cannot be exempted from the fatal sentence. "In weighing
our sins," says Augustine, "let us not use a deceitful balance, weighing at our own discretion what we will, and how we will, calling this
heavy and that light: but let us use the divine balance of the Holy
Scriptures, as taken from the treasury of the Lord, and by it weigh
every offence, nay, not weigh, but rather recognise what has been
already weighed by the Lord" (August. De Bapt. cont. Donatist.
Lib. ii. chap. 6). And what saith the Scripture? Certainly when
Paul says, that "the wages of sin is death" (Rom. vi. 23), he shows
that he knew nothing of this vile distinction. As we are but too
prone to hypocrisy, there was very little occasion for this sop to
soothe our torpid consciences.

Marginalia: No such thing as a "minor" or "venial" sin.

---

[1] The French is, " Ces folastres sans propos prennent un grand mystére en ce mot
de Loy;" these foolish fellows absurdly find a great mystery in this term Law.

[2] See Book III. chap. iv. sec. 28, where it is also shown that this is not the dogma
of the Stoics—that all sins are equal.

59. I wish they would consider what our Saviour meant when he said, "Whosoever shall break one of these least commandments, and shall teach men so, he shall be called the least in the kingdom of heaven" (Matth. v. 19). Are they not of this number when they presume to extenuate the transgression of the Law, as if it were unworthy of death? The proper course had been to consider not simply what is commanded, but who it is that commands, because every least transgression of his Law derogates from his authority. Do they count it a small matter to insult the majesty of God in any one respect? Again, since God has explained his will in the Law, everything contrary to the Law is displeasing to him. Will they feign that the wrath of God is so disarmed that the punishment of death will not forthwith follow upon it? He has declared plainly (if they could be induced to listen to his voice, instead of darkening his clear truth by their insipid subtleties), "The soul that sinneth it shall die" (Ezek. xviii. 20). Again, in the passage lately quoted, "The wages of sin is death." What these men acknowledge to be sin, because they are unable to deny it, they contend is not mortal. Having already indulged this madness too long, let them learn to repent; or, if they persist in their infatuation, taking no further notice of them, let the children of God remember that all sin is mortal, because it is rebellion against the will of God, and necessarily provokes his anger; and because it is a violation of the Law, against every violation of which, without exception, the judgment of God has been pronounced. The faults of the saints are indeed venial, not, however, in their own nature, but because, through the mercy of God, they obtain pardon.

CHAPTER IX.

CHRIST, THOUGH KNOWN TO THE JEWS UNDER THE LAW, YET ONLY
MANIFESTED UNDER THE GOSPEL.

There are three principal heads in this chapter. I. Preparatory to a consideration
of the knowledge of Christ, and the benefits procured by him; the 1st and 2d sections
are occupied with the dispensation of this knowledge, which, after the manifestation
of Christ in the flesh, was more clearly revealed than under the Law. II. A refutation of the profane dream of Servetus, that the promises are entirely abrogated, sec.
3. Likewise, a refutation of those who do not properly compare the Law with the
Gospel, sec. 4. III. A necessary and brief exposition of the ministry of John Baptist,
which occupies an intermediate place between the Law and the Gospel.

Sections.

1. The holy fathers under the Law saw the day of Christ, though obscurely. He is
more fully revealed to us under the Gospel. A reason for this, confirmed by the
testimony of Christ and his Apostles.
2. The term Gospel, used in its most extensive sense, comprehends the attestations of
mercy which God gave to the fathers. Properly, however, it means the promulgation of grace exhibited in the God-man Jesus Christ.
3. The notion of Servetus, that the promises are entirely abolished, refuted. Why we
must still trust to the promises of God. Another reason. Solution of a difficulty.
4. Refutation of those who do not properly compare the Law and the Gospel. Answer
to certain questions here occurring. The Law and the Gospel briefly compared.
5. Third part of the chapter. Of the ministry of John the Baptist.

1. SINCE God was pleased (and not in vain) to testify in ancient
times, by means of expiations and sacrifices, that he was a Father,
and to set apart for himself a chosen people, he was doubtless known
even then in the same character in which he is now fully revealed to
us. Accordingly, Malachi, having enjoined the Jews to attend to
the Law of Moses (because after his death there was to be an interruption of the prophetical office), immediately after declares that the
Sun of righteousness should arise (Mal. iv. 2); thus intimating, that
though the Law had the effect of keeping the pious in expectation of
the coming Messiah, there was ground to hope for much greater light
on his advent. For this reason, Peter, speaking of the ancient prophets, says, "Unto whom it was revealed, that not unto themselves,
but unto us, they did minister the things which are now reported
unto you by them that have preached the gospel unto you, with the
Holy Ghost sent down from heaven" (1 Pet. i. 12). Not that the
prophetical doctrine was useless to the ancient people, or unavailing
to the prophets themselves, but that they did not obtain possession of
the treasure which God has transmitted to us by their hands. The

grace of which they testified is now set familiarly before our eyes. They had only a slight foretaste ; to us is given a fuller fruition. Our Saviour, accordingly, while he declares that Moses testified of him, extols the superior measure of grace bestowed upon us (John v. 46). Addressing his disciples, he says, " Blessed are your eyes, for they see, and your ears, for they hear. For verily I say unto you, That many prophets and righteous men have desired to see those things which ye see, and have not seen them, and to hear those things which ye hear, and have not heardthem " (Matth. xiii. 16 ; Luke x. 23). It is no small commendation of the gospel revelation, that God has preferred us to holy men of old, so much distinguished for piety. There is nothing in this view inconsistent with another passage, in which our Saviour says, " Your father Abraham rejoiced to see my day, and he saw it and was glad" (John viii. 56). For though the event being remote, his view of it was obscure, he had full assurance that it would one day be accomplished ; and hence the joy which the holy patriarch experienced even to his death. Nor does John Baptist, when he says, " No man hath seen God at any time ; the only begotten Son, which is in the bosom of the Father, he hath declared him " (John i. 18), exclude the pious who had previously died from a participation in the knowledge and light which are manifested in the person of Christ ; but comparing their condition with ours, he intimates that the mysteries which they only beheld dimly under shadows are made clear to us ; as is well explained by the author of the Epistle to the Hebrews, in these words, " God, who at sundry times and in divers manners spake in time past unto the fathers by the prophets, hath in these last days spoken unto us by his Son " (Heb. i. 1, 2). Hence, although this only begotten Son, who is now to us the brightness of his Father's glory and the express image of his person, was formerly made known to the Jews, as we have else- where shown from Paul, that he was the Deliverer under the old dis- pensation ; it is nevertheless true, as Paul himself elsewhere declares, that " God, who commanded the light to shine out of darkness, hath shined in our hearts, to give the light of the knowledge of the glory of God in the face of Jesus Christ " (2 Cor. iv. 6); because, when he appeared in this his image, he in a manner made himself visible, his previous appearance having been shadowy and obscure. More shame- ful and more detestable, therefore, is the ingratitude of those who walk blindfold in this meridian light. Accordingly, Paul says that " the god of this world hath blinded their minds, lest the light of the glorious gospel of Christ should shine unto them " (2 Cor. iv. 4).

2. By the Gospel, I understand the clear manifestation of the mys- tery of Christ. I confess, indeed, that inasmuch as the term Gospel is applied by Paul to the doctrine of faith (2 Tim. iv. 10), it includes all the promises by which God reconciles men to himself, and which occur throughout the Law. For Paul there opposes faith to those terrors which vex and torment the conscience when salvation is sought

by means of works. Hence it follows, that *Gospel*, taken in a large sense, comprehends the evidences of mercy and paternal favour which God bestowed on the Patriarchs. Still, by way of excellence, it is applied to the promulgation of the grace manifested in Christ. This is not only founded on general use, but has the sanction of our Saviour and his Apostles. Hence it is described as one of his peculiar characteristics, that he preached the Gospel of the kingdom (Matth. iv. 23 ; ix. 35 ; Mark i. 14). Mark, in his preface to the Gospel, calls it " *The beginning of the Gospel of Jesus Christ.*" There is no use of collecting passages to prove what is already perfectly known. Christ at his advent " brought life and immortality to light through the Gospel" (2 Tim. i. 10). Paul does not mean by these words that the Fathers were plunged in the darkness of death before the Son of God became incarnate ; but he claims for the Gospel the honourable distinction of being a new and extraordinary kind of embassy, by which God fulfilled what he had promised, these promises being realised in the person of the Son. For though believers have at all times experienced the truth of Paul's declaration, that " all the promises of God in him are yea and amen," inasmuch as these promises were sealed upon their hearts ; yet because he hath in his flesh completed all the parts of our salvation, this vivid manifestation of realities was justly entitled to this new and special distinction. Accordingly, Christ says, " Hereafter ye shall see heaven open, and the angels of God ascending and descending upon the Son of man." For though he seems to allude to the ladder which the Patriarch Jacob saw in vision, he commends the excellence of his advent in this, that it opened the gate of heaven, and gave us familiar access to it.

3. Here we must guard against the diabolical imagination of Servetus, who, from a wish, or at least the pretence of a wish, to extol the greatness of Christ, abolishes the promises entirely, as if they had come to an end at the same time with the Law. He pretends, that by the faith of the Gospel all the promises have been fulfilled ; as if there was no distinction between us and Christ. I lately observed that Christ had not left any part of our salvation incomplete ; but from this it is erroneously inferred, that we are now put in possession of all the blessings purchased by him ; thereby implying, that Paul was incorrect in saying, " We are saved by hope" (Rom. iii. 24). I admit, indeed, that by believing in Christ we pass from death unto life ; but we must at the same time remember the words of John, that though we know we are " the sons of God," " it doth not yet appear what we shall be : but we know that, when he shall appear, we shall be like him ; for we shall see him as he is" (1 John iii. 2). Therefore, although Christ offers us in the Gospel a present fulness of spiritual blessings, fruition remains in the keeping of hope,[1] until

---

[1] " Sub custodia spei."—French, " sous la garde, et comme sous le cachet d'espoir;" under the guard, and, as it were, under the seal of hope.

we are divested of corruptible flesh, and transformed into the glory of him who has gone before us. Meanwhile, in leaning on the promises, we obey the command of the Holy Spirit, whose authority ought to have weight enough with us to silence all the barkings of that impure dog. We have it on the testimony of Paul, that "Godliness is profitable unto all things, having promise of the life that now is, and of that which is to come" (1 Tim. iv. 8); for which reason, he glories in being "an apostle of Jesus Christ, according to the promise of life which is in Christ Jesus" (2 Tim. i. 1). And he elsewhere reminds us, that we have the same promises which were given to the saints in ancient time (2 Cor. vii. 1). In fine, he makes the sum of our felicity consist in being sealed with the Holy Spirit of promise. Indeed, we have no enjoyment of Christ, unless by embracing him as clothed with his own promises. Hence it is, that he indeed dwells in our hearts, and yet we are as pilgrims in regard to him, because "we walk by faith, not by sight" (2 Cor. v. 6, 7). There is no inconsistency in the two things—viz. that in Christ we possess everything pertaining to the perfection of the heavenly life, and yet that faith is only a vision "of things not seen" (Heb. xi. 1). Only there is this difference to be observed in the nature or quality of the promises, that the Gospel points with the finger to what the Law shadowed under types.

4. Hence, also, we see the error of those who, in comparing the Law with the Gospel, represent it merely as a comparison between the merit of works, and the gratuitous imputation of righteousness. The contrast thus made is by no means to be rejected, because, by the term Law, Paul frequently understands that rule of holy living in which God exacts what is his due, giving no hope of life unless we obey in every respect; and, on the other hand, denouncing a curse for the slightest failure. This Paul does when showing that we are freely accepted of God, and accounted righteous by being pardoned, because that obedience of the Law to which the reward is promised is nowhere to be found. Hence he appropriately represents the righteousness of the Law and the Gospel as opposed to each other. But the Gospel has not succeeded the whole Law in such a sense as to introduce a different method of salvation. It rather confirms the Law, and proves that everything which it promised is fulfilled. What was shadow, it has made substance. When Christ says that the Law and the Prophets were until John, he does not consign the fathers to the curse, which, as the slaves of the Law, they could not escape. He intimates that they were only imbued with the rudiments, and remained far beneath the height of the Gospel doctrine. Accordingly Paul, after calling the Gospel "the power of God unto salvation to every one that believeth," shortly after adds, that it was "witnessed by the Law and the Prophets" (Rom. i. 16; iii. 21). And in the end of the same Epistle, though he describes "the preaching of Jesus Christ" as "the revelation of the mystery which was kept secret since

the world began," he modifies the expression by adding, that it is "now made manifest" "by the scriptures of the prophets" (Rom. xvi. 25, 26). Hence we infer, that when the whole Law is spoken of, the Gospel differs from it only in respect of clearness of manifestation. Still, on account of the inestimable riches of grace set before us in Christ, there is good reason for saying, that by his advent the kingdom of heaven was erected on the earth (Matth. xii. 28).

5. John stands between the Law and the Gospel, holding an intermediate office allied to both. For though he gave a summary of the Gospel when he pronounced Christ to be "the Lamb of God who taketh away the sin of the world," yet, inasmuch as he did not unfold the incomparable power and glory which shone forth in his resurrection, Christ says that he was not equal to the Apostles. For this is the meaning of the words: "Among them that are born of woman, there hath not risen a greater than John the Baptist: notwithstanding, he that is least in the kingdom of heaven is greater than he" (Matth. xi. 11). He is not there commending the persons of men, but after preferring John to all the Prophets, he gives the first place to the preaching of the Gospel, which is elsewhere designated by the kingdom of heaven. When John himself, in answer to the Jews, says that he is only "a voice" (John i. 23), as if he were inferior to the Prophets, it is not in pretended humility, but he means to teach that the proper embassy was not intrusted to him, that he only performed the office of a messenger, as had been foretold by Malachi, "Behold, I will send you Elijah the prophet, before the coming of the great and dreadful day of the Lord" (Mal. iv. 5). And, indeed, during the whole course of his ministry, he did nothing more than prepare disciples for Christ. He even proves from Isaiah that this was the office to which he was divinely appointed. In this sense, he is said by Christ to have been "a burning and a shining light" (John v. 35), because full day had not yet appeared. And yet this does not prevent us from classing him among the preachers of the Gospel, since he used the same baptism which was afterwards committed to the Apostles. Still, however, he only began that which had freer course under the Apostles, after Christ was taken up into the heavenly glory.

CHAPTER X.

THE RESEMBLANCE BETWEEN THE OLD TESTAMENT AND THE NEW.[1]

This chapter consists of four parts. I. The sum, utility, and necessity of this discussion, sec. 1. II. A proof that, generally speaking, the old and new dispensations are in reality one, although differently administered. Three points in which the two dispensations entirely agree, sec. 2—4. III. The Old Testament, as well as the New, had regard to the hope of immortality and a future life, whence two other resemblances or points of agreement follow—viz that both were established by the free mercy of God, and confirmed by the intercession of Christ. This proved by many arguments, passages of Scripture, and examples, sec. 5—23. IV. Conclusion of the whole chapter, where, for fuller confirmation, certain passages of Scripture are produced. Refutation of the cavils of the Sadducees and other Jews.

Sections.

1. Introduction, showing the necessity of proving the similarity of both dispensations in opposition to Servetus and the Anabaptists.
2. This similarity in general. Both covenants truly one, though differently administered. Three things in which they entirely agree.
3. First general similarity, or agreement—viz. that the Old Testament, equally with the New, extended its promises beyond the present life, and held out a sure hope of immortality. Reason for this resemblance. Objection answered.
4. The other two points of resemblance—viz. that both covenants were established in the mercy of God, and confirmed by the mediation of Christ.
5. The first of these points of resemblance being the foundation of the other two, a lengthened proof is given of it. The first argument taken from a passage, in which Paul, showing that the sacraments of both dispensations had the same meaning, proves that the condition of the ancient church was similar to ours.
6. An objection from John vi. 49—viz. that the Israelites ate manna in the wilderness, and are dead, whereas Christians eat the flesh of Christ, and die not. Answer reconciling this passage of the Evangelist with that of the Apostle.
7. Another proof from the Law and the Prophets—viz. the power of the divine word in quickening souls before Christ was manifested. Hence the believing Jews were raised to the hope of eternal life.
8. Third proof from the form of the covenant, which shows that it was in reality one both before and after the manifestation of Christ in the flesh.
9. Confirmation of the former proof from the clear terms in which the form is expressed. Another confirmation derived from the former and from the nature of God.
10. Fourth proof from examples. Adam, Abel, and Noah, when tried with various temptations, neglecting the present, aspired with living faith and invincible hope to a better life. They, therefore, had the same aim as believers under the Gospel.
11. Continuation of the fourth proof from the example of Abraham, whose call and whole course of life shows that he ardently aspired to eternal felicity. Objection disposed of.
12. Continuation of the fourth proof from the examples of Isaac and Jacob.
13. Conclusion of the fourth proof. Adam, Abel, Noah, Abraham, Isaac, Jacob, and others under the Law, looked for the fulfilment of the divine promises not on the earth, but in heaven. Hence they termed this life an earthly pilgrimage, and desired to be buried in the land of Canaan, which was a figure of eternal happiness.

[1] As to the agreement of both dispensations, see August. Lib. de Moribus Eccles. Lat., especially cap. xxviii.

14. A fifth proof from Jacob's earnestness to obtain the birthright. This shows a prevailing desire of future life. This perceived in some degree by Balaam.
15. A sixth proof from David, who expects such great things from the Lord, and yet declares the present life to be mere vanity.
16. A seventh proof also from David. His descriptions of the happiness of believers could only be realised in a future state.
17 An eighth proof from the common feeling and confession of all the pious who sought by faith and hope to obtain in heaven what they did not see in the present shadowy life.
18. A continuation and confirmation. of the former proof from the exultation of the righteous, even amid the destruction of the world.
19. A ninth proof from Job, who spoke most distinctly of this hope. Two objections disposed of.
20. A tenth proof from the later Prophets, who taught that the happiness of the righteous was placed beyond the limits of the present life.
21. This clearly established by Ezekiel's vision of the dry bones, and a passage in Isaiah.
22. Last proof from certain passages in the Prophets, which clearly show the future immortality of the righteous in the kingdom of heaven.
23. Conclusion of the whole discussion concerning the similarity of both dispensations. For fuller confirmation, four passages of Scripture produced. Refutation of the error of the Sadducees and other Jews, who denied eternal salvation and the sure hope of the Church.

1. FROM what has been said above, it must now be clear, that all whom, from the beginning of the world, God adopted as his peculiar people, were taken into covenant with him on the same conditions, and under the same bond of doctrine, as ourselves; but as it is of no small importance to establish this point, I will here add it by way of appendix, and show, since the Fathers were partakers with us in the same inheritance, and hoped for a common salvation through the grace of the same Mediator, how far their condition in this respect was different from our own. For although the passages which we have collected from the Law and the Prophets for the purpose of proof, make it plain that there never was any other rule of piety and religion among the people of God; yet as many things are written on the subject of the difference between the Old and New Testaments in a manner which may perplex ordinary readers, it will be proper here to devote a special place to the better and more exact discussion of this subject. This discussion, which would have been most useful at any rate, has been rendered necessary by that monstrous miscreant Servetus, and some madmen of the sect of the Anabaptists, who think of the people of Israel just as they would do of some herd of swine, absurdly imagining that the Lord gorged them with temporal blessings here, and gave them no hope of a blessed immortality.[1] Let us guard pious minds against this pestilential error, while we at the same time remove all the difficulties which are wont to start up when mention is made of the difference between the Old and the New Testaments. By the way also, let us consider what resemblance and what difference there is between the covenant which the Lord

---

1 The French is, " Veu qu'ils pensent que notre Seigneur l'ait voulu seulement engraisser en terre comme en une auge, sans esperance aucune de l'immortalité celeste;" —seeing they think that our Lord only wished to fatten them on the earth as in a sty, without any hope of heavenly immortality.

made with the Israelites before the advent of Christ, and that which he has made with us, now that Christ is manifested.

2. It is possible, indeed, to explain both in one word. The covenant made with all the fathers in so far from differing from ours in reality and substance, that it is altogether one and the same: still the administration differs. But because this brief summary is insufficient to give any one a full understanding of the subject, our explanation to be useful must extend to greater length. It were superfluous, however, in showing the similarity, or rather identity, of the two dispensations, again to treat of the particulars which have already been discussed, as it were unseasonable to introduce those which are still to be considered elsewhere. What we propose to insist upon here may be reduced to three heads:—*First*, That temporal opulence and felicity was not the goal to which the Jews were invited to aspire, but that they were admitted to the hope of immortality, and that assurance of this adoption was given by immediate communications, by the Law and by the Prophets. *Secondly*, That the covenant by which they were reconciled to the Lord was founded on no merits of their own, but solely on the mercy of God, who called them ; and, *thirdly*, That they both had and knew Christ the Mediator, by whom they were united to God, and made capable of receiving his promises. The second of these, as it is not yet perhaps sufficiently understood, will be fully considered in its own place (Book III. chap. xv.—xviii). For we will prove by many clear passages in the Prophets, that all which the Lord has ever given or promised to his people is of mere goodness and indulgence. The third also has, in various places, been not obscurely demonstrated. Even the first has not been left unnoticed.

3. As the first is most pertinent to the present subject, and is most controverted, we shall enter more fully into the consideration of it, taking care, at the same time, where any of the others require explanation, to supply it by the way, or afterwards add it in its proper place. The Apostle, indeed, removes all doubt when he says that the Gospel which God gave concerning his Son, Jesus Christ, " he had promised aforetime by his prophets in the holy Scriptures " (Rom. i. 2). And again, that " the righteousness of God without the law is manifested, being witnessed by the law and the prophets " (Rom. iii. 21). For the Gospel does not confine the hearts of men to the enjoyment of the present life, but raises them to the hope of immortality ; does not fix them down to earthly delights, but announcing that there is a treasure laid up in heaven, carries the heart thither also. For in another place he thus explains, " After that ye believed [the Gospel], ye were sealed with that Holy Spirit of promise, which is the earnest of our inheritance unto the redemption of the purchased possession " (Eph. i. 13, 14). Again, " Since we heard of your faith in Jesus Christ, and of the love which ye have to all the saints, for the hope which is laid up for you in heaven, whereof ye

heard before in the word of the truth of the Gospel" (Col. i. 4). Again, "Whereunto he called you by our Gospel to the obtaining of the glory of our Lord Jesus Christ" (2 Thess. ii. 14). Whence also it is called the word of salvation and the power of God, with salvation to every one that believes, and the kingdom of heaven.[1] But if the doctrine of the Gospel is spiritual, and gives access to the possession of incorruptible life, let us not suppose that those to whom it was promised and declared altogether neglected the care of the soul, and lived stupidly like cattle in the enjoyment of bodily pleasures. Let no one here quibble and say, that the promises concerning the Gospel, which are contained in the Law and the Prophets, were designed for a new people.[2] For Paul, shortly after making that statement concerning the Gospel promised in the Law, adds, that "whatsoever things the law saith, it saith to those who are under the law." I admit, indeed, he is there treating of a different subject, but when he said that everything contained in the Law was directed to the Jews, he was not so oblivious as not to remember what he had said a few verses before of the Gospel promised in the Law. Most clearly, therefore, does the Apostle demonstrate that the Old Testament had special reference to the future life, when he says that the promises of the Gospel were comprehended under it.

4. In the same way we infer that the Old Testament was both established by the free mercy of God and confirmed by the intercession of Christ. For the preaching of the Gospel declares nothing more than that sinners, without any merit of their own, are justified by the paternal indulgence of God. It is wholly summed up in Christ. Who, then, will presume to represent the Jews as destitute of Christ, when we know that they were parties to the Gospel covenant, which has its only foundation in Christ? Who will presume to make them aliens to the benefit of gratuitous salvation, when we know that they were instructed in the doctrine of justification by faith? And not to dwell on a point which is clear, we have the remarkable saying of our Lord, " Your father Abraham rejoiced to see my day, and he saw it and was glad" (John viii. 56). What Christ here declares of Abraham, an apostle shows to be applicable to all believers, when he says that Jesus Christ is the " same yesterday, to-day, and for ever" (Heb. xiii. 8). For he is not there speaking merely of the eternal divinity of Christ, but of his power, of which believers had always full proof. Hence both the blessed Virgin[3] and Zachariah, in their hymns, say that the salvation revealed in Christ was a fulfilment of the mercy promised " to our fathers, to Abraham, and to his seed for ever" (Luke i. 55, 72). If, by manifesting Christ, the Lord fulfilled

---

1 Acts xiii. 26; Rom. i. 16; 1 Cor. i. 18; Matth. iii. 2, 4, 17, &c., especially xiii.
2 " Novo populo." French, "au peuple du Nouveau Testament"—the people of the New Dispensation.
3 " Beata Virgo." French, " la Vierge Marie;"—the Virgin Mary.

his ancient oath, it cannot be denied that the subject of that oath [1] must ever have been Christ and eternal life.

5. Nay, the Apostle makes the Israelites our equals, not only in the grace of the covenant, but also in the signification of the Sacraments. For employing the example of those punishments, which the Scripture states to have been of old inflicted on the Jews, in order to deter the Corinthians from falling into similar wickedness, he begins with premising that they have no ground to claim for themselves any privilege which can exempt them from the divine vengeance which overtook the Jews, since the Lord not only visited them with the same mercies, but also distinguished his grace among them by the same symbols : as if he had said, If you think you are out of danger, because the Baptism which you received, and the Supper of which you daily partake, have excellent promises, and if, in the mean time, despising the goodness of God, you indulge in licentiousness, know that the Jews, on whom the Lord inflicted his severest · judgments, possessed similiar symbols. They were baptised in passing through the sea, and in the cloud which protected them from the burning heat of the sun. It is said, that this passage was a carnal baptism, corresponding in some degree to our spiritual baptism. But if so, there would be a want of conclusiveness in the argument of the Apostle, whose object is to prevent Christians from imagining that they excelled the Jews in the matter of baptism. Besides, the cavil cannot apply to what immediately follows—viz. that they did "all eat the same spiritual meat ; and did all drink the same spiritual drink : for they drank of that spiritual Rock that followed them : and that Rock was Christ" (1 Cor. x. 3, 4).

6. To take off the force of this passage of Paul, an objection is founded on the words of our Saviour, " Your fathers did eat manna in the wilderness, and are dead." " If any man eat of this bread, he shall live for ever " (John vi. 49, 51). There is no difficulty in reconciling the two passages. The Lord, as he was addressing hearers who only desired to be filled with earthly food, while they cared not for the true food of the soul, in some degree adapts his speech to their capacity, and, in particular, to meet their carnal view, draws a comparison between manna and his own body. They called upon him to prove his authority by performing some miracle, such as Moses performed in the wilderness when he obtained manna from heaven. In this manna they saw nothing but a relief of the bodily hunger from which the people were then suffering ; they did not penetrate to the sublimer mystery to which Paul refers. Christ, therefore, to demonstrate that the blessing which they ought to expect from him was more excellent than the lauded one which Moses had bestowed upon their fathers, draws this comparison : If, in your opinion, it was a great and memorable miracle when the Lord, by

---

1 " Ejus finis." French, " la fin du Vieil Testament ;"—the end of the Old Testament.

Moses, supplied his people with heavenly food that they might be supported for a season, and not perish in the wilderness from famine; from this infer how much more excellent is the food which bestows immortality. We see why our Lord omitted to mention what was of principal virtue in the manna, and mentioned only its meanest use. Since the Jews had, as it were by way of upbraiding, cast up Moses to him as one who had relieved the necessity of the people by means of manna, he answers, that he was the minister of a much larger grace, one compared with which the bodily nourishment of the people, on which they set so high a value, ought to be held worthless. Paul, again, knowing that the Lord, when he rained manna from heaven, had not merely supplied their bodies with food, but had also dispensed it as containing a spiritual mystery to typify the spiritual quickening which is obtained in Christ, does not overlook that quality which was most deserving of consideration. Wherefore it is surely and clearly proved, that the same promises of celestial and eternal life, which the Lord now gives to us, were not only communicated to the Jews, but also sealed by truly spiritual sacraments. This subject is copiously discussed by Augustine in his work against Faustus the Manichee.

7. But if my readers would rather have passages quoted from the Law and the Prophets, from which they may see, as we have already done from Christ and the Apostles, that the spiritual covenant was common also to the Fathers, I will yield to the wish, and the more willingly, because opponents will thus be more surely convinced, that henceforth there will be no room for evasion. And I will begin with a proof which, though I know it will seem futile and almost ridiculous to supercilious Anabaptists, will have very great weight with the docile and sober-minded. I take it for granted that the word of God has such an inherent efficacy, that it quickens the souls of all whom he is pleased to favour with the communication of it. Peter's statement has ever been true, that it is an incorruptible seed, "which liveth and abideth for ever" (1 Peter i. 23), as he infers from the words of Isaiah (Is. xl. 6). Now when God, in ancient times, bound the Jews to him by this sacred bond, there cannot be a doubt that he separated them unto the hope of eternal life. When I say that they embraced the word which brought them nearer to God, I refer not to that general method or communication which is diffused through heaven and earth, and all the creatures of the world, and which, though it quickens all things, each according to its nature, rescues none from the bondage of corruption. I refer to that special mode of communication by which the minds of the pious are both enlightened in the knowledge of God, and, in a manner, linked to him. Adam, Abel, Noah, Abraham, and the other patriarchs, having been united to God by this illumination of the word, I say there cannot be the least doubt that entrance was given them into the immortal kingdom of God. They had that solid participation in God which cannot exist without the blessing of everlasting life.

8. If the point still seems somewhat involved, let us pass to the form of the covenant, which will not only satisfy calm thinkers, but sufficiently establish the ignorance of gainsayers. The covenant which God always made with his servants was this, " I will walk among you, and will be your God, and ye shall be my people" (Lev. xxvi. 12). These words, even as the prophets are wont to expound them, comprehend life and salvation, and the whole sum of blessedness. For David repeatedly declares, and with good reason, " Happy is that people whose God is the Lord." " Blessed is the nation whose God is the Lord ; and the people whom he hath chosen for his own inheritance" (Psalm cxliv. 15 ; xxxiii. 12) ; and this not merely in respect of earthly happiness, but because he rescues from death, constantly preserves, and, with eternal mercy, visits those whom he has adopted for his people. As is said in other prophets, " Art not thou from everlasting, O Lord my God, mine Holy One ? we shall not die." " The Lord is our judge, the Lord is our lawgiver, the Lord is our king; he will save us." " Happy art thou, O Israel : who is like unto thee, O people saved by the Lord ?" (Hab. 1, 12 ; Isaiah xxxiii. 22 ; Deut. xxxiii. 29.) But not to labour superfluously, the prophets are constantly reminding us that no good thing, and, consequently, no assurance of salvation, is wanting, provided the Lord is our God. And justly. For if his face, the moment it hath shone upon us, is a perfect pledge of salvation, how can he manifest himself to any one as his God, without opening to him the treasures of salvation ? The terms on which God makes himself ours is to dwell in the midst of us, as he declared by Moses (Lev. xxvi. 11). But such presence cannot be enjoyed without life being, at the same time, possessed along with it. And though nothing more had been expressed, they had a sufficiently clear promise of spiritual life in these words, " I am your God" (Exod. vi. 7). For he declared that he would be a God not to their bodies only, but specially to their souls. Souls, however, if not united to God by righteousness, remain estranged from him in death. On the other hand, that union, wherever it exists, will bring perpetual salvation with it.

9. To this we may add, that he not only declared he was, but also promised that he would be, their God. By this their hope was extended beyond present good, and stretched forward into eternity. Moreover, that this observance of the future had the effect, appears from the many passages in which the faithful console themselves not only in their present evils, but also for the future, by calling to mind that God was never to desert them. Moreover, in regard to the second part of the promise—viz. the blessing of God, its extending beyond the limits of the present life was still more clearly confirmed by the words, I will be the God of your seed after you (Gen. xvii. 7). If he was to manifest his favour to the dead by doing good to their posterity, much less would he deny his favour to themselves. God is not like men, who transfer their love to the children of their

friends, because the opportunity of bestowing kind offices as they wished upon themselves is interrupted by death. But God, whose kindness is not impeded by death, does not deprive the dead of the benefit of his mercy, which, on their account, he continues to a thousand generations. God, therefore, was pleased to give a striking proof of the abundance and greatness of his goodness which they were to enjoy after death, when he described it as overflowing to all their posterity (Exod. xx. 6). The truth of this promise was sealed, and in a manner completed, when, long after the death of Abraham, Isaac, and Jacob, he called himself their God (Exod. xx. 6). And why? Was not the name absurd if they had perished? It would have been just the same as if he had said, I am the God of men who exist not. Accordingly, the Evangelists relate that, by this very argument, our Saviour refuted the Sadducees (Matth. xxii. 23 ; Luke xx. 32), who were, therefore, unable to deny that the resurrection of the dead was attested by Moses, inasmuch as he had taught them that all the saints are in his hand (Deut. xxxiii. 3). Whence it is easy to infer that death is not the extinction of those who are taken under the tutelage, guardianship, and protection of him who is the disposer of life and death.

10. Let us now see (and on this the controversy principally turns) whether or not believers themselves were so instructed by the Lord, as to feel that they had elsewhere a better life, and to aspire to it while disregarding the present. First, the mode of life which heaven had imposed upon them made it a constant exercise, by which they were reminded, that if in this world only they had hope, they were of all men the most miserable. Adam, most unhappy even in the mere remembrance of his lost felicity, with difficulty supplies his wants by anxious labours ; and that the divine curse might not be restricted to bodily labour, his only remaining solace becomes a source of the deepest grief. Of two sons, the one is torn from him by the parricidal hand of his brother ; while the other, who survives, causes detestation and horror by his very look. Abel, cruelly murdered in the very flower of his days, is an example of the calamity which had come upon man. While the whole world are securely living in luxury, Noah, with much fatigue, spends a great part of his life in building an ark. He escapes death, but by greater troubles than a hundred deaths could have given. Besides his ten months' residence in the ark, as in a kind of sepulchre, nothing could have been more unpleasant than to have remained so long pent up among the filth of beasts. After escaping these difficulties he falls into a new cause of sorrow. He sees himself mocked by his own son, and is forced, with his own mouth, to curse one whom, by the great kindness of God, he had received safe from the deluge.

11. Abraham alone ought to be to us equal to tens of thousands if we consider his faith, which is set before us as the best model of believing, to whose race also we must be held to belong in order that

we may be the children of God.[1] What could be more absurd than
that Abraham should be the father of all the faithful, and not even
occupy the meanest corner among them ? He cannot be denied a
place in the list ; nay, he cannot be denied one of the most honourable places in it, without the destruction of the whole Church. Now,
as regards his experience in life, the moment he is called by the command of God, he is torn away from friends, parents, and country,
objects in which the chief happiness of life is deemed to consist, as if
it had been the fixed purpose of the Lord to deprive him of all the
sources of enjoyment. No sooner does he enter the land in which
he was ordered to dwell, than he is driven from it by famine. In the
country to which he retires to obtain relief, he is obliged, for his personal safety, to expose his wife to prostitution. This must have been
more bitter than many deaths. After returning to the land of his
habitation, he is again expelled by famine. What is the happiness
of inhabiting a land where you must so often suffer from hunger,
nay, perish from famine, unless you flee from it ? Then, again, with
Abimelech, he is reduced to the same necessity of saving his head
by the loss of his wife (Gen. xii. 12). While he wanders up and
down uncertain for many years, he is compelled, by the constant
quarrelling of servants, to part with his nephew, who was to him as
a son. This departure must doubtless have cost him a pang something like the cutting off of a limb. Shortly after, he learns that his
nephew is carried off captive by the enemy. Wherever he goes, he
meets with savage-hearted neighbours, who will not even allow him
to drink of the wells which he has dug with great labour. For he
would not have purchased the use from the king of Gerar if he had
not been previously prohibited. After he had reached the verge of
life, he sees himself childless (the bitterest and most unpleasant feeling to old age), until, beyond expectation, Ishmael is born ; and yet
he pays dearly for his birth in the reproaches of Sarah, as if he was
the cause of domestic disturbance by encouraging the contumacy of a
female slave. At length Isaac is born, but in return, the first-born
Ishmael is displaced, and almost hostilely driven forth and abandoned.
Isaac remains alone, and the good man, now worn out with age, has
his heart upon him, when shortly after he is ordered to offer him up
in sacrifice. What can the human mind conceive more dreadful than
for the father to be the murderer of his son ? Had he been carried
off by disease, who would not have thought the old man much to be
pitied in having a son given to him in mockery, and in having his
grief for being childless doubled to him ? Had he been slain by some
stranger, this would, indeed, have been much worse than natural
death. But all these calamities are little compared with the murder
of him by his father's hand. Thus, in fine, during the whole course
of his life, he was harassed and tossed in such a way, that any one

1 Calv. in Genes. cap. xii. 11—15.

desirous to give a picture of a calamitous life could not find one more appropriate. Let it not be said that he was not so very distressed, because he at length escaped from all these tempests. He is not said to lead a happy life who, after infinite difficulties during a long period, at last laboriously works out his escape, but he who calmly enjoys present blessings without any alloy of suffering.

12. Isaac is less afflicted, but he enjoys very few of the sweets of life. He also meets with those vexations which do not permit a man to be happy on the earth. Famine drives him from the land of Canaan ; his wife is torn from his bosom ; his neighbours are ever and anon annoying and vexing him in all kinds of ways, so that he is even obliged to fight for water. At home, he suffers great annoyance from his daughters-in-law ; he is stung by the dissension of his sons, and has no other cure for this great evil than to send the son whom he had blessed into exile (Gen. xxvi. xxvii.). Jacob, again, is nothing but a striking example of the greatest wretchedness. His boyhood is passed most uncomfortably at home amidst the threats and alarms of his elder brother, and to these he is at length forced to give way (Gen. xxvii. xxviii.). A fugitive from his parents and his native soil, in addition to the hardships of exile, the treatment he receives from his uncle Laban is in no respect milder and more humane (Gen. xxix.). As if it had been little to spend seven years of hard and rigorous servitude, he is cheated in the matter of a wife. For the sake of another wife, he must undergo a new servitude, during which, as he himself complains, the heat of the sun scorches him by day, while in frost and cold he spends the sleepless night (Gen. xxxi. 40, 41). For twenty years he spends this bitter life, and daily suffers new injuries from his father-in-law. Nor is he quiet at home, which he sees disturbed and almost broken up by the hatreds, quarrels, and jealousies of his wives. When he is ordered to return to his native land, he is obliged to take his departure in a manner resembling an ignominious flight. Even then he is unable to escape the injustice of his father-in-law, but in the midst of his journey is assailed by him with contumely and reproach (Gen. xxxi. 20.[1]) By-and-by a much greater difficulty befalls him (Gen. xxxii. xxxiii.). For as he approaches his brother, he has as many forms of death in prospect as a cruel foe could invent. Hence, while waiting for his arrival, he is distracted and excruciated by direful terrors ; and when he comes into his sight, he falls at his feet like one half dead, until he perceives him to be more placable than he had ventured to hope. Moreover, when he first enters the land, he is bereaved of Rachel his only beloved

---

[1] The French is, " Et encore ne peut il pas ainsi eviter l'iniquité de son beau père, qu'il ne soit de lui persecuté, et atteint au milieu du chemin ; et pourceque Dieu ne permettoit point qu'il lui advint pis, il est vexé de beaucoup d'opprobres et contumelies, par celui du quel il avoit bonne matiere de se plaindre."—Even thus he cannot escape the injustice of his father-in-law, but is persecuted by him, and attacked in the midst of his journey ; and because God did not allow worse to happen, he is assailed with much contumely and reproach by one of whom he had good cause to complain.

wife. Afterwards he hears that the son whom she had borne him, and whom he loved more than all his other children, is devoured by a wild beast (Gen. xxxvii. 33). How deep the sorrow caused by his death he himself evinces, when, after long tears, he obstinately refuses to be comforted, declaring that he will go down to the grave to his son mourning. In the mean time, what vexation, anxiety, and grief, must he have received from the carrying off and dishonour of his daughter, and the cruel revenge of his sons, which not only brought him into bad odour with all the inhabitants of the country, but exposed him to the greatest danger of extermination? (Gen. xxxiv.) Then follows the horrid wickedness of Reuben his first-born, wickedness than which none could be committed more grievous (Gen. xxxvi. 22). The dishonour of a wife being one of the greatest of calamities, what must be said when the atrocity is perpetrated by a son? Some time after, the family is again polluted with incest (Gen. xxxviii. 18). All these disgraces might have crushed a mind otherwise the most firm and unbroken by misfortune. Towards the end of his life, when he seeks relief for himself and his family from famine, he is struck by the announcement of a new misfortune, that one of his sons is detained in prison, and that to recover him he must intrust to others his dearly beloved Benjamin (Gen. xlii. xliii.). Who can think that in such a series of misfortunes, one moment was given him in which he could breathe secure? Accordingly, his own best witness, he declares to Pharaoh, " Few and evil have the days of the years of my life been" (Gen. xlvii. 9). In declaring that he had spent his life in constant wretchedness, he denies that he had experienced the prosperity which had been promised him by the Lord. Jacob, therefore, either formed a malignant and ungrateful estimate of the Lord's favour, or he truly declared that he had lived miserable on the earth. If so, it follows that his hope could not have been fixed on earthly objects.

13. If these holy Patriarchs expected a happy life from the hand of God (and it is indubitable that they did), they viewed and contemplated a different happiness from that of a terrestrial life. This is admirably shown by an Apostle, " By faith, he [Abraham] sojourned in the land of promise, as in a strange country, dwelling in tabernacles with Isaac and Jacob, the heirs with him of the same promise : for he looked for a city which hath foundations, whose builder and maker is God." " These all died in faith, not having received the promises, but having seen them afar off, and were persuaded of them, and embraced them, and confessed that they were strangers and pilgrims on the earth. For they that say such things declare plainly that they seek a country. And truly, if they had been mindful of that country from whence they came out, they might have had opportunity to have returned. But now they desire a better country, that is, an heavenly : wherefore God is not ashamed to be called their God : for he hath prepared for them a city " (Heb. xi. 9, 10, 13–16). They had been duller than blocks in so pertinaciously pursuing promises,

no hope of which appeared upon the earth, if they had not expected their completion elsewhere. The thing which the Apostle specially urges, and not without reason, is, that they called this world a pilgrimage, as Moses also relates (Gen. xlvii. 9). If they were pilgrims and strangers in the land of Canaan, where is the promise of the Lord which appointed them heirs of it? It is clear, therefore, that the promise of possession which they had received looked farther. Hence, they did not acquire a footbreadth in the land of Canaan, except for sepulture; thus testifying that they hoped not to receive the benefit of the promise till after death. And this is the reason why Jacob set so much value on being buried there, that he took Joseph bound by oath to see it done; and why Joseph wished that his bones should some ages later, long after they had mouldered into dust, be carried thither (Gen. xlvii. 29, 30; 1. 25).

14. In short, it is manifest, that in the whole course of their lives, they had an eye to future blessedness. Why should Jacob have aspired so earnestly to primogeniture, and intrigued for it at so much risk, if it was to bring him only exile and destitution, and no good at all, unless he looked to some higher blessing? And that this was his feeling, he declared in one of the last sentences he uttered, " I have waited for thy salvation, O God" (Gen. xlix. 18). What salvation could he have waited for, when he felt himself breathing his last, if he did not see in death the beginning of a new life? And why talk of saints and the children of God, when even one, who otherwise strove to resist the truth, was not devoid of some similar impression? For what did Balaam mean when he said, " Let me die the death of the righteous, and let my last end be like his" (Num. xxiii. 10), unless he felt convinced of what David afterward declares, " Precious in the sight of the Lord is the death of his saints" (Ps. cxvi. 15; xxxiv. 12). If death were the goal and ultimate limit, no distinction could be observed between the righteous and the wicked. The true distinction is the different lot which awaits them after death.

15. We have not yet come farther down than the books of Moses whose only office, according to our opponents, was to induce the people to worship God, by setting before them the fertility of the land, and its general abundance; and yet to every one who does not voluntarily shun the light, there is clear evidence of a spiritual covenant. But if we come down to the Prophets, the kingdom of Christ and eternal life are there exhibited in the fullest splendour. First, David, as earlier in time, in accordance with the order of the Divine procedure, spoke of heavenly mysteries more obscurely than they, and yet with what clearness and certainty does he point to it in all he says. The value he put upon his earthly habitation is attested by these words, " I am a stranger with thee, and a sojourner, as all my fathers were. Verily every man at his best estate is altogether vanity. Surely every man walketh in a vain show. And now, Lord, what

wait I for? my hope is in thee" (Ps. xxxix. 12, 5, 6, 7). He who confesses that there is nothing solid or stable on the earth, and yet firmly retains his hope in God, undoubtedly contemplates a happiness reserved for him elsewhere. To this contemplation he is wont to invite believers whenever he would have them to be truly comforted. For, in another passage, after speaking of human life as a fleeting and evanescent show, he adds, "The mercy of the Lord is from everlasting to everlasting upon them that fear him" (Ps. ciii. 17). To this there is a corresponding passage in another psalm, "Of old thou hast laid the foundation of the earth; and the heavens are the work of thy hands. They shall perish, but thou shalt endure; yea, all of them shall wax old like a garment; as a vesture shalt thou change them, and they shall be changed; but thou art the same, and thy years shall have no end. The children of thy servants shall continue, and their seed shall be established before thee" (Ps. cii. 25–28). If, notwithstanding of the destruction of the heavens and the earth, the godly cease not to be established before God, it follows, that their salvation is connected with his eternity. But this hope could have no existence, if it did not lean upon the promise as expounded by Isaiah, "The heavens shall vanish away like smoke, and the earth shall wax old like a garment, and they that dwell therein shall die in like manner; but my salvation shall be for ever, and my righteousness shall not be abolished" (Isa. li. 6). Perpetuity is here attributed to righteousness and salvation, not as they reside in God, but as they are experienced by men.

16. Nor can those things which are everywhere said as to the prosperous success of believers be understood in any other sense than as referring to the manifestation of celestial glory. Of this nature are the following passages: "He preserveth the souls of his saints; he delivereth them out of the hand of the wicked. Light is sown for the righteous, and gladness for the upright in heart." "His righteousness endureth for ever; his horn shall be exalted with honour— the desire of the wicked shall perish." "Surely the righteous shall give thanks unto thy name; the upright shall dwell in thy presence." "The righteous shall be in everlasting remembrance." "The Lord redeemeth the soul of his servants." [1] But the Lord often leaves his servants, not only to be annoyed by the violence of the wicked, but to be lacerated and destroyed; allows the good to languish in obscurity and squalid poverty, while the ungodly shine forth, as it were, among the stars; and even by withdrawing the light of his countenance does not leave them lasting joy. Wherefore, David by no means disguises the fact, that if believers fix their eyes on the present condition of the world, they will be grievously tempted to believe that with God integrity has neither favour nor reward; so much does impiety prosper and flourish, while the godly are oppressed with ignominy,

---

[1] Ps. xcvii. 10, 11; cxii. 9, 10; cxl. 13; cxii. 6; xxxiv. 22.

poverty, contempt, and every kind of cross. The Psalmist says, "But as for me, my feet were almost gone; my steps had well nigh slipped. For I was envious of the foolish, when I saw the prosperity of the wicked." At length, after a statement of the case, he concludes, "When I thought to know this, it was too painful for me : until I went into the sanctuary of God; then understood I their end" (Ps. lxxiii. 2, 3, 16, 17).

17. Therefore, even from this confession of David, let us learn that the holy fathers under the Old Testament were not ignorant that in this world God seldom or never gives his servants the fulfilment of what is promised them, and therefore has directed their minds to his sanctuary, where the blessings not exhibited in the present shadowy life are treasured up for them. This sanctuary was the final judgment of God, which, as they could not at all discern it by the eye, they were contented to apprehend by faith. Inspired with this confidence, they doubted not that whatever might happen in the world, a time would at length arrive when the divine promises would be fulfilled. This is attested by such expressions as these : "As for me, I will behold thy face in righteousness : I shall be satisfied, when I awake, with thy likeness" (Psalm xvii. 15). "I am like a green olive tree in the house of God" (Psalm lii. 8). Again, "The righteous shall flourish like the palm tree : he shall grow like a cedar in Lebanon. Those that be planted in the house of the Lord shall flourish in the courts of our God. They shall still bring forth fruit in old age; they shall be fat and flourishing" (Psalm xcii. 12—14). He had exclaimed a little before, "O Lord, how great are thy works! and thy thoughts are very deep." "When the wicked spring as the grass, and when all the workers of iniquity do flourish : it is that they shall be destroyed for ever." Where was this splendour and beauty of the righteous, unless when the appearance of this world was changed by the manifestation of the heavenly kingdom ? Lifting their eyes to the eternal world, they despised the momentary hardships and calamities of the present life, and confidently broke out into these exclamations : "He shall never suffer the righteous to be moved. But thou, O God, shalt bring them down into the pit of destruction : bloody and deceitful men shall not live out half their days" (Psalm. lv. 22, 23). Where in this world is there a pit of eternal destruction to swallow up the wicked, of whose happiness it is elsewhere said, "They spend their days in wealth, and in a moment go down to the grave"? (Job xxi. 13). Where, on the other hand, is the great stability of the saints, who, as David complains, are not only disturbed, but everywhere utterly bruised and oppressed ? It is here. He set before his eyes not merely the unstable vicissitudes of the world, tossed like a troubled sea, but what the Lord is to do when he shall one day sit to fix the eternal constitution of heaven and earth, as he in another place elegantly describes : "They that trust in their wealth, and boast themselves in the multitude of their

riches; none of them can by any means redeem his brother, nor give to God a ransom for him." "For he seeth that wise men die, likewise the fool and the brutish person perish, and leave their wealth to others. Their inward thought is, that their houses shall continue for ever, and their dwelling-places to all generations; they call their lands after their own names. Nevertheless, man being in honour abideth not: he is like the beasts that perish. This their way is their folly: yet their posterity approve their sayings. Like sheep they are laid in the grave; death shall feed on them; and the upright shall have dominion over them in the morning; and their beauty shall consume in the grave from their dwelling" (Psalm xlix. 6, 7, 10—14). By this derision of the foolish for resting satisfied with the slippery and fickle pleasures of the world, he shows that the wise must seek for a very different felicity. But he more clearly unfolds the hidden doctrine of the resurrection when he sets up a kingdom to the righteous after the wicked are cast down and destroyed. For what, pray, are we to understand by the "morning," unless it be the revelation of a new life, commencing when the present comes to an end?

18. Hence the consideration which believers employed as a solace for their sufferings, and a remedy for their patience: "His anger endureth but a moment: in his favour is life" (Psalm xxx. 5). How did their afflictions, which continued almost throughout the whole course of life, terminate in a moment? Where did they see the long duration of the divine benignity, of which they had only the slightest taste? Had they clung to earth, they could have found nothing of the kind; but looking to heaven, they saw that the period during which the Lord afflicted his saints was but a moment, and that the mercies with which he gathers them are everlasting: on the other hand, they foresaw that for the wicked, who only dreamed of happiness for a day, there was reserved an eternal and never-ending destruction. Hence those expressions: "The memory of the just is blessed, but the name of the wicked shall rot" (Prov. x. 7). "Precious in the sight of the Lord is the death of his saints (Psalm cxvi. 15). Again in Samuel: "The Lord will keep the feet of his saints, and the wicked shall be silent in darkness" (1 Sam. ii. 9); showing they knew well, that however much the righteous might be tossed about, their latter end was life and peace; that how pleasant soever the delights of the wicked, they gradually lead down to the chambers of death. They accordingly designated the death of such persons as the death "of the uncircumcised," that is, persons cut off from the hope of resurrection (Ezek. xxviii. 10; xxxi. 18). Hence David could not imagine a greater curse than this: "Let them be blotted out of the book of the living, and not be written with the righteous" (Psalm lxix. 28).

19. The most remarkable passage of all is that of Job: "I know that my Redeemer liveth, and that he shall stand at the latter day

upon the earth: and though after my skin worms destroy this body, yet in my flesh shall I see God: whom I shall see for myself, and mine eyes shall behold, and not another" (Job xix. 25—27). Those who would make a display of their acuteness, pretend that these words are to be understood not of the last resurrection, but of the day when Job expected that God would deal more gently with him. Granting that this is partly meant, we shall, however, compel them, whether they will or not, to admit that Job never could have attained to such fulness of hope if his thoughts had risen no higher than the earth. It must, therefore, be confessed, that he who saw that the Redeemer would be present with him when lying in the grave, must have raised his eyes to a future immortality. To those who think only of the present life, death is the extremity of despair; but it could not destroy the hope of Job. "Though he slay me," said he, "yet will I trust in him" (Job xiii. 15). Let no trifler here burst in with the objection that these are the sayings of a few, and do not by any means prove that there was such a doctrine among the Jews. To this my instant answer is, that these few did not in such passages give utterance to some hidden wisdom, to which only distinguished individuals were admitted privately and apart from others, but that having been appointed by the Holy Spirit to be the teachers of the people, they openly promulgated the mysteries of God, which all in common behoved to learn as the principles of public religion. When, therefore, we hear that those passages in which the Holy Spirit spoke so distinctly and clearly of the spiritual life were public oracles in the Jewish Church, it were intolerably perverse to confine them entirely to a carnal covenant relating merely to the earth and earthly riches.

20. When we descend to the later prophets, we have it in our power to expatiate freely as in our own field. If, when David, Job, and Samuel were in question, the victory was not difficult, much easier is it here; for the method and economy which God observed in administering the covenant of his mercy was, that the nearer the period of its full exhibition approached, the greater the additions which were daily made to the light of revelation. Accordingly, at the beginning, when the first promise of salvation was given to Adam (Gen. iii. 15), only a few slender sparks beamed forth: additions being afterwards made, a greater degree of light began to be displayed, and continued gradually to increase and shine with greater brightness, until at length, all the clouds being dispersed, Christ the Sun of righteousness arose, and with full refulgence illumined all the earth (Mal. iv). In appealing to the Prophets, therefore, we can have no fear of any deficiency of proof; but as I see an immense mass of materials, which would occupy us much longer than is compatible with the nature of our present work (the subject, indeed, would require a large volume), and as I trust that, by what has already been said, I have paved the way, so that every reader of the very least discernment may proceed without stumbling, I will avoid a

prolixity, for which at present there is little necessity; only reminding my readers to facilitate the entrance by means of the key which was formerly put into their hands (*supra*, Chap. IV. sec. 3, 4)— namely, that whenever the Prophets make mention of the happiness of believers (a happiness of which scarcely any vestiges are discernible in the present life), they must have recourse to this distinction : that the better to commend the Divine goodness to the people, they used temporal blessings as a kind of lineaments to shadow it forth, and yet gave such a portrait as might lift their minds above the earth, the elements of this world, and all that will perish, and compel them to think of the blessedness of a future and spiritual life.

21. One example will suffice. When the Israelites were carried away to Babylon, their dispersion seemed to be the next thing to death, and they could scarcely be dissuaded from thinking that Ezekiel's prophecy of their restoration (Ezek. xxxvii. 4) was a mere fable, because it seemed to them the same thing as if he had prophesied that putrid carcases would be raised to life. The Lord, in order to show that, even in that case, there was nothing to prevent him from making room for his kindness, set before the prophet in vision a field covered with dry bones, to which, by the mere power of his word, he in one moment restored life and strength. The vision served, indeed, to correct the unbelief of the Jews at the time, but it also reminded them how much farther the power of the Lord extended than to the bringing back of the people, since by a single nod it could so easily give life to dry scattered bones. Wherefore, the passage may be fitly compared with one in Isaiah, "Thy dead men shall live, together with my dead body shall they arise. Awake and sing, ye that dwell in dust : for thy dew is as the dew of herbs, and the earth shall cast out the dead. Come, my people, enter thou into thy chambers, and shut thy doors about thee : hide thyself as it were for a little moment, until the indignation be overpast. For, behold, the Lord cometh out of his place to punish the inhabitants of the earth for their iniquity: the earth also shall disclose her blood, and shall no more cover her slain" (Isa. xxvi. 19—21).

22. It were absurd, however, to interpret all the passages on a similar principle ; for there are several which point without any veil to the future immortality which awaits believers in the kingdom of heaven. Some of them we have already quoted, and there are many others, but especially the following two. The one is in Isaiah, "As the new heavens and the new earth, which I will make, shall remain beforeme, saith the Lord, so shall your seed and your name remain. And it shall come to pass, that from one new moon to another, and from one sabbath to another, shall all flesh come to worship before me, saith the Lord. And they shall go forth, and look upon the carcases of the men that have transgressed against me : for their worm shall not die, neither shall their fire be quenched ; and they shall be an abhorring unto all flesh" (Isa. lxvi. 22—24). The other passage

is in Daniel. " At that shall Michael stand up, the great prince which standeth for the children of thy people : and there shall be a time of trouble, such as there never was since there was a nation even to that same time : and at that time thy people shall be delivered, every one shall be found written in the book. And many of them that sleep in the dust of the earth shall awake, some to everlasting life, and some to shame and everlasting contempt" (Dan. xii. 1, 2).

23. In proving the two remaining points—viz. that the Patriarchs had Christ as the pledge of their covenant, and placed all their hope of blessing in him—as they are clearer, and not so much controverted, I will be less particular. Let us then lay it down confidently as a truth which no engines of the devil can destroy—that the Old Testament, or covenant which the Lord made with the people of Israel, was not confined to earthly objects, but contained a promise of spiritual and eternal life, the expectation of which behoved to be impressed on the minds of all who truly consented to the covenant. Let us put far from us the senseless and pernicious notion, that the Lord proposed nothing to the Jews, or that they sought nothing but full supplies of food, carnal delights, abundance of wealth, external influence. a numerous offspring, and all those things which our animal nature deems valuable. For, even now, the only kingdom of heaven which our Lord Jesus Christ promises to his followers, is one in which they may sit down with Abraham, and Isaac, and Jacob (Matth. viii. 11) ; and Peter declared of the Jews of his day, that they were heirs of gospel grace because they were the sons of the prophets, and comprehended in the covenant which the Lord of old made with his people (Acts iii. 25). And that this might not be attested by words merely, our Lord also approved it by act (Matth. xxvii. 52). At the moment when he rose again, he deigned to make many of the saints partakers of his resurrection, and allowed them to be seen in the city ; thus giving a sure earnest, that everything which he did and suffered in the purchase of eternal salvation, belonged to believers under the Old Testament just as much as to us. Indeed, as Peter testifies, they were endued with the same spirit of faith by which we are regenerated to life (Acts xv. 8). When we hear that that spirit, which is, as it were, a kind of spark of immortality in us (whence it is called the " earnest" of our inheritance, Eph. i. 14), dwelt in like manner in them, how can we presume to deny them the inheritance ? Hence, it is the more wonderful how the Sadducees of old fell into such a degree of sottishness as to deny both the resurrection and the substantive existence[1] of spirits, both of which were attested to them by so many striking passages of Scripture. Nor would the stupidity of the whole nation in the present day, in expecting an earthly reign of the Messiah, be less wonderful, had not the Scriptures foretold this long before as the punishment which they were to suffer for rejecting the

---

[1] " Animarum substantiam." French, "immortalité des ames ;"—immortality of souls.

Gospel, God, by a just judgment, blinding minds which voluntarily invite darkness, by rejecting the offered light of heaven. They read, and are constantly turning over the pages of Moses, but a veil prevents them from seeing the light which beams forth in his countenance (2 Cor. iii. 14) ; and thus to them he will remain covered and veiled until they are converted to Christ, between whom and Moses they now study, as much as in them lies, to maintain a separation.

CHAPTER XI.

THE DIFFERENCE BETWEEN THE TWO TESTAMENTS.

This chapter consists principally of three parts. I. Five points of difference between the Old and the New Testaments, sec. 1–11. II. The last of these points being, that the Old Testament belonged to the Jews only, whereas the New Testament belongs to all; the calling of the Gentiles is shortly considered, sec. 12. III. A reply to two objections usually taken to what is here taught concerning the difference between the Old and the New Testaments, sec. 13, 14.

Sections.

1. Five points of difference between the Old and the New Testaments. These belong to the mode of administration rather than the substance. First difference. In the Old Testament the heavenly inheritance is exhibited under temporal blessings; in the New, aids of this description are not employed.
2. Proof of this first difference from the simile of an heir in pupillarity, as in Gal. iv. 1.
3. This the reason why the Patriarchs, under the Law, set a higher value on this life, and the blessings of it, and dreaded the punishments, these being even more striking. Why severe and sudden punishments existed under the Law.
4. A second difference. The Old Testament typified Christ under ceremonies. The New exhibits the immediate truth and the whole body. The scope of the Epistle to the Hebrews in explaining this difference. Definition of the Old Testament.
5. Hence the Law our Schoolmaster to bring us unto Christ.
6. Notwithstanding, among those under the Law, some of the strongest examples of faith are exhibited, their equals being scarcely to be found in the Christian Church. The ordinary method of the divine dispensation to be here attended to. These excellent individuals placed under the Law, and aided by ceremonies, that they might behold and hail Christ afar off.
7. Third difference. The Old Testament is literal, the New spiritual. This difference considered first generally.
8. Next treated specially, on a careful examination of the Apostle's text. A threefold antithesis. The Old Testament is literal, deadly, temporary. The New is spiritual, quickening, eternal. Difference between the letter and the spirit.
9. Fourth difference. The Old Testament belongs to bondage, the New to liberty. This confirmed by three passages of Scripture. Two objections answered.
10. Distinction between the three last differences and the first. Confirmation of the above from Augustine. Condition of the patriarchs under the Old Testament.
11. Fifth difference. The Old Testament belonged to one people only, the New to all.
12. The second part of the chapter depending on the preceding section. Of the calling of the Gentiles. Why the calling of the Gentiles seemed to the Apostles so strange and new.
13. The last part of the chapter. Two objections considered. 1. God being immutable cannot consistently disapprove what he once ordered. Answer confirmed by a passage of Scripture.
14. Objections. 2. God could at first have transacted with the Jews as he now does with Christians. Answer, showing the absurdity of this objection. Another answer founded on a just consideration of the divine will and the dispensation of grace.

1. WHAT, then? you will say, Is there no difference between the Old and the New Testaments? What is to become of the many

passages of Scripture in which they are contrasted as things differing most widely from each other? I readily admit the differences which are pointed out in Scripture, but still hold that they derogate in no respect from their established unity, as will be seen after we have considered them in their order. These differences (so far as I have been able to observe them and can remember) seem to be chiefly four, or if you choose to add a fifth, I have no objections. I hold, and think I will be able to show, that they all belong to the mode of administration rather than to the substance. In this way, there is nothing in them to prevent the promises of the Old and New Testament from remaining the same, Christ being the foundation of both. The first difference then is, that though, in old time, the Lord was pleased to direct the thoughts of his people, and raise their minds to the heavenly inheritance, yet, that their hope of it might be the better maintained, he held it forth, and, in a manner, gave a foretaste of it under earthly blessings, whereas the gift of future life, now more clearly and lucidly revealed by the gospel, leads our minds directly to meditate upon it, the inferior mode of exercise formerly employed in regard to the Jews being now laid aside. Those who attend not to the divine purpose in this respect, suppose that God's ancient people ascended no higher than the blessings which were promised to the body. They hear the land of Canaan so often named as the special, and as it were the only, reward of the Divine Law to its worshippers; they hear that the severest punishment which the Lord denounces against the transgressors of the Law is expulsion from the possession of that land and dispersion into other countries; they see that this forms almost the sum of the blessings and curses declared by Moses; and from these things they confidently conclude that the Jews were separated from other nations not on their own account, but for another reason—viz. that the Christian Church might have an emblem in whose outward shape might be seen an evidence of spiritual things. But since the Scripture sometimes demonstrates that the earthly blessings thus bestowed were intended by God himself to guide them to a heavenly hope, it shows great unskilfulness, not to say dulness, not to attend to this mode of dispensation. The ground of controversy is this: our opponents hold that the land of Canaan was considered by the Israelites as supreme and final happiness, and now, since Christ was manifested, typifies to us the heavenly inheritance; whereas we maintain that, in the earthly possession which the Israelites enjoyed, they beheld, as in a mirror, the future inheritance which they believed to be reserved for them in heaven.

2. This will better appear from the similitude which Paul uses in Galatians (Gal. iv. 1). He compares the Jewish nation to an heir in pupillarity, who, as yet unfit to govern himself, follows the direction of a tutor or guide to whose charge he has been committed. Though this simile refers especially to ceremonies, there is nothing to prevent us from applying it most appropriately here also. The

same inheritance was destined to them as to us, but from nonage they were incapable of entering to it, and managing it. They had the same Church, though it was still in puerility. The Lord, therefore, kept them under this tutelage, giving them spiritual promises, not clear and simple, but typified by earthly objects. Hence, when he chose Abraham, Isaac, and Jacob, and their posterity, to the hope of immortality, he promised them the land of Canaan for an inheritance, not that it might be the limit of their hopes, but that the view of it might train and confirm them in the hope of that true inheritance, which, as yet, appeared not. And, to guard against delusion, they received a better promise, which attested that this earth was not the highest measure of the divine kindness. Thus, Abraham is not allowed to keep down his thoughts to the promised land: by a greater promise his views are carried upward to the Lord. He is thus addressed, " Fear not, Abram: I am thy shield, and thy exceeding great reward" (Gen. xv. 1). Here we see that the Lord is the final reward promised to Abraham, that he might not seek a fleeting and evanescent reward in the elements of this world, but look to one which was incorruptible. A promise of the land is afterwards added for no other reason than that it might be a symbol of the divine benevolence, and a type of the heavenly inheritance, as the saints declare their understanding to have been. Thus David rises from temporal blessings to the last and highest of all, " My flesh and my heart faileth: but God is the strength of my heart, and my portion for ever." " My heart and my flesh crieth out for the living God" (Ps. lxxiii. 26 ; lxxxiv. 2). Again, " The Lord is the portion of mine inheritance and of my cup: thou maintainest my lot" (Ps. xvi. 5). Again, " I cried unto thee, O Lord: I said, Thou art my refuge and my portion in the land of the living" (Ps. cxlii. 5). Those who can venture to speak thus, assuredly declare that their hope rises beyond the world and worldly blessings. This future blessedness, however, the prophets often describe under a type which the Lord had taught them. In this way are to be understood the many passages in Job (Job xviii. 17) and Isaiah, to the effect, That the righteous shall inherit the earth, that the wicked shall be driven out of it, that Jerusalem will abound in all kinds of riches, and Sion overflow with every species of abundance. In strict propriety, all these things obviously apply not to the land of our pilgrimage, nor to the earthly Jerusalem, but to the true country, the heavenly city of believers, in which the Lord hath commanded blessing and life for evermore (Ps. cxxxiii. 3).

3. Hence the reason why the saints under the Old Testament set a higher value on this mortal life and its blessings than would now be meet. For, though they well knew that in their race they were not to halt at it as the goal, yet, perceiving that the Lord, in accommodation to their feebleness, had there imprinted the lineaments of his favour, it gave them greater delight than it could have done if considered only in itself. For as the Lord, in testifying his good-will

towards believers by means of present blessings, then exhibited spiritual felicity under types and emblems, so, on the other hand, by temporal punishments he gave proofs of his judgment against the reprobate. Hence, by earthly objects, the favour of the Lord was displayed, as well as his punishment inflicted. The unskilful, not considering this analogy and correspondence (if I may so speak) between rewards and punishments, wonder that there is so much variance in God, that those who, in old time, were suddenly visited for their faults with severe and dreadful punishments, he now punishes much more rarely and less severely, as if he had laid aside his former anger ; and, for this reason, they can scarcely help imagining, like the Manichees, that the God of the Old Testament was different from that of the New. But we shall easily disencumber ourselves of such doubts if we attend to that mode of divine administration to which I have adverted—that God was pleased to indicate and typify both the gift of future and eternal felicity by terrestrial blessings, as well as the dreadful nature of spiritual death by bodily punishments, at that time when he delivered his covenant to the Israelites as under a kind of veil.

4. Another distinction between the Old and New Testaments is in the types, the former exhibiting only the image of truth, while the reality was absent, the shadow instead of the substance, the latter exhibiting both the full truth and the entire body. Mention is usually made of this, whenever the New Testament is contrasted with the Old,[1] but it is nowhere so fully treated as in the Epistle to the Hebrews (chap. vii.—x.). The Apostle is there arguing against those who thought that the observances of the Mosaic Law could not be abolished without producing the total ruin of religion. In order to refute this error, he adverts to what the Psalmist had foretold concerning the priesthood of Christ (Ps. cx. 4). Seeing that an eternal priesthood is assigned to him, it is clear that the priesthood in which there was a daily succession of priests is abolished. And he proves that the institution of this new Priest must prevail, because confirmed by an oath. He afterwards adds, that a change of the priest necessarily led to a change of the covenant. And the necessity of this he confirms by the reason, that the weakness of the law was such, that it could make nothing perfect. He then goes on to show in what this weakness consists—namely, that it had external carnal observances which could not render the worshippers perfect in respect of conscience, because its sacrifices of beasts could neither take away sins nor procure true holiness. He therefore concludes that it was a shadow of good things to come, and not the very image of the things,

---

[1] The French is, " et à icelle se doivent reduire quasi tous les passages, auxquels le vieil Testament est opposé au Nouveau par comparaison."—And to this ought in a manner to be referred all the passages in which the Old Testament is, by way of comparison, opposed to the New.

and accordingly had no other office than to be an introduction to the better hope which is exhibited in the Gospel.

Here we may see in what respect the legal is compared with the evangelical covenant, the ministry of Christ with that of Moses. If the comparison referred to the substance of the promises, there would be a great repugnance between the two covenants; but since the nature of the case leads to a different view, we must follow it in order to discover the truth. Let us, therefore, bring forward the covenant which God once ratified as eternal and unending. Its completion, whereby it is fixed and ratified, is Christ. Till such completion takes place, the Lord, by Moses, prescribes ceremonies which are, as it were, formal symbols of confirmation. The point brought under discussion was, Whether or not the ceremonies ordained in the Law behoved to give way to Christ. Although these were merely accidents of the covenant, or at least additions and appendages, and, as they are commonly called, accessories, yet because they were the means of administering it, the name of covenant is applied to them, just as is done in the case of other sacraments.[1] Hence, in general, the Old Testament is the name given to the solemn method of confirming the covenant comprehended under ceremonies and sacrifices. Since there is nothing substantial in it, until we look beyond it, the Apostle contends that it behoved to be annulled and become antiquated (Heb. vii. 22), to make room for Christ, the surety and mediator of a better covenant, by whom the eternal sanctification of the elect was once purchased, and the transgressions which remained under the Law wiped away. But if you prefer it, take it thus: the covenant of the Lord was old, because veiled by the shadowy and ineffectual observance of ceremonies; and it was therefore temporary, being, as it were, in suspense until it received a firm and substantial confirmation. Then only did it become new and eternal when it was consecrated and established in the blood of Christ. Hence the Saviour, in giving the cup to his disciples in the last supper, calls it the cup of the new testament in his blood; intimating, that the covenant of God was truly realised, made new, and eternal, when it was sealed with his blood.

5. It is now clear in what sense the Apostle said (Gal. iii. 24; iv. 1), that by the tutelage of the Law the Jews were conducted to Christ, before he was exhibited in the flesh. He confesses that they were sons and heirs of God, though, on account of nonage, they were placed under the guardianship of a tutor. It was fit, the Sun of Righteousness not yet having risen, that there should neither be so much light of revelation nor such clear understanding. The Lord dispensed the light of his word, so that they could behold it at a distance, and

---

[1] " Qualiter et aliis Sacramentis dari solet." French, " comme l'Escriture a coustume d'attribuer aux sacremens le nom des choses qu'ils representent;"—just as Scripture is wont to give sacraments the names of the things which they represent.

obscurely. Accordingly, this slender measure of intelligence is designated by Paul by the term *childhood*, which the Lord was pleased to train by the elements of this world, and external observances, until Christ should appear. Through him the knowledge of believers was to be matured. This distinction was noted by our Saviour himself when he said that the Law and the Prophets were until John, that from that time the gospel of the kingdom was preached (Matth. xi. 13). What did the Law and the Prophets deliver to the men of their time? They gave a foretaste of that wisdom which was one day to be clearly manifested, and showed it afar off. But where Christ can be pointed to with the finger, there the kingdom of God is manifested. In him are contained all the treasures of wisdom and understanding, and by these we penetrate almost to the very shrine of heaven.

6. There is nothing contrary to this in the fact, that in the Christian Church scarcely one is to be found who, in excellence of faith, can be compared to Abraham, and that the Prophets were so distinguished by the power of the Spirit, that even in the present day they give light to the whole world. For the question here is, not what grace the Lord conferred upon a few, but what was the ordinary method which he followed in teaching the people, and which even was employed in the case of those very prophets who were endued with special knowledge above others. For their preaching was both obscure as relating to distant objects, and was included in types. Moreover, however wonderful the knowledge displayed in them, as they were under the necessity of submitting to the tutelage common to all the people, they must also be ranked among children. Lastly, none of them ever had such a degree of discernment as not to savour somewhat of the obscurity of the age. Whence the words of our Saviour, " Many kings and prophets have desired to see the things which you see, and have not seen them ; and to hear the things which ye hear, and have not heard them. Blessed are your eyes, for they see ; and your ears, for they hear " (Matth. xiii. 17). And it was right that the presence of Christ should have this distinguishing feature, that by means of it the revelation of heavenly mysteries should be made more transparent. To the same effect is the passage which we formerly quoted from the First Epistle of Peter, that to them it was revealed that their labour should be useful not so much to themselves as to our age.

7. I proceed to the third distinction, which is thus expressed by Jeremiah : " Behold, the days come, saith the Lord, that I will make a new covenant with the house of Israel, and with the house of Judah : not according to the covenant that I made with their fathers in the day that I took them by the hand to bring them out of the land of Egypt ; which my covenant they brake, although I was an husband unto them, saith the Lord : but this shall be the covenant that I will make with the house of Israel ; After those days, saith the Lord, I

will put my law in their inward parts, and write it in their hearts ; and will be their God, and they shall be my people. And they shall teach no more every man his neighbour, and every man his brother, saying, Know the Lord : for they shall all know me, from the least of them unto the greatest of them " (Jer. xxxi. 31—34). From these words, the Apostle took occasion to institute a comparison between the Law and the Gospel, calling the one a doctrine of the letter, the other a doctrine of the spirit ; describing the one as formed on tables of stone, the other on tables of the heart; the one the preaching of death, the other of life ; the one of condemnation, the other of justification ; the one made void, the other permanent (2 Cor. iii. 5, 6). The object of the Apostle being to explain the meaning of the Prophet, the words of the one furnish us with the means of ascertaining what was understood by both. And yet there is some difference between them. For the Apostle speaks of the Law more disparagingly than the Prophet. This he does not simply in respect of the Law itself, but because there were some false zealots of the Law who, by a perverse zeal for ceremonies, obscured the clearness of the Gospel, he treats of the nature of the Law with reference to their error and foolish affection. It will, therefore, be proper to attend to this peculiarity in Paul. Both, however, as they are contrasting the Old and New Testament, consider nothing in the Law but what is peculiar to it. For example, the Law everywhere [1] contains promises of mercy ; but as these are adventitious to it, they do not enter into the account of the Law as considered only in its own nature. All which is attributed to it is, that it commands what is right, prohibits crimes, holds forth rewards to the cultivators of righteousness, and threatens transgressors with punishment, while at the same time it neither changes nor amends that depravity of heart which is naturally inherent in all.

8. Let us now explain the Apostle's contrast step by step. The Old Testament is literal, because promulgated without the efficacy of the Spirit : the New spiritual, because the Lord has engraven it on the heart. The second antithesis is a kind of exposition of the first. The Old is deadly, because it can do nothing but involve the whole human race in a curse ; the New is the instrument of life, because those who are freed from the curse it restores to favour with God. The former is the ministry of condemnation, because it charges the whole sons of Adam with transgression ; the latter the ministry of righteousness, because it unfolds the mercy of God, by which we are justified. The last antithesis must be referred to the Ceremonial Law. Being a shadow of things to come, it behoved in time to perish and vanish away ; whereas the Gospel, inasmuch as it exhibits the very body, is firmly established for ever. Jeremiah, indeed, calls the Moral Law also a weak and fragile covenant ; but for another

---

1 " Passim." French, " çá et lá ; "—here and there.

reason—namely, because it was immediately broken by the sudden defection of an ungrateful people; but as the blame of such violation is in the people themselves, it is not properly alleged against the covenant. The ceremonies, again, inasmuch as through their very weakness they were dissolved by the advent of Christ, had the cause of weakness from within. Moreover, the difference between the spirit and the letter must not be understood as if the Lord had delivered his Law to the Jews without any good result ; *i.e.* as if none had been converted to him. It is used comparatively to commend the riches of the grace with which the same Lawgiver, assuming, as it were, a new character, honoured the preaching of the Gospel. When we consider the multitude of those whom, by the preaching of the Gospel, he has regenerated by his Spirit, and gathered out of all nations into the communion of his Church, we may say that those of ancient Israel who, with sincere and heartfelt affection, embraced the covenant of the Lord, were few or none, though the number is great when they are considered in themselves without comparison.

9. Out of the third distinction a fourth arises. In Scripture, the term bondage is applied to the Old Testament, because it begets fear, and the term freedom to the New, because productive of confidence and security. Thus Paul says to the Romans, " Ye have not received the spirit of bondage again to fear ; but ye have received the Spirit of adoption, whereby we cry, Abba, Father" (Rom. viii. 15). To the same effect is the passage in the Hebrews, " For ye are not come unto the mount that might be touched, and that burned with fire, nor unto blackness, and darkness, and tempest, and the sound of a trumpet, and the voice of words ; which voice they that heard entreated that the word should not be spoken to them any more (for they could not endure that which was commanded, And if so much as a beast touch the mountain, it shall be stoned, or thrust through with a dart : and so terrible was the sight, that Moses said, I exceedingly fear and quake) : but ye are come unto Mount Sion, and unto the city of the living God, the heavenly Jerusalem," &c. (Heb. xii. 18—22). What Paul briefly touches on in the passage which we have quoted from the Romans, he explains more fully in the Epistle to the Galatians, where he makes an allegory of the two sons of Abraham in this way : " Agar is mount Sinai in Arabia, and answereth to Jerusalem which now is, and is in bondage with her children. But Jerusalem which is above is free, which is the mother of us all" (Gal. iv. 25, 26). As the offspring of Agar was born in slavery, and could never attain to the inheritance, while that of Sara was free and entitled to the inheritance, so by the Law we are subjected to slavery, and by the Gospel alone regenerated into liberty. The sum of the matter comes to this : The Old Testament filled the conscience with fear and trembling, the New inspires it with gladness. By the former the conscience is held in bondage, by the latter it is manumitted and made free. If it be objected, that the holy fathers among the Israel-

ites, as they were endued with the same spirit of faith, must also have been partakers of the same liberty and joy, we answer, that neither was derived from the Law; but feeling that by the Law they were oppressed like slaves, and vexed with a disquieted conscience, they fled for refuge to the Gospel; and, accordingly, the peculiar advantage of the Gospel was, that, contrary to the common rule of the Old Testament, it exempted those who were under it from those evils. Then, again, we deny that they did possess the spirit of liberty and security in such a degree as not to experience some measure of fear and bondage. For however they might enjoy the privilege which they had obtained through the grace of the Gospel, they were under the same bonds and burdens of observances as the rest of their nation. Therefore, seeing they were obliged to the anxious observance of ceremonies (which were the symbols of a tutelage bordering on slavery, and handwritings by which they acknowledged their guilt, but did not escape from it), they are justly said to have been, comparatively, under a covenant of fear and bondage, in respect of that common dispensation under which the Jewish people were then placed.

10. The three last contrasts to which we have adverted (sec. 4, 7, 9), are between the Law and the Gospel, and hence in these the Law is designated by the name of the Old, and the Gospel by that of the New Testament. The first is of wider extent (sec. 1), comprehending under it the promises which were given even before the Law. When Augustine maintained that these were not to be included under the name of the Old Testament (August. ad Bonifac. Lib. iii. c. 14), he took a most correct view, and meant nothing different from what we have now taught; for he had in view those passages of Jeremiah and Paul in which the Old Testament is distinguished from the word of grace and mercy. In the same passage, Augustine, with great shrewdness, remarks, that from the beginning of the world the sons of promise, the divinely regenerated, who, through faith working by love, obeyed the commandments, belonged to the New Testament; entertaining the hope not of carnal, earthly, temporal, but spiritual, heavenly, and eternal blessings, believing especially in a Mediator, by whom they doubted not both that the Spirit was administered to them, enabling them to do good, and pardon imparted as often as they sinned. The thing which he thus intended to assert was, that all the saints mentioned in Scripture, from the beginning of the world, as having been specially selected by God, were equally with us partakers of the blessing of eternal salvation. The only difference between our division and that of Augustine is, that ours (in accordance with the words of our Saviour, "All the prophets and the law prophesied until John," Matth. xi. 13) distinguishes between the gospel light and that more obscure dispensation of the word which preceded it, while the other division simply distinguishes between the weakness of the Law and the strength of the Gospel. And here also, with regard to the holy

fathers, it is to be observed, that though they lived under the Old Testament, they did not stop there, but always aspired to the New, and so entered into sure fellowship with it. Those who, contented with existing shadows, did not carry their thoughts to Christ, the Apostle charges with blindness and malediction. To say nothing of other matters, what greater blindness can be imagined, than to hope for the expiation of sin from the sacrifice of a beast, or to seek mental purification in external washing with water, or to attempt to appease God with cold ceremonies, as if he were greatly delighted with them? Such are the absurdities into which those fall who cling to legal observances, without respect to Christ.

11. The fifth distinction which we have to add consists in this, that until the advent of Christ, the Lord set apart one nation, to which he confined the covenant of his grace. Moses says, " When the Most High divided to the nations their inheritance, when he separated the sons of Adam, he set the bounds of the people according to the number of the children of Israel. For the Lord's portion is his people ; Jacob is the lot of his inheritance" (Deut. xxxii. 8, 9). In another passage he thus addresses the people : " Behold, the heaven and the heaven of heavens is the Lord's thy God, the earth also, with all that therein is. Only the Lord had a delight in thy fathers to love them, and he chose their seed, after them, even you, above all people, as it is this day" (Deut. x. 14, 15). That people, therefore, as if they had been the only part of mankind belonging to him, he favoured exclusively with the knowledge of his name, depositing his covenant, as it were, in their bosom, manifesting to them the presence of his divinity, and honouring them with all privileges. But to say nothing of other favours, the only one here considered is his binding them to him by the communion of his word, so that he was called and regarded as their God. Meanwhile other nations, as if they had had no kind of intercourse with him, he allowed to wander in vanity, not even supplying them with the only means of preventing their destruction—viz. the preaching of his word. Israel was thus the Lord's favourite child, the others were aliens. Israel was known and admitted to trust and guardianship, the others left in darkness ; Israel was made holy, the others were profane ; Israel was honoured with the presence of God, the others kept far aloof from him. But on the fulness of the time destined to renew all things, when the Mediator between God and man was manifested, the middle wall of partition, which had long kept the divine mercy within the confines of Israel, was broken down, peace was preached to them who were afar off, as well as to those who were nigh, that being together reconciled to God, they might unite as one people. Wherefore, there is now no respect of Jew or Greek, of circumcision or uncircumcision, but Christ is all and in all. To him the heathen have been given for his inheritance, and the uttermost parts of the earth for his possession (Ps. ii. 8), that he may rule

without distinction "from sea to sea, and from the river unto the ends of the earth" (Ps. lxxii. 8).

12. The calling of the Gentiles, therefore, is a distinguishing feature illustrative of the superiority of the New over the Old Testament. This, it is true, had been previously declared by the prophets, in passages both numerous and clear, but still the fulfilment of it was deferred to the reign of the Messiah. Even Christ did not acknowledge it at the very outset of his ministry, but delayed it until having completed the whole work of redemption in all its parts, and finished the period of his humiliation, he received from the Father "a name which is above every name, that at the name of Jesus every knee should bow" (Philip. ii. 9, 10). Hence the period being not yet completed, he declared to the woman of Canaan, "I am not sent but unto the lost sheep of the house of Israel" (Matth. xv. 24). Nor in his first commission to the Apostles does he permit them to pass the same limits, "Go not into the way of the Gentiles, and into any city of the Samaritans enter ye not: but go rather to the lost sheep of the house of Israel" (Matth. x. 5, 6). However plainly the thing may have been declared in numerous passages, when it was announced to the Apostles, it seemed to them so new and extraordinary, that they were horrified at is as something monstrous. At length, when they did act upon it, it was timorously, and not without reluctance. Nor is this strange ; for it seemed by no means in accordance with reason, that the Lord, who for so many ages had selected Israel from the rest of the nations, should suddenly, as it were, change his purpose, and abandon his choice. Prophecy, indeed, had foretold it, but they could not be so attentive to prophecies, as not to be somewhat startled by the novel spectacle thus presented to their eye. It was not enough that God had in old times given specimens of the future calling of the Gentiles. Those whom he had so called were very few in number, and, moreover, he in a manner adopted them into the family of Abraham, before allowing them to approach his people. But by this public call, the Gentiles were not only made equal to the Jews, but seemed to be substituted into their place, as if the Jews had been dead.[1] We may add, that any strangers whom God had formerly admitted into the body of the Church, had never been put on the same footing with the Jews. Wherefore, it is not without cause that Paul describes it as "the mystery which hath been hid from ages and from generations, but now is made manifest to his saints" (Col. i. 26).

13. The whole difference between the Old and New Testaments has, I think, been fully and faithfully explained, under these four or five heads, in so far as requisite for ordinary instruction. But since this variety in governing the Church, this diversity in the mode

---

[1] "In demortuorum locum." The French is simply, "en leur lieu ; "—into their place.

of teaching, this great change in rites and ceremonies, is regarded
by some as an absurdity, we must reply to them before passing to
other matters. And this can be done briefly, because the objections
are not so strong[1] as to require a very careful refutation. It is unreasonable, they say, to suppose that God, who is always consistent
with himself, permitted such a change as afterwards to disapprove
what he had once ordered and commended. I answer, that God
ought not to be deemed mutable, because he adapts different forms
to different ages, as he knows to be expedient for each. If the husbandman prescribes one set of duties to his household in winter, and
another in summer, we do not therefore charge him with fickleness,
or think he deviates from the rules of good husbandry, which depends
on the regular course of nature. In like manner, if a father of a
family, in educating, governing, and managing his children, pursues
one course in boyhood, another in adolescence, and another in manhood, we do not therefore say that he is fickle, or abandons his
opinions. Why, then, do we charge God with inconstancy, when he
makes fit and congruous arrangements for diversities of times? The
latter similitude ought to be completely satisfactory. Paul likens
the Jews to children, and Christians to grown men (Gal. iv. 1).
What irregularity is there in the Divine arrangement, which confined
them to the rudiments which were suitable to their age, and trains
us by a firmer and more manly discipline? The constancy of God
is conspicuous in this, that he delivered the same doctrine to all ages,
and persists in requiring that worship of his name which he commanded at the beginning. His changing the external form and
manner does not show that he is liable to change. In so far he has
only accommodated himself to the mutable and diversified capacities
of man.

14. But it is said, Whence this diversity, save that God chose to
make it? Would it not have been as easy for him from the first, as
after the advent of Christ, to reveal eternal life in clear terms without any figures, to instruct his people by a few clear sacraments, to
bestow his Holy Spirit, and diffuse his grace over the whole globe?
This is very much the same as to bring a charge against God,
because he created the world at so late a period, when he could have
done it at the first, or because he appointed the alternative changes
of summer and winter, of day and night. With the feeling common
to every pious mind, let us not doubt that everything which God
has done has been done wisely and justly, although we may be
ignorant of the cause which required that it should be so done.
We should arrogate too much to ourselves were we not to concede to God that he may have reasons for his counsel, which we
are unable to discern. It is strange, they say, that he now repudiates
and abominates the sacrifices of beasts, and the whole apparatus of

1 " Firmæ," French, " Ne si fortes, ne si urgentes;"—neither so strong, nor so
pressing.

that Levitical priesthood in which he formerly delighted. As if those external and transient matters could delight God, or affect him in any way![1] It has already been observed, that he appointed none of these things on his own account, but instituted them all for the salvation of men. If a physician, adopting the best method, effects a cure upon a youth, and afterwards, when the same individual has grown old, and is again subject to the same disease, employs a different method of cure, can it be said that he repudiates the method which he formerly approved? Nay, continuing to approve of it, he only adapts himself to the different periods of life. In l ke manner, it was necessary in representing Christ in his absence, and predicting his future advent, to employ a different set of signs from those which are employed, now that his actual manifestation is exhibited. It is true, that since the advent of Christ, the calling of God is more widely addressed to all nations, and the graces of the Spirit more liberally bestowed than they had previously been. But who, I ask, can deny the right of God to have the free and uncontrolled disposal of his gifts, to select the nations which he may be pleased to illuminate, the places which he may be pleased to illustrate by the preaching of his word, and the mode and measure of progress and success which he may be pleased to give to his doctrine,—to punish the world for its ingratitude, by withdrawing the knowledge of his name for certain ages, and again, when he so pleases, to restore it in mercy? We see, then, that in the calumnies which the ungodly employ in this matter, to perplex the minds of the simple, there is nothing that ought to throw doubt either on the justice of God or the veracity of Scripture.

1 " Aut ullo modo afficiant." French, " ou comme si jamais il s'y fust arreté ;"—or as if he could ever have stopped at them.

CHAPTER XII.

CHRIST, TO PERFORM THE OFFICE OF MEDIATOR, BEHOVED TO BECOME MAN.

The two divisions of this chapter are, I. The reasons why our Mediator behoved to be very God, and to become man, sec. 1—3. II. Disposal of various objections by some fanatics, and especially by Osiander, to the orthodox doctrine concerning the Mediator, sec. 4—7.

Sections.

1. Necessary, not absolutely, but by divine decree, that the Mediator should be God, and become man. Neither man nor angel, though pure, could have sufficed. The Son of God behoved to come down. Man in innocence could not penetrate to God without a Mediator, much less could he after the fall.
2. A second reason why the Mediator behoved to be God and man—viz. that he had to convert those who were heirs of hell into children of God.
3. Third reason, that in our flesh he might yield a perfect obedience, satisfy the divine justice, and pay the penalty of sin. Fourth reason, regarding the consolation and confirmation of the whole Church.
4. First objection against the orthodox doctrine: Answer to it. Confirmation from the sacrifices of the Law, the testimony of the Prophets, Apostles, Evangelists, and even Christ himself.
5. Second objection: Answer: Answer confirmed. Third objection: Answer. Fourth objection by Osiander: Answer.
6. Fifth objection, forming the basis of Osiander's errors on this subject: Answer. Nature of the divine image in Adam. Christ the head of angels and men.
7. Sixth objection: Answer. Seventh objection: Answer. Eighth objection: Answer. Ninth objection: Answer. Tenth objection: Answer. Eleventh objection: Answer. Twelfth objection: Answer. The sum of the doctrine.

1. IT deeply concerned us, that he who was to be our Mediator should be very God and very man. If the necessity be inquired into, it was not what is commonly termed simple or absolute, but flowed from the divine decree on which the salvation of man depended. What was best for us, our most merciful Father determined. Our iniquities, like a cloud intervening between Him and us, having utterly alienated us from the kingdom of heaven, none but a person reaching to him could be the medium of restoring peace. But who could thus reach to him? Could any of the sons of Adam? All of them, with their parent, shuddered at the sight of God. Could any of the angels? They had need of a head, by connection with which they might adhere to their God entirely and inseparably. What then? The case was certainly desperate, if the Godhead itself did not descend to us, it being impossible for us to ascend. Thus the Son of God behoved to become our Emmanuel, *i.e.* God with us; and in such a way, that by mutual union his divinity and our nature might be com-

bined; otherwise, neither was the proximity near enough, nor the affinity strong enough, to give us hope that God would dwell with us; so great was the repugnance between our pollution and the spotless purity of God. Had man remained free from all taint, he was of too humble a condition to penetrate to God without a Mediator. What, then, must it have been, when by fatal ruin he was plunged into death and hell, defiled by so many stains, made loathsome by corruption; in fine, overwhelmed with every curse? It is not without cause, therefore, that Paul, when he would set forth Christ as the Mediator, distinctly declares him to be man. There is, says he, " one Mediator between God and man, the man Christ Jesus" (1 Tim. ii. 5). He might have called him God, or at least, omitting to call him God, he might also have omitted to call him man: but because the Spirit, speaking by his mouth, knew our infirmity, he opportunely provides for it by the most appropriate remedy, setting the Son of God familiarly before us as one of ourselves. That no one, therefore, may feel perplexed where to seek the Mediator, or by what means to reach him, the Spirit, by calling him man, reminds us that he is near, nay, contiguous to us, inasmuch as he is our flesh. And, indeed, he intimates the same thing in another place, where he explains at greater length that he is not a high priest who " cannot be touched with the feeling of our infirmities; but was in all points tempted like as we are, yet without sin" (Heb. iv. 15).

2. This will become still clearer if we reflect, that the work to be performed by the Mediator was of no common description : being to restore us to the divine favour, so as to make us, instead of sons of men, sons of God ; instead of heirs of hell, heirs of a heavenly kingdom. Who could do this unless the Son of God should also become the Son of man, and so receive what is ours as to transfer to us what is his, making that which is his by nature to become ours by grace ? Relying on this earnest, we trust that we are the sons of God, because the natural Son of God assumed to himself a body of our body, flesh of our flesh, bones of our bones, that he might be one with us ; he declined not to take what was peculiar to us, that he might in his turn extend to us what was peculiarly his own, and thus might be in common with us both Son of God and Son of man. Hence that holy brotherhood which he commends with his own lips, when he says, " I ascend to my Father, and your Father, to my God, and your God " (John xx. 17). In this way, we have a sure inheritance in the heavenly kingdom, because the only Son of God, to whom it entirely belonged, has adopted us as his brethren; and if brethren, then partners with him in the inheritance (Rom. viii. 17). Moreover, it was especially necessary for this cause also that he who was to be our Redeemer should be truly God and man. It was his to swallow up death: who but Life could do so ? It was his to conquer sin: who could do so save Righteousness itself? It was his to put to flight the powers of the air and the world : who could do so but the mighty power superior

to both ? But who possesses life and righteousness, and the dominion and government of heaven, but God alone ? Therefore God, in his infinite mercy, having determined to redeem us, became himself our Redeemer in the person of his only-begotten Son.

3. Another principal part of our reconciliation with God was, that man, who had lost himself by his disobedience, should by way of remedy, oppose to it obedience, satisfy the justice of God, and pay the penalty of sin. Therefore, our Lord came forth very man, adopted the person of Adam, and assumed his name, that he might in his stead obey the Father ; that he might present our flesh as the price of satisfaction to the just judgment of God, and in the same flesh pay the penalty which we had incurred. Finally, since as God only he could not suffer, and as man only could not overcome death, he united the human nature with the divine, that he might subject the weakness of the one to death as an expiation of sin, and by the power of the other, maintaining a struggle with death, might gain us the victory. Those, therefore, who rob Christ of divinity or humanity, either detract from his majesty and glory, or obscure his goodness. On the other hand, they are no less injurious to men, undermining and subverting their faith, which, unless it rest on this foundation, cannot stand. Moreover, the expected Redeemer was that son of Abraham and David whom God had promised in the Law and in the Prophets. Here believers have another advantage. Tracing up his origin in regular series to David and Abraham, they more distinctly recognise him as the Messiah celebrated by so many oracles. But special attention must be paid to what I lately explained, namely, that a common nature is the pledge of our union with the Son of God ; that, clothed with our flesh, he warred to death with sin that he might be our triumphant conqueror ; that the flesh which he received of us he offered in sacrifice, in order that by making expiation he might wipe away our guilt, and appease the just anger of his Father.

4. He who considers these things with due attention, will easily disregard vague speculations, which attract giddy minds and lovers of novelty. One speculation of this class is, that Christ, even though there had been no need of his interposition to redeem the human race, would still have become man. I admit that in the first ordering of creation, while the state of nature was entire, he was appointed head of angels and men ; for which reason Paul designates him " the first-born of every creature " (Col. i. 15). But since the whole Scripture proclaims that he was clothed with flesh in order to become a Redeemer, it is presumptuous to imagine any other cause or end. We know well why Christ was at first promised—viz. that he might renew a fallen world, and succour lost man. Hence under the Law he was typified by sacrifices, to inspire believers with the hope that God would be propitious to them after he was reconciled by the expiation of their sins. Since from the earliest age, even before the Law was promulgated, there was never any promise of a Mediator without

blood, we justly infer that he was destined in the eternal counsel of God to purge the pollution of man, the shedding of blood being the symbol of expiation. Thus, too, the prophets, in discoursing of him, foretold that he would be the Mediator between God and man. It is sufficient to refer to the very remarkable prophecy of Isaiah (Is. liii. 4, 5), in which he foretells that he was "smitten for our iniquities;" that "the chastisement of our peace was upon him;" that as a priest "he was made an offering for sin:" "that by his stripes we are healed;" that as all "like lost sheep have gone astray," "it pleased the Lord to bruise him, and put him to grief," that he might "bear our iniquities." After hearing that Christ was divinely appointed to bring relief to miserable sinners, whoso overleaps these limits gives too much indulgence to a foolish curiosity.

Then when he actually appeared, he declared the cause of his advent to be, that by appeasing God he might bring us from death unto life. To the same effect was the testimony of the Apostles concerning him (John i. 9; x. 14). Thus John, before teaching that the Word was made flesh, narrates the fall of man. But above all, let us listen to our Saviour himself when discoursing of his office: "God so loved the world, that he gave his only-begotten Son, that whosoever believeth in him should not perish, but have everlasting life." Again, "The hour is coming, and now is, when the dead shall hear the voice of the Son of God: and they that hear shall live." "I am the resurrection and the life: he that believeth in me, though he were dead, yet shall he live." "The Son of man is come to save that which was lost." Again, "They that be whole need not a physician."[1] I should never have done were I to quote all the passages. Indeed, the Apostles, with one consent, lead us back to this fountain; and assuredly, if he had not come to reconcile God, the honour of his priesthood would fall, seeing it was his office as priest to stand between God and men, and "offer both gifts and sacrifices for sins" (Heb. v. 1); nor could he be our righteousness, as having been made a propitiation for us in order that God might not impute to us our sins (2 Cor. v. 19). In short, he would be stript of all the titles with which Scripture invests him. Nor could Paul's doctrine stand. "What the law could not do, in that it was weak through the flesh, God sending his own Son in the likeness of sinful flesh, and for sin, condemned sin in the flesh" (Rom. viii. 3). Nor what he states in another passage: "The grace of God that bringeth salvation hath appeared to all men"(Tit. ii. 11). In fine, the only end which the Scripture uniformly assigns for the Son of God voluntarily assuming our nature, and even receiving it as a command from the Father, is, that he might propitiate the Father to us by becoming a victim. "Thus it is written, and thus it behoved Christ to suffer;"—"and that repentance and remission of sins should be preached in his name."

---

[1] John iii. 16; v. 25; xi. 25; Matth. xviii. 11; ix. 12.

" Therefore doth my Father love me, because I lay down my life, that I might take it again." " This commandment have I received of my Father." " As Moses lifted up the serpent in the wilderness, even so must the Son of man be lifted up." " Father, save me from this hour: but for this cause came I unto this hour. Father, glorify thy name."[1] Here he distinctly assigns as the reason for assuming our nature, that he might become a propitiatory victim to take away sin. For the same reason Zacharias declares (Luke i. 79), that he came " to perform the mercy promised to our fathers," " to give light to them that sit in darkness, and in the shadow of death." Let us remember that all these things are affirmed of the Son of God, in whom, as Paul elsewhere declares, were " hid all the treasures of wisdom and knowledge," and save whom it was his determination " not to know anything" (Col. ii. 3: 1 Cor. ii. 2).

5. Should any one object, that in this there is nothing to prevent the same Christ who redeemed us when condemned from also testifying his love to us when safe by assuming our nature, we have the brief answer, that when the Spirit declares that by the eternal decree of God the two things were connected together—viz. that Christ should be our Redeemer, and, at the same time, a partaker of our nature, it is unlawful to inquire further. He who is tickled with a desire of knowing something more, not contented with the immutable ordination of God, shows also that he is not even contented with that Christ who has been given us as the price of redemption. And, indeed, Paul not only declares for what end he was sent, but rising to the sublime mystery of predestination, seasonably represses all the wantonness and pruriency of the human mind. " He hath chosen us in him before the foundation of the world, that we should be holy and without blame before him in love: having predestinated us unto the adoption of children by Jesus Christ to himself, according to the good pleasure of his will, to the praise of the glory of his grace, wherein he hath made us accepted in the Beloved: In whom we have redemption through his blood" (Eph. i. 4–7). Here certainly the fall of Adam is not presupposed as anterior in point of time, but our attention is directed to what God predetermined before all ages, when he was pleased to provide a cure for the misery of the human race. If, again, it is objected that this counsel of God depended on the fall of man, which he foresaw, to me it is sufficient and more to reply, that those who propose to inquire, or desire to know more of Christ than God predestinated by his secret decree, are presuming with impious audacity to invent a new Christ. Paul, when discoursing of the proper office of Christ, justly prays for the Ephesians that God would strengthen them " by his Spirit in the inner man," that they might " be able to comprehend with all saints what is the breadth and length, and depth and height; and to know the love of Christ

1 Luke xxiv. 46; John x. 17; iii. 14; xii. 27, 28.

which passeth knowledge" (Eph. iii. 16, 18); as if he intended of set purpose to set barriers around our minds, and prevent them from declining one iota from the gift of reconciliation whenever mention is made of Christ. Wherefore, seeing it is as Paul declares it to be, "a faithful saying, and worthy of all acceptation, that Christ Jesus came into the world to save sinners" (1 Tim. i. 15), in it I willingly acquiesce. And since the same Apostle elsewhere declares that the grace which is now manifested by the Gospel "was given us in Christ Jesus before the world began" (2 Tim. i. 9), I am resolved to adhere to it firmly even to the end. This moderation is unjustly vituperated by Osiander, who has unhappily, in the present day, again agitated this question, which a few had formerly raised. He brings a charge of overweening confidence against those who deny that the Son of God would have appeared in the flesh if Adam had not fallen, because this notion is not repudiated by any passage of Scripture. As if Paul did not lay a curb on perverse curiosity when, after speaking of the redemption obtained by Christ, he bids us "avoid foolish questions" (Tit. iii. 9). To such insanity have some proceeded in their preposterous eagerness to seem acute, that they have made it a question whether the Son of God might not have assumed the nature of an ass. This blasphemy, at which all pious minds justly shudder with detestation, Osiander excuses by the pretext that it is nowhere distinctly refuted in Scripture; as if Paul, when he counted nothing valuable or worth knowing "save Jesus Christ and him crucified" (1 Cor. ii. 2), were admitting that the author of salvation is an ass. He who elsewhere declares that Christ was by the eternal counsel of the Father appointed "head over all things to the church," would never have acknowledged another to whom no office of redemption had been assigned.

6. The principle on which Osiander founds is altogether frivolous. He will have it that man was created in the image of God, inasmuch as he was formed on the model of the future Messiah, in order to resemble him whom the Father had already determined to clothe with flesh. Hence he infers, that though Adam had never fallen from his first and pure original, Christ would still have been man. How silly and distorted this view is, all men of sound judgment will at once discern; still he thinks he was the first to see what the image of God was— namely, that not only did the divine glory shine forth in the excellent endowments with which he was adorned, but God dwelt in him essentially. But while I grant that Adam bore the image of God, inasmuch as he was united to God (this being the truest and highest perfection of dignity), yet I maintain, that the likeness of God is to be sought for only in those marks of superiority with which God has distinguished Adam above the other animals. All, likewise, with one consent, acknowledge that Christ was even then the image of God, and, accordingly, whatever excellence was engraven on Adam had its origin in this, that by means of the only begotten Son he ap-

proximated to the glory of his Maker. Man, therefore, was created in the image of God (Gen. i. 27), and in him the Creator was pleased to behold, as in a mirror, his own glory. To this degree of honour he was exalted by the kindness of the only-begotten Son. But I add, that, as the Son was the common head both of men and angels, so the dignity which was conferred on man belonged to the angels also. For when we hear them called the sons of God (Ps. lxxxii. 6), it would be incongruous to deny that they were endued with some quality in which they resembled the Father. But if he was pleased that his glory should be represented in men and angels, and made manifest in both natures, it is ignorant trifling in Osiander to say, that angels were postponed to men, because they did not bear the image of Christ. They could not constantly enjoy the immediate presence of God if they were not like to him ; nor does Paul teach (Col. iii. 10) that men are renewed in the image of God in any other way than by being associated with angels, that they may be united together under one head. In fine, if we believe Christ, our felicity will be perfected when we shall have been received into the heavens, and made like the angels. But if Osiander is entitled to infer that the primary type of the image of God was in the man Christ, on the same ground may any one maintain that Christ behoved to partake of the angelic nature, seeing that angels also possess the image of God.

7. Osiander has no reason to fear that God would be found a liar, if the decree to incarnate the Son was not previously immutably fixed in his mind. Even had Adam not lost his integrity, he would, with the angels, have been like to God ; and yet it would not therefore have been necessary that the Son of God should become either a man or an angel. In vain does he entertain the absurd fear, that unless it had been determined by the immutable counsel of God, before man was created, that Christ should be born, not as the Redeemer, but as the first man, he might lose his precedence, since he would not have been born, except for an accidental circumstance—namely, that he might restore the lost race of man ; and in this way would have been created in the image of Adam. For why should he be alarmed at what the Scripture plainly teaches, that " he was in all points tempted like as we are, yet without sin ?" (Heb. iv. 15.) Hence Luke, also, hesitates not to reckon him in his genealogy as a son of Adam (Luke iii. 38). I should like to know why Christ is termed by Paul the second Adam (1 Cor. xv. 47), unless it be that a human condition was decreed him, for the purpose of raising up the ruined posterity of Adam. For if in point of order, that condition was antecedent to creation, he ought to have been called the first Adam. Osiander confidently affirms, that because Christ was in the purpose of God foreknown as man, men were formed after him as their model. But Paul, by calling him the second Adam, gives that revolt which made it necessary to restore nature to its primitive condition an intermediate place between its original formation and the restitution which we

obtain by Christ: hence it follows, that it was this restitution which made the Son of God be born, and thereby become man. Moreover, Osiander argues ill and absurdly, that as long as Adam maintained his integrity, he would have been the image of himself, and not of Christ. I maintain, on the contrary, that although the Son of God had never become incarnate, nevertheless the image of God was conspicuous in Adam, both in his body and his soul ; in the rays of this image it always appeared that Christ was truly head, and had in all things the pre-eminence. In this way we dispose of the futile sophism put forth by Osiander, that the angels would have been without this head, had not God purposed to clothe his Son with flesh, even independent of the sin of Adam. He inconsiderately assumes what no rational person will grant, that Christ could have had no supremacy over the angels, so that they might enjoy him as their prince, unless in so far as he was man. But it is easy to infer from the words of Paul (Col. i. 15), that inasmuch as he is the eternal Word of God, he is the first-born of every creature, not because he is created, or is to be reckoned among the creatures, but because the entire structure of the world, such as it was from the beginning, when adorned with exquisite beauty, had no other beginning ; then, inasmuch as he was made man, he is the first-born from the dead. For in one short passage (Col. i. 16—18), the Apostle calls our attention to both views : that by the Son all things were created, so that he has dominion over angels ; and that he became man, in order that he might begin to be a Redeemer. Owing to the same ignorance, Osiander says that men would not have had Christ for their king unless he had been a man ; as if the kingdom of God could not have been established by his eternal Son, though not clothed with human flesh, holding the supremacy, while angels and men were gathered together to participate in his celestial life and glory. But he is always deluded, or imposes upon himself by this false principle, that the church would have been ἀκέφαλον—without a head—had not Christ appeared in the flesh. In the same way as angels enjoyed him for their head, could he not by his divine energy preside over men, and by the secret virtue of his Spirit quicken and cherish them as his body, until they were gathered into heaven to enjoy the same life with the angels ? The absurdities which I have been refuting, Osiander regards as infallible oracles. Taking an intoxicating delight in his own speculations, his wont is to extract ridiculous pæans out of nothing. He afterwards says that he has a much stronger passage to produce—namely, the prophecy of Adam, who, when the woman was brought to him, said, " This is now bone of my bone, and flesh of my flesh " (Gen. ii. 23). But how does he prove it to be a prophecy ? Because in Matthew Christ attributes the same expression to God ! as if everything which God has spoken by man contained a prophecy. On the same principle, as the law proceeded from God, let Osiander in each precept find a prophecy. Add, that our Saviour's exposition would have been harsh and grovelling, had he confined himself to the literal meaning. He was not referring to the mystical union with which he has honoured the Church, but only to conjugal fidelity, and states, that the reason why God declared man and wife to be one flesh, was to prevent any one from violating that indissoluble tie by divorce. If this simple meaning is too low for Osiander, let him censure Christ for not leading his disciples to the hidden sense, by interpreting his Father's words with more subtlety. Paul gives no countenance to Osiander's dream, when, after saying that "we are members of his body, of his flesh, and of his bones," he immediately adds, "This is a great mystery" (Eph. v. 30—32). For he meant not to refer to the sense in which Adam used the words, but sets forth, under the figure and similitude of marriage, the sacred union which makes us one with Christ. His words have this meaning; for reminding us that he is speaking of Christ and the Church, he, by way of correction, distinguishes between the marriage tie and the spiritual union of Christ with his Church. Wherefore, this subtlety vanishes at once. I deem it unnecessary to discuss similar absurdities: for from this very brief refutation, the vanity of them all will be discovered. Abundantly sufficient for the solid nurture of the children of God is this sober truth, that "when the fulness of the time was come, God sent forth his Son, made of a woman, made under the law, to redeem them who were under the law" (Gal. iv. 4, 5).

CHAPTER XIII.

CHRIST CLOTHED WITH THE TRUE SUBSTANCE OF HUMAN NATURE.

The heads of this chapter are, I. The orthodox doctrine as to the true humanity of our Saviour, proved from many passages of Scripture, sec. 1. II. Refutation of the impious objections of the Marcionites, Manichees, and similar heretics, sec. 2–4.

Sections.

1. Proof of the true humanity of Christ, against the Manichees and Marcionites.
2. Impious objections of heretics farther discussed. Six objections answered.
3. Other eight objections answered.

1. OF the divinity of Christ, which has elsewhere been established by clear and solid proofs, I presume it were superfluous again to treat. It remains, therefore, to see how, when clothed with our flesh, he fulfilled the office of Mediator. In ancient times, the reality of his human nature was impugned by the Manichees and Marcionites, the latter figuring to themselves a phantom instead of the body of Christ, and the former dreaming of his having been invested with celestial flesh. The passages of Scripture contradictory to both are numerous and strong. The blessing is not promised in a heavenly seed, or the mask of a man, but the seed of Abraham and Jacob ; nor is the everlasting throne promised to an aërial man but to the Son of David, and the fruit of his loins. Hence, when manifested in the flesh, he is called the Son of David and Abraham, not because he was born of a virgin, and yet created in the air, but because, as Paul explains, he was "made of the seed of David, according to the flesh" (Rom. i. 3), as the same apostle elsewhere says, that he came of the Jews (Rom. ix. 5). Wherefore, our Lord himself, not contented with the name of man, frequently calls himself the Son of man, wishing to express more clearly that he was a man by true human descent. The Holy Spirit having so often, by so many organs, with so much care and plainness, declared a matter which in itself is not abstruse, who could have thought that mortals would have had the effrontery to darken it with their glosses? Many other passages are at hand, were it wished to produce more : for instance, that one of Paul, that " God sent forth his Son, made of a woman" (Gal. iv. 4), and innumerable others, which show that he was subject to hunger, thirst, cold, and the other infirmities of our nature. But from the many we must chiefly select those which may conduce to build up our minds in true faith, as when it is said, " Verily, he took not on

him the nature of angels, but he took on him the seed of Abraham," "that through death he might destroy him that had the power of death" (Heb. ii. 16, 14). Again, " Both he that sanctifieth and they who are sanctified are all of one: for which cause he is not ashamed to call them brethren." " Wherefore in all things it behoved him to be made like unto his brethren, that he might be a merciful and faithful high priest" (Heb. ii. 11, 17). Again, " We have not an high priest which cannot be touched with the feeling of our infirmities" (Heb. iv. 15), and the like. To the same effect is the passage to which we lately referred, in which Paul distinctly declares, that the sins of the world behoved to be expiated in our flesh (Rom. viii. 3). And certainly everything which the Father conferred on Christ pertains to us for this reason, that " he is the head," that from him the whole body is " fitly joined together, and compacted by that which every joint supplieth" (Eph. iv. 16). Nay, in no other way could it hold true as is said, that the Spirit was given to him without measure (John i. 16), and that out of his fulness have all we received ; since nothing could be more absurd than that God, in his own essence, should be enriched by an adventitious gift. For this reason also, Christ himself elsewhere says, " For their sakes I sanctify myself" (John xvii. 19).

2. The passages which they produce in confirmation of their error are absurdly wrested, nor do they gain anything by their frivolous subtleties when they attempt to do away with what I have now adduced in opposition to them. Marcion imagines that Christ, instead of a body, assumed a phantom, because it is elsewhere said, that he was made in the likeness of man, and found in fashion as a man. Thus he altogether overlooks what Paul is then discussing (Philip. ii. 7). His object is not to show what kind of body Christ assumed, but that, when he might have justly asserted his divinity, he was pleased to exhibit nothing but the attributes of a mean and despised man. For, in order to exhort us to submission by his example, he shows, that when as God he might have displayed to the world the brightness of his glory, he gave up his right, and voluntarily emptied himself; that he assumed the form of a servant, and, contented with that humble condition, suffered his divinity to be concealed under a veil of flesh. Here, unquestionably, he explains not what Christ was, but in what way he acted. Nay, from the whole context, it is easily gathered, that it was in the true nature of man that Christ humbled himself. For what is meant by the words, he was " found in fashion as a man," but that for a time, instead of being resplendent with divine glory, the human form only appeared in a mean and abject condition ? Nor would the words of Peter, that he was " put to death in the flesh, but quickened by the Spirit" (1 Pet. iii. 18), hold true, unless the Son of God had become weak in the nature of man. This is explained more clearly by Paul, when he declares that " he was crucified through weakness" (2 Cor. xiii. 4). And

hence his exaltation ; for it is distinctly said, that Christ acquired new glory after he humbled himself. This could fitly apply only to a man endued with a body and a soul. "Manes" dreams of an aërial body, because, Christ is called the second Adam, the Lord from heaven. But the apostle does not there speak of the essence of his body as heavenly, but of the spiritual life which, derived from Christ, quickens us (1 Cor. xv. 47). This life Paul and Peter, as we have seen, separate from his flesh. Nay, that passage admirably confirms the doctrine of the orthodox, as to the human nature of Christ. If his body were not of the same nature with ours, there would be no soundness in the argument which Paul pursues with so much earnestness,—If Christ is risen, we shall rise also ; if we rise not, neither hath Christ risen. Whatever be the cavils by which the ancient Manichees, or their modern disciples, endeavour to evade this, they cannot succeed. It is a frivolous and despicable evasion to say, that Christ is called the Son of man, because he was promised to men ; it being obvious that, in the Hebrew idiom, the Son of man means a true man : and Christ, doubtless, retained the idiom of his own tongue.[1] Moreover, there cannot be a doubt as to what is to be understood by the sons of Adam. Not to go farther, a passage in the eighth psalm, which the apostles apply to Christ, will abundantly suffice : "What is man, that thou art mindful of him ? and the son of man, that thou visitest him ?" (Ps. viii. 4). Under this figure is expressed the true humanity of Christ. For although he was not immediately descended of an earthly father, yet he originally sprang from Adam. Nor could it otherwise be said in terms of the passage which we have already quoted, "Forasmuch, then, as the children are partakers of flesh and blood, he also himself likewise took part of the same ;" these words plainly proving that he was an associate and partner in the same nature with ourselves. In this sense also it is said, that "both he that sanctifieth and they who are sanctified are all of one." The context proves that this refers to a community of nature ; for it is immediately added, "For which cause he is not ashamed to call them brethren" (Heb. ii. 11). Had he said at first that believers are of God, where could there have been any ground for being ashamed of persons possessing such dignity ? But when Christ of his boundless grace associates himself with the mean and ignoble, we see why it was said that "he is not ashamed." It is vain to object, that in this way the wicked will be the brethren of Christ ; for we know that the children of God are not born of flesh and blood, but of the Spirit through faith. Therefore, flesh alone does not constitute the union of brotherhood. But although the apostle assigns to believers only the honour of being one with Christ, it does not, however, follow, that unbelievers have not the same origin accordingly to the flesh ; just as when we say that Christ became

---

[1] The last clause of the sentence is omited in the French.

man, that he might make us sons of God, the expression does not extend to all classes of persons; the intervention of faith being necessary to our being spiritually ingrafted into the body of Christ. A dispute is also ignorantly raised as to the term *first-born*. It is alleged that Christ ought to have been the first son of Adam, in order that he might be the first-born among the brethren (Rom. viii. 29). But primogeniture refers not to age, but to degree of honour and preeminence of virtue. There is just as little colour for the frivolous assertion that Christ assumed the nature of man, and not that of angels (Heb. ii. 16), because it was the human race that he restored to favour. The apostle, to magnify the honour which Christ has conferred upon us, contrasts us with the angels, to whom we are in this respect preferred. And if due weight is given to the testimony of Moses (Gen. iii. 15), when he says that the seed of the woman would bruise the head of the serpent, the dispute is at an end. For the words there used refer not to Christ alone, but to the whole human race. Since the victory was to be obtained for us by Christ. God declares generally, that the posterity of the woman would overcome the devil. From this it follows, that Christ is a descendant of the human race, the purpose of God in thus addressing Eve being to raise her hopes, and prevent her from giving way to despair.

3. The passages in which Christ is called the seed of Abraham, and the fruit of the loins of David, those persons, with no less folly than wickedness, wrap up in allegory. Had the term *seed* been used allegorically, Paul surely would not have omitted to notice it, when he affirms clearly, and without figure, that the promise was not given "to seeds, as of many; but as of one, And to thy seed, which is Christ" (Gal. iii. 16). With similar absurdity they pretend that he was called the Son of David, for no other reason but because he had been promised, and was at length in due time manifested. For Paul, after he had called him the Son of David, by immediately subjoining *according to the flesh*, certainly designates his nature. So also (Rom. ix. 5), while declaring him to be " God blessed for ever," he mentions separately, that, " as concerning the flesh, he was descended from the Jews." Again, if he had not been truly begotten of the seed of David, what is the meaning of the expression, that he is the "fruit of his loins;" or what the meaning of the promise, " Of the fruit of thy body will I set upon thy throne?" (Ps. cxxxii. 11). Moreover, their mode of dealing with the genealogy of Christ, as given by Matthew, is mere sophistry; for though he reckons up the progenitors not of Mary, but of Joseph, yet as he was speaking of a matter then generally understood, he deems it enough to show that Joseph was descended from the seed of David, since it is certain that Mary was of the same family. Luke goes still farther, showing that the salvation brought by Christ is common to the whole human race, inasmuch as Christ, the author of salvation, is descended from Adam, the common father of us all. I confess, indeed, that the genealogy proves Christ

to be the Son of David, only as being descended of the Virgin; but the new Marcionites, for the purpose of giving a gloss to their heresy—namely, to prove that the body which Christ assumed was unsubstantial, too confidently maintain that the expression as to seed is applicable only to males, thus subverting the elementary principles of nature. But as this discussion belongs not to theology, and the arguments which they adduce are too futile to require any laboured refutation, I will not touch on matters pertaining to philosophy and the medical art. It will be sufficient to dispose of the objection drawn from the statement of Scripture, that Aaron and Jehoiadah married wives out of the tribe of Judah, and that thus the distinction of tribes was confounded, if proper descent could come through the female. It is well known, that in regard to civil order, descent is reckoned through the male; and yet the superiority on his part does not prevent the female from having her proper share in the descent. This solution applies to all the genealogies. When Scripture gives a list of individuals, it often mentions males only. Must we therefore say that females go for nothing? Nay, the very children know that they are classified with men. For this reason, wives are said to give children to their husbands, the name of the family always remaining with the males. Then, as the male sex has this privilege, that sons are deemed of noble or ignoble birth, according to the condition of their fathers, so, on the other hand, in slavery, the condition of the child is determined by that of the mother, as lawyers say, *partus sequitur ventrem.* Whence we may infer, that offspring is partly procreated by the seed of the mother. According to the common custom of nations, mothers are deemed progenitors, and with this the divine law agrees, which could have had no ground to forbid the marriage of the uncle with the niece, if there was no consanguinity between them. It would also be lawful for a brother and sister uterine to intermarry, when their fathers are different. But while I admit that the power assigned to the woman is passive, I hold that the same thing is affirmed indiscriminately of her and of the male. Christ is not said to have been made by a woman, but of a woman (Gal. iv. 4). But some of this herd, laying aside all shame, publicly ask whether we mean to maintain that Christ was procreated of the proper seed of a Virgin.[1] I, in my turn, ask, whether they are not forced to admit that he was nourished to maturity in the Virgin's womb. Justly, therefore, we infer from the words of Matthew, that Christ, inasmuch as he was begotten of Mary, was procreated of her seed; as a similar generation is denoted when Boaz is said to have been begotten of Rachab (Matth. i. 5, 16). Matthew does not here describe the Virgin as the channel through which Christ flowed, but distinguishes his miraculous from an ordinary birth, in that Christ was begotten by her of the seed of David. For the same reason for

---

[1] Latin, "An dicere velimus ex semine menstruali virginis procreatur esse Christum."

which Isaac is said to be begotten of Abraham, Joseph of Jacob, Solomon of David, is Christ said to have been begotten of his mother. The Evangelist has arranged his discourse in this way. Wishing to prove that Christ derives his descent from David, he deems it enough to state, that he was begotten of Mary. Hence it follows, that he assumed it as an acknowledged fact, that Mary was of the same lineage as Joseph.

4. The absurdities which they wish to fasten upon us are mere puerile calumnies. They reckon it base and dishonouring to Christ to have derived his descent from men ; because, in that case, he could not be exempted from the common law which includes the whole offspring of Adam, without exception, under sin. But this difficulty is easily solved by Paul's antithesis, " As by one man sin entered into the world, and death by sin "—" even so by the righteousness of one the free gift came upon all men unto justification of life" (Rom. v. 12, 18). Corresponding to this is another passage, " The first man is of the earth, earthy : the second man is the Lord from heaven" (1 Cor. xv. 47). Accordingly, the same apostle, in another passage, teaching that Christ was sent " in the likeness of sinful flesh, that the righteousness of the law might be fulfilled in us," distinctly separates him from the common lot, as being true man, and yet without fault and corruption (Rom. viii. 3). It is childish, trifling to maintain, that if Christ is free from all taint, and was begotten of the seed of Mary, by the secret operation of the Spirit, it is not therefore the seed of the woman that is impure, but only that of the man. We do not hold Christ to be free from all taint, merely because he was born of a woman unconnected with a man, but because he was sanctified by the Spirit, so that the generation was pure and spotless, such as it would have been before Adam's·fall. Let us always bear in mind, that wherever Scripture adverts to the purity of Christ, it refers to his true human nature, since it were superfluous to say that God is pure. Moreover, the sanctification of which John speaks in his seventeenth chapter is inapplicable to the divine nature. This does not suggest the idea of a twofold seed in Adam, although no contamination extended to Christ, the generation of man not being in itself vicious or impure, but an accidental circumstance of the fall. Hence, it is not strange that Christ, by whom our integrity was to be restored, was exempted from the common corruption. Another absurdity which they obtrude upon us—viz. that if the Word of God became incarnate, it must have been enclosed in the narrow tenement of an earthly body, is sheer petulance. For although the boundless essence of the Word was united with human nature into one person, we have no idea of any enclosing. The Son of God descended miraculously from heaven, yet without abandoning heaven ; was pleased to be conceived miraculously in the Virgin's womb, to live on the earth, and hang upon the cross, and yet always filled the world as from the beginning.

CHAPTER XIV.

HOW TWO NATURES CONSTITUTE THE PERSON OF THE MEDIATOR.

This chapter contains two principal heads : I. A brief exposition of the doctrine of Christ's two natures in one person, sec. 1—4. II. A refutation of the heresies of Servetus, which destroy the distinction of natures in Christ, and the eternity of the divine nature of the Son.

Sections.

1. Proof of two natures in Christ—a human and a divine. Illustrated by analogy, from the union of body and soul. Illustration applied.
2. Proof from passages of Scripture which distinguish between the two natures. Proof from the communication of properties.
3. Proof from passages showing the union of both natures. A rule to be observed in this discussion.
4. Utility and use of the doctrine concerning the two natures. The Nestorians. The Eutychians. Both justly condemned by the Church.
5. The heresies of Servetus refuted. General answer or sum of the orthodox doctrine concerning Christ. What meant by the hypostatic union. Objections of Servetus to the deity of Christ. Answer.
6. Another objection and answer. A twofold filiation of Christ.
7. Other objections answered.
8. Conclusion of the former objections. Other pestilential heresies of Servetus.

1. WHEN it is said that the Word was made flesh, we must not understand it as if he were either changed into flesh, or confusedly intermingled with flesh, but that he made choice of the Virgin's womb as a temple in which he might dwell. He who was the Son of God became the Son of man, not by confusion of substance, but by unity of person. For we maintain, that the divinity was so conjoined and united with the humanity, that the entire properties of each nature remain entire, and yet the two natures constitute only one Christ. If, in human affairs, anything analogous to this great mystery can be found, the most apposite similitude[1] seems to be that of man, who obviously consists of two substances, neither of which, however, is so intermingled with the other as that both do not retain their own properties. For neither is soul body, nor is body soul. Wherefore that is said separately of the soul which cannot in any way apply to the body; and that, on the other hand, of the body which is altogether inapplicable to the soul ; and that, again, of the whole man, which cannot be affirmed without absurdity either of the body or of the soul separately. Lastly, the properties of the soul are

[1] Augustine employs the same similitude, Epist. cii.

transferred to the body, and the properties of the body to the soul, and yet these form only one man, not more than one. Such modes of expression intimate both that there is in man one person formed of two compounds, and that these two different natures constitute one person. Thus the Scriptures speak of Christ. They sometimes attribute to him qualities which should be referred specially to his humanity, and sometimes qualities applicable peculiarly to his divinity, and sometimes qualities which embrace both natures, and do not apply specially to either. This combination of a twofold nature in Christ they express so carefully, that they sometimes communicate them with each other, a figure of speech which the ancients termed ἰδιωμάτων κοινωνία (a communication of properties).

2. Little dependence could be placed on these statements, were it not proved by numerous passages throughout the sacred volume that none of them is of man's devising. What Christ said of himself, " Before Abraham was I am " (John xiii. 58), was very foreign to his humanity. I am not unaware of the cavil by which erroneous spirits distort this passage—viz. that he was before all ages, inasmuch as he was foreknown as the Redeemer, as well in the counsel of the Father as in the minds of believers. But seeing he plainly distinguishes the period of his manifestation from his eternal existence, and professedly founds on his ancient government, to prove his precedence to Abraham, he undoubtedly claims for himself the peculiar attributes of divinity. Paul's assertion that he is "the first-born of every creature," that " he is before all things, and by him all things consist" (Col. i. 15, 17); his own declaration, that he had glory with the Father before the world was, and that he worketh together with the Father, are equally inapplicable to man. These and similar properties must be specially assigned to his divinity. Again, his being called the servant of the Father, his being said to grow in stature, and wisdom, and favour with God and man, not to seek his own glory, not to know the last day, not to speak of himself, not to do his own will, his being seen and handled,[1] apply entirely to his humanity; since, as God, he cannot be in any respect said to grow, works always for himself, knows everything, does all things after the counsel of his own will, and is incapable of being seen or handled. And yet he not merely ascribes these things separately to his human nature, but applies them to himself as suitable to his office of Mediator. There is a communication of ἰδιωμάτα, or properties, when Paul says, that God purchased the Church " with his own blood" (Acts xx. 28), and that the Jews crucified the Lord of glory (1 Cor. ii. 8). In like manner, John says, that the Word of God was " handled." God certainly has no blood, suffers not, cannot be touched with hands ; but since that Christ, who was true God and true man, shed

---

[1] Isaiah xli. 1, &c.; John v. 17; Luke ii. 52; John viii. 50; Mark xiii. 32; John xiv. 10; vi. 38; Luke xxiv. 39.

his blood on the cross for us, the acts which were performed in his human nature are transferred improperly, but not causelessly, to his divinity. We have a similar example in the passage where John says that God laid down his life for us (1 John iii. 16). Here a property of his humanity is communicated with his other nature. On the other hand, when Christ, still living on the earth, said, "No man hath ascended up to heaven, but he that came down from heaven, even the Son of man, which is in heaven" (John iii. 13), certainly regarded as man in the flesh which he had put on, he was not then in heaven, but inasmuch as he was both God and man, he, on account of the union of a twofold nature, attributed to the one what properly belonged to the other.

3. But, above all, the true substance of Christ is most clearly declared in those passages which comprehend both natures at once. Numbers of these exist in the Gospel of John. What we there read as to his having received power from the Father to forgive sins; as to his quickening whom he will; as to his bestowing righteousness, holiness, and salvation; as to his being appointed judge both of the quick and the dead; as to his being honoured even as the Father,[1] are not peculiar either to his Godhead or his humanity, but applicable to both. In the same way he is called the Light of the world, the good Shepherd, the Door, the true Vine. With such prerogatives the Son of God was invested on his manifestation in the flesh, and though he possessed the same with the Father before the world was created, still it was not in the same manner or respect; neither could they be attributed to one who was a man and nothing more. In the same sense we ought to understand the saying of Paul, that at the end Christ shall deliver up "the kingdom to God, even the Father" (1 Cor. xv. 24). The kingdom of God assuredly had no beginning, and will have no end: but because he was hid under a humble clothing of flesh, and took upon himself the form of a servant, and humbled himself (Phil. ii. 8), and laying aside the insignia of majesty, became obedient to the Father; and after undergoing this subjection was at length crowned with glory and honour (Heb. ii. 7), and exalted to supreme authority, that at his name every knee should bow (Phil. ii. 10); so at the end he will subject to the Father both the name and the crown of glory, and whatever he received of the Father, that God may be all in all (1 Cor. xv. 28). For what end were that power and authority given to him, save that the Father might govern us by his hand? In the same sense, also, he is said to sit at the right hand of the Father. But this is only for a time, until we enjoy the immediate presence of his Godhead. And here we cannot excuse the error of some ancient writers, who, by not attending to the office of Mediator, darken the genuine meaning of almost the whole doctrine which we read in the Gospel of John, and entangle themselves in many snares.

1 John i. 29; v. 21—23; ix. 5; x. 9—11; xv. 1.

Let us, therefore, regard it as the key of true interpretation, that those things which refer to the office of Mediator are not spoken of the divine or human nature simply.[1] Christ, therefore, shall reign until he appear to judge the world, inasmuch as, according to the measure of our feeble capacity, he now connects us with the Father. But when, as partakers of the heavenly glory, we shall see God as he is, then Christ, having accomplished the office of Mediator, shall cease to be the vicegerent of the Father, and will be content with the glory which he possessed before the world was. Nor is the name of Lord specially applicable to the person of Christ in any other respect than in so far as he holds a middle place between God and us. To this effect are the words of Paul, " To us there is but one God, the Father, of whom are all things, and we in him; and one Lord Jesus Christ, by whom are all things, and we by him" (1 Cor. viii. 6); that is, to the letter a temporary authority has been committed by the Father until his divine majesty shall be beheld face to face. His giving up of the kingdom to the Father, so far from impairing his majesty, will give a brighter manifestation of it. God will then cease to be the head of Christ, and Christ's own Godhead will then shine forth of itself, whereas it is now in a manner veiled.

4. This observation, if the readers apply it properly, will be of no small use in solving a vast number of difficulties. For it is strange how the ignorant, nay, some who are not altogether without learning, are perplexed by these modes of expression which they see applied to Christ, without being properly adapted either to his divinity or his humanity, not considering their accordance with the character in which he was manifested as God and man, and with his office of Mediator. It is very easy to see how beautifully they accord with each other, provided they have a sober interpreter, one who examines these great mysteries with the reverence which is meet. But there is nothing which furious and frantic spirits cannot throw into confusion.[2] They fasten on the attributes of humanity to destroy his divinity; and, on the other hand, on those of his divinity to destroy his humanity: while those which, spoken conjointly of the two natures, apply to neither, they employ to destroy both. But what else is this than to contend that Christ is not man because he is God, not God because he is man, and neither God nor man because he is both at once. Christ, therefore, as God and man, possessing natures which are united but not confused, we conclude that he is our Lord and the true Son of God, even according to his humanity, though not by means of his humanity. For we must put far from us the heresy of Nestorius, who, presuming to dissect rather than distinguish between the two natures, devised a double Christ. But we see the Scripture loudly protesting against this, when the name of the Son of God is given to him who is born of a Virgin, and the Virgin herself is called the

---

1 *Vide* Calv. Epist. ad Polonos adversus Stancarum.
2 See August. in Enchir. ad Laurent. c. 36.

mother of our Lord (Luke i. 32, 43). We must beware also of the insane fancy of Eutyches, lest, when we would demonstrate the unity of person, we destroy the two natures. The many passages we have already quoted, in which the divinity is distinguished from the humanity, and the many other passages existing throughout Scripture, may well stop the mouth of the most contentious. I will shortly add a few observations, which will still better dispose of this fiction. For the present, one passage will suffice—Christ would not have called his body a temple (John ii. 19), had not the Godhead distinctly dwelt in it. Wherefore, as Nestorius had been justly condemned in the Council of Ephesus, so afterwards was Eutyches in those of Constantinople and Chalcedon, it being not more lawful to confound the two natures of Christ than to divide them.

5. But in our age, also, has arisen a not less fatal monster, Michael Servetus, who for the Son of God has substituted a figment composed of the essence of God, spirit, flesh, and three uncreated elements. First, indeed, he denies that Christ is the Son of God, for any other reason than because he was begotten in the womb of the Virgin by the Holy Spirit. The tendency of this crafty device is to make out, by destroying the distinction of the two natures, that Christ is somewhat composed of God and man, and yet is not to be deemed God and man. His aim throughout is to establish, that before Christ was manifested in the flesh there were only shadowy figures in God, the truth or effect of which existed for the first time, when the Word who had been destined to that honour truly began to be the Son of God. We indeed acknowledge that the Mediator who was born of the Virgin is properly the Son of God. And how could the man Christ be a mirror of the inestimable grace of God, had not the dignity been conferred upon him both of being and of being called the only-begotten Son of God ? Meanwhile, however, the definition of the Church stands unmoved, that he is accounted the Son of God, because the Word begotten by the Father before all ages assumed human nature by hypostatic union,—a term used by ancient writers to denote the union which of two natures constitutes one person, and invented to refute the dream of Nestorius, who pretended that the Son of God dwelt in the flesh in such a manner as not to be at the same time man. Servetus calumniously charges us with making the Son of God double, when we say that the eternal Word before he was clothed with flesh was already the Son of God: as if we said anything more than that he was manifested in the flesh. Although he was God before he became man, he did not therefore begin to be a new God. Nor is there any greater absurdity in holding that the Son of God, who by eternal generation ever had the property of being a Son, appeared in the flesh. This is intimated by the angel's words to Mary : " That holy thing which shall be born of thee shall be called the Son of God " (Luke i. 35); as if he had said said that the name of Son, which was more obscure under the law, would become

celebrated and universally known.   Corresponding to this is the passage of Paul, that being now the sons of God by Christ, we "have received the Spirit of adoption, whereby we cry, Abba, Father" (Rom. viii. 15).   Were not also the holy patriarchs of old reckoned among the sons of God?   Yea, trusting to this privilege, they invoked God as their Father.   But because ever since the only-begotten Son of God came forth into the world, his celestial paternity has been more clearly manifested, Paul assigns this to the kingdom of Christ as its distinguishing feature.   We must, however, constantly hold, that God never was a Father to angels and men save in respect of his only-begotten Son : that men, especially, who by their iniquity were rendered hateful to God, are sons by gratuitous adoption, because he is a Son by nature.   Nor is there anything in the assertion of Servetus, that this depends on the filiation which God had decreed with himself.   Here we deal not with figures, as expiation by the blood of beasts was shown to be ; but since they could not be the sons of God in reality, unless their adoption was founded in the head, it is against all reason to deprive the head of that which is common to the members.   I go farther : since the Scripture gives the name of sons of God to the angels, whose great dignity in this respect depended not on the future redemption, Christ must in order take precedence of them that he may reconcile the Father to them. I will again briefly repeat and add the same thing concerning the human race.   Since angels as well as men were at first created on the condition that God should be the common Father of both ; if it is true, as Paul says, that Christ always was the head, " the first-born of every creature—that in all things he might have the pre-eminence" (Col. i. 15, 18), I think I may legitimately infer, that he existed as the Son of God before the creation of the world.

6. But if his filiation (if I may so express it) had a beginning at the time when he was manifested in the flesh, it follows that he was a Son in respect of human nature also.   Servetus, and others similarly frenzied, hold that Christ who appeared in the flesh is the Son of God, inasmuch as but for his incarnation he could not have possessed this name.   Let them now answer me, whether, according to both natures, and in respect of both, he is a Son?   So indeed they prate ; but Paul's doctrine is very different.   We acknowledge, indeed, that Christ in human nature is called a Son, not like believers by gratuitous adoption merely, but the true, natural, and, therefore, only Son, this being the mark which distinguishes him from all others. Those of us who are regenerated to a new life God honours with the name of sons ; the name of true and only-begotten Son he bestows on Christ alone.   But how is he an only Son in so great a multitude of brethren, except that he possesses by nature what we acquire by gift ?   This honour we extend to his whole character of Mediator, so that He who was born of a Virgin, and on the cross offered himself in sacrifice to the Father, is truly and properly the Son of God ; but

still in respect of his Godhead: as Paul teaches when he says, that he "was separated unto the gospel of God (which he had promised afore by his prophets in the Holy Scriptures), concerning his Son Jesus Christ our Lord, which was made of the seed of David according to the flesh; and declared to be the Son of God with power" (Rom. i. 1—4). When distinctly calling him the Son of David according to the flesh, why should he also say that he was "declared to be the Son of God," if he meant not to intimate, that this depended on something else than his incarnation? For in the same sense in which he elsewhere says, that "though he was crucified through weakness, yet he liveth by the power of God" (2 Cor. xiii. 4), so he now draws a distinction between the two natures. They must certainly admit, that as on account of his mother he is called the Son of David, so, on account of his Father, he is the Son of God, and that in some respect differing from his human nature. The Scripture gives him both names, calling him at one time the Son of God, at another the Son of Man. As to the latter, there can be no question that he is called a Son in accordance with the phraseology of the Hebrew language, because he is of the offspring of Adam   On the other hand, I maintain that he is called a Son on account of his Godhead and eternal essence, because it is no less congruous to refer to his divine nature his being called the Son of God, than to refer to his human nature his being called the Son of Man. In fine, in the passage which I have quoted, Paul does not mean that he who, according to the flesh, was begotten of the seed of David, was declared to be the Son of God in any other sense than he elsewhere teaches that Christ, who, descended of the Jews according to the flesh, is "over all, God blessed for ever" (Rom. ix. 5). But if in both passages the distinction of two natures is pointed out, how can it be denied, that he who according to the flesh is the Son of Man, is also in respect of his divine nature the Son of God?

7. They indeed find a blustering defence of their heresy in its being said, that "God spared not his own Son," and in the communication of the angel, that He who was to be born of the Virgin should be called the "Son of the Highest" (Rom. viii. 32; Luke i. 32). But before pluming themselves on this futile objection, let them for a little consider with us what weight there is in their argument. If it is legitimately concluded, that at conception he began to be the Son of God, because he who has been conceived is called a Son, it will follow, that he began to be the Word after his manifestation in the flesh, because John declares, that the Word of life of which he spoke was that which "our hands have handled" (1 John i. 1). In like manner we read in the prophet, "Thou, Bethlehem Ephratah, though thou be little among the thousands of Israel, yet out of thee shall he come forth that is to be a ruler in Israel; whose goings forth have been from of old, from everlasting" (Mic. v. 2). How will they be forced to interpret if they will follow such a method of arguing?

I have declared that we by no means assent to Nestorius, who imagined a twofold Christ, when we maintain that Christ, by means of brotherly union, made us sons of God with himself, because in the flesh, which he took from us, he is the only-begotten Son of God. And Augustine wisely reminds us,[1] that he is a bright mirror of the wonderful and singular grace of God, because as man he obtained honour which he could not merit. With this distinction, therefore, according to the flesh, was Christ honoured even from the womb —viz. to be the Son of God. Still, in the unity of person we are not to imagine any intermixture which takes away from the Godhead what is peculiar to it. Nor is it more absurd that the eternal Word of God and Christ, uniting the two natures in one person, should in different ways be called the Son of God, than that he should in various respects be called at one time the Son of God, at another the Son of Man. Nor are we more embarrased by another cavil of Servetus—viz. that Christ, before he appeared in the flesh, is nowhere called the Son of God, except under a figure. For though the description of him was then more obscure, yet it has already been clearly proved, that he was not otherwise the eternal God, than as he was the Word begotten of the eternal Father. Nor is the name applicable to the office of Mediator which he undertook, except in that he was God manifest in the flesh. Nor would God have thus from the beginning been called a Father, had there not been even then a mutual relation to the Son, "of whom the whole family in heaven and earth is named" (Eph. iii. 15). Hence it is easy to infer, that under the Law and the Prophets he was the Son of God before this name was celebrated in the Church. But if we are to dispute about the word merely, Solomon, speaking of the incomprehensibility of God, affirms that his Son is like himself, incomprehensible: "What is his name, and what is his Son's name, if thou canst tell"? (Prov. xxx. 4). I am well aware that with the contentious this passage will not have sufficient weight; nor do I found much upon it, except as showing the malignant cavils of those who affirm that Christ is the Son of God only in so far as he became man. We may add, that all the most ancient writers, with one mouth and consent, testified the same thing so plainly, that the effrontery is no less ridiculous than detestable, which dares to oppose us with Irenæus and Tertullian, both of whom acknowledge that He who was afterwards visibly manifested was the invisible Son of God.[2]

8. But though Servetus heaped together a number of horrid dogmas, to which, perhaps, others would not subscribe, you will find, that all who refuse to acknowledge the Son of God except in the flesh, are obliged, when urged more closely, to admit that he was a Son,

---

1 See August. De Corruptione et Gratia. cap. xi., et De Civitate Dei, lib. x. cap 29, et alibi　See also cap. xvii. s. 1.

2 See Irenæus, lib. iv. cap 14 et 37; Tertullian adversus Praxeam. The above passages from The Proverbs is quoted by Augustine, Ep 49, Quæs. 5.

for no other reason than because he was conceived in the womb of the Virgin by the Holy Spirit ; just like the absurdity of the ancient Manichees, that the soul of man was derived by transfusion from God, from its being said, that he breathed into Adam's nostrils the breath of life (Gen. ii. 7). For they lay such stress on the name of Son that they leave no distinction between the natures, but babblingly maintain that the man Christ is the Son of God, because, according to his human nature, he was begotten of God. Thus, the eternal generation of Wisdom, celebrated by Solomon (Prov. viii. 22, seq.), is destroyed, and no kind of Godhead exists in the Mediator : or a phantom is substituted instead of man. The grosser delusions of Servetus, by which he imposed upon himself and some others, it were useful to refute, that pious readers might be warned by the example, to confine themselves within the bounds of soberness and modesty: however, I deem it superfluous here, as I have already done it in a special treatise.[1] The whole comes to this, that the Son of God was from the beginning an idea, and was even then a preordained man, who was to be the essential image of God. Nor does he acknowledge any other word of God except in external splendour. The generation he interprets to mean, that from the beginning a purpose of generating the Son was begotten in God, and that this purpose extended itself by act to creation. Meanwhile, he confounds the Spirit with the Word, saying that God arranged the invisible Word and Spirit into flesh and soul. In short, in his view the typifying of Christ occupies the place of generation ; but he says, that he who was then in appearance a shadowy Son, was at length begotten by the Word, to which he attributes a generating power. From this it will follow, that dogs and swine are not less sons of God, because created of the original seed of the Divine Word. But although he compounds Christ of three uncreated elements, that he may be begotten of the essence of God, he pretends that he is the first-born among the creatures, in such a sense that, according to their degree, stones have the same essential divinity. But lest he should seem to strip Christ of his Deity, he admits that his flesh is ὁμοούσιον, of the same substance with God, and that the Word was made man, by the conversion of flesh into Deity. Thus, while he cannot comprehend that Christ was the Son of God, until his flesh came forth from the essence of God and was converted into Deity, he reduces the eternal personality (*hypostasis*) of the Word to nothing, and robs us of the Son of David, who was the promised Redeemer. It is true, he repeatedly declares that the Son was begotten of God by knowledge and predestination, but that he was at length made man out of that matter which, from the beginning, shone with God in the three elements, and afterwards appeared in the first light of the world, in

---

[1] Vide Calv. Defensio Orthodoxæ Fidei Sacræ Trinitatis adversus Prodigiosos Errores Michaelis Serveti Hispani.

the cloud and pillar of fire.   How shamefully inconsistent with himself he ever and anon becomes, it were too tedious to relate.   From this brief account sound readers will gather, that by the subtle ambiguities of this infatuated man, the hope of salvation was utterly extinguished.   For if the flesh were the Godhead itself, it would cease to be its temple.   Now, the only Redeemer we can have is He who being begotten of the seed of Abraham and David according to the flesh, truly became man.   But he erroneously insists on the expression of John, " The Word was made flesh."   As these words refute the heresy of Nestorius, so they give no countenance to the impious fiction of which Eutyches was the inventor, since all that the Evangelist intended was to assert a unity of person in two natures.

CHAPTER XV.

THREE THINGS CHIEFLY TO BE REGARDED IN CHRIST—VIZ.
HIS OFFICES OF PROPHET, KING, AND PRIEST.

The principal parts of this chapter are—I. Of the Prophetical Office of Christ, its dignity and use, sec. 1, 2. II. The nature of the Kingly power of Christ, and the advantage we derive from it, sec. 3—5. III. Of the Priesthood of Christ, and the efficacy of it, sec. 6.

Sections.

1. Among heretics and false Christians, Christ is found in name only ; but by those who are truly and effectually called of God, he is acknowledged as a Prophet, King, and Priest. In regard to the Prophetical Office, the Redeemer of the Church is the same from whom believers under the Law hoped for the full light of understanding.
2. The unction of Christ, though it has respect chiefly to the Kingly Office, refers also to the Prophetical and Priestly Offices. The dignity, necessity, and use of this unction.
3. From the spirituality of Christ's kingdom its eternity is inferred. This twofold, referring both to the whole body of the Church, and to its individual members.
4. Benefits from the spiritual kingdom of Christ. 1. It raises us to eternal life. 2. It enriches us with all things necessary to salvation. 3. It makes us invincible by spiritual foes. 4. It animates us to patient endurance. 5. It inspires confidence and triumph. 6. It supplies fortitude and love.
5. The unction of our Redeemer heavenly. Symbol of this unction. A passage in the apostle reconciled with others previously quoted, to prove the eternal kingdom of Christ.
6. What necessary to obtain the benefit of Christ's Priesthood. We must set out with the death of Christ. From it follows, 1. His intercession for us. 2. Confidence in prayer. 3. Peace of conscience. 4. Through Christ, Christians themselves become priests. Grievous sin of the Papists in pretending to sacrifice Christ.

1. THOUGH heretics pretend the name of Christ, truly does Augustine affirm (Enchir. ad Laurent. cap. v.), that the foundation is not common to them with the godly, but belongs exclusively to the Church: for if those things which pertain to Christ be diligently considered, it will be found that Christ is with them in name only, not in reality. Thus, in the present day, though the Papists have the words, Son of God, Redeemer of the world, sounding in their mouths, yet, because contented with an empty name, they deprive him of his virtue and dignity ; what Paul says of "not holding the head," is truly applicable to them (Col. ii. 19). Therefore, that faith may find in Christ a solid ground of salvation, and so rest in him, we must set out with this principle, that the office which he received from the Father consists of three parts. For he was ap-

pointed both Prophet, King, and Priest; though little were gained by holding the names unaccompanied by a knowledge of the end and use. These, too, are spoken of in the Papacy, but frigidly, and with no great benefit, the full meaning comprehended under each title not being understood. We formerly observed, that though God, by supplying an uninterrupted succession of prophets, never left his people destitute of useful doctrine, such as might suffice for salvation; yet the minds of believers were always impressed with the conviction that the full light of understanding was to be expected only on the advent of the Messiah. This expectation, accordingly, had reached even the Samaritans, to whom the true religion had never been made known. This is plain from the expression of the woman, "I know that Messias cometh, which is called Christ: when he is come, he will tell us all things" (John iv. 25). Nor was this a mere random presumption which had entered the minds of the Jews. They believed what sure oracles had taught them. One of the most remarkable passages is that of Isaiah, "Behold, I have given him for a witness to the people, a leader and commander to the people" (Is. lv. 4); that is, in the same way in which he had previously in another place styled him "Wonderful, Counsellor" (Is. ix. 6).[1] For this reason the apostle, commending the perfection of gospel doctrine, first says that "God, at sundry times and in divers manners spake in times past unto the prophets," and then adds, that he "hath in these last days spoken unto us by his Son" (Heb. i. 1, 2). But as the common office of the prophets was to hold the Church in suspense, and at the same time support it until the advent of the Mediator; we read, that the faithful, during the dispersion, complained that they were deprived of that ordinary privilege. "We see not our signs: there is no more any prophet, neither is there among us any that knoweth how long" (Ps. lxxiv. 9). But when Christ was now not far distant, a period was assigned to Daniel "to seal up the vision and prophecy" (Daniel ix. 24), not only that the authority of the prediction there spoken of might be established, but that believers might, for a time, patiently submit to the want of the prophets, the fulfilment and completion of all the prophecies being at hand.

2. Moreover, it is to be observed, that the name *Christ* refers to those three offices: for we know that under the Law, prophets as well as priests and kings were anointed with holy oil. Whence, also, the celebrated name of Messiah was given to the promised Mediator. But although I admit (as, indeed, I have elsewhere shown) that he was so called from a view to the nature of a kingly office, still the prophetical and sacerdotal unctions have their proper place, and must not be overlooked. The former is expressly mentioned by Isaiah in these words; "The Spirit of the Lord God is upon me: because the

---

[1] Calvin translates, "Angelum vel Interpretem magni consilii;"—"the Angel or interpreter of the great counsel."

Lord hath anointed me to preach good tidings unto the meek ; he hath sent me to bind up the broken-hearted, to proclaim liberty to the captive, and the opening of the prison to them that are bound ; to proclaim the acceptable year of the Lord" (Is. lx. 1, 2). We see that he was anointed by the Spirit to be a herald and witness of his Father's grace, and not in the usual way ; for he is distinguished from other teachers who had a similar office. And here, again, it is to be observed, that the unction which he received, in order to perform the office of teacher, was not for himself, but for his whole body, that a corresponding efficacy of the Spirit might always accompany the preaching of the Gospel. This, however, remains certain, that by the perfection of doctrine which he brought, an end was put to all the prophecies, so that those who, not contented with the Gospel, annex somewhat extraneous to it, derogate from its authority. The voice which thundered from heaven, " This is my beloved Son, hear him," gave him a special privilege above all other teachers. Then from him, as head, this unction is diffused through the members, as Joel has foretold, " Your sons and your daughters shall prophesy, your old men shall dream dreams, and your young men shall see visions " (Joel ii. 28). Paul's expressions, that he was "made unto us wisdom" (1 Cor. i. 30), and elsewhere that in him " are hid all the treasures of wisdom and knowledge" (Col. ii. 3), have a somewhat different meaning—namely, that out of him there is nothing worth knowing, and that those who, by faith, apprehend his true character, possess the boundless immensity of heavenly blessings. For which reason, he elsewhere says, " I determined not to know anything among you, save Jesus Christ and him crucified" (1 Cor. ii. 2). And most justly : for it is unlawful to go beyond the simplicity of the Gospel. The purpose of this prophetical dignity in Christ is to teach us, that in the doctrine which he delivered is substantially included a wisdom which is perfect in all its parts.

3. I come to the Kingly office, of which it were in vain to speak, without previously reminding the reader that its nature is spiritual ; because it is from thence we learn its efficacy, the benefits it confers, its whole power and eternity. Eternity, moreover, which in Daniel an angel attributes to the office of Christ (Dan. ii. 44), in Luke an angel justly applies to the salvation of his people (Luke i. 33). But this is also twofold, and must be viewed in two ways ; the one pertains to the whole body of the Church, the other is proper to each member. To the former is to be referred what is said in the Psalms, " Once have I sworn by my holiness, that I will not lie unto David. His seed shall endure for ever, and his throne as the sun before me. It shall be established for ever, as the moon, and as a faithful witness in heaven" (Ps. lxxxix. 35, 37). There can be no doubt that God here promises that he will be, by the hand of his Son, the eternal governor and defender of the Church. In none but Christ will the fulfilment of this prophecy be found ; since immediately after Solo-

mon's death the kingdom in a great measure lost its dignity, and, with ignominy to the family of David, was transferred to a private individual. Afterwards decaying by degrees, it at length came to a sad and dishonourable end. In the same sense are we to understand the exclamation of Isaiah, "Who shall declare his generation?" (Isaiah liii. 8). For he asserts that Christ will so survive death as to be connected with his members. Therefore, as often as we hear that Christ is armed with eternal power, let us learn that the perpetuity of the Church is thus effectually secured; that amid the turbulent agitations by which it is constantly harassed, and the grievous and fearful commotions which threaten innumerable disasters, it still remains safe. Thus, when David derides the audacity of the enemy who attempt to throw off the yoke of God and his anointed, and says, that kings and nations rage "in vain" (Ps. ii. 2—4), because he who sitteth in the heaven is strong enough to repel their assaults, assuring believers of the perpetual preservation of the Church, he animates them to have good hope whenever it isoccasionally oppressed. So, in another place, when speaking in the person of God, he says, "The Lord said unto my Lord, Sit thou at my right hand, until I make thine enemies thy footstool" (Ps. cx. 1), he reminds us, that however numerous and powerful the enemies who conspire to assault the Church, they are not possessed of strength sufficient to prevail against the immortal decree by which he appointed his Son eternal King. Whence it follows that the devil, with the whole power of the world, can never possibly destroy the Church, which is founded on the eternal throne of Christ. Then in regard to the special use to be made by each believer, this same eternity ought to elevate us to the hope of a blessed immortality. For we see that everything which is earthly, and of the world, is temporary, and soon fades away. Christ, therefore, to raise our hope to the heavens, declares that his kingdom is not of this world (John xviii. 36). In fine, let each of us, when he hears that the kingdom of Christ is spiritual, be roused by the thought to entertain the hope of a better life, and to expect that as it is now protected by the hand of Christ, so it will be fully realised in a future life.

4. That the strength and utility of the kingdom of Christ cannot, as we have said, be fully perceived, without recognising it as spiritual, is sufficiently apparent, even from this, that having during the whole course of our lives to war under the cross, our condition here is bitter and wretched. What then would it avail us to be ranged under the government of a heavenly King, if its benefits were not realised beyond the present earthly life? We must, therefore, know that the happiness which is promised to us in Christ does not consist in external advantages—such as leading a joyful and tranquil life, abounding in wealth, being secure against all injury, and having an affluence of delights, such as the flesh is wont to long for—but properly belongs to the heavenly life. As in the world the prosperous and desirable

condition of a people consists partly in the abundance of temporal good and domestic peace, and partly in the strong protection which gives security against external violence; so Christ also enriches his people with all things necessary to the eternal salvation of their souls, and fortifies them with courage to stand unassailable by all the attacks of spiritual foes. Whence we infer, that he reigns more for us than for himself, and that both within us and without us; that being replenished, in so far as God knows to be expedient, with the gifts of the Spirit, of which we are naturally destitute, we may feel from their first fruits, that we are truly united to God for perfect blessedness; and then trusting to the power of the same Spirit, may not doubt that we shall always be victorious against the devil, the world, and everything that can do us harm. To this effect was our Saviour's reply to the Pharisees, "The kingdom of God is within you." "The kingdom of God cometh not with observation" (Luke xvii. 21, 22). It is probable that on his declaring himself to be that King under whom the highest blessing of God was to be expected, they had in derision asked him to produce his insignia. But to prevent those who were already more than enough inclined to the earth from dwelling on its pomp, he bids them enter into their consciences, for "the kingdom of God" is "righteousness, and peace, and joy in the Holy Ghost" (Rom. xiv. 17). These words briefly teach what the kingdom of Christ bestows upon us. Not being earthly or carnal, and so subject to corruption, but spiritual, it raises us even to eternal life, so that we can patiently live at present under toil, hunger, cold, contempt, disgrace, and other annoyances; contented with this, that our King will never abandon us, but will supply our necessities until our warfare is ended, and we are called to triumph: such being the nature of his kingdom, that he communicates to us whatever he received of his Father. Since then he arms and equips us by his power, adorns us with splendour and magnificence, enriches us with wealth, we here find most abundant cause of glorying, and also are inspired with boldness, so that we can contend intrepidly with the devil, sin, and death. In fine, clothed with his righteousness, we can bravely surmount all the insults of the world: and as he replenishes us liberally with his gifts, so we can in our turn bring forth fruit unto his glory.

5. Accordingly, his royal unction is not set before us as composed of oil or aromatic perfumes; but he is called the Christ of God, because "the Spirit of the Lord" rested upon him; "the Spirit of wisdom and understanding, the Spirit of counsel and might, the Spirit of knowledge and of the fear of the Lord" (Isaiah xi. 2). This is the oil of joy with which the Psalmist declares that he was anointed above his fellows (Ps. xlv. 7). For, as has been said, he was not enriched privately for himself, but that he might refresh the parched and hungry with his abundance. For as the Father is said to have given the Spirit to the Son without measure (John iii. 34), so the reason is

expressed, that we might all receive of his fulness, and grace for grace (John i. 16). From this fountain flows the copious supply (of which Paul makes mention, Eph. iv. 7) by which grace is variously distributed to believers according to the measure of the gift of Christ. Here we have ample confirmation of what I said, that the kingdom of Christ consists in the Spirit, and not in earthly delights or pomp, and that hence, in order to be partakers with him, we must renounce the world. A visible symbol of this grace was exhibited at the baptism of Christ, when the Spirit rested upon him in the form of a dove. To designate the Spirit and his gifts by the term *unction*, is not new, and ought not to seem absurd (see 1 John ii. 20, 27), because this is the only quarter from which we derive life; but especially in what regards the heavenly life, there is not a drop of vigour in us save what the Holy Spirit instils, who has chosen his seat in Christ, that thence the heavenly riches, of which we are destitute, might flow to us in copious abundance. But because believers stand invincible in the strength of their King, and his spiritual riches abound towards them, they are not improperly called Christians. Moreover, from this eternity of which we have spoken, there is nothing derogatory in the expression of Paul, " Then cometh the end, when he shall have delivered up the kingdom to God, even the Father" (1 Cor. xv. 24); and also, " Then shall the Son also himself be subject unto him that put all things under him, that God may be all in all" (1 Cor. xv. 28); for the meaning merely is, that, in that perfect glory, the administration of the kingdom will not be such as it now is. For the Father hath given all power to the Son, that by his hand he may govern, cherish, sustain us, keep us under his guardianship, and give assistance to us. Thus, while we wander far as pilgrims from God, Christ interposes, that he may gradually bring us to full communion with God. And, indeed, his sitting at the right hand of the Father has the same meaning as if he was called the vicegerent of the Father, intrusted with the whole power of government. For God is pleased, mediately (so to speak) in his person to rule and defend the Church. Thus also his being seated at the right hand of the Father is explained by Paul, in the Epistle to the Ephesians, to mean that " he is the head over all things to the Church, which is his body" (Eph. i. 20, 22). Nor is this different in purport from what he elsewhere teaches, that God hath "given him a name which is above every name; that at the name of Jesus every knee shall bow, of things in heaven, and things in earth, and things under the earth, and that every tongue should confess that Jesus Christ is Lord, to the glory of God the Father" (Phil. ii. 9—11). For in these words, also, he commends an arrangement in the kingdom of Christ, which is necessary for our present infirmity. Thus Paul rightly infers that God will then be the only Head of the Church, because the office of Christ, in defending the Church, shall then have been completed. For the same reason, Scripture throughout calls him *Lord*, the Father having appointed him over us for the express purpose of exercising his government through him. For though many lordships are celebrated in the world, yet Paul says, " To us there is but one God, the Father, of whom are all things, and we in him ; and one Lord Jesus Christ, by whom are all things, and we by him" (1 Cor. viii. 6). Whence it is justly inferred that he is the same God who, by the mouth of Isaiah, declared, " The Lord is our Judge, the Lord is our Lawgiver, the Lord is our King : he will save us" (Isaiah xxxiii. 22). For though he everywhere describes all the power which he possesses as the benefit and gift of the Father, the meaning simply is, that he reigns by divine authority, because his reason for assuming the office of Mediator was, that descending from the bosom and incomprehensible glory of the Father, he might draw near to us. Wherefore there is the greater reason that we all should with one consent prepare to obey, and with the greatest alacrity yield implicit obedience to, his will. For as he unites the offices of King and Pastor towards believers, who voluntarily submit to him, so, on the other hand, we are told that he wields an iron sceptre to break and bruise all the rebellious like a potter's vessel (Ps. ii. 9). We are also told that he will be the Judge of the Gentiles, that he will cover the earth with dead bodies, and level down every opposing height (Ps. cx. 6). Of this examples are seen at present, but full proof will be given at the final judgment, which may be properly regarded as the last act of his reign.

6. With regard to his Priesthood, we must briefly hold its end and use to be, that as a Mediator, free from all taint he may by his own holiness procure the favour of God for us. But because a deserved curse obstructs the entrance, and God in his character of Judge is hostile to us, expiation must necessarily intervene, that as a priest employed to appease the wrath of God, he may reinstate us in his favour. Wherefore, in order that Christ might fulfil this office, it behoved him to appear with a sacrifice. For even under the law of the priesthood it was forbidden to enter the sanctuary without blood, to teach the worshipper that however the priest might interpose to deprecate, God could not be propitiated without the expiation of sin. On this subject the Apostle discourses at length in the Epistle to the Hebrews, from the seventh almost to the end of the tenth chapter. The sum comes to this, that the honour of the priesthood was competent to none but Christ, because, by the sacrifice of his death, he wiped away our guilt, and made satisfaction for sin. Of the great importance of this matter, we are reminded by that solemn oath which God uttered, and of which he declared he would not repent, " Thou art a priest for ever, after the order of Melchizedek" (Ps. cx. 4). For, doubtless, his purpose was to ratify that point on which he knew that our salvation chiefly hinged. For, as has been said, there is no access to God for us or for our prayers until the priest, purging away our defilements, sanctify us, and obtain for

us that favour of which the impurity of our lives and hearts deprives us. Thus we see, that if the benefit and efficacy of Christ's priesthood is to reach us, the commencement must be with his death. Whence it follows, that he by whose aid we obtain favour, must be a perpetual intercessor. From this again arises not only confidence in prayer, but also the tranquillity of pious minds, while they recline in safety on the paternal indulgence of God, and feel assured, that whatever has been consecrated by the Mediator is pleasing to him. But since God under the Law ordered sacrifices of beasts to be offered to him, there was a different and new arrangement in regard to Christ —viz. that he should be at once victim and priest, because no other fit satisfaction for sin could be found, nor was any one worthy of the honour of offering an only-begotten son to God. Christ now bears the office of priest, not only that by the eternal law of reconciliation he may render the Father favourable and propitious to us, but also admit us into this most honourable alliance. For we, though in ourselves polluted, in him being priests (Rev. i. 6), offer ourselves and our all to God, and freely enter the heavenly sanctuary, so that the sacrifices of prayer and praise which we present are grateful and of sweet odour before him. To this effect are the words of Christ, " For their sakes I sanctify myself" (John xvii. 19) ; for being clothed with his holiness, inasmuch as he has devoted us to the Father with himself (otherwise we were an abomination before him), we please him as if we were pure and clean, nay, even sacred. Hence that unction of the sanctuary of which mention is made in Daniel (Dan. ix. 24). For we must attend to the contrast between this unction and the shadowy one which was then in use ; as if the angel had said, that when the shadows were dispersed, there would be a clear priesthood in the person of Christ. The more detestable, therefore, is the fiction of those who, not content with the priesthood of Christ, have dared to take it upon themselves to sacrifice him, a thing daily attempted in the Papacy, where the mass is represented as an immolation of Christ.

CHAPTER XVI.

HOW CHRIST PERFORMED THE OFFICE OF REDEEMER IN PROCURING OUR SALVATION. THE DEATH, RESURRECTION, AND ASCENSION OF CHRIST.

This chapter contains four leading heads—I. A general consideration of the whole subject, including a discussion of a necessary question concerning the justice of God and his mercy in Christ, sec. 1—4. II. How Christ fulfilled the office of Redeemer in each of its parts, sec. 5—17. His death, burial, descent to hell, resurrection, ascension, to heaven, seat at the right hand of the Father, and return to judgment. III. A great part of the Creed being here expounded, a statement is given of the view which ought to be taken of the Creed commonly ascribed to the Apostles, sec. 18. IV. Conclusion, setting forth the doctrine of Christ the Redeemer, and the use of the doctrine, sec. 19.

Sections.

1. Everything needful for us exists in Christ. How it is to be obtained.
2. Question as to the mode of reconciling the justice with the mercy of God. Modes of expression used in Scripture to teach us how miserable our condition is without Christ.
3. Not used improperly; for God finds in us ground both of hatred and love.
4. This confirmed from passages of Scripture and from Augustine.
5. The second part of the chapter, treating of our redemption by Christ. First generally. Redemption extends to the whole course of our Saviour's obedience, but is specially ascribed to his death. The voluntary subjection of Christ. His agony. His condemnation before Pilate. Two things observable in his condemnation. 1. That he was numbered among transgressors. 2. That he was declared innocent by the judge. Use to be made of this.
6. Why Christ was crucified. This hidden doctrine typified in the Law, and completed by the Apostles and Prophets. In what sense Christ was made a curse for us. The cross of Christ connected with the shedding of his blood.
7. Of the death of Christ. Why he died. Advantages from his death. Of the burial of Christ. Advantages.
8. Of the descent into hell. This article gradually introduced into the Church. Must not be rejected, nor confounded with the previous article respecting burial.
9. Absurd exposition concerning the Limbus Patrum. This fable refuted.
10. The article of the descent to hell more accurately expounded. A great ground of comfort.
11. Confirmation of this exposition from passages of Scripture and the works of ancient Theologians. An objection refuted. Advantages of the doctrine.
12. Another objection that Christ is insulted, and despair ascribed to him in its being said that he feared. Answer, from the statements of the Evangelists, that he did fear, was troubled in spirit, amazed, and tempted in all respects as we are, yet without sin. Why Christ was pleased to become weak. His fear without sin. Refutation of another objection, with an answer to the question, Did Christ fear death, and why? When did Christ descend to hell, and how? What has been said refutes the heresy of Apollinaris and of the Monothelites.
13. Of the resurrection of Christ. The many advantages from it. 1. Our righteousness in the sight of God renewed and restored. 2. His life the basis of our life and hope, also the efficacious cause of new life in us. 3. The pledge of our future resurrection.
14. Of the ascension of Christ. Why he ascended. Advantages derived from it.
15. Of Christ's seat at the Father's right hand. What meant by it.

16. Many advantages from the ascension of Christ. 1. He gives access to the kingdom which Adam had shut up. 2. He intercedes for us with the Father. 3. His virtue being thence transfused into us, he works effectually in us for salvation.
17. Of the return of Christ to judgment. Its nature. The quick and dead who are to be judged. Passages apparently contradictory reconciled. Mode of judgment.
18. Advantages of the doctrine of Christ's return to judgment. Third part of the chapter, explaining the view to be taken of the Apostles' Creed. Summary of the Apostles' Creed.
19. Conclusion of the whole chapter, showing that in Christ the salvation of the elect in all its parts is comprehended.

1. ALL that we have hitherto said of Christ leads to this one result, that condemned, dead, and lost in ourselves, we must in him seek righteousness, deliverance, life, and salvation, as we are taught by the celebrated words of Peter, "Neither is there salvation in any other: for there is none other name under heaven given among men whereby we must be saved" (Acts iv. 12). The name of Jesus was not given him at random, or fortuitously, or by the will of man, but was brought from heaven by an angel, as the herald of the supreme decree;[1] the reason also being added, "for he shall save his people from their sins" (Matt. i. 21). In these words attention should be paid to what we have elsewhere observed, that the office of Redeemer was assigned him in order that he might be our Saviour. Still, however, redemption would be defective if it did not conduct us by an uninterrupted progression to the final goal of safety. Therefore, the moment we turn aside from him in the minutest degree, salvation, which resides entirely in him, gradually disappears; so that all who do not rest in him voluntarily deprive themselves of all grace. The observation of Bernard well deserves to be remembered: The name of Jesus is not only light but food also, yea, oil, without which all the food of the soul is dry; salt, without which as a condiment whatever is set before us is insipid; in fine, honey in the mouth, melody in the ear, joy in the heart, and, at the same time, medicine; every discourse where this name is not heard is absurd (Bernard in Cantica., Serm. 15). But here it is necessary diligently to consider in what way we obtain salvation from him, that we may not only be persuaded that he is the author of it, but having embraced whatever is sufficient as a sure foundation of our faith, may eschew all that might make us waver. For seeing no man can descend into himself, and seriously consider what he is, without feeling that God is angry and at enmity with him, and therefore anxiously longing for the means of regaining his favour (this cannot be without satisfaction), the certainty here required is of no ordinary description,—sinners, until freed from guilt, being always liable to the wrath and curse of God, who, as he is a just judge, cannot permit his law to be violated with impunity, but is armed for vengeance.

2. But before we proceed farther, we must see in passing, how can

---

[1] Latin, "Supremi decreti." French, "Decret eternel et inviolable;"—Eternal and inviolable decree.

it be said that God, who prevents us with his mercy, was our enemy until he was reconciled to us by Christ. For how could he have given us in his only-begotten Son a singular pledge of his love, if he had not previously embraced us with free favour? As there thus arises some appearance of contradiction, I will explain the difficulty. The mode in which the Spirit usually speaks in Scripture is, that God was the enemy of men until they were restored to favour by the death of Christ (Rom. v. 10); that they were cursed until their iniquity was expiated by the sacrifice of Christ (Gal. iii. 10, 13); that they were separated from God, until by means of Christ's body they were received into union (Col. i. 21, 22). Such modes of expression are accommodated to our capacity, that we may the better understand how miserable and calamitous our condition is without Christ. For were it not said in clear terms, that Divine wrath, and vengeance, and eternal death, lay upon us, we should be less sensible of our wretchedness without the mercy of God, and less disposed to value the blessing of deliverance. For example, let a person be told, Had God at the time you were a sinner hated you, and cast you off as you deserved, horrible destruction must have been your doom; but spontaneously and of free indulgence he retained you in his favour, not suffering you to be estranged from him, and in this way rescued you from danger,—the person will indeed be affected, and made sensible in some degree how much he owes to the mercy of God. But again, let him be told, as Scripture teaches, that he was estranged from God by sin, an heir of wrath, exposed to the curse of eternal death, excluded from all hope of salvation, a complete alien from the blessing of God, the slave of Satan, captive under the yoke of sin; in fine, doomed to horrible destruction, and already involved in it; that then Christ interposed, took the punishment upon himself, and bore what by the just judgment of God was impending over sinners; with his own blood expiated the sins which rendered them hateful to God, by this expiation satisfied and duly propitiated God the Father, by this intercession appeased his anger, on this basis founded peace between God and men, and by this tie secured the Divine benevolence toward them; will not these considerations move him the more deeply, the more strikingly they represent the greatness of the calamity from which he was delivered? In short, since our mind cannot lay hold of life through the mercy of God with sufficient eagerness, or receive it with becoming gratitude, unless previously impressed with fear of the Divine anger, and dismayed at the thought of eternal death, we are so instructed by divine truth, as to perceive that without Christ God is in a manner hostile to us, and has his arm raised for our destruction. Thus taught, we look to Christ alone for divine favour and paternal love.

3. Though this is said in accommodation to the weakness of our capacity, it is not said falsely. For God, who is perfect righteousness, cannot love the iniquity which he sees in all. All of us, there-

fore, have that within which deserves the hatred of God. Hence, in respect, first, of our corrupt nature; and, secondly, of the depraved conduct following upon it, we are all offensive to God, guilty in his sight, and by nature the children of hell. But as the Lord wills not to destroy in us that which is his own, he still finds something in us which in kindness he can love. For though it iŝ by our own fault that we are sinners, we are still his creatures; though we have brought death upon ourselves, he had created us for life. Thus, mere gratuitous love prompts him to receive us into favour. But if there is a perpetual and irreconcilable repugnance between righteousness and iniquity, so long as we remain sinners we cannot be completely received. Therefore, in order that all ground of offence may be removed, and he may completely reconcile us to himself, he, by means of the expiation set forth in the death of Christ, abolishes all the evil that is in us, so that we, formerly impure and unclean, now appear in his sight just and holy. Accordingly, God the Father, by his love, prevents and anticipates our reconciliation in Christ. Nay, it is because he first loves us, that he afterwards reconciles us to himself. But because the iniquity, which deserves the indignation of God, remains in us until the death of Christ comes to our aid, and that iniquity is in his sight accursed and condemned, we are not admitted to full and sure communion with God, unless in so far as Christ unites us. And, therefore, if we would indulge the hope of having God placable and propitious to us, we must fix our eyes and minds on Christ alone, as it is to him alone it is owing that our sins, which necessarily provoked the wrath of God, are not imputed to us.

4. For this reason Paul says, that God "hath blessed us with all spiritual blessings in heavenly places in Christ: according as he hath chosen us in him before the foundation of the world" (Eph. i. 3, 4). These things are clear and conformable to Scripture, and admirably reconcile the passages in which it is said, that "God so loved the world, that he gave his only-begotten Son" (John iii. 16); and yet that it was "when we were enemies we were reconciled to God by the death of his Son" (Rom. v. 10). But to give additional assurance to those who require the authority of the ancient Church, I will quote a passage of Augustine to the same effect: "Incomprehensible and immutable is the love of God. For it was not after we were reconciled to him by the blood of his Son that he began to love us, but he loved us before the foundation of the world, that with his only-begotten Son we too might be sons of God before we were anything at all. Our being reconciled by the death of Christ must not be understood as if the Son reconciled us, in order that the Father, then hating, might begin to love us, but that we were reconciled to him already, loving, though at enmity with us because of sin. To the truth of both propositions we have the attestation of the Apostle, 'God commendeth his love toward us, in that while we were yet sinners, Christ died for us' (Rom. v. 8). Therefore he had this love

towards us even when, exercising enmity towards him, we were the workers of iniquity. Accordingly, in a manner wondrous and divine, he loved even when he hated us. For he hated us when we were such as he had not made us, and yet because our iniquity had not destroyed his work in every respect, he knew in regard to each one of us, both to hate what we had made, and love what he had made." Such are the words of Augustine (Tract in Jo. 110).

5. When it is asked then how Christ, by abolishing sin, removed the enmity between God and us, and purchased a righteousness which made him favourable and kind to us, it may be answered generally, that he accomplished this by the whole course of his obedience. This is proved by the testimony of Paul, "As by one man's disobedience many were made sinners, so by the obedience of one shall many be made righteous" (Rom. v. 19). And indeed he elsewhere extends the ground of pardon which exempts from the curse of the law to the whole life of Christ, "When the fulness of the time was come, God sent forth his Son, made of a woman, made under the law, to redeem them that were under the law" (Gal. iv. 4, 5). Thus even at his baptism he declared that a part of righteousness was fulfilled by his yielding obedience to the command of the Father. In short, from the moment when he assumed the form of a servant, he began, in order to redeem us, to pay the price of deliverance. Scripture, however, the more certainly to define the mode of salvation, ascribes it peculiarly and specially to the death of Christ. He himself declares that he gave his life a ransom for many (Matth. xx. 28). Paul teaches that he died for our sins (Rom. iv. 25). John Baptist exclaimed, "Behold the Lamb of God, which taketh away the sin of the world" (John i. 29). Paul in another passage declares, "that we are justified freely by his grace, through the redemption that is in Christ Jesus: whom God hath set forth to be a propitiation through faith in his blood" (Rom. iii. 25). Again, being "justified by his blood, we shall be saved from wrath through him" (Rom. v. 9). Again, "He hath made him to be sin for us, who knew no sin; that we might be made the righteousness of God in him" (2 Cor. v. 21). I will not search out all the passages, for the list would be endless, and many are afterwards to be quoted in their order. In the Confession of Faith, called the Apostles' Creed, the transition is admirably made from the birth of Christ to his death and resurrection, in which the completion of a perfect salvation consists. Still there is no exclusion of the other part of obedience which he performed in life. Thus Paul comprehends, from the beginning even to the end, his having assumed the form of a servant, humbled himself, and become obedient to death, even the death of the cross (Phil. ii. 7). And, indeed, the first step in obedience was his voluntary subjection; for the sacrifice would have been unavailing to justification if not offered spontaneously. Hence our Lord, after testifying, "I lay down my life for the sheep," distinctly adds, "No man taketh it from me"

(John x. 15, 18). In the same sense Isaiah says, "Like a sheep before her shearers is dumb, so he opened not his mouth" (Is. liii. 7). The Gospel History relates that he came forth to meet the soldiers; and in presence of Pilate, instead of defending himself, stood to receive judgment. This, indeed, he did not without a struggle, for he had assumed our infirmities also, and in this way it behoved him to prove that he was yielding obedience to his Father. It was no ordinary example of incomparable love towards us to struggle with dire terrors, and amid fearful tortures to cast away all care of himself that he might provide for us. We must bear in mind, that Christ could not duly propitiate God without renouncing his own feelings, and subjecting himself entirely to his Father's will. To this effect the Apostle appositely quotes a passage from the Psalms, "Lo, I come (in the volume of the book it is written of me) to do thy will, O God" (Heb. x. 5.; Ps. xl. 7, 8). Thus, as trembling consciences find no rest without sacrifice and ablution by which sins are expiated, we are properly directed thither, the source of our life being placed in the death of Christ. Moreover, as the curse consequent upon guilt remained for the final judgment of God, one principal point in the narrative is his condemnation before Pontius Pilate, the governor of Judea, to teach us, that the punishment to which we were liable was inflicted on that Just One. We could not escape the fearful judgment of God; and Christ, that he might rescue us from it, submitted to be condemned by a mortal, nay, by a wicked and profane man. For the name of Governor is mentioned not only to support the credibility of the narrative, but to remind us of what Isaiah says, that "the chastisement of our peace was upon him;" and that "with his stripes we are healed" (Is. liii. 5). For, in order to remove our condemnation, it was not sufficient to endure any kind of death. To satisfy our ransom, it was necessary to select a mode of death in which he might deliver us, both by giving himself up to condemnation, and undertaking our expiation. Had he been cut off by assassins, or slain in a seditious tumult, there could have been no kind of satisfaction in such a death. But when he is placed as a criminal at the bar, where witnesses are brought to give evidence against him, and the mouth of the judge condemns him to die, we see him sustaining the character of an offender and evil-doer. Here we must attend to two points which had both been foretold by the prophets, and tend admirably to comfort and confirm our faith. When we read that Christ was led away from the judgment-seat to execution, and was crucified between thieves, we have a fulfilment of the prophecy which is quoted by the Evangelist, "He was numbered with the transgressors" (Is. liii. 12; Mark xv. 28). Why was it so? That he might bear the character of a sinner, not of a just or innocent person, inasmuch as he met death on account not of innocence, but of sin. On the other hand, when we read that he was acquitted by the same lips that condemned him (for Pilate was forced once and again to bear public testimony to his innocence), let us call to mind what is said by another prophet, "I restored that which I took not away" (Ps. lxix. 4). Thus we perceive Christ representing the character of a sinner and a criminal, while, at the same time, his innocence shines forth, and it becomes manifest that he suffers for another's and not for his own crime. He therefore suffered under Pontius Pilate, being thus, by the formal sentence of the judge, ranked among criminals, and yet he is declared innocent by the same judge, when he affirms that he finds no cause of death in him. Our acquittal is in this—that the guilt which made us liable to punishment was transferred to the head of the Son of God (Is. liii. 12). We must specially remember this substitution in order that we may not be all our lives in trepidation and anxiety, as if the just vengeance, which the Son of God transferred to himself, were still impending over us.

6. The very form of the death embodies a striking truth. The cross was cursed not only in the opinion of men, but by the enactment of the Divine Law. Hence Christ, while suspended on it, subjects himself to the curse. And thus it behoved to be done, in order that the whole curse, which on account of our iniquities awaited us, or rather lay upon us, might be taken from us by being transferred to him. This was also shadowed in the Law, since אשמות, the word by which sin itself is properly designated, was applied to the sacrifices and expiations offered for sin. By this application of the term, the Spirit intended to intimate, that they were a kind of καθαρμάτων (purifications), bearing, by substitution, the curse due to sin. But that which was represented figuratively in the Mosaic sacrifices is exhibited in Christ the archetype. Wherefore, in order to accomplish a full expiation, he made his soul אשם, i.e., a propitiatory victim for sin (as the prophet says, Is. liii. 5, 10), on which the guilt and penalty being in a manner laid, ceases to be imputed to us. The Apostle declares this more plainly when he says, that " he made him to be sin for us, who knew no sin ; that we might be made the righteousness of God in him " (2 Cor. v. 21). For the Son of God, though spotlessly pure, took upon him the disgrace and ignominy of our iniquities, and in return clothed us with his purity. To the same thing he seems to refer, when he says, that he " condemned sin in the flesh " (Rom. viii. 3), the Father having destroyed the power of sin when it was transferred to the flesh of Christ. This term, therefore, indicates that Christ, in his death, was offered to the Father as a propitiatory victim ; that, expiation being made by his sacrifice, we might cease to tremble at the divine wrath. It is now clear what the prophet means when he says that " the Lord hath laid upon him the iniquity of us all " (Is. liii. 6) ; namely, that as he was to wash away the pollution of sins, they were transferred to him by imputation. Of this the cross to which he was nailed was a symbol, as the Apostle declares, " Christ hath redeemed us from the curse of the law, being made a curse for us : for it is written, Cursed is every one that hangeth

on a tree: that the blessing of Abraham might come on the Gentiles through Jesus Christ" (Gal. iii. 13, 14). In the same way Peter says, that he "bare our sins in his own body on the tree" (1 Peter ii. 24), inasmuch as from the very symbol of the curse, we perceive more clearly that the burden with which we were oppressed was laid upon him. Nor are we to understand that by the curse which he endured he was himself overwhelmed, but rather that by enduring it he repressed, broke, annihilated all its force. Accordingly, faith apprehends acquittal in the condemnation of Christ, and blessing in his curse. Hence it is not without cause that Paul magnificently celebrates the triumph which Christ obtained upon the cross, as if the cross, the symbol of ignominy, had been converted into a triumphal chariot. For he says, that he blotted out the handwriting of ordinances that was against us, which was contrary to us, and took it out of the way, nailing it to his cross : that, "having spoiled principalities and powers, he made a show of them openly, triumphing over them in it" (Col. ii. 14, 15). Nor is this to be wondered at ; for, as another Apostle declares, Christ, " through the eternal Spirit, offered himself without spot to God" (Heb. ix. 14), and hence that transformation of the cross which were otherwise against its nature. But that these things may take deep root and have their seat in our inmost hearts, we must never lose sight of sacrifice and ablution. For, were not Christ a victim, we could have no sure conviction of his being ἀπολύτρωσις, ἀντίλυτρον, και ἱλαστηριον, *our substitute-ransom and propitiation.* And hence mention is always made of blood whenever Scripture explains the mode of redemption: although the shedding of Christ's blood was available not only for propitiation, but also acted as a laver to purge our defilements.

7. The Creed next mentions, that he "was dead and buried." Here again it is necessary to consider how he substituted himself in order to pay the price of our redemption. Death held us under its yoke, but he in our place delivered himself into its power, that he might exempt us from it. This the Apostle means when he says, "that he tasted death for every man" (Heb. ii. 9). By dying he prevented us from dying; or (which is the same thing) he by his death purchased life for us (see Calvin in Psychopann). But in this he differed from us, that in permitting himself to be overcome of death, it was not so as to be ingulfed in its abyss, but rather to annihilate it, as it must otherwise have annihilated us ; he did not allow himself to be so subdued by it as to be crushed by its power; he rather laid it prostrate, when it was impending over us, and exulting over us as already overcome. In fine, his object was, "that through death he might destroy him that had the power of death, that is, the devil, and deliver them who through fear of death were all their lifetime subject to bondage" (Heb. ii. 14, 15). This is the first fruit which his death produced to us. Another is, that by fellowship with him he mortifies our earthly members, that they may

not afterwards exert themselves in action, and kills the old man, that he may not hereafter be in vigour and bring forth fruit. An effect of his burial, moreover, is, that we as his fellows are buried to sin. For when the Apostle says, that we are ingrafted into the likeness of Christ's death, and that we are buried with him unto sin, that by his cross the world is crucified unto us and we unto the world, and that we are dead with him, he not only exhorts us to manifest an example of his death, but declares that there is an efficacy in it which should appear in all Christians, if they would not render his death unfruitful and useless. Accordingly, in the death and burial of Christ a twofold blessing is set before us—viz. deliverance from death, to which we were enslaved, and the mortification of our flesh (Rom. vi. 5 ; Gal. ii. 19, vi. 14 ; Col. iii. 3).

8. Here we must not omit the descent to hell, which was of no little importance to the accomplishment of redemption. For although it is apparent from the writings of the ancient Fathers, that the clause which now stands in the Creed was not formerly so much used in the churches, still, in giving a summary of doctrine, a place must be assigned to it, as containing a matter of great importance which ought not by any means to be disregarded. Indeed, some of the ancient Fathers do not omit it,[1] and hence we may conjecture, that having been inserted in the Creed after a considerable lapse of time, it came into use in the Church not immediately but by degrees.[2] This much is uncontroverted, that it was in accordance with the general sentiment of all believers, since there is none of the Fathers who does not mention Christ's descent into hell, though they have various modes of explaining it. But it is of little consequence by whom and at what time it was introduced. The chief thing to be attended to in the Creed is, that it furnishes us with a full and every way complete summary of faith, containing nothing but what has been derived from the infallible word of God. But should any still scruple to give it admission into the Creed, it will shortly be made plain, that the place which it holds in a summary of our redemption is so important, that the omission of it greatly detracts from the benefit of Christ's death. There are some again who think that the article contains nothing new, but is merely a repetition in different words of what was previously said respecting burial, the word Hell (Infernis) being often used in Scripture for sepulchre. I admit the truth of what they allege with regard to the not unfrequent use of the term *infernis* for *sepulchre ;* but I cannot adopt their opinion, for two obvious reasons. First, What folly would it have been, after explaining a matter attended with no difficulty in clear and unambiguous terms, afterwards

---

1 It is not adverted to by Augustine, Lib. i. De Symbolo de Catechumenos.

2 The French of this sentence is, " Dont on peut conjecturer qu'il a esté tantost aprés le tems des Apostres adjousté ; mais que peu a peu il est venu en usage."—Whence we may conjecture that it was added some time after the days of the Apostles, but gradually came into use.

to involve rather than illustrate it by clothing it in obscure phraseology? When two expressions having the same meaning are placed together, the latter ought to be explanatory of the former. But what kind of explanation would it be to say, the expression, *Christ was buried*, means, that *he descended into hell?* My second reason is, the improbability that a superfluous tautology of this description should have crept into this compendium, in which the principal articles of faith are set down summarily in the fewest possible number of words. I have no doubt that all who weigh the matter with some degree of care will here agree with me.

9. Others interpret differently—viz. That Christ descended to the souls of the Patriarchs who died under the law, to announce his accomplished redemption, and bring them out of the prison in which they were confined. To this effect they wrest the passage [1] in the Psalms, "He hath broken the gates of brass, and cut the bars of iron in sunder" (Ps. cvii. 16); and also the passage in Zechariah, "I have sent forth thy prisoners out of the pit wherein is no water" (Zech. ix. 11). But since the psalm foretells the deliverance of those who were held captive in distant lands, and Zechariah comparing the Babylonish disaster into which the people had been plunged to a deep dry well or abyss, at the same time declares, that the salvation of the whole Church was an escape from a profound pit, I know not how it comes to pass, that posterity imagined it to be a subterraneous cavern, to which they gave the name of *Limbus*. Though this fable has the countenance of great authors, and is now also seriously defended by many as truth,[2] it is nothing but a fable. To conclude from it that the souls of the dead are in prison is childish. And what occasion was there that the soul of Christ should go down thither to set them at liberty? I readily admit that Christ illumined them by the power of his Spirit, enabling them to perceive that the grace of which they had only had a foretaste was then manifested to the world. And to this not improbably the passage of Peter may be applied, wherein he says, that Christ "went and preached to the spirits that were in prison" (or rather "a watch-tower") (1 Pet. iii. 19). The purport of the context is, that believers who had died before that time were partakers of the same grace with ourselves: for he celebrates the power of Christ's death, in that he penetrated even to the dead, pious souls obtaining an immediate view of that visitation for which they had anxiously waited; while, on the other hand, the reprobate were more clearly convinced that they were completely excluded from salvation. Although the passage in Peter is not perfectly definite, we

1 The French is, "Pour colorer leur fantaisie, ils tirent par les cheveux quelques temoignages."—To colour their fancy, they pull by the hair (violently wrest) certain passages.

2 See Justin, Ambrose, Jerome. The opinions of the Fathers and Rabbis on Hell and Limbus are collected by Peter Martyr, Loci Communes, Lib. iii. Loc. xvi. sect. 8: see Augustine, Ep. 99.

must not interpret as if he made no distinction between the righteous and the wicked : he only means to intimate, that the death of Christ was made known to both.

10. But, apart from the Creed, we must seek for a surer exposition of Christ's descent to hell : and the word of God furnishes us with one not only pious and holy, but replete with excellent consolation. Nothing had been done if Christ had only endured corporeal death. In order to interpose between us and God's anger, and satisfy his righteous judgment, it was necessary that he should feel the weight of divine vengeance. Whence also it was necessary that he should engage, as it were, at close quarters with the powers of hell and the horrors of eternal death. We lately quoted from the Prophet that the "chastisement of our peace was laid upon him," that he "was bruised for our iniquities," that he "bore our infirmities;" expressions which intimate, that, like a sponsor and surety for the guilty, and, as it were, subjected to condemnation, he undertook and paid all the penalties which must have been exacted from them, the only exception being, that the pains of death could not hold him. Hence there is nothing strange in its being said that he descended to hell, seeing he endured the death which is inflicted on the wicked by an angry God. It is frivolous and ridiculous to object that in this way the order is perverted, it being absurd that an event which preceded burial should be placed after it. But after explaining what Christ endured in the sight of man, the Creed appropriately adds the invisible and incomprehensible judgment which he endured before God, to teach us that not only was the body of Christ given up as the price of redemption, but that there was a greater and more excellent price—that he bore in his soul the tortures of condemned and ruined man.

11. In this sense, Peter says that God raised up Christ, "having loosed the pains of death : because it was not possible he should be holden of it" (Acts ii. 24). He does not mention death simply, but says that the Son of God endured the pains produced by the curse and wrath of God, the source of death. How small a matter had it been to come forth securely, and as it were in sport to undergo death. Herein was a true proof of boundless mercy, that he shunned not the death he so greatly dreaded. And there can be no doubt that, in the Epistle to the Hebrews, the Apostle means to teach the same thing when he says that he "was heard in that he feared" (Heb. v. 7). Some, instead of "feared," use a term meaning reverence or piety, but how inappropriately, is apparent both from the nature of the thing and the form of expression.[1] Christ then praying in a loud voice, and with tears, is heard in that he feared, not so as to be ex-

---

[1] French, "Les autres translatent Reverence ou Piété; mais la Grammaire et la matiere qui est la tracté monstrent que c'est mal à propos."—Others translate Reverence or Piety; but Grammar and the subject-matter show that they do it very unseasonably

empted from death, but so as not to be swallowed up of it like a sinner, though standing as our representative. And certainly no abyss can be imagined more dreadful than to feel that you are abandoned and forsaken of God, and not heard when you invoke him, just as if he had conspired your destruction. To such a degree was Christ dejected, that in the depth of his agony he was forced to exclaim, " My God, my God, why hast thou forsaken me ?" The view taken by some, that he here expressed the opinion of others rather than his own conviction, is most improbable ; for it is evident that the expression was wrung from the anguish of his inmost soul. We do not, however, insinuate that God was ever hostile to him or angry with him.[1] How could he be angry with the beloved Son, with whom his soul was well pleased ? or how could he have appeased the Father by his intercession for others if He were hostile to himself? But this we say, that he bore the weight of the divine anger, that, smitten and afflicted, he experienced all the signs of an angry and avenging God. Hence Hilary argues, that to this descent we owe our exemption from death. Nor does he dissent from this view in other passages, as when he says, " The cross, death, hell, are our life." And again, " The Son of God is in hell, but man is brought back to heaven." And why do I quote the testimony of a private writer, when an Apostle asserts the same thing, stating it as one fruit of his victory that he delivered "them who through fear of death were all their lifetime subject to bondage?" (Heb. ii. 15). He behoved, therefore, to conquer the fear which incessantly vexes and agitates the breasts of all mortals ; and this he could not do without a contest. Moreover, it will shortly appear with greater clearness that his was no common sorrow, was not the result of a trivial cause. Thus by engaging with the power of the devil, the fear of death, and the pains of hell, he gained the victory, and achieved a triumph, so that we now fear not in death those things which our Prince has destroyed.[2]

12. Here some miserable creatures, who, though unlearned, are however impelled more by malice than ignorance, cry out that I am offering an atrocious insult to Christ, because it were most incongruous to hold that he feared for the safety of his soul. And then in harsher terms they urge the calumnious charge that I attribute despair to the Son of God, a feeling the very opposite of faith. First, they wickedly raise a controversy as to the fear and dread which Christ felt, though these are openly affirmed by the Evangelists. For before the hour of his death arrived, he was troubled in spirit, and affected with grief ; and at the very onset began to be exceedingly amazed. To speak of these feelings as merely assumed, is a shameful evasion. It becomes us, therefore (as Ambrose truly teaches), boldly

1 See Cyril. Lib. ii. De Recta Fide ad Reginas ; Item, Hilarius de Trinitate, Lib. iv c. 2 and 3.
2 Vide Luther, tom. i. in Concione de Morte, fol. 87.

to profess the agony of Christ, if we are not ashamed of the cross. And certainly had not his soul shared in the punishment, he would have been a Redeemer of bodies only. The object of his struggle was to raise up those who were lying prostrate; and so far is this from detracting from his heavenly glory, that his goodness, which can never be sufficiently extolled, becomes more conspicuous in this, that he declined not to bear our infirmities. Hence also that solace to our anxieties and griefs which the Apostle sets before us: "We have not an high priest who cannot be touched with the feeling of our infirmities; but was in all respects tempted like as we are, yet without sin" (Heb. iv. 15). These men pretend that a thing in its nature vitious is improperly ascribed to Christ; as if they were wiser than the Spirit of God, who in the same passage reconciles the two things —viz. that he was tempted in all respects like as we are, and yet was without sin. There is no reason, therefore, to take alarm at infirmity in Christ, infirmity to which he submitted not under the constraint of violence and necessity, but merely because he loved and pitied us. Whatever he spontaneously suffered, detracts in no degree from his majesty. One thing which misleads these detractors is, that they do not recognise in Christ an infirmity which was pure and free from every species of taint, inasmuch as it was kept within the limits of obedience. As no moderation can be seen in the depravity of our nature, in which all affections with turbulent impetuosity exceed their due bounds, they improperly apply the same standard to the Son of God. But as he was upright, all his affections were under such restraint as prevented everything like excess. Hence he could resemble us in grief, fear, and dread, but still with this mark of distinction. Thus refuted. they fly off to another cavil, that although Christ feared death, yet he feared not the curse and wrath of God, from which he knew that he was safe. But let the pious reader consider how far it is honourable to Christ to make him more effeminate and timid than the generality of men. Robbers and other malefactors contumaciously hasten to death, many men magnanimously despise it, others meet it calmly. If the Son of God was amazed and terror-struck at the prospect of it, where was his firmness or magnanimity? We are even told, what in a common death would have been deemed most extraordinary, that in the depth of his agony his sweat was like great drops of blood falling to the ground. Nor was this a spectacle exhibited to the eyes of others, since it was from a secluded spot that he uttered his groans to his Father. And that no doubt may remain, it was necessary that angels should come down from heaven to strengthen him with miraculous consolation. How shamefully effeminate would it have been (as I have observed) to be so excruciated by the fear of an ordinary death as to sweat drops of blood, and not even be revived by the presence of angels? What? Does not that prayer, thrice repeated, "Father, if it be possible, let this cup pass from me" (Matth. xxvi. 39), a prayer dictated by incredible bitterness of soul, show that Christ had a fiercer and more arduous struggle than with ordinary death?

Hence it appears that these triflers, with whom I am disputing, presume to talk of what they know not, never having seriously considered what is meant and implied by ransoming us from the justice of God. It is of consequence to understand aright how much our salvation cost the Son of God. If any one now ask, Did Christ descend to hell at the time when he deprecated death? I answer, that this was the commencement, and that from it we may infer how dire and dreadful were the tortures which he endured when he felt himself standing at the bar of God as a criminal in our stead. And although the divine power of the Spirit veiled itself for a moment, that it might give place to the infirmity of the flesh, we must understand that the trial arising from feelings of grief and fear was such as not to be at variance with faith. And in this was fulfilled what is said in Peter's sermon as to having been loosed from the pains of death, because "it was not possible he could be holden of it" (Acts ii. 24). Though feeling, as it were, forsaken of God, he did not cease in the slightest degree to confide in his goodness. This appears from the celebrated prayer in which, in the depth of his agony, he exclaimed, "My God, my God, why hast thou forsaken me?" (Matth. xxvii. 46). Amid all his agony he ceases not to call upon his God, while exclaiming that he is forsaken by him. This refutes the Apollinarian heresy, as well as that of those who are called Monothelites. Apollinaris pretended, that in Christ the eternal Spirit supplied the place of a soul, so that he was only half a man; as if he could have expiated our sins in any other way than by obeying the Father. But where does the feeling or desire of obedience reside but in the soul? and we know that his soul was troubled in order that ours, being free from trepidation, might obtain peace and quiet. Moreover, in opposition to the Monothelites, we see that in his human he felt a repugnance to what he willed in his divine nature. I say nothing of his subduing the fear of which we have spoken by a contrary affection. This appearance of repugnance is obvious in the words, "Father, save me from this hour: but for this cause came I unto this hour. Father, glorify thy name" (John xii. 27, 28). Still, in this perplexity, there was no violent emotion, such as we exhibit while making the strongest endeavours to subdue our own feelings.

13. Next follows the resurrection from the dead, without which all that has hitherto been said would be defective. For seeing that in the cross, death and burial of Christ, nothing but weakness appears, faith must go beyond all these, in order that it may be provided with full strength. Hence, although in his death we have an effectual completion of salvation, because by it we are reconciled to God, satisfaction is given to his justice, the curse is removed, and the penalty paid; still it is not by his death, but by his resurrection, that we are said to be begotten again to a living hope (1 Pet. i. 3): because, as

he, by rising again, became victorious over death, so the victory of our faith consists only in his resurrection. The nature of it is better expressed in the words of Paul, " Who (Christ) was delivered for our offences, and was raised again for our justification" (Rom. iv. 25); as if he had said, By his death sin was taken away, by his resurrection righteousness was renewed and restored. For how could he by dying have freed us from death, if he had yielded to its power? how could he have obtained the victory for us, if he had fallen in the contest?

Our salvation may be thus divided between the death and the resurrection of Christ: by the former, sin was abolished and death annihilated; by the latter, righteousness was restored and life revived, the power and efficacy of the former being still bestowed upon us by means of the latter. Paul accordingly affirms, that he was declared to be the Son of God by his resurrection (Rom. i. 4), because he then fully displayed that heavenly power which is both a bright mirror of his divinity, and a sure support of our faith; as he also elsewhere teaches, that "though he was crucified through weakness, yet he liveth by the power of God" (2 Cor. xiii. 4). In the same sense, in another passage, treating of perfection, he says, " That I may know him and the power of his resurrection" (Phil. iii. 10). Immediately after he adds, "being made conformable unto his death." In perfect accordance with this is the passage in Peter, that God "raised him up from the dead, and gave him glory, that your faith and hope might be in God" (1 Pet. i. 21). Not that faith founded merely on his death is vacillating, but that the divine power by which he maintains our faith is most conspicuous in his resurrection. Let us remember, therefore, that when death only is mentioned, everything peculiar to the resurrection is at the same time included, and that there is a like synecdoche in the term *resurrection*, as often as it is used apart from death, everything peculiar to death being included. But as, by rising again, he obtained the victory, and became the resurrection and the life, Paul justly argues, " If Christ be not raised, your faith is vain; ye are yet in your sins" (1 Cor. xv. 17). Accordingly, in another passage, after exulting in the death of Christ in opposition to the terrors of condemnation, he thus enlarges, " Christ that died, yea rather, that is risen again, who is even at the right hand of God, who also maketh intercession for us" (Rom. viii. 34). Then, as we have already explained that the mortification of our flesh depends on communion with the cross, so we must also understand, that a corresponding benefit is derived from his resurrection. For as the Apostle says, " Like as Christ was raised up from the dead by the glory of the Father, even so we also should walk in newness of life" (Rom. vi. 4). Accordingly, as in another passage, from our being dead with Christ, he inculcates, " Mortify therefore your members which are upon the earth" (Col. iii. 5); so from our being risen with Christ he infers, " seek those things which are above, where Christ sitteth at the right hand of God" (Col. iii. 1). In these words we are not only urged by the example of a risen Saviour to follow newness of life, but are taught that by his power we are renewed unto righteousness. A third benefit derived from it is, that, like an earnest, it assures us of our own resurrection, of which it is certain that his is the surest representation. This subject is discussed at length (1 Cor. xv). But it is to be observed, in passing, that when he is said to have "risen from the dead," these terms express the reality both of his death and resurrection, as if it had been said, that he died the same death as other men naturally die, and received immortality in the same mortal flesh which he had assumed.

14. The resurrection is naturally followed by the ascension into heaven. For although Christ, by rising again, began fully to display his glory and virtue, having laid aside the abject and ignoble condition of a mortal life, and the ignominy of the cross, yet it was only by his ascension to heaven that his reign truly commenced. This the Apostle shows, when he says he ascended "that he might fill all things" (Eph. iv. 10); thus reminding us that, under the appearance of contradiction, there is a beautiful harmony, inasmuch as though he departed from us, it was that his departure might be more useful to us than that presence which was confined in a humble tabernacle of flesh during his abode on the earth. Hence John, after repeating the celebrated invitation, "If any man thirst, let him come unto me and drink," immediately adds, "the Holy Ghost was not yet given; because that Jesus was not yet glorified" (John vii. 37, 39). This our Lord himself also declared to his disciples, "It is expedient for you that I go away: for if I go not away, the Comforter will not come unto you" (John xvi. 7). To console them for his bodily absence, he tells them that he will not leave them comfortless, but will come again to them in a manner invisible indeed, but more to be desired, because they were then taught by a surer experience that the government which he had obtained, and the power which he exercises, would enable his faithful followers not only to live well, but also to die happily. And, indeed, we see how much more abundantly his Spirit was poured out, how much more gloriously his kingdom was advanced, how much greater power was employed in aiding his followers and discomfiting his enemies. Being raised to heaven, he withdrew his bodily presence from our sight, not that he might cease to be with his followers, who are still pilgrims on the earth, but that he might rule both heaven and earth more immediately by his power; or rather, the promise which he made to be with us even to the end of the world, he fulfilled by this ascension, by which, as his body has been raised above all heavens, so his power and efficacy have been propagated and diffused beyond all the bounds of heaven and earth. This I prefer to explain in the words of Augustine rather than my own: "Through death Christ was to go to the right hand of the Father, whence he is to come to judge the quick and the dead, and

that in corporal presence, according to the sound doctrine and rule of faith. For, in spiritual presence, he was to be with them after his ascension" (August. Tract. in Joann. 109). In another passage he is more full and explicit: "In regard to ineffable and invisible grace, is fulfilled what he said, Lo, I am with you alway, even to the end of the world (Matth. xxviii. 20); but in regard to the flesh which the Word assumed, in regard to his being born of a Virgin, in regard to his being apprehended by the Jews, nailed to the tree, taken down from the cross, wrapt in linen clothes, laid in the sepulchre, and manifested on his resurrection, it may be said, Me ye have not always with you. Why? because, in bodily presence, he conversed with his disciples forty days, and leading them out where they saw, but followed not, he ascended into heaven, and is not here: for there he sits at the right hand of the Father: and yet he is here, for the presence of his Godhead was not withdrawn. Therefore, as regards his divine presence, we have Christ always: as regards his bodily presence, it was truly said to the disciples, Me ye have not always. For a few days the Church had him bodily present. Now, she apprehends him by faith, but sees him not by the eye" (August. Tract. 51).

15. Hence it is immediately added, that he "sitteth at the right hand of God the Father;" a similitude borrowed from princes, who have their assessors to whom they commit the office of ruling and issuing commands. Thus Christ, in whom the Father is pleased to be exalted, and by whose hand he is pleased to reign, is said to have been received up, and seated on his right hand (Mark xvi. 19); as if it had been said, that he was installed in the government of heaven and earth, and formally admitted to possession of the administration committed to him, and not only admitted for once, but to continue until he descend to judgment. For so the Apostle interprets, when he says, that the Father "set him at his own right hand in the heavenly places, far above all principality, and power, and might, and dominion, and every name that is named not only in this world, but also in that which is to come; and hath put all things under his feet, and given him to be the head over all things to the Church."[1] You see to what end he is so seated—namely, that all creatures both in heaven and earth should reverence his majesty, be ruled by his hand, do him implicit homage, and submit to his power. All that the Apostles intend, when they so often mention his seat at the Father's hand, is to teach that everything is placed at his disposal. Those therefore are in error, who suppose that his blessedness merely is indicated. We may observe, that there is nothing contrary to this doctrine in the testimony of Stephen, that he saw him standing (Acts vii. 56), the subject here considered being not the position of his body, but the majesty of his empire, *sitting* meaning nothing more than presiding on the judgment-seat of heaven.

[1] Ephes. i. 20; Phil. ii. 9; 1 Cor. xv. 27; Ephes. iv. 15; Acts ii. 33; iii. 21; Heb. i. 4.

16. From this doctrine faith derives manifold advantages.[1]   First, it perceives that the Lord, by his ascension to heaven, has opened up the access to the heavenly kingdom, which Adam had shut.   For having entered it in our flesh, as it were in our name, it follows, as the Apostle says, that we are in a manner now seated in heavenly places, not entertaining a mere hope of heaven, but possessing it in our head.   Secondly, faith perceives that his seat beside the Father is not without great advantage to us.   Having entered the temple not made with hands, he constantly appears as our advocate and intercessor in the presence of the Father ; directs attention to his own righteousness, so as to turn it away from our sins ; so reconciles him to us, as by his intercession to pave for us a way of access to his throne, presenting it to miserable sinners, to whom it would otherwise be an object of dread, as replete with grace and mercy.   Thirdly, it discerns his power, on which depend our strength, might, resources, and triumph over hell, " When he ascended up on high, he led captivity captive " (Eph. iv. 8).   Spoiling his foes, he gave gifts to his people, and daily loads them with spiritual riches.   He thus occupies his exalted seat, that, thence transferring his virtue unto us, he may quicken us to spiritual life, sanctify us by his Spirit, and adorn his Church with various graces, by his protection preserve it safe from all harm, and by the strength of his hand curb the enemies raging against his cross and our salvation ; in fine, that he may possess all power in heaven and earth, until he have utterly routed all his foes, who are also ours, and completed the structure of his Church.   Such is the true nature of the kingdom, such the power which the Father has conferred upon him, until he arrive to complete the last act by judging the quick and the dead.

17. Christ, indeed, gives his followers no dubious proofs of present power, but as his kingdom in the world is in a manner veiled by the humiliation of a carnal condition, faith is most properly invited to meditate on the visible presence which he will exhibit on the last day. For he will descend from heaven in visible form, in like manner as he was seen to ascend,[2] and appear to all, with the ineffable majesty of his kingdom, the splendour of immortality, the boundless power of divinity, and an attending company of angels.   Hence we are told to wait for the Redeemer against that day on which he will separate the sheep from the goats, and the elect from the reprobate, and when not one individual either of the living or the dead shall escape his judgment.   From the extremities of the universe shall be heard the clang of the trumpet summoning all to his tribunal ; both those whom that day shall find alive, and those whom death shall previously have removed from the society of the living.   There are some who take the words, *quick* and *dead*, in a different sense ;[3] and, indeed, some an-

---

1 August. de Fide et Symbolo, cap. 8 ; Eph. ii. 6 ; Heb. vii. 25 ; ix. 11.
2 Acts i. 11 ; Matth. xxiv. 30 ; xxv. 31 ; 1 Thess. iv. 16, 17.
3 The French is, " Il y en a aucuns qui exposent par les vivans et les morts, les bons

cient writers appear to have hesitated as to the exposition of them ; but our meaning being plain and clear, is much more accordant with the Creed, which was certainly written for popular use. There is nothing contrary to it in the Apostle's declaration, that it is appointed unto all men once to die. For though those who are surviving at the last day shall not die after a natural manner, yet the change which they are to undergo, as it shall resemble, is not improperly. called, death (Heb. ix. 27). "We shall not all sleep, but we shall all be changed" (1 Cor. xv. 51). What does this mean? Their mortal life shall perish and be swallowed up in one moment, and be transformed into an entirely new nature. Though no one can deny that that destruction of the flesh will be death, it still remains true that the quick and the dead shall be summoned to judgment (1 Thess. iv. 16): for "the dead in Christ shall rise first; then we which are alive and remain shall be caught up together with them in the clouds to meet the Lord in the air." Indeed, it is probable, that these words in the Creed were taken from Peter's sermon as related by Luke (Acts x. 42), and from the solemn charge of Paul to Timothy (2 Tim. iv. 1).

18. It is most consolatory to think, that judgment is vested in him who has already destined us to share with him in the honour of judgment (Matth. xix. 28) ; so far is it from being true, that he will ascend the judgment-seat for our condemnation. How could a most merciful prince destroy his own people ? how could the head disperse its own members ? how could the advocate condemn his clients ? For if the Apostle, when contemplating the interposition of Christ, is bold to exclaim, "Who is he that condemneth?" (Rom. viii. 33), much more certain is it that Christ, the intercessor, will not condemn those whom he has admitted to his protection. It certainly gives no small security, that we shall be sisted at no other tribunal than that of our Redeemer, from whom salvation is to be expected; and that he who in the Gospel now promises eternal blessedness, will then as judge ratify his promise.[1] The end for which the Father has honoured the Son by committing all judgment to him (John v. 22), was to pacify the consciences of his people when alarmed at the thought of judgment. Hitherto I have followed the order of the Apostles' Creed, because it states the leading articles of redemption in a few words, and may thus serve as a tablet in which the points of Christian doctrine, most deserving of attention, are brought separately and distinctly before us.[2] I call it the Apostles' Creed, though I am by no

---

et les mauvais."—There are some who, by the quick and the dead, understand the good and the bad.

[1] Vide Ambros. de Jac. et Vita Beata, Lib. i. c. 6.

[2] The French is, "Jusques ici j'ay suivi l'ordre du Symbole qu'on appelle des Apostres, pource que la nous pouvons voir comme en un tableau, par les articles qui y sont contenus, en quoy gist nostre salut : et par ce moyen aussi entendons a quelles choses il nous faut arrester pour obtenir salut en Jesus Christ."—Hitherto I have followed the order of what is called the Apostles' Creed, because there we may see, as in a tablet,

means solicitous as to its authorship. The general consent of ancient writers certainly does ascribe it to the Apostles, either because they imagined it was written and published by them for common use, or because they thought it right to give the sanction of such authority to a compendium faithfully drawn up from the doctrine delivered by their hands. I have no doubt that, from the very commencement of the Church, and, therefore, in the very days of the Apostles, it held the place of a public and universally received confession, whatever be the quarter from which it originally proceeded. It is not probable that it was written by some private individual, since it is certain that, from time immemorial, it was deemed of sacred authority by all Christians. The only point of consequence we hold to be incontrovertible—viz. that it gives, in clear and succinct order, a full statement of our faith, and in everything which it contains is sanctioned by the sure testimony of Scripture. This being understood, it were to no purpose to labour anxiously, or quarrel with any one as to the authorship, unless, indeed, we think it not enough to possess the sure truth of the Holy Spirit, without, at the same time, knowing by whose mouth it was pronounced, or by whose hand it was written.

19. When we see that the whole sum of our salvation, and every single part of it, are comprehended in Christ, we must beware of deriving even the minutest portion of it from any other quarter. If we seek salvation, we are taught by the very name of Jesus that he possesses it;[1] if we seek any other gifts of the Spirit, we shall find them in his unction ; strength in his government ; purity in his conception ; indulgence in his nativity, in which he was made like us in all respects, in order that he might learn to sympathise with us : if we seek redemption, we shall find it in his passion ; acquittal in his condemnation ; remission of the curse in his cross ; satisfaction in his sacrifice ; purification in his blood ; reconciliation in his descent to hell ; mortification of the flesh in his sepulchre ; newness of life in his resurrection ; immortality also in his resurrection ; the inheritance of a celestial kingdom in his entrance into heaven ; protection, security, and the abundant supply of all blessings, in his kingdom ; secure anticipation of judgment in the power of judging committed to him. In fine, since in him all kinds of blessings are treasured up; let us draw a full supply from him, and none from any other quarter. Those who, not satisfied with him alone, entertain various hopes from others, though they may continue to look to him chiefly, deviate from the right path by the simple fact, that some portion of their thought takes a different direction. No distrust of this description can arise when once the abundance of his blessings is properly known:

by the articles which are contained in it, wherein consists our salvation, and by this means also understand on what things we ought to dwell in order to obtain salvation in Jesus Christ.

[1] Acts iv. 12; 1 Cor. i. 30; Heb. ii. 17; Gal. iii. 8.

CHAPTER XVII.

CHRIST RIGHTLY AND PROPERLY SAID TO HAVE MERITED GRACE AND SALVATION FOR US.

The three leading divisions of this chapter are,—I. A proof from reason and from Scripture that the grace of God and the merit of Christ (the prince and author of our salvation) are perfectly compatible, sec. 1 and 2.   II. Christ, by his obedience, even to the death of the cross (which was the price of our redemption), merited divine favour for us, sec. 3—5.   III. The presumptuous rashness of the Schoolmen in treating this branch of doctrine.

Sections.

1. Christ not only the minister, but also the author and prince of salvation. Divine grace not obscured by this mode of expression. The merit of Christ not opposed to the mercy of God, but depends upon it.
2. The compatibility of the two proved by various passages of Scripture.
3. Christ by his obedience truly merited divine grace for us.
4. This grace obtained by the shedding of Christ's blood and his obedience even unto death.
5. In this way he paid our ransom.
6. The presumptuous manner in which the Schoolmen handle this subject.

1. A QUESTION must here be considered by way of supplement. Some men too much given to subtilty, while they admit that we obtain salvation through Christ, will not hear of the name of merit, by which they imagine that the grace of God is obscured ; and therefore insist that Christ was only the instrument or minister, not the author or leader, or prince of life, as he is designated by Peter (Acts iii. 15).   I admit that were Christ opposed simply, and by himself, to the justice of God, there could be no room for merit, because there cannot be found in man a worth which could make God a debtor ; nay, as Augustine says most truly,[1] "The Saviour, the man Christ Jesus, is himself the brightest illustration of predestination and grace : his character as such was not procured by any antecedent merit of works or faith in his human nature.   Tell me, I pray, how that man, when assumed into unity of person by the Word, co-eternal with the Father, as the only begotten Son of God, could merit this." —"Let the very fountain of grace, therefore, appear in our head, whence, according to the measure of each, it is diffused through all his members.   Every man, from the commencement of his faith, becomes a Christian, by the same grace by which that man from his

[1] August. de Prædest. Sanct. Lib. i. c. xv.; De Bono Perseverantia, cap. ult.   See supra, chapter xiv. sec. 7.

formation became Christ." Again, in another passage, " There is not a more striking example of predestination than the Mediator himself. He who made him (without any antecedent merit in his will) of the seed of David a righteous man never to be unrighteous, also converts those who are members of his head from unrighteous into righteous," and so forth. Therefore, when we treat of the merit of Christ, we do not place the beginning in him, but we ascend to the ordination of God as the primary cause, because of his mere good pleasure he appointed a Mediator to purchase salvation for us. Hence the merit of Christ is inconsiderately opposed to the mercy of God. It is a well-known rule, that principal and accessory are not incompatible, and therefore there is nothing to prevent the justification of man from being the gratuitous result of the mere mercy of God, and, at the same time, to prevent the merit of Christ from intervening in subordination to this mercy. The free favour of God is as fitly opposed to our works as is the obedience of Christ, both in their order : for Christ could not merit anything save by the good pleasure of God, but only inasmuch as he was destined to appease the wrath of God by his sacrifice, and wipe away our transgressions by his obedience : in one word, since the merit of Christ depends entirely on the grace of God (which provided this mode of salvation for us), the latter is no less appropriately opposed to all righteousness of men than is the former.

2. This distinction is found in numerous passages of Scripture : " God so loved the world, that he gave his only begotten Son, that whosoever believeth in him might not perish (John iii. 16). We see that the first place is assigned to the love of God as the chief cause or origin, and that faith in Christ follows as the second and more proximate cause. Should any one object that Christ is only the formal cause,[1] he lessens his energy more than the words justify. For if we obtain justification by a faith which leans on him, the groundwork of our salvation must be sought in him. This is clearly proved by several passages : " Herein is love, not that we loved God, but that he loved us, and sent his Son to be the propitiation for our sins " (1 John iv. 10). These words clearly demonstrate that God, in order to remove any obstacle to his love towards us, appointed the method of reconciliation in Christ. There is great force in this word *propitiation;* for in a manner which cannot be expressed, God, at the very time when he loved us, was hostile to us until reconciled in Christ. To this effect are all the following passages : " He is the propitiation for our sins ;" " It pleased the Father that in him should all fulness dwell, and having made peace by the blood of his cross, by him to reconcile all things unto himself ;" " God was in Christ reconciling the world unto himself, not imputing their trespasses

"appeasing" [margin note]

---

[1] The French adds, " C'est a dire, qui n'emporte en soy vrai effect ;"—that is to say, which in itself produces no true effect.

unto them ;" " He hath made us accepted in the Beloved," " That he might reconcile both into one body by the cross."[1] The nature of this mystery is to be learned from the first chapter to the Ephesians, where Paul, teaching that we were chosen in Christ, at the same time adds, that we obtained grace in him. How did God begin to embrace with his favour those whom he had loved before the foundation of the world, unless in displaying his love when he was reconciled by the blood of Christ ? As God is the fountain of all righteousness, he must necessarily be the enemy and judge of man so long as he is a sinner. Wherefore, the commencement of love is the bestowing of righteousness, as described by Paul : " He hath made him to be sin for us who knew no sin ; that we might be made the righteousness of God in him " (2 Cor. v. 21). He intimates, that by the sacrifice of Christ we obtain free justification, and become pleasing to God, though we are by nature the children of wrath, and by sin estranged from him. This distinction is also noted whenever the grace of Christ is connected with the love of God (2 Cor. xiii. 13); whence it follows, that he bestows upon us of his own which he acquired by purchase. For otherwise there would be no ground for the praise ascribed to him by the Father, that grace is his, and proceeds from him.

3. That Christ, by his obedience, truly purchased and merited grace for us with the Father, is accurately inferred from several passages of Scripture. I take it for granted, that if Christ satisfied for our sins, if he paid the penalty due by us, if he appeased God by his obedience; in fine, if he suffered the just for the unjust, salvation was obtained for us by his righteousness ; which is just equivalent to meriting. Now, Paul's testimony is, that we were reconciled, and received reconciliation through his death (Rom. v. 11). But there is no room for reconciliation unless where offence[2] has preceded. The meaning therefore is, that God, to whom we were hateful through sin, was appeased by the death of his Son, and made propitious to us. And the antithesis which immediately follows is carefully to be observed, " As by one man's disobedience many were made sinners, so by the obedience of one shall many be made righteous " (Rom. v. 19). For the meaning is—As by the sin of Adam we were alienated from God and doomed to destruction, so by the obedience of Christ we are restored to his favour as if we were righteous. The future tense of the verb does not exclude present righteousness, as is apparent from the context. For he had previously said, " the free gift is of many offences unto justification."

4. When we say, that grace was obtained for us by the merit of Christ, our meaning is, that we were cleansed by his blood, that his death was an expiation for sin, " His blood cleanses us from all sin."

[1] 1 John ii. 2; Col. i. 19, 20; 2 Cor. v. 19; Eph. i. 6; ii. 16.
[2] French, " Offense, haine, divorce ;"—offence, hatred, divorce.

"This is my blood, which is shed for the remission of sins" (1 John i. 7; Luke xxii. 20). If the effect of his shed blood is, that our sins are not imputed to us, it follows, that by that price the justice of God was satisfied. To the same effect are the Baptist's words, "Behold the Lamb of God, which taketh away the sin of the world" (John i. 29). For he contrasts Christ with all the sacrifices of the Law, showing that in him alone was fulfilled what these figures typified. But we know the common expression in Moses—Iniquity shall be expiated, sin shall be wiped away and forgiven. In short, we are admirably taught by the ancient figures what power and efficacy there is in Christ's death. And the Apostle, skilfully proceeding from this principle, explains the whole matter in the Epistle to the Hebrews, showing that without shedding of blood there is no remission (Heb. ix. 22). From this he infers, that Christ appeared once for all to take away sin by the sacrifice of himself. Again, that he was offered to bear the sins of many (Heb. ix. 28). He had previously said, that not by the blood of goats or of heifers, but by his own blood, he had once entered into the holy of holies, having obtained eternal redemption for us. Now, when he reasons thus, "If the blood of bulls and of goats, and the ashes of an heifer sprinkling the unclean, sanctifieth to the purifying of the flesh: how much more shall the blood of Christ, who through the eternal Spirit offered himself to God, purge your consciences from dead works to serve the living God?" (Heb. ix. 13, 14), it is obvious that too little effect is given to the grace of Christ, unless we concede to his sacrifice the power of expiating, appeasing, and satisfying: as he shortly after adds, "For this cause he is the mediator of the new testament, that by means of his death, for the redemption of the transgressions that were under the first testament, they which are called might receive the promise of eternal inheritance" (Heb. ix. 15). But it is especially necessary to attend to the analogy which is drawn by Paul as to his having been made a curse for us (Gal. iii. 13). It had been superfluous and therefore absurd, that Christ should have been burdened with a curse, had it not been in order that, by paying what others owed, he might acquire righteousness for them. There is no ambiguity in Isaiah's testimony, "He was wounded for our transgressions, he was bruised for our iniquities: the chastisement of our peace was laid upon him; and with his stripes we are healed" (Is. liii. 5). For had not Christ satisfied for our sins, he could not be said to have appeased God by taking upon himself the penalty which we had incurred. To this corresponds what follows in the same place, "for the transgression of my people was he stricken" (Is. liii. 8). We may add the interpretation of Peter, who unequivocally declares, that he "bare our sins in his own body on the tree" (1 Pet. ii. 24), that the whole burden of condemnation, of which we were relieved, was laid upon him.

5. The Apostles also plainly declare that he paid a price to ransom us from death: "Being justified freely by his grace, through the re-

demption that is in Christ Jesus: whom God hath set forth to be a propitiation through faith in his blood" (Rom. iii. 24, 25). Paul commends the grace of God, in that he gave the price of redemption in the death of Christ; and he exhorts us to flee to his blood, that having obtained righteousness, we may appear boldly before the judgment-seat of God. To the same effect are the words of Peter: "Forasmuch as ye know that ye were not redeemed with corruptible things, as silver and gold,"——" but with the precious blood of Christ, as of a lamb without blemish and without spot" (1 Pet. i. 18, 19). The antithesis would be incongruous if he had not by this price made satisfaction for sins. For which reason, Paul says, "Ye are bought with a price." Nor could it be elsewhere said, there is "one mediator between God and men, the man Christ Jesus; who gave himself a ransom for all" (1 Tim. ii. 5, 6), had not the punishment which we deserved been laid upon him. Accordingly, the same Apostle declares, that "we have redemption through his blood, even the forgiveness of sins" (Col. i. 14); as if he had said, that we are justified or acquitted before God, because that blood serves the purpose of satisfaction. With this another passage agrees—viz. that he blotted out "the handwriting of ordinances which was against us, which was contrary to us" (Col. ii. 14). These words denote the payment or compensation which acquits us from guilt. There is great weight also in these words of Paul: "If righteousness come by the law, then Christ is dead in vain" (Gal. ii. 21). For we hence infer, that it is from Christ we must seek what the Law would confer on any one who fulfilled it; or, which is the same thing, that by the grace of Christ we obtain what God promised in the Law to our works: "If a man do, he shall live in them" (Lev. xviii. 5). This is no less clearly taught in the discourse at Antioch, when Paul declares, "That through this man is preached unto you the forgiveness of sins; and by him all that believe are justified from all things, from which ye could not be justified by the law of Moses" (Acts xiii. 38, 39). For if the observance of the Law is righteousness, who can deny that Christ, by taking this burden upon himself, and reconciling us to God, as if we were the observers of the Law, merited favour for us? Of the same nature is what he afterwards says to the Galatians: "God sent forth his Son, made of a woman, made under the law, to redeem them that were under the law" (Gal. iv. 4, 5). For to what end that subjection, unless that he obtained justification for us by undertaking to perform what we were unable to pay? Hence that imputation of righteousness without works, of which Paul treats (Rom. iv. 5), the righteousness found in Christ alone being accepted as if it were ours. And certainly the only reason why Christ is called our "meat" (John vi. 55), is because we find in him the substance of life. And the source of this efficacy is just that the Son of God was crucified as the price of our justification; as Paul says, Christ "hath given himself for us an offering and a sacrifice to God for a sweet-smelling savour" (Eph. v. 2); and elsewhere, he "was delivered for our offences, and was raised again for our justification" (Rom. iv. 25). Hence it is proved not only that salvation was given us by Christ, but that on account of him the Father is now propitious to us. For it cannot be doubted that in him is completely fulfilled what God declares by Isaiah under a figure, "I will defend this city to save it for mine own sake, and for my servant David's sake" (Isaiah xxxvii. 35). Of this the Apostle is the best witness, when he says, "Your sins are forgiven you for his name's sake" (1 John. ii. 12). For although the name of Christ is not expressed, John, in his usual manner, designates him by the pronoun "He" (αὐτὸς). In the same sence also our Lord declares, "As the living Father hath sent me, and I live by the Father: so he that eateth me, even he shall live by me" (John vi. 57). To this corresponds the passage of Paul, "Unto you it is given in the behalf of Christ, not only to believe in him, but also to suffer for his sake" (Phil i. 29).

6. To inquire, as Lombard and the Schoolmen do (Sent. Lib. III. Dist. 18), whether he merited for himself, is foolish curiosity. Equally rash is their decision when they answer in the affirmative. How could it be necessary for the only Son of God to come down in order to acquire some new quality for himself? The exposition which God gives of his own purpose removes all doubt. The Father is not said to have consulted the advantage of his Son in his services, but to have given him up to death, and not spared him, because he loved the world (Rom. viii). The prophetical expressions should be observed: "To us a Son is born;" "Rejoice greatly, O daughter of Zion: shout, O daughter of Jerusalem: behold, thy King cometh unto thee" (Isaiah ix. 6; Zech. ix. 9). It would otherwise be a cold commendation of love which Paul describes, when he says, "God commendeth his love toward us, in that, while we were yet sinners, Christ died for us" (Rom. v. 8). Hence, again, we infer that Christ had no regard to himself; and this he distinctly affirms, when he says, "For their sakes I sanctify myself" (John xvii. 19). He who transfers the benefit of his holiness to others, testifies that he acquires nothing for himself. And surely it is most worthy of remark, that Christ, in devoting himself entirely to our salvation, in a manner forgot himself. It is absurd to wrest the testimony of Paul to a different effect: "Wherefore God hath highly exalted him, and given him a name which is above every name" (Phil. ii. 9).[1] By what services could a man merit to become the judge of the world, the head of angels, to obtain the supreme government of God, and become the residence of that majesty of which all the virtues of men and angels

---

[1] The sentence stands thus in the French:—"Les Sorbonnistes pervertissent le passage de S. Paul, l'appliquans a ce propos c'est que pource que Jesus Christ s'est humilié, le Pere l'a exalté et lui donné un nom souverain:"—The Sorbonnists pervert the passage of St Paul, and apply it in this way—that because Christ humbled himself, the Father exalted him, and gave him a sovereign name.

cannot attain one thousandth part? The solution is easy and complete. Paul is not speaking of the cause of Christ's exaltation, but only pointing out a consequence of it by way of example to us. The meaning is not much different from that of another passage: "Ought not Christ to have suffered these things, and to enter into his glory?" (Luke xxiv. 26.)

END OF THE SECOND BOOK.

INSTITUTES

OF

THE CHRISTIAN RELIGION.

BOOK THIRD

THE MODE OF OBTAINING THE GRACE OF CHRIST.
THE BENEFITS IT CONFERS, AND THE
EFFECTS RESULTING FROM IT.

SUBJECT.

The two former Books treated of God the Creator and Redeemer. This Book, which contains a full exposition of the Third Part of the Apostles' Creed, treats of the mode of procuring the grace of Christ, the benefits which we derive and the effects which follow from it, or of the operations of the Holy Spirit in regard to our salvation.

The subject is comprehended under seven principal heads, which almost all point to the same end—namely, the doctrine of faith.

I. As it is by the secret and special operation of the Holy Spirit that we enjoy Christ and all his benefits, the First Chapter treats of this operation, which is the foundation of faith, new life, and all holy exercises.

II. Faith being, as it were, the hand by which we embrace Christ the Redeemer' offered to us by the Holy Spirit, Faith is fully considered in the Second Chapter.

III. In further explanation of Saving Faith, and the benefits derived from it, it is mentioned that true repentance always flows from true faith. The doctrine of Repentance is considered generally in the Third Chapter, Popish repentance in the Fourth Chapter, Indulgences and Purgatory in the Fifth Chapter. Chapters Sixth to Tenth are devoted to a special consideration of the different parts of true Repentance—viz., mortification of the flesh, and quickening of the Spirit.

IV. More clearly to show the utility of this Faith, and the effects resulting from it, the doctrine of Justification by Faith is explained in the Eleventh Chapter, and certain questions connected with it explained from the Twelfth to the Eighteenth Chapter. Christian liberty a kind of accessory to Justification, is considered in the Nineteenth Chapter.

V. The Twentieth Chapter is devoted to Prayer, the principal exercise of faith, and, as it were, the medium or instrument through which we daily procure blessings from God.

VI. As all do not indiscriminately embrace the fellowship of Christ offered in the Gospel, but those only whom the Lord favours with the effectual and special grace of his Spirit, lest any should impugn this arrangement, Chapters Twenty-First to Twenty-Fourth are occupied with a necessary and apposite discussion of the subject of Election.

VII. Lastly, As the hard warfare which the Christian is obliged constantly to wage may have the effect of disheartening him, it is shown how it may be alleviated by meditating on the final resurrection. Hence the subject of the Resurrection is considered in the Twenty-Fifth Chapter.

INSTITUTES

OF

THE CHRISTIAN RELIGION.

BOOK THIRD.

THE MODE OF OBTAINING THE GRACE OF CHRIST. THE BENEFITS IT CONFERS, AND THE EFFECTS RESULTING FROM IT.

CHAPTER I.

THE BENEFITS OF CHRIST MADE AVAILABLE TO US BY THE SECRET OPERATION OF THE SPIRIT.

The three divisions of this chapter are,—I. The secret operation of the Holy Spirit, which seals our salvation, should be considered first in Christ the Mediator as our Head, sec. 1 and 2. II. The titles given to the Holy Spirit show that we become members of Christ by his grace and energy, sec. 3. III. As the special influence of the Holy Spirit is manifested in the gift of faith, the former is a proper introduction to the latter, and thus prepares for the second chapter, sec. 4.

Sections.

1. The Holy Spirit the bond which unites us with Christ. This the result of faith produced by the secret operation of the Holy Spirit. This obvious from Scripture.
2. In Christ the Mediator the gifts of the Holy Spirit are to be seen in all their fulness. To what end. Why the Holy Spirit is called the Spirit of the Father and the Son.
3. Titles of the Spirit,—1. The Spirit of adoption. 2. An earnest and seal. 3. Water. 4. Life. 5 Oil and unction. 6. Fire. 7. A fountain. 8. The word of God. Use of these titles.
4. Faith being the special work of the Holy Spirit, the power and efficacv of the Holy Spirit usually ascribed to it.

1. WE must now see in what way we become possessed of the blessings which God has bestowed on his only begotten Son, not for

private use, but to enrich the poor and needy. And the first thing to be attended to is, that so long as we are without Christ and separated from him, nothing which he suffered and did for the salvation of the human race is of the least benefit to us. To communicate to us the blessings which he received from the Father, he must become ours and dwell in us. Accordingly, he is called our Head, and the first-born among many brethren, while, on the other hand, we are said to be ingrafted into him and clothed with him,[1] all which he possesses being, as I have said, nothing to us until we become one with him. And although it is true that we obtain this by faith, yet since we see that all do not indiscriminately embrace the offer of Christ which is made by the gospel, the very nature of the case teaches us to ascend higher, and inquire into the secret efficacy of the Spirit, to which it is owing that we enjoy Christ and all his blessings. I have already treated of the eternal essence and divinity of the Spirit (Book I. chap. xiii. sect. 14, 15); let us at present attend to the special point, that Christ came by water and blood, as the Spirit testifies concerning him, that we might not lose the benefits of the salvation which he has purchased. For as there are said to be three witnesses in heaven, the Father, the Word, and the Spirit, so there are also three on the earth—namely, water, blood, and Spirit. It is not without cause that the testimony of the Spirit is twice mentioned, a testimony which is engraven on our hearts by way of seal, and thus seals the cleansing and sacrifice of Christ. For which reason, also, Peter says, that believers are "elect" "through sanctification of the Spirit, unto obedience and sprinkling of the blood of Jesus Christ" (1 Pet. i. 2). By these words he reminds us, that if the shedding of his sacred blood is not to be in vain, our souls must be washed in it by the secret cleansing of the Holy Spirit. For which reason, also, Paul, speaking of cleansing and purification, says, "But ye are washed, but ye are sanctified, but ye are justified in the name of the Lord Jesus, and by the Spirit of our God" (1 Cor. vi. 11). The whole comes to this; that the Holy Spirit is the bond by which Christ effectually binds us to himself. Here we may refer to what was said in the last Book concerning his anointing.

2. But in order to have a clearer view of this most important subject, we must remember that Christ came provided with the Holy Spirit after a peculiar manner—namely, that he might separate us from the world, and unite us in the hope of an eternal inheritance. Hence the Spirit is called the Spirit of sanctification, because he quickens and cherishes us, not merely by the general energy which is seen in the human race, as well as other animals, but because he is the seed and root of heavenly life in us. Accordingly, one of the highest commendations which the prophets give to the kingdom of Christ is, that under it the Spirit would be poured out in richer abundance. One

1 Eph. iv. 15; Rom. vi. 5; xi. 17; viii. 29; Gal. iii. 27.

of the most remarkable passages is that of Joel, "It shall come to pass afterward, that I will pour out my Spirit upon all flesh" (Joel ii. 28). For although the prophet seems to confine the gifts of the Spirit to the office of prophesying, he yet intimates, under a figure, that God will, by the illumination of his Spirit, provide himself with disciples who had previously been altogether ignorant of heavenly doctrine. Moreover, as it is for the sake of his Son that God bestows the Holy Spirit upon us, and yet has deposited him in all his fulness with the Son, to be the minister and dispenser of his liberality, he is called at one time the Spirit of the Father, at another the Spirit of the Son: "Ye are not in the flesh but in the Spirit, if so be that the Spirit of God dwell in you. Now, if any man have not the Spirit of Christ, he is none of his" (Rom. viii. 9); and hence he encourages us to hope for complete renovation: "If the Spirit of him that raised up Jesus from the dead dwell in you, he that raised up Christ from the dead shall also quicken your mortal bodies by his Spirit that dwelleth in you" (Rom. viii. 11). There is no inconsistency in ascribing the glory of those gifts to the Father, inasmuch as he is the author of them, and, at the same time, ascribing them to Christ, with whom they have been deposited, that he may bestow them on his people. Hence he invites all the thirsty to come unto him and drink (John vii. 37). And Paul teaches, that "unto every one of us is given grace, according to the measure of the gift of Christ" (Eph. iv. 7). And we must remember that the Spirit is called the Spirit of Christ, not only inasmuch as the eternal Word of God is with the Father united with the Spirit, but also in respect of his office of Mediator; because, had he not been endued with the energy of the Spirit, he had come to us in vain. In this sense he is called the "last Adam," and said to have been sent from heaven "a quickening Spirit" (1 Cor. xv. 45), where Paul contrasts the special life which Christ breathes into his people, that they may be one with him, with the animal life which is common even to the reprobate. In like manner, when he prays that believers may have "the grace of our Lord Jesus Christ, and the love of God," he at the same time adds, "the communion of the Holy Ghost," without which no man shall ever taste the paternal favour of God, or the benefits of Christ. Thus, also, in another passage he says, "The love of God is shed abroad in our hearts by the Holy Ghost, which is given unto us" (Rom. v. 5).

3. Here it will be proper to point out the titles which the Scripture bestows on the Spirit, when it treats of the commencement and entire renewal of our salvation. First, he is called the "Spirit of adoption," because he is witness to us of the free favour with which God the Father embraced us in his well-beloved and only-begotten Son, so as to become our Father, and give us boldness of access to him; nay, he dictates the very words, so that we can boldly cry, "Abba, Father." For the same reason, he is said to have "sealed us, and given the earnest of the Spirit in our hearts," because, as

[margin note: Titles bestowed by Scripture upon the Holy Spirit.]

pilgrims in the world, and persons in a manner dead, he so quickens us from above as to assure us that our salvation is safe in the keeping of a faithful God. Hence, also, the Spirit is said to be "life because of righteousness." But since it is his secret irrigation that makes us bud forth and produce the fruits of righteousness, he is repeatedly described as *water*. Thus in Isaiah, "Ho, every one that thirsteth, come ye to the waters." Again, "I will pour water upon him that is thirsty, and floods upon the dry ground." Corresponding to this are the words of our Saviour, to which I lately referred, "If any man thirst, let him come unto me and drink." Sometimes, indeed, he receives this name from his energy in cleansing and purifying, as in Ezekiel, where the Lord promises, "Then will I sprinkle you with clean water, and ye shall be clean." As those sprinkled with the Spirit are restored to the full vigour of life, he hence obtains the names of *"Oil"* and *"Unction."* On the other hand, as he is constantly employed in subduing and destroying the vices of our concupiscence, and inflaming our hearts with the love of God and piety, he hence receives the name of *Fire*. In fine, he is described to us as a *Fountain*, whence all heavenly riches flow to us; or as the *Hand* by which God exerts his power, because by his divine inspiration he so breathes divine life into us, that we are no longer acted upon by ourselves, but ruled by his motion and agency, so that everything good in us is the fruit of his grace, while our own endowments without him are mere darkness of mind and perverseness of heart. Already, indeed, it has been clearly shown, that until our minds are intent on the Spirit, Christ is in a manner unemployed, because we view him coldly without us, and so at a distance from us. Now we know that he is of no avail save only to those to whom he is a head and the first-born among the brethren, to those, in fine, who are clothed with him.[1] To this union alone it is owing that, in regard to us, the Saviour has not come in vain. To this is to be referred that sacred marriage, by which we become bone of his bone, and flesh of his flesh, and so one with him (Eph. v. 30), for it is by the Spirit alone that he unites himself to us. By the same grace and energy of the Spirit we become his members, so that he keeps us under him, and we in our turn possess him.

4. But as faith is his principal work, all those passages which express his power and operations are, in a great measure, referred to it, as it is only by faith that he brings us to the light of the Gospel, as John teaches, that to those who believe in Christ is given the privilege " to become the Sons of God, even to them that believe in his name, which were born not of blood, nor of the will of the flesh, nor of the will of man, but of God" (John i. 12). Opposing *God* to *flesh and blood*, he declares it to be a supernatural gift, that those

[margin note: Faith is the principal work of the spirit.]

---

[1] Rom. viii. 15; Gal. iv. 6; 2 Cor. i. 22; Eph. i. 13, 14; Rom. viii. 10; Isa. lv. 1; xliv. 3; John viii. 37; Ezek. xxxvi. 25; John ii. 14; 1 John ii. 20, 27; Luke iii. 16; Acts xi. 21.

The Spirit is the internal teacher

who would otherwise remain in unbelief receive Christ by faith. Similar to this is our Saviour's reply to Peter, " Flesh and blood hath not revealed it unto thee, but my Father which is in heaven " (Matt. xvi. 17). These things I now briefly advert to, as I have fully considered them elsewhere. To the same effect Paul says to the Ephesians, " Ye were sealed with that Holy Spirit of promise " (Eph. i. 13); thus showing that he is the internal teacher, by whose agency the promise of salvation, which would otherwise only strike the air or our ears, penetrates into our minds. In like manner, he says to the Thessalonians, " God hath from the beginning chosen you to salvation, through sanctification of the Spirit and belief of the truth " (2 Thess. ii. 13) ; by this passage briefly reminding us, that faith itself is produced only by the Spirit. This John explains more distinctly, " We know that he abideth in us, by the Spirit which he hath given us ;" again, " Hereby know we that we dwell in him and he in us, because he hath given us of his Spirit " (1 John iii. 24 ; iv. 13). Accordingly, to make his disciples capable of heavenly wisdom, Christ promised them " the Spirit of truth, whom the world cannot receive " (John xiv. 17). And he assigns it to him, as his proper office, to bring to remembrance the things which he had verbally taught ; for in vain were light offered to the blind, did not that Spirit of understanding open the intellectual eye ; so that he himself may be properly termed the key by which the treasures of the heavenly kingdom are unlocked, and his illumination, the eye of the mind by which we are enabled to see : hence Paul so highly commends the ministry of the Spirit[1] (2 Cor. iii. 6), since teachers would cry aloud to no purpose, did not Christ, the internal teacher, by means of his Spirit, draw to himself those who are given him of the Father. Therefore, as we have said that salvation is perfected in the person of Christ, so, in order to make us partakers of it, he baptises us " with the Holy Spirit and with fire " (Luke iii. 16), enlightening us into the faith of his Gospel, and so regenerating us to be new creatures. Thus cleansed from all pollution, he dedicates us as holy temples to the Lord.

Spirit is the key to the treasures of the heavenly kingdom

[1] The French adds, " qui vaut autant a dire comme la predication ayant avec soy vivacité spirituelle ;"—that is to say, preaching carrying spiritual quickening along. with it.

CHAPTER II.

OF FAITH. THE DEFINITION OF IT. ITS PECULIAR PROPERTIES.

This chapter consists of three principal parts.—I. A brief explanation of certain matters pertaining to the doctrine of Faith, sec. 1—14. First, of the object of faith, sec. 1. Second, of Implicit Faith, sec. 2—6. Third, Definition of Faith, sec. 7. Fourth, the various meanings of the term Faith, sec. 8—13. II. A full exposition of the definition given in the seventh section, sec. 14—40. III. A brief confirmation of the definition by the authority of an Apostle. The mutual relation between faith, hope, and charity, sec. 41—43.

Sections.

1. A brief recapítulation of the leading points of the whole discussion. The scope of this chapter. The necessity of the doctrine of faith. This doctrine obscured by the Schoolmen, who make God the object of faith, without referring to Christ. The Schoolmen refuted by various passages.
2. The dogma of implicit faith refuted. It destroys faith, which consists in a knowledge of the divine will. What this will is, and how necessary the knowledge of it.
8. Many things are and will continue to be implicitly believed. Faith, however, consists in the knowledge of God and Christ, not in a reverence for the Church. Another refutation from the absurdities to which this dogma leads.
4. In what sense our faith may be said to be implicit. Examples in the Apostles, in the holy women, and in all believers.
5. In some, faith is implicit, as being a preparation for faith. This, however, widely different from the implicit faith of the Schoolmen.
6. The word of God has a similar relation to faith, the word being, as it were, the source and basis of faith, and the mirror in which it beholds God. Confirmation from various passages of Scripture. Without the knowledge of the word there can be no faith. Sum of the discussion of the Scholastic doctrine of implicit faith.
7. What faith properly has respect to in the word of God—namely, the promise of grace offered in Christ, provided it be embraced with faith. Proper definition of faith.
8. Scholastic distinction between faith formed and unformed, refuted by a consideration of the nature of faith, which, as the gift of the Spirit, cannot possibly be disjoined from pious affection.
9. Objection from a passage of Paul. Answer to it. Error of the Schoolmen in giving only one meaning to faith, whereas it has many meanings. The testimony of faith improperly ascribed to two classes of men.
10. View to be taken of this. Who those are that believe for a time. The faith of hypocrites. With whom they may be compared.
11. Why faith attributed to the reprobate. Objection. Answer. What perception of grace in the reprobate. How the elect are distinguished from the reprobate.
12. Why faith is temporary in the reprobate, firm and perpetual in the elect. Reason in the case of the reprobate. Example. Why God is angry with his children. In what sense many are said to fall from faith.
13. Various meanings of the term faith. 1. Taken for soundness in the faith. 2. Sometimes restricted to a particular object. 3. Signifies the ministry or testimony by which we are instructed in the faith.
14. Definition of faith explained under six principal heads. 1. What meant by *Knowledge* in the definition.

40. A third objection, impugning the final perseverance of the elect. Answer by an Apostle. Summary of the refutation.
41. The definition of faith accords with that given by the Apostle in the Hebrews. Explanation of this definition. Refutation of the scholastic error, that charity is prior to faith and hope.
42. Hope the inseparable attendant of true faith. Reason. Connection between faith and hope. Mutually support each other. Obvious from the various forms of temptation, that the aid of hope necessary to establish faith.
43. The terms faith and hope sometimes confounded. Refutation of the Schoolmen, who attribute a twofold foundation to hope—viz. the grace of God and the merit of works.

1. ALL these things will be easily understood after we have given a clearer definition of faith, so as to enable the readers to apprehend its nature and power. Here it is of importance to call to mind what was formerly taught, first, That since God by his Law prescribes what we ought to do, failure in any one respect subjects us to the dreadful judgment of eternal death, which it denounces. Secondly, Because it is not only difficult, but altogether beyond our strength and ability, to fulfil the demands of the Law, if we look only to ourselves and consider what is due to our merits, no ground of hope remains, but we lie forsaken of God under eternal death. Thirdly, That there is only one method of deliverance which can rescue us from this miserable calamity—viz. when Christ the Redeemer appears, by whose hand our heavenly Father, out of his infinite goodness and mercy, has been pleased to succour us, if we with true faith embrace this mercy, and with firm hope rest in it. It is now proper to consider the nature of this faith, by means of which, those who are adopted into the family of God obtain possession of the heavenly kingdom. For the accomplishment of so great an end, it is obvious that no mere opinion or persuasion is adequate. And the greater care and diligence is necessary in discussing the true nature of faith, from the pernicious delusions which many, in the present day, labour under with regard to it. Great numbers, on hearing the term, think that nothing more is meant than a certain common assent to the Gospel History; nay, when the subject of faith is discussed in the Schools, by simply representing God as its object, they by empty speculation, as we have elsewhere said (Book II. chap. vi. sec. 4), hurry wretched souls away from the right mark instead of directing them to it. For seeing that God dwells in light that is inaccessible, Christ must intervene. Hence he calls himself "the light of the world;" and in another passage, "the way, the truth, and the life." None cometh to the Father (who is the fountain of life), except by him; for "no man knoweth who the Father is but the Son, and he to whom the Son will reveal him." For this reason, Paul declares, "I count all things as loss for the excellency of the knowledge of Christ Jesus my Lord." In the twentieth chapter of the Acts, he states that he preached "faith towards our Lord Jesus Christ;" and in another passage, he introduces Christ as thus addressing him: "I have appeared unto thee for this purpose, to make thee a minister and a witness;" —— "delivering

thee from the people, and from the Gentiles, unto whom now I send thee,"——" that they may receive forgiveness of sins, and inheritance among them which are sanctified through faith which is in me." Paul further declares, that in the person of Christ the glory of God is visibly manifested to us, or, which is the same thing, we have "the light of the knowledge of the glory of God in the face of Jesus Christ."[1] It is true, indeed, that faith has respect to God only; but to this we should add, that it acknowledges Jesus Christ whom he hath sent. God would remain far off, concealed from us, were we not irradiated by the brightness of Christ. All that the Father had, he deposited with his only begotten Son, in order that he might manifest himself in him, and thus by the communication of blessings express the true image of his glory. Since, as has been said, we must be led by the Spirit, and thus stimulated to seek Christ, so must we also remember that the invisible Father is to be sought nowhere but in this image. For which reason Augustine, treating of the object of faith (De Civitate Dei, Lib. xi. c. 2), elegantly says, " The thing to be known is, whither we are to go, and by what way ;" and immediately after infers, that " the surest way to avoid all errors is to know him who is both God and man. It is to God we tend, and it is by man we go, and both of these are found only in Christ."[2] Paul, when he preaches faith towards God, surely does not intend to overthrow what he so often inculcates—viz. that faith has all its stability in Christ. Peter most appropriately connects both, saying, that by him " we believe in God" (1 Pet. i. 21).

2. This evil, therefore, must, like innumerable others, be attributed to the Schoolmen,[3] who have in a manner drawn a veil over Christ, to whom, if our eye is not directly turned, we must always wander through many labyrinths. But besides impairing, and almost annihilating, faith by their obscure definition, they have invented the fiction of implicit faith, with which name decking the grossest ignorance, they delude the wretched populace to their great destruction.[4] Nay, to state the fact more truly and plainly, this fiction not only buries true faith, but entirely destroys it. Is it faith to understand nothing, and merely submit your convictions implicitly to the Church? Faith consists not in ignorance, but in knowledge—knowledge not of God merely, but of the divine will. We do not obtain salvation either because we are prepared to embrace every dictate of the Church as true, or leave to the Church the province of inquiring and determining; but when we recognise God as a propitious Father through the reconciliation made by Christ, and Christ as given to us for

[1] 1 Tim. vi. 16; John viii. 12; xiv. 6; Luke x. 22; 1 Cor. ii. 2; Acts xx. 21; xxvi. 17, 18; 2 Cor. iv. 6.

[2] The French is, " Car nous tendons a Dieu, et par l'humanité de Jesus Christ, nous y sommes conduits ; "—For we tend to God, and by the humanity of Christ are conducted to him.

[3] French, " Theologiens Sorboniques ; "—Theologians of Sorbonne.

[4] In opposition to this ignorance, see Chrysostom in Joann. Homil. xvi.

righteousness, sanctification, and life. By this knowledge, I say, not by the submission of our understanding, we obtain an entrance into the kingdom of heaven. For when the Apostle says, "With the heart man believeth unto righteousness; and with the mouth confession is made unto salvation" (Rom. x. 10), he intimates, that it is not enough to believe implicitly without understanding, or even inquiring. The thing requisite is an explicit recognition of the divine goodness, in which our righteousness consists.

3. I indeed deny not (so enveloped are we in ignorance), that to us very many things now are and will continue to be completely involved until we lay aside this weight of flesh, and approach nearer to the presence of God. In such cases the fittest course is to suspend our judgment, and resolve to maintain unity with the Church. But under this pretext, to honour ignorance, tempered with humility, with the name of faith, is most absurd. Faith consists in the knowledge of God and Christ (John xvii. 3), not in reverence for the Church. And we see what a labyrinth they have formed out of this implicit faith—everything, sometimes even the most monstrous errors, being received by the ignorant as oracles without any discrimination, provided they are prescribed to them under the name of the Church. This inconsiderate facility, though the surest precipice to destruction, is, however, excused on the ground that it believes nothing definitely, but only with the appended condition, If such is the faith of the Church. Thus they pretend to find truth in error, light in darkness, true knowledge in ignorance. Not to dwell longer in refuting these views, we simply advise the reader to compare them with ours. The clearness of truth will itself furnish a sufficient refutation. For the question they raise is not, whether there may be an implicit faith with many remains of ignorance, but they maintain, that persons living and even indulging in a stupid ignorance duly believe, provided, in regard to things unknown, they assent to the authority and judgment of the Church: as if Scripture did not uniformly teach, that with faith understanding is conjoined.

4. We grant, indeed, that so long as we are pilgrims in the world faith is implicit, not only because as yet many things are hidden from us, but because, involved in the mists of error, we attain not to all. The highest wisdom, even of him who has attained the greatest perfection, is to go forward, and endeavour in a calm and teachable spirit to make further progress. Hence Paul exhorts believers to wait for further illumination in any matter in which they differ from each other (Phil. iii. 15).[1] And certainly experience teaches, that so long as we are in the flesh, our attainments are less than is to be desired. In our daily reading we fall in with many obscure passages which

[Marginalia: Faith consists of knowledge of God and Christ, and not in reverence for the church.]

[Marginalia: So long as we are pilgrims in the world, many things remain hidden from us.]

[1] See Augustin. Ep. 102, "Si propter eos solos Christus mortuus est, qui certa intelligentia possunt ista discernera, pæne frustra in ecclesia laboramus," &c.;—If Christ died for those only who are able to discern these things with true understanding, our labour in the Church is almost in vain.

Briefly,
it seems
that here
Calvin is
saying
that it
is man's
duty to
know as
much of
God as
He can,
and when
he reaches
the limits
of his
knowledge,
there a
trusting
faith
takes over.

convict us of ignorance. With this curb God keeps us modest, assigning to each a measure of faith, that every teacher, however excellent, may still be disposed to learn. Striking examples of this implicit faith may be observed in the disciples of Christ before they were fully illuminated. We see with what difficulty they take in the first rudiments, how they hesitate in the minutest matters, how, though hanging on the lips of their Master, they make no great progress; nay, even after running to the sepulchre on the report of the women, the resurrection of their Master appears to them a dream. As Christ previously bore testimony to their faith, we cannot say that they were altogether devoid of it; nay, had they not been persuaded that Christ would rise again, all their zeal would have been extinguished. Nor was it superstition that led the women to prepare spices to embalm a dead body of whose revival they had no expectation; but, although they gave credit to the words of one whom they knew to be true, yet the ignorance which still possessed their minds involved their faith in darkness, and left them in amazement. Hence they are said to have believed only when, by the reality, they perceive the truth of what Christ had spoken; not that they then began to believe, but the seed of a hidden faith, which lay as it were dead in their hearts, then burst forth in vigour. They had, therefore, a true but implicit faith, having reverently embraced Christ as the only teacher. Then, being taught by him, they felt assured that he was the author of salvation: in fine, believed that he had come from heaven to gather disciples, and take them thither through the grace of the Father. There cannot be a more familiar proof of this, than that in all men faith is always mingled with incredulity.

5. We may also call their faith implicit, as being properly nothing else than a preparation for faith. The Evangelists describe many as having believed, although they were only roused to admiration by the miracles, and went no farther than to believe that Christ was the promised Messiah, without being at all imbued with Evangelical doctrine. The reverence which subdued them, and made them willingly submit to Christ, is honoured with the name of faith, though it was nothing but the commencement of it. Thus the nobleman who believed in the promised cure of his son, on returning home, is said by the Evangelist (John iv. 53) to have again believed; that is, he had first received the words which fell from the lips of Christ as an oracular response, and thereafter submitted to his authority and received his doctrine. Although it is to be observed that he was docile and disposed to learn, yet the word "*believed*" in the former passage denotes a particular faith, and in the latter gives him a place among those disciples who had devoted themselves to Christ. Not unlike this is the example which John gives of the Samaritans, who believed the woman, and eagerly hastened to Christ; but, after they had heard him, thus express themselves, " Now we believe, not because of thy saying, for we have heard him ourselves, and know

that this is indeed the Christ, the Saviour of the world" (John iv. 42). From these passages it is obvious, that even those who are not yet imbued with the first principles, provided they are disposed to obey, are called *believers*, not properly indeed, but inasmuch as God is pleased in kindness so highly to honour their pious feeling. But this docility, with a desire of further progress, is widely different from the gross ignorance in which those sluggishly indulge who are contented with the implicit faith of the Papists. If Paul severely condemns those who are "ever learning, and never able to come to the knowledge of the truth," how much more sharply ought those to be rebuked who avowedly affect to know nothing?

6. The true knowledge of Christ consists in receiving him as he is offered by the Father—namely, as invested with his Gospel. For, as he is appointed as the end of our faith, so we cannot directly tend towards him except under the guidance of the Gospel. Therein are certainly unfolded to us treasures of grace. Did these continue shut, Christ would profit us little. Hence Paul makes faith the inseparable attendant of doctrine in these words, "Ye have not so learned Christ; if so be that ye have heard him, and have been taught by him, as the truth is in Jesus" (Eph. iv. 20, 21). Still I do not confine faith to the Gospel in such a sense as not to admit that enough was delivered to Moses and the Prophets to form a foundation of faith; but as the Gospel exhibits a fuller manifestation of Christ, Paul justly terms it the doctrine of faith (1 Tim. iv. 6). For which reason, also, he elsewhere says, that, by the coming of faith, the Law was abolished (Rom. x. 4), including under the expression a new and unwonted mode of teaching, by which Christ, from the period of his appearance as the great Master, gave a fuller illustration of the Father's mercy, and testified more surely of our salvation. But an easier and more appropriate method will be to descend from the general to the particular. First, we must remember, that there is an inseparable relation between faith and the word, and that these can no more be disconnected from each other than rays of light from the sun. Hence in Isaiah the Lord explains, "Hear, and your soul shall live" (Is. lv. 3). And John points to this same fountain of faith, in the following words, "These are written that ye might believe" (John xx. 31). The Psalmist also, exhorting the people to faith, says, "To-day, if ye will hear his voice" (Ps. xcv. 7), to *hear* being uniformly taken for to *believe*. In fine, in Isaiah the Lord distinguishes the members of the Church from strangers by this mark, "All thy children shall be taught of the Lord" (Is liv. 13); for if the benefit was indiscriminate, why should he address his words only to a few? Corresponding with this, the Evangelists uniformly employ the terms *believers* and *disciples* as synonymous. This is done especially by Luke in several passages of the Acts. He even applies the term *disciple* to a woman (Acts ix. 36). Wherefore, if faith declines in the least degree from the mark at which it ought to

Faith which does not steadfastly aim at the highest level of understanding becomes vague credulity

The word is a mirror in which faith beholds God.

Faith is the knowledge of the divine will in regards to us, as ascertained from his word.

It is the certainty of God's love and mercy that draw us to Him.

aim, it does not retain its nature, but becomes uncertain credulity and vague wandering of mind. The same word is the basis on which it rests and is sustained. Declining from it, it falls. Take away the word, therefore, and no faith will remain. We are not here discussing whether, in order to propagate the word of God by which faith is engendered, the ministry of man is necessary (this will be considered elsewhere); but we say that the word itself, whatever be the way in which it is conveyed to us, is a kind of mirror in which faith beholds God. In this, therefore, whether God uses the agency of man, or works immediately by his own power, it is always by his word that he manifests himself to those whom he designs to draw to himself. Hence Paul designates faith as the obedience which is given to the Gospel (Rom. i. 5); and writing to the Philippians, he commends them for the obedience of faith (Phil. ii. 17). For faith includes not merely the knowledge that God is, but also, nay chiefly, a perception of his will towards us. It concerns us to know not only what he is in himself, but also in what character he is pleased to manifest himself to us. We now see, therefore, that faith is the knowledge of the divine will in regard to us, as ascertained from his word. And the foundation of it is a previous persuasion of the truth of God. So long as your mind entertains any misgivings as to the certainty of the word, its authority will be weak and dubious, or rather it will have no authority at all. Nor is it sufficient to believe that God is true, and cannot lie or deceive, unless you feel firmly persuaded that every word which proceeds from him is sacred, inviolable truth.

7. But since the heart of man is not brought to faith by every word of God, we must still consider what it is that faith properly has respect to in the word. The declaration of God to Adam was, "Thou shalt surely die" (Gen. ii. 17); and to Cain, "The voice of thy brother's blood crieth unto me from the ground" (Gen. iv. 10); but these, so far from being fitted to establish faith, tend only to shake it. At the same time, we deny not that it is the office of faith to assent to the truth of God whenever, whatever, and in whatever way he speaks: we are only inquiring what faith can find in the word of God to lean and rest upon. When conscience sees only wrath and indignation, how can it but tremble and be afraid? and how can it avoid shunning the God whom it thus dreads? But faith ought to seek God, not shun him. It is evident, therefore, that we have not yet obtained a full definition of faith, it being impossible to give the name to every kind of knowledge of the divine will. Shall we, then, for *will*, which is often the messenger of bad news and the herald of terror, substitute the benevolence or mercy of God? In this way, doubtless, we make a nearer approach to the nature of faith. For we are allured to seek God when told that our safety is treasured up in him ; and we are confirmed in this when he declares that he studies and takes an interest in our welfare. Hence there is

need of the gracious promise, in which he testifies that he is a propitious Father; since there is no other way in which we can approach to him, the promise being the only thing on which the heart of man can recline. For this reason, the two things, mercy and truth, are uniformly conjoined in the Psalms as having a mutual connection with each other. For it were of no avail to us to know that God is true, did He not in mercy allure us to himself; nor could we of ourselves embrace his mercy did not He expressly offer it. "I have declared thy faithfulness and thy salvation: I have not concealed thy loving-kindness and thy truth. Withhold not thy tender mercies from me, O Lord: let thy loving-kindness and thy truth continually preserve me" (Ps. xl. 10, 11). "Thy mercy, O Lord, is in the heavens; and thy faithfulness reacheth unto the clouds" (Ps. xxxvi. 5). "All the paths of the Lord are mercy and truth unto such as keep his covenant and his testimonies" (Ps. xxv. 10). "His merciful kindness is great towards us: and the truth of the Lord endureth for ever" (Ps. cxvii. 2). "I will praise thy name for thy loving-kindness and thy truth" (Ps. cxxxviii. 2). I need not quote what is said in the Prophets, to the effect that God is merciful and faithful in his promises. It were presumptuous in us to hold that God is propitious to us, had we not his own testimony, and did he not prevent us by his invitation, which leaves no doubt or uncertainty as to his will. It has already been seen that Christ is the only pledge of love, for without him all things, both above and below, speak of hatred and wrath. We have also seen, that since the knowledge of the divine goodness cannot be of much importance unless it leads us to confide in it, we must exclude a knowledge mingled with doubt, —a knowledge which, so far from being firm, is continually wavering. But the human mind, when blinded and darkened, is very far from being able to rise to a proper knowledge of the divine will; nor can the heart, fluctuating with perpetual doubt, rest secure in such knowledge. Hence, in order that the word of God may gain full credit, the mind must be enlightened, and the heart confirmed, from some other quarter. We shall now have a full definition of faith [1] if we say that it is a firm and sure knowledge of the divine favour toward us, founded on the truth of a free promise in Christ, and revealed to our minds, and sealed on our hearts, by the Holy Spirit.

8. But before I proceed farther, it will be necessary to make some preliminary observations for the purpose of removing difficulties which might otherwise obstruct the reader. And first, I must refute the nugatory distinction of the Schoolmen as to formed and unformed faith.[2] For they imagine that persons who have no fear of God, and no sense of piety, may believe all that is necessary to be known for salvation; as if the Holy Spirit were not the witness of our adoption

---

1 This definition is explained, sections 14, 15, 28, 29, 32, 33, 31, of this chapter.
2 See Lombard, Lib. iii. Dist. 23. See the refutation in the middle of sections 41 42, 43, where it is shown that faith produces, and is inseparable from, hope and love.

by enlightening our hearts unto faith. Still, however, though the whole Scripture is against them, they dogmatically give the name of faith to a persuasion devoid of the fear of God. It is unnecessary to go farther in refuting their definition, than simply to state the nature of faith as declared in the word of God. From this it will clearly appear how unskilfully and absurdly they babble, rather than discourse, on this subject. I have already done this in part, and will afterwards add the remainder in its proper place. At present, I say that nothing can be imagined more absurd than their fiction. They insist that faith is an assent with which any despiser of God may receive what is delivered by Scripture. But we must first see whether any one can by his own strength acquire faith, or whether the Holy Spirit, by means of it, becomes the witness of adoption. Hence it is childish trifling in them to inquire whether the faith formed by the supervening quality of love be the same, or a different and new faith. By talking in this style, they show plainly that they have never thought of the special gift of the Spirit; since one of the first elements of faith is reconciliation implied in man's drawing near to God. Did they duly ponder the saying of Paul, "With the heart man believeth unto righteousness" (Rom. x. 10), they would cease to dream of that frigid quality. There is one consideration which ought at once to put an end to the debate—viz. that assent itself (as I have already observed, and will afterwards more fully illustrate) is more a matter of the heart than the head, of the affection than the intellect. For this reason, it is termed "the obedience of faith" (Rom. i. 5), which the Lord prefers to all other service, and justly, since nothing is more precious to him than his truth, which, as John Baptist declares, is in a manner signed and sealed by believers (John iii. 33). As there can be no doubt on the matter, we in one word conclude, that they talk absurdly when they maintain that faith is formed by the addition of pious affection as an accessory to assent, since assent itself, such at least as the Scripture describes, consists in pious affection. But we are furnished with a still clearer argument. Since faith embraces Christ as he is offered by the Father, and he is offered not only for justification, for forgiveness of sins and peace, but also for sanctification, as the fountain of living waters, it is certain that no man will ever know him aright without at the same time receiving the sanctification of the Spirit; or, to express the matter more plainly, faith consists in the knowledge of Christ; Christ cannot be known without the sanctification of his Spirit: therefore faith cannot possibly be disjoined from pious affection.

9. In their attempt to mar faith by divesting it of love, they are wont to insist on the words of Paul, "Though I have all faith, so that I could remove mountains, and have not charity, I am nothing" (1 Cor. xiii. 2). But they do not consider what the faith is of which the Apostle there speaks. Having, in the previous chapter, discoursed of the various gifts of the Spirit (1 Cor. xii. 10), including

diversity of tongues, miracles, and prophecy, and exhorted the Corinthians to follow the better gifts, in other words, those from which the whole body of the Church would derive greater benefit, he adds, "Yet show I unto you a more excellent way" (1 Cor. xii. 30). All other gifts, how excellent soever they may be in themselves, are of no value unless they are subservient to charity. They were given for the edification of the Church, and fail of their purpose if not so applied. To prove this he adopts a division, repeating the same gifts which he had mentioned before, but under different names. Miracles and faith are used to denote the same thing—viz. the power of working miracles. Seeing, then, that this miraculous power or faith is the particular gift of God, which a wicked man may possess and abuse, as the gift of tongues, prophecy, or other gifts, it is not strange that he separates it from charity. Their whole error lies in this, that while the term faith has a variety of meanings, overlooking this variety, they argue as if its meaning were invariably one and the same. The passage of James, by which they endeavour to defend their error, will be elsewhere discussed (*infra*, chap. xvii. sec. 11). Although, in discoursing of faith, we admit that it has a variety of forms ; yet, when our object is to show what knowledge of God the wicked possess, we hold and maintain, in accordance with Scripture, that the pious only have faith. Multitudes undoubtedly believe that God is, and admit the truth of the Gospel History, and the other parts of Scripture, in the same way in which they believe the records of past events, or events which they have actually witnessed. There are some who go even farther : they regard the Word of God as an infallible oracle ; they do not altogether disregard its precepts, but are moved to some degree by its threatenings and promises. To such the testimony of faith is attributed, but by *catachresis;* because they do not with open impiety impugn, reject, or contemn, the Word of God, but rather exhibit some semblance of obedience.

[margin note: Multitudes give intellectual assent without conviction in their hearts.]

10. But as this shadow or image of faith is of no moment, so it is unworthy of the name. How far it differs from true faith will shortly be explained at length. Here, however, we may just indicate it in passing. Simon Magus is said to have believed, though he soon after gave proof of his unbelief (Acts viii. 13–18). In regard to the faith attributed to him, we do not understand with some, that he merely pretended a belief which had no existence in his heart : we rather think that, overcome by the majesty of the Gospel, he yielded some kind of assent, and so far acknowledged Christ to be the author of life and salvation, as willingly to assume his name. In like manner, in the Gospel of Luke, those in whom the seed of the word is choked before it brings forth fruit, or in whom, from having no depth of earth, it soon withereth away, are said to believe for a time. Such, we doubt not, eagerly receive the word with a kind of relish, and have some feeling of its divine power, so as not only to impose upon men by a false semblance of faith, but even to impose upon them-

Assent which does not penetrate to the heart & stay there is of no value.

selves. They imagine that the reverence which they give to the word is genuine piety, because they have no idea of any impiety but that which consists in open and avowed contempt. But whatever that assent may be, it by no means penetrates to the heart, so as to have a fixed seat there. Although it sometimes seems to have planted its roots, these have no life in them. The human heart has so many recesses for vanity, so many lurking places for falsehood, is so shrouded by fraud and hypocrisy, that it often deceives itself. Let those who glory in such semblances of faith know that, in this respect, they are not a whit superior to devils. The one class, indeed, is inferior to them, inasmuch as they are able without emotion to hear and understand things, the knowledge of which makes devils tremble (James ii. 19). The other class equals them in this, that whatever be the impression made upon them, its only result is terror and consternation.

Those who are not among the elect may feel so close to the faith that they do not realize their lost condition.

11. I am aware it seems unaccountable to some how faith is attributed to the reprobate, seeing that it is declared by Paul to be one of the fruits of election;[1] and yet the difficulty is easily solved: for though none are enlightened into faith, and truly feel the efficacy of the Gospel, with the exception of those who are fore-ordained to salvation, yet experience shows that the reprobate are sometimes affected in a way so similar to the elect, that even in their own judgment there is no difference between them. Hence it is not strange, that by the Apostle a taste of heavenly gifts, and by Christ himself a temporary faith, is ascribed to them. Not that they truly perceive the power of spiritual grace and the sure light of faith; but the Lord, the better to convict them, and leave them without excuse, instils into their minds such a sense of his goodness as can be felt without the Spirit of adoption. Should it be objected, that believers have no stronger testimony to assure them of their adoption, I answer, that though there is a great resemblance and affinity between the elect of God and those who are impressed for a time with a fading faith, yet the elect alone have that full assurance which is extolled by Paul, and by which they are enabled to cry, Abba, Father. Therefore, as God regenerates the elect only for ever by incorruptible seed, as the seed of life once sown in their hearts never perishes, so he effectually seals in them the grace of his adoption, that it may be sure and stedfast. But in this there is nothing to prevent an inferior operation of the Spirit from taking its course in the reprobate. Meanwhile, believers are taught to examine themselves carefully and humbly, lest carnal security creep in and take the place of assurance of faith. We may add, that the reprobate never have any other than a confused sense of grace, laying hold of the shadow rather than the substance, because the Spirit properly seals the forgiveness of sins in the elect only, applying it by special faith to their use. Still it is correctly said, that

---

[1] 1 Thess. i. 3, 4; 2 Thess. ii. 13; Tit. i.

the reprobate believe God to be propitious to them, inasmuch as they accept the gift of reconciliation, though confusedly and without due discernment; not that they are partakers of the same faith or regeneration with the children of God; but because, under a covering of hypocrisy, they seem to have a principle of faith in common with them. Nor do I even deny that God illumines their minds to this extent, that they recognise his grace; but that conviction he distinguishes from the peculiar testimony which he gives to his elect in this respect, that the reprobate never obtain to the full result or to fruition. When he shows himself propitious to them, it is not as if he had truly rescued them from death, and taken them under his protection. He only gives them a manifestation of his present mercy.[1] In the elect alone he implants the living root of faith, so that they persevere even to the end. Thus we dispose of the objection, that if God truly displays his grace, it must endure for ever. There is nothing inconsistent in this with the fact of his enlightening some with a present sense of grace, which afterwards proves evanescent.

Only those who have the living root of faith persevere to the end & are among the elect.

12. Although faith is a knowledge of the divine favour towards us, and a full persuasion of its truth, it is not strange that the sense of the divine love, which though akin to faith differs much from it, vanishes in those who are temporarily impressed. The will of God is, I confess, immutable, and his truth is always consistent with itself; but I deny that the reprobate ever advance so far as to penetrate to that secret revelation which Scripture reserves for the elect only. I therefore deny that they either understand his will considered as immutable, or steadily embrace his truth, inasmuch as they rest satisfied with an evanescent impression; just as a tree not planted deep enough may take root, but will in process of time wither away, though it may for several years not only put forth leaves and flowers, but produce fruit. In short, as by the revolt of the first man, the image of God could be effaced from his mind and soul, so there is nothing strange in His shedding some rays of grace on the reprobate, and afterwards allowing these to be extinguished. There is nothing to prevent His giving some a' slight knowledge of his Gospel, and imbuing others thoroughly. Meanwhile, we must remember that however feeble and slender the faith of the elect may be, yet as the Spirit of God is to them a sure earnest and seal of their adoption, the impression once engraven can never be effaced from their hearts, whereas the light which glimmers in the reprobate is afterwards quenched.[2] Nor can it be said that the Spirit therefore deceives, because he does not quicken the seed which lies in their hearts, so as to make it ever remain incorruptible as in the elect. I go farther: seeing it is evident, from the doctrine of Scripture and from daily experience, that

Here, one certainly feels the axe hanging above his head.

1 The French adds, " Comme par une bouffee ,"—as by fits and starts.
2 See section 13, where it is said that this impression, sometimes existing in the reprobate, is called faith, but improperly.

the reprobate are occasionally impressed with a sense of divine grace, some desire of mutual love must necessarily be excited in their hearts. Thus for a time a pious affection prevailed in Saul, disposing him to love God. Knowing that he was treated with paternal kindness, he was in some degree attracted by it. But as the reprobate have no rooted conviction of the paternal love of God, so they do not in return yield the love of sons, but are led by a kind of mercenary affection. The Spirit of love was given to Christ alone, for the express purpose of conferring this Spirit upon his members; and there can be no doubt that the following words of Paul apply to the elect only: "The love of God is shed abroad in our hearts, by the Holy Ghost which is given unto us" (Rom. v. 5); namely, the love which begets that confidence in prayer to which I have above adverted. On the other hand, we see that God is mysteriously offended with his children, though he ceases not to love them. He certainly hates them not, but he alarms them with a sense of his anger, that he may humble the pride of the flesh, arouse them from lethargy, and urge them to repentance. Hence they, at the same instant, feel that he is angry with them for their sins, and also propitious to their persons. It is not from fictitious dread that they deprecate his anger, and yet they betake themselves to him with tranquil confidence. It hence appears that the faith of some, though not true faith, is not mere pretence. They are borne along by some sudden impulse of zeal, and erroneously impose upon themselves, sloth undoubtedly preventing them from examining their hearts with due care. Such probably was the case of those whom John describes as believing on Christ; but of whom he says, "Jesus did not commit himself unto them, because he knew all men, and needed not that any should testify of man: for he knew what was in man" (John ii. 24, 25). Were it not true that many fall away from the common faith (I call it common, because there is a great resemblance between temporary and living, ever-during faith), Christ would not have said to his disciples, "If ye continue in my word, then are ye my disciples indeed; and ye shall know the truth, and the truth shall make you free" (John viii. 31, 32). He is addressing those who had embraced his doctrine, and urging them to progress in the faith, lest by their sluggishness they extinguish the light which they have received. Accordingly, Paul claims faith as the peculiar privilege of the elect, intimating that many, from not being properly rooted, fall away (Tit. i. 1). In the same way, in Matthew, our Saviour says, "Every plant which my heavenly Father hath not planted shall be rooted up" (Matth. xvi. 13). Some who are not ashamed to insult God and man are more grossly false. Against this class of men, who profane the faith by impious and lying pretence, James inveighs (James ii. 14). Nor would Paul require the faith of believers to be unfeigned (1 Tim. i. 5), were there not many who presumptuously arrogate to themselves what they have not, deceiving others and sometimes even themselves, with empty show.   Hence he compares a good conscience to the ark in which faith is preserved, because many, by falling away, have in regard to it made shipwreck.

13. It is necessary to attend to the ambiguous meaning of the term: for *faith* is often equivalent in meaning to *sound doctrine*, as in the passage which we lately quoted, and in the same Epistle where Paul enjoins the deacons to hold " the mystery of the faith in a pure conscience ;" in like manner, when he denounces the defection of certain from the faith.   The meaning again is the same, when he says that Timothy had been brought up in the faith ; and in like manner, when he says that profane babblings and oppositions of science, falsely so called, lead many away from the faith.   Such persons he elsewhere calls reprobate as to the faith.   On the other hand, when he enjoins Titus, " Rebuke them sharply, that they may be sound in the faith;"[1] by soundness he means purity of doctrine, which is easily corrupted, and degenerates through the fickleness of men.   And indeed, since in Christ, as possessed by faith, are " hid all the treasures of wisdom and knowledge" (Col. i. 2, 3), the term *faith* is justly extended to the whole sum of heavenly doctrine, from which it cannot be separated.   On the other hand, it is sometimes confined to a particular object, as when Matthew says of those who let down the paralytic through the roof. that Jesus saw their faith (Matth. ix. 2); and Jesus himself exclaims in regard to the centurion, "I have not found so great faith, no, not in Israel" (Matth. viii. 10).   Now, it is probable that the centurion was thinking only of the cure of his son, by whom his whole soul was engrossed ;[2] but because he is satisfied with the simple answer and assurance of Christ, and does not request his bodily presence, this circumstance calls forth the eulogium on his faith. And we have lately shown how Paul uses the term faith for the gift of miracles—a gift possessed by persons who were neither regenerated by the Spirit of God, nor sincerely reverenced him.   In another passage, he uses faith for the doctrine by which we are instructed in the faith.   For when he says, that " that which is in part shall be done away" (1 Cor. xiii. 10), there can be no doubt that reference is made to the ministry of the Church, which is necessary in our present imperfect state ; in these forms of expression the analogy is obvious. But when the name of faith is improperly transferred to a false profession or lying assumption, the *catachresis* ought not to seem harsher than when the fear of God is used for vitious and perverse worship ; as when it is repeatedly said in sacred history, that the foreign nations which had been transported to Samaria and the neighbouring districts, feared false gods and the God of Israel : in other words, confounded heaven with earth.   But we have now been inquiring what the faith is which distinguishes the children of God from unbelievers, the faith

[1] 1 Tim. iii. 9 ; iv. 1, 6 ; 2 Tim. ii. 15; iii. 18; Tit. i. 13; ii. 2.
[2] The French adds, " Comme il montre par ses propos quel souci il en avoit;"—as ʒe shows by his urgency what anxiety he felt.

by which we invoke God the Father, by which we pass from death unto life, and by which Christ, our eternal salvation and life, dwells in us. Its power and nature have, I trust, been briefly and clearly explained.

14. Let us now again go over the parts of the definition separately: I should think that, after a careful examination of them, no doubt will remain. By knowledge we do not mean comprehension, such as that which we have of things falling under human sense. For that knowledge is so much superior, that the human mind must far surpass and go beyond itself in order to reach it. Nor even when it has reached it does it comprehend what it feels, but persuaded of what it comprehends not, it understands more from mere certainty of persuasion than it could discern of any human matter by its own capacity. Hence it is elegantly described by Paul as ability "to comprehend with all saints what is the breadth, and length, and depth, and height; and to know the love of Christ, which passeth knowledge" (Eph. iii. 18, 19). His object was to intimate, that what our mind embraces by faith is every way infinite, that this kind of knowledge far surpasses all understanding. But because the "mystery which hath been hid from ages and from generations" is now "made manifest to the saints" (Col. i. 26), *faith* is, for good reason, occasionally termed in Scripture *understanding* (Col. ii. 2); and *knowledge*, as by John (1 John iii. 2), when he declares that believers know themselves to be the sons of God. And certainly they do know, but rather as confirmed by a belief of the divine veracity than taught by any demonstration of reason. This is also indicated by Paul when he says, that "whilst we are at home in the body, we are absent from the Lord: (for we walk by faith, not by sight)" (2 Cor. v. 6, 7): thus showing that what we understand by faith is yet distant from us and escapes our view. Hence we conclude that the knowledge of faith consists more of certainty than discernment.

The knowledge of faith consists more of certainty than discernment.

15. We add, that it is *sure and firm*, the better to express strength and constancy of persuasion. For as faith is not contented with a dubious and fickle opinion, so neither is it contented with an obscure and ill-defined conception. The certainty which it requires must be full and decisive, as is usual in regard to matters ascertained and proved. So deeply rooted in our hearts is unbelief, so prone are we to it, that while all confess with the lips that God is faithful, no man ever believes it without an arduous struggle. Especially when brought to the test,[1] we by our wavering betray the vice which lurked within. Nor is it without cause that the Holy Spirit bears such distinguished testimony to the authority of God, in order that it may cure the disease of which I have spoken, and induce us to give full credit to the divine promises: "The words of the Lord"

Man cannot believe the faithfulness of God without an arduous struggle

---

Latin, "Præsentim ubi ad rem ventum est."—French, "Principalement quand les tentations nous pressent;"—especially when temptations press us.

(says David, Ps. xii. 6) " are pure words, as silver tried in a furnace of earth, purified seven times :" " The word of the Lord is tried: he is a buckler to all those that trust in him" (Ps. xviii. 30). And Solomon declares the same thing almost in the same words, " Every word of God is pure" (Prov. xxx. 5). But further quotation is superfluous, as the cxix. Psalm is almost wholly occupied with this subject. Certainly, whenever God thus recommends his word, he indirectly rebukes our unbelief, the purport of all that is said being to eradicate perverse doubt from our hearts. There are very many also who form such an idea of the divine mercy as yields them very little comfort. For they are harassed by miserable anxiety while they doubt whether God will be merciful to them. They think, indeed, that they are most fully persuaded of the divine mercy, but they confine it within too narrow limits. The idea they entertain is, that this mercy is great and abundant, is shed upon many, is offered and ready to be bestowed upon all; but that it is uncertain whether it will reach to them individually, or rather whether they can reach to it. Thus their knowledge stopping short leaves them only midway; not so much confirming and tranquillising the mind as harassing it with doubt and disquietude. Very different is that feeling of full assurance (πληροφορια) which the Scriptures uniformly attribute to faith—an assurance which leaves no doubt that the goodness of God is clearly offered to us. This assurance we cannot have without truly perceiving its sweetness, and experiencing it in ourselves. Hence from faith the Apostle deduces confidence, and from confidence boldness. His words are, " In whom (Christ) we have boldness and access with confidence by the faith of him" (Eph. iii. 12): thus undoubtedly showing that our faith is not true unless it enables us to appear calmly in the presence of God. Such boldness springs only from confidence in the divine favour and salvation. So true is this, that the term *faith* is often used as equivalent to *confidence*.

16. The principal hinge on which faith turns is this: We must not suppose that any promises of mercy which the Lord offers are only true out of us, and not at all in us: we should rather make them ours by inwardly embracing them. In this way only is engendered that confidence which he elsewhere terms peace (Rom. v. 1); though perhaps he rather means to make peace follow from it. This is the security which quiets and calms the conscience in the view of the judgment of God, and without which it is necessarily vexed and almost torn with tumultuous dread, unless when it happens to slumber for a moment, forgetful both of God and of itself. And verily it is but for a moment. It never long enjoys that miserable obliviousness, for the memory of the divine judgment, ever and anon recurring, stings it to the quick. In one word, he only is a true believer who, firmly persuaded that God is reconciled, and is a kind Father to him, hopes everything from his kindness, who, trusting to the promises of the divine favour, with undoubting confidence anti-

[margin note:] True faith is that faith which enables us to stand calmly in the presence of God.

[margin note:] The true believer is one who confidently, and without fear claims the loving, merciful promises of God, the Father

cipates salvation; as the Apostle shows in these words, "We are made partakers of Christ, if we hold the beginning of our confidence stedfast unto the end" (Heb. iii. 14). He thus holds, that none hope well in the Lord save those who confidently glory in being the heirs of the heavenly kingdom. No man, I say, is a believer but he who, trusting to the security of his salvation, confidently triumphs over the devil and death, as we are taught by the noble exclamation of Paul, "I am persuaded, that neither death, nor life, nor angels, nor principalities, nor powers, nor things present, nor things to come, nor height, nor depth, nor any other creature, shall be able to separate us from the love of God, which is in Christ Jesus our Lord" (Rom. viii. 38). In like manner, the same Apostle does not consider that the eyes of our understanding are enlightened unless we know what is the hope of the eternal inheritance to which we are called (Eph. i. 18). Thus he uniformly intimates throughout his writings, that the goodness of God is not properly comprehended when security does not follow as its fruit.

17. But it will be said that this differs widely from the experience of believers, who, in recognising the grace of God toward them, not only feel disquietude (this often happens), but sometimes tremble, overcome with terror,[1] so violent are the temptations which assail their minds. This scarcely seems consistent with certainty of faith. It is necessary to solve this difficulty, in order to maintain the doctrine above laid down. When we say that faith must be certain and secure, we certainly speak not of an assurance which is never affected by doubt, nor a security which anxiety never assails, we rather maintain that believers have a perpetual struggle with their own distrust, and are thus far from thinking that their consciences possess a placid quiet, uninterrupted by perturbation. On the other hand, whatever be the mode in which they are assailed, we deny that they fall off and abandon that sure confidence which they have formed in the mercy of God. Scripture does not set before us a brighter or more memorable example of faith than in David, especially if regard be had to the constant tenor of his life. And yet how far his mind was from being always at peace is declared by innumerable complaints, of which it will be sufficient to select a few. When he rebukes the turbulent movements of his soul, what else is it but a censure of his unbelief? "Why art thou cast down, my soul? and why art thou disquieted in me? hope thou in God" (Psalm xlii. 6). His alarm was undoubtedly a manifest sign of distrust, as if he thought that the Lord had forsaken him. In another passage we have a fuller confession: "I said in my haste, I am cut off from before thine eyes" (Psalm xxxi. 22). In another passage, in anxious and wretched perplexity, he debates with himself, nay, raises a question as to the

[1] As to the imperfection, strengthening, and increase of faith, see Book IV. chap. xiv. sec. 7, 8.

nature of God: "Hath God forgotten to be gracious? hath he in anger shut up his tender mercies?" (Psalm lxxvii. 9.) What follows is still harsher: "I said this is my infirmity; but I will remember the years of the right hand of the Most High."[1] As if desperate, he adjudges himself to destruction.[2] He not only confesses that he is agitated by doubt, but, as if he had fallen in the contest, leaves himself nothing in reserve,—God having deserted him, and made the hand which was wont to help him the instrument of his destruction. Wherefore, after having been tossed among tumultuous waves, it is not without reason he exhorts his soul to return to her quiet rest (Psalm cxvi. 7). And yet (what is strange) amid those commotions, faith sustains the believer's heart, and truly acts the part of the palm-tree, which supports any weights laid upon it, and rises above them; thus David, when he seemed to be overwhelmed, ceased not by urging himself forward to ascend to God. But he who, anxiously contending with his own infirmity, has recourse to faith, is already in a great measure victorious. This we may infer from the following passage, and others similar to it: "Wait on the Lord: be of good courage, and he shall strengthen thine heart: wait, I say, on the Lord" (Psalm xxvii. 14). He accuses himself of timidity, and repeating the same thing twice, confesses that he is ever and anon exposed to agitation. Still he is not only dissatisfied with himself for so feeling, but earnestly labours to correct it. Were we to take a nearer view of his case, and compare it with that of Ahaz, we should find a great difference between them. Isaiah is sent to relieve the anxiety of an impious and hypocritical king, and addresses him in those terms: "Take heed, and be quiet; fear not," &c. (Isaiah vii. 4). How did Ahaz act? As has already been said, his heart was shaken as a tree is shaken by the wind: though he heard the promise, he ceased not to tremble. This, therefore, is the proper hire and punishment of unbelief, so to tremble as in the day of trial to turn away from God, who gives access to himself only by faith. On the other hand, believers, though weighed down and almost overwhelmed with the burden of temptation, constantly rise up, though not without toil and difficulty; hence, feeling conscious of their own weakness, they pray with the Prophet, "Take not the word of truth utterly out of my mouth" (Psalm cxix. 43). By these words, we are taught that they at times become dumb, as if their faith were overthrown, and yet that they do not withdraw or turn their backs, but persevere in the contest, and by prayer stimulate their sluggishness, so as not to fall into stupor by giving way to it. (See Calv. in Psalm lxxxviii. 16.)

18. To make this intelligible, we must return to the distinction

---

[1] Calvin's Latin translation of the passage is, "Atque dixi, occidere meum est; mutationes dexteræ excelsi."—The French is, "J'ay dit, Il me faut mourir. Voicy un changement de la main de Dieu;"—I said I must die. Behold a change in the hand of God.

[2] See Calv adv. Pighium, near the commencement.

Two principles within the believer

1. Delight in divine goodness.

2. Bitter awareness of fallen state.

between flesh and spirit, to which we have already adverted, and which here becomes most apparent. The believer finds within himself two principles: the one filling him with delight in recognising the divine goodness, the other filling him with bitterness under a sense of his fallen state ; the one leading him to recline on the promise of the Gospel, the other alarming him by the conviction of his iniquity; the one making him exult with the anticipation of life, the other making him tremble with the fear of death. This diversity is owing to imperfection of faith, since we are never so well in the course of the present life as to be entirely cured of the disease of distrust, and completely replenished and engrossed by faith. Hence those conflicts : the distrust cleaving to the remains of the flesh rising up to assail the faith existing in our hearts. But if in the believer's mind certainty is mingled with doubt, must we not always be carried back to the conclusion that faith consists not of a sure and clear, but only of an obscure and confused, understanding of the divine will in regard to us? By no means. Though we are distracted by various thoughts, it does not

Momentary doubt does not divest us of faith.

follow that we are immediately divested of faith. Though we are agitated and carried to and fro by distrust, we are not immediately plunged into the abyss ; though we are shaken, we are not therefore driven from our place. The invariable issue of the contest is, that faith in the long-run surmounts the difficulties by which it was beset and seemed to be endangered.

19. The whole, then, comes to this : As soon as the minutest particle of faith is instilled into our minds, we begin to behold the face of God placid, serene, and propitious; far off, indeed, but still so distinctly as to assure us that there is no delusion in it. In proportion

A mind illumined by knowledge of God is at first involved in much ignorance. This, however, is gradually removed.

to the progress we afterwards make (and the progress ought to be uninterrupted), we obtain a nearer and surer view, the very continuance making it more familiar to us. Thus we see that a mind illumined with the knowledge of God is at first involved in much ignorance,— ignorance, however, which is gradually removed. Still this partial ignorance or obscure discernment does not prevent that clear knowledge of the divine favour which holds the first and principal part in faith. For as one shut up in a prison, where from a narrow opening he receives the rays of the sun indirectly and in a manner divided, though deprived of a full view of the sun, has no doubt of the source from which the light comes, and is benefited by it ; so believers, while bound with the fetters of an earthly body, though surrounded on all sides with much obscurity, are so far illumined by any slender light which beams upon them and displays the divine mercy as to feel secure.

20 The Apostle elegantly adverts to both in different passages. When he says, " We know in part, and we prophecy in part;" and " Now we see through a glass darkly " (1 Cor. xiii. 9, 12), he intimates how very minute a portion of divine wisdom is given to us in the present life. For although those expressions do not simply indicate that faith is imperfect so long as we groan under a weight of flesh, but

that the necessity of being constantly engaged in learning is owing to our imperfection, he at the same time reminds us, that a subject which is of boundless extent cannot be comprehended by our feeble and narrow capacities. This Paul affirms of the whole Church, each individual being retarded and impeded by his own ignorance from making so near an approach as were to be wished. But that the foretaste which we obtain from any minute portion of faith is certain, and by no means fallacious, he elsewhere shows, when he affirms that " We all, with open face beholding as in a glass the glory of the Lord, are changed into the same image, from glory to glory, even as by the Spirit of the Lord" (2 Cor. iii. 18). In such degrees of ignorance much doubt and trembling is necessarily implied, especially seeing that our heart is by its own natural bias prone to unbelief. To this we must add the temptations which, various in kind and infinite in number, are ever and anon violently assailing us. In particular, conscience itself, burdened with an incumbent load of sins, at one time complains and groans, at another accuses itself; at one time murmurs in secret, at another openly rebels. Therefore, whether adverse circumstances betoken the wrath of God, or conscience finds the subject and matter within itself, unbelief thence draws weapons and engines to put faith to flight, the aim of all its efforts being to make us think that God is adverse and hostile to us, and thus, instead of hoping for any assistance from him, to make us dread him as a deadly foe.

The vicissitudes of life try to make us believe that God is our enemy

21. To withstand these assaults, faith arms and fortifies itself with the word of God. When the temptation suggested is, that God is an enemy because he afflicts, faith replies, that while he afflicts he is merciful, his chastening proceeding more from love than anger. To the thought that God is the avenger of wickedness, it opposes the pardon ready to be bestowed on all offences whenever the sinner betakes himself to the divine mercy. Thus the pious mind, how much soever it may be agitated and torn, at length rises superior to all difficulties, and allows not its confidence in the divine mercy to be destroyed. Nay, rather, the disputes which exercise and disturb it tend to establish this confidence. A proof of this is, that the saints, when the hand of God lies heaviest upon them, still lodge their complaints with him, and continue to invoke him, when to all appearance he is least disposed to hear. But of what use were it to lament before him if they had no hope of solace? They never would invoke him did they not believe that he is ready to assist them. Thus the disciples, while reprimanded by their Master for the weakness of their faith in crying out that they were perishing, still implored his aid (Matth. viii. 25). And he, in rebuking them for their want of faith, does not disown them or class them with unbelievers, but urges them to shake off the vice. Therefore, as we have already said, we again maintain, that faith remaining fixed in the believer's breast never can be eradicated from it. However it may seem shaken and bent in this direction or in that, its flame is never so completely quenched as not at least to lurk under the embers.

Faith, however, arms us against this delusion.

Faith, then, can never be eradicated from the believer's breast.

In this way, it appears that the word, which is an incorruptible seed, produces fruit similar to itself. Its germ never withers away utterly and perishes. The saints cannot have a stronger ground for despair than to feel that, according to present appearances, the hand of God is armed for their destruction; and yet Job thus declares the strength of his confidence: " Though he slay me, yet will I trust in him." The truth is, that unbelief reigns not in the hearts of believers, but only assails them from without; does not wound them mortally with its darts, but annoys them, or, at the utmost, gives them a wound which can be healed. Faith, as Paul declares (Eph. vi. 16), is our shield, which receiving these darts, either wards them off entirely, or at least breaks their force, and prevents them from reaching the vitals. Hence when faith is shaken, it is just as when, by the violent blow of a javelin, a soldier standing firm is forced to step back and yield a little; and again, when faith is wounded, it is as if the shield were pierced, but not perforated by the blow. The pious mind will always rise, and be able to say with David, " Yea, though I walk through the valley of the shadow of death, I will fear no evil: for thou art with me" (Psalm. xxiii. 4). Doubtless it is a terrific thing to walk in the darkness of death, and it is impossible for believers, however great their strength may be, not to shudder at it; but since the prevailing thought is that God is present and providing for their safety, the feeling of security overcomes that of fear. As Augustine says,—whatever be the engines which the devil erects against us, as he cannot gain the heart where faith dwells, he is cast out. Thus, if we may judge by the event, not only do believers come off safe from every contest, so as to be ready, after a short repose, to descend again into the arena, but the saying of John, in his Epistle, is fulfilled, " This is the victory that overcometh the world, even our faith" (1 John v. 4). It is not said that it will be victorious in a single fight, or a few, or some one assault, but that it will be victorious over the whole world, though it should be a thousand times assailed.

22. There is another species of fear and trembling, which, so far from impairing the security of faith, tends rather to establish it—namely, when believers, reflecting that the examples of the divine vengeance on the ungodly are a kind of beacons warning them not to provoke the wrath of God by similar wickedness, keep anxious watch, or, taking a view of their own inherent wretchedness, learn their entire dependence on God, without whom they feel themselves to be fleeting and evanescent as the wind. For when the Apostle sets before the Corinthians the scourges which the Lord in ancient times inflicted on the people of Israel, that they might be afraid of subjecting themselves to similar calamities, he does not in any degree destroy the ground of their confidence; he only shakes off their carnal torpor which suppresses faith, but does not strengthen it. Nor when he takes occasion from the case of the Israelites to exhort, " Let him that thinketh he standeth take heed lest he fall" (1 Cor.

<!-- marginalia: Doubt only a temporary annoyance to real belief. -->
<!-- marginalia: Divine punishment of the unjust encourages the saints not to follow in their footsteps. -->

x. 12), he does not bid us waver, as if we had no security for our stedfastness: he only removes arrogance and rash confidence in our strength, telling the Gentiles not to presume because the Jews had been cast off, and they had been admitted to their place (Rom. xi. 20). In that passage, indeed, he is not addressing believers only, but also comprehends hypocrites, who gloried merely in external appearance; nor is he addressing individuals, but contrasting the Jews and Gentiles, he first shows that the rejection of the former was a just punishment of their ingratitude and unbelief, and then exhorts the latter to beware lest pride and presumption deprive them of the grace of adoption which had lately been transferred to them. For as in that rejection of the Jews there still remained some who were not excluded from the covenant of adoption, so there might be some among the Gentiles who, possessing no true faith were only puffed up with vain carnal confidence, and so abused the goodness of God to their own destruction. But though you should hold that the words were addressed to elect believers, no inconsistency will follow. It is one thing, in order to prevent believers from indulging vain confidence, to repress the temerity which, from the remains of the flesh, sometimes gains upon them, and it is another thing to strike terror into their consciences, and prevent them from feeling secure in the mercy of God.

[margin: God never terrorizes the faithful beyond their ability to stand]

23. Then, when he bids us work out our salvation with fear and trembling, all he requires is, that we accustom ourselves to think very meanly of our own strength, and confide in the strength of the Lord. For nothing stimulates us so strongly to place all our confidence and assurance on the Lord as self-diffidence, and the anxiety produced by a consciousness of our calamitous condition. In this sense are we to understand the words of the Psalmist: "I will come into thy house in the multitude of thy mercy: and in thy fear will I worship toward thy holy temple" (Ps. v. 7). Here he appropriately unites confident faith leaning on the divine mercy with religious fear, which of necessity we must feel whenever coming into the presence of the divine majesty, we are made aware by its splendour of the extent of our own impurity. Truly also does Solomon declare: "Happy is the man that feareth alway; but he that hardeneth his heart falleth into mischief" (Prov. xxviii. 14). The fear he speaks of is that which renders us more cautious, not that which produces despondency; the fear which is felt when the mind confounded in itself resumes its equanimity in God, downcast in itself, takes courage in God, distrusting itself, breathes confidence in God. Hence there is nothing inconsistent in believers being afraid, and at the same time possessing secure consolation as they alternately behold their own vanity, and direct their thoughts to the truth of God. How, it will be asked, can fear and faith dwell in the same mind? Just in the same way as sluggishness and anxiety can so dwell. The ungodly court a state of lethargy that the fear of God may not annoy them; and yet the

[margin: Nothing encourages us more to put our trust in the Lord more than our own calamitous condition]

[margin: There is, therefore, no inconsistency in believers being afraid while yet possessing secure consolation.]

judgment of God so urges that they cannot gain their desire.   In the same way God can train his people to humility, and curb them by the bridle of modesty, while yet fighting bravely.   And it is plain, from the context, that this was the Apostle's meaning, since he states, as the ground of fear and trembling, that it is God who worketh in us to will and to do of his good pleasure.   In the same sense must we understand the words of the Prophet, "The children of Israel" "shall fear the Lord and his goodness in the latter days" (Hos. iii. 5). For not only does piety beget reverence to God, but the sweet attractiveness of grace inspires a man, though desponding of himself, at once with fear and admiration, making him feel his dependence on God, and submit humbly to his power.

24. Here, however, we give no countenance to that most pestilential philosophy which some semi-papists are at present beginning to broach in corners.   Unable to defend the gross doubt inculcated by the Schoolmen, they have recourse to another fiction, that they may compound a mixture of faith and unbelief.   They admit, that whenever we look to Christ we are furnished with full ground for hope ; but as we are ever unworthy of all the blessings which are offered us in Christ, they will have us to fluctuate and hesitate in the view of our unworthiness.   In short, they give conscience a position between hope and fear, making it alternate, by successive turns, to the one and the other.   Hope and fear, again, they place in complete contrast,—the one falling as the other rises, and rising as the other falls. Thus Satan, finding the devices by which he was wont to destroy the certainty of faith too manifest to be now of any avail, is endeavouring, by indirect methods, to undermine it.[1]   But what kind of confidence is that which is ever and anon supplanted by despair ?   They tell you, if you look to Christ salvation is certain ; if you return to yourself damnation is certain.   Therefore, your mind must be alternately ruled by diffidence and hope ; as if we were to imagine Christ standing at a distance, and not rather dwelling in us.   We expect salvation from him—not because he stands aloof from us, but because ingrafting us into his body he not only makes us partakers of all his benefits, but also of himself.   Therefore, I thus retort the argument, If you look to yourself damnation is certain : but since Christ has been communicated to you with all his benefits, so that all which is his is made yours, you become a member of him, and hence one with him.   His righteousness covers your sins—his salvation extinguishes your condemnation ; he interposes with his worthiness, and so prevents your unworthiness from coming into the view of God.   Thus it truly is.   It will never do to separate Christ from us, nor us from

---

1 The French is, "Voila comme Satan, quand il voit que par mensonge clair et ouvert il ne peust plus destruire la certitude de la foy, s'efforce en cachette et comme par dessous terre la ruiner."—Behold how Satan, when he sees that by clear and open falsehood he can no longer destroy the certainty of faith, is striving in secret, and as it were below ground, to ruin it.

[Margin notes:]
The Schoolmen make of our conscience sort of a yo-yo-bobbing up and down between hope and dispair.

Since Christ has been communicated to us, all of His benifits are ours.

him; but we must, with both hands, keep firm hold of that alliance by which he has riveted us to himself. This the Apostle teaches us: "The body is dead because of sin; but the spirit is life because of righteousness" (Rom. viii. 10). According to the frivolous trifling of these objectors he ought to have said, Christ indeed has life in himself, but you, as you are sinners, remain liable to death and condemnation. Very different is his language. He tells us that the condemnation which we of ourselves deserve is annihilated by the salvation of Christ; and to confirm this he employs the argument to which I have referred—viz. that Christ is not external to us, but dwells in us; and not only unites us to himself by an undivided bond of fellowship, but by a wondrous communion brings us daily into closer connection, until he becomes altogether one with us. And yet I deny not, as I lately said, that faith occasionally suffers certain interruptions when, by violent assault, its weakness is made to bend in this direction or in that; and its light is buried in the thick darkness of temptation. Still happen what may, faith ceases not to long after God.

[margin note: Reiterates that according to his belief, hope and despair run together on parallel lines.]

25. The same doctrine is taught by Bernard when he treats professedly on this subject in his Fifth Homily on the Dedication of the Temple: "By the blessing of God, sometimes meditating on the soul, methinks I find in it as it were two contraries. When I look at it as it is in itself and of itself, the truest thing I can say of it is, that it has been reduced to nothing. What need is there to enumerate each of its miseries? how burdened with sin, obscured with darkness, ensnared by allurements, teeming with lusts, ruled by passion, filled with delusions, ever prone to evil, inclined to every vice; lastly, full of ignominy and confusion. If all its righteousnesses, when examined by the light of truth, are but as filthy rags (Is. lxiv. 6), what must we suppose its unrighteousness to be? 'If, therefore, the light that is in thee be darkness, how great is that darkness?' (Matth. vi. 23.) What then? man doubtless has been made subject to vanity—man has been reduced to nothing—man is nothing. And yet how is he whom God exalts utterly nothing? How is he nothing to whom a divine heart has been given? Let us breathe again, brethren. Although we are nothing in our hearts, perhaps something of us may lurk in the heart of God. O Father of mercies! O Father of the miserable! how plantest thou thy heart in us? Where thy heart is, there is thy treasure also. But how are we thy treasure if we are nothing? All nations before thee are as nothing. Observe, *before* thee; not *within* thee. Such are they in the judgment of thy truth, but not such in regard to thy affection. Thou callest the things which be not as though they were; and they are not, because thou callest them 'things that be not:' and yet they are because thou callest them. For though they are not as to themselves, yet they are with thee according to the declaration of Paul: 'Not of works, but of him that calleth'" (Rom. ix. 11). He then goes on to

[margin note: Supports this argument by quoting Bernard.]

say that the connection is wonderful in both points of view. Certainly things which are connected together do not mutually destroy each other. This he explains more clearly in his conclusion in the following terms: "If, in both views, we diligently consider what we are,—in the one view our nothingness, in the other our greatness,—I presume our glorying will seem restrained; but perhaps it is rather increased and confirmed, because we glory not in ourselves, but in the Lord. Our thought is, if he determined to save us we shall be delivered; and here we begin again to breathe. But, ascending to a loftier height, let us seek the city of God, let us seek the temple, let us seek our home, let us seek our spouse. I have not forgotten myself when, with fear and reverence, I say, We are,—are in the heart of God. We are, by his dignifying, not by our own dignity."

26. Moreover, the fear of the Lord, which is uniformly attributed to all the saints, and which, in one passage, is called "the beginning of wisdom," in another *wisdom* itself, although it is one, proceeds from a twofold cause. God is entitled to the reverence of a Father and a Lord. Hence he who desires duly to worship him, will study to act the part both of an obedient son and a faithful servant. The obedience paid to God as a Father he by his prophet terms *honour;* the service performed to him as a master he terms *fear.* "A son honoureth his father, and a servant his master. If then I be a father, where is mine honour? and if I be a master, where is my fear?"[1] But while he thus distinguishes between the two, it is obvious that he at the same time confounds them. The fear of the Lord, therefore, may be defined reverence mingled with honour and fear. It is not strange that the same mind can entertain both feelings; for he who considers with himself what kind of a father God is to us, will see sufficient reason, even were there no hell, why the thought of offending him should seem more dreadful than any death. But so prone is our carnal nature to indulgence in sin, that, in order to curb it in every way, we must also give place to the thought that all iniquity is abomination to the Master under whom we live; that those who, by wicked lives, provoke his anger, will not escape his vengeance.

27. There is nothing repugnant to this in the observation of John: "There is no fear in love; but perfect love casteth out fear: because fear hath torment" (1 John iv. 18). For he is speaking of the fear of unbelief, between which and the fear of believers there is a wide difference. The wicked do not fear God from any unwillingness to offend him, provided they could do so with impunity; but knowing that he is armed with power for vengeance, they tremble in dismay on hearing of his anger. And they thus dread his anger, because they think it is impending over them, and they every moment expect it to fall upon their heads. But believers, as has been said, dread the offence even more than the punishment. They are not alarmed

[1] Ps. cxi. 10; Prov. i. 7, ix. 10, xv. 24; Job xxviii. 28; Mal. i. 6.

by the fear of punishment, as if it were impending over them,[1] but are rendered the more cautious of doing anything to provoke it. Thus the Apostle addressing believers says, " Let no man deceive you with vain words ; for because of these things, the wrath of God cometh upon the children of disobedience" (Eph. v. 6 ; Col. iii. 6). He does not threaten that wrath will descend upon them ; but he admonishes them, while they think how the wrath of God is prepared for the wicked, on account of the crimes which he had enumerated, not to run the risk of provoking it.   It seldom happens that mere threatenings have the effect of arousing the reprobate ; nay, becoming more callous and hardened when God thunders verbally from heaven, they obstinately persist in their rebellion.   It is only when actually smitten by his hand that they are forced, whether they will or not, to fear.   This fear the sacred writers term *servile*, and oppose to the free and voluntary fear which becomes sons.   Some, by a subtle distinction, have introduced an intermediate species, holding that that forced and servile fear sometimes subdues the mind, and leads spontaneously to proper fear.

[margin: The wrath of God must fall upon the repro- bate be- fore they turn and fear Him.]

28. The divine favour to which faith is said to have respect, we understand to include in it the possession of salvation and eternal life. For if, when God is propitious, no good thing can be wanting to us, we have ample security for our salvation when assured of his love. " Turn us again, O God, and cause thy face to shine," says the Prophet, " and we shall be saved" (Ps. lxxx. 3).   Hence the Scriptures make the sum of our salvation to consist in the removal of all enmity, and our admission into favour ; thus intimating, that when God is reconciled all danger is past, and everything good will befall us. Wherefore, faith apprehending the love of God has the promise both of the present and the future life, and ample security for all blessings (Eph. ii. 14).   The nature of this must be ascertained from the word. Faith does not promise us length of days, riches, and honours (the Lord not having been pleased that any of these should be appointed us); but is contented with the assurance, that however poor we may be in regard to present comforts, God will never fail us.   The chief security lies in the expectation of future life, which is placed beyond doubt by the word of God.   Whatever be the miseries and calamities which await the children of God in this world, they cannot make his favour cease to be complete happiness.   Hence, when we were desirous to express the sum of blessedness, we designated it by the favour of God, from which, as their source, all kinds of blessings flow.   And we may observe throughout the Scriptures, that they refer us to the love of God, not only when they treat of our eternal salvation, but of any blessing whatever.   For which reason David sings, that the loving-kindness of God experienced by the pious heart is sweeter and more to be desired than life itself (Ps. lxiii. 3).   In short, if we have

[margin: Faith does not promise us worldly wealth, but rather, the presence of God. The chief security lies in the expectation of the future life.]

---

[1] Latin, " acsi cervicibus suis impenderet."—French, " comme si l'enfer leur etoit desia present pour les englouter;"—as if hell were already present to engulfthem.

Without God, worldly possessions mean nothing. With God, even our miseries become blessings.

every earthly comfort to a wish, but are uncertain whether we have the love or the hatred of God, our felicity will be cursed, and therefore miserable. But if God lift on us the light of his fatherly countenance, our very miseries will be blessed, inasmuch as they will become helps to our salvation. Thus Paul, after bringing together all kinds of adversity, boasts that they cannot separate us from the love of God: and in his prayers he uniformly begins with the grace of God as the source of all prosperity. In like manner, to all the terrors which assail us David opposes merely the favour of God,— "Yea, though I walk through the valley of the shadow of death, I will fear no evil: for thou art with me" (Ps. xxiii. 4). And we feel that our minds always waver until, contented with the grace of God, we in it seek peace, and feel thoroughly persuaded of what is said in the psalm, "Blessed is the nation whose God is the Lord, and the people whom he hath chosen for his own inheritance" (Ps. xxxiii. 12).

Free promise is the foundation of faith.

29. Free promise we make the foundation of faith, because in it faith properly consists. For though it holds that God is always true, whether in ordering or forbidding, promising or threatening; though it obediently receive his commands, observe his prohibitions, and give heed to his threatenings; yet it properly begins with promise, continues with it, and ends with it. It seeks life in God, life which is not found in commands or the denunciations of punishment, but in the promise of mercy. And this promise must be gratuitous; for a conditional promise, which throws us back upon our works, promises life only in so far as we find it existing in ourselves. Therefore, if we would not have faith to waver and tremble, we must support it with the promise of salvation, which is offered by the Lord spontaneously and freely, from a regard to our misery, rather than our worth. Hence the Apostle bears this testimony to the Gospel, that it is the word of faith (Rom. x. 8). This he concedes not either to the precepts or the promises of the Law, since there is nothing which can establish our faith, but that free embassy by which God reconciles the world to himself. Hence he often uses faith and the Gospel as correlative terms, as when he says, that the ministry of the Gospel was committed to him for "obedience to the faith;" that "it

Mercy is the object to which faith must look

is the power of God unto salvation to every one that believeth;" that "therein is the righteousness of God revealed from faith to faith" (Rom. i. 5, 16, 17). No wonder: for seeing that the Gospel is "the ministry of reconciliation" (2 Cor. v. 18), there is no other sufficient evidence of the divine favour, such as faith requires to know. Therefore, when we say, that faith must rest on a free promise, we deny not that believers accept and embrace the word of God in all its parts, but we point to the promise of mercy as its special object. Believers, indeed, ought to recognise God as the judge and avenger of wickedness; and yet mercy is the object to which they properly look, since he is exhibited to their contemplation as "good and ready to forgive," "plenteous in mercy," "slow to anger," "good to all," and shedding "his tender mercies over all his works" (Ps. lxxxvi. 5; ciii. 8; cxlv. 8, 9).

30. I stay not to consider the rabid objections of Pighius, and others like-minded, who inveigh against this restriction, as rending faith, and laying hold of one of its fragments. I admit, as I have already said, that the general object of faith (as they express it) is the truth of God, whether he threatens or gives hope of his favour. Accordingly, the Apostle attributes it to faith in Noah, that he feared the destruction of the world, when as yet it was not seen (Heb. xi. 17). If fear of impending punishment was a work of faith, threatenings ought not to be excluded in defining it. This is indeed true; but we are unjustly and calumniously charged with denying that faith has respect to the whole word of God. We only mean to maintain these two points,—that faith is never decided until it attain to a free promise; and that the only way in which faith reconciles us to God is by uniting us with Christ. Both are deserving of notice. We are inquiring after a faith which separates the children of God from the reprobate, believers from unbelievers. Shall every man, then, who believes that God is just in what he commands, and true in what he threatens, be on that account classed with believers? Very far from it. Faith, then, has no firm footing until it stand in the mercy of God. Then what end have we in view in discoursing of faith? Is it not that we may understand the way of salvation? But how can faith be saving, unless in so far as it engrafts us into the body of Christ? There is no absurdity, therefore, when, in defining it, we thus press its special object, and, by way of distinction, add to the generic character the particular mark which distinguishes the believer from the unbeliever. In short, the malicious have nothing to carp at in this doctrine, unless they are to bring the same censure against the Apostle Paul, who specially designates the Gospel as "the word of faith" (Rom. x. 8).

31. Hence again we infer, as has already been explained, that faith has no less need of the word than the fruit of a tree has of a living root; because, as David testifies, none can hope in God but those who know his name (Ps. ix. 10). This knowledge, however, is not left to every man's imagination, but depends on the testimony which God himself gives to his goodness. This the same Psalmist confirms in another passage, "Thy salvation according to thy word" (Ps. cxix. 41). Again, "Save me," "I hoped in thy word" (Ps. cxix. 146, 147). Here we must attend to the relation of faith to the word, and to salvation as its consequence. Still, however, we exclude not the power of God. If faith cannot support itself in the view of this power, it never will give Him the honour which is due. Paul seems to relate a trivial or very ordinary circumstance with regard to Abraham, when he says, that he believed that God, who had given him the promise of a blessed seed, was able also to perform it (Rom. iv. 21). And in like manner, in another passage, he says of himself, "I

[margin note:] Faith is never decided until it attain to a free Promise

[margin note:] Faith has no firm footing until it stand in the mercy of God.

know whom I have believed, and am persuaded that he is able to keep that which I have committed unto him against that day" (2 Tim. i. 12). But let any one consider with himself, how he is ever and anon assailed with doubts in regard to the power of God, and he will readily perceive, that those who duly magnify it have made no small progress in faith. We all acknowledge that God can do whatsoever he pleases; but while every temptation, even the most trivial, fills us with fear and dread, it is plain that we derogate from the power of God, by attaching less importance to his promises than to Satan's threatenings against them.[1]

This is the reason why Isaiah, when he would impress on the hearts of the people the certainty of faith, discourses so magnificently of the boundless power of God. He often seems, after beginning to speak of the hope of pardon and reconciliation, to digress, and unnecessarily take a long circuitous course, describing how wonderfully God rules the fabric of heaven and earth, with the whole course of nature; and yet he introduces nothing which is not appropriate to the occasion; because, unless the power of God, to which all things are possible, is presented to our eye, our ears malignantly refuse admission to the word, or set no just value upon it. We may add, that an effectual power is here meant; for piety, as it has elsewhere been seen, always makes a practical application of the power of God; in particular, keeps those works in view in which he has declared himself to be a Father. Hence the frequent mention in Scripture of redemption; from which the Israelites might learn, that he who had once been the author of salvation would be its perpetual guardian. By his own example, also, David reminds us, that the benefits which God has bestowed privately on any individual, tend to confirm his faith for the time to come; nay, that when God seems to have forsaken us, we ought to extend our view farther, and take courage from his former favours, as is said in another Psalm, "I remember the days of old: I meditate on all thy works" (Ps. cxliii. 5). Again, "I will remember the works of the Lord; surely I will remember thy wonders of old" (Ps. lxxvii. 11). But because all our conceptions of the power and works of God are evanescent without the word, we are not rash in maintaining, that there is no faith until God present us with clear evidence of his grace.

Here, however, a question might be raised as to the view to be taken of Sarah and Rebekah, both of whom, impelled as it would seem by zeal for the faith, went beyond the limits of the word. Sarah, in her eager desire for the promised seed, gave her maid to her husband. That she sinned in many respects is not to be denied; but the only fault to which I now refer is her being carried away by zeal, and not confining herself within the limits prescribed by the

1 The French adds, "Combien que nous ayons les promesses de Dieu pour nous munir à l'encontre;"—although we have the promise of God to strengthen us for the encounter.

word. It is certain, however, that her desire proceeded from faith. Rebekah, again, divinely informed of the election of her son Jacob, procures the blessing for him by a wicked stratagem ; deceives her husband, who was a witness and minister of divine grace ; forces her son to lie ; by various frauds and impostures corrupts divine truth ; in fine, by exposing his promise to scorn, does what in her lies to make it of no effect. And yet this conduct, however vicious and reprehensible, was not devoid of faith. She must have overcome many obstacles before she obtained so strong a desire of that which, without any hope of earthly advantage, was full of difficulty and danger. In the same way, we cannot say that the holy patriarch Isaac was altogether void of faith, in that, after he had been similarly informed of the honour transferred to the younger son, he still continues his predilection in favour of his first-born, Esau. These examples certainly show that error is often mingled with faith ; and yet that when faith is real, it always obtains the pre-eminence. For as the particular error of Rebekah did not render the blessing of no effect, neither did it nullify the faith which generally ruled in her mind, and was the principle and cause of that action. In this, nevertheless, Rebekah showed how prone the human mind is to turn aside whenever it gives itself the least indulgence. But though defect and infirmity obscure faith, they do not extinguish it. Still they admonish us how carefully we ought to cling to the word of God, and at the same time confirm what we have taught—viz. that faith gives way when not supported by the word, just as the minds of Sarah, Isaac, and Rebekah, would have lost themselves in devious paths, had not the secret restraint of Providence kept them obedient to the word.

32. On the other hand, we have good ground for comprehending all the promises in Christ, since the Apostle comprehends the whole Gospel under the knowledge of Christ, and declares that all the promises of God are in him, yea, and amen.[1] The reason for this is obvious. Every promise which God makes is evidence of his good will. This is invariably true, and is not inconsistent with the fact, that the large benefits which the divine liberality is constantly bestowing on the wicked are preparing them for heavier judgment. As they neither think that these proceed from the hand of the Lord, nor acknowledge them as his, or if they do so acknowledge them, never regard them as proofs of his favour, they are in no respect more instructed thereby in his mercy than brute beasts, which, according to their condition, enjoy the same liberality, and yet never look beyond it. Still it is true, that by rejecting the promises generally offered to them, they subject themselves to severer punishment. For though it is only when the promises are received in faith that their efficacy is manifested, still their reality and power are never extinguished by our infidelity or ingratitude. Therefore, when the Lord by his pro-

[Marginal note: Error is often mingled with faith, and yet when faith is real, it always obtains the pre-eminence.]

[Marginal note: Though defect and infirmity obscure faith, they do not extinguish it.]

---

[1] Rom. i. 3; 1 Cor. ii. 2; 2 Cor. i. 20.

God's promises are declarations of His love.

mises invites us not only to enjoy the fruits of his kindness, but also to meditate upon them, he at the same time declares his love. Thus we are brought back to our statement, that every promise is a manifestation of the divine favour toward us. Now, without controversy, God loves no man out of Christ. He is the beloved Son, in whom the love of the Father dwells, and from whom it afterwards extends to us. Thus Paul says, " In whom he hath made us accepted in the Beloved" (Eph. i. 6). It is by his intervention, therefore, that love is diffused so as to reach us. Accordingly, in another passage, the Apostle calls Christ "our peace" (Eph. ii. 14), and also represents him as the bond by which the Father is united to us in paternal affection (Rom. viii. 3). It follows, that whenever any promise is

whenever any promise is made to us, we must turn our eyes toward Christ.

made to us, we must turn our eyes toward Christ. Hence, with good reason, Paul declares that in him all the promises of God are confirmed and completed (Rom. xv. 8). Some examples are brought forward as repugnant to this view. When Naaman the Syrian made inquiry at the prophet as to the true mode of worshipping God, we cannot (it is said) suppose that he was informed of the Mediator, and yet he is commended for his piety (2 Kings v. 17—19). Nor could Cornelius, a Roman heathen, be acquainted with what was not known to all the Jews, and at best known obscurely. And yet his alms and prayers were acceptable to God (Acts x. 31), while the prophet by his answer approved of the sacrifices of Naaman. In both, this must have been the result of faith. In like manner, the eunuch to whom Philip was sent, had he not been endued with some degree of faith, never would have incurred the fatigue and expense of a long and difficult journey to obtain an opportunity of worship (Acts viii. 27, 31); and yet we see how, when interrogated by Philip, he betrays his ignorance of the Mediator. I admit that, in some respect, their faith was not explicit either as to the person of Christ, or the power and office assigned him by the Father. Still it is certain that they were imbued with principles which might give some, though a slender, foretaste of Christ. This should not be thought strange ; for the eunuch would not have hastened from a distant country to Jerusalem to an unknown God ; nor could Cornelius, after having once embraced the Jewish religion, have lived so long in Judea without becoming acquainted with the rudiments of sound doctrine. In regard to Naaman, it is absurd to suppose that Elisha, while he gave him many minute precepts, said nothing of the principal matter. Therefore, although their knowledge of Christ may have been obscure, we cannot suppose that they had no such knowledge at all. They used the sacrifices of the Law, and must have distinguished them from the spurious sacrifices of the Gentiles, by the end to which they referred—viz. Christ.

33. A simple external manifestation of the word ought to be amply sufficient to produce faith, did not our blindness and perverseness prevent. But such is the proneness of our mind to vanity, that it

can never adhere to the truth of God, and such its dulness, that it is always blind even in his light. Hence without the illumination of the Spirit the word has no effect; and hence also it is obvious that faith is something higher than human understanding. Nor were it sufficient for the mind to be illumined by the Spirit of God unless the heart also were strengthened and supported by his power. Here the Schoolmen go completely astray, dwelling entirely in their consideration of faith, on the bare simple assent of the understanding, and altogether overlooking confidence and security of heart. Faith is the special gift of God in both ways,—in purifying the mind so as to give it a relish for divine truth, and afterwards in establishing it therein. For the Spirit does not merely originate faith, but gradually increases it, until by its means he conducts us into the heavenly kingdom. "That good thing which was committed unto thee," says Paul, "keep by the Holy Ghost which dwelleth in us" (2 Tim. i. 14). In what sense Paul says (Gal. iii. 2), that the Spirit is given by the hearing of faith, may be easily explained. If there were only a single gift of the Spirit, he who is the author and cause of faith could not without absurdity be said to be its effect; but after celebrating the gifts with which God adorns his church, and by successive additions of faith leads it to perfection, there is nothing strange in his ascribing to faith the very gifts which faith prepares us for receiving. It seems to some paradoxical, when it is said that none can believe Christ save those to whom it is given; but this is partly because they do not observe how recondite and sublime heavenly wisdom is, or how dull the mind of man in discerning divine mysteries, and partly because they pay no regard to that firm and stable constancy of heart which is the chief part of faith.

34.[1] But as Paul argues, "What man knoweth the things of a man, save the spirit of man which is in him? even so the things of God knoweth no man but the Spirit of God" (1 Cor. ii. 11). If in regard to divine truth we hesitate even as to those things which we see with the bodily eye, how can we be firm and stedfast in regard to those divine promises which neither the eye sees nor the mind comprehends? Here human discernment is so defective and lost, that the first step of advancement in the school of Christ is to renounce it (Matth. xi. 25; Luke x. 21). Like a veil interposed, it prevents us from beholding divine mysteries, which are revealed only to babes. "Flesh and blood" doth not reveal them (Matth. xvi. 17). "The natural man receiveth not the things of the Spirit of God: for they are foolishness unto him; neither can he know them, for they are spiritually discerned" (1 Cor. ii. 14). The supplies of the Holy Spirit are therefore necessary, or rather his agency is here the only strength. "For who hath known the mind of the Lord? or who hath been his counsellor?" (Rom. xi. 34;) but "The Spirit searcheth

1 The French thus begins the section: "Lequel erreur est facile a convaincre;"— This error is easily refuted

all things, yea, the deep things of God" (1 Cor. ii. 10). Thus it is that we attain to the mind of Christ: "No man can come to me, except the Father which hath sent me draw him: and I will raise him up at the last day." "Every man therefore that hath heard, and learned of the Father, cometh unto me. Not that any man hath seen the Father, save he which is of God, he hath seen the Father" (John vi. 44, 45, 46). Therefore, as we cannot possibly come to Christ unless drawn by the Spirit, so when we are drawn we are both in mind and spirit exalted far above our own understanding. For the soul, when illumined by him, receives as it were a new eye, enabling it to contemplate heavenly mysteries, by the splendour of which it was previously dazzled. And thus, indeed, it is only when the human intellect is irradiated by the light of the Holy Spirit that it begins to have a taste of those things which pertain to the kingdom of God; previously it was too stupid and senseless to have any relish for them. Hence our Saviour, when clearly declaring the mysteries of the kingdom to the two disciples, makes no impression till he opens their minds to understand the Scriptures (Luke xxiv. 27, 45). Hence also, though he had taught the Apostles with his own divine lips, it was still necessary to send the Spirit of truth to instil into their minds the same doctrine which they had heard with their ears. The word is, in regard to those to whom it is preached, like the sun which shines upon all, but is of no use to the blind, In this matter we are all naturally blind; and hence the word cannot penetrate our mind unless the Spirit, that internal teacher, by his enlightening power make an entrance for it.

35. Having elsewhere shown more fully, when treating of the corruption of our nature, how little able men are to believe (Book II. c. ii. iii.), I will not fatigue the reader by again repeating it. Let it suffice to observe, that the spirit of faith is used by Paul as synonymous with the very faith which we receive from the Spirit, but which we have not naturally (2 Cor. iv. 13). Accordingly, he prays for the Thessalonians, "that our God would count you worthy of this calling, and fulfil all the good pleasure of his goodness, and the work of faith with power" (2 Thess. i. 2). Here, by designating faith the *work* of God, and distinguishing it by way of epithet, appropriately calling it his *good pleasure*, he declares that it is not of man's own nature; and not contented with this, he adds, that it is an illustration of divine power. In addressing the Corinthians, when he tells them that faith stands not "in the wisdom of man, but in the power of God" (1 Cor. ii. 4), he is no doubt speaking of external miracles; but as the reprobate are blinded when they behold them, he also includes that internal seal of which he elsewhere makes mention. And the better to display his liberality in this most excellent gift, God does not bestow it upon all promiscuously, but, by special privilege, imparts it to whom he will. To this effect we have already quoted passages of Scripture, as to which Augustine, their faithful expositor,

exclaims (De Verbo Apost. Serm. ii.), "Our Saviour, to teach that *Christ,* faith in him is a gift, not a merit, says, 'No man can come to me, *when he* except the Father, which hath sent me, draw him' (John vi. 44). It *produces* is strange when two persons hear, the one despises, the other ascends. *faith in us* Let him who despises impute it to himself; let him who ascends not *by the* arrogate it to himself." In another passage, he asks, "Wherefore is *agency of* it given to the one, and not to the other? I am not ashamed to say, *His Spirit,* This is one of the deep things of the cross. From some unknown *at the* depth of the judgments of God, which we cannot scrutinise, all our *same time* ability proceeds. I see that I am able; but how I am able I see *ingrafts us* not:—this far only I see, that it is of God. But why the one, and *into his* not the other? This is too great for me: it is an abyss, a depth of *body, that* the cross. I can cry out with wonder; not discuss and demonstrate." *we may be-* The whole comes to this, that Christ, when he produces faith in us *come par-* by the agency of his Spirit, at the same time ingrafts us into his body, *takers of* that we may become partakers of all blessings. *all bless-*

36. The next thing necessary is, that what the mind has imbibed *ings.* be transferred into the heart. The word is not received in faith when it merely flutters in the brain, but when it has taken deep root in the heart, and become an invincible bulwark to withstand and repel all the assaults of temptation. But if the illumination of the Spirit is *The* the true source of understanding in the intellect, much more manifest *Spirit* is his agency in the confirmation of the heart; inasmuch as there is *seals* more distrust in the heart than blindness in the mind; and it is more *upon our* difficult to inspire the soul with security than to imbue it with know- *hearts* ledge. Hence the Spirit performs the part of a seal, sealing upon our *the pro-* hearts the very promises, the certainty of which was previously im- *mises of* pressed upon our minds. It also serves as an earnest in establishing *God.* and confirming these promises. Thus the Apostle says, "In whom also, after that ye believed, ye were sealed with that holy Spirit of promise, which is the earnest of our inheritance" (Eph. i. 13, 14). You see how he teaches that the hearts of believers are stamped with the Spirit as with a seal, and calls it the Spirit of promise, because it ratifies the gospel to us. In like manner he says to the Corinthians, "God hath also sealed us, and given the earnest of the Spirit in our hearts" (2 Cor. i. 22). And again, when speaking of a full and con- fident hope, he founds it on the "earnest of the Spirit" (2 Cor. v. 5).

37. I am not forgetting what I formerly said, and experience brings daily to remembrance—viz. that faith is subject to various doubts,[1] so that the minds of believers are seldom at rest, or at least are not always tranquil. Still, whatever be the engines by which they are shaken, they either escape from the whirlpool of temptation, or remain stedfast in their place. Faith finds security and protection in the words of the psalm, "God is our refuge and strength, a very present help in trouble; therefore will not we fear, though the earth be

---

1 French, "Doutes, solicitudes, et detresses;"—doubts, anxieties, and distresses.

removed, and the mountains be carried into the midst of the sea" (Ps. xlvi. 1, 2). This delightful tranquillity is elsewhere described: "I laid me down and slept; I awaked, for the Lord sustained me" (Ps. iii. 5). Not that David was uniformly in this joyful frame; but in so far as the measure of his faith made him sensible of the divine favour, he glories in intrepidly despising everything that could disturb his peace of mind. Hence the Scripture, when it exhorts us to faith, bids us be at peace. In Isaiah it is said, "In quietness and in confidence shall be your strength" (Is. xxx. 15); and in the psalm, "Rest in the Lord, and wait patiently for him." Corresponding to this is the passage in the Hebrews, "Ye have need of patience," &c. (Heb. x. 36).

38. Hence we may judge how pernicious is the scholastic dogma,[1] that we can have no stronger evidence of the divine favour toward us than moral conjecture, according as each individual deems himself not unworthy of it. Doubtless, if we are to determine by our works in what way the Lord stands affected towards us, I admit that we cannot even get the length of a feeble conjecture: but since faith should accord with the free and simple promise, there is no room left for ambiguity. With what kind of confidence, pray, shall we be armed if we reason in this way—God is propitious to us, provided we deserve it by the purity of our lives? But since we have reserved this subject for discussion in its proper place, we shall not prosecute it farther at present, especially seeing it is already plain that nothing is more adverse to faith than conjecture, or any other feeling akin to doubt. Nothing can be worse than their perversion of the passage of Ecclesiastes, which is ever in their mouths: "No man knoweth either love or hatred by all that is before them" (Eccl. ix. 1).[2] For without insisting that the passage is erroneously rendered in the common version—even a child cannot fail to perceive what Solomon's meaning is—viz. that any one who would ascertain, from the present state of things, who are in the favour or under the displeasure of God, labours in vain, and torments himself to no useful purpose, since "all things come alike to all;" "to him that sacrificeth, and to him that sacrificeth not:" and hence God does not always declare his love to those on whom he bestows uninterrupted prosperity, nor his hatred against those whom he afflicts. And it tends to prove the vanity of the human intellect, that it is so completely in the dark as to matters which it is of the highest importance to know. Thus Solomon had said a little before, "That which befalleth the sons of men befalleth beasts; even one thing befalleth them: as the one dieth, so dieth the other" (Eccl. iii. 19). Were any one thence to infer that we hold the immortality of the soul by conjecture merely, would he not justly be deemed insane? Are those then sane who

[margin note: Against the schoolmen.]

---

[1] French, "La doctrine des theologiens sophistes;"—the doctrine of sophistical theologians.

[2] See Bernard, Serm. ii. in Die Ascensionis, and Serm. ii. in Octava Paschæ.

cannot obtain any certainty of the divine favour, because the carnal eye is now unable to discern it from the present appearance of the world?

39. But, they say, it is rash and presumptuous to pretend to an undoubted knowledge of the divine will. I would grant this, did we hold that we were able to subject the incomprehensible counsel of God to our feeble intellect. But when we simply say with Paul, " We have received not the spirit of the world, but the Spirit which is of God; that we might know the things that are freely given to us of God" (1 Cor. ii. 12), what can they oppose to this, without offering insult to the Spirit of God? But if it is sacrilege to charge the revelation which he has given us with falsehood, or uncertainty, or ambiguity, how can we be wrong in maintaining its certainty? But they still exclaim, that there is great temerity in our presuming to glory in possessing the Spirit of God.[1] Who could believe that these men, who desire to be thought the masters of the world, could be so stupid as to err thus grossly in the very first principles of religion? To me, indeed, it would be incredible, did not their own writings make it manifest. Paul declares that those only are the sons of God who are led by his Spirit (Rom. viii. 14); these men would have those who are the sons of God to be led by their own, and void of the divine Spirit. He tells us that we call God our Father in terms dictated by the Spirit, who alone bears witness with our spirit that we are the sons of God (Rom. viii. 16); they, though they forbid us not to invoke God, withdraw the Spirit, by whose guidance he is duly invoked. He declares that those only are the servants of Christ who are led by the Spirit of Christ (Rom. viii. 9); they imagine a Christianity which has no need of the Spirit of Christ. He holds out the hope of a blessed resurrection to those only who feel His Spirit dwelling in them (Rom. viii. 11); they imagine hope when there is no such feeling. But perhaps they will say, that they deny not the necessity of being endued with the Spirit, but only hold it to be the part of modesty and humility not to recognise it. What, then, does Paul mean, when he says to the Corinthians, " Examine yourselves whether ye be in the faith: prove your ownselves. Know ye not your ownselves, that Jesus Christ is in you, except ye be reprobates?" (2 Cor. xiii. 5.) John, moreover, says, " Hereby we know that he abideth in us by the Spirit which he hath given us" (1 John iii. 24). And what else is it than to bring the promises of Christ into doubt, when we would be deemed servants of Christ without having his Spirit, whom he declared that he would pour out on all his people? (Isa. xliv. 3.) What! do we not insult the Holy Spirit, when we separate faith, which is his peculiar work, from himself? These being the first rudiments of religion, it is the most wretched blindness to charge Christians with arrogance, for presum-

The Schoolmen imagine a Christianity which has no need of the Spirit of Christ

---

1 The French adds, " En quoy ils demonstrent grandement leur betise;"—In this they give a great demonstration of their stupidity.

ing to glory in the presence of the Holy Spirit ; a glorying without which Christianity itself does not exist. The example of these men illustrates the truth of our Saviour's declaration, that his Spirit "the world cannot receive, because it seeth him not, neither knoweth him ; but ye know him, for he dwelleth with you, and shall be in you" (John xiv. 17).

40. That they may not attempt to undermine the certainty of faith in one direction only, they attack it in another—viz. that though it be lawful for the believer, from his actual state of righteousness, to form a judgment as to the favour of God, the knowledge of final perseverance still remains in suspense. An admirable security, indeed, is left us, if, for the present moment only, we can judge from moral conjecture that we are in grace, but know not how we are to be to-morrow ! Very different is the language of the Apostle, "I am persuaded that neither death, nor life, nor angels, nor principalities, nor powers, nor things present nor things to come, nor height, nor depth, nor any other creature, shall be able to separate us from the love of God, which is in Christ Jesus our Lord" (Rom. viii. 38). They endeavour to evade the force of this by frivolously pretending that the Apostle had this assurance by special revelation. They are too well caught thus to escape ; for in that passage he is treating not of his individual experience, but of the blessings which all believers in common derive from faith. But then Paul in another passage alarms us by the mention of our weakness and inconstancy, " Let him that thinketh he standeth take heed lest he fall" (1 Cor. x. 12). True ; but this he says not to inspire us with terror, but that we may learn to humble ourselves under the mighty hand of God, as Peter explains (1 Pet. v. 6). Then how preposterous is it to limit the certainty of faith to a point of time ; seeing it is the property of faith to pass beyond the whole course of this life, and stretch forward to a future immortality ? Therefore, since believers owe it to the favour of God, that, enlightened by his Spirit, they, through faith, enjoy the prospect of heavenly life ; there is so far from an approach to arrogance in such glorying, that any one ashamed to confess it, instead of testifying modesty or submission, rather betrays extreme ingratitude, by maliciously suppressing the divine goodness.

41. Since the nature of faith could not be better or more clearly evinced than by the substance of the promise on which it leans as its proper foundation, and without which it immediately falls or rather vanishes away, we have derived our definition from it—a definition, however, not at all at variance with that definition, or rather description, which the Apostle accommodates to his discourse, when he says that faith is "the substance of things hoped for, the evidence of things not seen" (Heb. xi. 1). For by the term substance (ὑπόστασις), he means a kind of prop on which the pious mind rests and leans. As if he had said, that faith is a kind of certain and secure possession of those things which are promised to us by God; unless we prefer

taking ὑπόστασις for confidence. I have no objection to this, though I am more inclined to adopt the other interpretation, which is more generally received. Again, to intimate that until the last day, when the books will be opened (Dan. vii. 10; Rev. xx. 12), the things pertaining to our salvation are too lofty to be perceived by our sense, seen by our eyes, or handled by our hands, and that in the meantime there is no possible way in which these can be possessed by us, unless we can transcend the reach of our own intellect, and raise our eye above all worldly objects; in short, surpass ourselves, he adds that this certainty of possession relates to things which are only hoped for, and therefore not seen. For as Paul says (Rom. viii. 24), "hope that is seen is not hope," that we "hope for that we see not." When he calls it the evidence or proof, or, as Augustine repeatedly renders it (see Hom. in Joann. 79 and 95), the convictions of things not present, the Greek term being ἔλεγχος, it is the same as if he had called it the appearance of things not apparent, the sight of things not seen, the clearness of things obscure, the presence of things absent, the manifestation of things hid. For the mysteries of God (and to this class belong the things which pertain to our salvation) cannot be discerned in themselves, or, as it is expressed, in their own nature; but we behold them only in his word, of the truth of which we ought to be as firmly persuaded as if we held that everything which it says were done and completed. But how can the mind rise to such a perception and foretaste of the divine goodness, without being at the same time wholly inflamed with love to God? The abundance of joy which God has treasured up for those who fear him cannot be truly known without making a most powerful impression. He who is thus once affected is raised and carried entirely towards him. Hence it is not strange that no sinister perverse heart ever experiences this feeling, by which, transported to heaven itself, we are admitted to the most hidden treasures of God, and the holiest recesses of his kingdom, which must not be profaned by the entrance of a heart that is impure. For what the Schoolmen say as to the priority of love to faith and hope is a mere dream (see Sent. Lib. iii. Dist. 25, &c.), since it is faith alone that first engenders love. How much better is Bernard, "The testimony of conscience, which Paul calls 'the rejoicing' of believers, I believe to consist in three things. It is necessary, first of all, to believe that you cannot have remission of sins except by the indulgence of God; secondly, that you cannot have any good work at all unless he also give it; lastly, that you cannot by any works merit eternal life unless it also be freely given" (Bernard, Serm. i. in Annuntiatione). Shortly after he adds, "These things are not sufficient, but are a kind of commencement of faith; for while believing that your sins can only be forgiven by God, you must also hold that they are not forgiven until persuaded by the testimony of the Holy Spirit that salvation is treasured up for us; that as God pardons sins, and gives merits, and after merits rewards, you cannot halt at that beginning." But these and other topics will be considered in their own place; let it suffice at present to understand what faith is.

42. Wherever this living faith exists, it must have the hope of eternal life as its inseparable companion, or rather must of itself beget and manifest it; where it is wanting, however clearly and elegantly we may discourse of faith, it is certain we have it not. For if faith is (as has been said) a firm persuasion of the truth of God—a persuasion that it can never be false, never deceive, never be in vain, those who have received this assurance must at the same time expect that God will perform his promises, which in their conviction are absolutely true; so that in one word hope is nothing more than the expectation of those things which faith previously believes to have been truly promised by God. Thus, faith believes that God is true; hope expects that in due season he will manifest his truth. Faith believes that he is our Father; hope expects that he will always act the part of a Father towards us. Faith believes that eternal life has been given to us; hope expects that it will one day be revealed. Faith is the foundation on which hope rests; hope nourishes and sustains faith. For as no man can expect anything from God without previously believing his promises, so, on the other hand, the weakness of our faith, which might grow weary and fall away, must be supported and cherished by patient hope and expectation. For this reason Paul justly says, "We are saved by hope" (Rom. viii. 24). For while hope silently waits for the Lord, it restrains faith from hastening on with too much precipitation, confirms it when it might waver in regard to the promises of God or begin to doubt of their truth, refreshes it when it might be fatigued, extends its view to the final goal, so as not to allow it to give up in the middle of the course, or at the very outset. In short, by constantly renovating and reviving, it is ever and anon furnishing more vigour for perseverance. On the whole, how necessary the reinforcements of hope are to establish faith will better appear if we reflect on the numerous forms of temptation by which those who have embraced the word of God are assailed and shaken. First, the Lord often keeps us in suspense, by delaying the fulfilment of his promises much longer than we could wish. Here the office of hope is to perform what the prophet enjoins, "Though it tarry, wait for it" (Hab. ii. 3). Sometimes he not only permits faith to grow languid, but even openly manifests his displeasure. Here there is still greater necessity for the aid of hope, that we may be able to say with another prophet, "I will wait upon thet Lord that hideth his face from the house of Jacob, and I will look for him" (Isaiah viii. 17). Scoffers also rise up, as Peter tells us, and ask, "Where is the promise of his coming? for since the fathers fell asleep, all things continue as they were from the beginning of the creation" (2 Pet. iii. 4). Nay, the world and the flesh insinuate the same thing. Here faith must be supported by the patience of hope,

and fixed on the contemplation of eternity, consider that "one day is with the Lord as a thousand years, and a thousand years as one day" (2 Pet. iii. 8; Ps. xc. 4).

43. On account of this connection and affinity Scripture sometimes confounds the two terms, faith and hope. For when Peter says that we are "kept by the power of God through faith until salvation, ready to be revealed in the last time" (1 Pet. i. 5), he attributes to faith what more properly belongs to hope. And not without cause, since we have already shown that hope is nothing else than the food and strength of faith. Sometimes the two are joined together, as in the same Epistle, "That your faith and hope might be in God" (1 Pet. i. 21). Paul, again, in the Epistle to the Philippians, from hope deduces expectation (Phil. i. 20), because in hoping patiently we suspend our wishes until God manifest his own time. The whole of this subject may be better understood from the tenth chapter of the Epistle to the Hebrews, to which I have already adverted. Paul, in another passage, though not in strict propriety of speech, expresses the same thing in these words, "For we through the Spirit wait for the hope of righteousness by faith" (Gal. v. 5); that is, after embracing the testimony of the Gospel as to free love, we wait till God openly manifest what is now only an object of hope. It is now obvious how absurdly Peter Lombard lays down a double foundation of hope—viz. the grace of God and the merit of works (Sent. Lib. iii. Dist. 26). Hope cannot have any other object than faith has. But we have already shown clearly that the only object of faith is the mercy of God, to which, to use the common expression, it must look with both eyes. But it is worth while to listen to the strange reason which he adduces. If you presume, says he, to hope for anything without merit, it should be called not hope, but presumption. Who, dear reader, does not execrate the gross stupidity[1] which calls it rashness and presumption to confide in the truth of God? The Lord desires us to expect everything from his goodness, and yet these men tell us it is presumption to rest in it. O teacher, worthy of the pupils whom you found in these insane raving schools! Seeing that, by the oracles of God, sinners are enjoined to entertain the hope of salvation, let us willingly presume so far on his truth as to cast away all confidence in our works, and trusting in his mercy, venture to hope. He who hath said, "According to your faith be it unto you" (Matth. ix. 29), will never deceive.

(margin note: Hope is nothing else than the food and strength of faith)

(margin note: Hope can have no other object than faith has.)

1 Latin, "Quis non merito, amice lector, tales bestias execretur?" French, "Je vous prie, mes amis, qui se tiendra de maudire telles bestes?"—I pray you, my friends, who can refrain from execrating such beasts?

CHAPTER III.

REGENERATION BY FAITH. OF REPENTANCE.

This chapter is divided into five parts. I. The title of the chapter seems to promise a treatise on Faith, but the only subject here considered is Repentance, the inseparable attendant of faith. And, first, various opinions on the subject of repentance are stated, sec. 1—4. II. An exposition of the orthodox doctrine of Repentance, sec. 5—9. III. Reasons why repentance must be prolonged to the last moment of life, sec. 10—14. IV. Of the fruits of repentance, or its object and tendency, sec. 15—20. V. The source whence repentance proceeds, sec. 21—24. Of the sin against the Holy Spirit, and the impenitence of the reprobate, sec. 25.

Sections.

1. Connection of this chapter with the previous one and the subsequent chapters. Repentance follows faith, and is produced by it. Reason. Error of those who take a contrary view.
2. Their First Objection. Answer. In what sense the origin of Repentance ascribed to Faith. Cause of the erroneous idea that faith is produced by repentance. Refutation of it. The hypocrisy of Monks and Anabaptists in assigning limits to repentance exposed.
3. A second opinion concerning repentance considered.
4. A third opinion, assigning two forms to repentance, a legal and an Evangelical. Examples of each.
5. The orthodox doctrine of Repentance. 1. Faith and Repentance to be distinguished, not confounded or separated. 2. A consideration of the name. 3. A definition of the thing, or what repentance is. Doctrine of the Prophets and Apostles.
6. Explanation of the definition. This consists of three parts. 1. Repentance is a turning of our life unto God. This described and enlarged upon.
7. 2. Repentance produced by fear of God. Hence the mention of divine judgment by the Prophets and Apostles. Example. Exposition of the second branch of the definition from a passage in Paul. Why the fear of God is the first part of Repentance.
8. 3. Repentance consists in the mortification of the flesh and the quickening of the Spirit. These required by the Prophets. They are explained separately.
9. How this mortification and quickening are produced. Repentance just a renewal of the divine image in us. Not completed in a moment, but extends to the last moment of life.
10. Reasons why repentance must so extend. Augustine's opinion as to concupiscence in the regenerate examined. A passage of Paul which seems to confirm that opinion.
11. Answer. Confirmation of the answer by the Apostle himself. Another confirmation from a precept of the law. Conclusion.
12. Exception, that those desires only are condemned which are repugnant to the order of God. Desires not condemned in so far as natural, but in so far as inordinate. This held by Augustine.
13. Passages from Augustine to show that this was his opinion. Objection from a passage in James.
14. Another objection of the Anabaptists and Libertines to the continuance of repentance throughout the present life. An answer disclosing its impiety. Another answer, founded on the absurdities to which it leads. A third answer, contrasting sincere Christian repentance with the erroneous view of the objectors. Confirmation from the example and declaration of an Apostle.

1. ALTHOUGH we have already in some measure shown how faith possesses Christ, and gives us the enjoyment of his benefits, the subject would still be obscure were we not to add an exposition of the effects resulting from it. The sum of the Gospel is, not without good reason, made to consist in repentance and forgiveness of sins; and, therefore, where these two heads are omitted, any discussion concerning faith will be meagre and defective, and indeed almost useless. Now, since Christ confers upon us, and we obtain by faith, both free reconciliation and newness of life, reason and order require that I should here begin to treat of both. The shortest transition, however, will be from faith to repentance ; for repentance being properly understood, it will better appear how a man is justified freely by faith alone, and yet that holiness of life, *real* holiness, as it is called, is inseparable from the free imputation of righteousness.[1] That repentance not only always follows faith, but is produced by it, ought to be without controversy (see Calvin in Joann. i. 13). For since pardon and forgiveness are offered by the preaching of the Gospel, in order that the sinner, delivered from the tyranny of Satan, the yoke of sin, and the miserable bondage of iniquity, may pass into

---

[1] The French adds in explanation, " C'est à dire, que cela s'accorde bien, que nous ne soyons pas sans bonnes œuvres, et toutesfois que nous soyons reputés justes sans bonnes œuvres ;"—That is to say, that the two propositions are quite consistent—viz. that we are not without good works, and yet that we are accounted righteous without works.

the kingdom of God, it is certain that no man can embrace the grace of the Gospel without betaking himself from the errors of his former life into the right path and making it his whole study to practise repentance. Those who think that repentance precedes faith instead of flowing from, or being produced by it, as the fruit by the tree, have never understood its nature, and are moved to adopt that view on very insufficient grounds.

2. Christ and John. it is said, in their discourses, first exhort the people to repentance, and then add, that the kingdom of heaven is at hand (Matth. iii. 2; iv. 17). Such, too, is the message which the Apostles received, and such the course which Paul followed, as is narrated by Luke (Acts xx. 21). But clinging superstitiously to the juxta-position of the syllables, they attend not to the coherence of meaning in the words. For when our Lord and John begin their preaching thus, "Repent, for the kingdom of heaven is at hand" (Matth. iii. 2), do they not deduce repentance as a consequence of the offer of grace and promise of salvation? The force of the words, therefore, is the same as if it were said, As the kingdom of heaven is at hand, for that reason repent. For Matthew, after relating that John so preached, says that therein was fulfilled the prophecy concerning the voice of one crying in the desert, "Prepare ye the way of the Lord, make straight in the desert a highway for our God" (Isaiah xl. 3). But in the Prophet that voice is ordered to commence with consolation and glad tidings. Still, when we attribute the origin of repentance to faith, we do not dream of some period of time in which faith is to give birth to it: we only wish to show that a man cannot seriously engage in repentance unless he know that he is of God. But no man is truly persuaded that he is of God until he have embraced his offered favour. These things will be more clearly explained as we proceed. Some are perhaps misled by this, that not a few are subdued by terror of conscience, or disposed to obedience before they have been imbued with a knowledge, nay, before they have had any taste of the divine favour (see Calvin in Acts xx. 21). This is that initial fear[1] which some writers class among the virtues, because they think it approximates to true and genuine obedience. But we are not here considering the various modes in which Christ draws us to himself, or prepares us for the study of piety: All I say is, that no righteousness can be found where the Spirit, whom Christ received in order to communicate it to his members, reigns not. Then, according to the passage in the Psalms, "There is forgiveness with thee, that thou mayest be feared" (Psalm cxxx. 4), no man will ever reverence God who does not trust that God is propitious to him, no man will ever willingly set himself to observe the Law who is not persuaded that his services are pleas-

---

[1] Latin, "Initialis timor," which is thus paraphrased by the French: "Et c'est une crainte comme on la voit aux petits enfans, qui ne sont point gouvernés par raison;"—And it is a fear such as we see in little children, who are not governed by reason.

ing to God. The indulgence of God in tolerating and pardoning our iniquities is a sign of paternal favour. This is also clear from the exhortation in Hosea, " Come, and let us return unto the Lord : for he hath torn, and he will heal us; he hath smitten, and he will bind us up" (Hos. vi. 1); the hope of pardon is employed as a stimulus to prevent us from becoming reckless in sin. But there is no semblance of reason in the absurd procedure of those who, that they may begin with repentance, prescribe to their neophytes certain days during which they are to exercise themselves in repentance, and after these are elapsed, admit them to communion in Gospel grace. I allude to great numbers of Anabaptists, those of them especially who plume themselves on being spiritual, and their associates the Jesuits, and others of the same stamp. Such are the fruits which their giddy spirit produces, that repentance, which in every Christian man lasts as long as life, is with them completed in a few short days.

3. Certain learned men, who lived long before the present day, and were desirous to speak simply and sincerely, according to the rule of Scripture, held that repentance consists of two parts, mortification and quickening. By mortification they mean, grief of soul and terror, produced by a conviction of sin and a sense of the divine judgment. For when a man is brought to a true knowledge of sin, he begins truly to hate and abominate sin. He also is sincerely dissatisfied with himself, confesses that he is lost and undone, and wishes he were different from what he is. Moreover, when he is touched with some sense of the divine justice (for the one conviction immediately follows the other), he lies terror-struck and amazed, humbled and dejected, desponds and despairs. This, which they regarded as the first part of repentance, they usually termed *contrition*. By quickening they mean, the comfort which is produced by faith, as when a man prostrated by a consciousness of sin, and smitten with the fear of God, afterwards beholding his goodness, and the mercy, grace, and salvation obtained through Christ, looks up, begins to breathe, takes courage, and passes, as it were, from death unto life. I admit that these terms, when rightly interpreted, aptly enough express the power of repentance; only I cannot assent to their using the term *quickening*, for the joy which the soul feels after being calmed from perturbation and fear. It more properly means, that desire of pious and holy living which springs from the new birth ; as if it were said, that the man dies to himself that he may begin to live unto God.

4. Others seeing that the term is used in Scripture in different senses, have set down two forms of repentance, and, in order to distinguish them, have called the one Legal repentance; or that by which the sinner, stung with a sense of his sin, and overwhelmed with fear of the divine anger, remains in that state of perturbation, unable to escape from it. The other they term Evangelical repent-

ance ; or that by which the sinner, though grievously downcast in himself, yet looks up and sees in Christ the cure of his wound, the solace of his terror, the haven of rest from his misery. They give Cain, Saul, and Judas,[1] as examples of legal repentance. Scripture, in describing what is called their repentance, means that they perceived the heinousness of their sins, and dreaded the divine anger; but, thinking only of God as a judge and avenger, were overwhelmed by the thought. Their repentance, therefore, was nothing better than a kind of threshold to hell, into which having entered even in the present life, they began to endure the punishment inflicted by the presence of an offended God. Examples of evangelical repentance we see in all those who, first stung with a sense of sin, but afterwards raised and revived by confidence in the divine mercy, turned unto the Lord.[2] Hezekiah was frightened on receiving the message of his death, but praying with tears, and beholding the divine goodness, regained his confidence. The Ninevites were terrified at the fearful announcement of their destruction ; but clothing themselves in sackcloth and ashes, they prayed, hoping that the Lord might relent and avert his anger from them. David confessed that he had sinned greatly in numbering the people, but added, "Now, I beseech thee, O Lord, take away the iniquity of thy servant." When rebuked by Nathan, he acknowledged the crime of adultery, and humbled himself before the Lord ; but he, at the same time, looked for pardon. Similar was the repentance of those who, stung to the heart by the preaching of Peter, yet trusted in the divine goodness, and added, "Men and brethren, what shall we do?" Similar was the case of Peter himself, who indeed wept bitterly, but ceased not to hope.

5. Though all this is true, yet the term *repentance* (in so far as I can ascertain from Scripture) must be differently taken. For in comprehending faith under repentance, they are at variance with what Paul says in the Acts, as to his "testifying both to the Jews and also to the Greeks, repentance toward God, and faith toward our Lord Jesus Christ" (Acts xx. 21). Here he mentions faith and repentance as two different things. What then? Can true repentance exist without faith? By no means. But although they cannot be separated, they ought to be distinguished. As there is no faith without hope, and yet faith and hope are different, so repentance and faith, though constantly linked together, are only to be united, not confounded. I am not unaware that under the term *repentance* is comprehended the whole work of turning to God, of which not the least important part is faith; but in what sense this is done will be perfectly obvious, when its nature and power shall have been explained. The term repentance is derived in the Hebrew from con-

[1] Gen. iv. 13; 1 Sam. xv. 30; Matt. xxvii. 3, 4.
[2] 2 Kings xx. 2; Isa. xxxviii. 2; Jonah iii. 5; 2 Sam. xxiv. 10; xii. 13, 16; Acts ii. 37; Matth. xxvi 75; Luke xxii. 62.

Repentance is: A real conversion of our life unto God, proceeding from sincere and serious fear of God; and consisting in the mortification of our flesh and the old man, and the quickening by the Spirit.

version, or turning again; and in the Greek from a change of mind and purpose; nor is the thing meant inappropriate to both derivations, for it is substantially this, that withdrawing from ourselves we turn to God, and laying aside the old, put on a new mind. Wherefore, it seems to me, that repentance may be not inappropriately defined thus: A real conversion of our life unto God, proceeding from sincere and serious fear of God; and consisting in the mortification of our flesh and the old man, and the quickening of the Spirit. In this sense are to be understood all those addresses in which the prophets first, and the apostles afterwards, exhorted the people of their time to repentance. The great object for which they laboured was, to fill them with confusion for their sins and dread of the divine judgment, that they might fall down and humble themselves before him whom they had offended, and, with true repentance, betake themselves to the right path. Accordingly, they use indiscriminately in the same sense, the expressions, turning, or returning to the Lord; repenting, doing repentance.[1] Whence, also, the sacred history describes it as repentance towards God, when men who disregarded him and wantoned in their lusts begin to obey his word, and are prepared to go whithersoever he may call them. And John Baptist and Paul, under the expression, bringing forth fruits meet for repentance, described a course of life exhibiting and bearing testimony, in all its actions, to such a repentance.

6. But before proceeding farther, it will be proper to give a clearer exposition of the definition which we have adopted. There are three things, then, principally to be considered in it. First, in the conversion of the life to God, we require a transformation not only in external works, but in the soul itself, which is able only after it has put off its old habits to bring forth fruits conformable to its renovation. The prophet, intending to express this, enjoins those whom he calls to repentance to make them "a new heart and a new spirit" (Ezek. xviii. 31). Hence Moses, on several occasions, when he would show how the Israelites were to repent and turn to the Lord, tells them that it must be done with the whole heart, and the whole soul (a mode of expression of frequent recurrence in the prophets), and by terming it the circumcision of the heart, points to the internal affections. But there is no passage better fitted to teach us the genuine nature of repentance than the following: "If thou wilt return, O Israel, saith the Lord, return unto me." "Break up your fallow ground, and sow not among thorns. Circumcise yourselves to the Lord, and take away the foreskins of your heart" (Jer. iv. 1—4). See how he declares to them that it will be of no avail to commence the study of righteousness unless impiety shall first have been eradicated from their inmost heart. And to make the deeper impression, he reminds them that they have to do with God, and can gain nothing by deceit,

We require not only a transformation in external works, but in the soul itself.

because he hates a double heart. For this reason Isaiah derides the preposterous attempts of hypocrites, who zealously aimed at an external repentance by the observance of ceremonies, but in the meanwhile cared not " to loose the bands of wickedness, to undo the heavy burdens, and to let the oppressed go free" (Isaiah lviii. 6). In these words he admirably shows wherein the acts of unfeigned repentance consist.

Repentance proceeds from a sincere fear of God.

7 The second part of our definition is, that repentance proceeds from a sincere fear of God. Before the mind of the sinner can be inclined to repentance, he must be aroused by the thought of divine judgment; but when once the thought that God will one day ascend his tribunal to take an account of all words and actions has taken possession of his mind, it will not allow him to rest, or have one moment's peace, but will perpetually urge him to adopt a different plan of life, that he may be able to stand securely at that judgment-seat. Hence the Scripture, when exhorting to repentance, often introduces the subject of judgment as in Jeremiah, " Lest my fury come forth like fire, and burn that none can quench it, because of the evil of your doings" (Jer. iv. 4). Paul, in his discourse to the Athenians, says, " The times of this ignorance God winked at; but now commandeth all men everywhere to repent : because he hath appointed a day, in the which he will judge the world in righteousness" (Acts xvii. 30, 31). The same thing is repeated in several other passages. Sometimes God is declared to be a judge, from the punishments already inflicted, thus leading sinners to reflect that worse awaits them if they do not quickly repent. There is an example of this in the xxixth chapter of Deuteronomy. As repentance begins with dread and hatred of sin, the Apostle sets down godly sorrow as one of its causes (2 Cor vii. 10). By godly sorrow he means when we not only tremble at the punishment, but hate and abhor the sin, because we know it is displeasing to God. It is not strange that this should be, for unless we are stung to the quick, the sluggishness of our carnal nature cannot be corrected; nay, no degree of pungency would suffice for our stupor and sloth, did not God lift the rod and strike deeper. There is, moreover, a rebellious spirit which must be broken as with hammers. The stern threatenings which God employs are extorted from him by our depraved dispositions. For while we are asleep it were in vain to allure us by soothing measures. Passages to this effect are everywhere to be met with, and I need not quote them. But there is another reason why the

Common virtues not enough in the eyes of God.

fear of God lies at the root of repentance—viz. that though the life of man were possessed of all kinds of virtue, still if they do not bear reference to God, how much soever they may be lauded in the world, they are mere abomination in heaven, inasmuch as it is the principal part of righteousness to render to God that service and honour of which he is impiously defrauded, whenever it is not our express purpose to submit to his authority.

8. We must now explain the third part of the definition, and show

what is meant when we say that repentance consists of two parts— viz. the mortification of the flesh, and the quickening of the Spirit. The prophets, in accommodation to a carnal people, express this in simple and homely terms, but clearly, when they say, " Depart from evil, and do good " (Ps. xxxiv. 14). " Wash you, make you clean, put away the evil of your doings from before mine eyes ; cease to do evil ; learn to do well ; seek judgment ; relieve the oppressed," &c. (Isaiah i. 16, 17). In dissuading us from wickedness they demand the entire destruction of the flesh, which is full of perverseness and malice. It is a most difficult and arduous achievement to renounce ourselves, and lay aside our natural disposition. For the flesh must not be thought to be destroyed unless everything that we have of our own is abolished. But seeing that all the desires of the flesh are enmity against God (Rom. viii. 7), the first step to the obedience of his law is the renouncement of our own nature. Renovation is afterwards manifested by the fruits produced by it—viz. justice, judgment, and mercy. Since it were not sufficient duly to perform such acts, were not the mind and heart previously endued with sentiments of justice, judgment, and mercy, this is done when the Holy Spirit, instilling his holiness into our souls, so inspires them with new thoughts and affections, that they may justly be regarded as new. And, indeed, as we are naturally averse to God, unless self-denial precede, we shall never tend to that which is right. Hence we are so often enjoined to put off the old man, to renounce the world and the flesh, to forsake our lusts, and be renewed in the spirit of our mind. Moreover, the very name *mortification* reminds us how difficult it is to forget our former nature, because we hence infer that we cannot be trained to the fear of God, and learn the first principles of piety, unless we are violently smitten with the sword of the Spirit and annihilated, as if God were declaring, that to be ranked among his sons there must be a destruction of our ordinary nature.

9. Both of these we obtain by union with Christ. For if we have true fellowship in his death, our old man is crucified by his power, and the body of sin becomes dead, so that the corruption of our original nature is never again in full vigour (Rom. vi. 5, 6). If we are partakers in his resurrection, we are raised up by means of it to newness of life which conforms us to the righteousness of God. In one word, then, by repentance I understand regeneration,[1] the only aim of which is to form in us anew the image of God, which was sullied, and all but effaced by the transgression of Adam. So the Apostle teaches when he says, " We all with open face beholding as in a glass the glory of the Lord, are changed into the same image from glory to glory, as by the Spirit of the Lord." Again, " Be renewed in the spirit of your mind," and " put ye on the new man, which after God is created in righteousness and true holiness." Again, " Put ye on

---

1 French, " une regeneration spirituelle ;"—a spiritual regeneration.

[Margin annotations: Self-denial must pre-ceed, then acts of Justice, Judgement, and mercy follow. This done when the Holy Spirit instills new thoughts into our minds. By repentance, I understand regeneration, the only aim of which is to form in us anew the image of God sullied by Adam.]

the new man, which is renewed in knowledge after the image of him that created him."[1] Accordingly through the blessing of Christ we are renewed by that regeneration into the righteousness of God from which we had fallen through Adam, the Lord being pleased in this manner to restore the integrity of all whom he appoints to the inheritance of life. This renewal, indeed, is not accomplished in a moment, a day, or a year, but by uninterrupted, sometimes even by slow, progress God abolishes the remains of carnal corruption in his elect, cleanses them from pollution, and consecrates them as his temples, restoring all their inclinations to real purity, so that during their whole lives they may practise repentance, and know that death is the only termination to this warfare. The greater is the effrontery of an impure raver and apostate, named Staphylus, who pretends that I confound the condition of the present life with the celestial glory, when, after Paul, I make the image of God to consist in righteousness and true holiness ; as if in every definition it were not necessary to take the thing defined in its integrity and perfection. It is not denied that there is room for improvement ; but what I maintain is that the nearer any one approaches in resemblance to God, the more does the image of God appear in him. That believers may attain to it, God assigns repentance as the goal towards which they must keep running during the whole course of their lives.

10. By regeneration the children of God are delivered from the bondage of sin, but not as if they had already obtained full possession of freedom, and no longer felt any annoyance from the flesh. Materials for an unremitting contest remain, that they may be exercised, and not only exercised, but may better understand their weakness. All writers of sound judgment agree in this, that, in the regenerate man, there is still a spring of evil which is perpetually sending forth desires that allure and stimulate him to sin. They also acknowledge that the saints are still so liable to the disease of concupiscence, that, though opposing it, they cannot avoid being ever and anon prompted and incited to lust, avarice, ambition, or other vices. It is unnecessary to spend much time in investigating the sentiments of ancient writers. Augustine alone may suffice, as he has collected all their opinions with great care and fidelity.[2] Any reader who is desirous to know the sense of antiquity may obtain it from him. There is this difference apparently between him and us, that while he admits that believers, so long as they are in the body, are so liable to concupiscence that they cannot but feel it, he does not venture to give this disease the name of sin. He is contented with giving it the name of infirmity, and says, that it only becomes sin when either external act or consent is added to conception or apprehension ; that is, when the will yields to the first desire. We

---

[1] 2 Cor. iii. 18; Eph. iv. 23, 24; Col. iii. 10; 2 Cor. iv. 16.
[2] See August. ad Bonif. Lib. iv. et cont. Julianum, Lib. i. and ii. See also Serm. 6, de Verbis Apost. See also Calv. cont. Pighium, and Calv. ad Conc. Trident.

again regard it as sin whenever man is influenced in any degree by any desire contrary to the law of God; nay, we maintain that the very pravity which begets in us such desires is sin. Accordingly, we hold that there is always sin in the saints, until they are freed from their mortal frame, because depraved concupiscence resides in their flesh, and is at variance with rectitude. Augustine himself does not always refrain from using the name of sin, as when he says, "Paul gives the name of sin to that carnal concupiscence from which all sins arise. This in regard to the saints loses its dominion in this world, and is destroyed in heaven." In these words he admits that believers, in so far as they are liable to carnal concupiscence, are chargeable with sin.

11. When it is said that God purifies his Church, so as to be "holy and without blemish" (Eph. v. 26, 27), that he promises this cleansing by means of baptism, and performs it in his elect, I understand that reference is made to the guilt rather than to the matter of sin. In regenerating his people God indeed accomplishes this much for them; he destroys the dominion of sin,[1] by supplying the agency of the Spirit, which enables them to come off victorious from the contest. Sin, however, though it ceases to reign, ceases not to dwell in them. Accordingly, though we say that the old man is crucified, and the law of sin is abolished in the children of God (Rom. vi. 6), the remains of sin survive, not to have dominion, but to humble them under a consciousness of their infirmity. We admit that these remains, just as if they had no existence, are not imputed, but we, at the same time, contend that it is owing to the mercy of God that the saints are not charged with the guilt which would otherwise make them sinners before God. It will not be difficult for us to confirm this view, seeing we can support it by clear passages of Scripture. How can we express our view more plainly than Paul does in Rom. vii. 6? We have elsewhere shown, and Augustine by solid reasons proves, that Paul is there speaking in the person of a regenerated man. I say nothing as to his use of the words evil and sin. However those who object to our view may quibble on these words, can any man deny that aversion to the law of God is an evil, and that hinderance to righteousness is sin? In short, who will not admit that there is guilt where there is spiritual misery? But all these things Paul affirms of this disease. Again, the law furnishes us with a clear demonstration by which the whole question may be quickly disposed of. We are enjoined to love God with all our heart, with all our soul, with all our strength. Since all the faculties of our soul ought thus to be engrossed with the love of God, it is certain that the commandment is not fulfilled by those who receive the smallest desire into their heart, or admit into their minds any thought whatever which may lead them away from the love of God to vanity. What

---

[1] Latin, "Reatus."—French, "l'imputation du peché;"—the imputation of sin.

then? Is it not through the faculties of mind that we are assailed with sudden motions, that we perceive sensual, or form conceptions of mental objects? Since these faculties give admission to vain and wicked thoughts, do they not show that to that extent they are devoid of the love of God? He, then, who admits not that all the desires of the flesh are sins, and that that disease of concupiscence, which they call a stimulus, is a fountain of sin, must of necessity deny that the transgression of the law is sin.

12. If any one thinks it absurd thus to condemn all the desires by which man is naturally affected, seeing they have been implanted by God the author of nature, we answer, that we by no means condemn those appetites which God so implanted in the mind of man at his first creation, that they cannot be eradicated without destroying human nature itself, but only the violent lawless movements which war with the order of God. But as, in consequence of the corruption of nature, all our faculties are so vitiated and corrupted, that a perpetual disorder and excess is apparent in all our actions, and as the appetites cannot be separated from this excess, we maintain that therefore they are vicious; or, to give the substance in fewer words, we hold that all human desires are evil, and we charge them with sin not in as far as they are natural, but because they are inordinate, and inordinate because nothing pure and upright can proceed from a corrupt and polluted nature. Nor does Augustine depart from this doctrine in reality so much as in appearance. From an excessive dread of the invidious charge with which the Pelagians assailed him, he sometimes refrains from using the term sin in this sense; but when he says (ad Bonif.) that *the law of sin remaining in the saints, the guilt only is taken away*, he shows clearly enough that his view is not very different from ours.

13. We will produce some other passages to make it more apparent what his sentiments were. In his second book against Julian, he says, " This law of sin is both remitted in spiritual regeneration and remains in the mortal flesh; remitted, because the guilt is forgiven in the sacrament by which believers are regenerated, and yet remains, inasmuch as it produces desires against which believers fight." Again, " Therefore the law of sin (which was in the members of this great Apostle also) is forgiven in baptism, not ended." Again, " The law of sin, the guilt of which, though remaining, is forgiven in baptism, Ambrose called iniquity, for it is iniquitous for the flesh to lust against the Spirit." Again, " Sin is dead in the guilt by which it bound us; and until it is cured by the perfection of burial, though dead it rebels." In the fifth book he says still more plainly, "As blindness of heart is the sin by which God is not believed; and the punishment of sin, by which a proud heart is justly punished; and the cause of sin, when through the error of a blinded heart any evil is committed: so the lust of the flesh, against which the good Spirit wars, is also sin, because disobedient to the authority of the mind; and the punish-

ment of sin, because the recompense rendered for disobedience; and the cause of sin, consenting by revolt or springing up through contamination." He here without ambiguity calls it sin, because the Pelagian heresy being now refuted, and the sound doctrine confirmed, he was less afraid of calumny. Thus, also, in his forty-first Homily on John, where he speaks his own sentiments without controversy, he says, "If with the flesh you serve the law of sin, do what the Apostle himself says, 'Let not sin, therefore, reign in your mortal body, that ye should obey it in the lusts thereof' (Rom. vi. 12). He does not say, *Let it not be*, but *Let it not reign*. As long as you live there must be sin in your members; but at least let its dominion be destroyed; do not what it orders." Those who maintain that concupiscence is not sin, are wont to found on the passage of James, "Then, when lust hath conceived, it bringeth forth sin" (James i. 15). But this is easily refuted: for unless we understand him as speaking only of wicked works or actual sins, even a wicked inclination will not be accounted sin. But from his calling crimes and wicked deeds the fruits of lust, and also giving them the name of sins, it does not follow that the lust itself is not an evil, and in the sight of God deserving of condemnation.

14. Some Anabaptists in the present age mistake some indescribable sort of frenzied excess for the regeneration of the Spirit, holding that the children of God are restored to a state of innocence, and, therefore, need give themselves no anxiety about curbing the lust of the flesh; that they have the Spirit for their guide, and under his agency never err.[1] It would be incredible that the human mind could proceed to such insanity, did they not openly and exultingly give utterance to their dogma. It is indeed monstrous, and yet it is just, that those who have resolved to turn the word of God into a lie, should thus be punished for their blasphemous audacity. Is it indeed true, that all distinction between base and honourable, just and unjust, good and evil, virtue and vice, is abolished? The distinction, they say, is from the curse of the old Adam, and from this we are exempted by Christ. There will be no difference, then, between whoredom and chastity, sincerity and craft, truth and falsehood, justice and robbery. Away with vain fear! (they say), the Spirit will not bid you do anything that is wrong, provided you sincerely and boldly leave yourself to his agency. Who is not amazed at such monstrous doctrines? And yet this philosophy is popular with those who, blinded by insane lusts, have thrown off common sense. But what kind of Christ, pray, do they fabricate? what kind of Spirit do they belch forth? We acknowledge one Christ, and his one Spirit, whom the prophets foretold and the Gospel proclaims as actually manifested, but we hear nothing of this kind respecting him. That Spirit is not the patron of murder, adultery, drunkenness, pride, contention, avarice, and fraud,

[margin: Against the spiritualism of the Anabaptists.]

---

1 See Calvin, adv. Libertinos, cap. xviii.

but the author of love, chastity, sobriety, modesty, peace, moderation, and truth. He is not a Spirit of giddiness, rushing rashly and precipitately, without regard to right and wrong, but full of wisdom and understanding, by which he can duly distinguish between justice and injustice. He instigates not to lawless and unrestrained licentiousness, but, discriminating between lawful and unlawful, teaches temperance and moderation. But why dwell longer in refuting that brutish frenzy? To Christians the Spirit of the Lord is not a turbulent phantom, which they themselves have produced by dreaming, or received ready-made by others; but they religiously seek the knowledge of him from Scripture, where two things are taught concerning him: *first*, that he is given to us for sanctification, that he may purge us from all iniquity and defilement, and bring us to the obedience of divine rigteousness, an obedience which cannot exist unless the lusts to which these men would give loose reins are tamed and subdued; *secondly*, that though purged by his sanctification, we are still beset by many vices and much weakness, so long as we are enclosed in the prison of the body. Thus it is, that placed at a great distance from perfection, we must always be endeavouring to make some progress, and daily struggling with the evil by which we are entangled. Whence, too, it follows that, shaking off sloth and security, we must be intently vigilant, so as not to be taken unawares in the snares of our flesh; unless, indeed, we presume to think that we have made greater progress than the Apostle, who was buffeted by a messenger of Satan, in order that his strength might be perfected in weakness, and who gives in his own person a true, not a fictitious representation, of the strife between the Spirit and the flesh (2 Cor. xii. 7, 9; Rom. vii. 6).

15. The Apostle, in his description of repentance (2 Cor. vii. 2), enumerates seven causes, effects, or parts belonging to it, and that on the best grounds. These are carefulness, excuse, indignation, fear, desire, zeal, revenge. It should not excite surprise that I venture not to determine whether they ought to be regarded as causes or effects: both views may be maintained. They may also be called affections conjoined with repentance; but as Paul's meaning may be ascertained without entering into any of these questions, we shall be contented with a simple exposition. He says then that godly sorrow produces *carefulness*. He who is really dissatisfied with himself for sinning against his God, is, at the same time, stimulated to care and attention, that he may completely disentangle himself from the chains of the devil, and keep a better guard against his snares, so as not afterwards to lose the guidance of the Holy Spirit, or be overcome by security. Next comes *excuse*, which in this place means not defence, in which the sinner to escape the judgment of God either denies his fault or extenuates it, but apologising, which trusts more to intercession than to the goodness of the cause; just as children not altogether abandoned, while they acknowledge and confess their

errors, yet employ deprecation; and to make room for it, testify, by every means in their power, that they have by no means cast off the reverence which they owe to their parents; in short, endeavour by excuse not to prove themselves righteous and innocent, but only to obtain pardon. Next follows *indignation*, under which the sinner inwardly murmurs, expostulates, and is offended with himself on recognising his perverseness and ingratitude to God. By the term *fear* is meant that trepidation which takes possession of our minds whenever we consider both what we have deserved, and the fearful severity of the divine anger against sinners. Accordingly, the exceeding disquietude which we must necessarily feel, both trains us to humility and makes us more cautious for the future. But if the carefulness or anxiety which he first mentioned is the result of fear, the connection between the two becomes obvious. *Desire* seems to me to be used as equivalent to diligence in duty, and alacrity in doing service, to which the sense of our misdeeds ought to be a powerful stimulus. To this also pertains *zeal*, which immediately follows; for it signifies the ardour with which we are inflamed when such goads as these are applied to us. "What have I done? Into what abyss had I fallen had not the mercy of God prevented?" The last of all is *revenge*, for the stricter we are with ourselves, and the severer the censure we pass upon our sins, the more ground we have to hope for the divine favour and mercy. And certainly when the soul is overwhelmed with a dread of divine judgment, it cannot but act the part of an avenger in inflicting punishment upon itself. Pious men, doubtless, feel that there is punishment in the shame, confusion, groans, self-displeasure, and other feelings produced by a serious review of their sins. Let us remember, however, that moderation must be used, so that we may not be overwhelmed with sadness, there being nothing to which trembling consciences are more prone than to rush into despair. This, too, is one of Satan's artifices. Those whom he sees thus overwhelmed with fear he plunges deeper and deeper into the abyss of sorrow, that they may never again rise. It is true that the fear which ends in humility without relinquishing the hope of pardon cannot be in excess. And yet we must always beware, according to the apostolic injunction, of giving way to extreme dread, as this tends to make us shun God while he is calling us to himself by repentance. Wherefore, the advice of Bernard is good, "Grief for sins is necessary, but must not be perpetual. My advice is to turn back at times from sorrow and the anxious remembrance of your ways, and escape to the plain, to a calm review of the divine mercies. Let us mingle honey with wormwood, that the salubrious bitter may give health when we drink it tempered with a mixture of sweetness: while you think humbly of yourselves, think also of the goodness of the Lord" (Bernard in Cant. Serm. xi.).

16. We can now understand what are the fruits of repentance— viz. offices of piety towards God, and love towards men, general holi-

ness and purity of life. In short, the more a man studies to conform his life to the standard of the divinè law, the surer signs he gives of his repentance. Accordingly, the Spirit, in exhorting us to repentance, brings before us at one time each separate precept of the law ; at another the duties of the second table ; although there are also passages in which, after condemning impurity in its fountain in the heart, he afterwards descends to external marks, by which repentance is proved to be sincere. A portraiture of this I will shortly set before the eye of the reader when I come to describe the Christian life (*infra*, chapter vi.). I will not here collect the passages from the prophets in which they deride the frivolous observances of those who labour to appease God with ceremonies, and show that they are mere mockery ; or those in which they show that outward integrity of conduct is not the chief part of repentance, seeing that God looks at the heart. Any one moderately versant in Scripture will understand by himself, without being reminded by others, that when he has to do with God, nothing is gained without beginning with the internal affections of the heart. There is a passage of Joel which will avail not a little for the understanding of others : " Rend your heart, and not your garments " (Joel ii. 13). Both are also briefly expressed by James in these words : "Cleanse your hands, ye sinners ; and purify your hearts, ye double-minded" (James iv. 8). Here, indeed, the accessory is set down first ; but the source and principle is afterwards pointed out—viz. that hidden defilements must be wiped away, and an altar erected to God in the very heart. There are, moreover, certain external exercises which we employ in private as remedies to humble us and tame our flesh, and in public, to testify our repentance. These have their origin in that revenge of which Paul speaks (2 Cor. vii. 2), for when the mind is distressed it naturally expresses itself in sackcloth, groans, and tears, shuns ornament and every kind of show, and abandons all delights. Then he who feels how great an evil the rebellion of the flesh is, tries every means of curbing it. Besides, he who considers aright how grievous a thing it is to have offended the justice of God, cannot rest until, in his humility, he have given glory to God. Such exercises are often mentioned by ancient writers when they speak of the fruits of repentance. But although they by no means place the power of repentance in them, yet my readers must pardon me for saying what I think— they certainly seem to insist on them more than is right. Any one who judiciously considers the matter will, I trust, agree with me that they have exceeded in two ways ; first, by so strongly urging and extravagantly commending that corporal discipline, they indeed succeeded in making the people embrace it with greater zeal ; but they in a manner obscured what they should have regarded as of much more serious moment. Secondly, the inflictions which they enjoined were considerably more rigorous than ecclesiastical mildness demands, as will be elsewhere shown.

[Margin notes: Repentance must begin within the heart and not with vain ceremonies]

17. But as there are some who, from the frequent mention of sackcloth, fasting, and tears, especially in (Joel ii. 12), think that these constitute the principal part of repentance, we must dispel their delusion. In that passage the proper part of repentance is described by the words, "turn ye even to me with your whole heart;" "rend your heart, and not your garments." The "fasting," "weeping," and "mourning," are introduced not as invariable or necessary effects, but as special circumstances.[1] Having foretold that most grievous disasters were impending over the Jews, he exhorts them to turn away the divine anger, not only by repenting, but by giving public signs of sorrow. For as a criminal, to excite the commiseration of the judge, appears in a supplicating posture, with a long beard, uncombed hair, and coarse clothing, so should those who are charged at the judgment-seat of God deprecate his severity in a garb of wretchedness. But although sackcloth and ashes were perhaps more conformable to the customs of these times,[2] yet it is plain that weeping and fasting are very appropriate in our case whenever the Lord threatens us with any defeat or calamity. In presenting the appearance of danger, he declares that he is preparing, and, in a manner, arming himself for vengeance. Rightly, therefore, does the Prophet *Rend* exhort those, on whose crimes he had said a little before that vengeance was to be executed, to weeping and fasting,—that is, to the *your* mourning habit of criminals. Nor in the present day do ecclesiastical teachers act improperly when, seeing ruin hanging over the *heart* necks of their people,[3] they call aloud on them to hasten with weep- *and not* ing and fasting: only they must always urge, with greater care and earnestness, "rend your hearts, and not your garments." It is *your* beyond doubt that fasting is not always a concomitant of repentance, *garments* but is specially destined for seasons of calamity.[4] Hence our Saviour connects it with mourning (Matth. ix. 15), and relieves the Apostles of the necessity of it until, by being deprived of his presence, they were filled with sorrow. I speak of formal fasting. For the life of Christians ought ever to be tempered with frugality and sobriety, so that the whole course of it should present some appearance of fasting. As this subject will be fully discussed when the discipline of the Church comes to be considered, I now dwell less upon it.

18. This much, however, I will add: when the name *repentance* is applied to the external profession, it is used improperly, and not

---

[1] French, "Circonstances qui convenoyent specialement alors;"—circumstances which were then specially suitable.

[2] French, "Fust la coustume de ce temps-la, et ne nous appartienne aujourdhui de rien;"—was the custom of that time, and we have nowadays nothing to do with it.

[3] The French adds, "Soit de guerre, de famine, ou de pestilence;"—whether of war, famine, or pestilence.

[4] Latin, "Calamitosis temporibus peculiariter destinari."—French, "Convient particulierement a ceux qui veulent testifier quils se recognoissant avoir merité l'ire de Dieu, et neantmoins requierent pardon de sa clemence;"—is particularly suitable to those who acknowledge they have deserved the wrath of God, and yet seek pardon of his mercy.

in the genuine meaning as I have explained it. For that is not so much a turning unto God as the confession of a fault accompanied with deprecation of the sentence and punishment. Thus to repent in sackcloth and ashes (Matth. xi. 21 ; Luke x. 13), is just to testify self-dissatisfaction when God is angry with us for having grievously offended him. It is, indeed, a kind of public confession by which, condemning ourselves before angels and the world, we prevent the judgment of God. For Paul, rebuking the sluggishness of those who indulge in their sins, says, " If we would judge ourselves, we should not be judged " (1 Cor xi. 31). It is not always necessary, however, openly to inform others, and make them the witnesses of our repentance ; but to confess privately to God is a part of true repentance which cannot be omitted. Nothing were more incongruous than that God should pardon the sins in which we are flattering ourselves, and hypocritically cloaking that he may not bring them to light. We must not only confess the sins which we daily commit, but more grievous lapses ought to carry us farther, and bring to our remembrance things which seemed to have been long ago buried. Of this David sets an example before us in his own person (Ps. li). Filled with shame for a recent crime he examines himself, going back to the womb, and acknowledging that even then he was corrupted and defiled. This he does not to extenuate his fault, as many hide themselves in the crowd, and catch at impunity by involving others along with them. Very differently does David, who ingenuously makes it an aggravation of his sin, that being corrupted from his earliest infancy he ceased not to add iniquity to iniquity. In another passage, also, he takes a survey of his past life, and implores God to pardon the errors of his youth (Ps. xxv. 7). And, indeed, we shall not prove that we have thoroughly shaken off our stupor until, groaning under the burden, and lamenting our sad condition, we seek relief from God. It is, moreover, to be observed, that the repentance which we are enjoined assiduously to cultivate, differs from that which raises, as it were, from death those who had fallen more shamefully, or given themselves up to sin without restraint, or by some kind of open revolt, had thrown off the authority of God. For Scripture, in exhorting to repentance, often speaks of it as a passage from death unto life, and when relating that a people had repented, means that they had abandoned idolatry, and other forms of gross wickedness. For which reason Paul denounces woe to sinners, "who have not repented of the uncleanness, and fornication, and lasciviousness which they have committed" (2 Cor. xii. 21). This distinction ought to be carefully observed, lest when we hear of a few individuals having been summoned to repent we indulge in supine security, as if we had nothing to do with the mortification of the flesh ; whereas, in consequence of the depraved desires which are always enticing us, and the iniquities which are ever and anon springing from them, it must engage our unremitting care. The special repentance enjoined upon those whom the devil has entangled in deadly snares, and withdrawn from the fear of God, does not abolish that ordinary repentance which the corruption of nature obliges us to cultivate during the whole course of our lives.

19. Moreover, if it is true, and nothing can be more certain, than that a complete summary of the Gospel is included under these two heads—viz. repentance and the remission of sins—do we not see that the Lord justifies his people freely, and at the same time renews them to true holiness by the sanctification of his Spirit? John, the messenger sent before the face of Christ to prepare his ways, proclaimed, "Repent, for the kingdom of heaven is at hand" (Matth. xi. 10; iii. 2). By inviting them to repentance, he urged them to acknowledge that they were sinners, and in all respects condemned before God, that thus they might be induced earnestly to seek the mortification of the flesh, and a new birth in the Spirit. By announcing the kingdom of God, he called for faith, since by the kingdom of God which he declared to be at hand, he meant forgiveness of sins, salvation, life, and every other blessing which we obtain in Christ; wherefore we read in the other Evangelists, "John did baptise in the wilderness, and preach the baptism of repentance for the remission of sins" (Mark i. 4; Luke iii. 3). What does this mean, but that, weary and oppressed with the burden of sin, they should turn to the Lord, and entertain hopes of forgiveness and salvation?[1] Thus, too, Christ began his preaching, "The kingdom of God is at hand: repent ye, and believe the Gospel" (Mark i. 15). First, he declares that the treasures of the divine mercy were opened in him; next, he enjoins repentance; and, lastly, he encourages confidence in the promises of God. Accordingly, when intending to give a brief summary of the whole Gospel, he said that he behoved "to suffer, and to rise from the dead the third day, and that repentance and remission of sins should be preached in his name among all nations" (Luke xxiv. 26, 46). In like manner, after his resurrection the Apostles preached, "Him hath God exalted with his right hand, to be a Prince and a Saviour, for to give repentance to Israel and forgiveness of sins" (Acts v. 31). Repentance is preached in the name of Christ, when men learn, through the doctrines of the Gospel, that all their thoughts, affections, and pursuits, are corrupt and vicious; and that, therefore, if they would enter the kingdom of God they must be born again. Forgiveness of sins is preached when men are taught that Christ "is made unto us wisdom, and righteousness, and sanctification, and redemption" (1 Cor. i. 30), that on his account they are freely deemed righteous and innocent in the sight of God. Though both graces are obtained by faith (as has been shown elsewhere), yet as the goodness of God, by which sins are forgiven, is the proper object of faith, it was proper carefully to distinguish it from repentance.

[1] The French adds, "pource qu'il lui est propre, et comme naturel, de sauver ce que est perdu;"—because it is proper, and, as it were, natural to him to save that which is lost.

Repenta-
nce a
lifetime
proposit-
ion.

20. Moreover, as hatred of sin, which is the beginning of repentance, first gives us access to the knowledge of Christ, who manifests himself to none but miserable and afflicted sinners, groaning, labouring, burdened, hungry, and thirsty, pining away with grief and wretchedness, so if we would stand in Christ, we must aim at repentance, cultivate it during our whole lives, and continue it to the last. Christ came to call sinners, but to call them to repentance. He was sent to bless the unworthy, but by "turning away every one" "from his iniquities." The Scripture is full of similar passages. Hence, when God offers forgiveness of 'sins, he in return usually stipulates for repentance, intimating that his mercy should induce men to repent. "Keep ye judgment," saith he, "and do justice: for my salvation is near to come." Again, "The Redeemer shall come to Zion, and unto them that turn from transgression in Jacob." Again, "Seek ye the Lord while he may be found, call ye upon him while he is near. Let the wicked forsake his way, and the unrighteous man his thoughts, and let him return unto the Lord, and he will have mercy upon him." "Repent ye, therefore, and be converted, that your sins may be blotted out."[1] Here, however, it is to be observed, that repentance is not made a condition in such a sense as to be a foundation for meriting pardon; nay, it rather indicates the end at which they must aim if they would obtain favour, God having resolved to take pity on men for the express purpose of leading them to repent. Therefore, so long as we dwell in the prison of the body, we must constantly struggle with the vices of our corrupt nature, and so with our natural disposition. Plato sometimes says,[2] that the life of the philosopher is to meditate on death. More truly may we say, that the life of a Christian man is constant study and exercise in mortifying the flesh, until it is certainly slain, and the Spirit of God obtains dominion in us. Wherefore, he seems to me to have made most progress who has learned to be most dissatisfied with himself. He does not, however, remain in the miry clay without going forward; but rather hastens and sighs after God, that, ingrafted both into the death and the life of Christ, he may constantly meditate on repentance. Unquestionably those who have a genuine hatred of sin cannot do otherwise: for no man ever hated sin without being previously enamoured of righteousness. This view, as it is the simplest of all, seemed to me also to accord best with Scripture truth.

21. Moreover, that repentance is a special gift of God, I trust is too well understood from the above doctrine to require any lengthened discourse. Hence the Church[3] extols the goodness of God, and looks on in wonder, saying, "Then hath God also to the Gentiles granted repentance unto life"(Acts xi. 18); and Paul, enjoining Timothy to

---

[1] Isaiah lvi. 1; lix. 20; lv. 6, 7; Acts ii. 38; iii. 19.
[2] This is to be found in different passages of his work, and often in the Phaido.
[3] French, "L'Eglise primitive du temps des Apostres;"—the primitive Church of the Apostles' time.

deal meekly and patiently with unbelievers, says, "If God peradventure will give them repentance to the acknowledging of the truth, and that they may recover themselves out of the snare of the devil"(2 Tim. ii. 25, 26). God indeed declares, that he would have all men to repent, and addresses exhortations in common to all; their efficacy, however, depends on the Spirit of regeneration. It were easier to create us at first, than for us by our own strength to acquire a more excellent nature. Wherefore, in regard to the whole process of regeneration, it is not without cause we are called God's " workmanship, created in Christ Jesus unto good works, which God hath before ordained that we should walk in them" (Eph. ii. 10).[1] Those whom God is pleased to rescue from death, he quickens by the Spirit of regeneration; not that repentance is properly the cause of salvation, but because, as already seen, it is inseparable from the faith and mercy of God; for, as Isaiah declares, " The Redeemer shall come to Zion, and unto them that turn from trangression in Jacob." This, indeed, is a standing truth, that wherever the fear of God is in vigour, the Spirit has been carrying on his saving work. Hence, in Isaiah, while believers complain and lament that they have been forsaken of God, they set down the supernatural hardening of the heart as a sign of reprobation. The Apostle also, intending to exclude apostates from the hope of salvation, states, as the reason, that it is impossible to renew them to repentance (Heb. vi. 6); that is, God by renewing those whom he wills not to perish, gives them a sign of paternal favour, and in a manner attracts them to himself, by the beams of a calm and reconciled countenance; on the other hand, by hardening the reprobate whose impiety is not to be forgiven, he thunders against them. This kind of vengeance the Apostle denounces against voluntary apostates, (Heb. x. 29), who, in falling away from the faith of the gospel, mock God, insultingly reject his favour, profane and trample under foot the blood of Christ, nay, as far as in them lies, crucify him afresh. Still, he does not, as some austere persons preposterously insist, leave no hope of pardon to voluntary sins, but shows that apostacy being altogether without excuse, it is not strange that God is inexorably rigorous in punishing sacrilegious contempt thus shown to himself. For, in the same Epistle, he says, that " it is impossible for those who were once enlightened, and have tasted of the heavenly gift, and were made partakers of the Holy Ghost, and have tasted the word of God, and the powers of the world to come, if they shall fall away to renew them again to repentance, seeing they crucify the Son of God afresh, and put him to an open shame" (Heb. vii. 4—6). And in another passage, " If we sin willingly, after that we have received the knowledge of the truth, there remaineth no more sacrifice for sins, but a certain fearful looking for of judgment," &c. (Heb. xi.

[1] The French adds, " Et ce non seulement au regard d'un jour. mais de tout le cours de notre vocation;"—and this in regard not only to a single day, but to the whole course of our vocation.

528 INSTITUTES OF THE BOOK III.

25, 26). There are other passages, from a misinterpretation of which the Novatians of old extracted materials for their heresy; so much so, that some good men taking offence at their harshness, have deemed the Epistle altogether spurious, though it truly savours in every part of it of the apostolic spirit. But as our dispute is only with those who receive the Epistle, it is easy to show that those passages give no support to their error. First, the Apostle must of necessity agree with his Master, who declares, that "all manner of sin and blasphemy shall be forgiven unto men, but the blasphemy against the Holy Ghost shall not be forgiven unto men," " neither in this world, neither in the world to come" (Matth. xii. 31; Luke xii. 10). We must hold that this was the only exception which the Apostle recognised, unless we would set him in opposition to the grace of God. Hence it follows, that to no sin is pardon denied save to one, which proceeding from desperate fury cannot be ascribed to infirmity, and plainly shows that the man guilty of it is possessed by the devil.

22. Here, however, it is proper to consider what the dreadful iniquity is which is not to be pardoned. The definition which Augustine somewhere gives [1]—viz. that it is obstinate perverseness, with distrust of pardon, continued till death—scarcely agrees with the words of Christ, that it shall not be forgiven in this world. For either this is said in vain, or it may be committed in this world. But if Augustine's definition is correct, the sin is not committed unless persisted in till death. Others say, that the sin against the Holy Spirit consists in envying the grace conferred upon a brother; but I know not on what it is founded. Here, however, let us give the true definition, which, when once it is established by sound evidence, will easily of itself overturn all the others. I say, therefore, that he sins against the Holy Spirit who, while so constrained by the power of divine truth that he cannot plead ignorance, yet deliberately resists, and that merely for the sake of resisting. For Christ, in explanation of what he had said, immediately adds, "Whosoever speaketh a word against the Son of man, it shall be forgiven him; but whosoever speaketh against the Holy Ghost, it shall not be forgiven him" (Matth. xii. 31). And Matthew uses the term spirit of blasphemy [2] for blasphemy against the Spirit. How can any one insult the Son, without at the same time attacking the Spirit? In this way. Those who in ignorance assail the unknown truth of God, and yet are so disposed that they would be unwilling to extinguish the truth of God when manifested to them, or utter one word against-him whom they knew to be the Lord's Anointed, sin against the Father and the Son. Thus there are many in the present day who have the greatest abhorrence to the doctrine of the Gospel, and yet, if they knew it to be the doctrine of the Gospel, would be prepared to venerate it with their

1 August. Lib. de Correp. et Gratia, cap. xii.
2 The Greek is, " τοῦ πνεύματος βλασφημία." This Calvin translates in Latin, "Spiritum blasphemiæ," and in French, "Esprit de blaspheme."

[Marginal handwritten notes:] To no sin is pardon denied, save one. He sins against the Holy Spirit who, while so constrained by the power of divine truth, that he cannot plead ignorance yet deliberately resists, and that merely for the sake of resisting.

whole heart. But those who are convinced in conscience that what they repudiate and impugn is the word of God, and yet cease not to impugn it, are said to blaspheme against the Spirit, inasmuch as they struggle against the illumination which is the work of the Spirit. Such were some of the Jews, who, when they could not resist the Spirit speaking by Stephen, yet were bent on resisting (Acts vi. 10). There can be no doubt that many of them were carried away by zeal for the law ; but it appears that there were others who maliciously and impiously raged against God himself, that is, against the doctrine which they knew to be of God. Such, too, were the Pharisees, on whom our Lord denounced woe. To depreciate the power of the Holy Spirit, they defamed him by the name of Beelzebub (Matth. ix. 3, 4 ; xii. 24). The spirit of blasphemy, therefore, is, when a man audaciously, and of set purpose, rushes forth to insult his divine name. This Paul intimates when he says, "but I obtained mercy, because I did it ignorantly in unbelief ;" otherwise he had deservedly been held unworthy of the grace of God.[1] If ignorance joined with unbelief made him obtain pardon, it follows that there is no room for pardon when knowledge is added to unbelief.

23. If you attend properly, you will perceive that the Apostle speaks not of one particular lapse or two, but of the universal revolt by which the reprobate renounce salvation. It is not strange that God should be implacable to those whom John, in his Epistle, declares not to have been of the elect, from whom they went out (1 John ii. 19). For he is directing his discourse against those who imagined that they could return to the Christian religion though they had once revolted from it. To divest them of this false and pernicious opinion, he says, as is most true, that those who had once knowingly and willingly cast off fellowship with Christ, had no means of returning to it. It is not, however, so cast off by those who merely, by the dissoluteness of their lives, transgress the word of the Lord, but by those who avowedly reject his whole doctrine. There is a paralogism in the expression *casting off* and *sinning*. *Casting off*, as interpreted by the Novatians, is when any one, notwithstanding of being taught by the Law of the Lord not to steal or commit adultery, refrains not from theft or adultery. On the contrary, I hold that there is a tacit antithesis, in which all the things, contrary to those which had been said, must be held to be repeated, so that the thing expressed is not some particular vice, but universal aversion to God, and (so to speak) the apostasy of the whole man. Therefore, when he speaks of those falling away "who were once enlightened, and have tasted of the heavenly gift, and were made partakers of the Holy Ghost, and have tasted of the good word of God, and the powers of the world to come," we must understand him as referring to those who, with deliberate impiety, have quenched the light of the Spirit, tasted of the heavenly

---

[1] The omission of this last clause in the French seems to be an improvement.

word and spurned it, alienated themselves from the sanctification
of the Spirit, and trampled under foot the word of God and the
powers of a world to come. The better to show that this was the
species of impiety intended, he afterwards expressly adds the term
wilfully. For when he says, " If we sin wilfully, after that we have
received the knowledge of the truth, there remaineth no more sacrifice
for sins," he denies not that Christ is a perpetual victim to expiate
the transgressions of saints (this the whole Epistle, in explaining the
priesthood of Christ, distinctly proclaims), but he says that there
remains no other sacrifice after this one is abandoned. And it is
abandoned when the truth of the Gospel is professedly abjured.

24. To some it seems harsh, and at variance with the divine
mercy, utterly to deny forgiveness to any who betake themselves to
it. This is easily disposed of. It is not said that pardon will be
refused if they turn to the Lord, but it is altogether denied that they
can turn to repentance, inasmuch as for their ingratitude they are
struck by the just judgment of God with eternal blindness. There
is nothing contrary to this in the application which is afterwards
made of the example of Esau, who tried in vain, by crying and tears,
to recover his lost birthright; nor in the denunciation of the Prophet, " They cried, and I would not hear." Such modes of expression do not denote true conversion or calling upon God, but that
anxiety with which the wicked, when in calamity, are compelled to
see what they before securely disregarded—viz. that nothing can
avail but the assistance of the Lord. This, however, they do not so
much implore as lament the loss of. Hence all that the Prophet
means by crying, and the Apostle by tears, is the dreadful torment
which stings and excruciates the wicked in despair. It is of consequence carefully to observe this : for otherwise God would be inconsistent with himself when he proclaims through the Prophet, that
" If the wicked will turn from all his sins that he hath committed,"
—" he shall surely live, he shall not die " (Ezek. xviii. 21, 22). And
(as I have already said) it is certain that the mind of man cannot be
changed for the better unless by his preventing grace. The promise
as to those who call upon him will never fail ; but the names of conversion and prayer are improperly given to that blind torment by
which the reprobate are distracted when they see that they must seek
God if they would find a remedy for their calamities, and yet shun
to approach him.

25. But as the Apostle declares that God is not appeased by
feigned repentance, it is asked how Ahab obtained pardon, and
averted the punishment denounced against him (1 Kings xxi. 28,
29), seeing, it appears, he was only amazed on the sudden, and
afterwards continued his former course of life. He, indeed, clothed
himself in sackcloth, covered himself with ashes, lay on the ground,
and (as the testimony given to him bears) humbled himself before
God. It was a small matter to rend his garments while his heart

continued obstinate and swollen with wickedness, and yet we see that God was inclined to mercy. I answer, that though hypocrites are thus occasionally spared for a time, the wrath of God still lies upon them, and that they are thus spared not so much on their own account as for a public example. For what did Ahab gain by the mitigation of his punishment except that he did not suffer it alive on the earth? The curse of God, though concealed, was fixed on his house, and he himself went to eternal destruction. We may see the same thing in Esau (Gen. xxvii. 38, 39). For though he met with a refusal, a temporal blessing was granted to his tears. But as, according to the declaration of God, the spiritual inheritance could be possessed only by one of the brothers, when Jacob was selected instead of Esau, that event excluded him from the divine mercy; but still there was given to him, as a man of a grovelling nature, this consolation, that he should be filled with the fatness of the earth and the dew of heaven. And this, as I lately said, should be regarded as done for the example of others, that we may learn to apply our minds, and exert ourselves with greater alacrity, in the way of sincere repentance, as there cannot be the least doubt that God will be ready to pardon those who turn to him truly and with the heart, seeing his mercy extends even to the unworthy, though they bear marks of his displeasure. In this way also, we are taught how dreadful the judgment is which awaits all the rebellious who with audacious brow and iron heart make it their sport to despise and disregard the divine threatenings. God in this way often stretched forth his hand to deliver the Israelites from their calamities, though their cries were pretended, and their minds double and perfidious, as he himself complains in the Psalms, that they immediately returned to their former course (Psalm lxxviii. 36, 37). But he designed thus by kindness and forbearance to bring them to true repentance, or leave them without excuse. And yet by remitting the punishment for a time, he does not lay himself under any perpetual obligation. He rather at times rises with greater severity against hypocrites, and doubles their punishment, that it may thereby appear how much hypocrisy displeases him. But, as I have observed, he gives some examples of his inclination to pardon, that the pious may thereby be stimulated to amend their lives, and the pride of those who petulantly kick against the pricks be more severely condemned.

CHAPTER IV.

PENITENCE, AS EXPLAINED IN THE SOPHISTICAL JARGON OF THE SCHOOLMEN, WIDELY DIFFERENT FROM THE PURITY REQUIRED BY THE GOSPEL. OF CONFESSION AND SATISFACTION.

The divisions of this chapter are,—I. The orthodox doctrine of repentance being already expounded, the false doctrine is refuted in the present chapter; a general summary survey being at the same time taken of the doctrine of the Schoolmen, sec. 1, 2. II. Its separate parts are afterwards examined. Contrition, sec. 2 and 3. Confession, sec. 4–20 Sanctification, from sec. 20 to the end of the chapter.

Sections.

1. Errors of the Schoolmen in delivering the doctrine of repentance. 1. Errors in defining it. Four different definitions considered. 2. Absurd division. 3. Vain and puzzling questions. 4. Mode in which they entangle themselves.
2. The false doctrine of the Schoolmen necessary to be refuted. Of contrition. Their view of it examined.
3. True and genuine contrition.
4. Auricular confession. Whether or not of divine authority. Arguments of Canonists and Schoolmen. Allegorical argument founded on Judaism. Two answers. Reason why Christ sent the lepers to the priests.
5. Another allegorical argument. Answer.
6. A third argument from two passages of Scripture. These passages expounded.
7. Confession proved not to be of divine authority. The use of it free for almost twelve hundred years after Christ. Its nature. When enacted into a law. Confirmation from the history of the Church. A representation of the ancient auricular confession still existing among the Papists, to bear judgment against them. Confession abolished in the Church of Constantinople.
8. This mode of confession disapproved by Chrysostom, as shown by many passages.
9. False confession being thus refuted, the confession enjoined by the word of God is considered. Mistranslation in the old version. Proof from Scripture that confession should be directed to God alone.
10. Effect of secret confession thus made to God. Another kind of confession made to men.
11. Two forms of the latter confession—viz. public and private. Public confession either ordinary or extraordinary. Use of each. Objection to confession and public prayer. Answer.
12. Private confession of two kinds. 1. On our own account. 2. On account of our neighbour. Use of the former. Great assistance to be obtained from faithful ministers of the Church. Mode of procedure. Caution to be used.
13. The use of the latter recommended by Christ. What comprehended under it. Scripture sanctions no other method of confession.
1   The power of the keys exercised in these three kinds of confession. The utility of this power in regard to public confession and absolution. Caution to be observed.
15. Popish errors respecting confession. 1. In enjoining on all the necessity of confessing every sin. 2. Fictitious keys. 3. Pretended mandate to loose and bind. 4. To whom the office of loosing and binding committed.
16. Refutation of the first error, from the impossibility of so confessing, as proved by the testimony of David.
17. Refuted farther from the testimony of conscience. Impossible to observe this most rigid obligation. Necessarily leads to despair or indifference. Confirmation of the preceding remarks by an appeal to conscience.

18. Another refutation of the first error from analogy. Sum of the whole refutation. Third refutation, laying down the surest rule of confession. Explanation of the rule. Three objections answered.
19. Fourth objection—viz. that auricular confession does no harm, and is even useful. Answer, unfolding the hypocrisy, falsehood, impiety, and monstrous abominations of the patrons of this error.
20. Refutation of the second error. 1. Priests not successors of the Apostles. 2. They have not the Holy Spirit, who alone is arbiter of the keys.
21. Refutation of the third error. 1. They are ignorant of the command and promise of Christ. By abandoning the word of God they run into innumerable absurdities.
22. Objection to the refutation of the third error. Answers, reducing the Papists to various absurdities.
23. Refutation of the fourth error. 1. Petitio principii. 2. Inversion of ecclesiastical discipline. Three objections answered.
24. Conclusion of the whole discussion against this fictitious confession.
25. Of satisfaction, to which the Sophists assign the third place in repentance. Errors and falsehoods. These views opposed by the terms,—1. Forgiveness. 2. Free forgiveness. 3. God destroying iniquities. 4. By and on account of Christ. No need of our satisfaction.
26. Objection, confining the grace and efficacy of Christ within narrow limits. Answers by both John the Evangelist and John the Baptist. Consequence of these answers.
27. Two points violated by the fiction of satisfaction. First, the honour of Christ impaired. Secondly, the conscience cannot find peace. Objection, confining the forgiveness of sins to Catechumens, refuted.
28. Objection, founded on the arbitrary distinction between venial and mortal sins. This distinction insulting to God and repugnant to Scripture. Answer, showing the true distinction in regard to venial sin.
29. Objection, founded on a distinction between guilt and the punishment of it. Answer, illustrated by various passages of Scripture. Admirable saying of Augustine.
30. Answer, founded on a consideration of the efficacy of Christ's death, and the sacrifices under the law. Our true satisfaction.
31. An objection, perverting six passages of Scripture. Preliminary observations concerning a twofold judgment on the part of God. 1. For punishment. 2. For correction.
32. Two distinctions hence arising. Objection, that God is often angry with his elect. Answer, God in afflicting his people does not take his mercy from them. This confirmed by his promise, by Scripture, and the uniform experience of the Church. Distinction between the reprobate and the elect in regard to punishment.
33. Second distinction. The punishment of the reprobate a commencement of the eternal punishment awaiting them ; that of the elect designed to bring them to repentance. This confirmed by passages of Scripture and of the Fathers.
34. Two uses of this doctrine to the believer. In affliction he can believe that God, though angry, is still favourable to him. In the punishment of the reprobate, he sees a prelude to their final doom.
35. Objection, as to the punishment of David, answered. Why all men here subjected to chastisement.
36. Objections, founded on five other passages, answered.
37. Answer continued.
38. Objection, founded on passages in the Fathers. •Answer, with passages from Chrysostom and Augustine.
39. These satisfactions had reference to the peace of the Church, and not to the throne of God. The Schoolmen have perverted the meaning of some absurd statements by obscure monks.

1. I COME now to an examination of what the scholastic sophists teach concerning repentance. This I will do as briefly as possible ; for I have no intention to take up every point, lest this work, which I am desirous to frame as a compendium of doctrine, should exceed

all bounds. They have managed to envelop a matter, otherwise not much involved, in so many perplexities, that it will be difficult to find an outlet if once you get plunged but a little way into their mire. And, first, in giving a definition, they plainly show they never understood what repentance means. For they fasten on some expressions in the writings of the Fathers which are very far from expressing the nature of repentance. For instance, that to *repent* is to deplore past sins and not commit what is to be deplored. Again, that it is to bewail past evils, and not again to do what is to be bewailed. Again, that it is a kind of grieving revenge, punishing in itself what it grieves to have committed. Again, that it is sorrow of heart and bitterness of soul for the evils which the individual has committed, or to which he has consented.[1] Supposing we grant that these things were well said by Fathers (though, if one were inclined to dispute, it were not difficult to deny it), they were not, however, said with the view of describing repentance, but only of exhorting penitents not again to fall into the same faults from which they had been delivered. But if all descriptions of this kind are to be converted into definitions, there are others which have as good a title to be added. For instance, the following sentence of Chrysostom: "Repentance is a medicine for the cure of sin, a gift bestowed from above, an admirable virtue, a grace surpassing the power of laws." Moreover, the doctrine which they[2] afterwards deliver is somewhat worse than their definition. For they are so keenly bent on external exercises, that all you can gather from immense volumes[3] is, that repentance is a discipline, and austerity, which serves partly to subdue the flesh, partly to chasten and punish sins: of internal renovation of mind, bringing with it true amendment of life, there is a strange silence.[4] No doubt, they talk much of contrition and attrition, torment the soul with many scruples, and involve it in great trouble and anxiety; but when they seem to have deeply wounded the heart, they cure all its bitterness by a slight sprinkling of ceremonies. Repentance thus shrewdly defined, they divide into contrition of the heart, confession of the mouth, and satisfaction of works.[5] This is not more logical than the definition, though they would be thought to have spent their whole lives in framing syllogisms.[6] But if any one argues from the definition (a

1 The first definition is that of Gregory, and is contained Sentent. Lib. iv. Dist. 14, c. 1. The second, which is that of Ambrose, is given same place, and also Decret. Dist. 3, de Pœnitentia C. Pœnit. Prior. The third is Augustine's, as stated in the same place, and C. Pœnit. Poster. The fourth is from Ambrose, and is given Dist. 1, de Pœnit. C. Vera Pœnitentia.

2 French, " Ces bons glosateurs ;"—these worthy glossers.

3 Latin, " Immensis voluminibus."—French, "Leur gros bobulaire de livres ;"—their large lumbering books.

4 Latin, "Mirum silentium."—French, "Il n'en est nulles nouuelles en leur quartier ;"—there are no news in their quarter.

5 Sent. Lib. iv. Dist. 16, cap. 1 ; De Pœnit. Dist. 1 ; C. Perfecta Pœnit.

6 French, " Combien qu'ils n'estudient autre chose en toute leur vie que la Dialectique, que ont l'art de definir et partir ;"—although they study nought else during their whole life but Dialectics, which is the art of defining and dividing.

mode of argument prevalent with dialecticians) that a man may weep over his past sins, and not commit things that cause weeping; may bewail past evils, and not commit things that are to be bewailed; may punish what he is grieved for having committed, though he does not confess it with the mouth,—how will they defend their division? For if he may be a true penitent and not confess, repentance can exist without confession. If they answer, that this division refers to repentance regarded as a sacrament, or is to be understood of repentance in its most perfect form, which they do not comprehend in their definitions, the mistake does not rest with me: let them blame themselves for not defining more purely and clearly. When any matter is discussed, I certainly am dull enough to refer everything to the definition as the hinge and foundation of the whole discussion. But granting that this is a licence which masters have, let us now survey the different parts in their order. In omitting as frivolous several things which they vend with solemn brow as mysteries, I do it not from ignorance. It were not very difficult to dispose of all those points which they plume themselves on their acuteness and subtilty in discussing: but I consider it a sacred duty not to trouble the reader to no purpose with such absurdities. It is certainly easy to see from the questions which they move and agitate, and in which they miserably entangle themselves, that they are prating of things they know not. Of this nature are the following: Whether repentance of one sin is pleasing to God, while there is an obstinate adherence to other sins. Again, whether punishments divinely inflicted are available for satisfaction. Again, whether repentance can be several times repeated for mortal sins, whereas they grossly and wickedly define that daily repentance has to do with none but venial sins. In like manner, with gross error, they greatly torment themselves with a saying of Jerome, that repentance is a second plank after shipwreck.[1] Herein they show that they have never awoke from brutish stupor, so as to obtain a distant view of the thousandth part of their sins.

2. I would have my readers to observe, that the dispute here relates not to a matter of no consequence;[2] but to one of the most important of all—viz. the forgiveness of sins. For while they require three things in repentance—viz. compunction of heart, confession of the mouth, and satisfaction of work[3]—they at the same time teach that these are necessary to obtain the pardon of sins. If there is anything in the whole compass of religion which it is of importance

---

1 Latin, "Secundam tabulam post naufragium."—French, "Une seconde planche, sur laquelle celui que estoit pour perir en la mer, nage pour venir au port;"—a second plank on which he who was on the point of perishing in the sea swims to gain the harbour.

2 Latin, "De asini umbra rixam."—French, "En un combat frivole;"—engaged in a frivolous combat.

3 Luther (adv. Bullam Antichristi, Art. vi.) shows that those who set down these three parts of repentance, speak neither according to Scripture nor the ancient Fathers.

to us to know, this certainly is one of the most important—viz. to perceive and rightly hold by what means, what rule, what terms, with what facility or difficulty, forgiveness of sins may be obtained. Unless our knowledge here is clear and certain, our conscience can have no rest at all, no peace with God, no confidence or security, but is continually trembling, fluctuating, boiling, and distracted; dreads, hates, and shuns the presence of God. But if forgiveness of sins depends on the conditions to which they bind it, nothing can be more wretched and deplorable than our situation. *Contrition* they represent as the first step in obtaining pardon; and they exact it as due, that is, full and complete: meanwhile, they decide not when one may feel secure of having performed this contrition in due measure. I admit that we are bound strongly and incessantly to urge every man bitterly to lament his sins, and thereby stimulate himself more and more to dislike and hate them. For this is the "repentance to salvation not to be repented of" (2 Cor. vii. 10). But when such bitterness of sorrow is demanded as may correspond to the magnitude of the offence, and be weighed in the balance with confidence of pardon, miserable consciences are sadly perplexed and tormented when they see that the contrition due for sin is laid upon them, and yet that they have no measure of what is due, so as to enable them to determine that they have made full payment. If they say we are to do what in us lies, we are always brought back to the same point;[1] for when will any man venture to promise himself that he has done his utmost in bewailing sin? Therefore, when consciences, after a lengthened struggle and long contests with themselves, find no haven in which they may rest, as a means of alleviating their condition in some degree, they extort sorrow and wring out tears, in order to perfect their contrition.

3. If they say that this is calumny on my part, let them come forward and point out a single individual who, by this doctrine of contrition, has not either been driven to despair, or has not, instead of true, opposed pretended fear to the justice of God. We have elsewhere observed, that forgiveness of sins never can be obtained without repentance, because none but the afflicted, and those wounded by a consciousness of sins, can sincerely implore the mercy of God; but we, at the same time, added, that repentance cannot be the cause of the forgiveness of sins: and we also did away with that torment of souls—the dogma that it must be performed as due. Our doctrine was, that the soul looked not to its own compunction or its own tears, but fixed both eyes on the mercy of God alone. Only we observed, that those who labour and are heavy laden are called by Christ, seeing he was sent " to preach good tidings to the meek;" " to bind up the broken-hearted; to proclaim liberty to the captives, and the opening of the prison to them that are bound;" " to comfort all that

[1] French, "Nous tournerons toujours en un même circuit";—we shall always revolve in the same circle.

mourn."[1] Hence the Pharisees were excluded, because, full of their own righteousness, they acknowledged not their own poverty; and despisers, because, regardless of the divine anger, they sought no remedy for their wickedness. Such persons neither labour nor are heavy laden, are not broken-hearted, bound, nor in prison. But there is a great difference between teaching that forgiveness of sins is merited by a full and complete contrition (which the sinner never can give), and instructing him to hunger and thirst after the mercy of God, that recognising his wretchedness, his .turmoil, weariness, and captivity, you may show him where he should seek refreshment, rest, and liberty; in fine, teach him in his humility to give glory to God.

4. *Confession* has ever been a subject of keen contest between the Canonists and the Scholastic Theologians; the former contending that confession is of divine authority—the latter insisting, on the contrary, that it is merely enjoined by ecclesiastical constitution. In this contest great effrontery has been displayed by the Theologians, who have corrupted and violently wrested every passage of Scripture they have quoted in their favour.[2] And when they saw that even thus they could not gain their object, those who wished to be thought particularly acute had recourse to the evasion that confession is of divine authority in regard to the substance, but that it afterwards received its form from positive enactment. Thus the silliest of these quibblers refer the citation to divine authority, from its being said, " Adam, where art thou ?" (Gen. iii. 9, 12); and also the exception from Adam having replied as if excepting, " The woman whom thou gavest to be with me," &c. ; but say that the form of both was appointed by civil law. Let us see by what arguments they prove that this confession, formed or unformed, is a divine commandment. The Lord, they say, sent the lepers to the priests (Matth. viii. 4). What? did he send them to confession ? Who ever heard tell that the Levitical priests were appointed to hear confession ? Here they resort to allegory. The priests were appointed by the Mosaic law to discern between leper and leper : sin is spiritual leprosy; therefore it belongs to the priests to decide upon it. Before I answer, I would ask, in passing, why, if this passage makes them judges of spiritual leprosy, they claim the cognisance of natural and carnal leprosy ? This, forsooth, is not to play upon Scripture![3] The law gives the cognisance of leprosy to the Levitical priests: let us usurp this to ourselves. Sin is spiritual leprosy: let us also have cognisance of sin. I now give my answer : There being a change of the priesthood, there must of necessity be a change of the law. All the sacer-

---

1 Matth. xi. 28; Is. lxi. 1 ; Luke iv. 18.

2 Erasmus, in a letter to the Augustine Steuchus in 1531, while flattering, at the same time laughs at him, for thinking that the fifth chapter of Numbers sufficiently proves, in opposition to Luther, that auricular confession is of God.

3 French, " N'est ce pas bien se jouer des Escritures, de les tourner en ceste façon ?" —is it not indeed to make game of Scripture, to turn it in this fashion ?

dotal functions were transferred to Christ, and in him fulfilled and ended (Heb. vii. 12). To him alone, therefore, all the rights and honours of the priesthood have been transferred: If they are so fond then of hunting out allegories, let them set Christ before them as the only priest, and place full and universal jurisdiction on his tribunal : this we will readily admit. Besides, there is an incongruity in their allegory: it classes a merely civil enactment among ceremonies. Why, then, does Christ send the lepers to the priests? Lest the priests should be charged with violating the law, which ordained that the person cured of leprosy should present himself before the priest, and be purified by the offering of a sacrifice, he orders the lepers who had been cleansed to do what the law required. " Go and show thyself to the priest, and offer for thy cleansing according as Moses commanded for a testimony unto them " (Luke v. 17). And assuredly this miracle would be a testimony to them : they had pronounced them lepers ; they now pronounce them cured. Whether they would or not, they are forced to become witnesses to the miracles of Christ. Christ allows them to examine the miracle, and they cannot deny it: yet, as they still quibble, they have need of a testimony. So it is elsewhere said, " This gospel of the kingdom shall be preached in all the world, for a witness unto all nations" (Matth. xxiv. 14). Again, " Ye shall be brought before governors and kings for my sake, for a testimony against them and the Gentiles" (Matth. x. 18) ; that is, in order that, in the judgment of God, they might be more fully convicted. But if they prefer taking the view of Chrysostom (Hom. xii. de Muliere Cananæa), he shows that this was done by Christ for the sake of the Jews also, that he might not be regarded as a violator of the law. But we are ashamed to appeal to the authority of any man in a matter so clear, when Christ declares that he left the legal right of the priests entire, as professed enemies of the Gospel, who were always intent on making a clamour if their mouths were not stopped. Wherefore, let the Popish priests, in order to retain this privilege, openly make common cause with those whom it was necessary to restrain, by forcible means, from speaking evil of Christ.[1] For there is here no reference to his true ministers.

5. They draw their second argument from the same fountain,—I mean allegory ; as if allegories were of much avail in confirming any doctrine. But, indeed, let them avail, if those which I am able to produce are not more specious than theirs. They say, then, that the Lord, after raising Lazarus, commanded his disciples to " loose him and let him go " (John xi. 44). Their first statement is untrue : we no where read that the Lord said this to the disciples ; and it is much more probable that he spoke to the Jews who were standing by, that from there being no suspicion of fraud the miracle might be more

1 The French is, " Car ce que Jesus Christ laisse aux Presˆtres de la loy, n'appartient en rien à ses vrais ministres;"—for that which Jesus Christ leaves to the Priests, belongs not in any respect to his truê ministers.

manifest, and his power might be the more conspicuous from his raising the dead without touching him, by a mere word. In the same way, I understand that our Lord, to leave no ground of suspicion to the Jews, wished them to roll back the stone, feel the stench, perceive the sure signs of death, see him rise by the mere power of a word, and first handle him when alive. And this is the view of Chrysostom (Serm. C. Jud. Gent. et Hæret.). But granting that it was said to the disciples, what can they gain by it? That the Lord gave the apostles the power of loosing? How much more aptly and dexterously might we allegorise and say, that by this symbol the Lord designed to teach his followers to loose those whom he raises up; that is, not to bring to remembrance the sins which he himself had forgotten not to condemn as sinners those whom he had acquitted, not still to upbraid those whom he had pardoned, not to be stern and severe in punishing, while he himself was merciful and ready to forgive. Certainly nothing should more incline us to pardon than the example of the Judge who threatens that he will be inexorable to the rigid and inhumane. Let them go now and vend their allegories.[1]

6. They now come to closer quarters, while they support their view by passages of Scripture which they think clearly in their favour.[2] Those who came to John's baptism confessed their sins, and James bids us confess our sins one to another (James v. 16). It is not strange that those who wished to be baptised confessed their sins. It has already been mentioned, that John preached the baptism of repentance, baptised with water unto repentance. Whom then could he baptise, but those who confessed that they were sinners? Baptism is a symbol of the forgiveness of sins; and who could be admitted to receive the symbol but sinners acknowledging themselves as such? They therefore confessed their sins that they might be baptised. Nor without good reason does James enjoin us to confess our sins one to another. But if they would attend to what immediately follows, they would perceive that this gives them little support. The words are, " Confess your sins one to another, and pray one for another." He joins together mutual confession and mutual prayer. If, then, we are to confess to priests only, we are also to pray for them only. What? It would even follow from the words of James, that priests alone can confess. In saying that we are to confess mutually, he must be addressing those only who can hear the confession of others. He says, ἀλλήλοις, mutually, by turns, or, if they prefer it, reciprocally. But those only can confess reciprocally who are fit to hear confession. This being a privilege which they bestow upon priests only, we also leave them the office of confessing to each other. Have done then with such frivolous absurdities, and let us receive the true meaning of the

---

1 French, " Qu'ils voisent maintenant, et facent un bouclier de leur allegories;"—let them go now and make a buckler of their allegories,
2 Augustin. Epist. 54.

apostle, which is plain and simple; *first*, That we are to deposit our infirmities in the breasts of each other, with the view of receiving mutual counsel, sympathy, and comfort; and, *secondly*, That mutually conscious of the infirmities of our brethren, we are to pray to the Lord for them. Why then quote James against us who so earnestly insist on acknowledgment of the divine mercy? No man can acknowledge the mercy of God without previously confessing his own misery. Nay, we pronounce every man to be anathema who does not confess himself a sinner before God, before his angels, before the Church; in short, before all men. " The Scripture hath concluded all under sin," "that every mouth may be stopped, and all the world may become guilty before God," that God alone may be justified and exalted (Gal. iii. 22 ; Rom. iii. 9, 19).

7. I wonder at their effrontery in venturing to maintain that the confession of which they speak is of divine authority. We admit that the use of it is very ancient; but we can easily prove that at one time it was free. It certainly appears, from their own records, that no law or constitution respecting it was enacted before the days of Innocent III. Surely if there had been a more ancient law they would have fastened on it, instead of being satisfied with the decree of the Council of Lateran, and so making themselves ridiculous even to children. In other matters, they hesitate not to coin fictitious decrees, which they ascribe to the most ancient Councils, that they may blind the eyes of the simple by veneration for antiquity. In this instance it has not occurred to them to practise this deception, and hence, themselves being witnesses, three centuries have not yet elapsed since the bridle was put, and the necessity of confession imposed by Innocent III. And to say nothing of the time, the mere barbarism of the terms used destroys the authority of the law. For when these worthy fathers enjoin that every person of *both sexes* (utriusque sexus) must once a-year confess his sins to his own priest, men of wit humorously object that the precept binds hermaphrodites only, and has no application to any one who is either a male or a female. A still grosser absurdity has been displayed by their disciples, who are unable to explain what is meant by one's own priest (proprius sacerdos). Let all the hired ravers of the Pope babble as they may,[1] we hold that Christ is not the author of this law, which compels men to enumerate their sins ; nay, that twelve hundred years elapsed after the resurrection of Christ before any such law was made, and that, consequently, this tyranny was not introduced until piety and doctrine were extinct, and pretended pastors had usurped to themselves unbridled licence. There is clear evidence in historians, and other ancient writers, to show that this was a politic discipline introduced by bishops, not a law enacted by Christ or the

---

1 French, " Quoy que tous les advocats et procureurs du Pape, et tous les caphars qu'il a à louage gazouillent ;"—whatever all the advocates and procurators of the Pope, and all the caphars whom he has in his pay may gabble.

Apostles. Out of many I will produce only one passage, which will be no obscure proof. Sozomen[1] relates,[2] that this constitution of the bishops was carefully observed in the Western churches, but especially at Rome; thus intimating that it was not the universal custom of all churches. He also says, that one of the presbyters was specially appointed to take charge of this duty. This abundantly confutes their falsehood as to the keys being given to the whole priesthood indiscriminately for this purpose, since the function was not common to all the priests, but specially belonged to the one priest whom the bishop had appointed to it. He it was (the same who at present in each of the cathedral churches has the name of pœnitentiary) who had cognisance of offences which were more heinous, and required to be rebuked for the sake of example. He afterwards adds, that the same custom extited at Constantinpole, until a certain matron, while prentending to confess, was discovered to have used it as a cloak to cover her intercourse with a deacon. In consequence of that crime, Nectarious, the bishop of that church—a man famous for learning and sanctity—abolished the custom of confessing. Here, then, let these asses prick up their ears. If auricular confession was a divine law, how could Nectarius have dared to abolish or remodel it? Nectarius, a holy man of God, approved by the suffrage of all antiquity, will they charge with heresy and schism? With the same vote they will condemn the church of Constantinople, in which Sozomen affirms that the custom of confessing was not only disguised for a time, but even in his own memory abolished. Nay, let them charge with defection, not only Constantinople, but all the Eastern churches, which (if they say true) disregarded an inviolable law enjoined on all Christians.

8. This abrogation is clearly attested in so many passages by Chrysostom, who lived at Constantinople, and was himself prelate of the church, that it is strange they can venture to maintain the contrary: "Tell your sins," says he, that you may efface them: if you blush to tell another what sins you have committed, tell them daily in your soul. I say not, tell them to your fellow-servant who may upbraid you, but tell them to God who cures them. Confess your sins upon your bed, that your conscience may there daily recognise its iniquities." Again, "Now, however, it is not necessary to confess before witnesses; let the examination of your faults be made in your own thought: let the judgment be without a witness: let God alone see you confessing." Again, "I do not lead you publicly into the view of your fellow-servants; I do not force you to disclose your sins to men; review and lay open your conscience before God. Show your wounds to the Lord, the best of physicians, and seek medicine from him. Show to him who upbraids not, but cures most kindly." Again, "Certainly tell it not to man lest he upbraid you. Nor must you

1 The French adds, "l'un des auteurs de l'Histoire Ecclesiastique;"—one of the authors of the Ecclesiastical History.
2 Eccles Hist. Lib. viii. cap. 17, et Trepont. Hist. Lib. ix.

confess to your fellow-servant, who may make it public; but show your wounds to the Lord, who takes care of you, who is kind and can cure." He afterwards introduces God speaking thus: "I oblige you not to come into the midst of a theatre, and have many witnesses; tell your sins to me alone in private, that I may cure the ulcer."[1] Shall we say that Chrysostom, in writing these and similar passages, carried his presumption so far as to free the consciences of men from those chains with which they are bound by the divine law? By no means; but knowing that it was not at all prescribed by the word of God, he dares not exact it as necessary.

9. But that the whole matter may be more plainly unfolded, we shall first honestly state the nature of confession as delivered in the word of God, and thereafter subjoin their inventions—not all of them indeed (who could drink up that boundless sea?), but those only which contain a summary of their secret confession. Here I am grieved to mention how frequently the old interpreter[2] has rendered the word *confess* instead of *praise*, a fact notorious to the most illiterate, were it not fitting to expose their effrontery in transferring to their tyrannical edict what was written concerning the praises of God. To prove that confession has the effect of exhilarating the mind, they obtrude the passage in the psalm, "with the voice of joy and praise" (Vulgate, *confessionis*) (Ps. xlii. 4). But if such a metamorphosis is valid, anything may be made of anything. But, as they have lost all shame, let pious readers reflect how, by the just vengeance of God, they have been given over to a reprobate mind, that their audacity may be the more detestable. If we are disposed to acquiesce in the simple doctrine of Scripture, there will be no danger of our being misled by such glosses. There one method of confessing is prescribed; since it is the Lord who forgives, forgets, and wipes away sins, to him let us confess them, that we may obtain pardon. He is the physician, therefore, let us show our wounds to him. He is hurt and offended, let us ask peace of him. He is the discerner of the heart, and knows all our thoughts; let us hasten to pour out our hearts before him. He it is, in fine, who invites sinners; let us delay not to draw near to him. "I acknowledge my sin unto thee," says David; "and mine iniquity have I not hid. I said, I will confess my transgressions unto the Lord; and thou forgavest the iniquity of my sin" (Ps. xxxii. 5). Another specimen of David's confession is as follows: "Have mercy upon me, O God, according to thy loving kindness" (Ps. li. 1). The following is Daniel's confession: "We have sinned, and have committed iniquity, and have done wickedly, and have rebelled, even by departing from thy precepts and thy judgments" (Dan. ix. 5). Other examples everywhere occur in Scripture:

---

[1] Chrysost. Hom. ii. in Psal. 1. Serm. de Pœnit. et Confess. Hom. v. De Incomprehensibili Dei. Nat. cont. Anomeos. Item, Hom. iv. de Lazaro.

[2] Latin, "Vetus interpres."—French, "Le translateur tant Grec qui Latin;"—the Greek as well as Latin translator.

the quotation of them would almost fill a volume. " If we confess our sins," says John, " he is faithful and just to forgive us our sins " (1 John i. 9). To whom are we to confess? to him surely;—that is, we are to fall down before him with a grieved and humbled heart, and, sincerely accusing and condemning ourselves, seek forgiveness of his goodness and mercy.

10. He who has adopted this confession from the heart and as in the presence of God, will doubtless have a tongue ready to confess whenever there is occasion among men to publish the mercy of God. He will not be satisfied to whisper the secret of his heart for once into the ear of one individual, but will often, and openly, and in the hearing of the whole world, ingenuously make mention both of his own ignominy, and of the greatness and glory of the Lord. In this way David, after he was accused by Nathan, being stung in his conscience, confesses his sin before God and men. " I have sinned unto the Lord," says he (2 Sam. xii. 13); that is, I have now no excuse, no evasion ; all must judge me a sinner ; and that which I wished to be secret with the Lord must also be made manifest to men. Hence the secret confession which is made to God is followed by voluntary confession to men, whenever that is conducive to the divine glory or our humiliation. For this reason the Lord anciently enjoined the people of Israel that they should repeat the words after the priest, and make public confession of their iniquities in the temple ; because he foresaw that this was a necessary help to enable each one to form a just idea of himself. And it is proper that, by confession of our misery, we should manifest the mercy of our God both among our-selves and before the whole world.

11. It is proper that this mode of confession should both be ordi-nary in the Church, and also be specially employed on extraordinary occasions, when the people in common happen to have fallen into any fault. Of this latter description we have an example in the solemn confession which the whole people made under the authority and guidance of Ezra and Nehemiah (Neh. i. 6, 7). For their long captivity, the destruction of the temple, and suppression of their religion, having been the common punishment of their defection, they could not make meet acknowledgment of the blessing of deliver-ance without previous confession of their guilt. And it matters not though in one assembly it may sometimes happen that a few are innocent, seeing that the members of a languid and sickly body cannot boast of soundness. Nay, it is scarcely possible that these few have not contracted some taint, and so bear part of the blame. Therefore, as often as we are afflicted with pestilence, or war, or famine, or any other calamity whatsoever, if it is our duty to betake ourselves to mourning, fasting, and other signs of guiltiness, confession also, on which all the others depend, is not to be neglected. That ordinary confession which the Lord has moreover expressly commended, no sober man, who has reflected on its usefulness, will venture to disap-

prove. Seeing that in every sacred assembly we stand in the view of God and angels, in what way should our service begin but in acknowledging our own unworthiness? But this you will say is done in every prayer; for as often as we pray for pardon, we confess our sins. I admit it. But if you consider how great is our carelessness, or drowsiness, or sloth, you will grant me that it would be a salutary ordinance if the Christian people were exercised in humiliation by some formal method of confession. For though the ceremony which the Lord enjoined on the Israelites belonged to the tutelage of the Law, yet the thing itself belongs in some respect to us also. And, indeed, in all well-ordered churches, in observance of an useful custom, the minister, each Lord's day, frames a formula of confession in his own name and that of the people, in which he makes a common confession of iniquity, and supplicates pardon from the Lord. In short, by this key a door of prayer is opened privately for each, and publicly for all.

12. Two other forms of private confession are approved by Scripture. The one is made on our own account, and to it reference is made in the passage in James, "Confess your sins one to another" (James v. 16); for the meaning is, that by disclosing our infirmities to each other, we are to obtain the aid of mutual counsel and consolation. The other is to be made for the sake of our neighbour, to appease and reconcile him if by our fault he has been in any respect injured. In the former, although James, by not specifying any particular individual into whose bosom we are to disburden our feelings, leaves us the free choice of confessing to any member of the church who may seem fittest; yet as for the most part pastors are to be supposed better qualified than others, our choice ought chiefly to fall upon them. And the ground of preference is, that the Lord, by calling them to the ministry, points them out as the persons by whose lips we are to be taught to subdue and correct our sins, and derive consolation from the hope of pardon. For as the duty of mutual admonition and correction is committed to all Christians, but is specially enjoined on ministers, so while we ought all to console each other mutually, and confirm each other in confidence in the divine mercy, we see that ministers, to assure our consciences of the forgiveness of sins, are appointed to be the witnesses and sponsors of it, so that they are themselves said to forgive sins and loose souls (Matth. xvi. 19 ; xviii. 18). When you hear this attributed to them, reflect that it is for your use. Let every believer, therefore, remember, that if in private he is so agonised and afflicted by a sense of his sins that he cannot obtain relief without the aid of others, it is his duty not to neglect the remedy which God provides for him—viz. to have recourse for relief to a private confession to his own pastor, and for consolation privately implore the assistance of him whose business it is, both in public and private, to solace the people of God with Gospel doctrine. But we are always to use moderation, lest in a matter as to

which God prescribes no certain rule, our consciences be burdened with a certain yoke. Hence it follows, first, that confession of this nature ought to be free so as not to be exacted of all, but only recommended to those who feel that they have need of it; and, secondly, even those who use it according to their necessity must neither be compelled by any precept, nor artfully induced to enumerate all their sins, but only in so far as they shall deem it for their interest, that they may obtain the full benefit of consolation. Faithful pastors, as they would both eschew tyranny in their ministry, and superstition in the people, must not only leave this liberty to churches, but defend and strenuously vindicate it.

13. Of the second form of confession, our Saviour speaks in Matthew. "If thou bring thy gift to the altar, and there remember that thy brother hath ought against thee; leave there thy gift before the altar; first be reconciled to thy brother, and then come and offer thy gift" (Matth. v. 23, 24). Thus love, which has been interrupted by our fault, must be restored by acknowledging and asking pardon for the fault. Under this head is included the confession of those who by their sin have given offence to the whole Church (*supra*, sec. 10). For if Christ attaches so much importance to the offence of one individual, that he forbids the sacrifice of all who have sinned in any respect against their brethren, until by due satisfaction they have regained their favour, how much greater reason is there that he, who by some evil example has offended the Church, should be reconciled to it by the acknowledgment of his fault? Thus the member of the Church of Corinth was restored to communion after he had humbly submitted to correction (2 Cor. ii. 6). This form of confession existed in the ancient Christian Church, as Cyprian relates: "They practise repentance," says he, "for a proper time, then they come to confession, and by the laying on of the hands of the bishop and clergy, are admitted to communion. Scripture knows nothing of any other form or method of confessing, and it belongs not to us to bind new chains upon consciences which Christ most strictly prohibits from being brought into bondage. Meanwhile, that the flock present themselves before the pastor whenever they would partake of the Holy Supper, I am so far from disapproving, that I am most desirous it should be everywhere observed. For both those whose conscience is hindered may thence obtain singular benefit, and those who require admonition thus afford an opportunity for it; provided always no countenance is given to tyranny and superstition."

14. The *power of the keys* has place in the three following modes of confession,—either when the whole Church, in a formal acknowledgment of its defects,[1] supplicates pardon; or when a private individual who has given public offence by some notable delinquency, testifies his repentance; or when he who from disquiet of conscience

---

[1] As to the form of repentance enjoined by the primitive Church for more flagrant offences, see Book IV. chap i. sec. 29.

needs the aid of his minister, acquaints him with his infirmity. With regard to the reparation of offence, the case is different. For though in this also provision is made for peace of conscience, yet the principal object is to suppress hatred, and reunite brethren in the bond of peace. But the benefit of which I have spoken is by no means to be despised, that we may the more willingly confess our sins. For when the whole Church stands as it were at the bar of God, confesses her guilt, and finds her only refuge in the divine mercy, it is no common or light solace to have an ambassador of Christ present, invested with the mandate of reconciliation, by whom she may hear her absolution pronounced. Here the utility of the keys is justly commended when that embassy is duly discharged with becoming order and reverence. In like manner, when he who has as it were become an alien from the Church receives pardon, and is thus restored to brotherly unity, how great is the benefit of understanding that he is pardoned by those to whom Christ said, " Whose soever sins ye remit, they are remitted unto them" (John xx. 23). Nor is private absolution of less benefit or efficacy when asked by those who stand in need of a special remedy for their infirmity. It not seldom happens, that he who hears general promises which are intended for the whole congregation of the faithful, nevertheless remains somewhat in doubt, and is still disquieted in mind, as if his own remission were not yet obtained. Should this individual lay open the secret wound of his soul to his pastor, and hear these words of the Gospel specially addressed to him, "Son, be of good cheer ; thy sins be forgiven thee" (Matth. ix. 2),[1] his mind will feel secure, and escape from the trepidation with which it was previously agitated. But when we treat of the keys, we must always beware of dreaming of any power apart from the preaching of the Gospel. This subject will be more fully explained, when we come to treat of the government of the Church (Book IV. chap. xi. xii.). There we shall see, that whatever privilege of binding and loosing Christ has bestowed on his Church is annexed to the word. This is especially true with regard to the ministry of the keys, the whole power of which consists in this, that the grace of the Gospel is publicly and privately sealed on the minds of believers by means of those whom the Lord has appointed ; and the only method in which this can be done is by preaching.

15. What say the Roman theologians ? That all persons of both sexes,[2] so soon as they shall have reached the years of discretion, must, once a-year at least, confess all their sins to their own priest ; that the sin is not discharged unless the resolution to confess has been firmly conceived ; that if this resolution is not carried into effect when

1 The French is, " Et que le Pasteur addressant sa parole à lui, l'assure comme lui appliquant en particulier la doctrine generale ;"—and when the Pastor, addressing his discourse to him, assures him as applying the general doctrine to him in particular.
2 " C Omnis utriusque sexus ;"—every one of both sexes. Innocent's decree is in the Lateran Council, De Summa Trinitate et Fide Cathol. It is also given Sent. Lib. iv. Dist. 14, cap. 2, et Dist. 18. cap. 2.

an opportunity offers, there is no entrance into Paradise; that the priest, moreover, has the power of the keys, by which he can loose and bind the sinner; because the declaration of Christ is not in vain: "Whatsoever ye shall bind on earth shall be bound in heaven" (Matth. xviii. 18). Concerning this power, however, they wage a fierce war among themselves. Some say there is only one key essentially—viz. the power of binding and loosing; that knowledge, indeed, is requisite for the proper use of it, but only as an accessory, not as essentially inherent in it. Others, seeing that this gave too unrestrained licence, have imagined two keys—viz. discernment and power. Others, again, seeing that the licence of priests was curbed by such restraint, have forged other keys (infra, sec. 21), the authority of discerning to be used in defining, and the power to carry their sentences into execution; and to these they add knowledge as a counsellor. This binding and loosing, however, they do not venture to interpret simply, to forgive and wipe away sins, because they hear the Lord proclaiming by the prophet, "I, even I, am the Lord; and beside me there is no saviour." "I, even I, am he that blotteth out thy transgressions" (Isaiah xliii. 11, 25). But they say it belongs to the priest to declare who are bound or loosed, and whose sins are remitted or retained; to declare, moreover, either by confession, when he absolves and retains sins, or by sentence, when he excommunicates or admits to communion in the Sacraments. Lastly, perceiving that the knot is not yet untied, because it may always be objected that persons are often undeservedly bound and loosed, and therefore not bound or loosed in heaven; as their ultimate resource, they answer, that the conferring of the keys must be taken with limitation, because Christ has promised that the sentence of the priest, properly pronounced, will be approved at his judgment-seat according as the bound or loosed asked what they merited. They say, moreover, that those keys which are conferred by bishops at ordination were given by Christ to all priests, but that the free use of them is with those only who discharge ecclesiastical functions; that with priests excommunicated or suspended the keys themselves indeed remain, but tied and rusty. Those who speak thus may justly be deemed modest and sober compared with others, who on a new anvil have forged new keys, by which they say that the treasury of heaven is locked up: these we shall afterwards consider in their own place (chap. v. sec. 2).

16. To each of these views I will briefly reply. As to their binding the souls of believers by their laws, whether justly or unjustly, I say nothing at present, as it will be seen at the proper place; but their enacting it as a law, that all sins are to be enumerated; their denying that sin is discharged except under the condition that the resolution to confess has been firmly conceived; their pretence that there is no admission into Paradise if the opportunity of confession has been neglected, are things which it is impossible to bear. Are all sins to be enumerated? But David, who, I presume, had honestly pondered

with himself as to the confession of his sins, exclaimed, "Who can understand his errors? cleanse thou me from secret faults" (Ps. xix. 12); and in another passage, "Mine iniquities are gone over my head: as a heavy burden they are too heavy for me" (Ps. xxxviii. 4). He knew how deep was the abyss of our sins, how numerous the forms of wickedness, how many heads the hydra carried, how long a tail it drew. Therefore, he did not sit down to make a catalogue, but from the depth of his distress cried unto the Lord, "I am overwhelmed, and buried, and sore vexed; the gates of hell have encircled me: let thy right hand deliver me from the abyss into which I am plunged, and from the death which I am ready to die." Who can now think of a computation of his sins when he sees David's inability to number his?

17. By this ruinous procedure, the souls of those who were affected with some sense of God have been most cruelly racked. First, they betook themselves to calculation, proceeding according to the formula given by the Schoolmen, and dividing their sins into boughs, branches, twigs, and leaves; then they weighed the qualities, quantities, and circumstances; and in this way, for some time, matters proceeded. But after they had advanced farther, when they looked around, nought was seen but sea and sky; no road, no harbour. The longer the space they ran over, a longer still met the eye; nay, lofty mountains began to rise, and there seemed no hope of escape; none at least till after long wanderings. They were thus brought to a dead halt, till at length the only issue was found in despair. Here these cruel murderers, to ease the wounds which they had made, applied certain fomentations. Every one was to do his best. But new cares again disturbed, nay, new torments excruciated their souls. "I have not spent enough of time; I have not exerted myself sufficiently: many things I have omitted through negligence: forgetfulness proceeding from want of care is not excusable." Then new drugs were supplied to alleviate their pains. "Repent of your negligence; and provided it is not done supinely, it will be pardoned." All these things, however, could not heal the wound, being not so much alleviations of the sore as poison besmeared with honey, that its bitterness might not at once offend the taste, but penetrate to the vitals before it could be detected. The dreadful voice, therefore, was always heard pealing in their ears, "Confess all your sins," and the dread thus occasioned could not be pacified without sure consolation. Here let my readers consider whether it be possible to take an account of the actions of a whole year, or even to collect the sins committed in a single day, seeing every man's experience convinces him that at evening, in examining the faults of that single day, memory gets confused, so great is the number and variety presented. I am not speaking of dull and heartless hypocrites, who, after animadverting on three or four of their grosser offences, think the work finished; but of the true worshippers of God, who, after they have performed their examination,

feeling themselves overwhelmed, still add the words of John : " If our heart condemn us, God is greater than our heart, and knoweth all things" (1 John iii. 20); and, therefore, tremble at the thought of that Judge whose knowledge far surpasses our comprehension.

18. Though a good part of the world rested in these soothing suggestions, by which this fatal poison was somewhat tempered, it was not because they thought that God was satisfied, or they had quite satisfied themselves; it was rather like an anchor cast out in the middle of the deep, which for a little interrupts the navigation, or a weary, worn-out traveller, who lies down by the way.[1] I give myself no trouble in proving the truth of this fact. Every one can be his own witness. I will mention generally what the nature of this law is. First, The observance of it is simply impossible; and hence its only result is to destroy, condemn, confound, to plunge into ruin and despair. Secondly, By withdrawing sinners from a true sense of their sins, it makes them hypocritical, and ignorant both of God and themselves. For, while they are wholly occupied with the enumeration of their sins, they lose sight of that lurking hydra, their secret iniquities and internal defilements, the knowledge of which would have made them sensible of their misery. But the surest rule of confession is, to acknowledge and confess our sins to be an abyss so great as to exceed our comprehension. On this rule we see the confession of the publican was formed, " God be merciful to me, a sinner" (Luke xviii. 13); as if he had said, How great, how very great a sinner, how utterly sinful I am ! the extent of my sins I can neither conceive nor express. Let the depth of thy mercy ingulf the depth of sin ! What ! you will say, are we not to confess every single sin ? Is no confession acceptable to God but that which is contained in the words, "I am a sinner"? Nay, our endeavour must rather be, as much as in us lies, to pour out our whole heart before the Lord. Nor are we only in one word to confess ourselves sinners, but truly and sincerely acknowledge ourselves as such; to feel with our whole soul how great and various the pollutions of our sins are; confessing not only that we are impure, but what the nature of our impurity is, its magnitude and its extent; not only that we are debtors, but what the debts are which burden us, and how they were incurred; not only that we are wounded, but how numerous and deadly are the wounds. When thus recognising himself, the sinner shall have poured out his whole heart before God, let him seriously and sincerely reflect that a greater number of sins still remains, and that their recesses are too deep for him thoroughly to penetrate. Accordingly, let him exclaim with

---

1 The French is, "Mais comme les nautonniers fichans l'anchre au milieu de la mer, se reposent du trauail de leur navigation ; ou comme un pelerin lassé ou defaillant se sied au milieu de la voye pour reposer : en telle maniere ils prenoyent ce repos, combien qu'il ne leur fust suffisant;"—but as mariners casting anchor in the midst of the sea, repose from the toil of navigation; or as a pilgrim, weary or faint, sits down in the middle of the way·to rest himself: in this way they took this rest, though it was not sufficient for them.

David, "Who can understand his errors? cleanse thou me from secret faults" (Ps. xix. 12). But when the Schoolmen affirm that sins are not forgiven, unless the resolution to confess has been firmly conceived, and that the gate of Paradise is closed on him who has neglected the opportunity of confessing when offered, far be it from us to concede this to them. The remission of sins is not different now from what it has ever been. In all the passages in which we read that sinners obtained forgiveness from God, we read not that they whispered into the ear of some priest.[1] Indeed, they could not then confess, as priests were not then confessionaries, nor did the confessional itself exist. And for many ages afterwards, this mode of confession, by which sins were forgiven on this condition, was unheard of. But not to enter into a long discussion, as if the matter were doubtful, the word of God, which abideth for ever, is plain, "When the wicked shall turn away from all his sins that he hath committed, and keep all my statutes, and do that which is lawful and right, he shall surely live, he shall not die" (Ezek. xviii. 21). He who presumes to add to this declaration binds not sins, but the mercy of God. When they contend that judgment cannot be given unless the case is known, the answer is easy, that they usurp the right of judging, being only self-created judges. And it is strange, how confidently they lay down principles, which no man of sound mind will admit. They give out, that the office of binding and loosing has been committed to them, as a kind of jurisdiction annexed to the right of inquiry. That the jurisdiction was unknown to the Apostles their whole doctrine proclaims. Nor does it belong to the priest to know for certainty whether or not a sinner is loosed, but to Him from whom acquittal is asked; since he who only hears can ever know whether or not the enumeration is full and complete. Thus there would be no absolution, without restricting it to the words of him who is to be judged. We may add, that the whole system of loosing depends on faith and repentance, two things which no man can know of another, so as to pronounce sentence. It follows, therefore, that the certainty of binding and loosing is not subjected to the will of an earthly judge, because the minister of the word, when he duly executes his office, can only acquit conditionally, when, for the sake of the sinner, he repeats the words, "Whose soever sins ye remit;" lest he should doubt of the pardon, which, by the command and voice of God, is promised to be ratified in heaven.

19. It is not strange, therefore, that we condemn that auricular confession, as a thing pestilent in its nature, and in many ways injurious to the Church, and desire to see it abolished. But if the thing were in itself indifferent, yet, seeing it is of no use or benefit.

---

1 "Tous ceux que nous lisons avoir obtenu de Christ la remission de leurs pechez, ne sont pas dits s'etre confessés à l'aureille de quelque Messire Jean;"—None of whom we read as having obtained the forgiveness of their sins from Christ, are said to have confessed in the ear of some Mess John.

and has given occasion to so much impiety, blasphemy, and error, who does not think that it ought to be immediately abolished? They enumerate some of its uses, and boast of them as very beneficial, but they are either fictitious or of no importance. One thing they specially commend, that the blush of shame in the penitent is a severe punishment, which makes him more cautious for the future, and anticipates divine punishment, by his punishing himself. As if a man was not sufficiently humbled with shame when brought under the cognisance of God at his supreme tribunal. Admirable proficiency—if we cease to sin because we are ashamed to make one man acquainted with it, and blush not at having God as the witness of our evil conscience! The assertion, however, as to the effect of shame, is most unfounded, for we may everywhere see, that there is nothing which gives men greater confidence and licence in sinning than the idea, that after making confession to priests, they can *wipe their lips and say, I have not done it.* And not only do they during the whole year become bolder in sin, but, secure against confession for the remainder of it, they never sigh after God, never examine themselves, but continue heaping sins upon sins, until, as they suppose, they get rid of them all at once. And when they have got rid of them, they think they are disburdened of their load, and imagine they have deprived God of the right of judging, by giving it to the priest; have made God forgetful, by making the priest conscious. Moreover, who is glad when he sees the day of confession approaching? Who goes with a cheerful mind to confess, and does not rather, as if he were dragged to prison with a rope about his neck, go unwillingly, and, as it were, struggling against it? with the exception, perhaps, of the priests themselves, who take a fond delight in the mutual narrative of their own misdeeds, as a kind of merry tales. I will not pollute my page by retailing the monstrous abominations with which auricular confession teems; I only say, that if that holy man (Nectarius, of whom *supra*, sec. 7) did not act unadvisedly, when for one rumour of whoredom he banished confession from his church, or rather from the memory of his people, the innumerable acts of prostitution, adultery, and incest, which it produces in the present day, warns us of the necessity of abolishing it.

20. As to the pretence of the confessionaries respecting the power of the keys, and their placing in it, so to speak, the sum and substance of their kingdom, we must see what force it ought to have. Were the keys, then (they ask), given without a cause? Was it said without a cause, "Whatsoever ye shall bind on earth shall be bound in heaven, and whatsoever ye shall loose on earth shall be loosed in heaven"? (Matth. xviii. 18.) Do we make void the word of Christ? I answer, that there was a weighty reason for giving the keys, as I lately explained, and will again show at greater length when I come to treat of Excommunication (Book IV. cap. 12). But what if I should cut off the handle for all such questions with one sword—

viz. that priests are neither vicars nor successors of the Apostles? But that also will be elsewhere considered (Book IV. 6). Now, at the very place where they are most desirous to fortify themselves, they erect a battering-ram, by which all their own machinations are overthrown. Christ did not give his Apostles the power of binding and loosing before he endued them with the Holy Spirit. I deny, therefore, that any man, who has not previously received the Holy Spirit, is competent to possess the power of the keys. I deny that any one can use the keys, unless the Holy Spirit precede, teaching and dictating what is to be done. They pretend, indeed, that they have the Holy Spirit, but by their works deny him ; unless, indeed, we are to suppose that the Holy Spirit is some vain thing of no value, as they certainly do feign, but we will not believe them. With this engine they are completely overthrown ; whatever be the door of which they boast of having the key, we must always ask, whether they have the Holy Spirit, who is arbiter and ruler of the keys ? If they reply, that they have, we must again ask, whether the Holy Spirit can err ? This they will not venture to say distinctly, although by their doctrine they indirectly insinuate it. Therefore, we must infer, that no priestlings have the power of the keys, because they everywhere and indiscriminately loose what the Lord was pleased should be bound, and bind what he has ordered to be loosed.

21. When they see themselves convicted on the clearest evidence, of loosing and binding worthy and unworthy without distinction, they lay claim to power without knowledge. And although they dare not deny that knowledge is requisite for the proper use, they still affirm that the power itself has been given to bad administrators. This, however, is the power, " Whatsoever ye shall bind on earth shall be bound in heaven, and whatsoever ye shall loose on earth shall be loosed in heaven." Either the promise of Christ must be false, or those who are endued with this power bind and loose properly. There is no room for the evasion, that the words of Christ are limited, according to the merits of him who is loosed or bound. We admit, that none can be bound or loosed but those who are worthy of being bound or loosed. But the preachers of the Gospel and the Church have the word by which they can measure this worthiness. By this word preachers of the Gospel can promise forgiveness of sins to all who are in Christ by faith, and can declare a sentence of condemnation against all, and upon all, who do not embrace Christ. In this word the Church declares, that " neither fornicators, nor idolators, nor adulterers," " nor thieves, nor covetous, nor drunkards, nor revilers, nor extortioners, shall inherit the kingdom of God" (1 Cor. vi. 9, 10). Such it binds in sure fetters. By the same word it looses and consoles the penitent. But what kind of power is it which knows not what is to be bound or loosed? You cannot bind or loose without knowledge. Why, then, do they say, that they absolve by authority given to them, when absolution is uncertain ? As regards us, this

power is merely imaginary, if it cannot be used. Now, I hold, either that there is no use, or one so uncertain as to be virtually no use at all. For when they confess that a good part of the priests do not use the keys duly, and that power without the legitimate use is ineffectual, who is to assure me, that the one by whom I am loosed is a good dispenser of the keys? But if he is a bad one, what better has he given me than this nugatory dispensation,—What is to be bound or loosed in you I know not, since I have not the proper use of the keys; but if you deserve it, I absolve you? As much might be done, I say not by a laic, (since they would scarcely listen to such a statement), but by the Turk or the devil. For it is just to say, I have not the word of God, the sure rule for loosing, but authority has been given me to absolve you, if you deserve it. We see, therefore, what their object was, when they defined (see sec. 16) the keys as authority to discern and power to execute; and said, that knowledge is added as a counsellor, and counsels the proper use; their object was to reign libidinously and licentiously, without God and his word.

22. Should any one object, first, that the lawful ministers of Christ will be no less perplexed in the discharge of their duty, because the absolution, which depends on faith, will always be equivocal; and, secondly, that sinners will receive no comfort at all, or cold comfort, because the minister, who is not a fit judge of their faith, is not certain of their absolution, we are prepared with an answer. They say that no sins are remitted by the priest, but such sins as he is cognisant of; thus, according to them, remission depends on the judgment of the priest, and unless he accurately discriminate as to who are worthy of pardon, the whole procedure is null and void. In short, the power of which they speak is a jurisdiction annexed to examination, to which pardon and absolution are restricted. Here no firm footing can be found, nay, there is a profound abyss; because, where confession is not complete, the hope of pardon also is defective; next, the priest himself must necessarily remain in suspense, while he knows not whether the sinner gives a faithful enumeration of his sins; lastly, such is the rudeness and ignorance of priests, that the greater part of them are in no respect fitter to perform this office than a cobbler to cultivate the fields, while almost all the others have good reason to suspect their own fitness. Hence the perplexity and doubt as to the Popish absolution, from their choosing to found it on the person of the priest, and not on his person only, but on his knowledge, so that he can only judge of what is laid before him, investigated, and ascertained. Now, if any should ask at these good doctors, Whether the sinner is reconciled to God when some sins are remitted? I know not what answer they could give, unless that they should be forced to confess, that whatever the priest pronounces with regard to the remission of sins which have been enumerated to him will be unavailing, so long as others are not exempted from condemnation. On the

part of the penitent, again, it is hence obvious in what a state of pernicious anxiety his conscience will be held; because, while he leans on what they call the discernment of the priest, he cannot come to any decision from the word of God. From all these absurdities the doctrine which we deliver is completely free. For absolution is conditional, allowing the sinner to trust that God is propitious to him, provided he sincerely seek expiation in the sacrifice of Christ, and accept of the grace offered to him. Thus, he cannot err who, in the capacity of a herald, promulgates what has been dictated to him from the word of God. The sinner, again, can receive a clear and sure absolution when, in regard to embracing the grace of Christ, the simple condition annexed is in terms of the general rule of our Master himself,—a rule impiously spurned by the Papacy,—"According to your faith be it unto you" (Matth. ix. 29).

23. The absurd jargon which they make of the doctrine of Scripture concerning the power of the keys, I have promised to expose elsewhere; the proper place will be in treating of the Goverment of the Church (Book IV. c. 12). Meanwhile let the reader remember how absurdly they wrest to auricular and secret confession what was said by Christ partly of the preaching of the Gospel, and partly of excommunication. Wherefore, when they object that the power of loosing was given to the Apostles, and that this power priests exercise by remitting sins acknowledged to them, it is plain that the principle which they assume is false and frivolous: for the absolution which is subordinate to faith is nothing else than an evidence of pardon, derived from the free promise of the Gospel, while the other absolution, which depends on the discipline of the Church, has nothing to do with secret sins; but is more a matter of example for the purpose of removing the public offence given to the Church. As to their diligence in searching up and down for passages by which they may prove that it is not sufficient to confess sins to God alone, or to laymen, unless the priest take cognisance, it is vile and disgraceful. For when the ancient fathers advise sinners to disburden themselves to their pastor, we cannot understand them to refer to a recital which was not then in use. Then, so unfair are Lombard and others likeminded, that they seem intentionally to have devoted themselves to spurious books, that they might use them as a cloak to deceive the simple. They, indeed, acknowledge truly, that as forgiveness always accompanies repentance, no obstacle properly remains after the individual is truly penitent, though he may not have actually confessed; and, therefore, that the priest does not so much remit sins, as pronounce and declare that they are remitted; though in the term *declaring*, they insinuate a gross error, surrogating ceremony[1] in place of doctrine. But in pretending that he who has already obtained pardon before God is acquitted in the face of the Church, they

1 Latin simply, "ceremoniam." French, "la ceremonie de faire une croix sur le dos;"—the ceremony of making a cross upon the back

unseasonably apply to the special use of every individual, that which we have already said was designed for common discipline when the offence of a more heinous and notorious trangression was to be removed. Shortly after they pervert and destroy their previous moderation, by adding that there is another mode of remission—namely, by the infliction of penalty and satisfaction, in which they arrogate to their priests the right of dividing what God has everywhere promised to us entire. While He simply requires repentance and faith, their division or exception is altogether blasphemous. For it is just as if the priest, assuming the office of tribune, were to interfere with God,[1] and try to prevent him from admitting to his favour by his mere liberality any one who had not previously lain prostrate at the tribunicial bench, and there been punished.

24. The whole comes to this,[2] when they wish to make God the author of this fictitious confession their vanity is proved, as I have shown their falsehood in expounding the few passages which they cite. But while it is plain, that the law was imposed by men, I say that it is both tyrannical and insulting to God, who, in binding consciences to his word, would have them free from human rule. Then when confession is prescribed as necessary to obtain pardon, which God wished to be free, I say that the sacrilege is altogether intolerable, because nothing belongs more peculiarly to God than the forgiveness of sins, in which our salvation consists. I have, moreover, shown that this tyranny was introduced when the world was sunk in shameful barbarism.[3] Besides, I have proved that the law is pestiferous, inasmuch as when the fear of God exists, it plunges men into despair, and when there is security soothing itself with vain flattery, it blunts it the more. Lastly, I have explained that all the mitigations which they employ have no other tendency than to entangle, obscure, and corrupt the pure doctrine, and cloak their iniquities with deceitful colours.

25. In repentance they assign the third place to satisfaction, all their absurd talk as to which can be refuted in one word. They say,[4] that it is not sufficient for the penitent to abstain from past sins, and change his conduct for the better, unless he satisfy God for what he has done; and that there are many helps by which we may redeem sins, such as tears, fastings, oblations,[5] and offices of charity; that by them the Lord is to be propitiated; by them the

---

[1] French, "Car cela vaut autant comme si les prestres se faisoyent contrerolleurs de Dieu;"—for that is as much as if the priests made themselves controllers of God.

[2] See on the subject of this section, Calv. ad Concil. Trident. Also Vera Ecclesiæ Reformandæ Ratio, Epist. ad Sadoletum· Epist. adversus Theologos Parisienses. De Scandalis. De Necessitate Reformandæ Ecclesiæ, Lib. iv.

[3] French, "une barbarie si vileine que rien plus;"—a barbarism so vile that nothing could be more so.

[4] See Lombard, Sent. Lib. iv. Dist. 10, c. 4. C. Non sufficit. de Pœnit. C. (middle of same Dist.) C. Nullus (same Dist.). See also on the subject of satisfaction, infra, s. 29, and chap. xvi. 4.

[5] The French adds, "aumosnes;"—alms.

debts due to divine justice are to be paid; by them our faults are to be compensated; by them pardon is to be deserved: for though in the riches of his mercy he has forgiven the guilt, he yet, as a just discipline, retains the penalty, and that this penalty must be bought off by satisfaction. The sum of the whole comes to this: that we indeed obtain pardon of our sins from the mercy of God, but still by the intervention of the merit of works, by which the evil of our sins is compensated, and due satisfaction made to divine justice. To such false views I oppose the free forgiveness of sins, one of the doctrines most clearly taught in Scripture.[1] First, what is forgiveness but a gift of mere liberality? A creditor is not said to forgive when he declares, by granting a discharge, that the money has been paid to him; but when, without any payment, through voluntary kindness he expunges the debt. And why is the term *gratis* (free) afterwards added, but to take away all idea of satisfaction? With what confidence, then, do they still set up their satisfactions, which are thus struck down as with a thunderbolt? What? When the Lord proclaims by Isaiah, "I, even I, am he that blotteth out thy transgressions for mine own sake, and will not remember thy sins," does he not plainly declare, that the cause and foundation of forgiveness is to be sought from his goodness alone? Besides, when the whole of Scripture bears this testimony to Christ, that through his name the forgiveness of sins is to be obtained (Acts x. 43), does it not plainly exclude all other names? How then do they teach that it is obtained by the name of satisfaction? Let them not deny that they attribute this to satisfactions, though they bring them in as subsidiary aids.[2] For when Scripture says, *by the name of Christ*, it means, that we are to bring nothing, pretend nothing of our own, but lean entirely on the recommendation of Christ. Thus Paul, after declaring that "God was in Christ reconciling the world unto himself, not imputing their trespasses unto them," immediately adds the reason and the method, "For he hath made him to be sin for us who knew no sin" (2 Cor. v. 19, 20).

26. But with their usual perverseness, they maintain that both the forgiveness of sins and reconciliation take place at once when we are received into the favour of God through Christ in baptism; that in lapses after baptism we must rise again by means of satisfactions; that the blood of Christ is of no avail unless in so far as it is dispensed by the keys of the Church. I speak not of a matter as to which there can be any doubt; for this impious dogma is declared in the plainest terms, in the writings not of one or two, but of the whole Schoolmen. Their master (Sent. Lib. iii. Dist. 9), after acknow-

---

[1] Isa. lii. 3; Rom. v. 8; Col. ii. 14; Tit. iii. 5.
[2] The French is, "Et ne faut pas qu'ils disent, que combien que les satisfactions en soyent moyens, neantmoins ce n'est pas en leur nom, mais au nom de Jesus Christ;" —and they must not say that though satisfactions are the means, nevertheless it is not in their name, but in the name of Jesus Christ.

ledging, according to the doctrine of Peter, that Christ "bare our sins in his own body on the tree" (1 Pet. ii. 24), immediately modifies the doctrine by introducing the exception, that in baptism all the temporal penalties of sin are relaxed; but that after baptism they are lessened by means of repentance, the cross of Christ and our repentance thus co-operating together. St John speaks very differently, "If any man sin, we have an advocate with the Father, Jesus Christ the righteous; and he is the propitiation for our sins." "I write unto you, little children, because your sins are forgiven you for his name's sake" (1 John ii. 1, 2, 12). He certainly is addressing believers, and while setting forth Christ as the propitiation for sins, shows them that there is no other satisfaction by which an offended God can be propitiated or appeased. He says not: God was once reconciled to you by Christ; now, seek other methods; but he makes him a perpetual advocate, who always, by his intercession, reinstates us in his Father's favour—a perpetual propitiation by which sins are expiated. For what was said by another John will ever hold true, "Behold the Lamb of God, which taketh away the sins of the world" (John i. 29). He, I say, takes them away, and no other; that is, since he alone is the Lamb of God, he alone is the offering for our sins; he alone is expiation; he alone is satisfaction. For though the right and power of pardoning properly belongs to the Father, when he is distinguished from the Son, as has already been seen, Christ is here exhibited in another view, as transferring to himself the punishment due to us, and wiping away our guilt in the sight of God. Whence it follows, that we could not be partakers of the expiation accomplished by Christ, were he not possessed of that honour of which those who try to appease God by their compensations seek to rob him.

27. Here it is necessary to keep two things in view: that the honour of Christ be preserved entire and unimpaired, and that the conscience, assured of the pardon of sin, may have peace with God. Isaiah says that the Father "hath laid on him the iniquity of us all;" that "with his stripes we are healed" (Isa. liii. 5, 6). Peter repeating the same thing, in other words says, that he "bare our sins in his own body on the tree" (1 Pet. ii. 24). Paul's words are, "God sending his own Son in the likeness of sinful flesh, and for sin condemned sin in the flesh," "being made a curse for us" (Rom. viii. 3; Gal. iii. 13); in other words, the power and curse of sin was destroyed in his flesh when he was offered as a sacrifice, on which the whole weight of our sins was laid, with their curse and execration, with the fearful judgment of God, and condemnation to death. Here there is no mention of the vain dogma, that after the initial cleansing no man experiences the efficacy of Christ's passion in any other way than by means of satisfying penance: we are directed to the satisfaction of Christ alone for every fall. Now call to mind their pestilential dogma: that the grace of God is effective only in the first

forgiveness of sins ; but if we afterwards fall, our works co-operate in obtaining the second pardon. If these things are so, do the properties above attributed to Christ remain entire ? How immense the difference between the two propositions—that our iniquities were laid upon Christ, that in his own person he might expiate them, and that they are expiated by our works ; that Christ is the propitiation for our sins, and that God is to be propitiated by works. Then, in regard to pacifying the conscience, what pacification will it be to be told that sins are redeemed by satisfactions ? How will it be able to ascertain the measure of satisfaction ? It will always doubt whether God is propitious ; will always fluctuate, always tremble. Those who rest satisfied with petty satisfactions form too contemptible an estimate of the justice of God, and little consider the grievous heinousness of sin, as shall afterwards be shown. Even were we to grant that they can buy off some sins by due satisfaction, still what will they do while they are overwhelmed with so many sins, that not even a hundred lives, though wholly devoted to the purpose, could suffice to satisfy for them ? We may add, that all the passages in which the forgiveness of sins is declared refer not only to catechumens,[1] but to the regenerate children of God ; to those who have long been nursed in the bosom of the Church. That embassy which Paul so highly extols, " we pray you in Christ's stead, be ye reconciled to God " (2 Cor. v. 20), is not directed to strangers, but to those who had been regenerated long before. Setting satisfactions altogether aside, he directs us to the cross of Christ. Thus when he writes to the Colossians that Christ had " made peace through the blood of his cross," " to reconcile all things unto himself," he does not restrict it to the moment at which we are received into the Church, but extends it to our whole course. This is plain from the context, where he says that in him " we have redemption by his blood, even the forgiveness of sins" (Col. i. 14). It is needless to collect more passages, as they are ever occurring.

28. Here they take refuge in the absurd distinction that some sins are *venial*, and others *mortal;* that for the latter a weighty satisfaction is due, but that the former are purged by easier remedies ; by the Lord's Prayer, the sprinkling of holy water, and the absolution of the Mass. Thus they insult and trifle with God.[2] And yet, though they have the terms venial and mortal sin continually in their mouth, they have not yet been able to distinguish the one from the other, except by making impiety and impurity of heart[3] to be venial sin. We, on the contrary, taught by the Scripture standard of righteousness and unrighteousness, declare that " the wages of sin

---

1 Latin, " Catechumenos."—French, " Ceux qui ne sont point encore baptisez;"—those who are not yet baptised.

2 See on this Section, Book II. chap. viii. s. 58, 59.

3 The French adds, " Qui est le plus horrible peché devant Dieu;"—which is the most heinous sin in the sight of God.

is death;" and that "the soul that sinneth, it shall die" (Rom. vi. 23; Ezek. xviii. 20). The sins of believers are venial, not because they do not merit death, but because by the mercy of God there is "now no condemnation to those which are in Christ Jesus," their sin being not imputed, but effaced by pardon. I know how unjustly they calumniate this our doctrine; for they say it is the paradox of of the Stoics concerning the equality of sins: but we shall easily convict them out of their own mouths. I ask them whether, among those sins which they hold to be mortal, they acknowledge a greater and a less? If so, it cannot follow, as a matter of course, that all sins which are mortal are equal. Since Scripture declares that the wages of sin is death,—that obedience to the law is the way to life, —the transgression of it the way to death,—they cannot evade this conclusion. In such a mass of sins, therefore, how will they find an end to their satisfactions? If the satisfaction for one sin requires one day, while preparing it they involve themselves in more sins; since no man, however righteous, passes one day without falling repeatedly. While they prepare themselves for their satisfactions, number, or rather numbers without number, will be added.[1] Confidence in satisfaction being thus destroyed, what more would they have? how do they still dare to think of satisfying?

29. They endeavour, indeed, to disentangle themselves, but it is impossible. They pretend a distinction between penalty and guilt, holding that the guilt is forgiven by the mercy of God; but that though the guilt is remitted, the punishment which divine justice requires to be paid remains. Satisfactions then properly relate to the remission of the penalty. How ridiculous this levity! They now confess that the remission of guilt is gratuitous; and yet they are ever and anon telling us to merit it by prayers and tears, and other preparations of every kind. Still the whole doctrine of Scripture regarding the remission of sins is diametrically opposed to that distinction. But although I think I have already done more than enough to establish this, I will subjoin some other passages, by which these slippery snakes will be so caught as to be afterwards unable to writhe even the tip of their tail: "Behold, the days come, saith the Lord, that I will make a new covenant with the house of Israel, and with the house of Judah." "I will forgive their iniquity, and I will remember their sin no more" (Jer. xxxi. 31, 34). What this means we learn from another Prophet, when the Lord says, "When the righteous turneth away from his righteousness," "all his righteousness that he hath done shall not be mentioned." "Again, when the wicked man turneth away from his wickedness that he hath committed, and doth that which is lawful and right, he shall save his soul alive"

---

[1] French, "Et quand ils voudront satisfaire pour plusieurs, ils en commettront encore davantage jusques à venir à un abysme sans fin. Je traite encore des plus justes;"—And when they would satisfy for several sins, they will commit still more, until they come at last to a bottomless abyss. I am still speaking of the best.

(Ezek. xviii. 24, 27). When he declares that he will not remember righteousness, the meaning is, that he will take no account of it to reward it. In the same way, not to remember sins is not to bring them to punishment. The same thing is denoted in other passages,[1] by casting them behind his back, blotting them out as a cloud, casting them into the depths of the sea, not imputing them, hiding them. by such forms of expression the Holy Spirit has explained his meaning not obscurely, if we would lend a willing ear. Certainly if God punishes sins, he imputes them; if he avenges, he remembers; if he Brings them to judgment, he has not hid them; if he examines, he has not cast them behind his back; if he investigates, he has not blotted them out like a cloud; if he exposes them, he has not thrown them into the depths of the sea. In this way Augustine clearly interprets: " If God has covered sins, he willed not to advert to them; if he willed not to advert, he willed not to animadvert; if he willed not to animadvert, he willed not to punish: he willed not to take knowledge of them, he rather willed to pardon them. Why then did he say that sins were hid? Just that they might not be seen. What is meant by God seeing sins but punishing them?" (August. in Ps. xxxii. 1.) But let us hear from another prophetical passage on what terms the Lord forgives sins: " Though your sins be as scarlet, they shall be white as snow; though they be red like crimson, they shall be as wool" (Isa. i. 18). In Jeremiah again we read: " In those days, and in that time, saith the Lord, the iniquity of Israel shall be sought for, and there shall be none; and the sins of Judah, they shall not be found: for I will pardon them whom I reserve" (Jer. l. 20). Would you briefly comprehend the meaning of these words? Consider what, on the contrary, is meant by these expressions, " that transgression is sealed up in a bag;" "that the iniquity of Ephraim is bound up; his sin is hid;" that " the sin of Judah is written with a pen of iron, and with the point of a diamond."[2] If they mean, as they certainly do, that vengeance will be recompensed, there can be no doubt that, by the contrary passages, the Lord declares that he renounces all thought of vengeance. Here I must entreat the reader not to listen to any glosses of mine, but only to give some deference to the word of God.

30. What, pray, did Christ perform for us if the punishment of sin is still exacted? For when we say that he " bare our sins in his own body on the tree" (1 Pet. ii. 24), all we mean is, that he endured the penalty and punishment which was due to our sins. This is more significantly declared by Isaiah, when he says that the " chastisement (or correction) of our peace was upon him" (Isaiah liii. 5). But what is the correction of our peace, unless it be the punishment due to our sins, and to be paid by us before we could be reconciled to God, had he not become our substitute? Thus you clearly see that

[1] Isa. xxxviii. 17; xliv. 22; Micah vii. 19; Ps. xxxii. 1.
[2] Job xiv. 17; Hos. xiii. 12; Jer. xxii. 1.

Christ bore the punishment of sin that he might thereby exempt his people from it. And whenever Paul makes mention of the redemption procured by him,[1] he calls it ἀπολύτρωσις, by which he does not simply mean *redemption*, as it is commonly understood, but the very *price* and satisfaction of redemption.[2] For which reason, he also says, that Christ gave himself an ἀντίλυτρον (ransom) for us. " What is propitiation with the Lord (says Augustine) but sacrifice ? And what is sacrifice but that which was offered for us in the death of Christ ?" But we have our strongest argument in the injunctions of the Mosaic Law as to expiating the guilt of sin. The Lord does not there appoint this or that method of satisfying, but requires the whole compensation to be made by sacrifice, though he at the same time enumerates all the rites of expiation with the greatest care and exactness. How comes it that he does not at all enjoin works as the means of procuring pardon, but only requires sacrifices for expiation, unless it were his purpose thus to testify that this is the only kind of satisfaction by which his justice is appeased ? For the sacrifices which the Israelites then offered were not regarded as human works, but were estimated by their antitype, that is, the sole sacrifice of Christ. The kind of compensation which the Lord receives from us is elegantly and briefly expressed by Hosea : " Take with you words, and turn to the Lord : say unto him, Take away all iniquity, and receive us graciously," here is remission : " so will we render the calves of our lips," here is satisfaction (Hos. xiv. 2). I know that they have still a more subtile evasion,[3] by making a distinction between eternal and temporal punishment ; but as they define temporal punishment to be any kind of infliction with which God visits either the body or the soul, eternal death only excepted, this restriction avails them little. The passages which we have quoted above say expressly that the terms on which God receives us into favour are these—viz. he remits all the punishment which we deserved by pardoning our guilt. And whenever David or the other prophets ask pardon for their sins, they deprecate punishment. Nay, a sense of the divine justice impels them to this. On the other hand, when they promise mercy from the Lord, they almost always discourse of punishments and the forgiveness of them. Assuredly, when the Lord declares in Ezekiel, that he will put an end to the Babylonish captivity, not " for your sakes, O house of Israel, but for mine holy name's sake" (Ezek. xxxvi. 22), he sufficiently demonstrates that both are gratuitous. In short, if we are freed from guilt by Christ, the punishment consequent upon guilt must cease with it.

31. But since they also arm themselves with passages of Scripture, let us see what the arguments are which they employ. David, they

---

[1] Rom. iii. 24 ; 1 Cor. i. 30 ; Eph. i. 7 ; Col. i. 14 ; 1 Tim ii. 6.
[2] The French adds, " Que nous appellons Rançon en François ;"—which we call Ransom in French.
[3] See Calvin, ad Concil. Tridentini, Sess. cap. i. ad xv.

say, when upbraided by Nathan the Prophet for adultery and murder, receives pardon of the sin, and yet by the death of the son born of adultery is afterwards punished (2 Sam. xii. 13, 14). Such punishments, which were to be inflicted after the remission of the guilt, we are taught to ransom by satisfactions. For Daniel exhorted Nebuchadnezzar : " Break off thy sins by righteousness, and thine iniquities by showing mercy to the poor" (Dan. iv. 27). And Solomon says, "By mercy and truth iniquity is purged" (Prov. xvi. 6); and again, "love covereth all sins" (Prov. x. 12). This sentiment is confirmed by Peter (1 Pet. iv. 8). Also in Luke, our Lord says of the woman that was a sinner, "Her sins, which are many, are forgiven ; for she loved much" (Luke vii. 47). How perverse and preposterous the judgment they ever form of the doings of God ![1] Had they observed, what certainly they ought not to have overlooked, that there are two kinds of divine judgment, they would have seen in the correction of David a very different form of punishment from that which must be thought designed for vengeance. But since it in no slight degree concerns us to understand the purpose of God in the chastisements by which he animadverts upon our sins, and how much they differ from the exemplary punishments which he indignantly inflicts on the wicked and reprobate, I think it will not be improper briefly to glance at it. For the sake of distinction, we may call the one kind of judgment *punishment*, the other *chastisement*. In judicial punishment, God is to be understood as taking vengeance on his enemies, by displaying his anger against them, confounding, scattering, and annihilating them. By divine punishment, properly so called, let us then understand punishment accompanied with indignation. In judicial chastisement, he is offended, but not in wrath ; he does not punish by destroying or striking down as with a thunderbolt. Hence it is not properly punishment or vengeance, but correction and admonition. The one is the act of a judge, the other of a father. When the judge punishes a criminal, he animadverts upon the crime, and demands the penalty. When a father corrects his son sharply, it is not to mulct or avenge, but rather to teach him, and make him more cautious for the future. Chrysostom in his writings employs a simile which is somewhat different, but the same in purport. He says, " A son is whipt, and a slave is whipt, but the latter is punished as a slave for his offence : the former is chastised as a free-born son, standing in need of correction." The correction of the latter is designed to prove and amend him ; that of the former is scourging and punishment.

32. To have a short and clear view of the whole matter, we must make two distinctions. First, whenever the infliction is designed to avenge, then the curse and wrath of God displays itself. This is never the case with believers. On the contrary, the chastening of

---

[1] For a full exposition of these passages, see *infra*, sec. 35–37.

God carries his blessing with it, and is an evidence of love, as Scripture teaches.[1] This distinction is plainly marked throughout the word of God. All the calamities which the wicked suffer in the present life are depicted to us as a kind of anticipation of the punishment of hell. In these they already see, as from a distance, their eternal condemnation: and so far are they from being thereby reformed, or deriving any benefit, that by such preludes they are rather prepared for the fearful doom which finally awaits them. The Lord chastens his servants sore, but does not give them over unto death (Ps. cxviii. 18). When afflicted, they acknowledge it is good for them, that they may learn his statutes (Ps. cxix. 71). But as we everywhere read that the saints received their chastisements with placid mind, so inflictions of the latter kind they always most earnestly deprecated. "O Lord, correct me," says Jeremiah, "but with judgment; not in thine anger, lest thou bring me to nothing. Pour out thy fury upon the heathen that know thee not, and upon the families that call not on thy name" (Jer. x. 24, 25). David says, "O Lord, rebuke me not in thine anger, neither chasten me in thy hot displeasure" (Ps. vi. 1). There is nothing inconsistent with this in its being repeatedly said, that the Lord is angry with his saints when he chastens them for their sins (Ps. xxxviii. 7). In like manner, in Isaiah, "And in that day thou shalt say, O Lord, I will praise thee: though thou wast angry with me, thine anger is turned away, and thou comfortedst me" (Isa. xii. 1). Likewise in Habakkuk, "In wrath remember mercy" (Hab. iii. 2); and in Micah, "I will bear the indignation of the Lord, because I have sinned against him" (Mic. vii. 9). Here we are reminded not only that those who are justly punished gain nothing by murmuring, but that believers obtain a mitigation of their pain by reflecting on the divine intention. For the same reason, he is said to profane his inheritance; and yet we know that he will never profane it. The expression refers not to the counsel or purpose of God in punishing, but to the keen sense of pain, endured by those who are visited with any measure of divine severity. For the Lord not only chastens his people with a slight degree of austerity, but sometimes so wounds them, that they seem to themselves on the very eve of perdition. He thus declares that they have deserved his anger, and it is fitting so to do, that they may be dissatisfied with themselves for their sins, may be more careful in their desires to appease God, and anxiously hasten to seek his pardon; still, at this very time, he gives clearer evidence of his mercy than of his anger. For He who cannot deceive has declared, that the covenant made with us in our true Solomon[2] stands fast and will never be broken, "If his children forsake my law, and walk not in my judgments; if they break my statutes, and keep not my commandments;

---

[1] Job. v. 17; Prov. iii. 11; Heb. xii. 5.
[2] French, "Car l'alliance qu'il a une fois faite avec Jesus Christ et ses membres;"—
For the covenant which he once made with Jesus Christ and his members.

then will I visit their transgressions with the rod, and their iniquity with stripes. Nevertheless, my loving-kindness will I not utterly take from him, nor suffer my faithfulness to fail" (Ps. lxxxix. 31–34). To assure us of this mercy, he says, that the *rod* with which he will chastise the posterity of Solomon will be the "rod of men," and "the stripes of the children of men" (2 Sam. vii. 14). While by these terms he denotes moderation and lenity, he, at the same time, intimates, that those who feel the hand of God opposed to them cannot but tremble and be confounded. How much regard he has to this lenity in chastening his Israel he shows by the Prophet, "Behold, I have refined thee, but not with silver; I have chosen thee in the furnace of affliction" (Isa. xlviii. 10). Although he tells them that they are chastisements with a view to purification, he adds, that even these are so tempered, that they are not to be too much crushed by them. And this is very necessary, for the more a man reveres God, and devotes himself to the cultivation of piety, the more tender he is in bearing his anger (Ps. xc. 11; and ibid. Calv.). The reprobate, though they groan under the lash,[1] yet, because they weigh not the true cause, but rather turn their back, as well upon their sins as upon the divine judgment, become hardened in their stupor; or, because they murmur and kick, and so rebel against their judge, their infatuated violence fills them with frenzy and madness. Believers, again, admonished by the rod of God, immediately begin to reflect on their sins, and, struck with fear and dread, betake themselves as suppliants to implore mercy. Did not God mitigate the pains by which wretched souls are excruciated, they would give way a hundred times, even at slight signs of his anger.

33. The second distinction is, that when the reprobate are brought under the lash of God, they begin in a manner to pay the punishment due to his justice; and though their refusal to listen to these proofs of the divine anger will not escape with impunity, still they are not punished with the view of bringing them to a better mind, but only to teach them by dire experience that God is a judge and avenger. The sons of God are beaten with rods, not that they may pay the punishment due to their faults, but that they may thereby be led to repent. Accordingly, we perceive that they have more respect to the future than to the past. I prefer giving this in the words of Chrysostom rather than my own: "His object in imposing a penalty upon us, is not to inflict punishment on our sins, but to correct us for the future" (Chrysost. Serm. de Pœnit. et Confess.). So also Augustine, "The suffering at which you cry, is medicine, not punishment; chastisement, not condemnation. Do not drive away the rod, if you would not be driven away from the inheritance. Know, brethren, that the whole of that misery of the human race, under which the world groans, is a medicinal pain, not a penal sentence"

---

[1] French, "Car combien les reprouvés souspirent ou grinçent les dents sous les coups;"—For though the reprobate sigh or gnash their teeth under the strokes.

(August. in Psal. cii. circa finem). It seemed proper to quote these passages, lest any one should think the mode of expression which I have used to be novel or uncommon. To the same effect are the indignant terms in which the Lord expostulates with his people, for their ingratitude in obstinately despising all his inflictions. In Isaiah he says, "Why should ye be stricken any more? ye will revolt more and more. The whole head is sick, and the whole heart faint" (Isa. i. 5, 6). But as such passages abound in the Prophets, it is sufficient briefly to have shown, that the only purpose of God in punishing his Church is to subdue her to repentance. Thus, when he rejected Saul from the kingdom, he punished in vengeance (1 Sam. xv. 23); when he deprived David of his child, he chastised for amendment (2 Sam. xii. 18). In this sense Paul is to be understood when he says, "When we are judged, we are chastened of the Lord, that we should not be condemned with the world" (1 Cor. xi. 32); that is, while we as sons of God are afflicted by our heavenly Father's hand, it is not punishment to confound, but only chastisement to train us. On this subject Augustine is plainly with us (De Peccator. Meritis ac Remiss. Lib. ii. cap. 33, 34). For he shows that the punishments with which men are equally chastened by God are to be variously considered; because the saints after the forgiveness of their sins have struggles and exercises, the reprobate without forgiveness are punished for their iniquity. Enumerating the punishments inflicted on David and other saints, he says, it was designed, by thus humbling them, to prove and exercise their piety. The passage in Isaiah, in which it is said, "Speak ye comfortably to Jerusalem, and cry unto her, that her warfare is accomplished, that her iniquity is pardoned; for she has received of the Lord's hands double for all her sins" (Isa. xl. 2), proves not that the pardon of sin depends on freedom from punishment. It is just as if he had said, sufficient punishment has now been exacted; as for their number and heinousness, you have long been oppressed with sorrow and mourning, it is time to send you a message of complete mercy, that your minds may be filled with joy on feeling me to be a Father. For God there assumes the character of a father who repents even of the just severity which he has been compelled to use towards his son.

34. These are the thoughts with which the believer ought to be provided in the bitterness of affliction, "The time is come that judgment must begin at the house of God," "the city which is called by my name" (1 Pet. iv. 17; Jer. xxv. 29). What could the sons of God do, if they thought that the severity which they feel was vengeance? He who, smitten by the hand of God, thinks that God is a judge inflicting punishment, cannot conceive of him except as angry and at enmity with him; cannot but detest the rod of God as curse and condemnation; in short, can never persuade himself that he is loved by God, while he feels that he is still disposed to inflict punishment upon him. He only profits under the divine chastening

who considers that God, though offended with his sins, is still propitious and favourable to him. Otherwise, the feeling must necessarily be what the Psalmist complains that he had experienced, "Thy wrath lieth hard upon me, and thou hast afflicted me with all thy waves." Also what Moses says, "For we are consumed by thine anger, and by thy wrath we are troubled. Thou hast set our iniquities before thee, our secret sins in the light of thy countenance. For all our days are passed away in thy wrath; we spend our years as a tale that is told" (Ps. xc. 7–9). On the other hand, David, speaking of fatherly chastisements, to show how believers are more assisted than oppressed by them, thus sings, " Blessed is the man whom thou chastenest, O Lord, and teachest him out of thy law; that thou mayest give him rest from the days of adversity, until the pit be digged for the wicked" (Ps. xciv. 12, 13). It is certainly a sore temptation, when God, sparing unbelievers and overlooking their crimes, appears more rigid towards his own people. Hence, to solace them, he adds the admonition of the law which teaches them, that their salvation is consulted when they are brought back to the right path, whereas the wicked are borne headlong in their errors, which ultimately lead to the pit. It matters not whether the punishment is eternal or temporary. For disease, pestilence, famine, and war are curses from God, as much as even the sentence of eternal death, whenever their tendency is to operate as instruments of divine wrath and vengeance against the reprobate.

35. All, if I mistake not, now see what view the Lord had in chastening David—namely, to prove that murder and adultery are most offensive to God, and to manifest this offensiveness in a beloved and faithful servant, that David himself might be taught never again to dare to commit such wickedness; still, however, it was not a punishment designed in payment of a kind of compensation to God. In the same way are we to judge of that other correction, in which the Lord subjects his people to a grievous pestilence, for the disobedience of David in forgetting himself so far as to number the people. He indeed freely forgave David the guilt of his sin; but because it was necessary, both as a public example to all ages and also to humble David himself, not to allow such an offence to go unpunished, he chastened him most sharply with his whip. We ought also to keep this in view in the universal curse of the human race. For since after obtaining grace we still continue to endure the miseries denounced to our first parent as the penalty of transgression, we ought thereby to be reminded, how offensive to God is the trangression of his law, that thus humbled and dejected by a consciousness of our wretched condition, we may aspire more ardently to true happiness. But it were most foolish in any one to imagine, that we are subjected to the calamities of the present life for the guilt of sin. This seems to me to have been Chrysostom's meaning when he said, "If the purpose of God in inflicting punishment is to bring those persisting in evil to

repentance, when repentance is manifested punishment would be superfluous" (Chrysos. Homil. iii. de Provid.). Wherefore, as he knows what the disposition of each requires, he treats one with greater harshness, and another with more indulgence. Accordingly, when he wishes to show that he is not excessive in exacting punishment, he upbraids a hard-hearted and obstinate people, because, after being smitten, they still continued in sin (Jer. v. 3). In the same sense he complains, that "Ephraim is a cake not turned" (Hos. vii. 8), because chastisement did not make a due impression on their minds, and, correcting their vices, make them fit to receive pardon. Surely he who thus speaks shows, that as soon as any one repents he will be ready to receive him, and that the rigour which he exercises in chastising faults is wrung from him by our perverseness, since we should prevent him by a voluntary correction. Such, however, being the hardness and rudeness of all hearts, that they stand universally in need of castigation, our infinitely wise Parent hath seen it meet to exercise all without exception, during their whole lives, with chastisement. It is strange how they fix their eyes so intently on the one example of David, and are not moved by the many examples in which they might have beheld the free forgiveness of sins. The publican is said to have gone down from the temple justified (Luke xviii. 14); no punishment follows. Peter obtained the pardon of his sin (Luke xxii. 61). "We read of his tears," says Ambrose, (Serm. 46, De Pœnit. Petri), "we read not of satisfaction." To the paralytic it is said, "Son, be of good cheer; thy sins be forgiven thee," (Matth. ix. 2); no penance is enjoined. All the acts of forgiveness mentioned in Scripture are gratuitous. The rule ought to be drawn from these numerous examples, rather than from one example which contains a kind of specialty.

36. Daniel, in exhorting Nebuchadnezzar to break off his sins by righteousness, and his iniquities by showing mercy to the poor (Dan. iv. 27), meant not to intimate, that righteousness and mercy are able to propitiate God and redeem from punishment (far be it from us to suppose that there ever was any other ἀπολύτρωσις (ransom) than the blood of Christ); but the breaking off referred to in that passage has reference to man rather than to God: as if he had said, O king, you have exercised an unjust and violent domination, you have oppressed the humble, spoiled the poor, treated your people harshly and unjustly; instead of unjust exaction, instead of violence and oppression, now practise mercy and justice. In like manner, Solomon says, that love covers a multitude of sins; not, however, with God, but among men. For the whole verse stands thus, "Hatred stirreth up strifes; out love covereth all sins" (Prov. x. 12). Here, after his manner, he contrasts the evils produced by hatred with the fruits of charity, in this sense, Those who hate are incessantly biting, carping at, upbraiding, lacerating each other, making everything a fault; but those who love mutually conceal each other's faults, wink at many,

forgive many: not that the one approves the vices of the other, but tolerates and cures by admonishing, rather than exasperates by assailing. That the passage is quoted by Peter (1 Pet. iv. 8) in the same sense we cannot doubt, unless we would charge him with corrupting or craftily wresting Scripture. When it is said that "by mercy and truth iniquity-is purged" (Prov. xvi. 6), the meaning is, not that by them compensation is made to the Lord, so that he being thus satisfied remits the punishment which he would otherwise have exacted; but intimation is made after the familiar manner of Scripture, that those who, forsaking their vices and iniquities, turn to the Lord in truth and piety, will find him propitious: as if he had said, that the wrath of God is calmed, and his judgment is at rest, whenever we rest from our wickedness. But, indeed, it is not the cause of pardon that is described, but rather the mode of true conversion; just as the Prophets frequently declare, that it is in vain for hypocrites to offer God fictitious rites instead of repentance, seeing his delight is in integrity and the duties of charity.[1] In like manner, also, the author of the Epistle to the Hebrews, commending kindness and humanity, reminds us, that "with such sacrifices God is well pleased" (Heb. xiii. 16). And indeed when Christ, rebuking the Pharisees because, intent merely on the outside of the cup and platter, they neglected purity of heart, enjoins them, in order that they may be clean in all respects, to give alms, does he exhort them to give satisfaction thereby? He only tells them what the kind of purity is which God requires. Of this mode of expression we have treated elsewhere (Matth. xxiii. 25; Luke xi. 39-41; see Calv. in Harm. Evang.).

37. In regard to the passage in Luke (Luke vii. 36, sq.) no man of sober judgment who reads the parable there employed by our Lord, will raise any controversy with us. The Pharisee thought that the Lord did not know the character of the woman whom he had so easily admitted to his presence. For he presumed that he would not have admitted her if he had known what kind of a sinner she was; and from this he inferred, that one who could be deceived in this way was not a prophet. Our Lord, to show that she was not a sinner, inasmuch as she had already been forgiven, spake this parable: "There was a certain creditor which had two debtors; the one owed five hundred pence, and the other fifty. And when they had nothing to pay he frankly forgave them both. Tell me, therefore, which of them will love him most? The Pharisee answers: "I suppose that he to whom he forgave most." Then our Saviour rejoins: "Her sins, which are many, are forgiven; for she loved much." By these words it is plain he does not make love the cause of forgiveness, but the proof of it. The similitude is borrowed from the case of a debtor, to whom a debt of five hundred pence had been forgiven. It is not said that the debt is forgiven because he loved much, but that he loved

[1] French, "Integrité, pitié, droiture, et choses semblables;"—integrity, pity, uprightness, and the like.

much because it was forgiven. The similitude ought to be applied in this way: You think this woman is a sinner; but you ought to have acknowledged her as not a sinner, in respect that her sins have been forgiven her. Her love ought to have been to you a proof of her having obtained forgiveness, that love being an expression of gratitude for the benefit received. It is an argument *a posteriori*, by which something is demonstrated by the results produced by it Our Lord plainly attests the ground on which she had obtained forgiveness, when he says, "Thy faith hath saved thee." By faith, therefore, we obtain forgiveness: by love we give thanks, and bear testimony to the loving-kindness of the Lord.

38. I am little moved by the numerous passages in the writings of the Fathers relating to satisfaction. I see indeed that some (I will frankly say almost all whose books are extant) have either erred in this matter, or spoken too roughly and harshly; but I cannot admit that they were so rude and unskilful as to write these passages in the sense in which they are read by our new satisfactionaries. Chrysostom somewhere says, "When mercy is implored, interrogation ceases; when mercy is asked, judgment rages not; when mercy is sought, there is no room for punishment; where there is mercy, no question is asked; where there is mercy, the answer gives pardon" (Chrysos. Hom. ii. in Psal. 1). How much soever these words may be twisted, they can never be reconciled with the dogmas of the Schoolmen. In the book *De Dogmatibus Ecclesiasticis*, which is attributed to Augustine, you read (cap. 54), "The satisfaction of repentance is to cut off the causes of sins, and not to indulge an entrance to their suggestions." From this it appears that the doctrine of satisfaction, said to be paid for sins committed, was everywhere derided in those ages; for here the only satisfaction referred to is caution, abstinence from sin for the future. I am unwilling to quote what Chrysostom says (Hom. x. in Genes.), that God requires nothing more of us than to confess our faults before him with tears, as similar sentiments abound both in his writings and those of others. Augustine indeed calls works of mercy remedies for obtaining forgiveness of sins (Enchir. ad Laur.); but lest any one should stumble at the expression, he himself, in another passage, obviates the difficulty. "The flesh of Christ," says he, "is the true and only sacrifice for sins—not only for those which are all effaced in baptism, but those into which we are afterwards betrayed through infirmity, and because of which the whole Church daily cries, 'Forgive us our debts' (Matth. vi. 12). And they are forgiven by that special sacrifice."

39. By satisfaction, however, they, for the most part, meant not compensation to be paid to God, but the public testimony, by which those who had been punished with excommunication, and wished again to be received into communion, assured the Church of their repentance. For those penitents were enjoined certain fasts and other things, by which they might prove that they were truly, and from

the heart, weary of their former life, or rather might obliterate the remembrance of their past deeds: in this way they were said to give satisfaction, not to God, but to the Church. The same thing is expressed by Augustine in a passage in his Enchiridion ad Laurentium, cap. 65.[1] From that ancient custom the satisfactions and confessions now in use took their rise. It is indeed a viperish progeny, not even a vestige of the better form now remaining. I know that ancient writers sometimes speak harshly ; nor do I deny, as I lately said, that they have perhaps erred ; but dogmas, which were tainted with a few blemishes, now that they have fallen into the unwashed hands of those men, are altogether defiled. And if we were to decide the contest by authority of the Fathers, what kind of Fathers are those whom they obtrude upon us? A great part of those, from whom Lombard their Coryphæus framed his centos, are extracted from the absurd dreams of certain monks passing under the names of Ambrose, Jerome, Augustine, and Chrysostom. On the present subject almost all his extracts are from the book of Augustine *De Pœnitentia*, a book absurdly compiled by some rhapsodist, alike from good and bad authors—a book which indeed bears the name of Augustine, but which no person of the least learning would deign to acknowledge as his. Wishing to save my readers trouble, they will pardon me for not searching minutely into all their absurdities. For myself it were not very laborious, and might gain some applause, to give a complete exposure of dogmas which have hitherto been vaunted as mysteries ; but as my object is to give useful instruction, I desist.

---

[1] It is quoted in the Decret. c. in Art. de Pœnit. Dist. i.

CHAPTER V.

OF THE MODES OF SUPPLEMENTING SATISFACTION—VIZ., INDULGENCES AND PURGATORY.

Divisions of the chapter,—I. A summary description and refutation of Popish indulgences, sec. 1, 2. II. Confutation by Leo and Augustine. Answer to two objections urged in support of them, sec. 3, 4. A profane love of filthy lucre on the part of the Pope. The origin of indulgences unfolded, sec. 5. III. An examination of Popish purgatory. Its horrible impiety, sec. 6. An explanation of five passages of Scripture by which Sophists endeavour to support that dream, sec. 7, 8. Sentiments of the ancient Theologians concerning purgatory, sec. 10.

Sections.

1. The dogma of satisfaction the parent of indulgences. Vanity of both. The reason of it. Evidence of the avarice of the Pope and the Romish clergy: also of the blindness with which the Christian world was smitten.
2. View of indulgences given by the Sophists. Their true nature. Refutation of them. Refutation confirmed by seven passages of Scripture.
3. Confirmed also by the testimony of Leo, a Roman Bishop, and by Augustine. Attempts of the Popish doctors to establish the monstrous doctrine of indulgences, and even support it by Apostolical authority. First answer.
4. Second answer to the passage of an Apostle adduced to support the dogma of indulgences. Answer confirmed by a comparison with other passages, and from a passage in Augustine, explaining the Apostle's meaning. Another passage from the same Apostle confirming this view.
5. The Pope's profane thirst for filthy lucre exposed. The origin of indulgences.
6. Examination of the fictitious purgatory of the Papists. 1. From the nature of the thing itself. 2. From the authority of God. 3. From the consideration of the merit of Christ, which is destroyed by this fiction. Purgatory, what it is. 4. From the impiety teeming from this fountain.
7. Exposition of the passages of Scripture quoted in support of purgatory. 1. Of the unpardonable sin, from which it is inferred that there are some sins afterwards to be forgiven. 2. Of the passage as to paying the last farthing.
8. 3. The passage concerning the bending of the knee to Christ by things under the earth. 4. The example of Judas Maccabæus in sending an oblation for the dead to Jerusalem.
9. 5. Of the fire which shall try every man's work. The sentiment of the ancient theologians. Answer, containing a *reductio ad absurdum.* Confirmation by a passage of Augustine. The meaning of the Apostle. What to be understood by fire. A clear exposition of the metaphor. The day of the Lord. How those who suffer loss are saved by fire.
10. The doctrine of purgatory ancient, but refuted by a more ancient Apostle. Not supported by ancient writers, by Scripture, or solid argument. Introduced by custom and a zeal not duly regulated by the word of God. Ancient writers, as Augustine, speak doubtfully in commending prayer for the dead. At all events, we must hold by the word of God, which rejects this fiction. A vast difference between the more ancient and the more modern builders of purgatory. This shown by comparing them.

1. FROM this dogma of satisfaction that of indulgences takes its rise. For the pretence is, that what is wanting to our own ability is

hereby supplied; and they go the insane length of defining them
to be a dispensation of the merits of Christ, and the martyrs which
the Pope makes by his bulls. Though they are fitter for hellebore
than for argument,—and it is scarcely worth while to refute these frivolous errors, which, already battered down, begin of their own accord
to grow antiquated, and totter to their fall;—yet, as a brief refutation
may be useful to some of the unlearned, I will not omit it. Indeed,
the fact that indulgences have so long stood safe and with impunity,
and wantoned with so much fury and tyranny, may be regarded as a
proof into how deep a night of ignorance mankind were for some
ages plunged. They saw themselves insulted openly, and without
disguise, by the Pope and his bull-bearers; they saw the salvation of
the soul made the subject of a lucrative traffic, salvation taxed at a
few pieces of money, nothing given gratuitously; they saw what was
squeezed from them in the form of oblations basely consumed on
strumpets, pimps, and gluttony, the loudest trumpeters of indulgences
being the greatest despisers; they saw the monsters stalking abroad,
and every day luxurating with greater licence, and that without end,
new bulls being constantly issued, and new sums extracted. Still
indulgences were received with the greatest reverence, worshipped,
and bought. Even those who saw more clearly than others deemed
them pious frauds, by which, even in deceiving, some good was
gained. Now, at length, that a considerable portion of the world
have begun to bethink themselves, indulgences grow cool, and gradually even begin to freeze, preparatory to their final extinction.

2. But since very many who see the vile imposture, theft, and
rapine (with which the dealers in indulgences have hitherto deluded
and sported with us), are not aware of the true source of the impiety,
it may be proper to show not only what indulgences truly are, but
also that they are polluted in every part.[1] They give the name of
treasury of the Church to the merits of Christ, the holy Apostles and
Martyrs. They pretend as I have said, that the radical custody of
the granary has been delivered to the Roman bishop, to whom the
dispensation of these great blessings belongs in such a sense, that he
can both exercise it by himself, and delegate the power of exercising it to
others. Hence we have from the Pope at one time plenary indulgences,
at another for certain years; from the cardinals for a hundred days,
and from the bishops for forty. These, to describe them truly, are a
profanation of the blood of Christ, and a delusion of Satan, by which
the Christian people are led away from the grace of God and the life
which is in Christ, and turned aside from the true way of salvation.
For how could the blood of Christ be more shamefully profaned than

---

1 French, "Il est expedient de monstrer ici non seulement quelles sont les indul
gences, comme ils en usent; mais du tout que c'est, à les prendre en leur propre et
meilleure nature, sans quelque qualité ou vice accidental;"—it is expedient here to
show not only what indulgences are as in use, but in themselves, taking them in their
proper and best form, without any qualification or accidental vice.

by denying its sufficiency for the remission of sins, for reconciliation and satisfaction, unless its defects, as if it were dried up and exhausted, are supplemented from some other quarter ? Peter's words are : " To him give all the prophets witness, that through his name whosoever believeth in him shall receive remissior. of sins" (Acts x. 43) ; but indulgences bestow the remission of sins through Peter, Paul, and the Martyrs. " The blood of Jesus Christ his Son cleanseth us from all sin," says John (1 John i. 7). Indulgences make the blood of the martyrs an ablution of sins. " He hath made him to be sin (*i.e.* a satisfaction for sin) for us who knew no sin," says Paul (2 Cor. v. 21), " that we might be made the righteousness of God in him." Indulgences make the satisfaction of sin to depend on the blood of the martyrs. Paul exclaimed and testified to the Corinthians, that Christ alone was crucified, and died for them (1 Cor. i. 13). Indulgences declare that Paul and others died for us. Paul elsewhere says that Christ purchased the Church with his own blood (Acts xx. 28). Indulgences assign another purchase to the blood of martyrs. " By one offering he hath perfected for ever them that are sanctified," says the Apostle (Heb. x. 14). Indulgences, on the other hand, insist that sanctification, which would otherwise be insufficient, is perfected by martyrs. John says that all the saints " have washed their robes, and made them white in the blood of the Lamb" (Rev. vii. 14). Indulgences tell us to wash our robes in the blood of saints.

3. There is an admirable passage in opposition to their blasphemies in Leo, a Roman Bishop (ad Palæstinos, Ep. 81). "Although the death of many saints was precious in the sight of the Lord (Ps. cxvi. 15), yet no innocent man's slaughter was the propitiation of the world. The just received crowns, did not give them ; and the fortitude of believers produced examples of patience, not gifts of righteousness ; for their deaths were for themselves ; and none by his final end paid the debt of another, except Christ our Lord, in whom alone all are crucified—all dead, buried, and raised up." This sentiment, as it was of a memorable nature, he has elsewhere repeated (Epist. 95). Certainly one could desire a clearer confutation of this impious dogma. Augustine introduces the same sentiment not less appositely : " Although brethren die for brethren, yet no martyr's blood is shed for the remission of sins : this Christ did for us, and in this conferred upon us not what we should imitate, but what should make us grateful," (August. Tract. in Joann. 84). Again, in another passage : " As he alone became the Son of God and the Son of man, that he might make us to be with himself sons of God, so he alone, without any ill desert, undertook the penalty for us, that through him we might, without good desert, obtain undeserved favour" (ad Bonif. Lib. iv. cap. 4). Indeed, as their whole doctrine is a patchwork of sacrilege and blasphemy, this is the most blasphemous of the whole. Let them acknowledge whether or not they hold the following dogmas : That the martyrs, by their death, performed more to God, and merited

more than was necessary for themselves, and they have a large surplus of merits which may be applied to others; that in order that this great good may not prove superfluous, their blood is mingled with the blood of Christ, and out of both is formed the treasury of the Church, for the forgiveness and satisfaction of sins; and that in this sense we must understand the words of Paul: "Who now rejoice in my sufferings, and fill up that which is behind of the afflictions of Christ in my flesh for his body's sake, which is the Church" (Col. i. 24). What is this but merely to leave the name of Christ, and at the same time make him a vulgar saintling, who can scarcely be distinguished in the crowd? He alone ought to be preached, alone held forth, alone named, alone looked to, whenever the subject considered is the obtaining of the forgiveness of sins, expiation, and sanctification. But let us hear their propositions. That the blood of martyrs may not be shed without fruit, it must be employed for the common good of the Church. Is it so? Was there no fruit in glorifying God by death? in sealing his truth with their blood? in testifying, by contempt of the present life, that they looked for a better? in confirming the faith of the Church, and at the same time disabling the pertinacity of the enemy by their constancy? But thus it is. They acknowledge no fruit if Christ is the only propitiation, if he alone died for our sins, if he alone was offered for our redemption. Nevertheless, they say, Peter and Paul would have gained the crown of victory though they had died in their beds a natural death. But as they contended to blood, it would not accord with the justice of God to leave their doing so barren and unfruitful. As if God were unable to augment the glory of his servants in proportion to the measure of his gifts. The advantage derived in common by the Church is great enough, when, by their triumphs, she is inflamed with zeal to fight.

4. How maliciously they wrest the passage in which Paul says, that he supplies in his body that which was lacking in the sufferings of Christ! (Col. i. 24). That defect or supplement refers not to the work of redemption, satisfaction, or expiation, but to those afflictions with which the members of Christ, in other words, all believers, behove to be exercised, so long as they are in the flesh. He says, therefore, that part of the sufferings of Christ still remains—viz. that what he suffered in himself he daily suffers in his members. Christ so honours us as to regard and count our afflictions as his own. By the additional words—for *the Church*, Paul means not for the redemption or reconciliation, or satisfaction of the Church, but for edification and progress. As he elsewhere says, " I endure all things for the elect's sakes, that they may also obtain the salvation which is in Christ Jesus with eternal glory" (2 Tim. ii. 10). He also writes to the Corinthians: " Whether we be afflicted, it is for your consolation and salvation, which is effectual in the enduring of the same sufferings which we also suffer" (2 Cor. i. 6). In the same place he immediately explains his meaning by adding, that he was made a minister

of the Church, not for redemption, but according to the dispensation which he received to preach the Gospel of Christ. But if they still desire another interpreter, let them hear Augustine: "The sufferings of Christ are in Christ alone, as in the head ; in Christ and the Church as in the whole body. Hence Paul, being one member, says, 'I fill up in my body that which is behind of the sufferings of Christ.' Therefore, O hearer, whoever you be, if you are among the members of Christ, whatever you suffer from those who are not members of Christ, was lacking to the sufferings of Christ" (August. in Ps. xvi.). He elsewhere explains the end of the sufferings of the Apostles undertaken for Christ: "Christ is my door to you, because ye are the sheep of Christ purchased by his blood : acknowledge your price, which is not paid by me, but preached by me" (August. Tract. in Joann. 47). He afterwards adds, "As he laid down his life, so ought we to lay down our lives for the brethren, to build up peace and maintain faith." Thus far Augustine. Far be it from us to imagine that Paul thought anything was wanting to the sufferings of Christ in regard to the complete fulness of righteousness, salvation, and life, or that he wished to make any addition to it, after showing so clearly and eloquently that the grace of Christ was poured out in such rich abundance as far to exceed all the power of sin (Rom. v. 15). All saints have been saved by it alone, not by the merit of their own life or death, as Peter distinctly testifies (Acts xv. 11) ; so that it is an insult to God and his Anointed to place the worthiness of any saint in anything save the mercy of God alone. But why dwell longer on this, as if the matter were obscure, when to mention these monstrous dogmas is to refute them ?

5. Moreover, to say nothing of these abominations, who taught the Pope to enclose the grace of Jesus Christ in lead and parchment, grace which the Lord is pleased to dispense by the word of the Gospel? Undoubtedly either the Gospel of God or indulgences must be false. That Christ is offered to us in the Gospel with all the abundance of heavenly blessings, with all his merits, all his righteousness, wisdom, and grace, without exception, Paul bears witness when he says, "Now then we are ambassadors for Christ, as though God did beseech you by us: we pray you in Christ's stead, be ye reconciled to God. For he hath made him to be sin for us, who knew no sin ; that we might be made the righteousness of God in him" (2 Cor. v. 20, 21). And what is meant by the fellowship (κοινωνία) of Christ, which, according to the same Apostle (1 Cor. i. 9), is offered to us in the Gospel, all believers know. On the contrary, indulgences, bringing forth some portion of the grace of God from the armoury of the Pope, fix it to lead, parchment, and a particular place, but dissever it from the word of God. When we inquire into the origin of this abuse, it appears to have arisen from this, that when in old times the satisfactions imposed on penitents were too severe to be borne, those who felt themselves burdened beyond measure by the penance imposed,

petitioned the Church for relaxation. The remission so given was called indulgence. But as they transferred satisfactions to God, and called them compensations by which men redeem themselves from the justice of God, they in the same way transferred indulgences, representing them as expiatory remedies which free us from merited punishment. The blasphemies to which we have referred have been feigned with so much effrontery that there is not the least pretext for them.

6. Their purgatory cannot now give us much trouble, since with this axe we have struck it, thrown it down, and overturned it from its very foundations. I cannot agree with some who think that we ought to dissemble in this matter, and make no mention of purgatory, from which (as they say) fierce contests arise, and very little edification can be obtained. I myself would think it right to disregard their follies did they not tend to serious consequences. But since purgatory has been reared on many, and is daily propped up by new blasphemies; since it produces many grievous offences, assuredly it is not to be connived at, however it might have been disguised for a time, that without any authority from the word of God, it was devised by prying audacious rashness, that credit was procured for it by fictitious revelations, the wiles of Satan, and that certain passages of Scripture were ignorantly wrested to its support. Although the Lord bears not that human presumption should thus force its way to the hidden recesses of his judgments; although he has issued a strict prohibition against neglecting his voice, and making inquiry at the dead (Deut. xviii. 11), and permits not his word to be so erroneously contaminated. Let us grant, however, that all this might have been tolerated for a time as a thing of no great moment; yet when the expiation of sins is sought elsewhere than in the blood of Christ, and satisfaction is transferred to others, silence were most perilous. We are bound, therefore, to raise our voice to its highest pitch, and cry aloud that purgatory is a deadly device of Satan; that it makes void the cross of Christ; that it offers intolerable insult to the divine mercy; that it undermines and overthrows our faith. For what is this purgatory but the satisfaction for sin paid after death by the souls of the dead? Hence when this idea of satisfaction is refuted, purgatory itself is forthwith completely overturned.[1] But if it is perfectly clear, from what was lately said, that the blood of Christ is the only satisfaction, expiation, and cleansing for the sins of believers, what remains but to hold that purgatory is mere blasphemy, horrid blasphemy against Christ? I say nothing of the sacrilege by which it is daily defended, the offences which it begets in religion, and the other innumerable evils which we see teeming forth from that fountain of impiety.

7. Those passages of Scripture on which it is their wont falsely and iniquitously to fasten, it may be worth while to wrench out of

---

1 French, " Tellement que si on ote la fantasie de satisfaire, leur purgatorie s'en va bas ; "—so that if the fancy of satisfying is taken away, down goes their purgatory.

their hands.[1] When the Lord declares that the sin against the Holy Ghost will not be forgiven either in this world or the world to come, he thereby intimates (they say) that there is a remission of certain sins hereafter. But who sees not that the Lord there speaks of the guilt of sin ? But if this is so, what has it to do with their purgatory, seeing they deny not that the guilt of those sins, the punishment of which is there expiated, is forgiven in the present life ? Lest, however, they should still object, we shall give a plainer solution. Since it was the Lord's intention to cut off all hope of pardon from this flagitious wickedness, he did not consider it enough to say, that it would never be forgiven, but in the way of amplification, employed a division by which he included both the judgment which every man's conscience pronounces in the present life, and the final judgment which will be publicly pronounced at the resurrection ; as if he had said, Beware of this malignant rebellion, as you would of instant destruction ; for he who of set purpose endeavours to extinguish the offered light of the Spirit, shall not obtain pardon either in this life, which has been given to sinners for conversion, or on the last day when the angels of God shall separate the sheep from the goats, and the heavenly kingdom shall be purged of all that offends. The next passage they produce is the parable in Matthew : " Agree with thine adversary quickly, whiles thou art in the way with him ; lest at any time the adversary deliver thee to the judge, and the judge deliver thee to the officer, and thou be cast into prison. Verily, I say unto thee, Thou shalt by no means come out thence, till thou hast paid the uttermost farthing" (Matth. v. 25, 26). If in this passage the judge means God, the adversary the devil, the officer an angel, and the prison purgatory, I give in at once. But if every man sees that Christ there intended to show to how many perils and evils those expose themselves who obstinately insist on their utmost right, instead of being satisfied with what is fair and equitable, that he might thereby the more strongly exhort his followers to concord, where, I ask, are we to find their purgatory ?[2]

8. They seek an argument in the passage in which Paul declares, that all things shall bow the knee to Christ, " things in heaven, and things in earth, and things under the earth" (Phil. ii. 10). They take it for granted, that by " things under the earth" cannot be meant those who are doomed to eternal damnation, and that the only remaining conclusion is, that they must be souls suffering in purgatory. They would not reason very ill if, by the bending of the knee, the Apostle designated true worship ; but since he simply says that Christ has received a dominion to which all creatures are subject, what pre-

---

1 Matth. xii. 32 ; Mark iii. 28 ; Luke xii. 10 ; Matth. v. 25.
2 The French adds the following sentence : " Brief, que le passage soit regardé et prins en sa simple intelligence, et il n'y sera rien trouvé de ce qu'ils pretendent ;"— In short, let the passage be looked at and taken in its simple meaning, and there will be nothing found in it of what they pretend.

vents us from understanding those "under the earth" to mean the devils, who shall certainly be sisted before the judgment-seat of God, there to recognise their Judge with fear and trembling? In this way Paul himself elsewhere interprets the same prophecy: "We shall all stand before the judgment-seat of Christ. For it is written, As I live, saith the Lord, every knee shall bow to me, and every tongue shall confess to God" (Rom. xiv. 10, 11). But we cannot in this way interpret what is said in the Apocalypse: "Every creature which is in heaven, and on the earth, and under the earth, and such as are in the sea, heard I saying, Blessing, and honour, and glory, and power, be unto him that sitteth upon the throne, and unto the Lamb, for ever and ever" (Rev. v. 13). This I readily admit; but what kinds of creatures do they suppose are here enumerated? It is absolutely certain, that both irrational and inanimate creatures are comprehended. All, then, which is affirmed is, that every part of the universe, from the highest pinnacle of heaven to the very centre of the earth, each in its own way proclaims the glory of the Creator.

To the passage which they produce from the history of the Maccabees (1 Maccab. xii. 43), I will not deign to reply, lest I should seem to include that work among the canonical books. But Augustine[1] holds it to be canonical. First, with what degree of confidence? "The Jews," says he, "do not hold the book of the Maccabees as they do the Law, the Prophets, and the Psalms, to which the Lord bears testimony as to his own witnesses, saying, Ought not all things which are written in the Law, and the Psalms, and the Prophets, concerning me be fulfilled? (Luke xxiv. 44.) But it has been received by the Church not uselessly, if it be read or heard with soberness." Jerome, however, unhesitatingly affirms, that it is of no authority in establishing doctrine; and from the ancient little book, *De Expositione Symboli,* which bears the name of Cyprian, it is plain that it was in no estimation in the ancient Church. And why do I here contend in vain? As if the author himself did not sufficiently show what degree of deference is to be paid him, when in the end he asks pardon for anything less properly expressed (2 Maccab. xv. 38). He who confesses that his writings stand in need of pardon, certainly proclaims that they are not oracles of the Holy Spirit. We may add, that the piety of Judas is commended for no other reason than for having a firm hope of the final resurrection, in sending his oblation for the dead to Jerusalem. For the writer of the history does not represent what he did as furnishing the price of redemption, but merely that they might be partakers of eternal life, with the other saints who had fallen for their country and religion. The act, indeed, was not free from superstition and misguided zeal; but it is mere fatuity to extend the legal sacrifice to us, seeing we are assured that the sacrifices then in use ceased on the advent of Christ.

[1] See August. contra Secundum Gaudentii Epistolam, cap. 23.

9. But, it seems, they find in Paul an invincible support, which cannot be so easily overthrown. His words are, "Now if any man build upon this foundation gold, silver, precious stones, wood, hay, stubble ; every man's work shall be made manifest : for the day shall declare it, because it shall be revealed by fire ; and the fire shall try every man's work of what sort it is. If any man's work shall be burnt, he shall suffer loss : but he himself shall be saved ; yet so as by fire " (1 Cor. iii. 12—15). What fire (they ask) can that be but the fire of purgatory, by which the defilements of sin are wiped away, in order that we may enter pure into the kingdom of God ? But most of the Fathers [1] give it a different meaning—viz. the tribulation or cross by which the Lord tries his people, that they may not rest satisfied with the defilements of the flesh. This is much more probable than the fiction of a purgatory. I do not, however, agree with them, for I think I see a much surer and clearer meaning to the passage. But, before I produce it, I wish they would answer me, whether they think the Apostle and all the saints have to pass through this purgatorial fire ? I am aware they will say, no ; for it were too absurd to hold that purification is required by those whose superfluous merits they dream of as applicable to all the members of the Church. But this the Apostle affirms ; for he says, not that the works of certain persons, but the works of all will be tried.[2] And this is not my argument, but that of Augustine, who thus impugns that interpretation.[3] And (what makes the thing more absurd) he says, not that they will pass through fire for certain works, but that even if they should have edified the Church with the greatest fidelity, they will receive their reward after their works shall have been tried by fire. First, we see that the Apostle used a metaphor when he gave the names of wood, hay, and stubble, to doctrines of man's device. The ground of the metaphor is obvious—viz. that as wood when it is put into the fire is consumed and destroyed, so neither will those doctrines be able to endure when they come to be tried. Moreover, every one sees that the trial is made by the Spirit of God. Therefore, in following out the thread of the metaphor, and adapting its parts properly to each other, he gave the name of fire to the examination of the Holy Spirit. For just as silver and gold, the nearer they are brought to the fire, give stronger proof of their genuineness and purity, so the Lord's truth, the more thoroughly it is submitted to spiritual examination, has its authority the better confirmed. As hay, wood, and stubble, when the fire is applied to them, are suddenly consumed, so the inventions of man, not founded on the word of God, cannot stand the trial of the Holy Spirit, but forthwith give way and perish. In fine, if spurious doc-

1 Chrysostom, Augustine, and others ; see August. Enchirid. ad Laurent. cap. 68.
2 The French adds, " auquel nombre universel sont enclos les Apostres ;"—in which universal number the Apostles are included.
3 French, " l'exposition que font aujourdhui nos adversaires ;"—the exposition which our opponents give in the present day.

trines are compared to wood, hay, and stubble, because, like wood, hay, and stubble, they are burned by fire and fitted for destruction, though the actual destruction is only completed by the Spirit of the Lord, it follows that the Spirit is that fire by which they will be proved. This proof Paul calls the *day of the Lord;* using a term common in Scripture. For the day of the Lord is said to take place whenever he in some way manifests his presence to men, his face being specially said to shine when his truth is manifested. It has now been proved, that Paul has no idea of any other fire than the trial of the Holy Spirit. But how are those who suffer the loss of their works saved by fire? This it will not be difficult to understand, if we consider of what kind of persons he speaks. For he designates them builders of the Church, who, retaining the proper foundation, build different materials upon it ; that is, who, not abandoning the principal and necessary articles of faith, err in minor and less perilous matters, mingling their own fictions with the word of God. Such, I say, must suffer the loss of their work by the destruction of their fictions. They themselves, however, are saved, yet so as by fire ; that is, not that their ignorance and delusions are approved by the Lord, but they are purified from them by the grace and power of the Holy Spirit. All those, accordingly, who have tainted the golden purity of the divine word with the pollution of purgatory, must necessarily suffer the loss of their work.

10. But the observance of it in the Church is of the highest antiquity. This objection is disposed of by Paul, when, including even his own age in the sentence, he declares, that all who in building the Church have laid up something not conformable to the foundation, must suffer the loss of their work. When, therefore, my opponents object, that it has been the practice for thirteen hundred years to offer prayers for the dead, I, in return, ask them, by what word of God, by what revelation, by what example it was done ? For here not only are passages of Scripture wanting, but in the examples of all the saints of whom we read, nothing of the kind is seen. We have numerous, and sometimes long narratives, of their mourning and sepulchral rites, but not one word is said of prayers.[1] But the more important the matter was, the more they ought to have dwelt upon it. Even those who in ancient times offered prayers for the dead, saw that they were not supported by the command of God and legitimate example. Why then did they presume to do it ? I hold that herein they suffered the common lot of man, and therefore maintain, that what they did is not to be imitated. Believers ought not to engage in any work without a firm conviction of its propriety, as Paul enjoins,

---

1 French, " L'Escriture raconte souventesfois et bien au long, comment les fideles ont pleuré la mort de leurs parens, et comment ils les ont ensevelis; mais qu'ils ayent prié pour eux, il n'en est nouvelles;"—Scripture relates oftentimes and at great length, how the faithful lamented the death of their relations, and how they buried them : but that they prayed for them is never hinted at.

(Rom. xiv. 23) ; and this conviction is expressly requisite in prayer. It is to be presumed, however, that they were influenced by some reason ; they sought a solace for their sorrow, and it seemed cruel not to give some attestation of their love to the dead, when in the presence of God. All know by experience how natural it is for the human mind thus to feel.

Received custom too was a kind of torch, by which the minds of many were inflamed. We know that among all the Gentiles, and in all ages, certain rites were paid to the dead, and that every year lustrations were performed for their manes. Although Satan deluded foolish mortals by these impostures, yet the means of deceiving were borrowed from a sound principle—viz. that death is not destruction, but a passage from this life to another. And there can be no doubt that superstition itself always left the Gentiles without excuse before the judgment-seat of God, because they neglected to prepare for that future life which they professed to believe. Thus, that Christians might not seem worse than heathens, they felt ashamed of paying no office to the dead, as if they had been utterly annihilated. Hence their ill-advised assiduity; because they thought they would expose themselves to great disgrace, if they were slow in providing funeral feasts and oblations. What was thus introduced by perverse rivalship, ever and anon received new additions, until the highest holiness of the Papacy consisted in giving assistance to the suffering dead. But far better and more solid comfort is furnished by Scripture when it declares, " Blessed are the dead that die in the Lord ;" and adds the reason, " for they rest from their labours " (Rev. xiv. 13). We ought not to indulge our love so far as to set up a perverse mode of prayer in the Church. Surely every person possessed of the least prudence easily perceives, that whatever we meet with on this subject in ancient writers, was in deference to public custom, and the ignorance of the vulgar. I admit they were themselves also carried away into error, the usual effect of rash credulity being to destroy the judgment. Meanwhile the passages themselves show, that when they recommended prayer for the dead, it was with hesitation. Augustine relates in his Confessions, that his mother Monica earnestly entreated to be remembered when the solemn rites at the altar were performed; doubtless an old woman's wish, which her son did not bring to the test of Scripture, but from natural affection wished others to approve. His book, *De Cura pro Mortuis Agenda, On showing Care for the Dead,* is so full of doubt, that its coldness may well extinguish the heat of a foolish zeal. Should any one, in pretending to be a patron of the dead, deal merely in probabilities, the only effect will be to make those indifferent who were formerly solicitous.[1]

---

[1] French, " Le liure qu'il à composé tout expres de cest argument, et qu'il a intitule. Du soin pour les morts, est envellopée en tant de doutes, qu'il doit suffire pour refroidir ceux qui y auroyent devotion ; pour le moins en voyant qu'il ne s'aide que de conjec-tures bien legeres et foibles, on verra qu'on ne se doit point fort empescher d'une chose

The only support of this dogma is, that as a custom of praying for the dead prevailed, the duty ought not to be despised. But granting that ancient ecclesiastical writers deemed it a pious thing to assist the dead, the rule which can never deceive is always to be observed —viz. that we must not introduce anything of our own into our prayers, but must keep all our wishes in subordination to the word of God, because it belongs to Him to prescribe what he wishes us to ask. Now, since the whole Law and Gospel do not contain one syllable which countenances the right of praying for the dead, it is a profanation of prayer to go one step farther than God enjoins. But, lest our opponents boast of sharing their error with the ancient Church, I say, that there is a wide difference between the two. The latter made a commemoration of the dead, that they might not seem to have cast off all concern for them; but they, at the same time, acknowledged that they were doubtful as to their state; assuredly they made no such assertion concerning purgatory as implied that they did not hold it to be uncertain. The former insist, that their dream of purgatory shall be received without question as an article of faith. The latter sparingly and in a perfunctory manner only commended their dead to the Lord, in the communion of the holy supper. The former are constantly urging the care of the dead, and by their importunate preaching of it, make out that it is to be preferred to all the offices of charity. But it would not be difficult for us to produce some passages from ancient writers,[1] which clearly overturn all those prayers for the dead which were then in use. Such is the passage of Augustine, in which he shows that the resurrection of the flesh and eternal glory is expected by all, but that rest which follows death is received by every one who is worthy of it when he dies. Accordingly, he declares that all the righteous, not less than the Apostles, Prophets, and Martyrs, immediately after death enjoy blessed rest. If such is their condition, what, I ask, will our prayers contribute to them?[2] I say nothing of those grosser superstitions by which they have fascinated the minds of the simple; and yet they are innumerable, and most of them so monstrous, that they cannot cover them with any cloak of decency. I say nothing, moreover, of those most shameful traffickings, which they plied as they listed while the world was stupified. For I would never come to an end; and, without enumerating them, the pious reader will here find enough to establish his conscience.

où il n'y a nulle importance;"—The book which he has composed expressly on this subject, and which he has entitled, Of Care for the Dead, is enveloped in so many doubts, that it should be sufficient to cool those who are devoted to it; at least, as he supports his view only by very slight and feeble conjectures, it will be seen, that we ought not to trouble ourselves much with a matter in which there is no importance.

[1] See August. Homil. in Joann. 49. De Civitate Dei, Lib. xxi. cap. xiii.–xxiv.

[2] The French of the latter clause of this sentence is, " et toutesfois il y aura matiere assez ample de les pourmener en cette campagne, veu qu'ils n'ont nulle couleur pour s'excuser, qu'ils ne soyent conveincus d'etre les plus vilains trompeurs qui furent jamais;"—and yet there is ample space to travel them over this field, seeing they have no colour of excuse, but must be convicted of being the most villanous deceivers that ever were.